MASTER VISUALLY®

Project 2003

Visual™

by Elaine J. Marmel

From

maranGraphics®

&

Wiley Publishing, Inc.

Master VISUALLY®
Project 2003

Published by
Wiley Publishing, Inc.
111 River Street
Hoboken, NJ 07030-5774

Published simultaneously in Canada

Library of Congress Control Number: 2004103155

ISBN: 0-7645-6879-5

Manufactured in the United States of America

10 9 8 7 6 5 4 3 2 1

IVH/QZ/QW/QU/IN

Trademark Acknowledgments

Important Numbers

For U.S. corporate orders, please call maranGraphics at 800-469-6616 or fax 905-890-9434.

For general information on our other products and services or to obtain technical support please contact our Customer Care Department within the U.S. at 800-762-2974, outside the U.S. at 317-572-3993 or fax 317-572-4002.

Permissions

WILEY

U.S. Corporate Sales	U.S. Trade Sales
Contact maranGraphics at (800) 469-6616 or fax (905) 890-9434.	Contact Wiley at (800) 762-2974 or fax (317) 572-4002.

Praise for Visual books...

"If you have to see it to believe it, this is the book for you!"
—*PC World*

"A master tutorial/reference – from the leaders in visual learning!"
—*Infoworld*

"A publishing concept whose time has come!"
—*The Globe and Mail*

"Just wanted to say THANK YOU to your company for providing books which make learning fast, easy, and exciting! I learn visually so your books have helped me greatly – from Windows instruction to Web page development. I'm looking forward to using more of your Master VISUALLY series in the future, as I am now a computer support specialist. Best wishes for continued success."
—*Angela J. Barker (Springfield, MO)*

"I have over the last 10-15 years purchased thousands of dollars worth of computer books but find your books the most easily read, best set out, and most helpful and easily understood books on software and computers I have ever read. Please keep up the good work."
—*John Gatt (Adamstown Heights, Australia)*

"I am an avid fan of your Visual books. If I need to learn anything, I just buy one of your books and learn the topic in no time. Wonders! I have even trained my friends to give me Visual books as gifts."
—*Illona Bergstrom (Aventura, FL)*

"The Greatest. This whole series is the best computer-learning tool of any kind I've ever seen."
—*Joe Orr (Brooklyn, NY)*

"What fantastic teaching books you have produced! Congratulations to you and your staff."
—*Bruno Tonon (Melbourne, Australia)*

"I have quite a few of your Visual books and have been very pleased with all of them. I love the way the lessons are presented!"
—*Mary Jane Newman (Yorba Linda, CA)*

"Like a lot of other people, I understand things best when I see them visually. Your books really make learning easy and life more fun."
—*John T. Frey (Cadillac, MI)*

"Your Visual books have been a great help to me. I now have a number of your books and they are all great. My friends always ask to borrow my Visual books - trouble is, I always have to ask for them back!"
—*John Robson (Brampton, Ontario, Canada)*

"I would like to take this time to compliment maranGraphics on creating such great books. I work for a leading manufacturer of office products, and sometimes they tend to NOT give you the meat and potatoes of certain subjects, which causes great confusion. Thank you for making it clear. Keep up the good work."
—*Kirk Santoro (Burbank, CA)*

"I write to extend my thanks and appreciation for your books. They are clear, easy to follow, and straight to the point. Keep up the good work! I bought several of your books and they are just right! No regrets! I will always buy your books because they are the best."
—*Seward Kollie (Dakar, Senegal)*

"You're marvelous! I am greatly in your debt."
—*Patrick Baird (Lacey, WA)*

maranGraphics is a family-run business
located near Toronto, Canada.

At maranGraphics, we believe in producing great computer books – one book at a time.

maranGraphics has been producing high-technology products for over 25 years, which enables us to offer the computer book community a unique communication process.

Our computer books use an integrated communication process, which is very different from the approach used in other computer books. Each spread is, in essence, a flow chart – the text and screen shots are totally incorporated into the layout of the spread. Introductory text

and helpful tips complete the learning experience.

maranGraphics' approach encourages the left and right sides of the brain to work together – resulting in faster orientation and greater memory retention.

Above all, we are very proud of the handcrafted nature of our books. Our carefully-chosen writers are experts in their fields, and spend countless hours researching and organizing the content for each topic. Our artists rebuild every screen shot to provide the best clarity possible, making our screen

shots the most precise and easiest to read in the industry. We strive for perfection, and believe that the time spent handcrafting each element results in the best computer books money can buy.

Thank you for purchasing this book. We hope you enjoy it!

Sincerely,
Robert Maran
President
maranGraphics
Rob@maran.com

www.maran.com

CREDITS

Project Editor
Maureen Spears

Acquisitions Editor
Tom Heine

Product Development Manager
Lindsay Sandman

Copy Editor
Kim Heusel

Technical Editor
Jim Peters

Permissions Editor
Laura Moss

Editorial Manager
Robyn Siesky

Manufacturing
Allan Conley
Linda Cook
Paul Gilchrist
Jennifer Guynn

Special Help
Tim Borek
Adrienne Porter

Indexer
Johnna Van Hoose

Book Design
maranGraphics®

Project Coordinator
Maridee Ennis

Layout
Beth Brooks
Carrie Foster
Jennifer Heliene
LeAndra Hosier
Kristin McMullan
Heather Pope

Screen Artist
Jill A. Proll

Illustrators
David E. Gregory
Ronda David-Burroughs

Proofreader
Vicki Broyles

Quality Control
John Greenough

Vice President and Executive Group Publisher
Richard Swadley

Vice President and Publisher
Barry Pruett

Composition Director
Debbie Stailey

ABOUT THE AUTHOR

Elaine Marmel is president of Marmel Enterprises, LLC, an organization that specializes in technical writing and software training. She routinely employs project management software and skills to manage critical business projects, and otherwise spends most of her time writing. Elaine has authored or coauthored more than 30 books about software, including Project, Word for Windows, Word for the Mac, Quicken for Windows, Quicken for DOS, 1-2-3 for Windows, Lotus Notes, and Excel. Elaine is a contributing editor to the monthly magazines *Peachtree Extra* and *QuickBooks Extra*.

Elaine left her native Chicago for the warmer climes of Florida (by way of Cincinnati, Ohio; Jerusalem, Israel; Ithaca, New York; and Washington, D.C.) where she gazes longingly out her window and dreams about basking in the sun (if she could ever find the time) with her dog, Josh, and her cats, Cato, Watson, and Buddy. Elaine also sings in the Toast of Tampa, an International Champion Sweet Adeline barbershop chorus.

AUTHOR'S ACKNOWLEDGMENTS

As all good project managers know, you can't do it all alone — every successful project is the product of many people's efforts. Thank you, Tom Heine, for the opportunity to write this book. Thank you, Maureen Spears, for your supportive guidance and understanding along the way. Thanks to Tim Borek, Kim Heusel, Adrian Porter, and all of the other unsung heroes at Wiley Publishing for helping to make this a better book.

Thank you, Jim Peters, for keeping me technically accurate and for the wonderful insights you added. It was a delight to work with you and I hope to have the opportunity again in the future. Jim is a Project Management Professional (PMP) and president of SoftwareMatters.com, Inc., a Microsoft Project Partner focused on integrating project management and software development methods with Microsoft's Enterprise Project Management solutions and tools. Jim has extensive experience designing and implementing enterprise project management software solutions, delivering project management training, and developing project management reporting systems. He can be reached by phone at (877) 257-1982 or by email at . For more information about SoftwareMatters.com, Inc., see their website, .

Last, thanks to the fellows at Project Server Support, Inc. and to Bob Woock — my "computer guy" — for being there when I needed you.

To my brother and sister-in-law, Jim and Mariann Marmel, who always believe in me, and to the memories of my mother, Susan Marmel (1914-2003) and my father, Harry Marmel (1914-1985), who always made me feel loved and cherished — I miss you.

WHAT'S INSIDE

IV TRACK THE PROJECT SCHEDULE AND COSTS

VI ADVANCED MICROSOFT OFFICE PROJECT

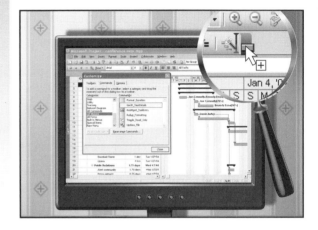

V WORK IN GROUPS

VII APPENDIX OVERVIEW PAGE

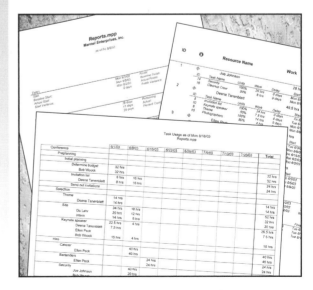

1 PROJECT MANAGEMENT BASICS

2

3) BUILD TASKS

FLEXIBLE-
Finish task in five days to
one week

INFLEXIBLE-
Deadline: May 3rd, 9:00 A.M.

4) CREATE RESOURCES

5) WORK WITH ESTIMATED PROJECT COSTS

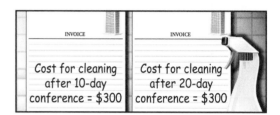

6) CUSTOMIZE VIEWS

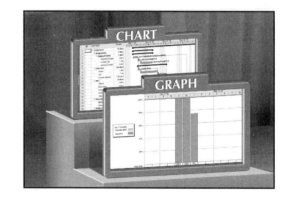

7) TABLES AND VIEWS

TABLE OF CONTENTS

8) ORGANIZE INFORMATION IN A VIEW

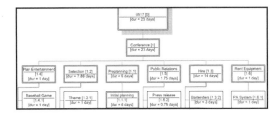

9) PROJECT AND CODES

3

RESOLVE CONFLICTS

10) RESOLVE SCHEDULING PROBLEMS

11) RESOLVE RESOURCE PROBLEMS

4

TRACK THE PROJECT SCHEDULE AND COSTS

12) ESTABLISH BASELINES

TABLE OF CONTENTS

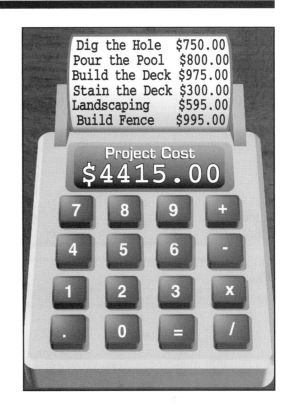

15) ANALYZE PROGRESS FINANCIALLY

5

WORK IN GROUPS

16) COORDINATE MULTIPLE PROJECTS OUTSIDE PROJECT SERVER

TABLE OF CONTENTS

17) PROJECT SERVER: BASIC SET UP ACTIVITIES

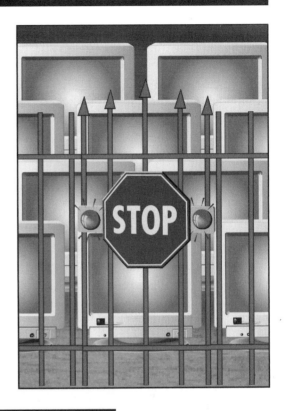

18) PROJECT SERVER AND THE PROJECT/RESOURCE MANAGER

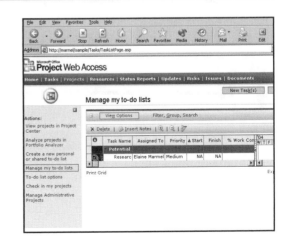

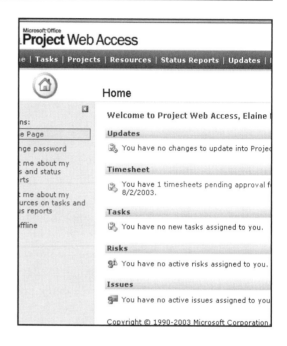

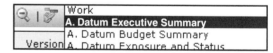

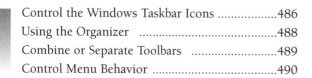

6

ADVANCED MICROSOFT OFFICE PROJECT

22) USING MACROS TO SPEED UP WORK

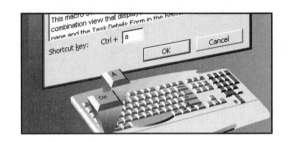

7

APPENDIXES

APPENDIX A) EXAMINE PROJECT VIEWS

APPENDIX B) REPORT SAMPLES

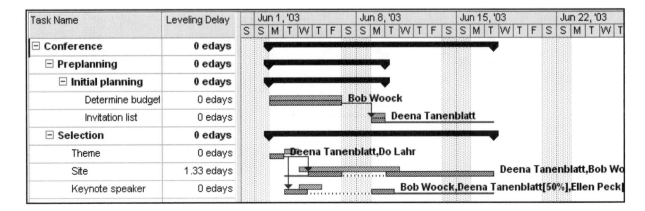
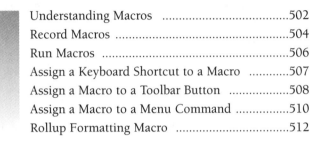

Master VISUALLY Project 2003 contains straightforward examples to teach you how to use the Microsoft Office Project programs.

This book is designed to help a reader receive quick access to any area of question. You can simply look up a subject within the Table of Contents or Index and go immediately to the task of concern. A *section* is a self-contained unit that walks you through a computer operation step-by-step. That is, with rare exception, all the information you need regarding an area of interest is contained within a section.

The Organization of Each Chapter

Each section contains an introduction, a set of screen shots with steps, and, if the steps goes beyond 1 page, a set of tips. The introduction tells why you want to perform the steps, the advantages and disadvantages of performing the steps, a general explanation of any procedures, and references to other related sections in the book. The screens, located on the bottom half of each page, show a series of steps that you must complete to perform a given task. The tips give you an opportunity to further understand the subject matter under discussion, to learn about other related sections in other areas of the book, or to apply more complicated or alternative methods.

A chapter may also contain an illustrated group of pages that gives you background information that you need to understand the sections in a chapter.

The General Organization of This Book

Master VISUALLY Project 2003 has 22 Chapters and 2 Appendix(es) and is divided into 6 Parts.

Part I: *Project Management Basics* explains the basic project management concepts and terminology that you need to learn Project.

In Part II: *Get Your Project Going*, you learn about the type of information that Project needs to do its job.

Part III: *Resolve Conflicts* shows you how to tweak things in your project before it starts to address potential problems.

Part IV: *Track the Project Schedule and Costs* shows you how to track and monitor your project's progress and costs from various perspectives after you set your basic schedule and the project begins.

PROJECT 2003

Part V: *Work in Groups* explains how teams of people use Project and Project Server, because most projects worth the effort of tracking are not done by a single person.

Part VI: *Advanced Microsoft Office Project* provides advice and information to make your use of Project easier.

Who This Book is For

Because project management is a discipline of its own, this book does not try to teach you project management, but it does include discussion of basic project management concepts, particularly addressing the way that Project handles them. This book is for the beginner, who is unfamiliar with the various Project \programs but who is familiar with project management concepts. It is also for more computer literate individuals with project management background who want to expand their knowledge of the different features that Project has to offer.

What You Need to Use This Book

Microsoft Office Project Professional, a computer with a minimum of an Intel Pentium 233-MHz processor (Pentium III recommended), 128 MB RAM, Super VGA (800 _ 600) resolution monitor, Windows 2000 with Service Pack 3 or Windows XP, and a CD-ROM.

To use Chapters 17-20, you need, at a minimum, a computer with a Pentium III processor that runs at 500 MHzand 512 MB RAM, a CD-ROM, a Super VGA (800x600) resolution monitor, and a mouse. On this computer, you need to install Windows Server 2003 with IIS enabled, SQL Server 2000 with Service Pack 3, SQL Analysis Services, Windows SharePoint Services, Internet Explorer 5.01 with Service Pack 3 or higher and the sample data from the Project Server CD.

Conventions When Using the Mouse

This book uses the following conventions to describe the actions you perform when using the mouse:

- **Click:** Press and release the left mouse button. You use a click to select an item on the screen.
- **Double-click:** Quickly press and release the left mouse button twice. You use a double-click to open a document or start a program.
- **Right-click:** Press and release the right mouse button. You use a right-click to display a shortcut menu, a list of commands specifically related to the selected item.

- **Click and Drag, and Release the Mouse:** Position the mouse pointer over an item on the screen and then press and hold down the left mouse button. Still holding down the button, move the mouse to where you want to place the item and then release the button. Dragging and dropping makes it easy to move an item to a new location.

The Conventions in This Book

A number of typographic and layout styles have been used throughout *Master Visually Project 2003* to distinguish different types of information.

- **Bold** indicates the information that you must type into a dialog box or code that you must type into the editing window.
- *Italics* indicates a new term being introduced.
- Numbered steps indicate that you must perform these steps in order to successfully perform the task.
- Bulleted steps give you alternative methods, explain various options, or present what a program will do in response to the numbered steps.
- Notes in the steps give you additional information to help you complete a task. The purpose of a note is three-fold: It can explain special conditions that may occur during the course of the task, warn you of potentially dangerous situations, or refer you to tasks in the same or a different chapter. References to tasks within the chapter are indicated by the phrase "See the section..." followed by the name of the task. References to other chapters are indicated by "See Chapter..." followed by the chapter number.
- Icons in the steps indicate a button that you must press.

 Most of the sections in this book are supplemented with a section called Master It. These are tips, hints, and tricks that extend your use of the section beyond what you learned by performing the steps in the section.

Operating System Difference

Most of this book was written using Windows XP; Chapters 17-20 were written using Windows 2003 Server. If you are using different versions of the Windows program, the screen shots that you view on-screen may vary from those shown in this book.

SECTION 1

WHAT IS A PROJECT?

Throughout the history of man, people have planned and managed projects. As civilizations arose, so did projects: cities to build, roads to connect them, land to manage, and legal and barter systems to write. People managed to create project timelines, locate materials and resources, and weigh project risks without the advanced tools, techniques, and methodologies available today.

The Definition of a Project

Dictionaries define the word project using words such as "design," "plan," and "group effort." At the Project Management Institute's Web site (www.pmi.org), you find the following definition of a project: "A project is a temporary endeavor undertaken to achieve a particular aim and to which project management can be applied, regardless of the project's size, budget, or timeline."

More simply put, a project involves a group of people with a common goal who work to perform a number of tasks within a certain time frame using the resources available to them.

People

A project involves a group of people: A project is not a simple one-person effort to perform a task, but rather a series of steps that are typically performed by more than one person.

Goals

A project has a specific and measurable goal. You know you have finished the project when you have successfully met the project's goal.

Timelines

A project has a specific time frame. You often need to complete a project by a specific date. You then measure the success of a project partially by whether you completed the project within the time frame allotted to it.

Tasks

A project has tasks: All projects consist of interdependent, yet individual, steps called tasks. Few portions of a project exist in a vacuum. If one task runs late or over budget, it typically affects other tasks, the overall schedule, and the total cost of the project.

Resources

Projects use resources. Resources are the people, machinery, materials, and other goods you need to complete the project. Another measure of a project's success or failure lies in the assessment of how well you utilize resources.

PROJECT MANAGEMENT OVERVIEW

Project management is a discipline that examines various aspects of projects and offers ways to control their progress. As defined in the 2000 edition of *A Guide to the Project Management Body of Knowledge (PMBOK® Guide)*,

"Project management is the application of knowledge, skills, tools, and techniques to a broad range of activities in order to meet the requirements of a particular project."

Editor's Note: The 2000 edition of *A Guide to the Project Management Body of Knowledge (PMBOK® Guide)* was designated an American

National Standard (ANSI/PMI 99-001-2000) by the American National Standards Institute in March 2001. It is considered representative of project management standard for the project management profession and describes standard principles and practices generally accepted and applicable in the field.

Who Uses Project Management?

The phrase *project management* emerged in the late 1950s and early 1960s when projects began to grow in size, scope, duration, and the amount of resources needed. Today, project management is used globally by everyone from corporations, governments, all branches of the military, to smaller profit and non-profit organizations as a means of meeting their customers' or constituents' needs. Project management helps all of these organizations standardize and reduce the basic tasks necessary to complete a project in the most effective and efficient manner while simultaneously utilizing available resources as effectively and efficiently as possible.

Project managers concern themselves with scheduling, budgeting, managing resources, and tracking and reporting progress and focus on organizing and systematizing the tasks in a project to minimize the number of surprises encountered.

Planning and Communication

Projects range from the simple to the complex; the more complex a project, the more you need to manage it to minimize problems. Good planning and communication can go a long way toward avoiding disaster. And although no amount of planning can prevent all possible problems, good project management enables project managers to deal efficiently with those inevitable twists and turns.

Up-to-Date Information

Projects tend to grow, change, and behave in ways that no one can predict. Consequently, project managers have to remain alert to the progress and vagaries of their projects to ensure the successful outcome of each project. Documentation and communication are the two key tools for staying on top of a project throughout its life.

PROJECT MANAGEMENT ACTIVITIES

Project management consists of several activities, and understanding the nature of each of these activities can help you relate the features of Microsoft Project to your own projects. Performing these activities can help you save time and money especially if your project is complex. The first step is to define your project's scope and goals. After setting these goals, you can begin planning your project. Once you start your project, you need to continually revise the schedule by having others review it. You can then monitor it to make sure that you are on track. After you plan the project and incorporate revisions into the schedule, you begin tracking the project. Using Microsoft Office Project, you also can compare your estimates to actual information to help you learn how to estimate better.

Identify the Project's Goal and Scope

Before you can begin to plan a project, you have to identify the goal — and identifying the project's goal is not always as simple and obvious as it sounds. Because projects involve the combined efforts of several individuals, you may find that various participants define a project's goal differently. In fact, many projects fail because the team members are unwittingly working toward different goals. For example, is the outcome for your project to produce a building design, or is it to construct the building? Take the time to write goal and scope statements and circulate them among the team members to make sure that you have gathered key data — such as deliverables, timing, and budget — and that everyone understands the common focus of the project.

To identify your goal, you can use various communication tools, such as meetings, status reports, e-mail, and conference calls. Most importantly, you should conduct a dialogue at various levels (from management through front-line personnel) that gets ideas on the table and answers questions. Be careful not to set a long-range goal that is likely to change before the project ends. Smaller projects or projects that have been broken into various phases are more manageable and more flexible.

A scope statement is a definition of more specific parameters or constraints for completing the project. Project constraints usually fall within the areas of time, quality, and cost, and they often relate directly to project deliverables. Keep your goal and scope statements brief. If you cannot explain your goal or scope in a sentence or two, you may have made your project overly ambitious and complex and you should consider breaking the project into smaller projects. For example, if Project A's goal is to launch a new cleaning product, the scope might include test-marketing the product, designing packaging, and creating and launching an advertising campaign before the end of the third quarter of 2004 with a cost not exceeding $750,000.

Project A's scope statement designates major phases of the project (conducting test marketing, designing packaging, and creating an ad campaign) and provides a starting point for planning the tasks in the project. In fact, you may eventually decide to break this project into smaller projects of conducting test marketing, designing packaging, and launching an advertising campaign. Writing the scope of the project may encourage you to redefine both the goal and the scope to make the project more manageable.

Plan the Project

Once you understand the goal and scope of a project, you can determine the steps that you need to take to reach the goal. Look for major phases first, and then break each phase into a logical sequence of steps. Some people find it easiest to identify the steps by working backwards from the end of the project.

In addition to identifying the steps to reach your goal, you must plan for the resources that accomplish the steps. Resources can include equipment of limited availability, materials, individual workers, and groups of workers. Remember to consider various scheduling issues, such as overtime, vacations, and resources that are shared among projects. Time, money, and resources are closely related: You can save time with more resources, but resources typically cost money. And, you need to understand your organization's order of priority among time, quality, and money, because there is truth to the old joke: Time, budget, or quality — pick two. Adding resources to a project schedule

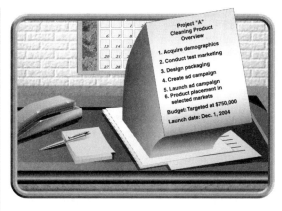

can decrease the time to complete the schedule, but additional resources also can introduce loss of quality control while simultaneously increasing the cost of the project. Similarly, lengthening the time frame of the project can improve quality but usually increases costs and introduces resource schedule conflicts.

You begin to enter data in Microsoft Project and see your project take shape while you are planning. The outline format of a Project schedule clearly shows the various phases of your project.

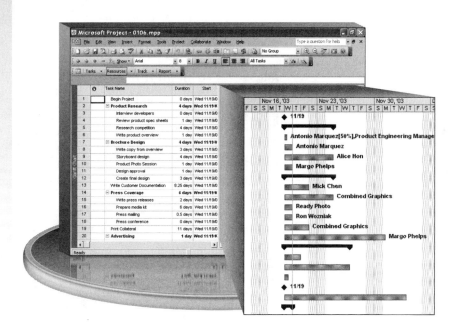

PROJECT MANAGEMENT ACTIVITIES (CONTINUED)

Revise the Schedule

In most organizations, project planners send an initial project schedule to various managers or coworkers for approval or input so that they can refine the schedule based on different factors. As a project planner, you can encourage the input of your colleagues using the reporting features of Microsoft Project.

You should welcome revisions to a project plan from your coworkers, because statistics show that people cooperate as part of a team — helping to ensure the success of the project — when they feel that their thoughts and ideas have been considered and accepted. As you revise your plan to incorporate the ideas of others, you can create and save multiple Project files to generate what-if scenarios based on the input that you receive. Seeing your plans from various perspectives is a great way to take advantage of Project's power.

Addressing Conflicts

Resolving conflicts in timing and resource allocation is another aspect of planning and revising. Project helps you pinpoint these conflicts, such as a team member or resource that is booked on several projects at once, a task that begins before another task that must precede it, or an unusually high use of expensive equipment in one phase that is upsetting your budget.

When your project plan seems solid, you can take a picture of it, called a *baseline,* against which you can track actual progress. See Chapter 8 to learn more about working with baselines.

Track Progress

You should try to solidify your tracking methods before your project begins. Ask yourself the following questions:

- How often do you want to track progress? Once a week? Once a month?

- Do project participants track their own work or merely report their progress to you?

- Do you want to roll those smaller reports into a single, less-detailed report for management?

The answers to these questions also can help you determine if you need to use Project Standard, Project Professional, or Project Server. See Chapter 2 for information on choosing the Project product that best suits your needs.

You can help your team establish efficient tracking mechanisms from the outset if you know how you are going to track your project's progress and who needs to know what and when.

When you begin tracking progress, you establish a baseline for the project, which is a snapshot of your project at the point in time you set the baseline. Then you can use the Tracking Gantt view in Project to show the baseline (the bottom bar of each task) tracked against actual progress (the top bar of each task). The darker portion of each upper task bar and the percentage figure to the right of each upper task bar indicate the percentage of each task that is complete.

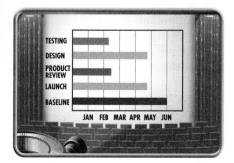

You can save interim baselines of a schedule at various points during your project. This approach helps you see where major shifts occurred and shows how you accommodated those shifts.

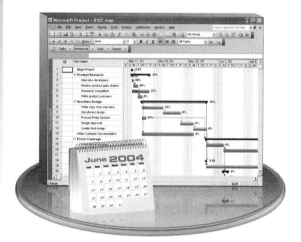

Trial and Error

Microsoft Project enables you to review your projects and to clearly see where you estimated correctly or incorrectly, made adjustments too quickly or too slowly, or created too many or too few tasks to effectively manage the project. Project keeps your original schedule's baseline in a single file, along with interim baselines and your final tracked schedule. When planning future projects, you can use these older baselines to help gauge the duration of tasks and the cost of certain items and to estimate an accurate number of resources to use.

In the end, you can become a more successful and efficient project manager. You can easily show your boss the specific actions that you have taken to avoid problems and provide solutions. In addition, you have the tools that you need to help you and your managers understand the issues that you face and to get the support that you need.

UNDERSTANDING PROJECT MANAGEMENT TERMS AND TOOLS

To manage the various aspects of projects, certain terminology has evolved, and you need an understanding of that terminology to succeed as a project manager and in using Microsoft Office Project. Knowing the difference between durations and milestones, or between resource-driven tasks and fixed-duration tasks, can help you better plan your project. Understanding what a critical path is can help you anticipate and prevent unwanted delays while knowing the importance of a dependency can help you determine what tasks you need to perform first in a project.

In addition to terminology used in the project management genre, tools in the form of various charts have also evolved to aid project managers visually understand project status. For example, the Gantt Chart shows the individual tasks, complete with milestones, in bar format, while the Network Diagram illustrates the relationships of tasks to each other.

Critical Path

The critical path highlights the series of tasks in a project that you must complete on time for the overall project to stay on schedule. Knowing where your critical path tasks are at any point during the project is crucial to staying on track.

Consider this simple example: Suppose that you are planning a birthday surprise party for your boss, and you have five days to plan the party. During this time, you need to get the card signed, order the food, reserve a room for the party, and buy a birthday gift. And, you estimate that it may take you five days to get the card signed, one day each to order the food and buy the birthday gift, and one hour to reserve the room.

The shortest task, reserving a room, takes only 1 hour. If you know that plenty of rooms are available for holding the party, you can delay reserving the room until the last hour of the third day. Delaying this task does not cause any delay in holding the party — as long as you complete this task by the end of the longest task, which is getting everyone to sign the birthday card. Therefore, the task of reserving a room is not on the critical path.

However, you cannot delay the task of signing the birthday card without delaying the party. Therefore, the card-signing task is on the critical path.

The critical path may change as the project progresses. You should closely monitor the tasks on the critical path to ensure that they do not run late and affect your overall schedule. The illustrations show the same schedule; one shows all tasks in the project, and the other shows the same project filtered to display only the tasks that are on the critical path. See Chapter 5 to learn how to display only critical tasks.

Slack

Slack (also called *float*) is the amount of time that you can delay a task before that task moves onto the critical path. In the preceding example, the 1-hour-long task — reserving a room — has slack. This task can slip a few hours, even a couple of days, and, if the other tasks are on time, the party will still happen on time. However, if you wait until the last hour of the fifth day to reserve a room, the task has used up its slack and will move onto the critical path.

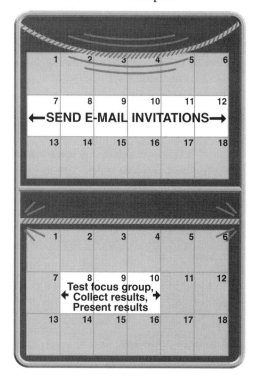

Dependencies

The final project management concept that you should understand is dependencies. The overall timing of a project is not simply the sum of the durations of all tasks. While some tasks can occur simultaneously — in the preceding example, you could have shopped

for the birthday gift while someone else ordered the food — other tasks must happen in a certain order. For example, when you build a home, you must pour the foundation first. You also need to build the walls and roof before you lay carpeting. In this project, no other task can start until you complete the Pour Foundation task. Likewise you cannot start the Install Carpeting task until you complete the Build Walls and Roof task. The relationships being described here are called *dependencies*. As part of the project planning process, project managers anticipate and establish dependencies among the tasks in a project. The overall timing of a project becomes clear after you create tasks, assign durations to them, and establish dependencies.

Please note that there are four different types of dependencies. You can learn more about them in Chapter 3.

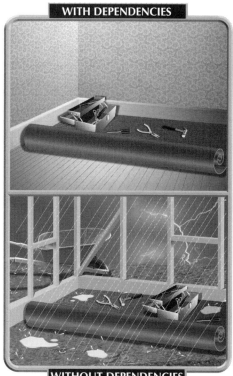

UNDERSTANDING PROJECT MANAGEMENT TERMS AND TOOLS (CONTINUED)

Durations

Tasks can take anywhere from 5 minutes to 5 months, but most tasks in a project take a specific amount of time to accomplish. *Duration* is the length of time you need to complete a task. You should always try to break the long tasks in a project into smaller tasks of shorter duration so that you can track their progress more accurately. For example, break a 6-month-long task into six 1-month tasks. Checking off the completion of the smaller tasks each month reduces the odds of a serious surprise 6 months down the road and provides the added side benefit of making you feel like you are accomplishing something.

Milestones

Some tasks have no (0) duration; these tasks are actually points in time that mark the start or completion of some phase of a project. For example, if your project involves designing a new car, you may consider the approval of the initial design a milestone. You can assign a duration to the process of routing the design to various people for review, but assigning a length of time to the moment when you have everyone's final approval is probably impossible. Therefore, the moment that you have everyone's approval has a duration of 0. Tasks that have no duration are called *milestones*; think of milestones as markers of key moments in a project.

Time to complete prototype: 2 months

DURATION

Approval for design: 0 months

PROJECT MILESTONE

Resource-Driven Schedules and Fixed-Duration Tasks

You can complete many tasks in a shorter period of time if you assign more resources to work on the task to complete it. For example, if one person needs four hours to mow a lawn, adding a second person and lawn mower can cut this time in half. The project still requires four hours of effort, but two resources can perform tasks simultaneously. Tasks whose durations are affected by the addition or subtraction of resources are called *resource-driven tasks.*

Note that in real-world projects, this calculation is seldom so exact. Because people have different skill levels and perform work at different speeds, two people do not always cut the time of a task exactly in half. In addition, when you add more people to a task, doing so may require more communication, cooperation, and training.

However, some tasks take the same amount of time no matter how many people or other resources you devote to them. Flying non-stop from Tampa to Phoenix is likely to take about five hours, regardless of the number of pilots or flight attendants on the plane. Pregnancy takes approximately nine months; you cannot speed it up or slow it down. These tasks have a *fixed duration,* meaning that their timing is set by the nature of the task. These tasks are also called *fixed duration tasks.*

TIME REQUIRED: 4 HOURS

TIME REQUIRED: 2 HOURS

NON-STOP FLIGHT TO LONDON: 6 HOURS 45 MINUTES

Visual Tools in Project Management

Gantt Charts and network diagrams are among the most popular visual tools of project management that have evolved over many years. Each tool presents a different view of your project, helping you track different aspects of your project. In Project, you can display your project information in a Gantt Chart view, a Network Diagram view, or several variations of either view.

If you have not already seen examples of a Microsoft Project Gantt Chart, they represent the tasks in a project with bars that reflect the duration of individual tasks. Milestones are shown as diamond-shaped objects. A Gantt Chart enables you to visualize and track the timing of a project.

You can also display a network diagram in Project. Network diagrams do not accurately detail the timing of a project. Instead, a network diagram shows the flow of tasks in a project and the relationships of tasks to each other. Each task is contained in a box called a *node*, and lines that flow among the nodes indicate the flow of tasks.

Some organizations use a work breakdown structure (WBS) chart. Although Microsoft Project does not include a WBS chart as one of its standard views, you can purchase WBS Chart Pro, a Project add-on product, to create a WBS chart from a Microsoft Project file. For more on WBS charts, see Chapter 9.

WHY USE PROJECT MANAGEMENT SOFTWARE?

As the size and complexity of projects has grown, so has the need for project management software. Before the advent of project management software, people managed projects with stacks of to-do lists and colorful hand-drawn wall charts. They scribbled notes on calendars in pencil because they anticipated changes in dates and tasks over time. They held numerous meetings to keep everyone in the project informed. Managers developed these simple organizational tools because their projects had so many bits and pieces that no one could possibly remember all of them.

Before people used computers to manage their projects, managers updated those charts and to-do lists by hand as the project progressed; you can imagine how difficult they were to read by the end of the project. Thankfully, project management software makes this information much easier to generate, update, and customize. To manage a project, you need a set of procedures. Project management software automates many of these procedures.

Plan Before You Begin

By actively planning the various elements of your project using Project 2004, you focus on the project's various elements; ultimately, you can estimate the time and resources that you require to complete the project more accurately than you would without making the effort to plan. If you have tasks that repeat throughout the life of a project, such as weekly meetings or regular reviews, you can create a single repeating task, and Project duplicates it for you. And, if you often do similar types of projects, Project enables you to create project templates with typical project tasks already in place; you can then modify the templates for individual projects. Project comes with templates to help you get started.

In Chapter 2, you read about setting up a project, including creating a project, including creating tasks, using calendars, moving tasks around in a project, and saving files and templates. Chapter 3 explores working with tasks further; you read about the various task types and see how to assign durations to tasks. You also read about task dependencies and constraints. In Chapter 4, you begin to discover resources; you learn how to create them and assign them to tasks, and you read about removing or replacing resource assignments. Chapter 5 begins to explain how Project gathers cost information and calculates costs. Chapters 6 through 8 help you manipulate information in Project using views, tables, sorting, groups, and filters.

Updating the Project

After you enter your basic project information into Microsoft Project, the ongoing maintenance of that data is far easier than generating handwritten to-do lists that become obsolete almost immediately. You can create projects from tasks that you set up in Outlook, or you can use Excel to start your project and then easily import the spreadsheet into Project. You can also download project tasks into Outlook from Project Web Access, work on them, record the work in Outlook, and then upload the updated information to Project Web Access. See Chapter 3 for more information about starting projects in Outlook and Excel and then moving them into Project 2003. See Chapter 17 for more information on Using Project Server to exchange task information with Outlook.

Chapters 10 through 13 help you put the finishing touches on a project before it begins by dealing with scheduling and resource conflicts, and then show you how to approach tracking.

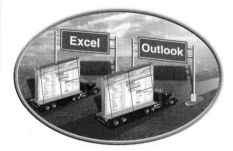

Monitoring the Project's Progress

By examining your progress on an ongoing basis from various perspectives, you can see whether you are likely to meet your goal. And, using Project makes it easy for you to quickly spot potential problems and to test alternative solutions. When you uncover time and resource conflicts early, you can try out various what-if scenarios to resolve them before the project gets out of hand. When you make adjustments to task timing and costs, Project automatically updates all other tasks in the project to reflect the changes.

Generating Professional-Looking Reports

You can create reports on the status of your project to help team members prioritize and to help management make informed decisions. The accuracy and professionalism of reports that you generate with Project can make the difference between a poorly managed project and a successful one. In addition, you can take advantage of Microsoft Visual Basic to build macros that automate repetitive tasks, such as generating weekly reports. Chapter 14 helps you produce reports in Project, and Chapter 15 helps you evaluate your progress financially. See Chapter 22 for more information about using macros to speed your work.

SELECT THE CORRECT EDITION OF PROJECT

Microsoft Office Project 2003 is available in three different editions — Project Standard, Project Professional, and Project Server.

Both Project Standard and Project Professional can be used as stand-alone products, and Project Server adds functionality to Project Professional. You need to select the

product or combination of products that best supports your needs. Please note that this book primarily covers Project Professional.

Project Standard

Using Project Standard 2003, project managers, business managers, and planners can manage schedules and resources independently, efficiently organizing and tracking tasks and resources. Project Standard 2003 integrates well with other Microsoft Office System programs like Microsoft Office PowerPoint 2003 and Microsoft Office Visio 2003, helping you present project status effectively.

Project Standard works well in environments where you plan projects independently and share resources on a limited basis.

Project Standard

Project Professional

Project Professional 2003 contains all the features you find in Project Standard, with the added advantage of supporting collaboration. Imagine a scenario where your organization manages many projects. Resource sharing is fairly extensive, and, at some point, management may want to know where things stand in a "big picture" way. Project Professional, in conjunction with Project Server, can support these needs.

Project Server

Project Server stores Microsoft Project Professional files in an SQL database on a Web server. Project and resource managers from

Project Server

all over your organization store their project information in the common Project Server database and manage the projects using a combination of Project Professional and Project Web Access, the browser-based interface for Project Server. Using Project Web Access contains features that enable resource managers to manage projects without Project Professional and team members anywhere in the world to update projects and communicate with project managers as needed and to receive, refuse, and delegate work assignments. The Project Server database supports an Enterprise Resource Pool so that you can share resources around the world. And, the Project Server database supports an Enterprise Global Template that enables you to enforce project management standards across your organization.

Optionally, your organization can use Windows SharePoint Services with the Project Server database to enable document, risk, and issue-tracking features in the Project Server database.

START PROJECT

You can start Project in several ways. You can use the Start menu or a desktop shortcut or even use the Windows Run command. When you first open Project, you see the task pane, which you find in all Office family products, as well as a blank project in the Gantt Chart view. On the left side of the Project window, you can enter task information into a table. On the right side of the default Gantt Chart view, Project displays bars that represent the duration of each task you record in the table.

The task pane in Project enables you to connect to the Office Online site, search Microsoft Project Help, open an existing project, or start a new project. Most of the choices in the task pane are hyperlinks and work similarly to links on Web pages. When you point the mouse at a link, Project displays a tip about the link; when you click a link, Project takes the action defined by the hyperlink.

How do I create a shortcut icon?

✔ Follow steps 1 to 3 in this section. For step 4, right-click Microsoft Office Project 2003 and click Send To. From the menu that appears, click Desktop (create shortcut).

START PROJECT

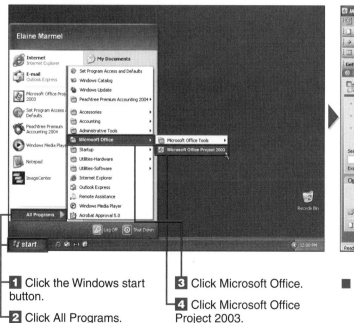

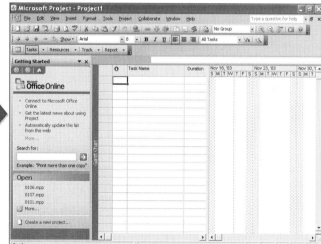

1 Click the Windows start button.

2 Click All Programs.

3 Click Microsoft Office.

4 Click Microsoft Office Project 2003.

■ Project opens.

FIRST LOOK AT PROJECT

The Project window contains several features that help you work efficiently while creating and editing projects. You can use the various toolbars and the scrollbar to navigate to the screens views that you need.

Title Bar

Displays the name of the program and current project.

Standard Toolbar

Contains buttons to help you select common commands, such as open a project or link two tasks.

Menu Bar

Lists the menu names.

Formatting Toolbar

Contains buttons to help you select formatting commands such as indent or outdent a task, or filter the project to show only certain types of tasks.

Project Guide Toolbar

Contains buttons that access various wizards to guide you through the use of Project, helping you plan and schedule tasks, add and edit resources, and track your project.

Scrollbars

Allows you to move vertically through the project and horizontally through the view's table or chart.

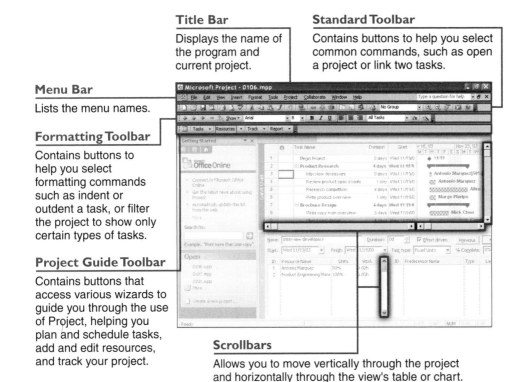

Entry Bar

Displays information already typed in a table field; you can edit information using the Entry Bar or directly in the table field.

View Area

Displays information about your project. The View Area contains, at a minimum, a table with field headings. If appropriate for the selected view, the View Area also contains a chart with a timescale.

Side Pane

Displays either the task pane that appears when you open Project or the Project Guide if you start a new project or click any of the buttons on the Project Guide toolbar.

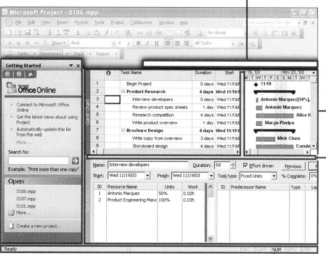

Split Bars

The vertical split bar allows you to view more of the table or the chart portion of a view. The horizontal split bar allows you to display more than one view on-screen at the same time.

Status Bar

The right side displays the current condition of the Extended Selection, Caps Lock, Num Lock, Scroll Lock, and Overtype modes. The middle section may display, if appropriate, one of two messages concerning the project's calculation mode or circular references that exist in the project.

CONTINUED ▶

FIRST LOOK AT PROJECT (CONTINUED)

Field Heading

Displays the title of each column in a table.

Select All Button

Click to Select all entries in the current table; right-click to change tables.

Active Pane Indicator

Displays the name of the active view when you display two views.

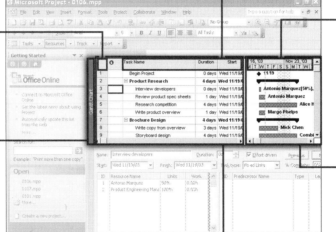

Timescale

Displays a calendar-like legend at the top of views containing time-related charts; the Gantt Chart, Task Usage, Resource Graph, and Resource Usage views.

Chart Area

The portion of a view that displays task information graphically.

Table Area

Each row displays information about a single task in a project, and each column displays a specific piece of information about that task. The intersection of a row and column is called a field.

UNDERSTANDING THE PROJECT GUIDE

The Project Guide appears automatically when you start a new project; it consists of a toolbar and a side pane area that contains a series of links that act like wizards and walk you through creating, updating, and reporting on a project.

Tasks Button

Displays links to various activities you perform relating to tasks in a project. Click ▾ to select a link or click the button to display the links in the side pane. Click a link to walk through the steps and complete the activity.

Resources Button

Displays links to various activities you perform relating to resources in a project. Click ▾ to select a link or click the button to display the links in the side pane. Click a link to walk through the steps and complete the activity.

Show/Hide Project Guide

Displays or hides the Project Guide.

Forward/Back Buttons

Click to move forward or backward through a selected link.

Side Pane

Contains a list of the activities you perform while creating, editing, or tracking a project and instructions for performing them. The list changes, depending on the Project Guide toolbar button you click.

Track Button

Displays links to various activities you perform relating to tracking in a project. Click ▾ to select a link or click the button to display the links in the side pane. Click a link to walk through the steps and complete the activity.

Report Button

Displays links to various activities you perform relating to reporting on a project. Click ▾ to select a link or click the button to display the links in the side pane. Click a link to walk through the steps and complete the activity.

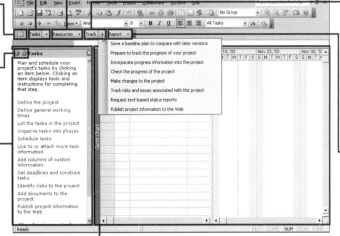

View Area

Displays Project views relevant to the activity that appears in the Side Pane. Please note that to keep screens as uncluttered as possible, this book does not show the Project Guide.

ESTABLISH BASIC SCHEDULING INFORMATION

You can use the Project Information dialog box to supply basic scheduling information for a project, such as a start date; if the project has already started, you can set the start date to a date in the past to accurately reflect the real start date. When you add new tasks, Project sets them to use the constraint type As Soon As Possible (ASAP).

While you plan a project, you can change the project's start date to try alternative what-if scenarios. As

you define tasks, Project indicates the finish date based on the length of your tasks and their timing relationships. When you are satisfied with the overall time frame, you can set the start date that works best.

Or, if you know the deadline date of the project, such as a Christmas party, you can schedule tasks by moving backward from the finish date. Be aware that Project cannot use tools, such as resource leveling, to resolve conflicts in your schedule

if you decide to schedule backward from the finish date; therefore, if possible, schedule the project from the start date. If you schedule from the project finish date, Project sets all new tasks to use the constraint type As Late As Possible (ALAP).

ESTABLISH BASIC SCHEDULING INFORMATION

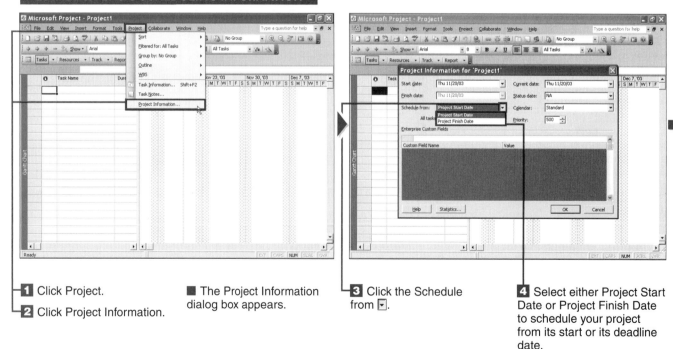

1 Click Project.

2 Click Project Information.

■ The Project Information dialog box appears.

3 Click the Schedule from ▾.

4 Select either Project Start Date or Project Finish Date to schedule your project from its start or its deadline date.

When do I use the Status Date ⏷?

✔ By default, Project sets the status date to your computer's current date setting. You change this date when you update the progress of your project or when you perform earned-value calculations. See Chapters 8 and 10 for more information.

What do the Priority numbers mean?

✔ A priority is a numerical value between 1 and 1,000 that you can assign to your project and to each task in the project. The project priority helps you to better control how resource leveling adjusts tasks in projects that use shared resources. See Chapter 7 for information on resource leveling.

What are Enterprise Custom Fields, and do I need them?

✔ Project Server lets you standardize projects by applying custom fields or outline codes uniformly. Custom fields and outline codes appear in the Project Information dialog box. You must assign values to any required custom field or outline code, which is identified by an asterisk (*) next to it.

Can I make the Project Information box appear automatically when I start a new project?

✔ Yes. Click Tools, and then click Options. On the General tab of the Options dialog box, select Prompt for project info for new projects (☐ changes to ✔).

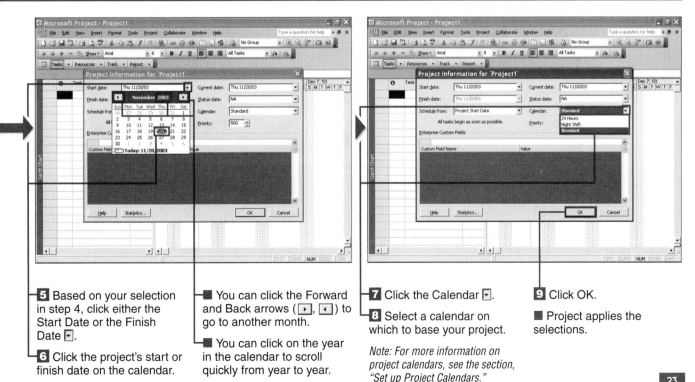

5 Based on your selection in step 4, click either the Start Date or the Finish Date ⏷.

6 Click the project's start or finish date on the calendar.

■ You can click the Forward and Back arrows (▶, ◀) to go to another month.

■ You can click on the year in the calendar to scroll quickly from year to year.

7 Click the Calendar ⏷.

8 Select a calendar on which to base your project.

Note: For more information on project calendars, see the section, "Set up Project Calendars."

9 Click OK.

■ Project applies the selections.

SET UP CALENDAR AND SCHEDULE OPTIONS

You can customize Project's handling of calendar and schedule options to match your work style. Project makes default assumptions about the base calendar that you select for your project, like a default week that contains five working days and 40 working hours. These options do not affect scheduling; Project uses them to convert durations into

corresponding time amounts. For example, if you enter 1mo for a task's duration, Project assumes that you are allotting 20 days — a working month — for that task. You can select any day of the week as your start day. You can change the fiscal year setting if your company uses a fiscal year other than the calendar year. You also can designate specific start and end

times for each day, the number of hours in a day and in a week, and the number of days in a month.

You also can control the default settings for entering tasks. You can change the default unit of time for entering task durations, which is either days, work time (hours), and whether new tasks start on the project start date or the current date.

SET UP CALENDAR AND SCHEDULE OPTIONS

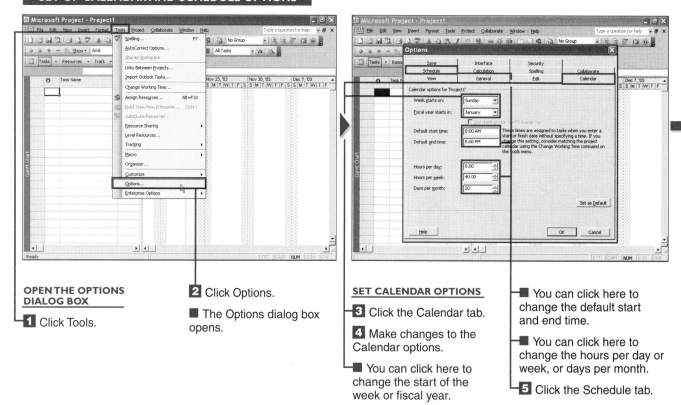

OPEN THE OPTIONS DIALOG BOX

1 Click Tools.

2 Click Options.

■ The Options dialog box opens.

SET CALENDAR OPTIONS

3 Click the Calendar tab.

4 Make changes to the Calendar options.

■ You can click here to change the start of the week or fiscal year.

■ You can click here to change the default start and end time.

■ You can click here to change the hours per day or week, or days per month.

5 Click the Schedule tab.

The options on the Calendar tab of the Options box refer to the project's calendar, but some of my tasks do not use the same schedule as the project's calendar. Can I set separate calendars for these tasks?

✔ Yes. Project supports both task calendars and resource calendars for use in setting exceptions to base calendar settings. You can set the options for the base calendar to manage the majority of tasks and resources on the project; you can use special task and resource calendars to handle exceptions. See Chapters 3 and 4, respectively, for more about task and resource calendars.

Do changes to calendar and schedule options apply to all my projects?

✔ Any changes that you make to these options apply to the current schedule only. To save your changes for all projects, click Set as Default.

Because my project information does not really have anything to do with accounting, why should I change the Fiscal year starts in setting?

✔ Making this setting match your company's fiscal year is especially useful when you generate reports that show costs per quarter or year.

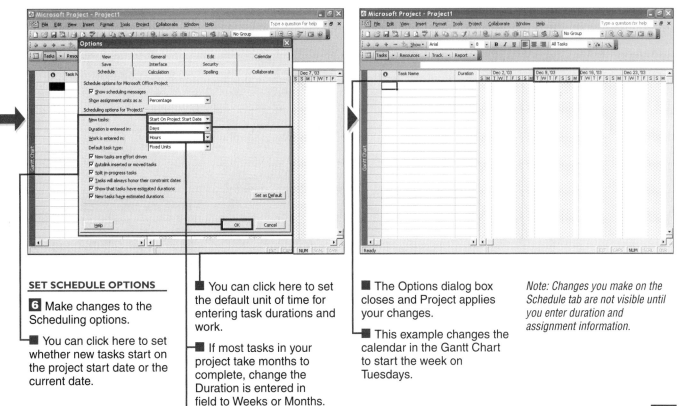

SET SCHEDULE OPTIONS

6 Make changes to the Scheduling options.

■ You can click here to set whether new tasks start on the project start date or the current date.

■ You can click here to set the default unit of time for entering task durations and work.

■ If most tasks in your project take months to complete, change the Duration is entered in field to Weeks or Months.

7 Click OK.

■ The Options dialog box closes and Project applies your changes.

■ This example changes the calendar in the Gantt Chart to start the week on Tuesdays.

Note: Changes you make on the Schedule tab are not visible until you enter duration and assignment information.

SET UP PROJECT CALENDARS

When you enter timing information for tasks in your project, Project calculates the schedule using the project's base calendar. You designate the project's calendar in the Project Information dialog box. For more information on setting the project's calendar, see the section "Establish Basic Project Scheduling Information" earlier in this chapter.

The Standard calendar assumes a Monday to Friday, 8 a.m. to 5 p.m., 40-hour workweek. However, the Standard calendar may not work for your project. If all the resources working on your project work from 11 a.m. to 8 p.m., you can change the project's working day to match the workday of your resources. Or, suppose that you run a print shop and each project that you complete requires you to use the printing press, but the press requires

cleaning and maintenance each week for two hours on Thursday afternoon. To make sure that each printing project considers the maintenance requirement of the printing press, you can create a Press calendar that considers the need to shut the press down for cleaning and maintenance. Then you can assign the Press calendar to the Press Time task that you eventually create for the project.

SET UP PROJECT CALENDARS

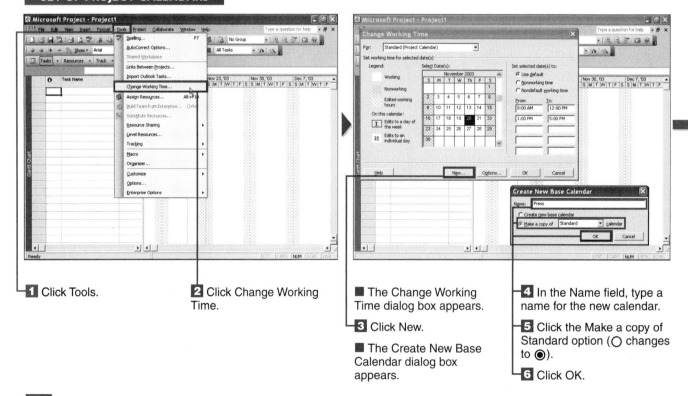

1 Click Tools.

2 Click Change Working Time.

■ The Change Working Time dialog box appears.

3 Click New.

■ The Create New Base Calendar dialog box appears.

4 In the Name field, type a name for the new calendar.

5 Click the Make a copy of Standard option (○ changes to ●).

6 Click OK.

How can I select contiguous or noncontiguous days?

✔ To select contiguous days, click the first day, press Shift, and click the last day that you want to select. To select noncontiguous days, press Ctrl and click each day that you want to select.

I accidentally changed Sunday to scheduled working time. How do I change it back to nonworking time?

✔ Reselecting a date and clicking the Use default option (◯ changes to ◉) returns the date to its originally scheduled time on that date. Therefore, selecting Sunday and clicking the Use default option tells Project not to schedule work on Sundays.

With Project Professional sometimes I can create my own calendar and at other times I cannot. Why?

✔ Your organization uses Project Server and Project Professional. Project Standard users can always set their own base calendars. Project Professional users can create their own base calendars if they work offline and store the project locally, and not in a Project Server database. For projects stored in a Project Server database, you can create base calendars only if the administrator gives you the rights to do so. Also, the privilege to create base calendars does not permit you to change the Standard calendar.

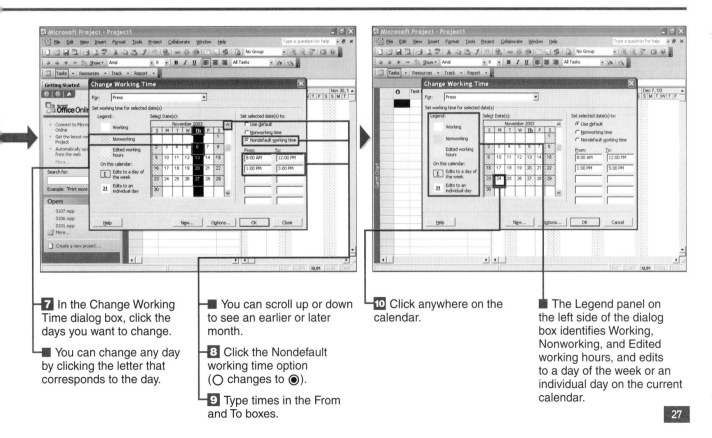

7 In the Change Working Time dialog box, click the days you want to change.

■ You can change any day by clicking the letter that corresponds to the day.

■ You can scroll up or down to see an earlier or later month.

8 Click the Nondefault working time option (◯ changes to ◉).

9 Type times in the From and To boxes.

10 Click anywhere on the calendar.

■ The Legend panel on the left side of the dialog box identifies Working, Nonworking, and Edited working hours, and edits to a day of the week or an individual day on the current calendar.

ADD TASKS AND SUBTASKS

You can build a project by entering, in the table portion of the Project window, descriptions of the major steps to reach your goal in roughly the same order that you expect them to occur. If you are not quite accurate about the sequence of events, you can easily reorganize or delete tasks in your schedule at any time. As you enter task names, Project assigns a duration in the Duration column and also displays a bar in the Gantt Chart representing the task's duration.

After you enter the major tasks in your project, you fill in the details by adding subordinate tasks, or *subtasks*, under the major tasks. When you add subtasks, the subtask appears indented under the major task that precedes it, and the major task becomes a summary task — a task comprised of other tasks. A *summary task* summarizes the duration required to complete all of its subtasks. Summary tasks and subtasks provide an easy-to-apply outline structure for your schedule.

If you start your project by entering the major tasks, then you will generally insert subtasks between tasks that already exist in the project. When you insert a new task, it appears above the currently selected task.

ADD TASKS AND SUBTASKS

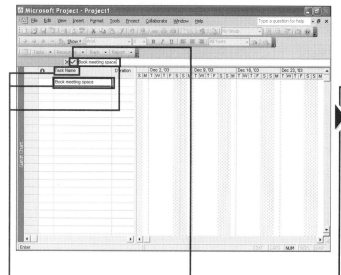

ADD A TASK

1 Click in the Task Name column.

2 Type a task description.

■ The description appears in the cell and Entry bar.

3 Press Enter or click the check mark (☑) in the Entry bar.

■ Project stores the task's description, its duration, and a Gantt bar for it.

Note: See the section "Set up Calendar and Schedule Options" for more on the durations Project assigns.

ADD A SUBTASK

4 Perform steps 1 to 3 in this section until the major tasks in the outline appear.

■ After typing a task name, you can press the Right Arrow key and type a duration, replacing the one that Project supplies.

5 Click the task that should appear below the task you want to insert.

What does the question mark (☐) in the Duration column mean?

✔ It represents an estimated duration assigned by Project using the settings stored on the Schedule tab of the Options dialog box to assign the estimated duration. When you see a ☐, you know that Project assigned the duration. Any duration that you type is not followed by a ☐.

How do I delete a task?

✔ Click the row number of the task you want to delete and press the Delete key.

How do I insert a task that is not a subtask?

✔ Follow the steps in this section to add the task in the correct location and then click the Outdent button ☐.

What do the two points on the end of the summary task bar represent?

✔ They represent the total amount of time required to complete all tasks that the summary task summarizes. Changing the timing of a subtask can make the summary task duration change also.

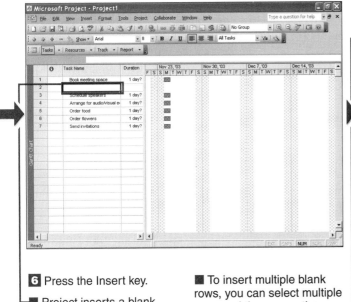

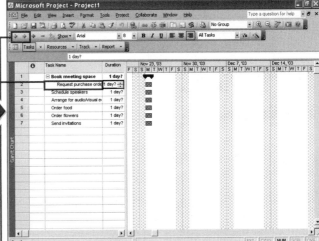

6 Press the Insert key.

■ Project inserts a blank row.

■ To insert multiple blank rows, you can select multiple rows and then press the Insert key.

7 Type the task description here.

8 Press the Tab key.

■ You can click these buttons to indent and create a subtask (☐), or outdent a task (☐).

■ Project changes the major task to a summary task.

■ The summary task appears in bold while the subtask appears in normal type.

MOVE OR COPY TASKS

You can easily move tasks in an outline using either the cut-and-paste or the drag-and-drop method. Typically, you list your tasks in the order that you intend to complete them. This helps you visually identify dependencies in the Gantt Chart. Therefore, you move tasks when their outline placement does not match their completion order. You copy tasks on occasion when you

have tasks with characteristics that closely match the characteristics of another task that you need to add to the outline.

When you move a summary task, its subtasks move with it. And, if you move a task at the highest level of the outline to a new location just below a task with subtasks, Project indents the task that you move. Similarly, if you move a subtask so that it appears below a task at the

highest level of the outline, Project outdents the subtask that you move.

You can copy tasks the same way that you move them; instead of using the Cut and Paste commands, use the Copy and Paste commands. If you prefer to drag and drop, hold down the Ctrl key while you drag the task(s) to another location. Release the mouse button to complete the copy.

MOVE OR COPY TASKS

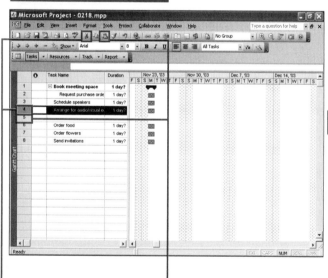

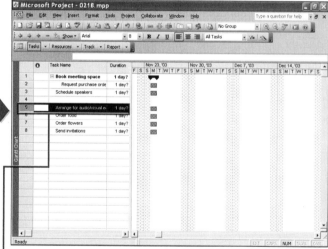

USING CUT AND PASTE

■1 Select the task that you want to move by clicking its ID number.

■2 Click the Cut button (🔳).

■ Project removes the task from the schedule.

■3 Select the row that you want to appear below the task you are moving.

■4 Click the Paste button (🔳).

■ Project moves the task you cut so that it appears above the task you selected before pasting.

■ The moved task appears selected.

Note: If you do not need the blank line, you can delete the row by clicking the row number and pressing the Delete key.

Is there an easy way to copy a summary task and all of its subtasks?

✔ Yes. To copy a summary task *and* its subtasks, you need only select the summary task and copy it. Project copies the subtasks with the summary task.

What if I make a mistake while copying or moving?

✔ Immediately undo your action. Project, unlike other Office products, contains only one level of undo. If you take any other action prior to undoing, you cannot undo; in that case, you can manually move tasks back to their original location or delete tasks that you inadvertently copied.

How do I select multiple tasks?

✔ To select several contiguous tasks, select the first task. Then hold down the Shift key and click the last task that you want to select. To select several noncontiguous tasks, hold down the Ctrl key as you select tasks.

How can I move or copy a summary task without moving or copying any of its subtasks?

✔ First, outdent all of the summary task's subtasks to the summary task's level. Then move or copy the summary task. For more on outdenting, see the section "Add Tasks and Subtasks."

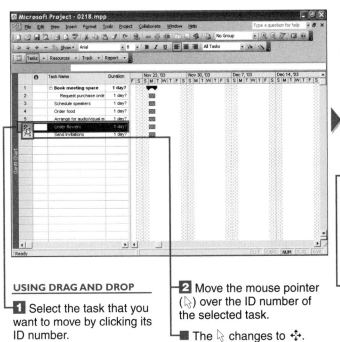

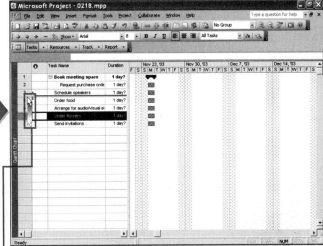

USING DRAG AND DROP

1 Select the task that you want to move by clicking its ID number.

2 Move the mouse pointer (↳) over the ID number of the selected task.

■ The ↳ changes to ✛.

3 Click and drag the task.

■ A horizontal gray line appears that represents the new position of the task.

4 Drag the task to its new location and release the mouse button.

■ The task appears in its new location.

REPEAT TASKS

You can save time by repeating tasks instead of copying them ten or 20 times. If you enter tasks in a project to test various versions of a compound to see which works best as a fixative, you may repeat the same series of tasks. For example, you may repeat the tasks Obtain compound sample, Test in various environments, and Write up test results several times.

You cannot repeat tasks that do not appear contiguously in the project schedule.

If I use the fill handle, does Project add rows or overwrite data?

✔ If the range where the new tasks will appear already contains information, Project overwrites the existing information. To avoid this, insert blank rows in the project before using the fill handle. See the section "Add Tasks and Subtasks" for more information about inserting tasks.

How do I select contiguous tasks?

✔ To select contiguous tasks, click the Task Name — not the ID — of the first task, hold down the Shift key and click the Task Name of the last task.

REPEAT TASKS

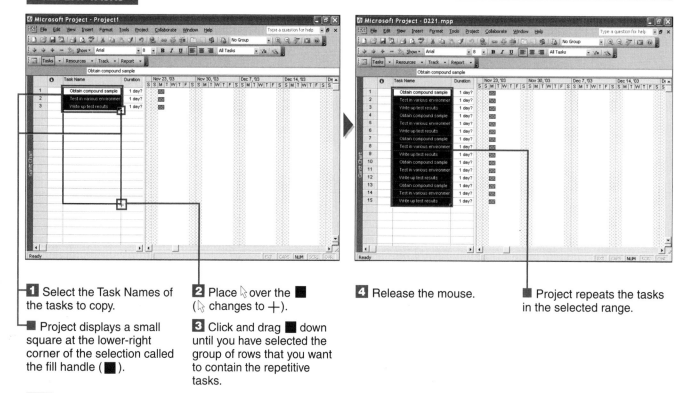

1 Select the Task Names of the tasks to copy.

■ Project displays a small square at the lower-right corner of the selection called the fill handle (■).

2 Place ⌘ over the ■ (⌘ changes to +).

3 Click and drag ■ down until you have selected the group of rows that you want to contain the repetitive tasks.

4 Release the mouse.

■ Project repeats the tasks in the selected range.

HIDE OR DISPLAY TASKS

You can manipulate the project outline structure to show more or less detail about your project by expanding or collapsing the summary tasks. By collapsing or expanding summary tasks, you essentially hide or show tasks in the project. You can use the hide and show features of Project to focus on just the amount of detail that you want. For example, you may want to show just the highest level of detail for a report to management to summarize project activity.

Using many levels of outline indentation makes it difficult to see your entire schedule on-screen. And, a very detailed project outline may indicate that you need to rethink the scope of the project and break it into smaller, more manageable projects.

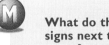

What do the minus and plus signs next to some tasks mean?

✔ A minus sign (⊟) to the left of each summary task indicates that all subtasks are in view. If you click ⊟, any subtasks disappear from view and a plus sign (⊞) replaces ⊟ next to the summary task name. The ⊞ indicates that the task is associated with some hidden detail tasks. You can click ⊞ to reveal the hidden subtasks.

HIDE OR DISPLAY TASKS

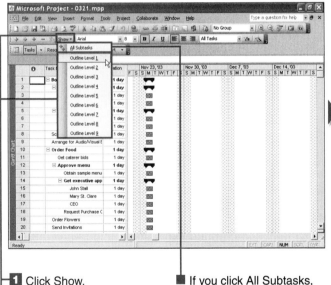

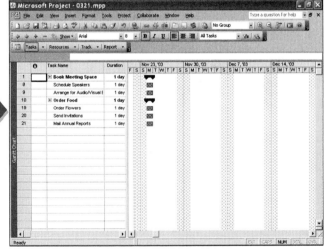

1 Click Show.

2 Select an outline level to view.

■ If you click All Subtasks, Project displays the entire project.

■ Project expands or contracts the outline as appropriate.

SAVE PROJECT FILES

You can save your project to store it for future use. With the often-mission-critical information that is stored in a Project file, you should always save your work frequently. If there is an equipment failure or power loss, you may lose the work you completed since the last time you saved the project.

The first time that you save a project, you assign it a name and a location. You should use a

descriptive name that helps you identify the project later. After the first time that you save the project, Project does not prompt you for a name and location.

For filenames, you can type up to 255 characters, including spaces, but you cannot use characters such as *, ^, colons (:), or semicolons (;). Project automatically assigns an extension of .mpp to each Project file.

Once you save a project, you can close it to remove it from your screen without exiting from Project. If you want to close Project, too, you can utilize the Close button in the upper-right corner of the Project window, or the Exit command in the File menu. If you do not save any open files, Project prompts you to do so.

SAVE PROJECT FILES

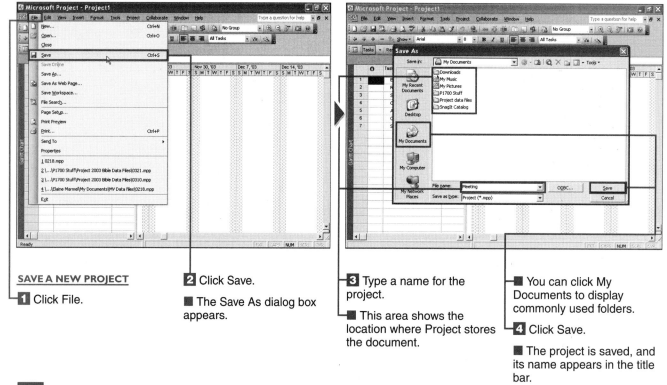

SAVE A NEW PROJECT

1 Click File.

2 Click Save.

■ The Save As dialog box appears.

3 Type a name for the project.

■ This area shows the location where Project stores the document.

■ You can click My Documents to display commonly used folders.

4 Click Save.

■ The project is saved, and its name appears in the title bar.

How do I save my Project 2003 file so that someone using Project 2000 can open it?

✔ You do not need to do anything differently. Project 2003, Project 2002, and Project 2000 share the same file format.

How do I save my Project 2003 file so that someone using Project 98 can open it?

✔ You can save a Project 2003 file in Project 98 format. In the Save As dialog box, click the Save As Type ⊡ and select Microsoft Project 98 (*.mpp).

I saved my project but want to change the filename. How can I do that?

✔ The easiest way is to open the project, click File, and then click Save As. In the Save As dialog box, you can supply a different filename.

Can I save a Project file as an Access database?

✔ Yes. You can also save a Project file as an Excel workbook or PivotTable. In the Save As dialog box, click the Save As Type ⊡ and select Microsoft Access Database, Microsoft Excel Workbook, or Microsoft Excel PivotTable.

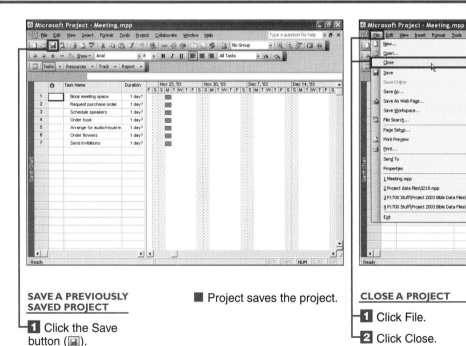

SAVE A PREVIOUSLY SAVED PROJECT

1 Click the Save button (🖫).

■ Project saves the project.

CLOSE A PROJECT

1 Click File.

2 Click Close.

■ Project closes the project file.

■ You also can click the Close button (☒) to close the Project.

Note: Be sure to click the button for the project window (☒), not the program window (☒).

PROTECT FILES

Some projects are top secret; as such, some people within the organization — and certainly people from outside the organization — should not have access to the details. If your project falls into this category, you can set up protection for it when you save it.

You can set up two different kinds of passwords for any given file. A protection password safeguards

the file from being opened. Only someone with the assigned password can open a file that you protect in this way. A Write reservation password allows others to open the file but does not permit viewers to make any changes to the file. That is, a Write reservation password allows anyone to open the file as a *read-only* file.

Project provides one other level of security for your files — you can set an option that displays a message when anyone opens the file, recommending that the user not make changes to the file. Be aware that this choice is merely a suggestion; it does not prevent someone from making changes.

PROTECT FILES

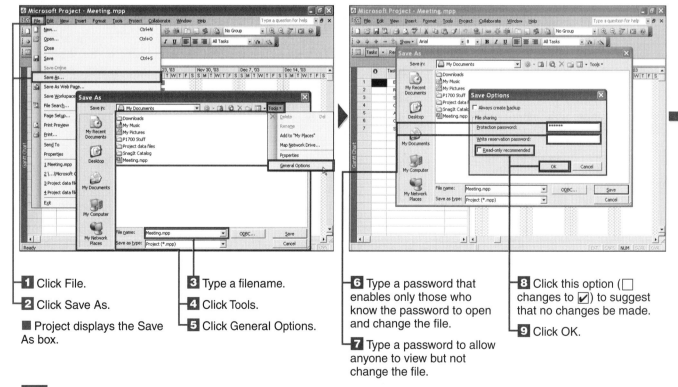

1 Click File.

2 Click Save As.

■ Project displays the Save As box.

3 Type a filename.

4 Click Tools.

5 Click General Options.

6 Type a password that enables only those who know the password to open and change the file.

7 Type a password to allow anyone to view but not change the file.

8 Click this option (☐ changes to ☑) to suggest that no changes be made.

9 Click OK.

What kind of passwords should I use?

✔ Consider two factors: You must be able to remember the password, and you must make it something that the average person is unlikely to guess. No password is perfect; if someone really wants to break into your files, it can be done. Try using passwords such as an address or phone number that you had as a child — information that you remember but others are not likely to know. Do not use your phone extension, birthday, or spouse's name as a password. Such passwords are much too easy to crack!

What do I do if I change my mind and do not want a password associated with the file?

✔ Repeat the steps as described, but delete the password(s).

Are passwords case-sensitive?

✔ Yes. Both the Protection password and Write reservation password are case-sensitive. If you assign a password of GayleK, you cannot open the file if you type **gaylek**.

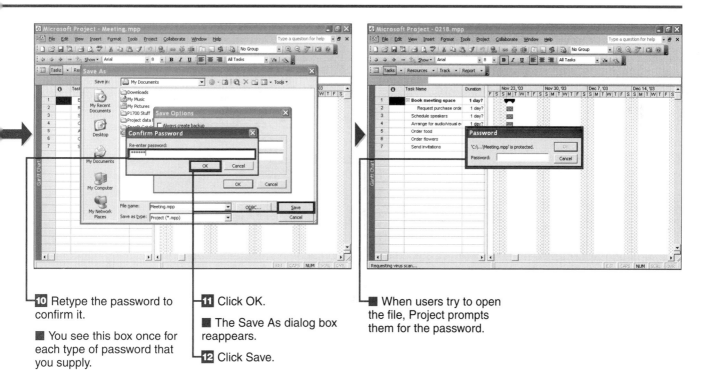

10 Retype the password to confirm it.

■ You see this box once for each type of password that you supply.

11 Click OK.

■ The Save As dialog box reappears.

12 Click Save.

■ When users try to open the file, Project prompts them for the password.

SAVE FILES AS TEMPLATES

Y ou can save Project files as templates; that is, files on which you can base other schedules. Template files have an .mpt extension.

The template feature is especially useful in project management because your projects are often similar to previous or future projects. A template file saves all the settings that you may have made for a particular project, such as formatting, commonly performed tasks, and calendar choices. Keeping template files on hand can save your coworkers, or you, from having to reinvent the wheel each time that you want to build a similar project.

Can I just save my previous project's file with a new name and use that for my next project?
✔ Yes, you can, but after you track progress on tasks, opening that final project file and stripping it back to its baseline settings is a cumbersome process — a project in and of itself. Saving the initial schedule as a template on which you can build new schedules is much easier.

If I am saving an existing project as a template, how do I get to the dialog box?
✔ Click File and then click Save As.

SAVE FILES AS TEMPLATES

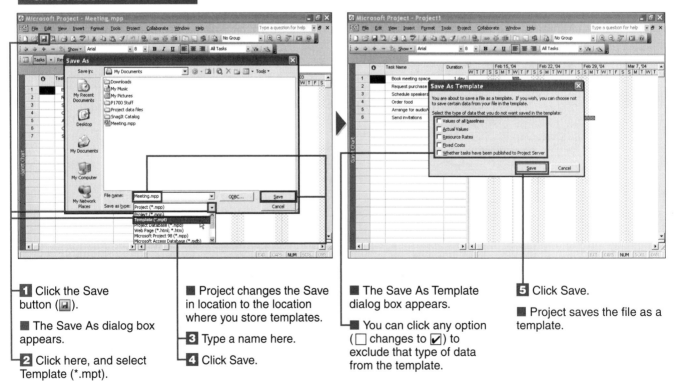

■1 Click the Save button (icon).

■ The Save As dialog box appears.

■2 Click here, and select Template (*.mpt).

■ Project changes the Save in location to the location where you store templates.

■3 Type a name here.

■4 Click Save.

■ The Save As Template dialog box appears.

■ You can click any option (☐ changes to ☑) to exclude that type of data from the template.

■5 Click Save.

■ Project saves the file as a template.

SAVE OPTIONS

You can speed up opening and saving projects if you specify the locations where you want to store Project files and Project templates. Using the locations you specify, Project, by default, displays those locations when you open or save a project or template or when you want to start a new project using a template. You can store your Project files and templates in any location you want — in any folder on any disk to which you have access.

By default, Project stores new projects in the My Documents folder on your C drive, and Project stores templates in the \Documents and Settings\ User Name\Application Data\Microsoft\Templates folder. Note that the predefined templates that come with Project are stored in the \Program Files\Microsoft Office\Templates\1033 folder.

What if I do not see the folder I want listed?
✔ You may need to click the Look in 🔽 to navigate through the drive and folder structure to find the folder. Or, you can create a new folder by clicking the Create New Folder button (🗁) at the top right of the Modify Location dialog box; type a folder name, and click OK.

SAVE OPTIONS

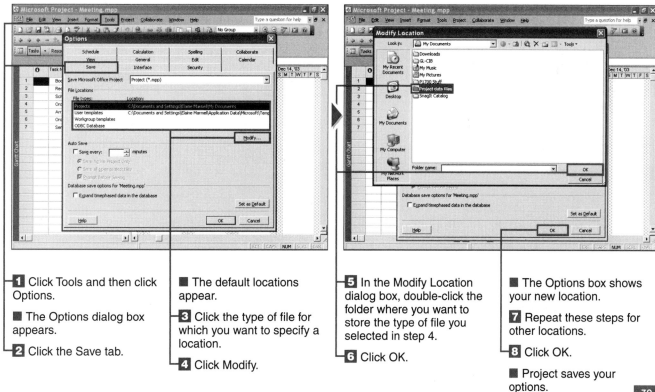

1 Click Tools and then click Options.

■ The Options dialog box appears.

2 Click the Save tab.

■ The default locations appear.

3 Click the type of file for which you want to specify a location.

4 Click Modify.

5 In the Modify Location dialog box, double-click the folder where you want to store the type of file you selected in step 4.

6 Click OK.

■ The Options box shows your new location.

7 Repeat these steps for other locations.

8 Click OK.

■ Project saves your options.

OPEN AN EXISTING PROJECT FILE

You can open a previously saved project in a couple of ways. You can use the Getting Started task pane that Project displays on the left side of the screen when you open the program. Or, you can use the Open dialog box.

The Getting Started task pane displays recently opened files; if the file you want to open appears in the

Getting Started pane, you can open the file by clicking it. Otherwise, use the Open dialog box.

If you use Project Server, Project displays the Open from Microsoft Project Server window so that you can select a project that is available through Project Server. If your project is not stored in the Project

Server database, use the Open from File option to displays the Open dialog box.

Using the Open dialog box, you can navigate to a particular drive and folder using the Places bar, which displays the contents of commonly used folders. Or, you can open the Look in list to display the drives and folders to which you have access.

OPEN AN EXISTING PROJECT FILE

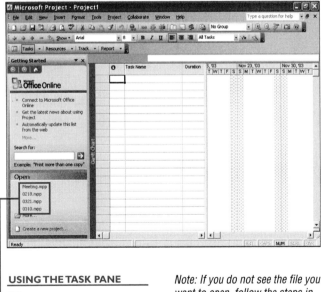

USING THE TASK PANE

1 Click the file you want to open.

Note: If you do not see the file you want to open, follow the steps in the subsection "Using a Dialog Box."

■ Project opens the file.

USING A DIALOG BOX

1 Click the Open button (■).

■ If you see the file you want to open in the Open portion of the Task Pane, follow the steps in the subsection, "Using the Task Pane."

■ You can click More in the Open section of the Getting Started task pane to display the Open dialog box

■ The Open dialog box appears.

I do not see the Getting Started task pane; I see the Project Guide pane. Can I display the Getting Started pane?

✔ Yes. Right-click any toolbar and select Task Pane.

I do not see the Getting Started task pane; I see the Search Results pane. Can I display the Getting Started pane?

✔ Yes. If you see the Search Results pane, the Help pane, or the New Project pane on the left side of the screen, click the task pane arrow (▾), and then click Getting Started.

Can I open a file I used recently without displaying the Task Pane?

✔ Yes. Project displays the names of the last four files you opened at the bottom of the File menu. To open one of these files, click File and then click the file you want to open. You can change the number of recently used file names that appear at the bottom of the File menu in the Options dialog box. Click Tools and then click Options. When the box appears, click the General tab and adjust the number that appears in the Recently used file box.

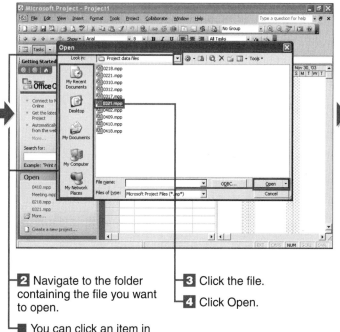

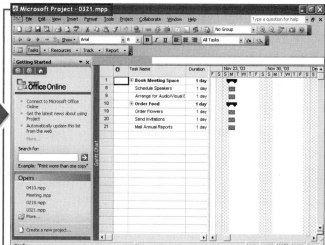

2 Navigate to the folder containing the file you want to open.

■ You can click an item in the Look in list to display a list of folders on your computer.

3 Click the file.

4 Click Open.

■ Project opens the file, and the filename appears in the title bar.

BASE A PROJECT ON A TEMPLATE

When you first start Project, you see a blank project that you can use to create a project. The blank project that you see is based on Project's default template, which includes settings for page margins, a default font, and other settings appropriate for a typical project. A template for your organization may include specific views, tables, filters, and groups, including custom views, tables, filters, and groups that you create to meet the needs of your environment. You can read more about creating custom views in Chapter 6, creating custom tables in Chapter 7, and creating custom filters and groups in Chapter 8.

To help you create a project more quickly, you can base your project on one of the predefined templates that first became available in Project 2000. These templates contain settings and tasks common to a particular kind of project. Instead of entering tasks, you may need only to edit tasks. You find templates installed on your computer, and you can search for additional templates at the Office Online Web site.

BASE A PROJECT ON A TEMPLATE

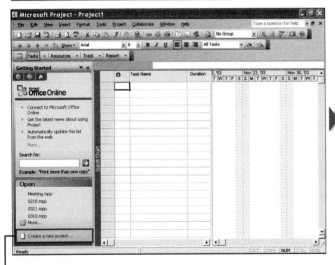

1 Click Create a new project.

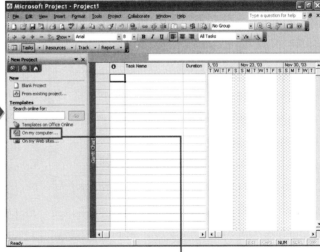

■ Project displays the New Project pane.

2 Click the On my computer link.

When should I create my own template?

✔ The template feature is especially useful in project management when the projects in your organization are similar to each other. In a template file, you can save features such as formatting, commonly performed tasks, calendar choices, specific views, tables, filters, and groups that you use on a regular basis. Creating template files keeps you from having to reinvent the wheel each time that you want to build a similar project.

Can I create my own templates?

✔ Yes. See the section "Save Files as Templates" earlier in this chapter for more on creating templates.

To create a project based on a template, do I need to close the blank project that Project first presents?

✔ No. You can open simultaneously as many projects as your computer's memory permits.

When I try to use a template, I receive a message about needing my Project 2003 CD. Why?

✔ Depending on the method you use to install Project, you may not have initially installed the templates. Insert your Project 2003 CD and Project installs the template.

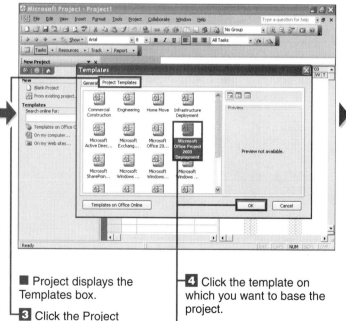

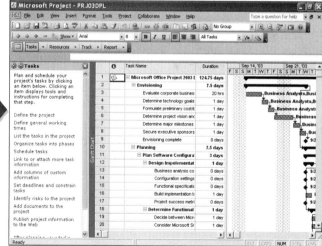

■ Project displays the Templates box.

3 Click the Project Templates tab.

4 Click the template on which you want to base the project.

5 Click OK.

■ Project displays a new project containing the content stored in the template.

GET HELP

You can get help on various aspects of Project using the Help system. In Help information, you often find the steps required to complete a procedure, a See Also hyperlink that takes you to related topics, and even demos.

To get Help, you can use the Type a question text box that appears at the right edge of the menu bar. You can use this box to search for help using keywords much the way you use the index of a book.

You can also open the Assistance pane on the left side of your screen via the Help menu on the Standard toolbar. The Search for box in the Assistance pane functions the same way that the Type a question box on the menu bar functions. When you search from either location, Project automatically searches both the Project Help file and online resources.

From the Assistance pane, you also can display the Help Table of Contents link. The Table of Contents is a good way to get help if you know the general topic that you want to learn about but perhaps do not know enough about the terminology to type a specific phrase or term in the Search box.

GET HELP

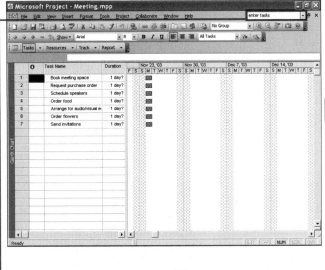

SEARCH THE INDEX

1 Click here and type a question or phrase.

2 Press Enter.

■ Help searches for topics online and on your computer.

■ Topics related to your question appear in the Search Results pane.

3 Click the link for a topic of interest.

■ The information for that topic appears in a Help window or on a Web page.

How do I navigate using the Assistance pane?

✔ Open the pane by clicking Help, and then Microsoft Project Help. Type a phrase in the Search for box and press Enter. You can click the buttons at the top of the pane to go back (🔘) and forward (🔘). Click the Home icon (🏠) to return to the Getting Started pane.

What happened to the Office Assistant?

✔ The Office Assistant is still available, but it is no longer installed by default. Most people use either the Type a question box on the menu bar or the Search for box on the Assistance pane.

What do the two kinds of icons next to topics signify?

✔ Help searches online and the Project Help file for topics and the icons distinguish between them. Icons in square pages (🔲) represent online topics, and icons in circles (🔘) represent Project Help file topics.

Can I prevent Help from searching online?

✔ Yes. Click the ⬇ on the Assistance pane to scroll down to the bottom of the pane. Click the Online Content Settings link to display the Service Options dialog box, where you can control online searching settings.

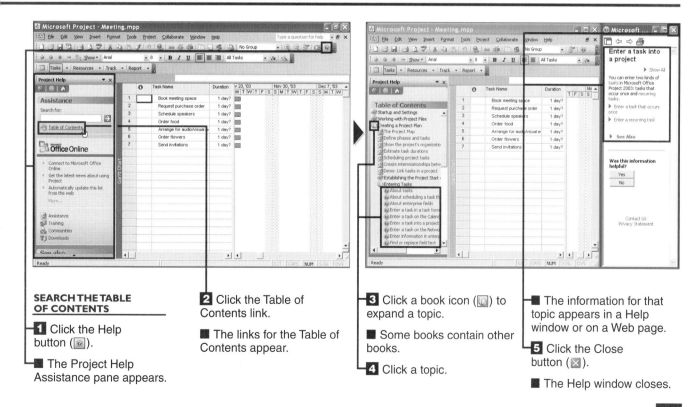

SEARCH THE TABLE OF CONTENTS

■1 Click the Help button (🔘).

■ The Project Help Assistance pane appears.

■2 Click the Table of Contents link.

■ The links for the Table of Contents appear.

■3 Click a book icon (📖) to expand a topic.

■ Some books contain other books.

■4 Click a topic.

■ The information for that topic appears in a Help window or on a Web page.

■5 Click the Close button (✕).

■ The Help window closes.

SECTION II

Project 2003 • Project 2003 • Project 2003 •

GET YOUR PROJECT GOING

HOW PROJECT HANDLES TASK TIMING

On projects, timing is everything. Understanding how Project handles timing helps you accurately plan. When you list the steps for your goal, Project assigns the default length of one estimated day to each task, and all tasks start on the same day. Without related timing constraints, the tasks in your schedule may as well be a shopping list. In Project, you establish how long each task takes by assigning a duration and how long the project takes by establishing task relationships, called *dependencies*.

You estimate the duration for a task in a project by making educated guesses. For example, to calculate the arrival time of a shipped product, you include the product's manufacturing and shipping time in your estimate. Accurately estimating durations in Project requires that you understand how Project handles specific task timing issues.

Duration is the working days portion of calendar time a task takes to complete, *work* is the amount of effort necessary to complete a task, and *units* are the number of resources, given as a percentage, that you assign to a task. For example, if it takes from start of day Monday to end of day Thursday to paint a room, the task duration is four days. Painting a room may take 96 hours of effort. If you assign three full time resources, units equal 300 percent. Project allows use of three types of tasks based on the duration, work, or units.

Fixed-Unit Tasks

By default, Project creates fixed-unit tasks for which the values, or units, of the assigned resources do not change if you change the amount of work or the task's duration.

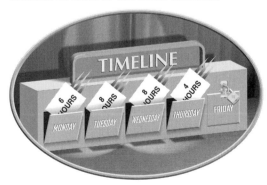

Fixed-Duration Tasks

With this type of task, the number of resources you assign does not affect the task's duration. For example, pregnancy takes approximately nine months — placing additional people on the job does not speed up the process. Likewise, you cannot change the duration of a week-long conference by adding people to work on it.

Fixed-Work Tasks

For this type of task, the effort — work — is a set amount that does not change; you set the duration of the task, and Project assigns a percentage of effort sufficient to complete the task in the time that you allot for each assigned resource. For example, if you assign two people to work on a one-day task, Project assigns each person 50 percent of his or her time on the task to complete it in one day. Similarly, if a task takes 32 hours to complete — its fixed-work value — then one resource, working eight hours a day, needs four days to complete the task. Two resources, working eight hours a day, need two days to complete the task.

Effort-Driven Tasks

By definition, Project's fixed-unit and fixed-duration tasks are effort-driven, but you can turn off this setting. When a fixed-unit task is effort-driven, the number of assigned resources affects the amount of time to complete the task. For example, one person cleaning a house may take four hours, but adding a second person decreases the total time to two hours. When the fixed-unit task is not effort-driven, the number of assigned resources does not affect the duration of the task; Project simply adds another person to the task.

You may not find the effort-driven, fixed-duration task as straightforward to understand as other task types because the duration does not change — and you may wonder how to make the fixed-duration task effort-driven. For example, if you create a non-effort-driven fixed-duration task requiring 100 percent effort from one person for four days, and add a second person, Project assumes that you need 200 percent effort to complete the task in four days and does not change the duration of the task. If, however, you create an effort-driven, fixed-

duration task requiring 100 percent effort from one person for four days, and you add another person to the task, Project reallocates the amount of effort to 50 percent from both assigned resources without changing the duration of the task.

Effort-driven scheduling kicks in after you assign resources to tasks, when you add or delete resource assignments. Note that Project calculates the time required on an effort-driven task mathematically, and does not consider that the personnel working on a task need time to communicate and hold meetings.

Padding

Because delays are inevitable, most project managers make accommodations for them in different ways. You can *pad*, or build in extra time at the task level, by adding a day or two to each task's duration; however, this can create an impossibly long schedule and raise questions if you allot two days to run a three-hour test. If you can justify your estimates — for example, you know that setting up the test parameters properly the first time is an error-prone process — you can make a case for building a project schedule based on a worst-case scenario.

Alternatively, you can add one long task at the end of the schedule that acts as a placeholder in the event that individual tasks run late. This approach can help you gauge how far behind a project is; if you scheduled two weeks for the final task and it is running a week late, you know that you have eaten up half of the slack that the task represents.

You can also build a schedule showing best-case timing, document any problems and delays that occur, and request additional time as needed. This works best for projects that you must complete quickly; however, best-case timing sets you up for potential missed deadlines.

ASSIGN DURATIONS

Using the information in the section "How Project Handles Task Timing," you can accurately enter durations for tasks because you understand how task timing relates resources expending effort on a task. The actual process of assigning durations is simple.

To assign a duration to a task, you can use one of three methods: you can use the Task Information dialog box to enter and view information

about all aspects of a task, including its timing, constraints, dependencies, resources, and priority in the overall project; you can enter a duration in the Duration column of the Gantt table; or you can use your mouse to change a task bar to the required length. Because Project displays the sum of all subtask time in summary tasks, you can only enter time for subtasks.

If you prefer to enter work values instead of durations, you can enter the work value after assigning the

resources to the task. Project then calculates task duration. See Chapter 4 for more information on assigning resources to tasks.

In addition to regular tasks, project managers use milestones to mark key events in a project, such as the completion of a phase or the approval of a product. In Project, milestones are tasks that usually have zero duration.

ASSIGN DURATIONS

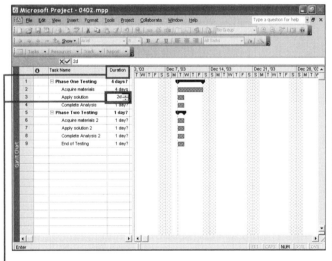

USING THE GANTT TABLE

1 Click the duration column.

2 Type a number, using h, d, w, or m for hours, days, weeks, or months.

Note: Project recognizes 3w, 3wks, 3weeks as three weeks.

3 Press Enter.

■ Project enters the duration, and the Gantt bar grows to reflect it.

USING THE MOUSE

1 Point the mouse (🖑) at the right edge of a task bar (the 🖑 changes to ↔).

2 Click and drag the bar to the right.

3 Release the mouse when you see the duration and finish date that you want in the box.

■ Project assigns the new duration.

How do I enter durations for summary tasks?

✔ You do not because they do not have any timing of their own. If three subtasks occur one after the other and each is three days long, their summary task takes nine days from beginning to end.

Does a milestone require a zero duration?

✔ No. You can mark any task as a milestone. On the Advanced tab of the Task Information dialog box, click the Mark task as milestone option (☐ changes to ☑). The task duration does not change to zero, but Project replaces the bar that represents the task in the Gantt Chart to a milestone diamond (◆).

Can I enter durations using the Start and Finish dates in the Task Information dialog box?

✔ Yes, but when you do, Project calculates the duration using only working days in that date range, without considering weekends and holidays. If you enter a duration, Project calculates the beginning and end of the task, taking into consideration weekends and holidays. These two methods can have different results.

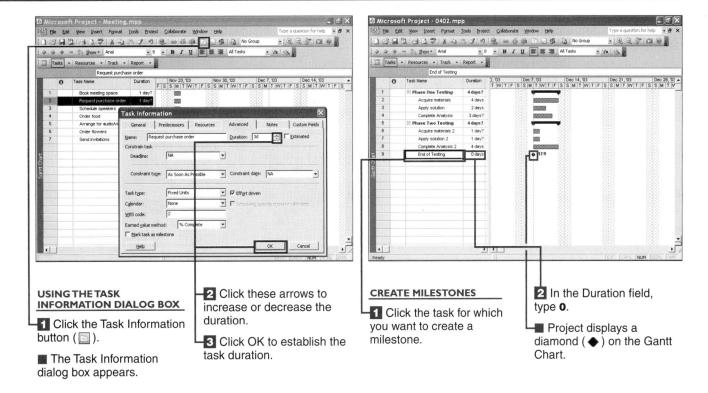

USING THE TASK INFORMATION DIALOG BOX

1 Click the Task Information button (▦).

■ The Task Information dialog box appears.

2 Click these arrows to increase or decrease the duration.

3 Click OK to establish the task duration.

CREATE MILESTONES

1 Click the task for which you want to create a milestone.

2 In the Duration field, type **0**.

■ Project displays a diamond (◆) on the Gantt Chart.

ESTABLISH DEADLINE DATES

You can set a deadline date for any task in a Project schedule. When you set a deadline date for a task, Project displays an indicator to alert you that you set the deadline. Project does not use the deadline date when calculating the schedule of a project. However, you can use the deadline indicator to display the deadline information.

Although deadline dates do not affect the calculation of a project schedule, they do affect a Late Finish date and the calculation of total slack for the project. In a project that you schedule from a beginning date, a deadline date has the same effect as a Finish No Later Than constraint. If you assign deadline dates to tasks in projects that you schedule from an ending

date, those tasks will finish on their deadline dates unless a constraint or a dependency pushes them to an earlier date. See the section "Establish Constraints" later in this chapter for information on constraints.

ESTABLISH DEADLINE DATES

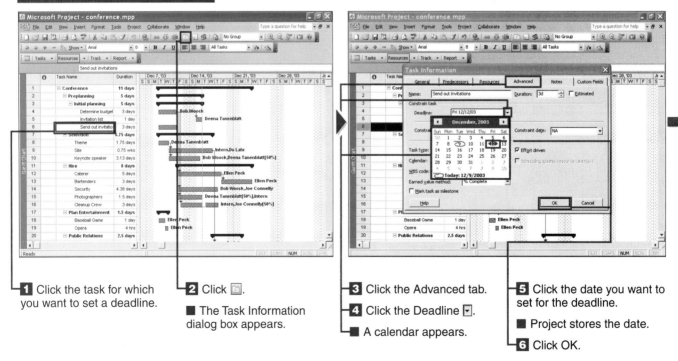

1 Click the task for which you want to set a deadline.

2 Click ▣.

■ The Task Information dialog box appears.

3 Click the Advanced tab.

4 Click the Deadline ▾.

■ A calendar appears.

5 Click the date you want to set for the deadline.

■ Project stores the date.

6 Click OK.

When should I use a deadline date instead of a milestone?

✔ Use deadline dates as visual reminders of completion dates for activities or milestones you hope to achieve. They provide an easy way to show the difference between the scheduled view of the world and the desired view. If the annual budget is due on December 15 but you want to finish it by December 1, set a December 1 deadline date. The budget document can appear as a milestone.

Are deadline dates and constraints related?

✔ Not really. Their major distinction is that Project uses constraints when calculating a project's schedule but does not use the deadline date when calculating a project's schedule.

When should I use a deadline date instead of a constraint?

✔ You do not need to make the choice. You can assign both a deadline date and a constraint to a task. Be aware, however, that constraints are not flexible because Project uses them to calculate the schedule.

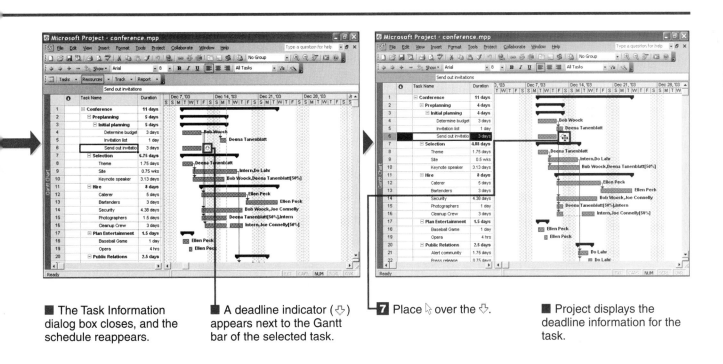

■ The Task Information dialog box closes, and the schedule reappears.

■ A deadline indicator (⟐) appears next to the Gantt bar of the selected task.

7 Place ⟐ over the ⟐.

■ Project displays the deadline information for the task.

ASSIGN A CALENDAR TO A TASK

By default, Project uses the project's standard calendar to calculate the project schedule. You may have situations, however, where the standard calendar works fine for the majority of the project, but does not work for certain tasks or resources. You can create and assign separate calendars to tasks and resources that take precedence over the project calendar for scheduling purposes. For more

information on assigning calendars to resources, see Chapter 4.

By default, Project uses the standard calendar, which assumes a 40-hour work week running Monday through Friday, beginning at 8 a.m. and ending at 5 p.m. While that work week may work for the majority of your project, it may not work for certain tasks in the project. Suppose that your project involves chemical mixtures that must react together for a

specified period of time, regardless of the hours that your resources work. You can create a special calendar for the chemical mixture reaction period and assign it to the task so that the chemical reaction works on a 24-hour schedule while the rest of your resources work on an eight-hour schedule.

You can create a task calendar the same way that you create a project calendar; see Chapter 2 for details.

ASSIGN A CALENDAR TO A TASK

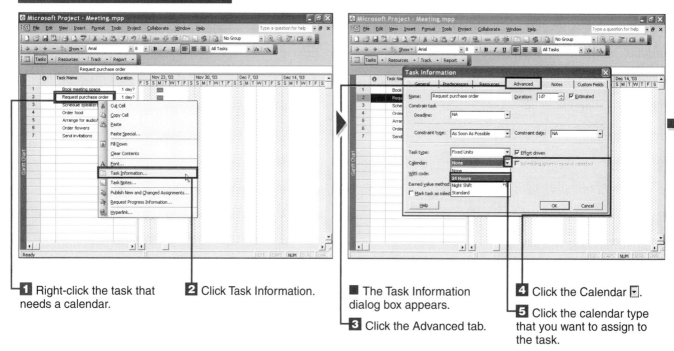

1 Right-click the task that needs a calendar.

2 Click Task Information.

■ The Task Information dialog box appears.

3 Click the Advanced tab.

4 Click the Calendar ▾.

5 Click the calendar type that you want to assign to the task.

What happens if I assign a task calendar without clicking the Scheduling ignores resource calendars option?

✔ Project schedules the task without considering the calendars of any assigned resources. If the resources are not available when Project applies the task calendar, you create a conflict because Project still schedules the task using the task calendar.

If I interrupt work on a project, should I use a task calendar and specify the interruption period as non-working time?

✔ You may prefer to use a split task, which provides a more visual representation of interrupted work. For more on split tasks, see Chapter 10.

In what order does Project use calendars when calculating the schedule?

✔ Project uses the project calendar first, the resource calendar next, and the task calendar last. If you do not assign resources or a task calendar to a task, Project schedules the task using the project calendar. If you assign resources to a task but do not assign a task calendar, Project schedules the task by first considering the resource calendars. If you assign resources and a task calendar, then Project's behavior depends on whether you selected the Scheduling ignores resource calendars option (☐ changes to ☑).

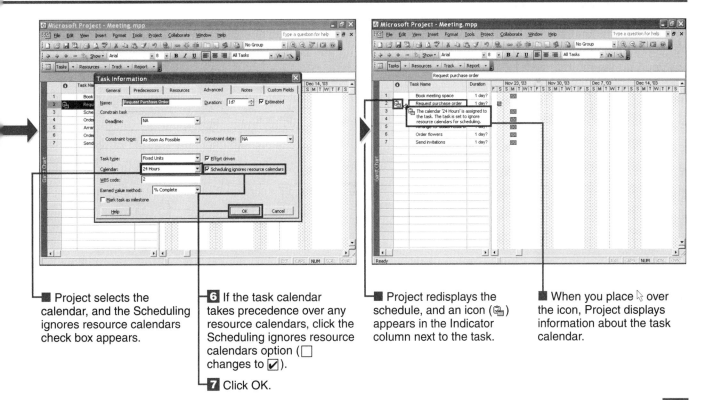

■ Project selects the calendar, and the Scheduling ignores resource calendars check box appears.

6 If the task calendar takes precedence over any resource calendars, click the Scheduling ignores resource calendars option (☐ changes to ☑).

7 Click OK.

■ Project redisplays the schedule, and an icon (🗓) appears in the Indicator column next to the task.

■ When you place ▷ over the icon, Project displays information about the task calendar.

ENTER AND PRINT TASK NOTES

Inevitably, you collect information that applies to specific tasks as you plan and track your project. You can attach notes to individual tasks to remind you of certain details of the task. For example, if a task involves several subcontractors, you can list their contact information. You can also use notes to document company regulations related to a procedure or to remind yourself to return a piece of rental equipment.

You can even store Web site addresses for easy access — Project formats the addresses as hyperlinks so that you can immediately visit the Web site.

You can format the information that appears in notes using typical word processing formatting. You can apply boldface, italics, or underline to the text, as well as select the font, font size, and font color. In addition, you can create bulleted lists and control paragraph

formatting by applying left, center, or right justification.

You can display the note on-screen or include it in a printed report. Once you activate the Print notes option in the Page Setup – Gantt Chart dialog box, Project prints all task notes the next time you print the Gantt Chart view. See Chapter 6 for information on printing your project.

ENTER AND PRINT TASK NOTES

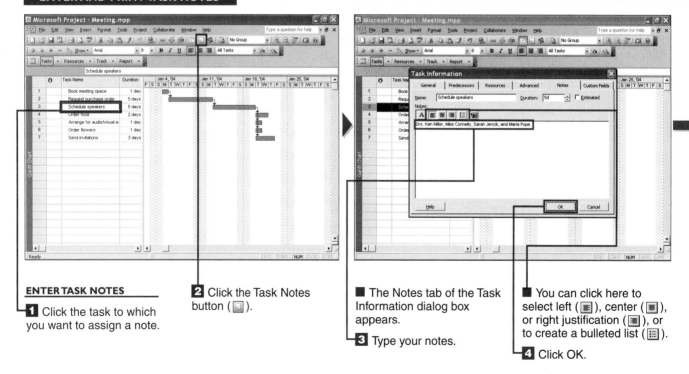

ENTER TASK NOTES

1 Click the task to which you want to assign a note.

2 Click the Task Notes button ( ).

■ The Notes tab of the Task Information dialog box appears.

3 Type your notes.

■ You can click here to select left ( ), center ( ), or right justification ( ), or to create a bulleted list ( ).

4 Click OK.

How do I change the font in my note?

✔ While viewing the Note tab of the Task Information dialog box, click the Format Font tool (▲) on the toolbar. Project displays the Font dialog box, where you can select the font and font size, and apply boldface, italics, underline, or color to the text.

How do I quickly remove notes that I added to several tasks without editing each task individually?

✔ There is an easy way. Select the tasks that contain the notes that you want to remove. Click Edit, Clear, and then Notes. Project deletes the notes.

Can I include a graphic image from my hard drive in a note?

✔ Yes. Click the Insert Object button (▣) on the toolbar above the area where you type the text. Project displays the Insert Object dialog box. Click the Create from File option (○ changes to ◉), and navigate to the file on your hard disk.

How do I store a hyperlink in a note?

✔ Type it on the Notes tab where you usually place text. To use the hyperlink, click the Notes tab of the Task Information dialog box, and click the link.

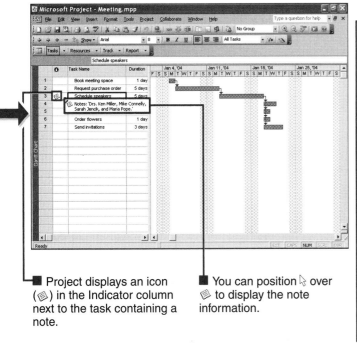

■ Project displays an icon (▣) in the Indicator column next to the task containing a note.

■ You can position ▷ over ▣ to display the note information.

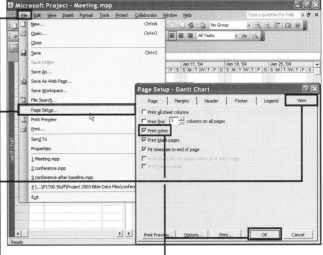

PRINT TASK NOTES

1 Click File.

2 Click Page Setup.

3 In the Page Setup – Gantt Chart dialog box, click the View tab.

4 Click the Print notes option (☐ changes to ☑).

5 Click OK.

■ The next time you print the Gantt Chart view, Project will also print all task notes.

CREATE RECURRING TASKS

I f a task occurs at regular intervals during the life of a project, you can save time by creating it as a recurring task. Weekly staff meetings, quarterly reports, monthly budget reviews, and repeatedly testing a product are all examples of events that you may want to create as recurring tasks. Creating a recurring task is also great when you want to remind

yourself to write any required and periodically occurring reports that show the progress of a project. You save time and effort by generating one task instead of 20 or so daily, weekly, monthly, or annual events over the life of a project. You can also assign a frequency and timing to the task.

If one of the occurrences of the task falls on a holiday, Project allows

you to skip the occurrence or to schedule it on the next working day. For example, you can schedule a test that you must repeat 16 times during the project to occur on the next working day to compensate for New Years, while you may skip a weekly staff meeting.

CREATE RECURRING TASKS

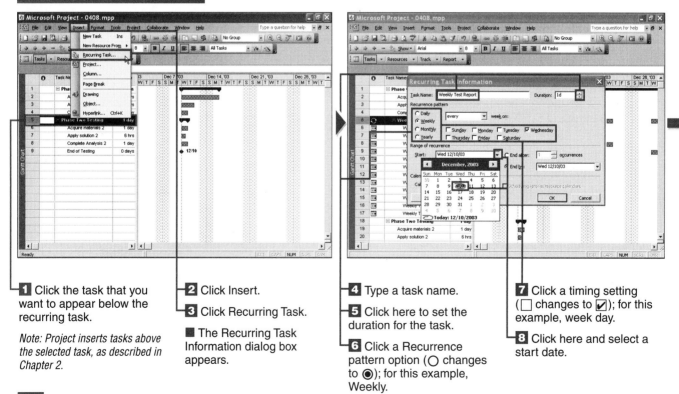

1 Click the task that you want to appear below the recurring task.

Note: Project inserts tasks above the selected task, as described in Chapter 2.

2 Click Insert.

3 Click Recurring Task.

■ The Recurring Task Information dialog box appears.

4 Type a task name.

5 Click here to set the duration for the task.

6 Click a Recurrence pattern option (○ changes to ◉); for this example, Weekly.

7 Click a timing setting (□ changes to ☑); for this example, week day.

8 Click here and select a start date.

MASTER IT

What kinds of settings for recurrence can I make for a daily task? An annual task?

✔ A list box that contains the same entries as the Every week list allows you to select all days or only work days. You can make the task recur on a specific date each year or on the first, second, third, fourth, or last day of the selected month.

How do I block out a specific time for a status meeting each week?

✔ Set up a recurring task, and add a calendar to the summary recurring task that specifies the hour.

How do I account for holidays when creating a recurring task?

✔ Set the End after number of occurrences to make Project calculate the date range required to complete that many occurrences of the task. The ending date automatically displays in the End by field. If one of the occurrences falls on a holiday, Project displays a box that allows you to skip the occurrence or to schedule it on the next working day.

How can I edit a recurring task to change the recurring settings?

✔ Double-click the icon (↻) that appears in the Indicator column to display the Recurring Task dialog box.

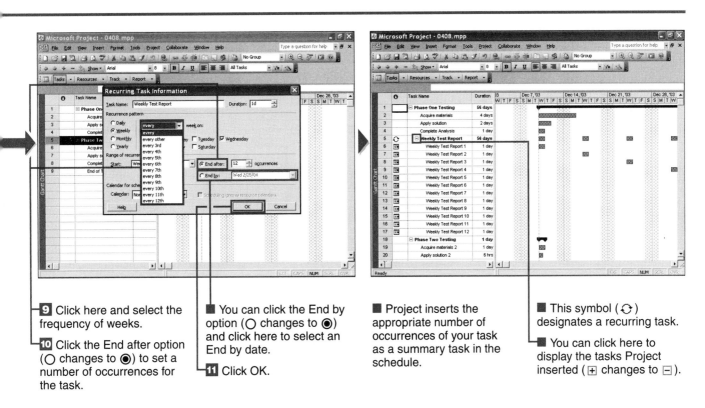

■9 Click here and select the frequency of weeks.

■10 Click the End after option (○ changes to ●) to set a number of occurrences for the task.

■ You can click the End by option (○ changes to ●) and click here to select an End by date.

■11 Click OK.

■ Project inserts the appropriate number of occurrences of your task as a summary task in the schedule.

■ This symbol (↻) designates a recurring task.

■ You can click here to display the tasks Project inserted (⊞ changes to ⊟).

VIEW DIFFERENT APPEARANCES OF TIMING

After you enter several tasks and task durations, you may find that you want to view more or less of your project. By manipulating the timescale, you can view different levels of detail about the information in your project.

The timescale is the gray band containing dates that appears at the top of the Gantt Chart view, the Task Usage view, the Resource

Usage view, and the Resource Graph view. For more information on views, see Chapter 5.

You can segment the timescale into top, middle, and bottom tiers. On each tier, you can display a different time measure. For example, you can display months on the top tier, weeks on the middle tier, and days on the bottom tier. By default, Project shows the middle and bottom tiers.

You also can format the tiers to display different increments of each time measure. For example, you can set the middle tier to weeks and view every other week. If you select these settings, your project appears compressed in the Gantt Chart, and you can view a longer time frame.

You also can control the appearance and format of non-working time. For more information, see Chapter 2.

VIEW DIFFERENT APPEARANCES OF TIMING

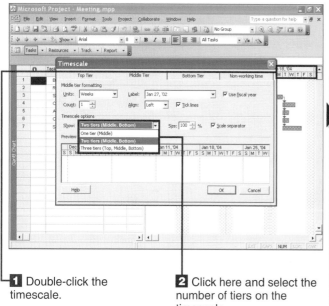

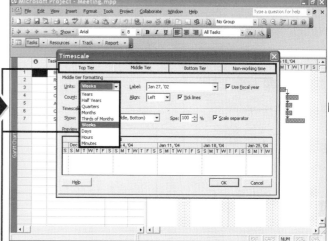

1 Double-click the timescale.

■ The Middle Tier tab of the Timescale dialog box appears.

2 Click here and select the number of tiers on the timescale.

■ Project applies your selection.

■ You can click any tier tab to establish settings for it.

3 Click here and select the units to appear on the tier.

■ Project applies your selection.

MASTER IT

Can I set the timescale to view more of my project, or enlarge the view?

✔ For two tiers, try setting the bottom tier to weeks and the middle tier to months. To enlarge the view click the Zoom In button (🔍). Click the Zoom Out button (🔍) to compress the view again. You find both buttons on the Standard Toolbar.

Is there an easy way to find a task's Gantt bar when I cannot see it on-screen?

✔ Yes. Select the task in the Task Name column and click the Go To Selected Task button (📋) on the Standard Toolbar.

What does the Count field do?

✔ The Count field controls where you see the vertical gray lines on the timescale for the selected tier. If you set the Count to 2 on a tier showing weeks, you see vertical gray lines every other week.

Can I change the formatting for non-working time independently for different calendars?

✔ No. The formatting you select for non-working time applies to all calendars. Use the Calendar list to see how your formatting selections look on each available calendar.

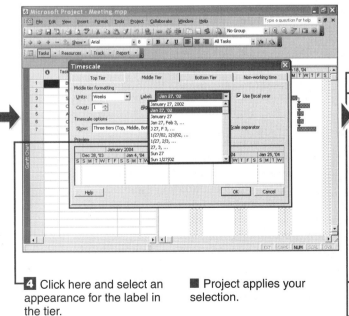

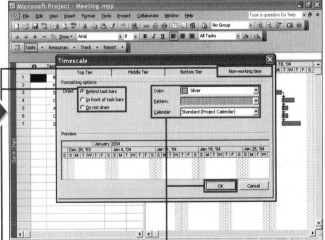

4 Click here and select an appearance for the label in the tier.

■ Project applies your selection.

5 Click the Non-working time tab.

6 Click a Draw option (○ changes to ◉).

■ You can hide non-working time or display it behind or in front of task bars.

■ You can also change the color and pattern of non-working time and display calendar formatting.

7 Click OK.

■ Project applies your changes.

61

UNDERSTANDING TASK CONSTRAINTS AND DEPENDENCIES

Dependencies work hand-in-hand with constraints and are central to visualizing the true length of a project.

Constraints tie tasks to the project start or end or to particular dates, while *dependencies* tie tasks to the timing of other tasks in the project.

Both constraints and dependencies drive the timing of a task.

What Is a Constraint?

Constraints are restrictions that you can place on tasks that affect how Project calculates the start or finish dates of the tasks in your project. You can learn more about constraints in the sections "Types of Contraints" and "Establish Constraints."

There are two general categories of constraints: flexible constraints and inflexible constraints. *Flexible constraints* do not tie a task to a specific date but only to some time frame. *Inflexible constraints* tie a task to an exact date. You use flexible constraints whenever possible because they give Project more freedom to accurately calculate your schedule using task durations and dependencies. If you use inflexible constraints, you may accidentally create artificial due dates for tasks.

What Is a Dependency?

Dependency refers to the relationship between two entities, and, in project management, dependency refers to the relationship between two tasks. A dependency exists between two tasks when the completion of one task cannot happen unless the other task either finishes or starts.

Dependencies exist because all tasks in a project rarely can happen simultaneously; usually, some tasks must start or finish before others can begin. Tasks overlap for many reasons; resources cannot do more than one task at a time or equipment is not available. Sometimes, the nature of the tasks themselves dictates the dependency. For example, you can't start construction until you receive a construction permit. You can't know the total time that you will need to complete a project until you establish durations and dependencies. For example, suppose that your project is comprised of five 5-day-long tasks with no dependencies among the tasks; in this case, the project takes 5 days to complete. But, suppose that the tasks must happen one after the other; in this case, the project takes 25 days to complete.

How Constraints and Dependencies Interrelate

Consider for a moment how constraints and dependencies may interact when you apply one of each to a task. Suppose that you have a task to open a new facility, and you have set up the task so that it must occur on June 6. Suppose that you then set up a dependency that indicates that the open facility task should begin after the fire inspection task that is scheduled for completion on June 10. When you try to set up such a dependency, Project displays a Planning Wizard dialog box that indicates a scheduling conflict. Project displays this dialog box when a conflict exists among dependencies or between constraints and dependencies.

Predecessors and Successors

A task that must occur before another task is a *predecessor task*, and the task that occurs later in the relationship is a *successor task*. Task A can have multiple predecessors because several tasks may need to start or complete before Task A can begin. Similarly, Task A can have many successors because many other tasks in the project may not be able to start or finish until Task A starts or finishes.

In Project, you *link* tasks that depend on one another. The Gantt Chart shows these links as lines running between task bars; an arrow at one end points to the successor task. Some dependency relationships are as simple as one task ending before another can begin. However, some relationships are much more complex. For example, if you move into a new office and the first task is assembling cubicles, you do not have to wait until all the cubicles are assembled to begin moving in furniture. You may work in tandem, using the first morning to set up cubicles on the first floor. Then you can begin to move chairs and bookcases into the first-floor cubicles while the setup task continues on the second floor.

Conflicts

If a conflict exists between a constraint and a dependency, the constraint drives the timing of the task; the task does not move from the constraint-imposed date. You can modify this functionality on the Schedule tab of the Options box. When you select the Tasks will always honor their constraint dates option, dependencies rather than constraints determine timing. You access the dialog box via the Options command in the Tools menu.

Overlaps and Delay

Many dependency relationships are relatively clear-cut, but some are more finely delineated. These relationships involve overlap and delay, and you can create these types of relationships in Project by adding lag time or lead time to the dependency relationship. See the section "Create Overlaps and Delays" later in this chapter for more information.

ESTABLISH CONSTRAINTS

Constraints are restrictions that you can place on tasks that affect how Project calculates the start or finish dates of the tasks in your project. For example, use a constraint when the billing of a major account must start no sooner than the first day of the next quarter to avoid accruing income this quarter, or when you must complete a budget no later than the last day of the fiscal year so that the new year can begin with the budget in place.

Project contains flexible and inflexible constraints and, by default, applies flexible constraints to tasks. Project calculates the schedule so that each task starts as early as possible or as late as possible and ends before the project finishes, barring other constraints and task dependencies in the schedule. For more information on task dependencies, see the section "Understanding Task Constraints and Dependencies."

Do flexible constraints have characteristics in common?

✔ Unlike inflexible constraints, which tie a task to an exact date, flexible constraints tie a task only to some time frame. Think of all the flexible constraints except for ASAP and ALAP as "soft" flexible constraints — you associated dates with them, but conditions in your project can move the dates.

ESTABLISH CONSTRAINTS

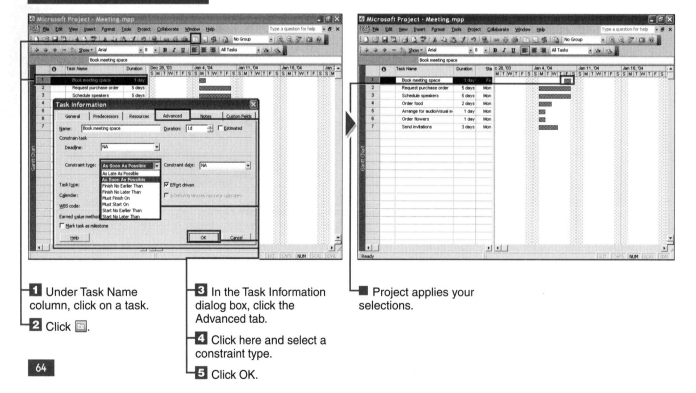

1 Under Task Name column, click on a task.

2 Click 🗄.

3 In the Task Information dialog box, click the Advanced tab.

4 Click here and select a constraint type.

5 Click OK.

■ Project applies your selections.

TYPES OF CONSTRAINTS

To help you understand how constraints work, this section lists all the constraints from which you can select. For more information on constraints and how to establish them, see the previous section.

Project contains flexible and inflexible constraints. Project's flexible constraints are: As Soon As Possible (ASAP), As Late As Possible (ALAP), Finish No Earlier

Than, Finish No Later Than, Start No Earlier Than, and Start No Later Than. Project's inflexible constraints are: Must Finish On, Must Start On, Finish No Earlier Than, Finish No Later Than, Start No Earlier Than, and Start No Later Than.

You use an inflexible constraint when you must account for an external factor, such as the availability of resources. As an alternative, instead of using

inflexible constraints when you want to target a particular date, use a flexible constraint and enter a deadline for the task.

When you assign a constraint other than an As Soon As Possible or an As Late As Possible constraint, an icon appears in the indicator column as a reminder that you set a constraint. You can place your mouse over the icon to see the constraint type and date.

As Soon As Possible

Starts a project on the nearest possible date.

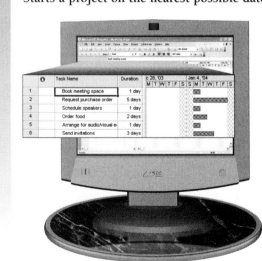

As Late As Possible

If you select an As Late As Possible constraint type, the one-day task starts in time to complete at the same time as the longest task in the schedule.

CONTINUED▶

TYPES OF CONSTRAINTS (CONTINUED)

Finish No Earlier Than

If you select a Finish No Earlier Than constraint
type and set the constraint date to January 7, the
one-day task starts and finishes on January 7.

Finish No Later Than

If you select a Finish No Later Than constraint
type and set the constraint date to January 5, the
one-day task starts and finishes on January 5.

Must Finish On

If you select a Must Finish On constraint
type and set the constraint date to January
12, the one-day task starts and finishes on
January 12.

Must Start On

If you select a Must Start On constraint type and set the constraint date to January 8, the one-day task starts and finishes on January 8.

Start No Earlier

If you select a Start No Earlier Than constraint type and set the constraint date to January 6, the one-day task starts and finishes on January 6.

Start No Later Than

If you select a Start No Later Than constraint type and set the constraint date to January 9, the one-day task starts as soon as possible, starting and finishing on January 5.

CREATE TASK DEPENDENCIES

Four types of dependencies enable you to deal with every variable of how tasks can relate to each other's timing. Each of these dependency relationships defines the relationship between the start and finish of tasks. Project uses four different dependencies: start-to-finish, finish-to-start, start-to-start, and finish-to-finish. The first timing mentioned in each relationship name relates to the

predecessor task and the second to the successor. Therefore, a finish-to-start relationship relates the finish of the predecessor to the start of the successor and a start-to-finish dependency relates the start of the predecessor to the finish of the successor. Project refers to dependencies as *links* and to dependency relationships by their initials, such as *SS* for a start-to-start relationship.

You can determine whether two tasks are linked when you see an arrow connecting their bars on the Gantt Chart. You can identify the type of dependency by noting the direction of the arrow that runs between the two dependent tasks. If you position the mouse pointer on the line that links the tasks, Project displays link information, including the type of link. This task shows an example of each dependency type.

CREATE TASK DEPENDENCIES

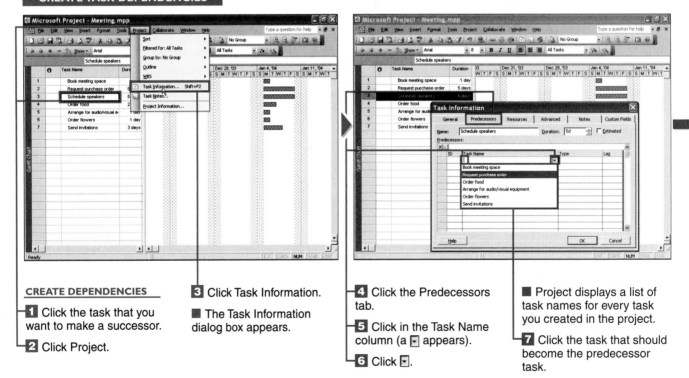

CREATE DEPENDENCIES

1 Click the task that you want to make a successor.

2 Click Project.

3 Click Task Information.

■ The Task Information dialog box appears.

4 Click the Predecessors tab.

5 Click in the Task Name column (a ⯆ appears).

6 Click ⯆.

■ Project displays a list of task names for every task you created in the project.

7 Click the task that should become the predecessor task.

Can I set dependencies between summary tasks?

✔ You can use a finish-to-start or a start-to-start dependency between two summary tasks or between a summary task and a subtask not summarized by the summary task. You cannot use any other type of dependency, and you cannot set dependencies between a summary task and any of its own subtasks.

What do you place in the Lag column of the Task Information dialog box?

✔ You use this column to create lag or lead time between tasks. See the section "Create Overlaps and Delays" for more information.

How are constraints and dependencies related in Project?

✔ Constraints and dependencies are closely related; constraints describe the relationship between a task and the project's start or finish date, while dependencies describe the relationship between the start and finish dates of tasks. If a conflict exists between a constraint and a dependency, Project, by default, uses the constraint to drive the timing of the task; the task does not move from the constraint-imposed date. See the section "Establish Constraints" earlier in this chapter for more information.

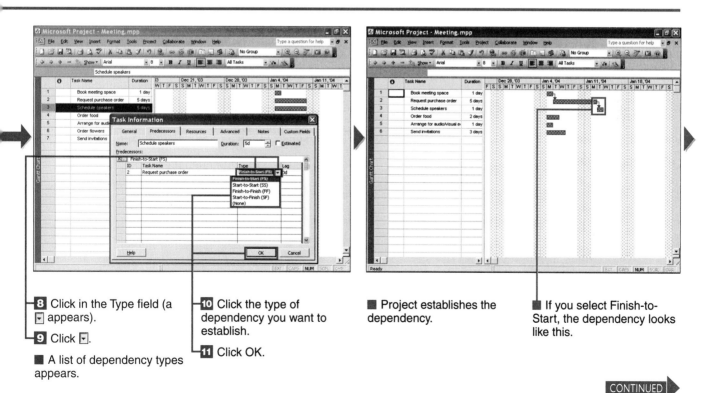

8 Click in the Type field (a ▾ appears).

9 Click ▾.

■ A list of dependency types appears.

10 Click the type of dependency you want to establish.

11 Click OK.

■ Project establishes the dependency.

■ If you select Finish-to-Start, the dependency looks like this.

CONTINUED

CREATE TASK
DEPENDENCIES (CONTINUED)

I n a finish-to-start relationship, the most common type of dependency — the successor task — cannot start until the predecessor task finishes. When would you use a finish-to-start dependency? You must write a report before you can edit it; or, you must have a computer before you can install your software.

With the start-to-finish relationship, the successor task cannot finish until the predecessor

task starts. For example, you can finish scheduling production crews only when you start receiving materials; or, employees can start using a new procedure only when they finish training for it.

In a start-to-start relationship, the successor cannot start until the predecessor starts. For example, when you start receiving results in an election, you can begin to compile them; or when the drivers start their engines, the flagger can start the race.

In the finish-to-finish dependency, the successor task cannot finish until the predecessor task finishes. For example, you finish installing computers at the same time that you finish moving employees into the building so that the employees can begin using the computers right away. Or, two divisions must finish retooling their production lines on the same day so that the CEO can inspect the lines at the same time.

CREATE TASK DEPENDENCIES (CONTINUED)

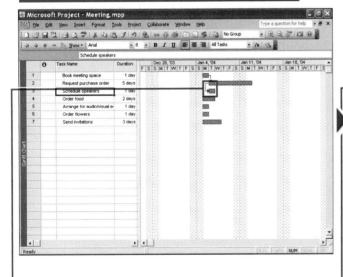

■ If you select Start-to-Start, the dependency looks like this.

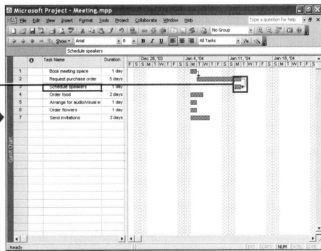

■ If you select Finish-to-Finish, the dependency looks like this.

In your example for a start-to-finish task, employees can start using a new procedure only when they finish training for it. Can you set up this relationship as a finish-to-start relationship?

✔ Not really. If the implementation of the new procedure is delayed, you also want to delay the training so that it occurs as late as possible before the implementation to allow no delay between training and implementation. If you start the new procedure only when the training finishes, the new procedure can start any time after the training ends.

Which type of dependency does Project assign by default?

✔ By default, Project assigns a finish-to-start dependency to each task you create. Because the finish-to-start dependency is most common, Project contains shortcuts to create this link. See the section "Shortcuts to Create and Change Links" for more information.

Can I link tasks in one project to tasks in another project?

✔ Yes. The process is called *external linking*, and most people use it when working with consolidated projects. See Chapter 11 for information on consolidated projects and linking them.

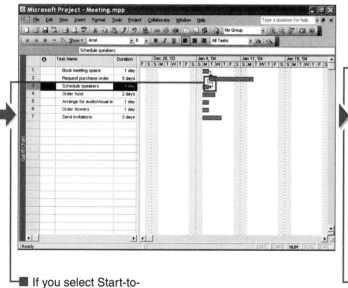

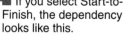 If you select Start-to-Finish, the dependency looks like this.

🔢 Position 👆 on the link line.

■ Project displays information about the link, including the type of link.

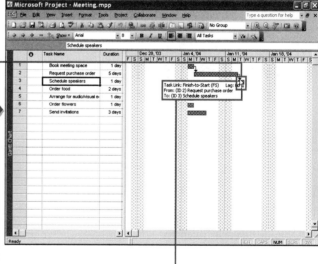

SHORTCUTS TO CREATE AND CHANGE LINKS

Because the finish-to-start link is the most commonly used link, you may expect to find some quick ways to assign this link type.

Suppose that you created a series of links and then discovered that your logic was a little faulty. Or, suppose that there was nothing wrong with your logic — you simply allowed Project to create finish-to-start links

to quickly establish the majority of the links you need. Now you need to change some dependencies in the project. You know that you can select the task and reopen the Task Information dialog box, as shown in the section "Create Task Dependencies," but you really want an easier way.

Project enables you to use the mouse in a couple of different ways

to create a finish-to-start link. And, you can quickly change links to a different link type by using the Task Dependency dialog box.

Most people tend to use the shortcuts first and only use the Predecessors tab of the Task Information dialog box to deal with tasks that do not have a finish-to-start relationship.

SHORTCUTS TO CREATE AND CHANGE LINKS

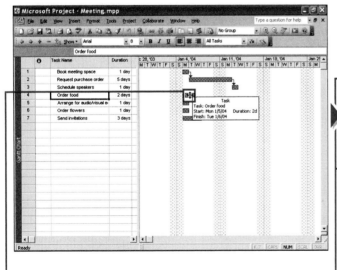
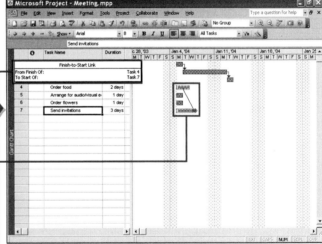

CREATE A FINISH-TO-START TASK DEPENDENCY

1 Position ▷ over the task bar of the predecessor task (▷ changes to ✣).

2 Click and drag ✣ to the second task (✣ changes to ⟲).

■ An information box describes the finish-to-start link that you are about to create.

3 Release the mouse button.

■ Project establishes the link.

Can I quickly create finish-to-finish, start-to-finish, or start-to-start relationships?

✔ Yes. Create the default finish-to-start relationship for the tasks. Double-click the link line to open the Task Dependency dialog box, and change the relationship.

Can I link more than one task at a time?

✔ Yes, if you use a finish-to-start link. To select adjacent tasks, click and drag through their ID numbers in the Gantt Chart table. To select nonadjacent tasks, press Ctrl as you click the ID numbers of each task that you want to link.

I do not like dragging the mouse. Is there another easy way to change a link?

✔ Yes. You can select two tasks and click the Link Tasks button (🖳). The first task that you select becomes the predecessor in the relationship.

What if I am in the middle of dragging to create a link and I change my mind?

✔ Project does not establish the relationship until you release the mouse button. If you have second thoughts while dragging, just drag 🔗 back to the predecessor task before releasing your mouse button.

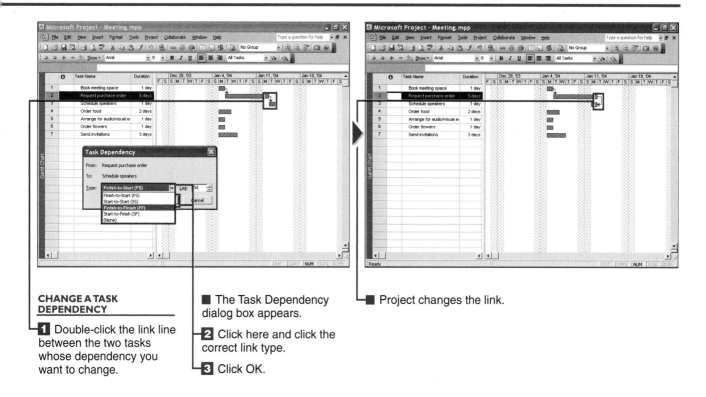

CHANGE A TASK DEPENDENCY

1 Double-click the link line between the two tasks whose dependency you want to change.

■ The Task Dependency dialog box appears.

2 Click here and click the correct link type.

3 Click OK.

■ Project changes the link.

CREATE OVERLAPS AND DELAYS

Not all dependency relationships are simple. In some cases, you must build in time for tasks to overlap or delay. In Project, you account for overlap and delay by adding lag time or lead time to the dependency relationship of the tasks.

For example, if your project tests a series of metals, your first task may apply a solution to the metal, and

the second may analyze the results. You may want the analysis to begin only after several days after an application. You build in a delay — lag time in Project — between the finish of the first task (the predecessor) and the start of the second task (the successor). In the Gantt Chart, you see the dependency line and some space between the finish of the first task

and the start of the second task; the gap between the tasks represents the lag time.

To follow the first example, in another test in your project, you may apply the solution for two days and then also apply heat. You can build in overlap — lead time in Project — between the two tasks so that the successor task where you apply heat begins three hours after the start of the predecessor task.

CREATE OVERLAPS AND DELAYS

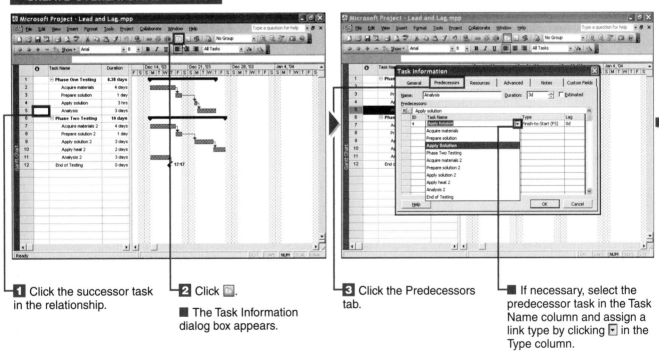

1 Click the successor task in the relationship.

2 Click 🖼.

■ The Task Information dialog box appears.

3 Click the Predecessors tab.

■ If necessary, select the predecessor task in the Task Name column and assign a link type by clicking ▼ in the Type column.

I want a more obvious reminder of lag time. What do you suggest?

✔ Try building a task to represent lag. For example, create a task called Solution Reaction Period, and create a simple dependency relationship between Solution Reaction Period and the analysis so that the analysis task does not begin until Solution Reaction Period is complete. Adding the lag tasks can generate a very long schedule with multiple tasks and relationships to track. But, in a simpler schedule, you can see relationships as task bars. You can try both methods and see which works best for you.

I need to set up lag time for a task that runs in only one day, but must make sure that the task runs through lunch time. How can I do that?

✔ Set up a task calendar that ignores lunchtime so that both tasks can continue uninterrupted. Icons in the Indicator column represent the task calendar. Also remember that when the timing is in hours instead of days or weeks, you may want to change the timescale so that you can see the hours of the day.

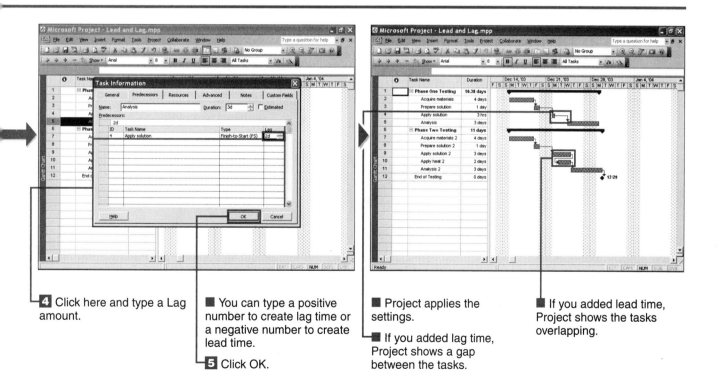

■4 Click here and type a Lag amount.

■ You can type a positive number to create lag time or a negative number to create lead time.

■5 Click OK.

■ Project applies the settings.

■ If you added lag time, Project shows a gap between the tasks.

■ If you added lead time, Project shows the tasks overlapping.

VIEW AND DELETE DEPENDENCIES

I t happens. You link tasks together in your schedule and circumstances determine that the tasks should not be linked. For example, you may link Tasks A and B, and then discover a third task, Task C, that actually belongs between Tasks A and B. You need to remove the link that connects Task A to Task B so that you can connect Task A to Task C and then Task C to Task B.

In other circumstances, you may need to delete a link because you must move tasks in your project. In some circumstances, when you move tasks, Project automatically makes new link assignments, but in other cases, Project retains the original assignment. Because this may not work for you, you must delete a dependency link.

Deleting a dependency is not difficult; you simply need to view it. Project provides a number of

ways to view and delete dependency information. When you delete a task dependency, Project reassigns the task's start date based on either the project's start date or other constraints that exist in the project.

Exercise caution when using the steps in Using the Task Bar; Project removes *all* links between the selected task and any other tasks.

VIEW AND DELETE DEPENDENCIES

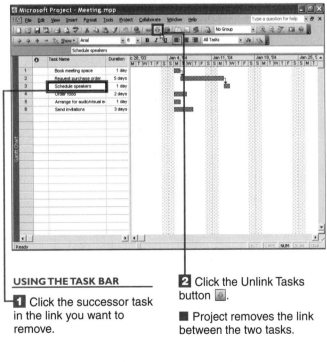

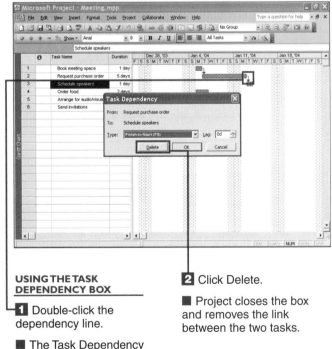

USING THE TASK BAR

1 Click the successor task in the link you want to remove.

2 Click the Unlink Tasks button 📊.

■ Project removes the link between the two tasks.

USING THE TASK DEPENDENCY BOX

1 Double-click the dependency line.

■ The Task Dependency dialog box appears.

2 Click Delete.

■ Project closes the box and removes the link between the two tasks.

MASTER IT

How can I easily remove more than one dependency?

✔ Select the names of the tasks whose dependencies you want to delete, and click the Unlink Tasks button 🖳.

My schedule does not work with the dependencies I set. Can I start over, without retyping all the task names?

✔ Yes. Click the title of the Task Name column to select everything in that column. Then, click 🖳. Before you make this change, save a backup of your project in case you decide to continue working with the original schedule.

If I move linked tasks in my project, do I need to delete the links and relink the tasks?

✔ You may. When you copy or move an entire task or resource, Project automatically reassigns task dependencies if the tasks are part of a series of consecutively linked tasks, the task dependencies are finish-to-start, and you have selected the Autolink inserted or moved tasks options (☐ changes to ☑) on the Schedule tab of the Options dialog box. Project retains the original dependencies if any of these conditions do not exist.

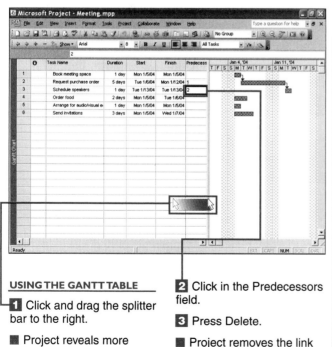

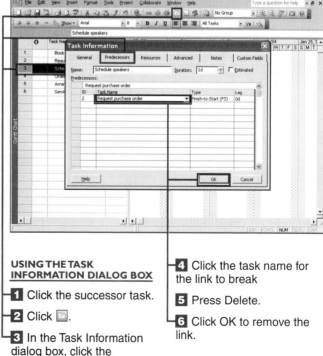

USING THE GANTT TABLE

1 Click and drag the splitter bar to the right.

■ Project reveals more columns of the table.

2 Click in the Predecessors field.

3 Press Delete.

■ Project removes the link between the two tasks.

USING THE TASK INFORMATION DIALOG BOX

1 Click the successor task.

2 Click 🗐.

3 In the Task Information dialog box, click the Predecessors tab.

4 Click the task name for the link to break

5 Press Delete.

6 Click OK to remove the link.

UNDERSTANDING RESOURCES

To finish a project, you need resources — people, supplies, and equipment — that enable you to complete the tasks in a project schedule. As a project manager, you need to identify the resources that you require for each task and then assign the resources to the tasks.

Some tasks require only people; other tasks may require people and equipment. In Project, you can define *work resources*, or people and equipment, and *material resources*, which are consumable materials. You can also define *generic resources*, which are not specific work or material resources but descriptions of resources that you need to finish a project. Take the opportunity in this section to learn more about these three types of resources, and how they figure into your project's cost and scheduling.

Work Resources

Work resources are equipment or people that consume time when working on a task. When you set up work resources, you define the amount of time that the resources spend on a project with 100 percent being full time. Similarly, when you assign a work resource to a task, you indicate the amount of time that you want the work resource to spend on the task; again, 100 percent is full time.

Material Resources

Material resources are items that are consumed while working on a project. Instead of using time, material resources use materials such as paper, gasoline, or wood. When you assign a material resource to a task, you specify the amount of the material resource that you intend to use in units that are appropriate for the material resource. You also can indicate whether the amount of material you use is based on time or is fixed. For example, when you water a lawn, the amount of material you use is based on time, because the number of gallons of water you consume depends on the amount of time that you run the water and the number of gallons per hour that flow from the faucet. The amount of material you use is fixed when you need five 2 x 4 pieces of wood to construct a bench; in this case, the amount of material you need has no connection to the time it takes you to build the bench.

Generic Resources

Project enables you to define generic resources. *Generic resources* are not specific people, equipment, or materials, but rather descriptions of the skills that you need for a task. You use generic resources when you do not know the specific resources that are available. Although the generic resource feature in Project was designed to work in conjunction with the Resource Substitution Wizard and Enterprise Resources available in Project Server, you may find generic resources handy even if you do not use Project Server. For example, you can use generic resources when you do not care who does the work — you simply want to track the work that is completed on a project.

If you use Project Server, you can also take advantage of three other related features. You can define Enterprise Resources, which are resources available company-wide for projects. You can use Team Builder to help you select resources for your project from the Enterprise Resource pool, and you can use the Resource Substitution Wizard to replace generic resources with actual resources. Read more about these features in Chapter 13.

How Resources Work

Resources cost money; when you assign resources to tasks in a project, you assign a cost to the project as a whole. Therefore, you need to know how Project uses those resource assignments to change the duration and length of your project.

By assigning resources to tasks, you can identify potential resource shortages that may force you to miss scheduled deadlines and possibly extend the duration of your project. You also can identify underutilized resources; if you reassign these resources, you may be able to shorten the project's schedule. You can also monitor the cost of the project. For more information on project costs, see Chapters 5 and 12.

When you assign resources to effort-driven tasks — and Project defines all new tasks as effort-driven by default — the resources that you assign to the task can affect the duration of the task. For example, if you assign two people to do a job, the job typically gets done in less time than if you assign only one person to the job. But, you ask, does the use of additional resources increase the project's cost? Perhaps yes, perhaps no. You may find that using more resources to complete the project in less time saves money because you can accept more projects. Or you may be eligible for a bonus if you complete the project earlier than expected, and the bonus may cover or exceed the cost of the additional resources that you use. Balancing the costs of resource usage is one of the primary jobs of the project manager.

How Resource Information Affects Schedules

For effort-driven tasks that are not fixed-duration tasks, Project uses the resource information that you provide to calculate the duration of the task and, consequently, the duration of the project. If the work assigned to a resource exceeds the available time, Project assigns the resource to the task and indicates that the reource is over allocated. However, if you set up a task with a fixed duration, Project ignores the resources that are assigned to the task when calculating the duration of the project. Similarly, if you do not assign resources, Project calculates the schedule using only the task duration and task dependency information that you provide. See Chapter 3 for information on task durations and task dependencies.

VIEW THE RESOURCE SHEET

The Resource Sheet is a table view in Project that you can use to define the resources in your project. Each cell in the table is a *field* into which you type information that describes some aspect of the resource. If you type a resource name, Project automatically fills in default information for the rest of the fields.

You cannot type in the Indicators field; instead, icons appear here from time to time. If you position your mouse over an indicator, Project displays the information that is associated with the icon.

Type

Use this column to specify whether you are defining a human or material resource. Project refers to human resources as Work resources. For more on resources, see the section "Understanding Resources."

Resource Name

Type the name of the resource. For a person, you can type the person's name or you can type a job description, such as Electrician 1 or Electrician 2.

Indicators

You cannot type in the Indicators field; instead, icons appear here from time to time. If you position your mouse over an indicator, Project displays the information that is associated with the icon.

Material Label

For material resources, you specify the unit of measure. You can set up any label that you want. For example, you can use minutes for long distance, feet for lumber, or miles for gasoline.

Initials

You can type initials for the resource, or accept the default that Project provides, which is the first letter of the resource name. This designation appears on any view to which you add the Initials field. Typically, a resource's name appears, but you can customize the view to display initials if you prefer.

Group

You can assign resources to groups if they share a common characteristic, such as job function. You can use this field as a filtering or sorting mechanism to display information about a group as opposed to a specific resource. Just type a name to create a group, making sure that you spell the group name the same way each time so that Projects can filter or sort by group.

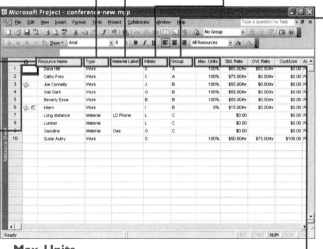

Max. Units

Project expresses the amount of work resource that you have available for assignment as a percentage. For example, 100 percent equals one unit, or the equivalent of one full-time resource; 50 percent equals one-half of a unit, or one-half of a full-time resource's time; and 200 percent equals two full-time resources. You cannot assign a value to this field for material resources.

Std. Rate

You charge the standard rate for regular work for a resource. Project uses the standard rate, the overtime rate, and the cost-per-use rate to calculate resource costs. To calculate the standard rate, Project multiplies the number of hours times the cost per hour. Project calculates the default rate in hours, but you can charge a resource's work in other time increments. For example, you may charge $100 per day for a trainer. For work resources, you can use minutes, days, weeks, or years. For material resources, think of the charge as per-unit based on the Material Label. To specify a time increment other than hours, type a forward slash and then the first letter of the word representing the time increment. For example, to charge a resource's use in days, type **/d** after the rate that you specify.

Ovt. Rate

You charge the overtime rate for overtime work for a work resource. Again, Project calculates the default rate in hours, but you can change the default unit the same way that you changed it for the standard rate.

Cost/Use

In the Cost/Use column — read as cost per use — supply a rate for costs that you charge for each use of the resource. The Cost/Use rate is a fixed fee that you charge for each use of the resource. For example, if you rent a piece of equipment that costs you $25 per hour plus a setup charge of $100, you assign a Std. Rate of $25/hour and a Cost/Use of $100.

Accrue At

This field specifies how and when Microsoft Office Project charges resource costs to a task at the standard or overtime rates. The default option is Prorated, but you also can select Start or End. If you select Start and assign that resource to a task, Project calculates the cost for a task as soon as the task begins. If you select End and assign that resource to a task, Project calculates the cost for the task when the task is completed. If you select Prorated and assign that resource to a task, Project accrues the cost of the task as you complete scheduled work.

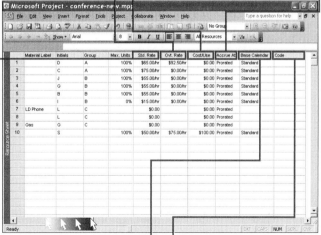

Base Calendar

Base calendar identifies the calendar that Project uses when scheduling the resource to identify working and non-working time. Project assumes that each resource uses the Standard calendar, but you can create calendars for resource groups, perhaps to handle shift work, or you can modify an individual resource's calendar to reflect vacation or other unavailable time, such as jury duty.

Code

Use this field as a catchall field to assign any information that you want to a resource, using an abbreviation of some sort. For example, if your company uses cost-center codes, you may want to supply the cost-center code for the resource in the Code field. You can sort and filter information by the abbreviations that you supply in the Code field.

CREATE A RESOURCE LIST

The Resource Sheet displays a list of the resources that are available to your project. Using the Resource Sheet is a safe way to define resources; the visual presentation helps you avoid accidentally creating the same resource twice. For example, if you define Mariann and Marianne, Project sees two resources, even if you simply misspelled the name the second time.

You can enter the basics for the resource by filling in the Resource Sheet. After you create a resource, Project displays the resource's ID number on the left edge of the Resource Sheet, to the left of the Indicator column.

You can customize the Resource Sheet by adding columns to show additional fields that you may want to set up for each resource. For

example, to enter notes for each resource, you can add the Notes column to the Resource Sheet. See Chapter 7 to find out how to insert a column in a table.

As part of the Project Guide, you can have Project walk you through the process of creating resources. The Resources page of the Project Guide appears when you display the Resource Sheet view.

CREATE A RESOURCE LIST

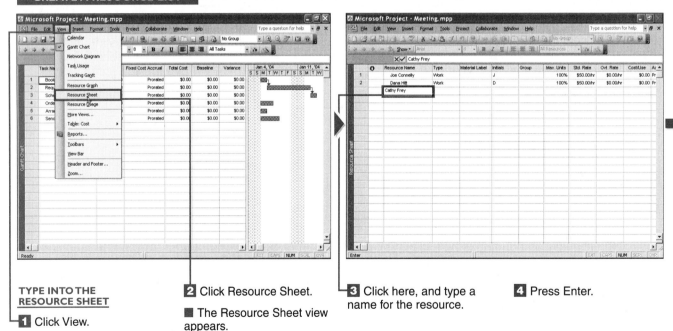

TYPE INTO THE RESOURCE SHEET

1 Click View.

2 Click Resource Sheet.

■ The Resource Sheet view appears.

3 Click here, and type a name for the resource.

4 Press Enter.

How does the Accrue At value affect the timing of the cost-per-use charge?

✔ Project uses the Accrue At field to determine when to apply the cost. If you select Start or Prorated, Project charges the Cost/Use amount at the beginning of the task. If you select End, Project charges the cost at the end of the task.

How can I add or change resource information that does not appear on the Resource Sheet without adding columns to the sheet?

✔ Open the Resource Information dialog box. In the Resource Sheet view, click Project and then Resource Information or double-click the resource name of the resource you want to edit.

What is the best way to set up a resource who does not work full time?

✔ Create a resource calendar for the resource. See the section "Create Resource Calendars" for more information.

I use the same resources over and over on my projects. Is there an easy way to set up resources so that I do not have to set them up in every project?

✔ Set up the resources in a special project that contains no tasks. Then use Project's resource pooling feature and your resource project to share resources across multiple projects. For more information about resource pooling, see Chapter 12.

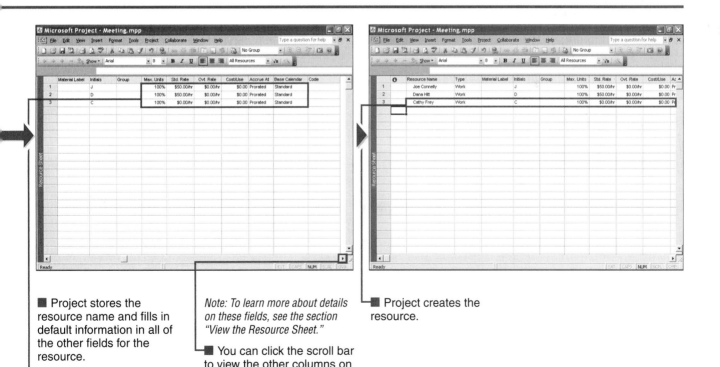

■ Project stores the resource name and fills in default information in all of the other fields for the resource.

5 Type to change default information as appropriate.

Note: To learn more about details on these fields, see the section "View the Resource Sheet."

■ You can click the scroll bar to view the other columns on the resource sheet and make changes as needed.

■ Project creates the resource.

CONTINUED ▶

CREATE A RESOURCE LIST (CONTINUED)

If you store all of the information about your resources in your Contact List in Outlook, you can use this information to create your resource list without retyping it into the Resource Sheet.

Note that the steps in this task assume that you use Outlook 2003. While you can use Outlook 2000's Contact List, the steps are different than described here.

The process is simple, but you may want to edit the information stored in your Contacts folder so that it

matches the information Project stores. For example, suppose that you have Joan Smith stored in your Contacts folder with an e-mail address of joan@hotmail. com. By default, Outlook displays Joan's name as Joan Smith (joan@ hotmail.com).

Project imports the displayed name of each contact as the resource name. In this example, Project records Joan's name in the Resource Sheet as Joan Smith (joan@hotmail.com). You may want to remove the e-mail address

from the displayed name before you import it into Project and you can edit the contact information in Outlook at the same time that you import it.

This section assumes that you are already in the Resource Sheet view. For more on accessing this view, see steps 1 and 2 on the previous page.

CREATE A RESOURCE LIST (CONTINUED)

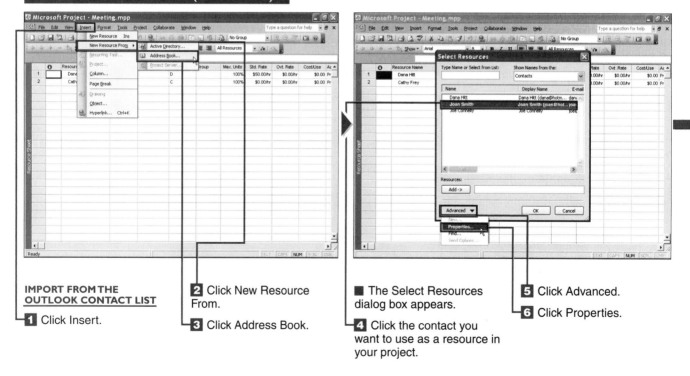

IMPORT FROM THE OUTLOOK CONTACT LIST

1 Click Insert.

2 Click New Resource From.

3 Click Address Book.

■ The Select Resources dialog box appears.

4 Click the contact you want to use as a resource in your project.

5 Click Advanced.

6 Click Properties.

Is there a way to store the e-mail address of the resource?

✔ Yes, but you must store the e-mail address in the E-mail field. Using the import method described in this section does not separate the name from the e-mail address, but you can easily import the information. For more, see the section "Store an E-mail Address with Resource Information."

How do I know if the resource I want to assign to my project is available?

✔ You can check availability as you assign the resource to tasks. See the section "Remove, or Replace Resource Assignments."

At my company, we share resources and I often do not know whom I want; instead, I know the skills I need for my project. Is there a way in Project to find a resource based on skills?

✔ Yes, if you use Project Server. Essentially, your company's resource pool contains skills for each resource. In your project, you create generic resources with specific skills and use Project Server's Resource Substitution Wizard to find resources that meet your needs. See Chapter 13 for information on using the Resource Substitution Wizard. Also see the section "Create a Generic Resource" later in this chapter.

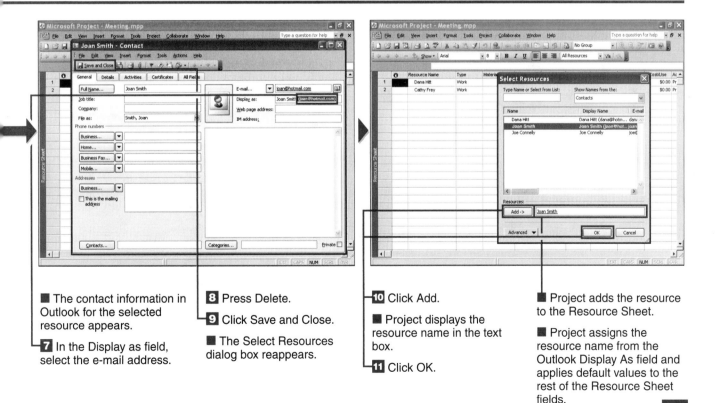

■ The contact information in Outlook for the selected resource appears.

7 In the Display as field, select the e-mail address.

8 Press Delete.

9 Click Save and Close.

■ The Select Resources dialog box reappears.

10 Click Add.

■ Project displays the resource name in the text box.

11 Click OK.

■ Project adds the resource to the Resource Sheet.

■ Project assigns the resource name from the Outlook Display As field and applies default values to the rest of the Resource Sheet fields.

STORE AN E-MAIL ADDRESS WITH RESOURCE INFORMATION

Yo u can store an e-mail address for each resource. If you are using any of Project Professional's collaboration features, you need the resource's e-mail address so that you can communicate. When you use Project collaboratively, resources can assign, accept, or decline work electronically.

Collaboration is an option that you can set in the Options dialog box. You can make a selection from the

Workgroup list to specify an electronic communication method.

Even if you do not use Project to collaborate, storing a resource's e-mail address can be effective because storing in one file all of the e-mail addresses for all resources working on the project makes them easily accessible.

Project gives you different methods for entering e-mail addresses. You can type the information for each

resource or, if you use Outlook and have stored the resource's e-mail address in the Contacts folder, you can import the information.

This section assumes that you are using Outlook 2003 and are already in the Resource Sheet view. For more on accessing this view, see the section "Create a Resource List." For more on the various fields of the Resource Sheet, see the section "View the Resource Sheet" earlier in this chapter.

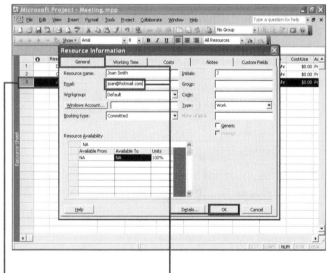

STORE AN E-MAIL ADDRESS WITH RESOURCE INFORMATION

TYPE AN E-MAIL ADDRESS

1 Double-click the resource whose e-mail address you want to add.

■ The Resource Information dialog box appears.

2 Click the General tab.

3 Click in the Email field, and type the e-mail address.

4 Click OK.

■ Project saves the resource's e-mail address.

IMPORT AN E-MAIL ADDRESS FROM OUTLOOK

1 Follow steps 1 to 2 in "Typing an E-mail Address" to open the Resource Information dialog box.

2 Click Details.

■ A message appears asking if you want to permit access to e-mail addresses stored in Outlook.

3 Click Yes.

I have all my resources in groups in Outlook. Can I import the Outlook group, or do I need to import individual names?

✔ You can import groups and distribution lists. Project is smart enough to create individual resources from a group or distribution list.

Can I import e-mail addresses from any other program besides Outlook?

✔ Yes. You can import from any MAPI-compliant, 32-bit e-mail system using the steps presented in this section.

What does the Workgroup option Default on the General tab of the Resource Information mean?

✔ In the Options dialog box of Project, on the Collaborate tab, you can set an option to define the type of collaboration you want to use for the project. If you set the Workgroup option on the General tab of the Resource Information dialog box to Default, the resource uses whatever collaboration method you set up for the project on the Collaborate tab of the Options dialog box.

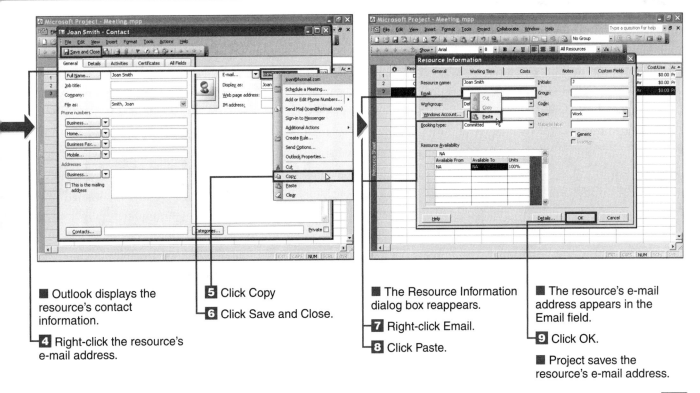

■ Outlook displays the resource's contact information.

4 Right-click the resource's e-mail address.

5 Click Copy

6 Click Save and Close.

■ The Resource Information dialog box reappears.

7 Right-click Email.

8 Click Paste.

■ The resource's e-mail address appears in the Email field.

9 Click OK.

■ Project saves the resource's e-mail address.

CREATE A GENERIC RESOURCE

A generic resource is a job description, not a person. An intern, a project manager, a computer programmer, and an editor are all examples of generic resources. You can use generic resources as placeholders in your project when you do not know the specific person who will work on the project, but you know you need a person.

Typically, you associate a set of skills with the generic resource that describes the skills needed to work on the project. If you are using Project Server, you can use the Build Team dialog box and the Resource Substitution Wizard to help you replace generic resources with real people who have the skills you need for your project. For more information on the Build Team dialog box and the Resource Substitution Wizard, see Chapter 17. For more on resources in

general, see the section "Understanding Resources." You can take advantage of the generic resource concept without using Project Server. If your project calls for three plumbers, you can define plumber as a generic resource and assign 300 percent for the maximum units. Project then uses other resource information that you define — such as cost and availability — when calculating the project schedule and costs.

CREATE A GENERIC RESOURCE

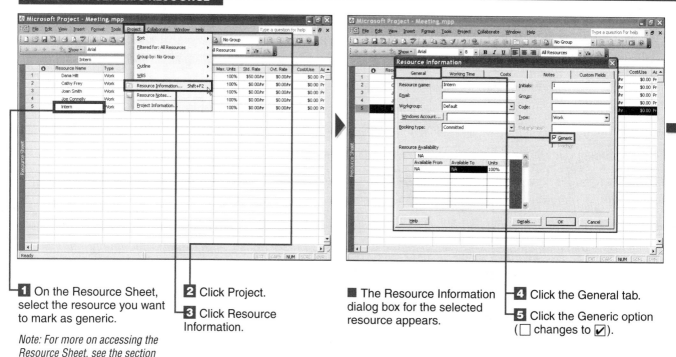

1 On the Resource Sheet, select the resource you want to mark as generic.

Note: For more on accessing the Resource Sheet, see the section "Create a Resource List."

2 Click Project.

3 Click Resource Information.

■ The Resource Information dialog box for the selected resource appears.

4 Click the General tab.

5 Click the Generic option (☐ changes to ☑).

When I click the Custom Fields tab, I do not see any fields. What am I doing wrong?

✔ Nothing. You must define custom fields before you see them on the tab. See Chapter 13 to learn how to create enterprise custom fields you use with Project Server. See Chapter 16 to learn how to create custom fields you use in stand-alone projects. You can use custom fields to make Project work the way your organization works; custom fields are very powerful and can help you standardize project management in your organization.

What is the purpose of the Booking type field on the General tab?

✔ Booking types are most useful in the Enterprise environment, where you utilize the Enterprise Resource Pool. When you select Committed in the Booking type field, you reserve time on the resource's calendar. When you select Proposed in the Booking type field, you leave the resource's calendar untouched by assignments in your project. For Proposed Booking types, another project manager can commit the resource to a different project for the same time frame, and Project does *not* mark the resource as overallocated.

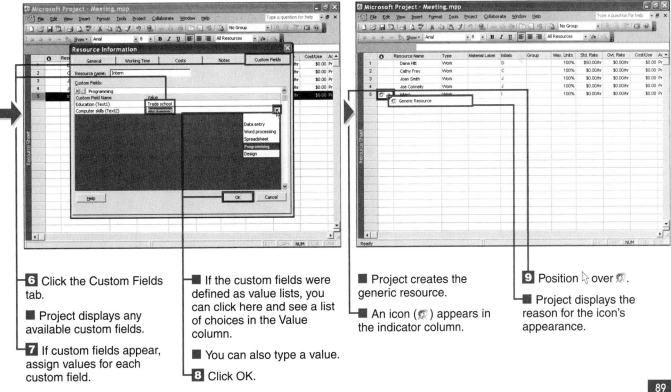

-6 Click the Custom Fields tab.

■ Project displays any available custom fields.

-7 If custom fields appear, assign values for each custom field.

■ If the custom fields were defined as value lists, you can click here and see a list of choices in the Value column.

■ You can also type a value.

-8 Click OK.

■ Project creates the generic resource.

■ An icon (🌼) appears in the indicator column.

-9 Position ⬚ over 🌼.

■ Project displays the reason for the icon's appearance.

SPECIFY RESOURCE AVAILABILITY

I f you share resources with other project managers, availability of resources is a constant concern. Project uses the term *availability* to identify when and how much of a resource's time you can schedule. For a specific person that works full time, the maximum time available is typically 100 percent. If your project calls for four electricians, you can schedule 400 percent of that resource. To identify a resource's availability, Project

considers the project's calendar, the resource's calendar, resource start and finish dates, and the amount of work already assigned to the resource.

Be careful not to confuse Resource Availability with a resource calendar. A particular resource may not be available for your project, but the resource may still be available to work. For example, you may have previously committed a resource to a different project for part of the

time during which your project runs. You can use the Resource Availability table of the Resource Information dialog box to determine if you have a time when the resource is available — or unavailable — for your project. You use a resource calendar to specify times, such as vacation, when the resource is unavailable for *all* projects. See the section "Create Resource Calendars" for more information on resource calendars.

SPECIFY RESOURCE AVAILABILITY

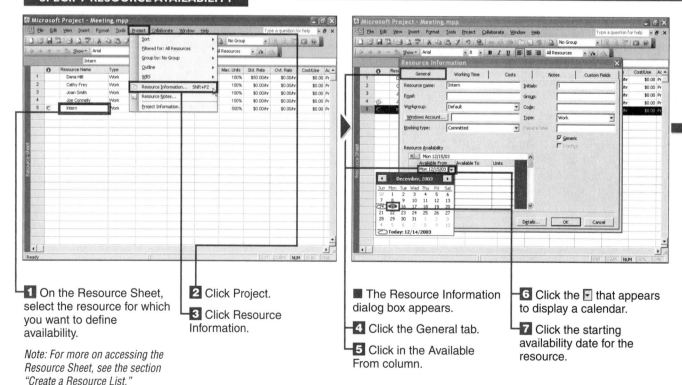

1 On the Resource Sheet, select the resource for which you want to define availability.

Note: For more on accessing the Resource Sheet, see the section "Create a Resource List."

2 Click Project.

3 Click Resource Information.

■ The Resource Information dialog box appears.

4 Click the General tab.

5 Click in the Available From column.

6 Click the ▾ that appears to display a calendar.

7 Click the starting availability date for the resource.

Do I use the Resource Availability table to indicate that a resource is available only three days per week?

✔ You can. In your example, assign the resource's availability units as 60 percent between the start and finish dates of your project.

Is there any easy way to tell that a resource is overallocated?

✔ Yes. In the Resource Sheet, an icon appears in the Indicator column and the resource appears in red.

Do the resource availability values have any effect on the resource's cost?

✔ No. Use cost rate tables to control differing resource rates over the life of your project.

If values appear in the Resource Availability table that indicate a resource is unavailable, does Project prohibit me from assigning the resource to work during that time?

✔ No. Project uses the resource availability information to determine when you overallocate a resource. Project considers the resource overallocated if you assign more work to the resource than the resource can complete in the available working time. You create an overallocated resource by assigning more units of the resource during a given time period than you have available.

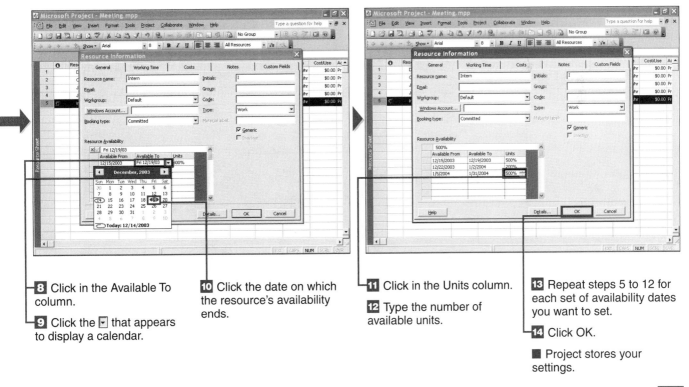

-8 Click in the Available To column.

-9 Click the ▼ that appears to display a calendar.

10 Click the date on which the resource's availability ends.

-11 Click in the Units column.

12 Type the number of available units.

13 Repeat steps 5 to 12 for each set of availability dates you want to set.

-14 Click OK.

■ Project stores your settings.

ENTER AND PRINT RESOURCE NOTES

Eventually, you collect information that applies to specific resources as you plan and track your project. You can attach notes to resources to remind you of certain parameters or details. For example, you may want to store a reminder about a resource's upcoming vacation or an explanation about resource availability. Or, if a resource brings certain information pertaining to

the project to your attention, along with information he finds on the Internet, you can store the Web site addresses for easy access. Project formats the addresses as hyperlinks so that you can click the link and immediately visit the Web site.

You can format the information that appears in notes using typical word processing formatting. You can apply boldface, italics, or

underline to the text, as well as select the font, font size, and font color. In addition, you can create bulleted lists and control paragraph formatting by applying left, center, or right justification.

When you add a note to a resource, you can display the note on-screen and include the note in a printed report.

ENTER AND PRINT RESOURCE NOTES

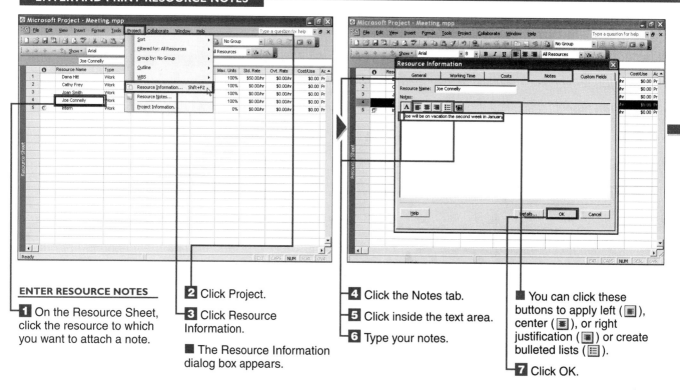

ENTER RESOURCE NOTES

1 On the Resource Sheet, click the resource to which you want to attach a note.

2 Click Project.

3 Click Resource Information.

■ The Resource Information dialog box appears.

4 Click the Notes tab.

5 Click inside the text area.

6 Type your notes.

■ You can click these buttons to apply left (▤), center (▤), or right justification (▤) or create bulleted lists (▤).

7 Click OK.

How can I change the font for the text in my note?

✔ While viewing the Notes tab of the Resource Information dialog box, click the Format Font tool (Ⓐ) on the toolbar. Project displays the Font dialog box. In this box, you can select the font and font size and also apply boldface, italics, underline, or color to the text.

How do I store a hyperlink in a note?

✔ Just type it on the Notes tab where you usually place text. To use the hyperlink, display the Notes tab of the Resource Information dialog box, and click the link.

In a note, can I include a graphic image stored on my hard drive?

✔ Yes. Click the Insert Object button (▣) on the toolbar above the area where you type text. The Insert Object dialog box appears. Click Create from File (○ changes to ◉), and navigate to the file on your hard drive.

Is there an easy way to delete notes I have placed in several resources, or must I edit each resource individually?

✔ There is an easy way. Select the resources that contain the notes that you want to clear. Click Edit, Clear, and then Notes. Project deletes the notes.

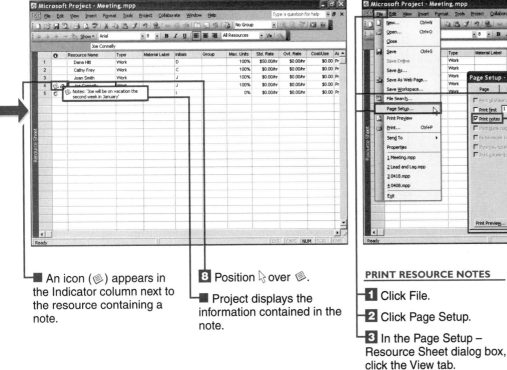

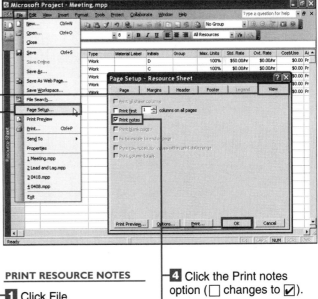

■ An icon (▤) appears in the Indicator column next to the resource containing a note.

8 Position ▷ over ▤.

■ Project displays the information contained in the note.

PRINT RESOURCE NOTES

1 Click File.

2 Click Page Setup.

3 In the Page Setup – Resource Sheet dialog box, click the View tab.

4 Click the Print notes option (☐ changes to ☑).

5 Click OK.

■ Project prints the report.

CREATE RESOURCE CALENDARS

By default, Project calculates the schedule using the Standard calendar as the project's base calendar, but that calendar does not take into consideration that you may not have all resources available at all times. To compensate, you can create resource calendars. See Chapter 2 for more information about establishing basic project scheduling information.

The Standard calendar assumes a Monday to Friday, 8 a.m. to 5 p.m., 40-hour workweek. When you

create a resource for your project, Project assigns the Standard calendar to the resource, assuming that the resource works eight-hour days and 40 hours per week. The entire project has a Standard calendar, and each resource has an individual calendar.

The individual resource calendar is rarely the same as the Standard calendar. First, human resources take time off from work. To avoid overallocating a person by assigning work during a vacation period, mark vacation days on the resource's

calendar. In addition, you may not have some resources available to you all day on one or more days. For example, you may have the high school age interns at your company who work from 1 p.m. to 6 p.m.

If necessary, modify the dates and working times that a resource is available.

CREATE RESOURCE CALENDARS

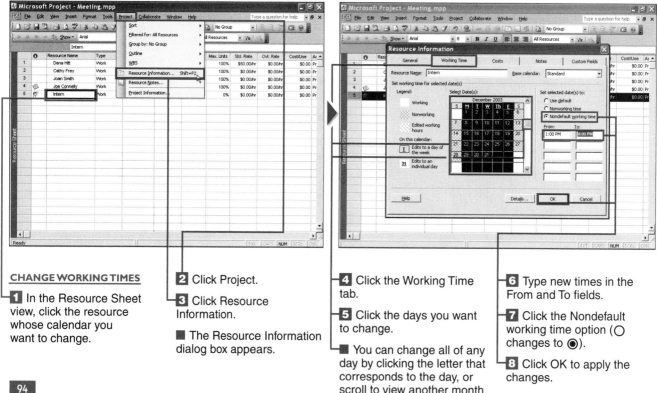

CHANGE WORKING TIMES

1 In the Resource Sheet view, click the resource whose calendar you want to change.

2 Click Project.

3 Click Resource Information.

■ The Resource Information dialog box appears.

4 Click the Working Time tab.

5 Click the days you want to change.

■ You can change all of any day by clicking the letter that corresponds to the day, or scroll to view another month.

6 Type new times in the From and To fields.

7 Click the Nondefault working time option (○ changes to ⦿).

8 Click OK to apply the changes.

How can I select contiguous or noncontiguous days?

✔ To select contiguous days, click the first day, press Shift and click the last day that you want to select. To select noncontiguous days, press Ctrl and click each day that you want to select.

Why is the Working Time tab of the Resource Information box gray and not available when I open the box?

✔ You selected a material resource before opening the box. Project does not use resource calendars for material resources; it is not logical to try to assign a calendar to paper or wood or gasoline.

I accidentally changed Sunday to scheduled working time. How do I change it back to nonworking time?

✔ Reselecting a date and clicking Use default returns the date to its originally scheduled time on that date.

What do I need to do to ensure that Project uses the modified resource calendar instead of the project calendar?

✔ Nothing. By default, Project schedules a task by checking both the project calendar and the resource calendars of resources assigned to the task.

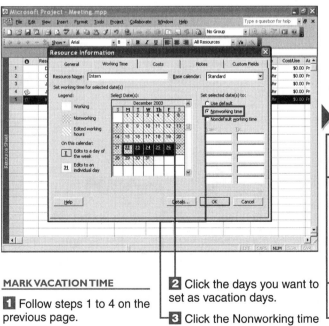

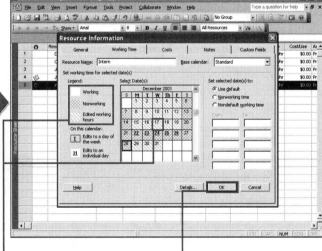

MARK VACATION TIME

1 Follow steps 1 to 4 on the previous page.

2 Click the days you want to set as vacation days.

3 Click the Nonworking time option (○ changes to ◉).

4 Click anywhere on the calendar.

■ The Legend panel identifies Working, Nonworking, and Edited working hours, as well as Edits to a day of the week or Edits to an individual day on the current calendar.

5 Click OK.

■ Project saves the resource calendar changes.

ASSIGN, FILTER, AND CHECK AVAILABILITY OF RESOURCES

You define resources because you need them to complete the tasks in a project schedule. Once you define resources, you need to assign them to tasks. Assigning resources involves designating a number of units, which you express as a percentage. For example, assigning a resource to work half time on a task means that you designate 50 percent of the resource. By default,

Project assigns 100 percent of a resource to a task if you do not assign a number of units.

Because you can consume material resources in two ways, fixed and variable, you must identify the consumption method when you assign material resources. *Fixed consumption* means that you use the same quantity of the material no matter how long the task lasts. *Variable consumption* means that

the length of the task does affect the amount of the material that you use. For example, building a swimming pool requires 2 tons of concrete, no matter how long it takes you to pour the concrete; the concrete is a fixed-consumption resource. When you mow the lawn with a gas mower, the amount of gas that you consume depends on how long you run the mower, making gas a variable-consumption resource.

ASSIGN, FILTER, AND CHECK AVAILABILITY OF RESOURCES

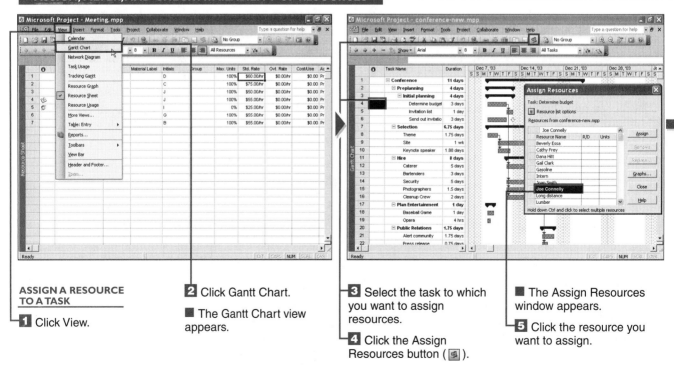

ASSIGN A RESOURCE TO A TASK

1 Click View.

2 Click Gantt Chart.

■ The Gantt Chart view appears.

3 Select the task to which you want to assign resources.

4 Click the Assign Resources button (▥).

■ The Assign Resources window appears.

5 Click the resource you want to assign.

Can I assign more than 100 percent of a resource?

✔ Yes. Assigning more than 100 percent may overallocate the resource, but Project will allow you to make the assignment.

When I type units, do I need to type the percent sign?

✔ No, Project assumes percentages. If you assign 100 percent of the resource, you do not need to type anything in the Units column; Project automatically assigns 100 percent of the resource. Type a value without the percent sign if you want to assign more or less than 100 percent of the resource.

What is the R/D column for?

✔ If you are using Project Server and you intend to use the Resource Substitution Wizard, in the R/D field, type **R** for Request to indicate that, considering other assignments already made to the task, any resource with the required skills can work on the task. You can type **D** for Demand to indicate that the selected resource is specifically required to work on the task. Leaving the column blank is the same as typing R except that Project does not consider any assignment already made to the task.

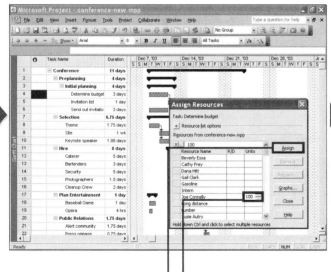

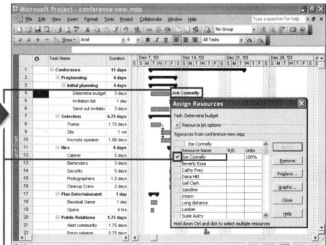

6 Click in the Units column next to the resource you have selected.

7 Type the percentage you want to assign.

8 Click Assign.

■ The check mark (☑) beside the resource's name indicates that Project assigned the units to the resource.

■ The resource's name appears at the right edge of the task bar.

■ You can repeat steps 1 to 8 to assign more resources to the task.

Note: The Assign Resources window remains open while you click another task and assign resources.

ASSIGN, FILTER, AND CHECK
AVAILABILITY OF RESOURCES (CONTINUED)

Y ou can leave the Assign
Resources window open as
you select different tasks
in your project to make resource
assignment much easier. The name
of the task to which you assign
resources appears at the top of
the Assign Resources window.

If you have trouble finding the
resource that you want to assign to
a task, you can have Project help
you. You can narrow the list of

resources that you see in the Assign
Resources window by filtering the
resources based on criteria that
you specify. For example, you can
search for only material resources
or you can search for resources in
a particular group. While Project
provides a fairly lengthy list of
filtering criteria, you can create
your own filter if you do not find
one that meets your needs. See
Chapter 6 to learn how to create
a custom filter.

You may not see the resource that
you want to assign to the task in
the Assign Resources window. In
this case, you may be able to add
the resource to your project from
Active Directory, from your address
book if you use a MAPI-compliant
e-mail program such as Microsoft
Outlook or Outlook Express, or
from Project Server.

ASSIGN, FILTER, AND CHECK AVAILABILITY OF RESOURCES (CONTINUED)

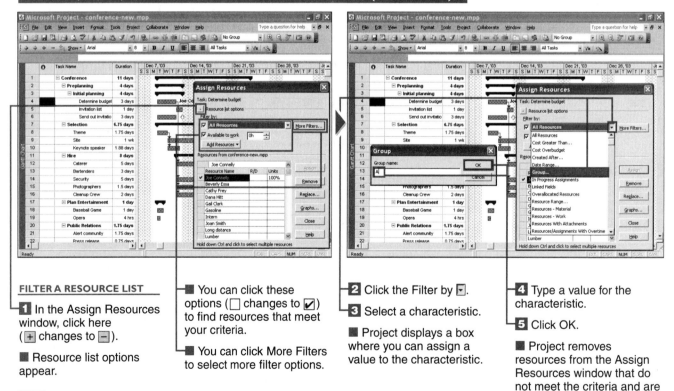

FILTER A RESOURCE LIST

1 In the Assign Resources
window, click here
(⊞ changes to ⊟).

■ Resource list options
appear.

■ You can click these
options (☐ changes to ☑)
to find resources that meet
your criteria.

■ You can click More Filters
to select more filter options.

2 Click the Filter by ▼.

3 Select a characteristic.

■ Project displays a box
where you can assign a
value to the characteristic.

4 Type a value for the
characteristic.

5 Click OK.

■ Project removes
resources from the Assign
Resources window that do
not meet the criteria and are
not assigned to the task.

If I need a resource for days instead of hours, do I need to convert the number of days to hours?

✔ No. Project makes the conversion for you. If you need a resource for nine days, type **9d** in the Available to work text field. Project converts the value to 72 hours.

When I click Add Resources, I see the Active Directory option. What is Active Directory?

✔ Active Directory is a Windows network feature used to control access to the network. In a Windows network, the administrator can set up Active Directory to contain a list of people and their contact information.

How does the Available to work option work?

✔ This option, which you access by clicking the Resource list options ⊞ (⊞ changes to ⊟), allows you to search for available resources for specific hours. When you select this option (☐ changes to ☑), Project calculates the remaining available hours of each resource for the duration of the task and compares the result with the number of hours that you specified. Resources with available hours equal to or greater than your value appear in the list, along with the resources that you have already assigned to the selected task.

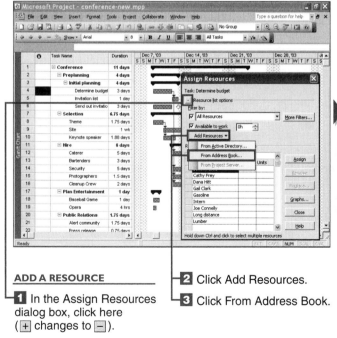

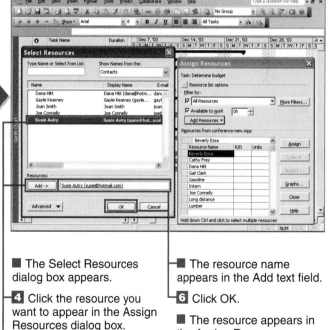

ADD A RESOURCE

1 In the Assign Resources dialog box, click here (⊞ changes to ⊟).

2 Click Add Resources.

3 Click From Address Book.

■ The Select Resources dialog box appears.

4 Click the resource you want to appear in the Assign Resources dialog box.

5 Click Add.

■ The resource name appears in the Add text field.

6 Click OK.

■ The resource appears in the Assign Resources window.

ASSIGN, FILTER, AND CHECK AVAILABILITY OF RESOURCES (CONTINUED)

As you make resource assignments, you may wonder if you are overallocating a resource; ideally, you want to know if you overallocate a resource *before* you assign the resource rather than having to fix the problem later.

Project contains three graphs that help you select the best resource for the job, and you can display these graphs without leaving the Assign Resources window. Be aware that none of these graphs relates particularly to a task for which you are considering a resource assignment; instead, the graphs focus on the resource.

The Work graph shows you, on a day-by-day basis, the amount of work that you have assigned to the selected resource, regardless of the task.

The Assignment Work graph breaks down the total workload of the resource under consideration by showing you the resource's workload on the selected task, other tasks, and the resource's total availability based on the calendar. Using this graph helps determine if you are overallocating the resource by assigning it to this task.

The Remaining Availability graph shows you the resource's unassigned time.

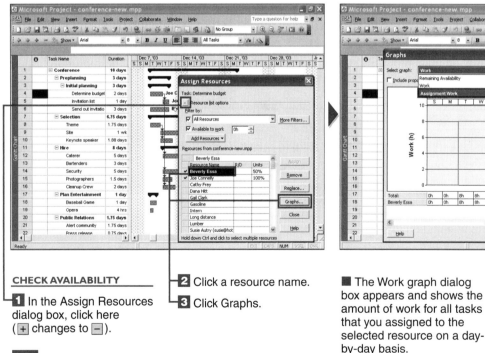

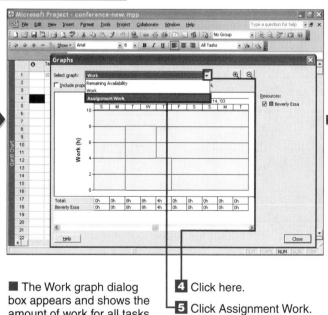

CHECK AVAILABILITY

1 In the Assign Resources dialog box, click here (⊞ changes to ⊟).

2 Click a resource name.

3 Click Graphs.

■ The Work graph dialog box appears and shows the amount of work for all tasks that you assigned to the selected resource on a day-by-day basis.

4 Click here.

5 Click Assignment Work.

MASTER IT

If I overallocate a resource, does the graph show a negative availability?
✔ No. If you overallocate a resource, you do not see a negative availability; the resource's availability is 0.

Besides the graphs, are there any other ways to recognize an overallocated resource?
✔ Yes. Project displays overallocated resources in red on the Resource Sheet view. To display the Resource Sheet view, see the section "View the Resource Sheet."

Can I graph more than one resource at a time?
✔ Yes, you can. To make the graph useful, select resources that have the same skill. Then you can see the remaining availability for all the resources — each with its own line.

How does Project calculate Available to work time?
✔ Project uses the resource's calendar, availability contour, and the duration of the task. Using the resource's calendar, Project calculates the number of working hours for the selected task. Project then multiplies available working hours by the availability contour value and subtracts existing assignment work hours to determine Available to work hours.

If I overallocate a resource, how do I fix the problem?
✔ Consider assigning a different resource, spreading the work out over a longer period of time by increasing the duration, or by changing the availability to 110-125 percent for a brief period to accommodate planned overtime (hopefully paid overtime!). Chapter 8 explains how to handle these problems in more detail.

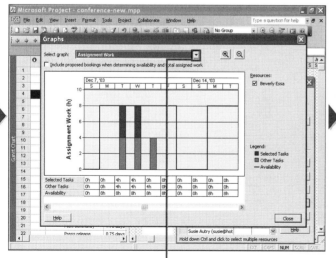

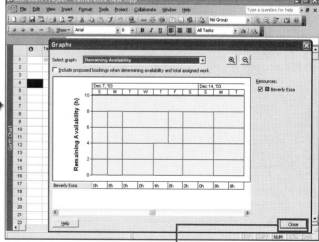

■ The Assignment Work graph appears in the Graphs dialog box and breaks down the total workload of the resource on the selected task and other tasks.

■ Using this graph helps you determine whether you will overallocate the resource by assigning it to this task.

6 Click here and select Remaining Availability.

■ The Remaining Availability graph appears in the Graphs dialog box.

■ The Remaining Availability graph shows you the resource's unassigned time.

7 Click Close.

■ The Assign Resources dialog box reappears.

REMOVE OR REPLACE RESOURCE ASSIGNMENTS

Y ou can be sure that at some point in your project you will want to change resource assignments. Perhaps you discover an overallocation that you want to correct, or perhaps a resource leaves the company. Perhaps the company hires a new resource that you want to assign in place of an existing resource because the new resource costs less to use.

Suppose, for example, that you are

planning a surprise party for your boss and, of course, you need to find a place to hold the party. After you complete that task and hire a caterer, the facility informs you that they had actually already had a commitment and you cannot hold the party there. In this case, you will need to replace the facility with a different facility, and you may need to hire a different caterer who is closer to the new facility

so that the food will not get cold. There are many reasons why you may need to change resource assignments.

You may want to remove an assignment completely, or you may want to switch the assignment to a different resource. Project enables you to easily switch assignments or remove them altogether.

REMOVE OR REPLACE RESOURCE ASSIGNMENTS

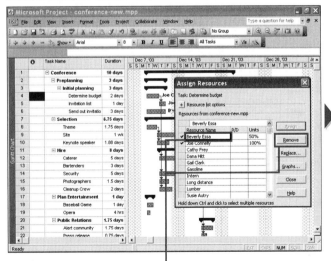

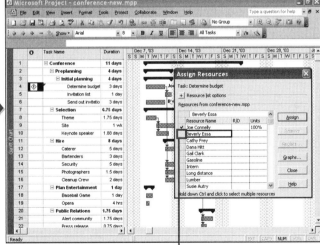

REMOVE A RESOURCE ASSIGNMENT

■1 Follow steps 1 to 4 on page 100.

■2 In the Assign Resources window, click the resource whose assignment you want to remove.

■3 Click Remove.

■ Project removes the resource assignment from the task.

■ Project removes the ☑ beside the resources name and moves the name below any remaining assignments.

Can I replace a work resource with a material resource?

✔ No. You also cannot replace a material resource with a work resource, but you can get around this issue. First, remove the work resource, then assign the material resource.

Can I replace one resource with several resources?

✔ Yes. In the Replace Resource dialog box, click each resource that you want to assign and supply a number of units for the resource. Project replaces one resource with many.

Can I replace one resource with more or less of another resource?

✔ Yes. If the task is effort-driven, changing the amount of the resource assignment affects the task's duration.

If I make a replacement, how does Project handle the assignment units and the work amounts?

✔ Project tries to maintain the assignment units and the work amounts for the replaced resource when possible, but the task type determines Project's behavior. See "How Project Handles Task Timing" in Chapter 3.

What happens if I replace one resource with several other resources and the percentages for the new resources do not equal the percentage for the original resource?

✔ If you change the assignments on an effort-driven task, Project adjusts the task's duration accordingly; a smart tag will appear, allowing you to adjust the Work or the Duration of the task.

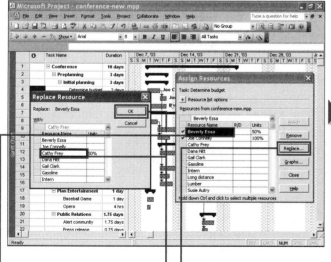

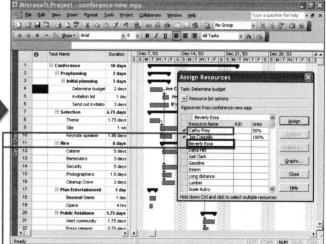

REPLACE AN ASSIGNMENT

1 Follow steps 1 to 4 on page 100.

2 In the Assign Resources window, click the resource whose assignment you want to replace.

3 Click Replace.

■ The Replace Resource dialog box appears.

4 Click each resource that you want to assign, and type a number of units.

5 Click OK.

■ Project switches the resource assignments.

HOW PROJECT GATHERS COST INFORMATION

Project gathers cost information from costs that you assign to a task. You can assign costs directly to a task, and you can assign costs to a resource that you then assign to tasks. Assigning costs enables you to monitor and control the money spent on a project. Project shows you where and how you are spending your money.

The cost-related information that Project provides helps you to verify the cost of resources and materials for any task, the cost of any phase of your project, and the cost of the entire project. This information can help you predict when a project's costs accrue, which, in turn, helps you to schedule your bill payments. Lastly, cost information that you gather on one project may help you to calculate bids for future projects.

Variable Task Costs

Most often, the cost of a task is a function of the cost of the resources assigned to the task and the amount of time that those resources take to complete the task. You generally assign a standard rate to the resource and, to determine the cost of the task, you multiply the resource's standard rate by the number of hours the resource takes to complete the task. The calculation is mathematical: Resource cost times the hours spent equals the cost of the task.

Fixed Task Costs

There are cases, however, where you cannot calculate the cost of a task in this simple, basic way. For example, some tasks are fixed-cost tasks. You know that the cost of a particular task stays the same regardless of the duration of the task or the work performed by any resources on the task. For tasks like these, you assign the cost directly to the task. If you assign a cost to a task, Project adds the fixed cost of the task to the cost of any resource work that you assign to the task when calculating costs for the project.

Remember that assigning a fixed cost to a task does not necessarily make the total cost of the task equal to the fixed cost that you assigned. You can, for example, assign more than one fixed cost as well as resource-based costs to a task.

To learn more about adding fixed costs to tasks, see "Assign Fixed Costs to Tasks" later in this chapter.

Standard Rates for Resources

When you create a resource, you can assign a standard rate, and if you want, an overtime rate as well as a cost-per-use rate to the resource. Once you assign rates to your resources and then assign the resources to tasks, Project calculates the cost of your project using these rates. As noted above, Project also adds any fixed task costs that you assign.

The *standard rate* that you assign to resources represents the rate for work performed by the resource during regular business hours. Typically, the standard rate is expressed as a cost per hour. To calculate a task cost using the standard rate, Project multiplies the number of hours worked by the resource times the resource's standard rate. Project calculates the default rate in hours, but you can charge a resource's work in other time increments. For example, you may charge $100 per day for a trainer. For work resources, you can use minutes, days, weeks, or years. For material resources, think of the charge as per unit based on the unit you specify for the Material Label field.

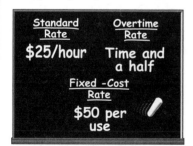

Overtime Rates for Resources

The *overtime rate* that you assign to resources represents the rate used in cost calculations for work performed by the resource outside of regular business hours. Again, Project calculates the default rate in hours, but you can change the default unit the same way that you changed it for the standard rate.

Fixed Costs for Resources

The *cost-per-use rate* that you can assign to a resource represents the rate to charge for each time you use the resource. You can think of the cost-per-use rate you assign to a resource as a fixed fee that is charged for each use of the resource.

To read more about the effects of fixed resource costs on tasks, see the section "Assign Fixed Costs to a Task" later in this chapter.

Accruing Costs

For each task fixed cost and each resource rate that you assign to a task or resource, you can control how and when Project charges the costs to a task. The Prorated option, which is the default option, tells Project to accrue the cost of the task as you complete scheduled work. You also can tell Project to accrue the cost either as soon as the task begins or when the task ends. Please note that you cannot prorate a per-use resource cost; instead, you assign an effective date for the cost.

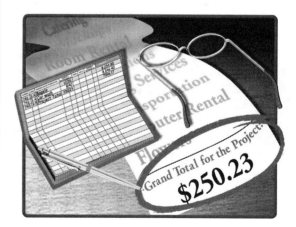

ASSIGN FIXED COSTS TO TASKS

You can create fixed-cost tasks in Project. A *fixed-cost task* is one for which the cost stays the same regardless of the duration of the task or the work that resources perform on the task. For example, if your catering service washes linens, you can assign the fixed cost of washing linens as an expense of a catering event. This cost may include the expense of detergent, fabric softener, water,

and electricity as well as the wear-and-tear costs to the machine — assuming that you own it — each time that you run a wash cycle. Likewise, renting a site for a meeting for a flat fee is a fixed-cost task in your project.

In cases like these, where the cost is static dependent on the task and not on resources assigned to the task, you assign the cost directly to

the task. Project adds the fixed task cost to the cost of any resource work assigned to the task when calculating costs for the task and, ultimately, for the project.

In this section, you can apply different tables to views comprised of a table and a chart. For more information on tables and views, see Chapter 6 and Appendix A.

ASSIGN FIXED COSTS TO TASKS

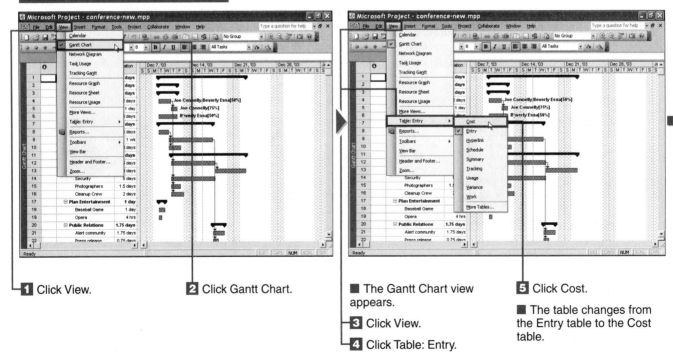

1 Click View.

2 Click Gantt Chart.

■ The Gantt Chart view appears.

3 Click View.

4 Click Table: Entry.

5 Click Cost.

■ The table changes from the Entry table to the Cost table.

What does the Fixed Cost Accrual column do?

✔ It helps you control when Project accrues the fixed cost for a task. Selecting Prorated tells Project to accrue the cost as you complete scheduled work. You also select Start or Finish to tell Project to accrue the cost as soon as the task begins or when the task ends.

Can I ensure that Project accrues all fixed costs consistently in my project?

✔ Yes. Click Tools and then click Options. Click the Calculation tab and click ⊡ next to Default fixed costs accrual to select Prorated, Start, or Finish. By default, Project prorates fixed costs.

Why is the total cost for the task not equal to the fixed cost I assigned?

✔ You assigned other fixed or variable costs to your task along with the fixed cost.

Can I set a fixed cost for the entire project?

✔ Yes. Click Tools and then click Options. On the View tab, under Outline options, click the Project summary task option (☐ changes to ☑), and click OK. On your project, click in the Fixed Cost field for the project summary task and type the cost.

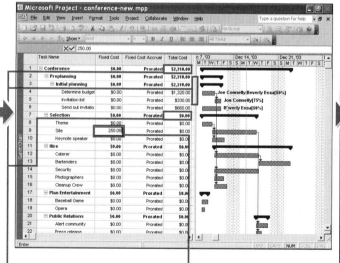

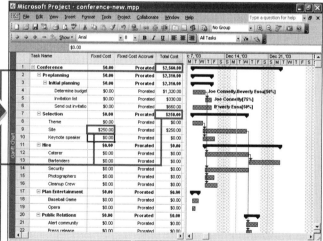

6 Click and drag the splitter bar to show more of the table.

7 Take note of the total cost of the summary task as well as the cost of the project.

8 Click the Fixed Cost field of the task to which you want to assign a fixed cost, and type the fixed cost.

9 Press Enter.

■ Project updates the cost of the task, the cost of the task's summary task, and the total cost of the project.

ASSIGN A FIXED-COST RESOURCE TO A TASK

If you assign a standard rate, an overhead rate, and a cost-per-use rate to a resource, Project can include the cost of using the resource when Project calculates the cost of your project. Project also adds any fixed task costs that you assign when calculating the cost of your project.

The *standard rate*, expressed as a cost per hour, represents the rate for work performed by the resource

during regular business hours. To calculate a task cost using the standard rate, Project multiplies the number of hours worked by the resource times the resource's standard rate.

The *overtime rate* represents the rate for work performed by the resource outside of regular business hours. Again, Project calculates overtime cost by multiplying the number of overtime hours times the cost per hour.

The *cost-per-use rate* represents a fixed resource cost. Fixed resource costs are fees that you charge each time you use the resource. For example, you may charge $200 each time you use a printing press to cover the cost of setting up the press.

For more on standard, overhead, and cost-per-use rates, see the section "How Project Gathers Cost Information" earlier in this chapter.

ASSIGN A FIXED-COST RESOURCE TO A TASK

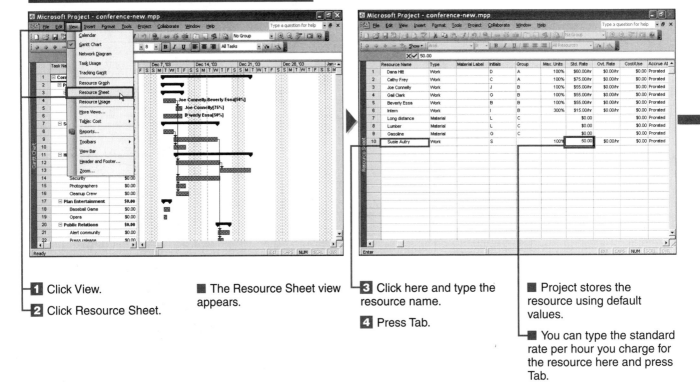

-1 Click View.

-2 Click Resource Sheet.

■ The Resource Sheet view appears.

-3 Click here and type the resource name.

4 Press Tab.

■ Project stores the resource using default values.

■ You can type the standard rate per hour you charge for the resource here and press Tab.

When do I use a fixed-cost resource?

✔ You use a fixed-cost resource whenever the cost of using the resource does not depend on any time factor or any per unit cost factor. For example, if you hire a consultant to perform a task for a fixed amount of money, you assign the consultant to the task as a fixed-cost resource.

What do I do if the cost of using the resource does depend on a time factor and a per-hour rate?

✔ Assign a standard rate, an overtime rate, and a cost-per-use rate.

Must I assign a standard rate and an overtime rate to the resource if I am going to assign a fixed cost?

✔ No. If you assign only a Cost/Use rate and do not assign a standard or overtime rate to the resource, Project assigns the Cost/Use rate to the task when you assign the resource to the task. In this case, Project ignores the number of hours the resource works on the task when calculating the cost of the task and the cost of your project.

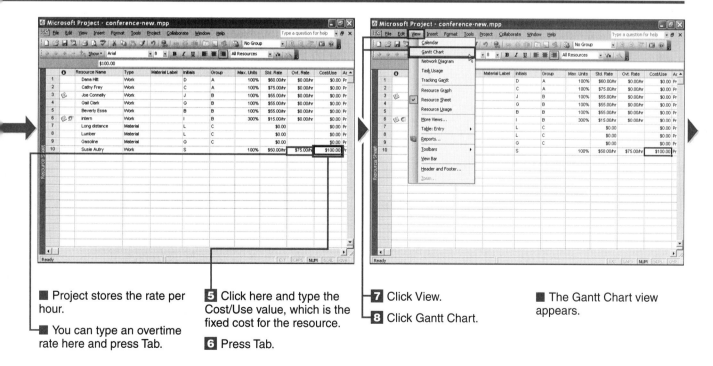

■ Project stores the rate per hour.

■ You can type an overtime rate here and press Tab.

5 Click here and type the Cost/Use value, which is the fixed cost for the resource.

6 Press Tab.

7 Click View.

8 Click Gantt Chart.

■ The Gantt Chart view appears.

CONTINUED ▶

ASSIGN A FIXED-COST RESOURCE TO A TASK (CONTINUED)

You can have a task comprised of a fixed-cost resource as well as other costs. When calculating the total cost of the task, Project adds a fixed resource cost to other resource and task costs, but the fixed resource cost does not depend on the time that the resource spends working on the task.

You can assign a fixed-cost resource to a task in two different ways. Project Help describes a method in which you use a split view, with the Gantt Chart appearing in the top portion of your screen, and the Task Form appearing in the bottom. In this view, you record 0% of the resource assigned to the task but supply a cost. While this method assigns a fixed-cost resource to the task, it also has

potential undesirable side effects. For example, when you assign only one resource to the task, Project turns the task into a Milestone; the duration of the task is lost, and Project does not apply future resource rate or availability changes to the task.

The method described here works also and has none of the side effects listed above.

ASSIGN A FIXED-COST RESOURCE TO A TASK (CONTINUED)

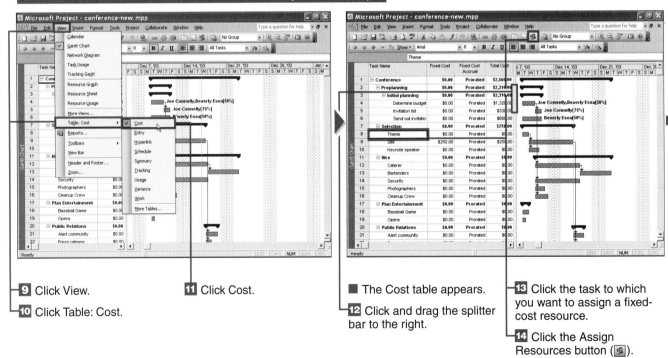

-9 Click View.

-10 Click Table: Cost.

11 Click Cost.

■ The Cost table appears.

12 Click and drag the splitter bar to the right.

13 Click the task to which you want to assign a fixed-cost resource.

14 Click the Assign Resources button (▣).

Was it necessary to switch to the Cost table to assign the fixed resource cost to the task?

✔ No, but switching to the Cost table enables you to see the impact on the cost of the task when you assign the resource.

What happens if I do not assign 100 percent of a resource with both a fixed and variable cost to the task?

✔ Project assigns the fixed cost of the resource to the task as a lump sum. The variable amount changes, because Project calculates the variable cost for the resource as (Units x Std. Rate) + (Units x Ovt. Rate).

In the example for this section, how did Project arrive at a cost of $500 for the Theme task when the fixed cost was $100?

✔ Susie Autry's rate per hour is $50, and she is assigned full time — 100 percent — to a one-day task. Using a calendar that specifies an eight-hour day, Susie spends eight hours on the task, making her variable cost $50 x 8 hours = $400. Project added Susie's fixed cost of $100 to her variable cost of $400 to arrive at a total cost for the task of $500.

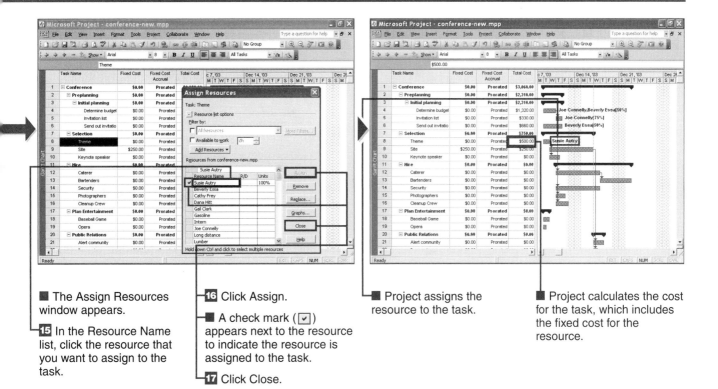

■ The Assign Resources window appears.

15 In the Resource Name list, click the resource that you want to assign to the task.

16 Click Assign.

■ A check mark (☑) appears next to the resource to indicate the resource is assigned to the task.

17 Click Close.

■ Project assigns the resource to the task.

■ Project calculates the cost for the task, which includes the fixed cost for the resource.

VIEW THE PROJECT'S ESTIMATED COST

O nce you assign costs to your project, you lay all the groundwork necessary to view the total estimated cost of your project. You can view the estimated cost of the project at any point; typically, you take a first look at estimated project cost after you have assigned costs to your project even if you still need to tweak your project before beginning work. Because management measures a project's success, in

part, by the cost, identifying the estimated cost of your project is important. For more on assigning costs to your project, see the previous sections in this chapter.

In this section, you take a look at estimated project costs for the first time — before you finish the planning phase and before you set a baseline. A *baseline* is a snapshot of your project at a point in time — typically set after you complete the

planning phase and just before you begin the tracking phase. You use baselines to compare estimates to actual information. For more information on what a baseline is and when and how to set one, see Chapter 12. Part IV covers tracking, recording work done, and analyzing and reporting on progress. Chapter 13 describes ways to view project costs once you have started tracking progress.

VIEW THE PROJECT'S ESTIMATED COST

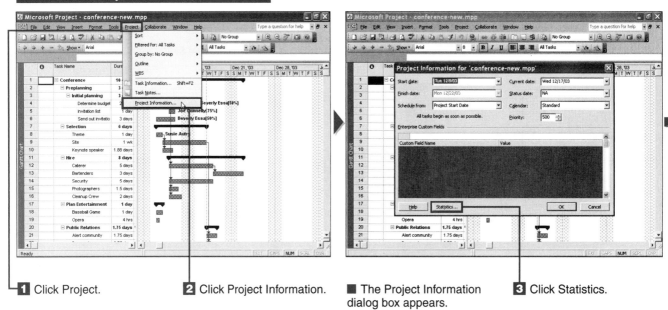

1 Click Project.

2 Click Project Information.

■ The Project Information dialog box appears.

3 Click Statistics.

Why are the Baseline and Actual values for Duration, Work, and Cost for the section example all 0?

✔ This project is still in the planning stages and has not yet been started. No baseline has been set yet, and no information has been recorded to reflect actual work performed on the project. At this point, Project has no information to provide about the baseline or actual duration, work assignments, or cost of the project.

Does it matter what view I use when I perform this task?

✔ No. The Project Information dialog box and the Project Statistics dialog box are available from all views.

What does Variance mean in the top of the Project Statistics box?

✔ Variance, calculated in days, represents the difference between the initial start or finish date estimate, which is called the baseline estimate, and the actual date you start or finish the task.

Why has Project set the Current Finish Date to 12/22/03 in the example for this section?

✔ The Current Duration value indicates that the project will last ten days. There are ten working days between December 9 and December 22.

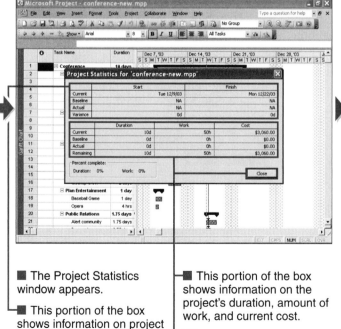

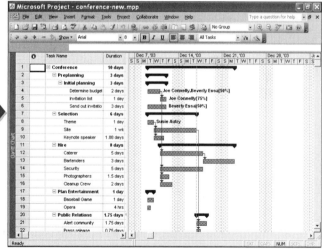

■ The Project Statistics window appears.

■ This portion of the box shows information on project dates.

■ This portion of the box shows information on the project's duration, amount of work, and current cost.

4 Click Close.

■ The project reappears.

ACCOUNT FOR RESOURCE RATE CHANGES

Life is rarely static, and neither are resource rates. Invariably, resource rates increase or decrease, and to accurately evaluate the cost of your project, you need to account for those changes.

Rate increases or decreases to resources are not the only rate changes for which you may need to account. For example, in some situations, you may need to charge

different rates on different tasks for the same resource. In Project, you handle these rate change situations using *cost rate tables*. When you set up cost rate tables, you define the various rates you need to assign to resources, and you identify an effective date for each rate. Project then uses the cost rate tables to accurately reflect resource costs as they change.

You can find the cost rate tables on the Costs tab of the Resource Information dialog box, where you find five tabs representing the cost rate tables. After establishing rates on the tables, you can assign a rate table to a task. Project checks the cost rate tables when calculating the cost of a task and calculates the cost of the task based on the cost rate table in effect during the dates of the task.

ACCOUNT FOR RESOURCE RATE CHANGES

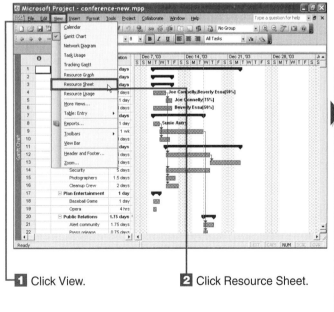

1 Click View.

2 Click Resource Sheet.

■ The Resource Sheet view appears.

3 Double-click a resource.

■ The Resource Information dialog box for the resource appears.

4 Click the Costs tab.

5 Click Effective Date ▾.

6 In the calendar that appears, select the date.

Can the dates I define on Tab A overlap with dates that I define on Tab B?

✔ Yes. By default, Project uses rates on Tab A when calculating a task's cost. If you assign different rates using the same dates on another tab, you must assign the appropriate cost rate table to the task. You cannot use the same dates on the same tab.

How many rates can I set up?

✔ You can identify up to 125 rates and associated effective dates for a single resource. Project enables you to store as many as 25 rates on each cost rate table.

Is there an easy way to specify a new rate as an increase or decrease of an existing rate?

✔ Yes. You can type the new rate as a percentage such as +10% or -10%, making sure that you enter the percent sign (%). When Project sees the percent sign, it calculates the value of the rate for you as a percentage of the existing rate.

Can I assign different Cost Accrual methods for each rate table?

✔ No. The Cost Accrual method applies to all cost rate tables.

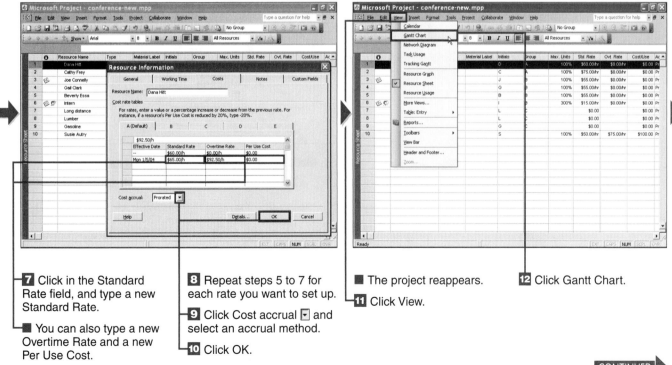

–7 Click in the Standard Rate field, and type a new Standard Rate.

■ You can also type a new Overtime Rate and a new Per Use Cost.

8 Repeat steps 5 to 7 for each rate you want to set up.

9 Click Cost accrual ▼ and select an accrual method.

–10 Click OK.

■ The project reappears.

–11 Click View.

12 Click Gantt Chart.

CONTINUED ▶

ACCOUNT FOR RESOURCE RATE CHANGES (CONTINUED)

The Cost tab of the Resource Information dialog box contains five tabs — Tabs A through E — that are, in fact, the cost rate tables. Each table contains many lines that you can fill with your various cost rates and their effective dates.

If you have many different cost rates to define, you may want to give some thought to organizing the

cost rate table tabs, because Project uses the rates on a particular tab to calculate the cost of the task. For example, if you charge different amounts for resources depending on the type of work that they perform, you may want to designate the costs on Tab A to represent one kind of work while the costs on Tab B represent a different kind of work.

The Task Usage view shows you the amount of time that a resource is assigned to a particular task. From the Task Usage view, you can identify the cost of a task and simultaneously specify the cost rate table that you want Project to use when calculating the cost of the task.

See Chapter 11 for more information on project costs.

ACCOUNT FOR RESOURCE RATE CHANGES (CONTINUED)

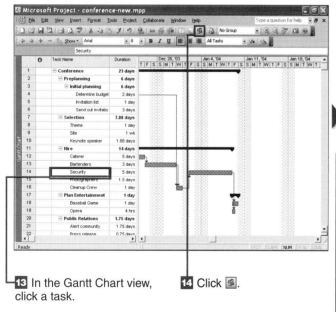

13 In the Gantt Chart view, click a task.

14 Click 🔄.

■ The Assign Resources window appears.

15 Click the resource you want to assign to the task.

■ In the Units column, you can type a value to assign less than 100 percent of the resource.

16 Click Assign.

■ A ✓ appears next to the resource.

17 Click Close.

For the section example, how did Project calculate a resource cost of $2560 for Dana Hitt?

✔ Dana is assigned to the Security task, which runs for five days between January 2 and January 8, skipping the holiday designated on the project calendar on January 1. Dana's rate change becomes effective on January 5, when her rate increases from $60 per hour to $65 per hour. Therefore, she will work on the Security task for eight hours at $60 per hour for a cost of $480 and for 32 hours at $65 per hour hour for a cost of $2080, bringing the total cost of her assignment on the task to $2560.

When I select a different cost rate table in the Assignment Information dialog box, the cost does not change. What did I do wrong?

✔ You need to save the change you made in the Assignment Information dialog box before Project reflects it. After you click the Cost rate table ⊡ and select a new cost table, click OK to save the change. When you reopen the Assignment Information dialog box, Project uses the new cost table that you selected to calculate the cost of the task.

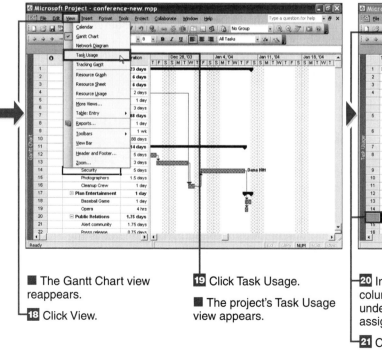

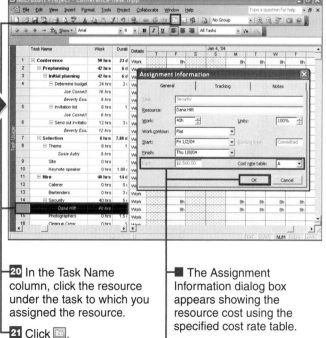

■ The Gantt Chart view reappears.

18 Click View.

19 Click Task Usage.

■ The project's Task Usage view appears.

20 In the Task Name column, click the resource under the task to which you assigned the resource.

21 Click 🗒.

■ The Assignment Information dialog box appears showing the resource cost using the specified cost rate table.

22 Click OK.

■ Project applies your changes.

UNDERSTANDING PROJECT VIEWS

Views in Project enable you to enter, organize, and examine project information in various ways. Using different views helps you focus on different aspects of the project while all project information remains stored in the project file, using different views allows you to see only the portions of the project information that you need to see. And, the same information appears on more than one view; for example, a task's duration appears on both the Gantt Chart view and the Task Sheet view.

Views may be comprised of a table and a chart, a table and a details section, only a table, or only a graph. See Appendix A for examples of the various views available in Project. You can categorize the views that you find in Project into three types, and Project often uses them in combination.

You may notice icons appearing in the leftmost column of table views; these icons are *indicators* that represent additional information about the row in which they appear. For example, you see a Notes indicator in the Indicator field on the resource sheet if you assign a note to a resource. See Chapter 4 for more information about assigning notes to resources.

If you see an indicator, you can position the mouse pointer over it to identify its purpose. Project tells you what the indicator means or displays additional information to remind you of important details. See the Project Help topic, "About Indicators," for a complete list of each indicator icon and its meaning.

Chart and Graph Views

Chart and graph views present information by using pictures. The Gantt Chart view is a chart view, and the Resource graph is a graph view.

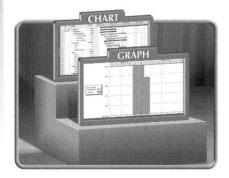

Sheet Views

Also called table views, sheet views present information in tables comprised of rows and columns, similar to the way information appears in a spreadsheet program. The Resource Sheet view is a sheet view, and each row on the sheet contains all the information about an individual resource in your project. Each column represents a field that identifies the information that you are storing about the resource.

Some sheet views, like the Resource Usage view, also contain a details section on the right side of the view. The details section is usually in table form, and Project enables you to add information to the details section; for example, you can simultaneously view both Work, which is the estimated effort to complete the task, and Actual Work, which is work already completed on a task.

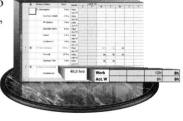

Forms

As you might expect, form views present information in a way that resembles a paper form. The Task Form displays information about a single task in your project.

You can find views that focus on task information, views that focus on resource information, and combination views that show both task and resource information; in a typical combination view, you see task information in the top portion of the view and resource information in the bottom portion of the view.

You can modify the default views by switching what appears on-screen. You also can create custom views and combination views.

Constraint Indicators

Constraint indicators identify the type of constraint that is assigned to a task. For example, a task can have a flexible constraint, such as Finish No Later Than, if the task is scheduled from the finish date. Or, a task can have an inflexible constraint, such as Must Start On, for tasks that are scheduled from the start date. Constraint indicators also show that the task has not been completed within the time frame of the constraint.

Task Type Indicators

These indicators may identify special conditions about a task, such as whether the task is a recurring task or whether the task has been completed. Task type indicators also identify the status of projects that are inserted in a task. You can find out more about inserted projects in Chapter 16.

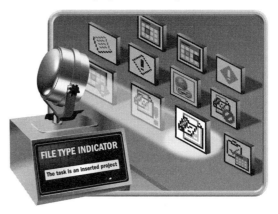

Workgroup Indicators

These indicators provide some information about the task and its resources. For example, a workgroup indicator can tell you that a task has been assigned but that the resource has not yet confirmed the assignment.

Contour Indicators

These indicators identify the type of contouring that is used to distribute the work assigned to the task. Read more about contouring in Chapter 12.

Miscellaneous Indicators

These indicators identify items, such as a note or a hyperlink, that you created; a calendar that you have assigned to a task; or a resource that needs leveling.

SWITCH VIEWS

Project has many built-in views that you can use to enter, organize, and examine project information in a variety of different ways. Viewing your project in different ways helps you focus on different aspects of the project, because views display the portion of the information in the project that is relevant to the view. While all project information remains stored in the project file, using views allows you see only the portion that you need to see.

Because Project gives you many different ways to look at your project, you need to know how to switch views. You can use two different methods. Project stores the views that most people use frequently on the View menu, so you can easily switch among the most popular views using a menu. To display the other views, you must utilize the More Views command on the Views menu.

Please note that the same information appears on more than one view. For example, you can see a task's duration on both the Gantt Chart and the Task Sheet views. See Appendix A, which contains examples of the various views available in Project, to see the different kinds of information that you will find on a particular view.

SWITCH VIEWS

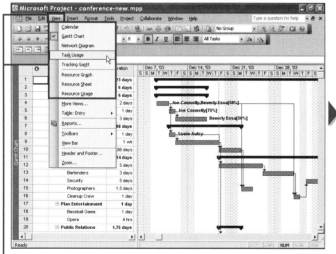

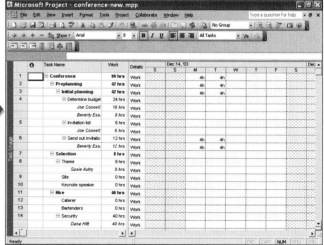

SELECT FROM THE MENU

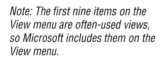 Click View.

2 Click the view you want to display.

Note: The first nine items on the View menu are often-used views, so Microsoft includes them on the View menu.

■ The view you clicked appears.

What do I do if I need to simultaneously see information that Project stores on two different views?

✔ You have two choices. You can use an existing combination view or you can create a new view. See the sections "Display and Change Combination Views" and "Create a New View" or "Create a New Combination View" later in this chapter to learn more about these options.

How do I know which view to select?

✔ Experience is the best teacher here. Study the figures in Appendix A to get a feel for the information Project displays in each view.

When I switch from the Resource Sheet to the Gantt Chart view, why do I not see the cost of my resources that I entered on the Resource Sheet?

✔ Each view focuses on providing a particular kind of information. Although you see the names of resources assigned to tasks on the Gantt Chart, the view helps you focus primarily on task timing and dependencies. On the other hand, the Resource Sheet view helps you focus exclusively on resource information and shows no task information at all to distract you.

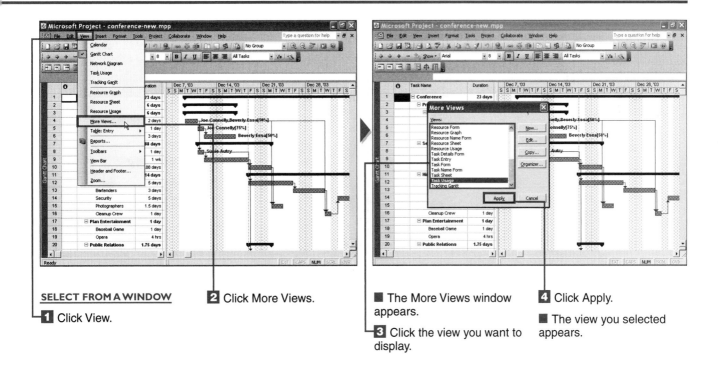

SELECT FROM A WINDOW

1 Click View.

2 Click More Views.

■ The More Views window appears.

3 Click the view you want to display.

4 Click Apply.

■ The view you selected appears.

CREATE A NEW VIEW

Views display a variety of information. Some views contain or are comprised of tables with several fields of data, while other views contain task bars or network diagram nodes. Project provides a plethora of views, meeting just about every information need.

Nevertheless, you may want to create a variation on one of those views to look at information from a different perspective. For example,

if you constantly find yourself modifying the Network Diagram so that it displays different information than the default Network Diagram shows, you can save time by creating a new view. In this case, create a second Network Diagram view in which you set the nodes to display the information that you need frequently, eliminating the need to modify the nodes in the original Network Diagram view each time to see the

information that you call on frequently. You can save time and effort by creating a new view.

Project makes it easy to create a new view. You can use an existing view as the foundation for your new view and change the information that Project displays by default to include only the information that you need.

CREATE A NEW VIEW

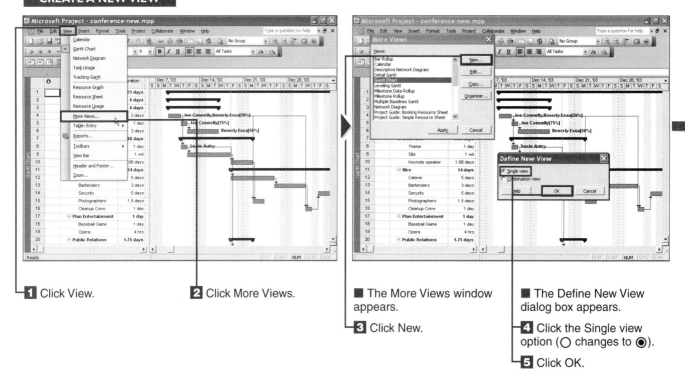

1 Click View.

2 Click More Views.

■ The More Views window appears.

3 Click New.

■ The Define New View dialog box appears.

4 Click the Single view option (○ changes to ●).

5 Click OK.

When should I define a Group in the View Definition dialog box?

✔ Use a group when you want to organize the information in a particular way. Project supplies different groups for tasks and resources; if you do not find a group that meets your needs, you can create your own group. See Chapter 8 for more information.

What does the Highlight filter option do?

✔ Project normally hides the tasks or resources that do not meet the filter criteria. When you select this option (□ changes to ☑), Project highlights tasks in the view that meet the filter criteria you defined for the view to make the filtered tasks easy to identify.

When do I use a Filter?

✔ You use a filter, which you select in the View Definition dialog box, when you want to limit the information that appears in the view. For example, in a task view, you may want to filter out all but the most critical tasks.

What does the Show in menu option do?

✔ If you find that you use a view frequently, select this option (□ changes to ☑) in the View Definition dialog box. Project displays the view name on the View menu so that you do not need to open the More Views window to apply the view.

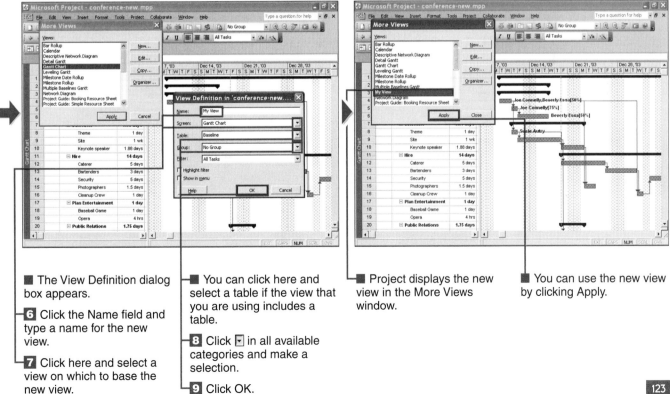

■ The View Definition dialog box appears.

6 Click the Name field and type a name for the new view.

7 Click here and select a view on which to base the new view.

■ You can click here and select a table if the view that you are using includes a table.

8 Click ▾ in all available categories and make a selection.

9 Click OK.

■ Project displays the new view in the More Views window.

■ You can use the new view by clicking Apply.

DELETE A VIEW

On occasion, you may find that you do not need a previously created view. If you do not want it to continue to clutter up the More Views window or even the View menu, you can delete the view.

Project stores views that you create in the project in which you create them. When you view the Organizer window, as shown in the example

for this section, you see all previously created or used views in your project in the list on the right side of the window. Deleting a view on the right side of the window is safe in that it does not affect any other project.

However, on the left side of the Organizer window, Project displays, by default, all views that it stores

in the global template file — global.mpt. These are the views that Project lists in the More Views window. Deleting any view from the global template file affects *all* projects, and that view becomes unavailable for any project.

The moral of the story? Unless you *really* know what you are doing, leave the left side of the window alone.

DELETE A VIEW

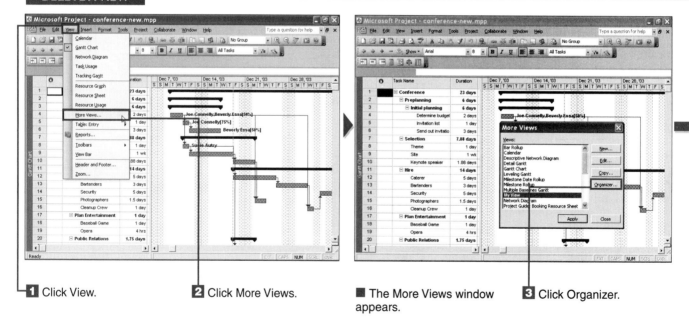

1 Click View.

2 Click More Views.

■ The More Views window appears.

3 Click Organizer.

I opened the Views available in the list box on the left side of the Organizer window, and I saw both the Global.mpt file and my project file. Why?

✔ The Views available in list boxes on both the left and right sides of the Organizer window display all open project files. You can select any open file to appear in either list, which is a handy feature when you want to copy a view or table from one project to another. See the section, "Copy a View from One Project to Another," later in this chapter for more information.

Can I delete a default view from the right side of the window?

✔ Although the views on the right have the same name as the default views, they may include changes you made to the default view. While you can delete any view that appears on the right, make sure that you have not customized the view before you delete it.

I deleted a view by accident. Can I get it back?

✔ If you copied it to the Global template or another project, you can copy it back. Otherwise, you need to use a backup of your file that contains the missing view.

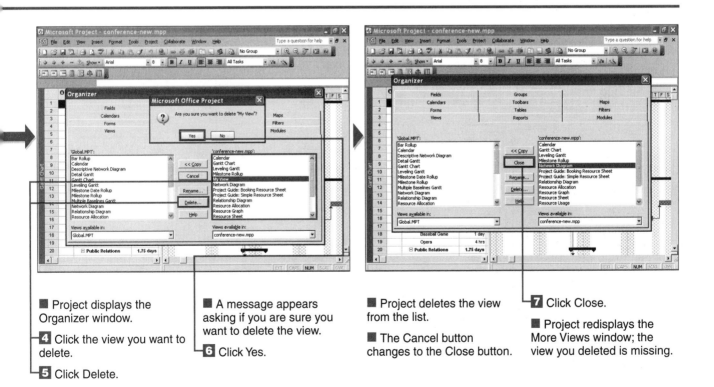

■ Project displays the Organizer window.

4 Click the view you want to delete.

5 Click Delete.

■ A message appears asking if you are sure you want to delete the view.

6 Click Yes.

■ Project deletes the view from the list.

■ The Cancel button changes to the Close button.

7 Click Close.

■ Project redisplays the More Views window; the view you deleted is missing.

EDIT A VIEW

I f Project contains a view that is similar but not quite the same as the view that you want to create, instead of creating your view from scratch, you can edit an existing view. For example, if you know that you want to group tasks on the Gantt Chart to show completed tasks separately from uncompleted tasks, you can edit the

default Gantt Chart and change its grouping. Or, if you want a view of the Resource Sheet that shows only overallocated resources, you can edit the default Resource Sheet and change its filter. Or, if you want a view of the Gantt Chart using the Variance table, you can edit the default Gantt Chart and change its table.

Editing a default view causes no harm if you know that you will never use Project's version of the view in your project. However, if you are not certain, you should make a copy of the default view instead of editing it. That way, you can leave the default view intact and available but still easily create the view you need.

EDIT A VIEW

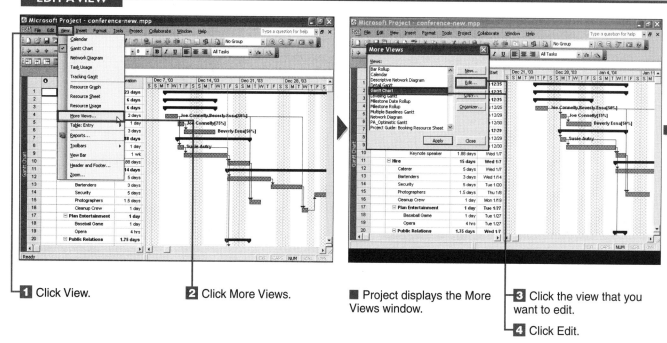

1 Click View.

2 Click More Views.

■ Project displays the More Views window.

3 Click the view that you want to edit.

4 Click Edit.

Can I edit one of the default views?
✔ Yes, but you really should not. Instead, copy the default view and make changes to the copy.

How do I copy a default View?
✔ In the More Views window, click the view you want to copy and then click Copy. The View Definition dialog box appears. Rename the view to something more meaningful than Copy of and then make your other changes. You cannot change the screen on which Project bases the copy, but you can make changes in all of the other fields.

When I copied a default view, why did the name that Project displayed include an ampersand (&)?
✔ The ampersand is the character Project uses to represent a menu command hot key — the key you press on your keyboard to execute the command without using your mouse. The hot key for any command is the underscored letter in the command name. When you include an ampersand before a character in a view name that you add to the View menu, be sure not to place the ampersand before a letter that Project already uses as a hot key on the View menu.

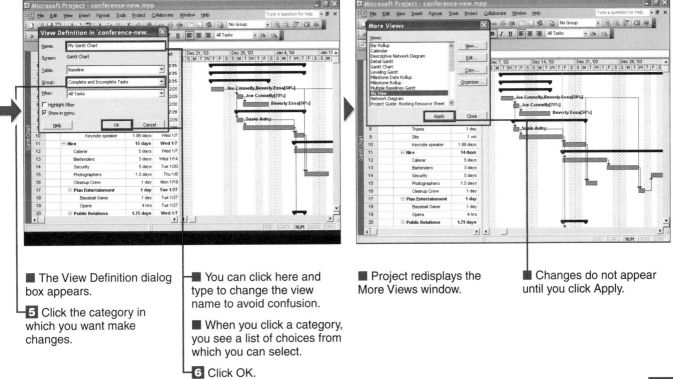

■ The View Definition dialog box appears.

5 Click the category in which you want make changes.

■ You can click here and type to change the view name to avoid confusion.

■ When you click a category, you see a list of choices from which you can select.

6 Click OK.

■ Project redisplays the More Views window.

■ Changes do not appear until you click Apply.

COPY A VIEW FROM ONE PROJECT TO ANOTHER

I f you work very hard to create a new view, getting it exactly the way you want it so it is a thing of wonder and beauty, and really want to use it in many other projects — in fact, you really want to make the view available to *all* projects, you can use the Organizer window to copy views from one project to another. This is especially useful when you have

put a lot of work into this view, and you do not want to re-create it for every project.

When you open the Organizer window, Project displays, by default, all of the elements that you have used on your project so far on the right side of the window. On the left side of the Organizer window are all of the elements stored in the global template file,

global.mpt, on which Project bases all new projects by default. If you copy your new view to the global template file, it appears in the More Views window and becomes available for you to use on every project.

You do not need to work in the project that contains the view you want to copy; you only need to open the project.

COPY A VIEW FROM ONE PROJECT TO ANOTHER

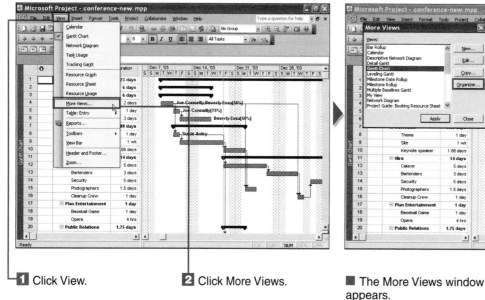

1 Click View.

2 Click More Views.

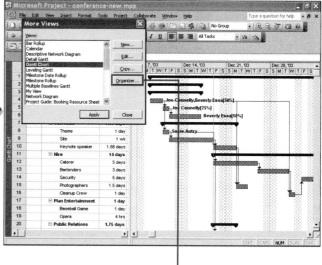

■ The More Views window appears.

3 Click Organizer.

You showed me how to copy to the global template file. How do I copy to another project file?

✔ Make sure that both the project containing the view you want to copy and the project to which you want to copy the view are open. Click the Views available in 🔽 on the left side of the Organizer window and select the project from which you are copying. Click the Views available in 🔽 on the right side of the Organizer window and select the project to which you are copying. Click Copy.

Why do I see more views on the right side of the Organizer window for some projects than for others?

✔ The right side of the Organizer window shows only the views you used in the selected project. If you used only a few views, you see only a few views. Do not confuse the views you see on the right side of the Organizer window with the views that are available to your project. All views in the global template file, which usually displays on the left side of the window, are available to your project.

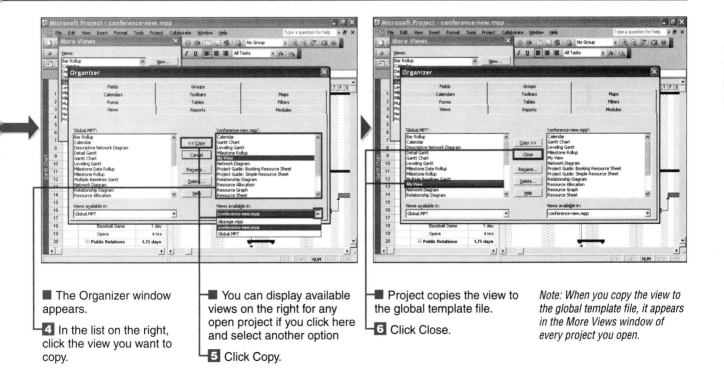

■ The Organizer window appears.

4 In the list on the right, click the view you want to copy.

■ You can display available views on the right for any open project if you click here and select another option

5 Click Copy.

■ Project copies the view to the global template file.

6 Click Close.

Note: When you copy the view to the global template file, it appears in the More Views window of every project you open.

DISPLAY AND CHANGE COMBINATION VIEWS

Project typically displays one view at a time, but you can display two views simultaneously. Called a *combination view*, Project splits the screen horizontally and displays one view in the top part of the screen and the other view in the bottom. Typically, the view in the bottom displays detailed information about the selected task or resource in the top view. Each

portion of the screen is referred to as a *pane* because it is part of a window, and only one pane is active at a time; you can identify the active pane if you look at the left edge of the screen. The view name that appears in the brighter bar identifies the active view.

Combination views are powerful tools. Suppose that you want to review the relationships and

dependencies for all tasks in the project. The Gantt Chart shows the list of tasks, but typically, you look at the Task Information form for details on predecessors. Use a combination view showing the Gantt Chart on top and the Task Form - Predecessor and Successors in the bottom to scroll to any task in the Gantt Chart and see all of the relationship details in the bottom pane.

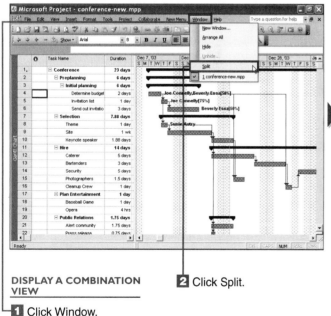

DISPLAY A COMBINATION VIEW

1 Click Window.

2 Click Split.

■ Project splits the screen with the original view on the top and a new view on the bottom.

I prefer to avoid menus; is there a way to split the view without using the menu?

✔ Yes. There are two ways, and both involve moving the mouse pointer (↳) over the splitter bar. When a single view appears on-screen, the splitter bar appears at the bottom edge of the right scroll bar. You can double-click the splitter bar, or you can click and drag it to split the view. To positively identify the splitter bar, see p. 18.

How do I remove a split view?

✔ You can click Window and then click Remove Split, or you can double-click the splitter bar.

I displayed a split view using the Gantt Chart and the Task Form view, and then I switched to the Resource Sheet, but only the top view changed. Why?

✔ Project retains the split view as you move from one view to another, and the new view you select replaces the view in the active pane unless you remove the split.

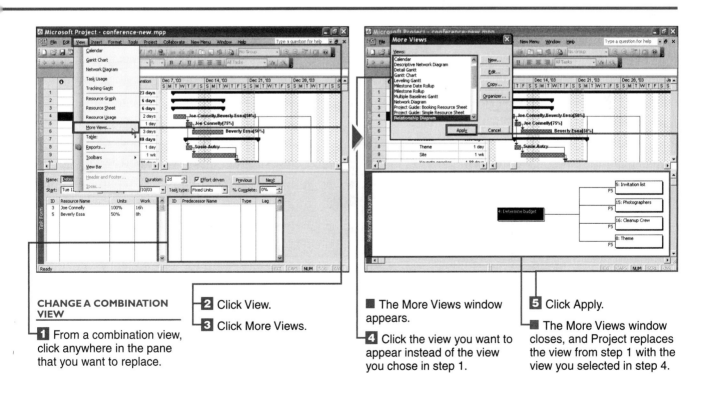

CHANGE A COMBINATION VIEW

■1 From a combination view, click anywhere in the pane that you want to replace.

■2 Click View.

■3 Click More Views.

■ The More Views window appears.

■4 Click the view you want to appear instead of the view you chose in step 1.

■5 Click Apply.

■ The More Views window closes, and Project replaces the view from step 1 with the view you selected in step 4.

CREATE A NEW COMBINATION VIEW

You can display two views at the same time on-screen. These views are called *combination views*. When you work in a combination view, Project splits the screen horizontally and displays one view in the top part of the screen and the other view in the bottom portion of the screen. Typically, the view in the bottom portion of the screen displays

detailed information about the task or resource you selected in the view in the top portion of the screen.

Suppose that you find yourself working with a particular combination of views on a regular basis. Instead of setting up the combination view each time you need to use it, you can save it as a combination view so that it will be available in the More Views window or from the View menu.

You can create a combination view using any two views in Project, and you can display your combination view at any time. Because you previously defined the combination view to consist of two particular views, Project replaces any view currently on-screen with the views defined in your combination view.

CREATE A NEW COMBINATION VIEW

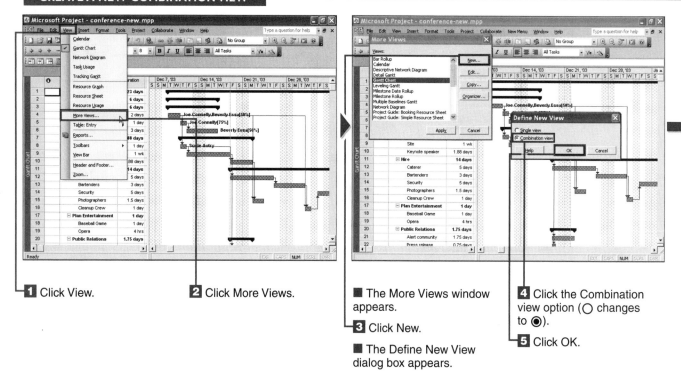

1 Click View.

2 Click More Views.

■ The More Views window appears.

3 Click New.

■ The Define New View dialog box appears.

4 Click the Combination view option (○ changes to ⊙).

5 Click OK.

What does the Show in menu option do, and when should I use it?

✔ You select this option (☐ changes to ☑) if you often use the view that you are creating. By selecting this option, you tell Project that you want your view to appear both in the More Views window and on the View menu.

When I finish using my combination view, what do I do?

✔ You can click Window and then click Remove Split, or you can double-click the split bar. Either action displays, full screen, the view in the active pane.

Can I display my combination view by double-clicking the split bar?

✔ No. When you double-click or drag the split bar to display a combination view, Project always displays either the Task Form or the Resource Form in the bottom pane, depending on the view that appears in the top pane. If a resource view appears in the top pane when you double-click, Project displays the Resource Form. If a task view appears in the top pane when you double-click, Project displays the Task Form.

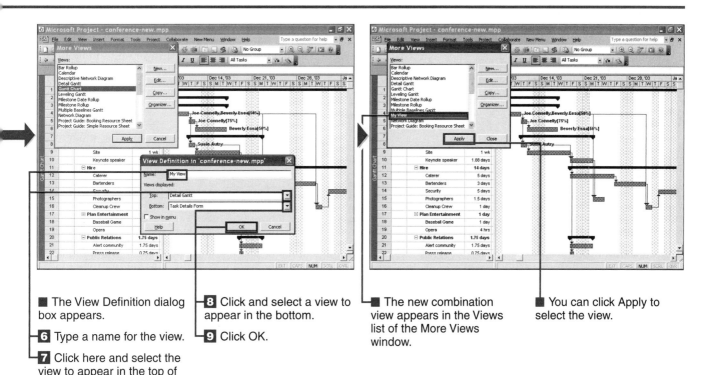

■ The View Definition dialog box appears.

6 Type a name for the view.

7 Click here and select the view to appear in the top of the combination view.

8 Click and select a view to appear in the bottom.

9 Click OK.

■ The new combination view appears in the Views list of the More Views window.

■ You can click Apply to select the view.

CHANGE THE DETAILS IN A VIEW

Using the various components of views, you can enter, organize, and examine project information in various ways. On some views, you find a details section. On form views, for example, the details section contains columns of information; you cannot change the details on form views. However, on the Task Usage and the Resource Usage views, the details section appears in a table, and you can add rows to the table to display additional information. For example, to use the Task Usage view to review both the work and the costs assigned to each resource on various tasks at the same time, you can view both pieces of information simultaneously by changing the details section.

You can add a field to the details section from a menu command; if the field you want to add does not appear on the menu, you can find it in a dialog box.

This section shows the steps that change the details section of the Task Usage view. To change the details section of the Task Usage view or the Resource Usage view, switch to the appropriate view before you begin. For help switching views, see the section, "Switch Views," earlier in this chapter.

CHANGE THE DETAILS IN A VIEW

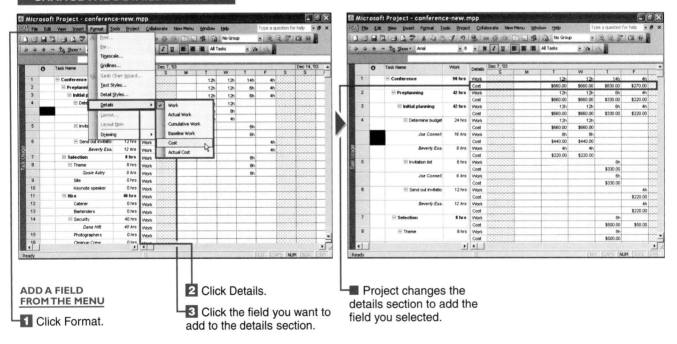

ADD A FIELD FROM THE MENU

1 Click Format.

2 Click Details.

3 Click the field you want to add to the details section.

■ Project changes the details section to add the field you selected.

Why are some of the fields on the Details section yellow and some white?

✔ In the Task Usage view, yellow fields are in the same row as tasks; the white fields appear in rows with resource names. You can type in either box, but if you type in a yellow box, you assign the value you type to the task and not to a specific resource.

How do I remove a row I added from the dialog box?

✔ Follow the steps in Add a Field from a Dialog Box. In step 5, click the field in the Show these fields list. In step 6, click Hide.

In the Detail Styles dialog box, what does the Show in menu option do?

✔ For every field that appears in the Available fields list, you have the option of selecting Show in menu option (☐ changes to ☑). This option displays the selected field on the menu that appears when you click Format and then click Details.

How do I remove a row I added from the menu?

✔ Follow the steps in Add a Field from the Menu subsection, and click the field you want to remove. Deselecting the field in the menu (☐ changes to ☑) removes it from the Usage Details.

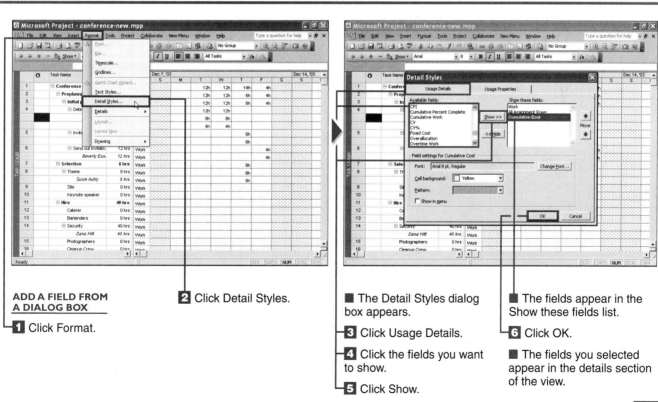

ADD A FIELD FROM A DIALOG BOX

1 Click Format.

2 Click Detail Styles.

■ The Detail Styles dialog box appears.

3 Click Usage Details.

4 Click the fields you want to show.

5 Click Show.

■ The fields appear in the Show these fields list.

6 Click OK.

■ The fields you selected appear in the details section of the view.

PRINT A VIEW

You can preview and print any view. Before you start, select the view that you want to print. See the section "Switch Views" earlier in this chapter for help.

If you print a sheet view, the number of columns that you see on-screen determines the number of columns that print. If the printed product requires more than one

page, Project prints down and across; that is, the entire left side of your project prints before the right side prints.

You can set the first page number of the printed product. For example, suppose that your project is ten pages long but you intend to print only pages 5 and 6. Typically, you would want to number those pages as 1 and 2, and you can do exactly that.

For the Task Usage and Resource Usage views, you can print column totals and row totals for values within the printed date range. When you print this information, Project calculates totals in memory and adds a row to the printed page showing totals for time-phased data as well as for sheet data. The totals lines print on the same page as the last rows or columns of data, before any Notes pages.

PRINT A VIEW

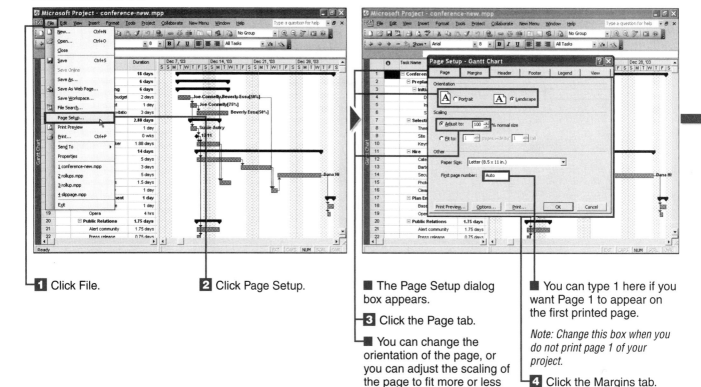

1 Click File.

2 Click Page Setup.

■ The Page Setup dialog box appears.

3 Click the Page tab.

■ You can change the orientation of the page, or you can adjust the scaling of the page to fit more or less onto a page.

■ You can type 1 here if you want Page 1 to appear on the first printed page.

Note: Change this box when you do not print page 1 of your project.

4 Click the Margins tab.

What can I set on the Header tab and the Footer tab?

✔ The tabs contain identical fields. You can type information on the left, center, and right portions of the header and footer that include project fields like % Complete and general items like the page number and the project title.

What can I set on the Legend tab?

✔ The Legend tab is available only when you print a Calendar, Gantt Chart, or Network Diagram view. The Legend tab works just like the Header and Footer tabs, and you can align and include the same kind of updating information.

On the View tab, what does the Fit timescale to end of page check box tab do?

✔ When you click this option (☐ changes to ☑), Project changes the width of the timescale units so that information prints on all available space on the page. You click this option for most views to fill the page.

Views are fine, but is there an easy way to pull information from views and print?

✔ Yes. Project contains a wide variety of reports. See Appendix B for samples. See Chapter 14 for details on how to print them.

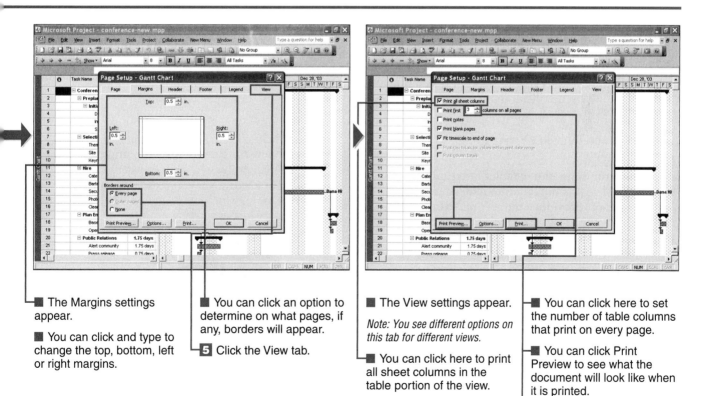

■ The Margins settings appear.

■ You can click and type to change the top, bottom, left or right margins.

■ You can click an option to determine on what pages, if any, borders will appear.

5 Click the View tab.

■ The View settings appear.

Note: You see different options on this tab for different views.

■ You can click here to print all sheet columns in the table portion of the view.

■ You can click here to set the number of table columns that print on every page.

■ You can click Print Preview to see what the document will look like when it is printed.

6 Click Print.

UNDERSTANDING TABLES

Most views in Project are comprised of a table and another element, such as a chart, a graph, or a details section. In their row-and-column format, tables can provide you with a variety of information about tasks and resources. Typically, each row in a table represents one task or one resource, while each column provides one piece of information about that task or resource.

Tables in Project give the project manager the flexibility to collect the data that is pertinent to a specific project management activity in one table, reducing both the time spent recording information and the potential for errors by not recording all necessary information. Most project managers need to update the status

of all of the tasks on which they have worked during the current week. Suppose that your organization does not use Project Server 2003 or Project Professional's workgroup features and wants you to record your updates weekly. You can spend a significant part of every week updating every task and resource assignment, because the process may involve updating percent complete for any tasks on which the staff has worked, adjusting the remaining hours when the staff determines that the originally planned hours are insufficient to complete the work, and updating the custom text field that was added to document the inspections done for each task. To streamline this updating process, you can create a table that shows only the

fields you need and then any other fields you want to use for easy reference. Adding a custom-designed table can significantly reduce the amount of time you need to spend to complete the weekly updates. The same custom-designed table can also help ensure that you do not forget to enter key information that your organization has identified and the chances of forgetting to enter key information.

Project does not limit you to using the tables as they appear, by default, in the software. You can edit the tables in all views in a variety of ways. For example, you can add or remove columns in the table or modify the height of the rows. You also can edit existing tables or create your own tables.

Switch the Table in a View

Before you start editing tables or creating new tables, it is important to understand that Project provides a number of default tables, and you can use each of these tables in any view that contains a table. Because different tables display different information, you can easily use one view but change your focus while evaluating project information. For example, you can view a Gantt Chart using the Entry table, which provides fields that help you enter task information. Or, you can view the Gantt Chart using the Cost table, which provides fields that identify various costs associated with tasks. You also can view the Resource Sheet using the Entry

table to help enter resource information, or you can view the Resource Sheet using the Cost table to evaluate resource costs. While working in a single view, you can switch to a different table, which can help you when you shift gears while evaluating project information.

Edit and Delete Tables

You can edit and delete tables in Project. Typically, instead of editing an existing default table, you should consider creating a copy of the table and editing the copy. In this way, you leave the original default table untouched so that you can use it when you need it, and use it as a foundation to create the table containing the fields you need. If you ever decide that you do not need a table, you can easily delete it.

Create New Tables

While Project contains some very useful standard tables, you may find that none of them contains enough information to form a foundation for the table you have decided you really need. If you cannot find an existing table in Project that contains the majority of the fields you need, you can create a new table; the process is simple, and you end up with the exact table that you want.

Modify the Appearance of Tables

In addition to creating, editing, and deleting tables, you can modify the appearance of tables. First, you can adjust the amount of the screen allocated to the table when compared to the chart, graph, or details section. In addition, tables consist of rows and columns; you can change the height of a row and the width of a column. You also can add columns to tables and remove columns that you do not need.

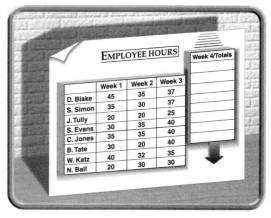

Suppose, for example, that Project's default Tracking table contains some fields that you use but others that you do not. And, you find that some fields you would like on the Tracking table are not included on the default Tracking table. In this case, make a copy of the Tracking table and, on the copy, delete the columns you do not need and add the columns that you would like to use. See Edit and Delete Tables for information on making a copy of a table, and see Hide and Insert Columns for information on adding and removing table columns.

SWITCH TABLES

Although each view shows a particular table by default, you can switch tables while remaining in the same view. Switching tables quickly helps you efficiently find the data you need to manage your project. There are two methods for switching tables: using the menu or using a window.

Only a very few views in Project do not contain tables. The Resource Graph and the Network Diagram

are two. But in most views, you find a table; the rows of the table represent either a task or a resource, while each column of the table provides one piece of information about the task or resource.

Project contains a rather long list of tables that you can apply to any view containing a table. Because different tables display different information, you can easily use the

same view but change the table to change your focus while evaluating project information. For example, you can view the Tracking Gantt using the Tracking table, which provides fields that help you enter tracking information for each task. Or, you can view the Tracking Gantt using the Schedule table, which provides fields that identify various dates associated with tasks, along with each task's free slack and total slack.

SWITCH TABLES

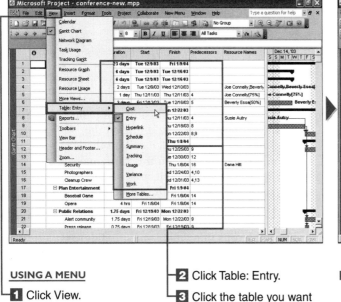

USING A MENU

1 Click View.

2 Click Table: Entry.

3 Click the table you want to display.

■ Project displays the table.

Why is the Apply button gray and not available when I click Resource in the More Tables dialog box?

✔ You were viewing a task view when you opened the More Tables dialog box. You cannot assign a resource table to a task view, and you cannot assign a task table to a resource view. Resource tables contain resource-related information such as the maximum units available that do not make sense while viewing a task view. Similarly, task tables contain task-related information such as task durations that do not make sense while viewing a resource view.

In a resource view, do I see different tables on the shortcut menu when I click the Select All button?

✔ Yes. You see the most commonly used resource tables.

What does the Calculate Project command on the shortcut menu do?

✔ By default, Project recalculates the changes to your project automatically. In large projects, recalculation after every change you make can be very time-consuming, so you can choose to manually recalculate the project. If you set your project to manual calculation, you can click Calculate Project when you want to recalculate the project. See Chapter 12 for details on setting Calcuation options.

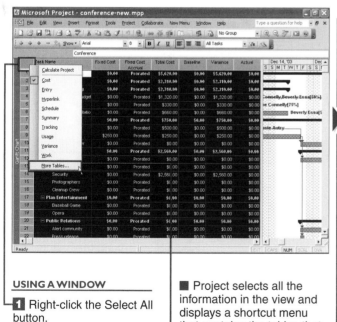

USING A WINDOW

1 Right-click the Select All button.

■ Project selects all the information in the view and displays a shortcut menu that contains the tables that appear on the View menu.

2 Click More Tables.

■ The More Tables window appears.

■ You can click the Task option (○ changes to ◉) to view task tables.

■ You can click Resource (○ changes to ◉) to view resource tables.

3 Click a table.

4 Click Apply.

■ Project applies the table you selected.

CREATE A NEW TABLE

What if you cannot find a table that displays the information you want in the way you want to display it? You can create a new table to solve the problem. When you add a new table to your project, you have the choice of creating an entirely new table or using an existing table as the foundation for your table and modifying it. If you can find a table that contains most of the

information you want on your table, copy it and edit it to meet your needs. See the section "Edit and Delete Tables" later in this chapter for detailed instructions.

If you create a table that contains only a few columns, or if you cannot find an existing table in Project that contains enough information to serve as the foundation for the table you need,

create a new table. For example, you can create a table that does nothing more than compare baseline durations to actual durations. Because it contains only two columns, this table is a candidate for a new table that is not based on an existing table.

When creating a task table, start in a task view; when creating a resource table, start in a resource view.

CREATE A NEW TABLE

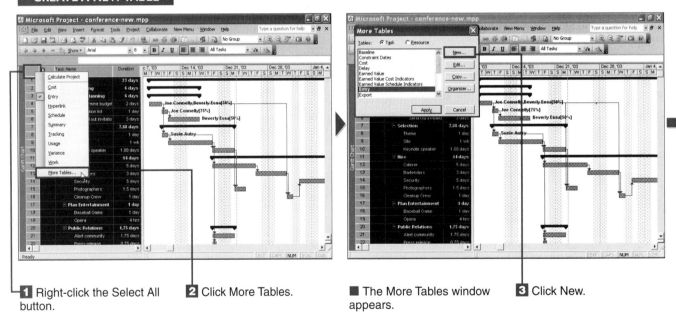

1 Right-click the Select All button.

2 Click More Tables.

■ The More Tables window appears.

3 Click New.

How do I know what width to assign to the columns so that I can see everything on-screen in the table?

✔ Do not worry about the column width at this point. You can accept the default value that Project assigns. Later, when you apply the table to a view, you can easily adjust column widths. For more information, see the section "Change Column Attributes."

Can I make my new table appear when I right-click the Select All button?

✔ Yes. In the Table Definition dialog box, click the Show in menu option (□ changes to ☑).

How do I decide whether to create a new table or modify an existing one?

✔ If you find a table that has several of the six fields that you want to include, copy that table, and delete, rearrange, modify, or add fields as needed. If you cannot find an appropriate model, you must create a new table.

Does my table appear in all projects?

✔ Yes, if you use the Organizer dialog box to copy it to the global template. Use the same techniques described in Chapter 6, but substitute the Table tab for the View tab.

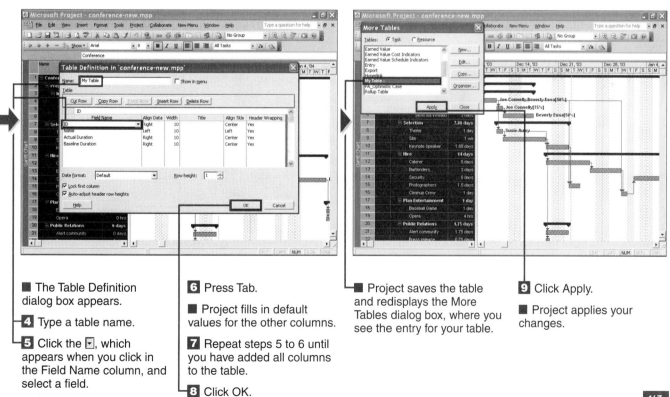

■ The Table Definition dialog box appears.

4 Type a table name.

5 Click the ▾, which appears when you click in the Field Name column, and select a field.

6 Press Tab.

■ Project fills in default values for the other columns.

7 Repeat steps 5 to 6 until you have added all columns to the table.

8 Click OK.

■ Project saves the table and redisplays the More Tables dialog box, where you see the entry for your table.

9 Click Apply.

■ Project applies your changes.

EDIT AND DELETE TABLES

Suppose that you find a table that contains the information you need, but you want the columns to appear in an order other than the order in which Project shows them. For example, many tables display all baseline fields and then all actual fields, resulting in this sequence of columns: Baseline Start, Baseline Finish, Actual Start, Actual Finish. You may find comparing this

information easier if you create a table that presents the information in this order: Baseline Start, Actual Start, Baseline Finish, Actual Finish, and so on.

You can add or delete columns in the table. Project displays the columns in a table from left to right to match the order of the field names listed from top to bottom in the rows of the Table Definition dialog box.

For any of these sections in this book, you can either edit an existing table or make a copy of it and edit the copy.

While you can delete a table, do not delete tables listed on the left side of the Organizer dialog box that appears in this section. The list on the left displays information stored in the Global template file.

EDIT AND DELETE TABLES

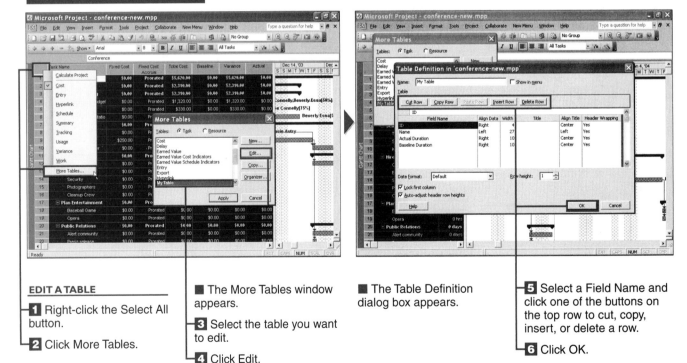

EDIT A TABLE

1 Right-click the Select All button.

2 Click More Tables.

■ The More Tables window appears.

3 Select the table you want to edit.

4 Click Edit.

■ The Table Definition dialog box appears.

5 Select a Field Name and click one of the buttons on the top row to cut, copy, insert, or delete a row.

6 Click OK.

How do I know which row to click when I want to add a column in a specific position in the table?

✔ To add a new column between columns 2 and 3, click row 3 in the Table Definition dialog box before clicking Insert Row. To add a new column between columns 3 and 4, click row 4 in the Table Definition dialog box before clicking Insert Row. Project inserts new rows above the selected row.

How do I copy a table?

✔ While viewing the More Tables dialog box, click the table you want to copy, and then click Copy.

When should I edit a table and when should I make a copy of a table to edit?

✔ If you share your schedule with others, copy a table and edit it. Others who use your project files expect the default tables to be available.

Can I delete a default table?

✔ You can, but you should not if you share your project with other people. If you delete one by accident, you can copy it from the Global template. See Chapter 6, and substitute the Table tab for the View tab.

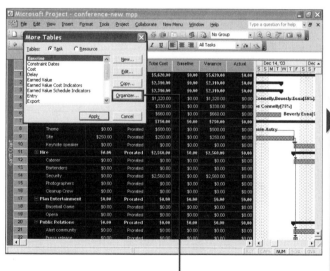

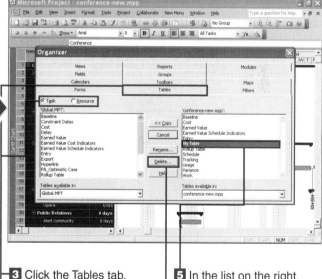

DELETE A TABLE

1 Perform steps 1 to 2 on the previous page.

■ The More Tables window appears.

2 Click Organizer.

■ The Organizer dialog box appears.

3 Click the Tables tab.

4 Click either the Task or Resource tables options (○ changes to ◉).

5 In the list on the right, click the table you want to delete.

6 Click Delete.

■ Project deletes the table.

REDISTRIBUTE SCREEN REAL ESTATE

Because most tables contain more columns than Project displays by default, you may periodically want to adjust the amount of space that Project devotes to the table portion of the screen so that you can see more or less of the columns in the table.

You have the option of controlling the amount of the screen that Project devotes to the right side or the left side of views comprised of two sides. Views comprised of two

sides usually have a table on the left side and a chart or details section on the right side. The Gantt Chart and its variations, such as the Tracking Gantt and the Detail Gantt, are comprised of a table on the left and a chart on the right. The Task Usage view and the Resource Usage view are examples of views that contain two sides, where the left side is a table and the right side is a details section.

Does the technique you describe in this section work if I display a combination view on-screen.

✔ Yes, if either pane contains a view comprised of a table and a chart or a table and a details section.

REDISTRIBUTE SCREEN REAL ESTATE

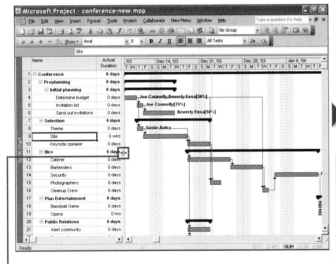

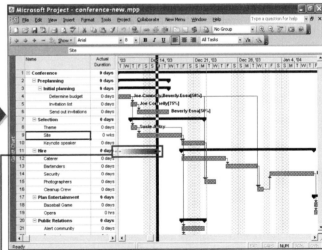

1 Position the mouse pointer (⌖) over the vertical split bar.

■ The ⌖ changes to a ↔.

2 Click and drag the splitter bar to the right to reveal more of the table and hide more of the chart.

■ You can also drag to the left to hide more of the table and devote more screen real estate to the chart.

■ When you release the ⌖, you see more or less of the table.

CHANGE ROW HEIGHT

When information is too wide to fit within a column, you can change the height of a row, and Project wraps the data in the column to fit within the taller row.

You can change the height of a single row or you can change the height of several rows at the same time. When you change multiple rows simultaneously, Project assigns a uniform height to the selected rows.

You can change row heights only in full row increments. In other words, you can make a row twice its original size but not one-and-a-half times its original size.

How do I change the height of more than one row at a time?

✓ To change the height of more than one row, press and hold Ctrl as you click the ID of each row that you want to change.

I do not want taller rows. Is there any other way to display text that I cannot see completely in a table?

✓ Yes. You can widen the column. See the section "Change Column Attributes" for more information.

CHANGE ROW HEIGHT

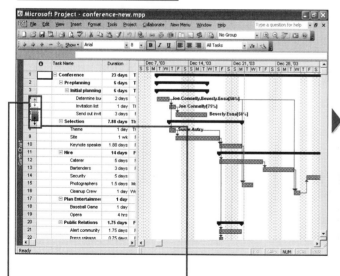

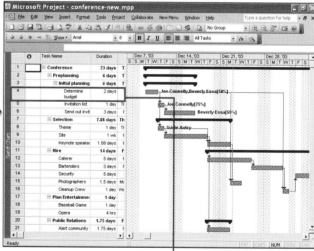

1 Position ⌐ in the Task ID number column at the bottom of the row you want to change.

■ The ⌐ changes to ↥.

2 Click and drag ↥ to below the Task ID number of the row immediately below.

Note: For example, if you are widening row 4, drag down below the number 5 in row 5.

3 Release the mouse.

■ The height of the row increases and any text wraps in that row that did not fit within its column.

CHANGE COLUMN ATTRIBUTES

To improve the appearance and layout of your tables, you can change the attributes of your columns. You make some changes out of necessity. For example, if you cannot see all of the information in a column or if you see pound signs (#) in a column, the column is not wide enough for Project to display the information in it, and you need to make the column wider.

You can modify the attributes of columns in a table in a variety of ways. You can adjust the width of columns in a table, or you can assign a title to a column that is different than the title that Project assigns by default. You also can change the alignment of the column title and the column data, and you can make these changes independently. For example, you can center the column title and

right-align the column data. You can even change the field displayed in a particular column of a table.

You can make some of these changes with your mouse. For other changes, you must open a dialog box. To make a row taller so that you can see all of the information in a cell, see the section "Change Row Height."

CHANGE COLUMN ATTRIBUTES

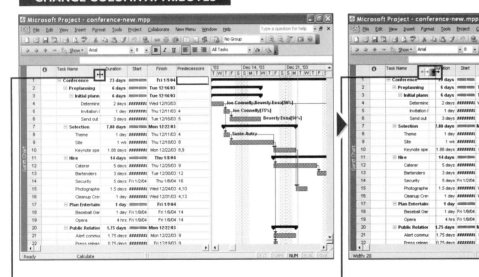

CHANGE COLUMN WIDTH

1 Position ⏰ over a column heading's right edge.

■ The ⏰ changes to a ↔.

2 Click and drag the column edge to the right or left.

■ You can drag to the right to make the column wider, or you can drag to the left to make it narrower.

3 Release the mouse.

■ The column width changes.

What does the Header Text Wrapping option do?

✔ This option controls the wrapping of the text that you type into the Title field of the Column Definition dialog box. When you deselect this option (☑ changes to ☐), Project does not wrap column heading text, and may prevent you from reading the entire column heading unless you adjust the width of the column.

Can Project automatically determine the width of the column so that I can see everything in it?

✔ Yes. In the Column Definition dialog box, click Best Fit. Or, double-click the right edge of the column's heading.

Can I change the order in which columns appear in the table?

✔ Yes. You can click the column heading to select it. Then, with ⌖ posititioned in the column heading, click and drag the column to a new position in the table. If you prefer, you can edit the table to reorder columns. Using the Table Definition dialog box, you can cut and paste to reorder table columns. See the section "Edit and Delete Tables" earlier in this chapter for details.

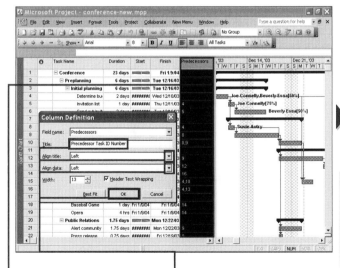

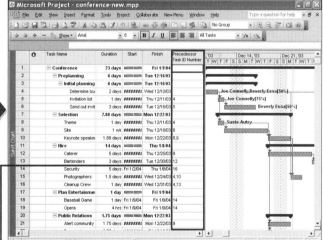

CHANGE A COLUMN TITLE

1 Double-click the heading of the column you want to change.

■ Project selects the column, and the Column Definition dialog box appears.

2 Click in the title field, and type a title to display for the field.

■ You can click here to change column and data alignment.

3 Click OK.

■ Project applies your changes to the column.

HIDE AND INSERT COLUMNS

Sometimes, a table contains most, but not all, of the information that you want to see. To display additional data, you can insert additional columns into the table at any position in the table that you want.

In the same way that a table may not display all of the information that you want to see, a table may

display *more* information than you need. In this case, you can hide columns in the table.

When you insert a column, Project shifts existing columns to the right to make room for the new column. When you hide a column, Project shifts existing columns to the left to fill up the space previously occupied by the hidden column.

By default, Project assigns a width of 10 characters to the column you insert. You can change this width as you insert the column or after you insert the column. To change the width as you insert the column, use the Column Definition dialog box that you see in this task. To change the width after you insert the column, see the section "Change Column Attributes" earlier in this chapter.

HIDE AND INSERT COLUMNS

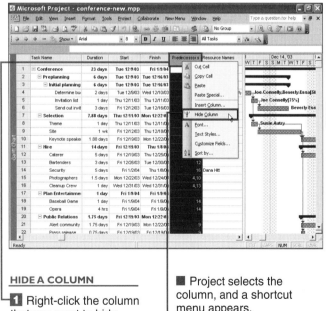

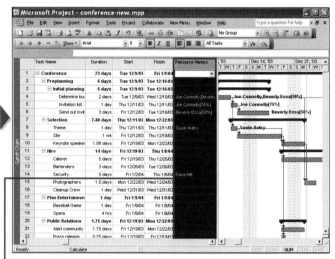

HIDE A COLUMN

1 Right-click the column that you want to hide.

■ Project selects the column, and a shortcut menu appears.

2 Click Hide Column.

■ Project hides the selected column and selects the column that appeared to the right of the hidden column.

I inserted the column, but I cannot read all of its title. What should I do?

✔ If you did not select the Header Text Wrapping option (☐ changes to ☑) in the Column Definition dialog box, double-click the column to reopen the dialog box and then click Header Text Wrapping. You can also make the column wider. See the section "Change Column Attributes" earlier in this chapter for details.

If I hide a column and immediately change my mind, can I undo the action and redisplay the column?

✔ No. To redisplay the column, you must reinsert it. To reinsert a column, follow the steps in the section "Insert a Column."

Can I hide a row?

✔ You cannot hide rows like you can hide columns. You can delete a row if you select the row and press the Delete key on your keyboard. Be aware, however, that Project permanently deletes all information stored in the row. You may be able to filter to hide rows; see Chapter 8 for more information.

When I hide a column, does Project delete the data?

✔ No. Project simply hides the information from view, but retains it in the file. You can redisplay it at any time if you reinsert the column.

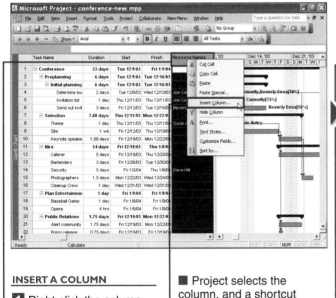

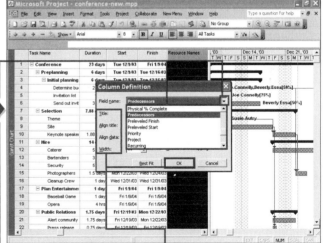

INSERT A COLUMN

1 Right-click the column that should appear to the right of the column you want to insert.

■ Project selects the column, and a shortcut menu appears.

2 Click Insert Column.

■ The Column Definition dialog box appears.

3 Click the Field here and select a column to insert.

■ You can change any other options for the field.

4 Click OK.

■ Project inserts the column to the left of the column you selected.

WAYS TO ORGANIZE INFORMATION

Some people define project management as the attempt to comprehend a large job by breaking the job into progressively smaller pieces until the job is a collection of tasks. When you finally break the job down to the task level, you want to organize the tasks so that you can estimate schedules, resource requirements, and costs. Project provides several ways to organize tasks.

Sort Tasks

Sometimes, sorting information in a different way helps you to see things that you may not have seen otherwise or even to get a better handle on a problem. In Project, you can sort a project from most views in almost any way that you want. For example, in the Gantt Chart view, Project automatically sorts tasks by ID. But you may find it easier to view your project information if you sort by Start Date or Finish Date. See "Sort Tasks in a View" for details.

Filter a Project

Filters help you to focus on specific aspects of your project. For example, suppose that you want to view the tasks that you assigned to only certain resources, or you want to display only the tasks that are on the critical path of your project. You can apply filters to views to limit the information that you see and to help you focus on a particular issue.

Project filters come in two varieties. Task filters enable you to view specific aspects of tasks, while resource filters enable you to view specific aspects of resources. The first table gives a description of the default task filters. Default resources filters are explained in the second table. Many of the filters perform similar functions. See the sections "Using Filters," "Create a New Filter," "Edit and Delete Filters," and "Using AutoFilters" for details.

Default Task Filters

Filter	Purpose
All Tasks	Displays all the tasks in your project
Completed Tasks	Displays all finished tasks
Confirmed	Displays the tasks on which specified resources have agreed to work when using Project Server
Cost Greater Than	Displays the tasks that exceed the cost you specify
Cost Overbudget	Calculated filter that displays all tasks with a cost that exceeds the baseline cost
Created After	Displays all tasks that you created in your project on or after the specified date
Critical	Displays all tasks on the critical path
Date Range	Interactive filter that prompts you for two dates and then displays all tasks that start after the earlier date and finish before the later date
In Progress Tasks	Displays all tasks that have started but have not finished
Incomplete Tasks	Displays all unfinished tasks
Late/Overbudget Tasks Assigned To	Prompts you to specify a resource. Then, Project displays tasks that meet either of two conditions: the tasks assigned to that resource that exceed the budget you allocated for them, or the unfinished tasks that will finish after the baseline finish date. Note that completed tasks do not appear when you apply this filter, even if you completed them after the baseline finish date.
Linked Fields	Displays tasks to which you have linked text from other programs
Milestones	Displays only milestones
Resource Group	Displays the tasks assigned to resources that belong to the group you specify
Should Start By	Prompts you for a date and then displays all tasks not yet begun that should have started by that date
Should Start/ Finish By	Prompts you for two dates: a start date and a finish date. Then Project uses the filter to display those tasks that have not started by the start date and those tasks that have not finished by the finish date.

Filter	Purpose
Slipped/Late Progress	Displays two types of tasks: those that have slipped behind their baseline scheduled finish date and those that are not progressing on schedule
Slipping Tasks	Displays all tasks that are behind schedule
Summary Tasks	Displays all tasks that have subtasks grouped below them
Task Range	Shows all tasks that have ID numbers within the range that you provide
Tasks With a Task Calendar Assigned	Shows tasks that have a task calendar assigned
Tasks with Attachments	Displays tasks that have objects attached or a note in the Notes box
Tasks with Deadlines	Displays all tasks to which you have assigned deadline dates
Tasks with Estimated Durations	Displays all tasks to which you have assigned an estimated duration
Tasks with Fixed Dates	Displays all tasks that have an actual start date and tasks to which you assign some constraint other than As Soon As Possible
Tasks/Assignments with Overtime	Displays the tasks or assignments that have overtime
Top Level Tasks	Displays the highest-level summary tasks
Unconfirmed	Displays the tasks on which specified resources have not agreed to work when using Project Server
Unstarted Tasks	Displays unstarted tasks
Update Needed	Displays tasks that have changes, such as revised start and finish dates or resource reassignments, and that you need to send to resources for update or confirmation when using Project Server
Using Resource	Displays all tasks that use the resource that you specify
Using Resource in Date Range	Displays the tasks that you assigned to a specified resource that start after the first date you specify and finish before the second date you specify
Work Overbudget	Displays all tasks with scheduled work greater than baseline work

CONTINUED

WAYS TO ORGANIZE INFORMATION (CONTINUED)

Default Resource Filters

Filter	Purpose
All Resources	Displays all the resources in your project
Confirmed Assignments	Available only in the Resource Usage view; displays only those tasks for which a resource has confirmed the assignment when using Project Server
Cost Greater Than	Displays the resources that exceed the cost that you specify
Cost Overbudget	Calculated filter that displays all resources with a cost that exceeds the baseline cost
Date Range	Interactive filter that prompts you for two dates and then displays all tasks and resources with assignments that start after the earlier date and finish before the later date
Enterprise Resources	Shows resources available in the enterprise resource pool when using Project Server
Group	Prompts you for a group and then displays all resources that belong to that group
In Progress Assignments	Displays all tasks that have started but have not finished
Linked Fields	Displays resources to which you have linked text from other programs
Overallocated Resources	Displays all resources that are scheduled to do more work than they have the capacity to do
Project Team Members	Displays team members of a specific project and that are applied to that project when multiple enterprise projects are open using Project Server
Resource Range	Interactive filter that prompts you for a range of ID numbers and then displays all resources within that range
Resources – Material	Displays all material resources

Filter	Purpose
Resources – Work	Displays all work resources such as people
Resources with Attachments	Displays resources that have objects attached or a note in the Notes box
Resources/ Assignments with Overtime	Displays the resources or assignments that have overtime
Should Start By	Prompts you for a date and then displays all tasks and resources with assignments not yet begun that should have started by that date
Should Start/ Finish By	Prompts you for two dates: a start date and a finish date. Then Project uses the filter to display those tasks or assignments that have not started by the start date and those tasks or assignments that have not finished by the finish date.
Slipped/Late Progress	Displays two types of resources: those that have slipped behind their baseline scheduled finish date and those that are not progressing on schedule
Slipping Assignments	Displays all resources with uncompleted tasks that are behind schedule because the tasks have been delayed from the original baseline plan
Unconfirmed Assignments	Displays the assignments for which requested resources have not yet agreed to work when using Project Server
Unstarted Assignments	Displays confirmed assignments that have not yet started
Work Complete	Displays resources that have completed all their assigned tasks
Work Incomplete	Displays all resources with baseline work greater than scheduled work
Work Overbudget	Displays all resources with scheduled work greater than baseline work

Group Tasks in the Project

You can use grouping as another way to organize information in your project. When you group tasks, you arrange tasks together on-screen using some common attribute. For example, grouping tasks together by duration to help identify shorter versus longer tasks may help you solve a problem.

As with filters, Project groups come in two varieties: task groups and resource groups. The first table describes default task groups; the second table describes default resource groups. See "Using Grouping" for details.

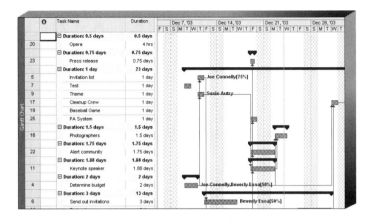

Default Task Groups

Filter	Purpose
No Group	Displays all the tasks in your project in the default order of the view
Complete and Incomplete Tasks	Groups tasks in % Work Complete groups of 0, 1-99, and 100. This grouping helps you quickly identify incomplete tasks.
Constraint Type	Groups tasks so that all tasks with the same type of constraint appear together. This grouping helps you quickly identify each task's constraint type.
Critical	Divides tasks into two groups: critical and not critical. These groups help you quickly see tasks on the critical path.
Duration	Groups tasks by the estimated time it takes to complete them
Duration then Priority	Groups tasks first by the estimated time it takes to complete them and then, within a duration group, by task priority
Milestones	Divides tasks into two groups: milestones and other tasks, helping you quickly identify milestones
Priority	Groups tasks in intervals of 100 from lowest to highest priority
Priority Keeping Outline Structure	Maintains project's outline structure and, within each outline heading group, organizes tasks by priority. You can use this grouping to maintain a work breakdown structure and view tasks within by priority within each outline heading.
Team Status Pending	Displays project tasks for which team members have been sent a request for status but have yet to respond. This view requires use of the collaboration features of Microsoft Office Project Server 2003.

Default Resource Groups

Filter	Purpose
No Group	Displays all the resources in your project in the default order of the view
Assignments Keeping Outline Structure	For each resource, view his or her assignments within the outline structure of your project. This grouping only works in the Resource Usage view.
Complete and Incomplete Resources	Groups resources in % Work Complete groups of 0, 1-99, and 100. This grouping helps you see how each of your resources is progressing on each of his or her assignments.
Resource Group	Groups resources by the information you stored about the resource in the Group box of the Resource Information dialog box
Standard Rate	Groups resources by their standard rates from lowest to highest
Work vs. Material Resources	Divides resources into two groups — work and material

SORT TASKS IN A VIEW

Y ou can sort information in a view in ways different than the default sort order Project provides for the view. Sorting the information differently helps you better understand a problem or identifies as yet unseen issues.

You can sort a project from most views in almost any way that you want. In the menus, you find five common sort keys, but you can sort by just about any field in the view using the Sort dialog box. From this dialog box, you can sort in ascending or descending order using up to three sort keys. When you use more than one sort key, Project breaks any ties it finds at the first sort level using a second sort key. Similarly, if you define a third sort key, Project breaks any ties it finds at the second sort level.

Sorting from the Sort dialog box, you can permanently reorder your project in the sort order you specify and control whether Project maintains the outline structure in your project when sorting.

Save your project before sorting; if you do not like the sorting results, you can close the project without saving and negate the effects of sorting without data loss.

SORT TASKS IN A VIEW

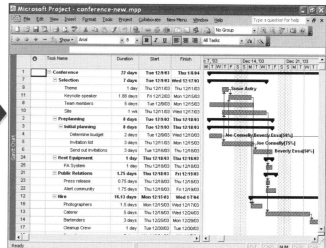

USING A DEFAULT SORT ORDER

1 Click Project.

2 Click Sort.

3 Click a sort order.

■ Project re-sorts the project in the order you selected.

What is the purpose of the Permanently renumber tasks option?

✔ When you do not select this option on the Sort window, Project sorts the tasks but the tasks retain their original ID numbers. If you select this option (☐ changes to ☑), Project sorts the tasks *and* renumbers them so that tasks that move due to sorting also receive a new ID number.

What if I do not like the sort order after I sort the project?

✔ Click Edit, and then click Undo. If the Undo command is not available, close your project without saving it.

What is the purpose of the Keep outline structure option?

✔ When you select this option (☐ changes to ☑), Project sorts tasks relative to their summary task only. That is, Project may reorder subtasks within their summary task, but Project keeps the subtasks with their summary tasks. If you unselect this option (☑ changes to ☐), Project moves subtasks in the project based on the criteria you set without regard for a subtask's summary task. Under these conditions, Project may separate a subtask from its summary task, and this may compromise the logic of your project outline.

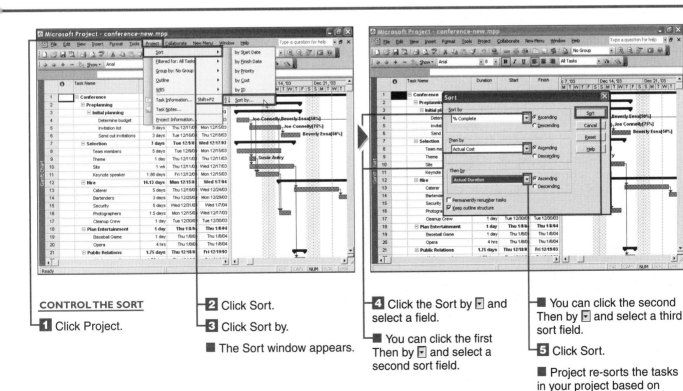

CONTROL THE SORT

■1 Click Project.

■2 Click Sort.

■3 Click Sort by.

■ The Sort window appears.

■4 Click the Sort by ▾ and select a field.

■ You can click the first Then by ▾ and select a second sort field.

■ You can click the second Then by ▾ and select a third sort field.

■5 Click Sort.

■ Project re-sorts the tasks in your project based on your selections.

USING FILTERS

Y ou can focus on specific aspects of your project when you use filters. You can apply filters to views to limit the information that you see and to help you focus on a particular issue.

For example, suppose that you want to display only the tasks that are on the critical path of your project or that you want to view only those tasks to which you

assigned a task calendar. You also can easily filter your project to tasks that should start by a particular date or tasks that are slipping. By applying a filter to a view, you specify criteria that Project uses to determine what tasks or resources should appear in that view. Project then selects information to display and either highlights the selected information or hides the rest of the information.

Some filters are interactive; that is, Project prompts you to supply a value for Project to use when filtering, and Project displays the tasks or resources that match the value. When you display only the tasks with ID numbers within a certain range, Project prompts you to supply the ID number range.

USING FILTERS

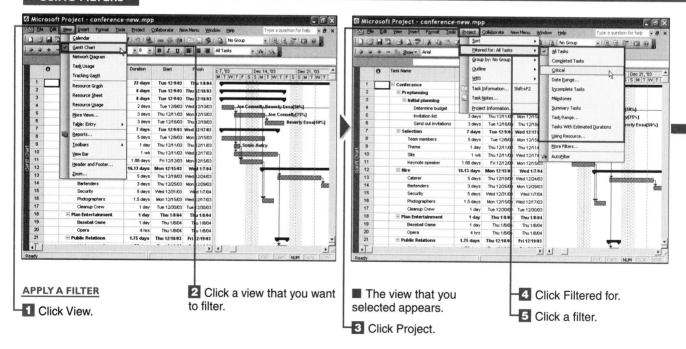

APPLY A FILTER

1 Click View.

2 Click a view that you want to filter.

■ The view that you selected appears.

3 Click Project.

4 Click Filtered for.

5 Click a filter.

When I apply a filter, does Project delete the information that meets the filter criteria?

✔ No. The information remains safely in your project file. When you filter a project, Project simply temporarily hides from view the information that meets the criteria. When you remove the filter, Project redisplays the information.

What if I cannot find a filter that meets my needs?

✔ Try the filters you see in the More Filters window. If none of them works for you, create your own filter. See the section "Create a New Filter" later in this chapter for more information.

I want to remove a filter I applied while viewing the Resource Usage view, but I cannot find the All Tasks command on the Filtered for menu. How do I remove the filter?

✔ Because Project enables you to apply task filters to task views only and resource filters to resource views only, the Filtered for menu shows either All Tasks or All Resources, depending on the view that you displayed before starting these steps. In your case, click All Resources to remove the filter.

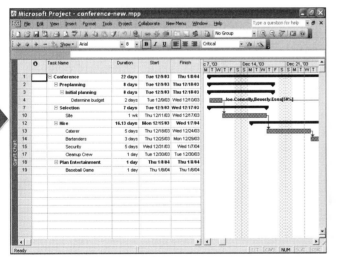

■ Only the tasks that meet the filter criteria appear.

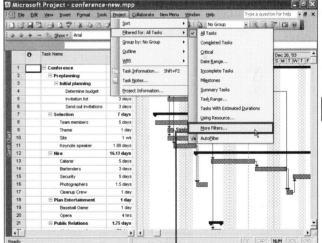

APPLY A HIGHLIGHTING FILTER

1 Follow steps 1 to 4 in "Apply a Filter."

2 Click More Filters.

CONTINUED ▶

USING FILTERS (CONTINUED)

Filters are very effective tools to help you focus on particular aspects of your project. As with tables and views, Project filters come in two varieties. Task filters enable you to view specific aspects of tasks, and resource filters enable you to view specific aspects of resources. In the section "Ways to Organize Information" earlier in this chapter, you find descriptions of the default task filters and the default resource filters. As you may expect, Project does not let you apply a task filter to a resource view or a resource filter to a task view.

When you apply a filter, you can let Project hide the tasks or resources that do not meet the filter criteria. Or you can have Project display all tasks or resources but show the tasks or resources that meet the filter criteria in a different color if you apply a highlighting filter.

When you no longer need to filter the project, you can easily remove the filter; removing a filter is not the same as deleting a filter. When you remove a filter, you simply apply no special criteria to the tasks or resources displayed on-screen.

USING FILTERS (CONTINUED)

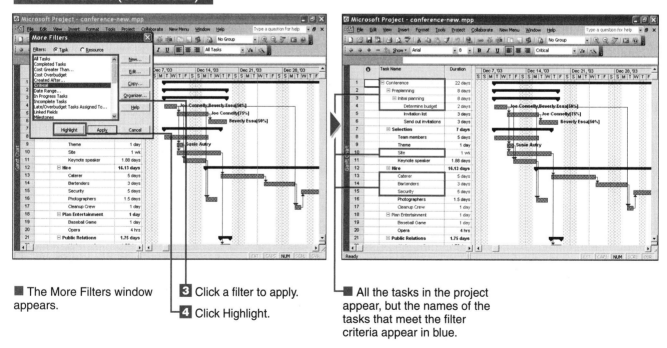

■ The More Filters window appears.

3 Click a filter to apply.

4 Click Highlight.

■ All the tasks in the project appear, but the names of the tasks that meet the filter criteria appear in blue.

What filter should I use if I want to display only those tasks on which a particular resource is working?

✔ Select the Using Resource filter that appears on the Filtered for menu. Project prompts you for the resource name using a box that contains the names of all resources in your project. Select the resource from the box and click OK. Any time you use an interactive filter, Project prompts you for the information it needs to filter your project appropriately.

The highlighting filter is not strong enough to suit me. Is there a way to change the font as well as the color?

✔ Instead of filtering, you can format the text style of tasks that meet certain criteria. Click Format and then click Text Styles. In the Text Styles dialog box, select the type of item you want to change — for example, all critical tasks — and then select a font, font style, size, and color. This technique works well if you print to a black-and-white printer and want to highlight certain kinds of tasks.

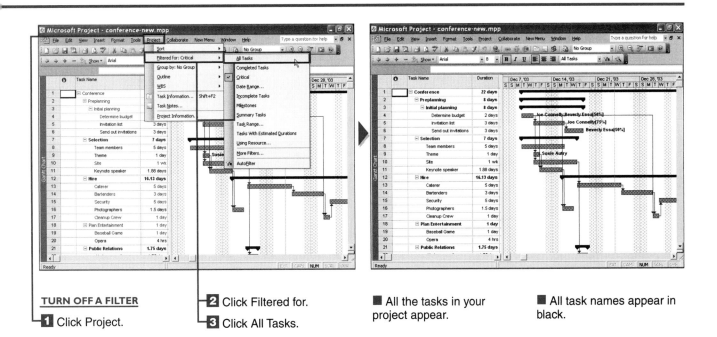

TURN OFF A FILTER

1 Click Project.

2 Click Filtered for.

3 Click All Tasks.

■ All the tasks in your project appear.

■ All task names appear in black.

CREATE A NEW FILTER

Suppose that you cannot find a filter that displays the information you want in the way you want to display it. You can create a new filter to solve your problem.

When you add a new filter to your project, you have the choice of creating an entirely new filter or using an existing filter as the foundation for your filter and modifying it. If you can find an

existing filter that contains most of the information you want in your filter, copy it and edit it to meet your needs. See the section "Edit and Delete Filters" later in this chapter for detailed instructions.

Each line that you create in the Filter Definition dialog box is called a *statement*. To evaluate certain statements together, but separate them from other statements in your filter, group the

statements into a set of criteria. To group statements, leave a blank line between sets of criteria, and select either operator in the And/Or field for the blank row.

Within a criteria group containing three or more statements, Project evaluates all And statements before evaluating Or statements. Across groups, Project evaluates And conditions in the order in which they appear.

CREATE A NEW FILTER

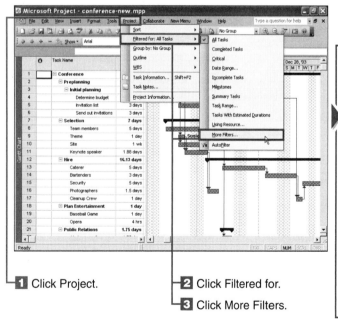

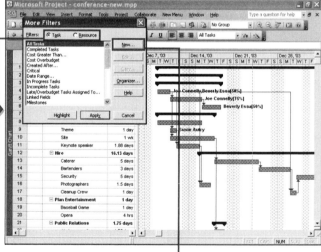

1 Click Project.

2 Click Filtered for.

3 Click More Filters.

■ The More Filters window appears.

4 Click either the Task option or the Resource option (○ changes to ●), depending on the type of filter you want to create.

5 Click New.

■ The Filter Definition dialog box appears.

When do I use the And/Or column?

✔ Use this column when you want to specify more than one criterion. You select And if the task or resource needs to meet *all* of the criteria. Select Or if the task or resource needs to meet *any* of the criteria.

How do I decide whether to create a new filter or modify an existing one?

✔ If you find a filter that has several of the criteria that you want to include, copy that filter and delete, rearrange, modify, or add fields as needed. If you cannot find an appropriate model, create a new filter.

In the Field Definition dialog box, how do I select a field?

✔ When you click in the Field Name column, a ⊡ appears that you use to select the field.

What are the Test field and the Value(s) field?

✔ You use the Test field to select a mathematical operator that compares the Field Name and the Value, which is either another Project field or a number that you type. For example, if you set up a task filter using Cost as the Field Name, is greater than as the test, and 500 for the value, Project displays tasks that cost more than $500.

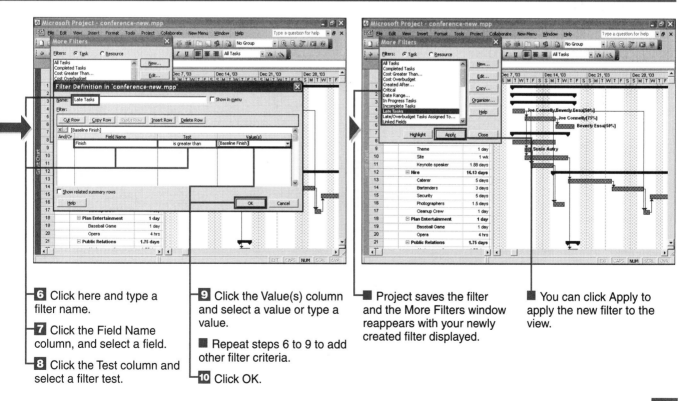

■ **6** Click here and type a filter name.

■ **7** Click the Field Name column, and select a field.

■ **8** Click the Test column and select a filter test.

■ **9** Click the Value(s) column and select a value or type a value.

■ Repeat steps 6 to 9 to add other filter criteria.

■ **10** Click OK.

■ Project saves the filter and the More Filters window reappears with your newly created filter displayed.

■ You can click Apply to apply the new filter to the view.

EDIT AND DELETE FILTERS

What if you find a filter that contains desired criteria, but you want the criteria to appear in a different order? What if a filter that contains most, but not all, of the desired criteria, or contains the desired criteria, but you want to change the test, or the value, or both? You can simply add, delete, change, or rearrange criteria using the Filter Definition dialog box and Project

applies filter criteria in the order you list them. A powerful way to modify a filter criteria is to change And to Or. By making this change, you include more information when Project filters your project.

For any of the sections in this chapter, you can either edit an existing filter or make a copy of it and edit the copy. If you edit a copy instead of an original, you

always have the original filter available to use.

When you can delete a filter, do not delete filters listed on the left side of the Organizer window because Project stores their information in the Global template file that is available to all projects; deleting something from the global template file makes it permanently unavailable to any project.

EDIT FILTERS

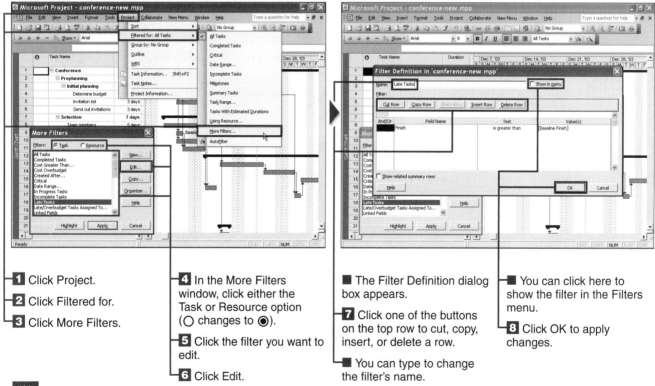

-1 Click Project.

-2 Click Filtered for.

-3 Click More Filters.

-4 In the More Filters window, click either the Task or Resource option (○ changes to ●).

-5 Click the filter you want to edit.

-6 Click Edit.

■ The Filter Definition dialog box appears.

-7 Click one of the buttons on the top row to cut, copy, insert, or delete a row.

■ You can type to change the filter's name.

■ You can click here to show the filter in the Filters menu.

-8 Click OK to apply changes.

Does my filter appear in all projects?

✔ Yes, if you use the Organizer window to copy it to the global template. Use the same techniques described in Chapter 6, but substitute the Filter tab for the View tab.

How do I copy a filter?

✔ While viewing the More Filters dialog box, select the filter and click Copy. Project displays a copy of the selected filter in the Filter Definition dialog box. Next, you can type a new name for the filter and update the filtering criteria as shown in the Edit Filters subsection.

Can I delete a default filter?

✔ Technically, you can, but you should not delete a default filter if you share your project with others. If you delete a filter by accident, you can copy it from the Global template. To copy a view from one project to another use the technique in Chapter 6, but substitute the Filter tab for the View tab.

DELETE A FILTER

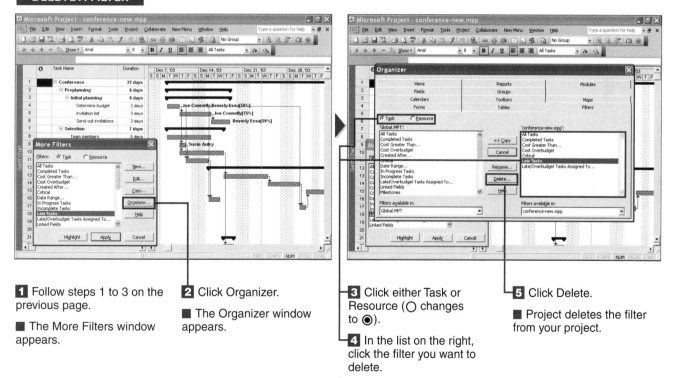

1 Follow steps 1 to 3 on the previous page.

■ The More Filters window appears.

2 Click Organizer.

■ The Organizer window appears.

3 Click either Task or Resource (○ changes to ⦿).

4 In the list on the right, click the filter you want to delete.

5 Click Delete.

■ Project deletes the filter from your project.

USING AUTOFILTERS

AutoFilters provide a quick and easy way to filter a sheet view. AutoFilters are similar to regular Project filters, but you can apply them directly on the sheet of any sheet view instead of using a menu or a dialog box. When you enable AutoFilters, an arrow appears at the right edge of every column name in a sheet view. You can use this arrow to display filters for the column. Because each column contains different

information, the filters you can apply vary from column to column.

By default, Project filters a field using only one condition when you use an AutoFilter. If you customize an AutoFilter, you can filter a field using a maximum of two conditions. If you need to filter using three or more conditions, or if you need to use calculated values as your criteria, you should apply a filter via the More Filters window.

See the section "Using Filters" earlier in this chapter for more information on filters.

By default, Project has the AutoFilters option off when you create a project, but you can turn it on at any time. Also, AutoFilters are not available on any form view or on the Calendar, Resource Graph, Network Diagram, and Relationship Diagram views.

USING AUTOFILTERS

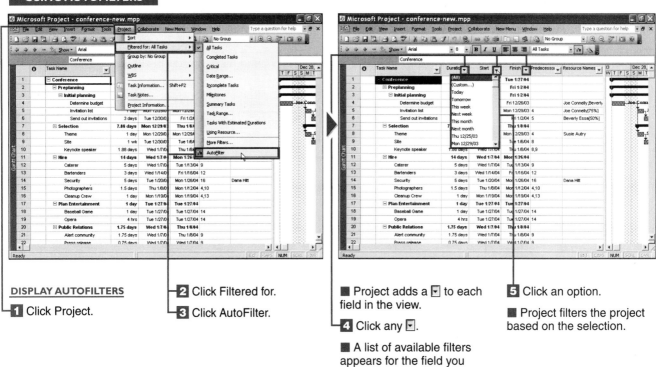

DISPLAY AUTOFILTERS

1 Click Project.

2 Click Filtered for.

3 Click AutoFilter.

■ Project adds a 🔽 to each field in the view.

4 Click any 🔽.

■ A list of available filters appears for the field you selected.

5 Click an option.

■ Project filters the project based on the selection.

Because AutoFilters provide a quick and easy way to filter a sheet, do I have a quick and easy way to make them visible?

✔ Yes. You can click the AutoFilter button ([▼]) on the Formatting toolbar.

Because I prefer AutoFilters, can I automatically have them on all the time for every project I create?

✔ Yes. You can can turn on AutoFilters automatically for new projects that you create. Click Tools and then click Options. On the General tab of the Options dialog box, click Set AutoFilter on for new projects (☐ changes to ☑).

Can I save the AutoFilter I set up to use on future projects?

✔ Yes. You can save filters from the Custom AutoFilter dialog box. Click the AutoFilter [▼] in the field heading, click Custom, and then click Save.

How do I turn AutoFilters off?

✔ You can repeat steps 1 to 3 in the subsection "Display AutoFilters," of this section, or you can click [▼] on the Formatting toolbar. Each time you click [▼], you toggle AutoFilters on or off.

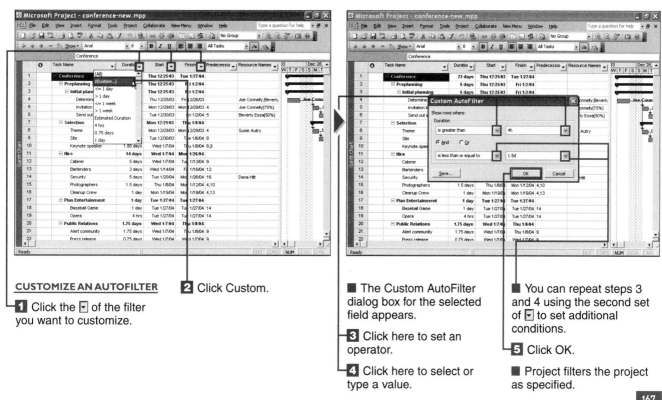

CUSTOMIZE AN AUTOFILTER

■1 Click the [▼] of the filter you want to customize.

■2 Click Custom.

■ The Custom AutoFilter dialog box for the selected field appears.

■3 Click here to set an operator.

■4 Click here to select or type a value.

■ You can repeat steps 3 and 4 using the second set of [▼] to set additional conditions.

■5 Click OK.

■ Project filters the project as specified.

USING GROUPING

Grouping is an alternative way to view information in your project. Project provides a wide variety of choices for grouping information. You can easily solve a problem if you group tasks by some common denominator. For example, if you want to find longer tasks so that you can concentrate on ways to shorten them, you can group your project by duration so that longer tasks appear together in a group.

Similarly, if you want to focus on reducing costs, you can group the tasks in your project by cost to see if you can find ways to reduce the cost of the more expensive tasks.

When you group information, Project reorganizes the information in your project so that data that falls within each group appear together on-screen and surrounded by yellow highlighting. You can apply grouping to most views in

Project; however, grouping is not available for the Relationship diagram or for form views.

Grouping operates on the current view at the time you select the group. Therefore, you must switch to the view you want to group before you start grouping. See Chapter 6 for instructions on switching views.

USING GROUPING

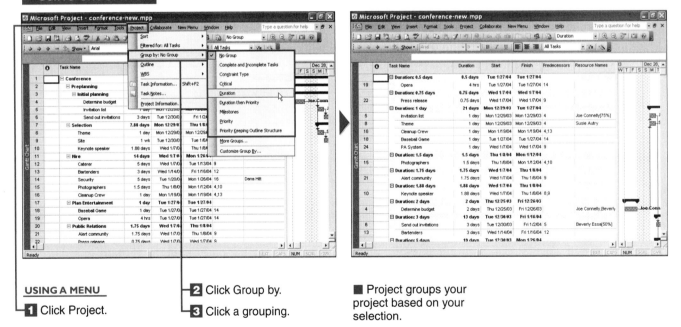

USING A MENU

■1 Click Project.

■2 Click Group by.

■3 Click a grouping.

■ Project groups your project based on your selection.

Why was the Apply button gray and not available when I clicked Resource in the More Groups window?

✔ You were viewing a task view when you opened the More Groups window. You cannot assign a resource group to a task view, and you cannot assign a task group to a resource view. Resource groups contain resource-related ways to group information such as the standard rate that do not make sense while viewing a task view. Similarly, task groups contain task-related ways to group information such as durations that do not make sense while viewing a resource view.

If I start in a resource view, do I see different groups on the Group by menu than I see if I start by viewing a task view?

✔ Yes. You see the most commonly used resource groups.

How do I remove a group?

✔ Click Project, Group by, and then No Group.

I do not see a cost group on the menu. Where can I find a cost group?

✔ Project does not contain a cost group by default, but you can create one. See the section "Create a New Group" for more information.

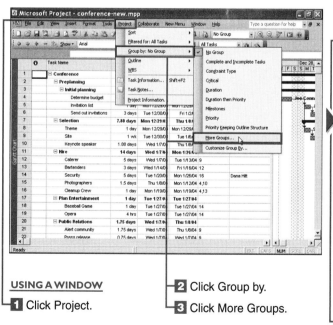

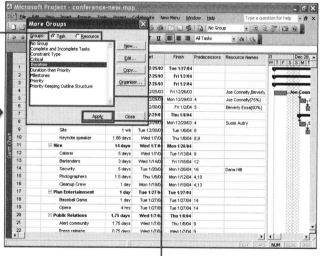

USING A WINDOW

1 Click Project.

2 Click Group by.

3 Click More Groups.

■ The More Groups window appears.

■ You can click either the Resource or Task option (○ changes to ⊙).

4 Click a group.

5 Click Apply.

■ Project applies the group you selected.

CREATE A NEW GROUP

Project contains a large number of predefined groups that you can apply to almost any group you create. Because different groups display information in different ways, you can easily use the same view but change the group to change your focus while evaluating project information. For example, if you want to focus on reducing costs, you can group the tasks in your

project by cost to find ways to reduce the cost of the more expensive tasks. Because Project does not contain a cost group, you can easily set one up.

If you cannot find a group that displays the information you want in the way you want it displayed, you can create a new group. When you add a new group to your project, you can create an entirely

new group or use an existing group as the foundation for your group and modify it. If you can find a group that contains most of the information you want in your group, you can copy it and edit it to meet your needs. See the section "Edit or Delete Groups" for detailed instructions.

CREATE A NEW GROUP

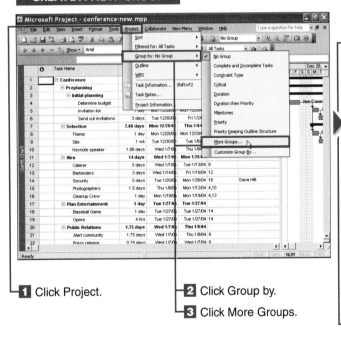

1 Click Project.

2 Click Group by.

3 Click More Groups.

■ The More Groups window appears.

4 Click either the Task option or Resource option (○ changes to ◉), depending on the type of group you want to create.

5 Click New.

What does the Customize Group By command on the Group by menu do?

✔ It provides an alternate way to regroup and optionally create a new group by opening the Custom Group dialog box, which is exactly the same as the Group Definition dialog box except that it contains two additional buttons — Save and Reset. Clicking Save lets you save the group you set up; Clicking Reset clears all the settings you make.

Can I make my new group appear on the Group by menu?

✔ Yes. In the Table Definition dialog box, click the Show in menu option (☐ changes to ☑).

Can I change the Field Type and Order while defining a new group?

✔ You can change the Order, but not the Field Type, which is based on the type of group, Task or Resource, you selected in the More Groups dialog box before you clicked New.

What does the Define Group Intervals button on the Group Definition dialog box do?

✔ It opens the Define Group Intervals dialog box, where you can define the range of values that appears in a group. For example, if you group cost, you can define the starting cost for the first group and the cost range of each group.

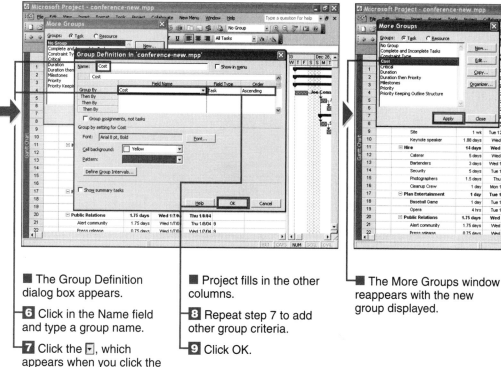

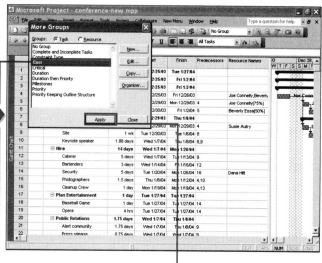

■ The Group Definition dialog box appears.

6 Click in the Name field and type a group name.

7 Click the ⏷, which appears when you click the Field Name column, and select a field.

■ Project fills in the other columns.

8 Repeat step 7 to add other group criteria.

9 Click OK.

■ The More Groups window reappears with the new group displayed.

■ You can click Apply to apply the new group to the view.

EDIT OR DELETE GROUPS

What if you find a group that contains the criteria that you need, but you want to group the criteria differently so that it appears in a different order than Project presently shows? Similarly, what if you find a group that contains most of your desired criteria, or that contains the desired criteria but has a different grouping order or a group behavior not quite to your specifications? To achieve the exact

grouping for your situation, you can add, delete, change, or rearrange criteria using the Group Definition dialog box. Project applies group criteria in the order you list the criteria in the Group Definition dialog box.

When editing, you can edit an existing group, or you can make a copy of the group and edit the copy. If you edit a copy instead of an original, you always have the original filter available to use.

While you can delete a group, do not delete groups listed on the left side of the Organizer window, which displays information that Project stores in the Global template file; because this information is available to all projects, deleting something from the Global template file makes it permanently unavailable to any project.

EDIT GROUPS

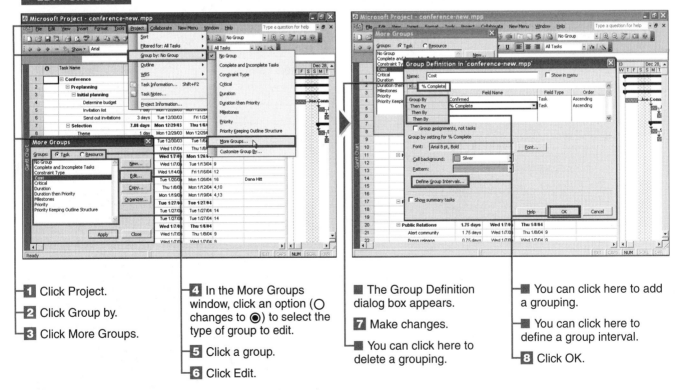

■1 Click Project.

■2 Click Group by.

■3 Click More Groups.

■4 In the More Groups window, click an option (○ changes to ◉) to select the type of group to edit.

■5 Click a group.

■6 Click Edit.

■ The Group Definition dialog box appears.

■7 Make changes.

■ You can click here to delete a grouping.

■ You can click here to add a grouping.

■ You can click here to define a group interval.

■8 Click OK.

Does my group appear in all projects?

✔ Yes, if you use the Organizer window to copy it to the Global template. Use the same techniques described in Chapter 6, but substitute the Group tab for the View tab.

When should I edit a group, and when should I make a copy of a group to edit?

✔ If you share your schedule with others, copy a group and edit it. Other people who use your project files expect the default groups to be available.

What happens when I do not select the Group assignments, not tasks option?

✔ If you are working in the Task Usage view, select this option to group by assignment instead of task. If you are working in the Resource Usage view, select this option to group by assignment instead of resource.

How do I copy a group?

✔ While viewing the More Groups dialog box, click the group you want to copy, and then click Copy. Project displays a copy of the selected group in the Group Definition dialog box. Change the name along with other modifications.

DELETE GROUPS

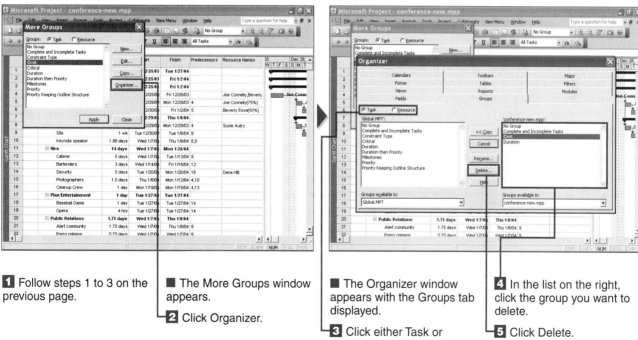

1 Follow steps 1 to 3 on the previous page.

■ The More Groups window appears.

2 Click Organizer.

■ The Organizer window appears with the Groups tab displayed.

3 Click either Task or Resource (○ changes to ◉).

4 In the list on the right, click the group you want to delete.

5 Click Delete.

■ Project deletes the group from your project.

UNDERSTANDING CUSTOM FIELDS AND CODES

Project includes extra fields that you can customize to store information that is unique to your organization. Project provides three unique kinds of fields and codes. With *custom fields* you can store costs, dates, durations, start dates, finish dates, flags, numbers, and text to display whatever kind of information you need. With *outline codes*, a special kind of custom field, you can create a hierarchical numbering structure to tasks in a project. With work breakdown structures (WBS), you can tie a graphic representation of a company organization chart to a numbered list of the tasks that you must complete to finish a project.

Custom Fields

In a custom field, you can create a formula that performs a calculation or compares Project fields and calculates a result that Project displays in the custom field. Or, instead of displaying the result of the calculation in the custom field, you can display graphical indicators to help you quickly determine, for example, when a value exceeds a specified number. You can create a list of values available to store in a custom field so that you can ensure speedy and accurate data entry.

You display custom fields on sheet views like you display other kinds of fields. After you define the custom field's function, you add a column to a sheet to display the custom field.

Outline Code

The outline code is a relative of the custom field, in that it is a special kind of custom field that you can create to assign a hierarchical structure to tasks in a project. For example, if you have a government contract for which you and the government have agreed to a numbering scheme, you can assign outline codes to each task in your project. Outline codes are completely *static* numbers that you can assign to each task in a project; they do not change if you move tasks around in your project because they are not tied to the outline structure of your project. For example, you can assign a department code to a task so that you can view your project organized by department. You may also want to assign a company cost code to a task so that you can view tasks by cost code.

Like custom fields, you can display outline codes after you define them by adding a column to a sheet view for the outline code field.

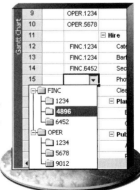

Work Breakdown Structure (WBS)

Work breakdown structure (WBS) codes, unlike their cousins the Custom Outline Codes, are very much tied to the structure of your project. The graphic representation of a WBS chart is reminiscent of a company organization chart and shows a numbered list of the tasks that you must complete to finish a project. The U.S. defense establishment initially developed the WBS chart, and you find it described in Section 1.6 of MIL-HDBK-881 (2 January 1998) as follows:

- A product-oriented family tree is composed of hardware, software, services, data, and facilities. The family tree structure results from systems engineering efforts during the acquisition of a defense material item.

- A WBS chart displays and defines the product, or products, to be developed and/or produced. It relates the elements of work to be accomplished to each other and to the end product.

You cannot produce a WBS graphic representation of your project in Project, but you can assign WBS codes to each task. If you have access to Visio 2000 or later, you can also use the Visio WBS Chart Wizard in Project 2003 to create a WBS chart in Visio from Project information. You find the Visio WBS Chart Wizard on the Analysis toolbar in Project. Or, you can use WBS Chart for Project, an add-on product for Project, to create a WBS chart from a Microsoft Project file. Visit www.criticaltools.com to learn more about WBS Chart for Project.

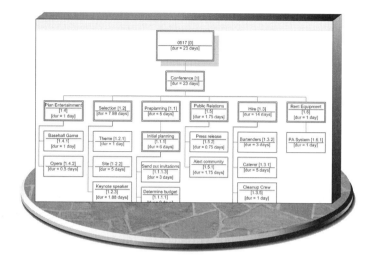

You can use any numbering system that you want for your WBS code structure when you add WBS codes to tasks in Project. You can make the WBS codes letters and numbers, or a combination of both, to help you identify the relationship among tasks and organize the project. WBS codes are *not static* like outline codes; if you move tasks around in your project and change the outline structure, the WBS codes renumber because they are tied to the outline structure of your project.

Like custom fields and outline codes, you display WBS codes after you define them by adding a column to a sheet view for the WBS code field.

USING CUSTOM FIELDS FOR DATA ENTRY

What if your boss wants your best guess on a task-by-task basis concerning whether you can maintain a schedule? You can set up a task-based custom field and provide the information on any sheet view of Project. *Custom fields* are extra fields in Project that you can customize to store information that is unique to your organization. Project contains custom fields that

can store costs, dates, durations, start dates, finish dates, flags, numbers, and text that display whatever kind of information you need.

In a custom field, you can create a formula that performs a calculation or compares Project fields and calculates a result that Project displays in the custom field. You can create a list of values available to store in a custom field so that

you can ensure speedy and accurate data entry. Customizing fields can help create standardization within your organization.

Using a custom field is a two-part process. First, you create a custom field, and then you display it on any sheet view. For the example in this section, the steps create a custom text called Best Guess that contains a list of three values: Yes, No, and Maybe.

USING CUSTOM FIELDS FOR DATA ENTRY

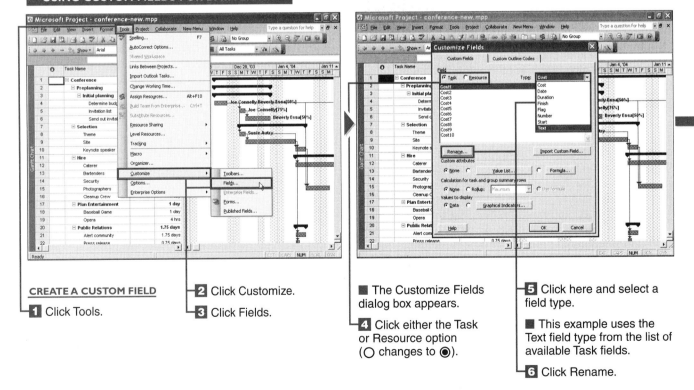

CREATE A CUSTOM FIELD

1 Click Tools.

2 Click Customize.

3 Click Fields.

■ The Customize Fields dialog box appears.

4 Click either the Task or Resource option (○ changes to ◉).

5 Click here and select a field type.

■ This example uses the Text field type from the list of available Task fields.

6 Click Rename.

What does the Import Custom Field button do?

✔ Located on the Customize Fields dialog box, this button displays the Import Custom Field box, which enables you to import any custom field from any open project or from the Global template.

Can I use a custom field to restrict the use of Priority values to 100, 200, 300, 400, and 500?

✔ No. You can create a Number custom field that allows the entry of only these five values in a sheet view. However, users can open the Task Information dialog box and assign any priority in the Priority field. The custom field is not substituting for the Priority field.

Can I select a wrong type of custom field? If so, what happens if I select the wrong type?

✔ The type that you select determines the values that you can include in the value list. You select Text to include only combinations of letters and numbers in the value list. If you select Date, Start, or Finish, you must include date-formatted numbers in the value list. If you select Number or Cost, you can include only numbers in the value list. If you select Flag, you can include only Yes or No in the value list.

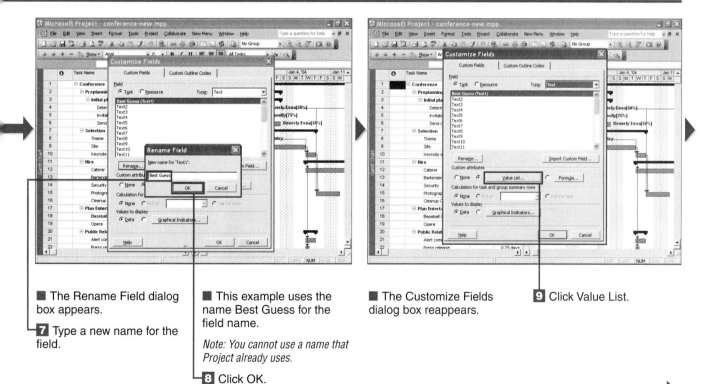

■ The Rename Field dialog box appears.

7 Type a new name for the field.

■ This example uses the name Best Guess for the field name.

Note: You cannot use a name that Project already uses.

8 Click OK.

■ The Customize Fields dialog box reappears.

9 Click Value List.

CONTINUED

USING CUSTOM FIELDS FOR DATA ENTRY (CONTINUED)

After you create any type of custom field, you display it on any sheet view or views simply by inserting a column on the sheet. Once the custom field appears on the sheet, you can use it like any other field. If you design the custom field to calculate something, you must enter information in the other fields that make up the calculation performed by the custom field. If the custom field is a data entry field, you must supply information.

For a custom field that you use for data entry, you can create a *value list*, which is a list of the valid values for the field; think of a value list as your own personal list field. You open a value list via a down arrow in the same way you open all list fields.

When you create a value list, Project sets up the value list by default to restrict data entry to values that appear in the list. This feature is useful because it ensures that users enter in the custom field only the values that you have identified as valid.

USING CUSTOM FIELDS FOR DATA ENTRY (CONTINUED)

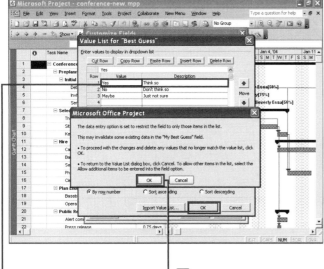

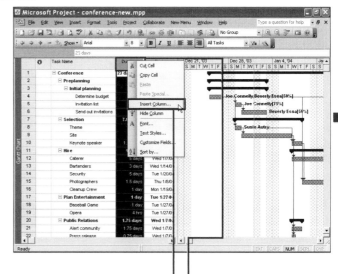

■ The Value List dialog box appears.

10 Click here and type a data entry value and a description of the value.

11 Repeat step 10 for each data entry value.

■ A message box appears.

12 Click OK twice to save the field.

DISPLAY A CUSTOM FIELD

1 Display the table in which you want to display the custom field.

Note: For more on switching tables, see Chapter 7.

2 Right-click the column title that you want to appear to the right of the custom field.

3 Click Insert Column.

Can I pick from the value list and also enter other values?

✔ Yes. In the Value List dialog box, click the Allow additional items to be entered into the field option (○ changes to ◉).

When should I restrict entries or allow other values into the list?

✔ You restrict list entries when you intend to use the entered information for grouping or integrating with other systems, where exact matches are important. The intent of list values is to increase the speed and accuracy of data entry. You can allow other values if you list the most common values but want to allow for new values.

In the Display order for dropdown list section of the Value List dialog box, what does By row number do?

✔ Using this option, Project displays values in the order listed in the Value List dialog box.

Must I create a value list for a custom field?

✔ No. You can simply create the field by clicking OK after step 8 in the subsection "Display a Custom Field." You can type any information you want into the custom field, as long as the information is consistent with the type of custom field you create. For example, you cannot enter text into a Cost custom field.

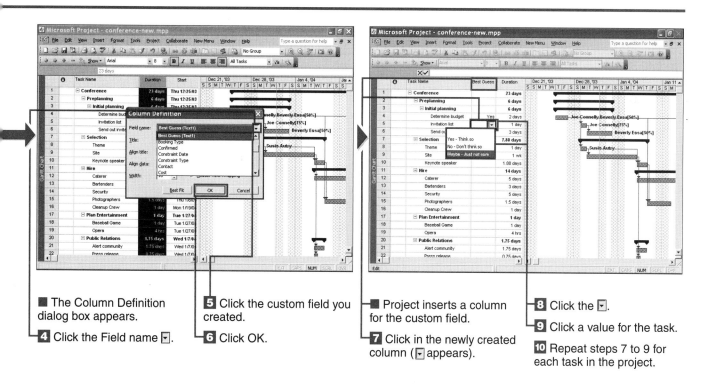

■ The Column Definition dialog box appears.

4 Click the Field name ▾.

5 Click the custom field you created.

6 Click OK.

■ Project inserts a column for the custom field.

7 Click in the newly created column (▾ appears).

8 Click the ▾.

9 Click a value for the task.

10 Repeat steps 7 to 9 for each task in the project.

USING CUSTOM FIELDS FOR FILTERS

You can use custom fields in filters. You can filter a project by a value that appears in a custom field, or you can use the custom field values in combination with other conditions that you establish. For more about filters, see Chapter 8.

If your custom field contains a value list, you can use AutoFilters

to set the criteria and display all tasks that contain one or two of the values in the value list. If you prefer, you can also create a custom filter that filters for three or more of the values in the value list, or your custom filter can filter for one of the values in the value list you created or any of the standard values available when creating a filter.

To use custom fields for filtering, you must first set up a custom field using the steps provided in the section "Using Custom Fields for Data Entry" earlier in this chapter. While you do not need to create a value list for the custom field, the example in this section uses a custom field with a value list because it gets the point across best.

USING CUSTOM FIELDS FOR FILTERS

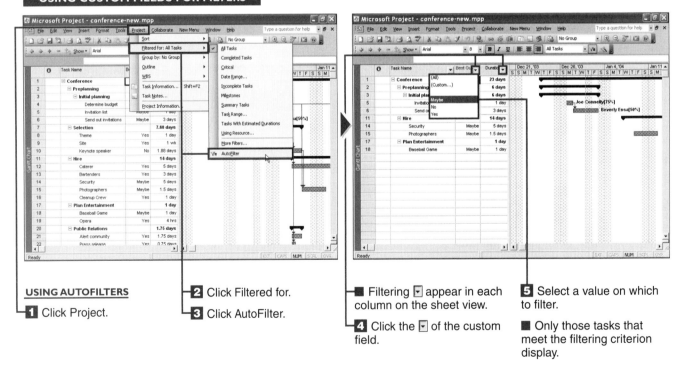

USING AUTOFILTERS

1 Click Project.

2 Click Filtered for.

3 Click AutoFilter.

■ Filtering ▾ appear in each column on the sheet view.

4 Click the ▾ of the custom field.

5 Select a value on which to filter.

■ Only those tasks that meet the filtering criterion display.

When I use the AutoFilter technique, can I filter on more than one field?

✔ Yes. By selecting values from more than one field, you set up an And filtering condition, where Project displays only those tasks that meet all filtering criteria you want. Selecting filtering criteria from multiple fields makes Project display less information than when you filter on only one field.

In the Field Definition dialog box, how do I select a field?

✔ When you click in the Field Name column, a ⬚ appears that you use to select the field.

How do I turn off AutoFilters?

✔ Click the AutoFilter button ( ) on the Formatting toolbar.

When do I use the And/Or column?

✔ Use this column when you specify more than one criterion. Select And if the task or resource needs to meet *all* of the criteria. Select Or if the task or resource needs to meet *any* of the criteria.

Can I make my filter appear in the Filtered For menu?

✔ Yes. In the Filter Definition dialog box, click the Show in menu option (⬚ changes to ☑).

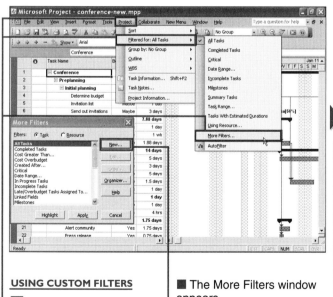

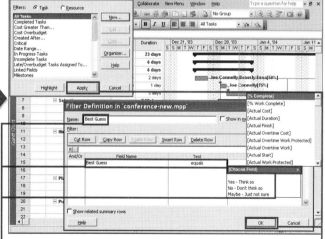

USING CUSTOM FILTERS

1 Click Project.

2 Click Filtered for.

3 Click More Filters.

■ The More Filters window appears.

4 Click New.

■ The Filter Definition dialog box appears.

5 Type a filter name.

6 Click to select a field name and a filter test.

7 Click here to select a value or type a value.

8 Repeat steps 5 to 8 to add other filter criteria.

9 Click OK.

■ You can click Apply to use the new filter.

USING FORMULAS IN CUSTOM FIELDS

Project contains custom fields that you can use to store and display costs, dates, durations, start dates, finish dates, flags, numbers, and text unique to your project. In any of these custom fields, you can create a formula that performs calculations or compares Project fields and calculates a result that Project displays in the custom field. You can compare the obvious — numbers — but you also can compare dates or text. Additionally, you can establish values for a custom field based on the true/false conditions established with Flag fields.

For example, what if your manager tells you that part of your evaluation in project management depends on the accuracy of your cost estimates? Under these circumstances, you may want to monitor the tasks for which actual cost exceeds baseline cost. You can set up a custom field to help you easily identify those tasks.

Using a custom field is a two-part process. First, you create a custom field containing the formula and then you display it on any sheet view. In this section, the steps create a cost custom field called Difference that calculates the difference between Actual Cost and the first Baseline Cost.

USING FORMULAS IN CUSTOM FIELDS

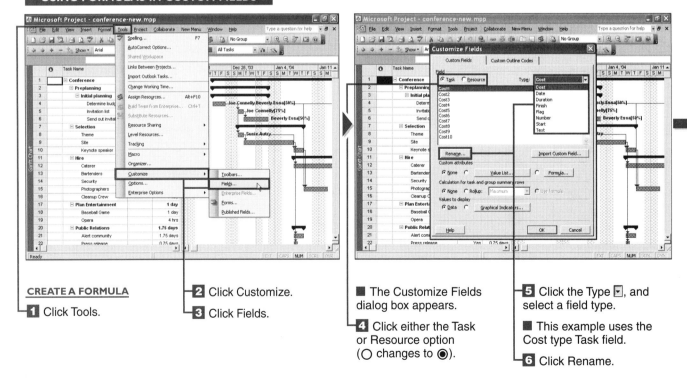

CREATE A FORMULA

1 Click Tools.

2 Click Customize.

3 Click Fields.

■ The Customize Fields dialog box appears.

4 Click either the Task or Resource option (○ changes to ●).

5 Click the Type ▾, and select a field type.

■ This example uses the Cost type Task field.

6 Click Rename.

What does the Import Formula button on the Formula dialog box do?

✓ Clicking this button displays the Import Formula dialog box from which you can import any formula from any field in any open project or from the Global template.

What does the Function button in the Formula dialog box do?

✓ Clicking this button makes the categories of functions that you can assign to formulas appear. These functions add to the calculation possibilities beyond the buttons that you see in the Formula dialog box below the calculation and include, among others, functions that use dates, times, or text to make calculations.

Will I have the same problems if I choose the wrong type of field when creating a formula as when I created a value list?

✓ No. The problems are different. If you select the wrong type when creating a value list, you cannot set up the appropriate values for the list. However, if you select a type that does not match what you try to calculate in a formula, Project lets you create the formula but displays #ERROR in the custom field column on the sheet because the formula does not make sense.

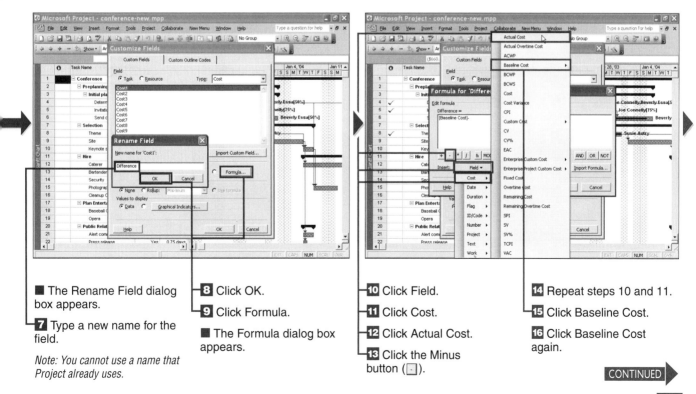

■ The Rename Field dialog box appears.

-7 Type a new name for the field.

Note: You cannot use a name that Project already uses.

-8 Click OK.

-9 Click Formula.

■ The Formula dialog box appears.

-10 Click Field.

-11 Click Cost.

-12 Click Actual Cost.

-13 Click the Minus button (⬚).

-14 Repeat steps 10 and 11.

-15 Click Baseline Cost.

-16 Click Baseline Cost again.

CONTINUED ▶

USING FORMULAS IN CUSTOM FIELDS (CONTINUED)

When you save a formula that you create for a custom field, Project displays a message that explains that the formula replaces all values previously stored in the custom field with the result of the calculation.

You can safely accept this message, because you just created a custom field that did not previously contain any data. If you

subsequently change the formula, pay attention to the message and make an informed decision about replacing the data in the custom field.

The custom field that contains the formula displays the results of the formula when you add the custom field to a table. The formula calculated in this section shows values only if you have saved a baseline for the project and then

recorded some tracking information about actual durations or actual finish dates.

In the formula that the steps in this section create, zeros or positive values in the final figure represent tasks where actual costs do not exceed baseline costs. Negative values in the Difference field indicate that the actual cost of the task exceeds the baseline cost.

USING FORMULAS IN CUSTOM FIELDS (CONTINUED)

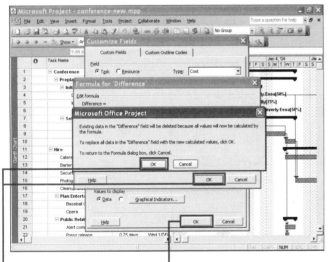

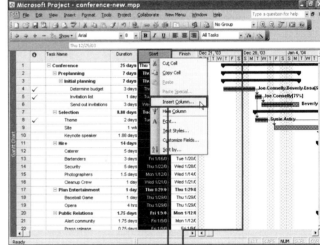

■ The formula that calculates the custom field displays in the Formula dialog box.

17 Click OK.

■ A message box appears.

18 Click OK.

■ Project saves the formula.

19 Click OK in the Customize Fields dialog box.

■ Project saves the custom field and redisplays your project.

DISPLAY A CUSTOM FIELD

1 Display the table in which you want to display the custom field.

Note: For more on switching tables, see Chapter 7.

2 Right-click the column that you want to appear to the right of the custom field.

3 Click Insert Column.

184

Should I use the Field button, the Function button, or the buttons on the Formula toolbar to create a formula?

✔ No. If you know the correct syntax, you can type the formula. Be aware, however, that the buttons help you avoid syntax mistakes.

What does the MOD button on the Formula toolbar do?

✔ It displays the remainder that results after you divide two integers. To distinguish MOD from /, which divides two values, you can express 9 MOD 2 equals 1 as 2 goes into 9 four times with 1 left over, while remembering that 9/2 equals 4.5.

What kinds of functions can I use when I create a formula?

✔ When you click Function in the Formula dialog box, a list of six categories of functions appears: Conversion functions convert values, Date/Time functions operate on or return dates and times, General functions do not fit in any other category, Math functions calculate values like a square root, Microsoft Office Project functions use Project fields to display values, and Text functions operate on text.

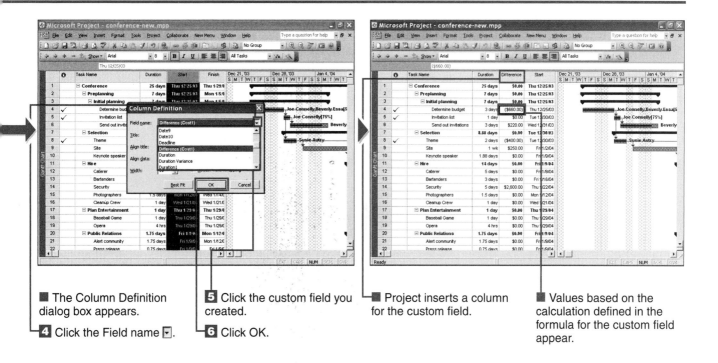

■ The Column Definition dialog box appears.

4 Click the Field name ▼.

5 Click the custom field you created.

6 Click OK.

■ Project inserts a column for the custom field.

■ Values based on the calculation defined in the formula for the custom field appear.

CONTINUED ▶

USING FORMULAS IN CUSTOM FIELDS (CONTINUED)

Up to this point, you have created a cost custom field that uses a formula to compare Actual Cost to Baseline Cost. You also have displayed the custom field; as you have seen, zeros or positive values represent tasks where actual costs do not exceed baseline costs. Negative values in the Difference field indicate that the actual cost of the task exceeds the baseline cost.

Suppose that the basic premise of the task is fine, but you want a custom field that shows you the difference between Actual Cost and Baseline Cost. Suppose, however, that you have decided that you do not want to read numbers or even look at numbers. You prefer for Project to alert you in some visual way to tasks that are over budget — that is, tasks for which Actual Cost exceeds Baseline Cost.

After all, you are a visual person or you would not have purchased this book! You want a custom field that uses a graphical indicator to get your attention when Actual Cost exceeds Baseline Cost.

You can modify the custom field called Difference that was created earlier in this task so that it displays an on-screen indicator instead of dollar values.

USING FORMULAS IN CUSTOM FIELDS (CONTINUED)

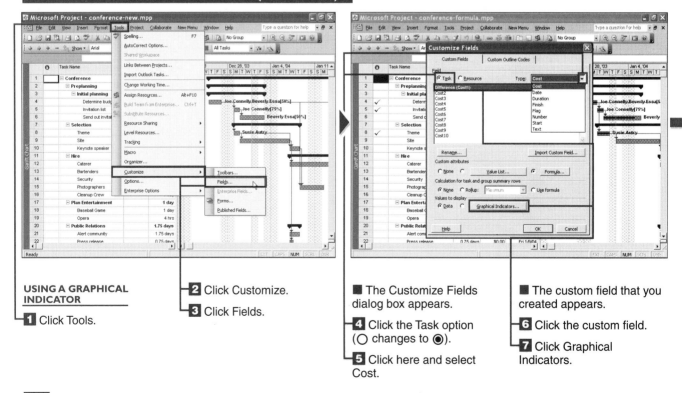

USING A GRAPHICAL INDICATOR

1 Click Tools.

2 Click Customize.

3 Click Fields.

■ The Customize Fields dialog box appears.

4 Click the Task option (○ changes to ⦿).

5 Click here and select Cost.

■ The custom field that you created appears.

6 Click the custom field.

7 Click Graphical Indicators.

How do you select a Test and an image for the first row in the Graphical Indicators dialog box? I do not see a ⊡.

✔ The ⊡ appears when you click in the appropriate box, and it disappears when you click somewhere else in the Graphical Indicators dialog box.

What if my formula calls for me to compare the result to a field?

✔ You can set the Value(s) column to the field you need. When you click in the Value(s) column, Project displays a list of all available fields.

Can I view both graphical indicators and actual values?

✔ You have two ways to approach this issue. You can display the Difference column twice in your table, or, in the Graphical Indicators dialog box, you can select the Show data values in ToolTips option (☐ changes to ☑). You cannot see the box in the steps for this section because the list for the Text column covers it. If you choose the second method, position the mouse over an indicator to make the dollar value associated with the indicator appear.

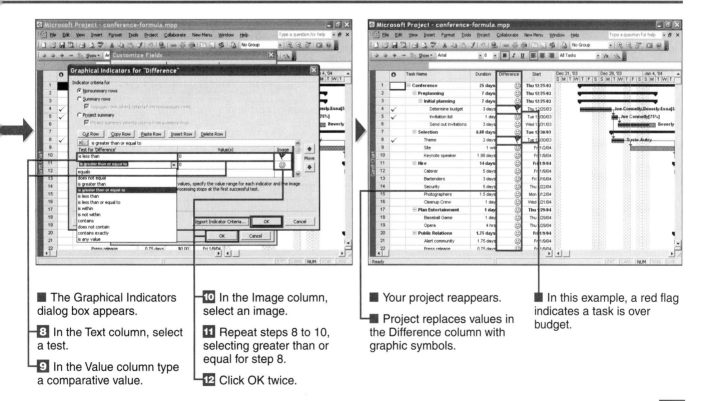

■ The Graphical Indicators dialog box appears.

8 In the Text column, select a test.

9 In the Value column type a comparative value.

10 In the Image column, select an image.

11 Repeat steps 8 to 10, selecting greater than or equal for step 8.

12 Click OK twice.

■ Your project reappears.

■ Project replaces values in the Difference column with graphic symbols.

■ In this example, a red flag indicates a task is over budget.

WORK WITH WBS CODES

The WBS chart, initially created by the U.S. defense establishment, displays and defines the products you want to develop. You use code structures, commonly called WBS codes, to establish relationships between each of the deliverables and to the end product. Government contracts often require you to create WBS codes in your project.

In Project, you can assign WBS codes, which tie to the structure of your project, to each task. To help you identify the relationship among deliverables and organize the project, you can use any numbering system for your WBS code structure or combinations of letters and numbers. Your WBS code can begin with a static prefix called the Project Code Prefix. To define the code, specify a format that describes your WBS code, including the number of levels the code will contain. For example, 1.1.1.1 contains four levels. The

example in this section creates a two-level WBS code that uses a Project Code Prefix followed by numeric values. The numeric values change as the outline level of the project changes. Like custom fields and outline codes, after defining WBS codes, you can define them by adding a column to a sheet view for the WBS code field.

WORK WITH WBS CODES

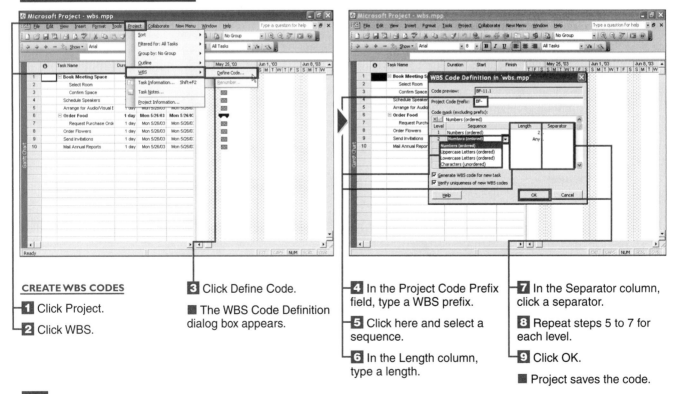

CREATE WBS CODES

1 Click Project.

2 Click WBS.

3 Click Define Code.

■ The WBS Code Definition dialog box appears.

4 In the Project Code Prefix field, type a WBS prefix.

5 Click here and select a sequence.

6 In the Length column, type a length.

7 In the Separator column, click a separator.

8 Repeat steps 5 to 7 for each level.

9 Click OK.

■ Project saves the code.

When should I use the Project Code Prefix box in the WBS Code Definition dialog box?

✔ You may want, for example, to start each WBS code with the initials of the project name. For a Project named Data Migration, you may use a prefix of DM.

What does the Generate WBS code for new task option do?

✔ If you click this option (☐ changes to ☑) in the WBS Code Defintion dialog box, you ensure that Project assigns a WBS code to all new tasks that you enter into the project.

What are the available choices for separators in the WBS Code Definition dialog box?

✔ You can select the period, the dash (-), the plus sign (+), or the slash (/) from the Separator list. You can also type a separator of your choice.

What does the Verify uniqueness of new WBS codes option do?

✔ Located in the WBS Code Definition dialog box, this option (☐ changes to ☑) double-checks each new WBS code to ensure that the code is unique and does not duplicate an existing WBS code.

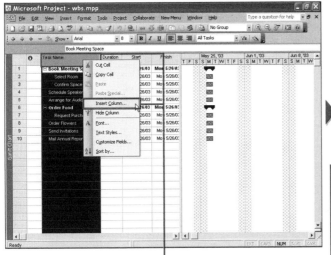

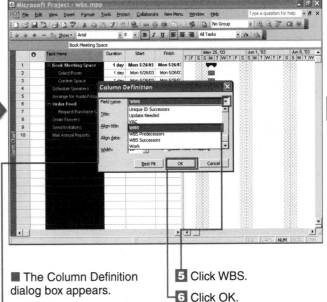

DISPLAY WBS CODES

1 Display the table in which you want the WBS codes to appear.

Note: For more on switching tables, see Chapter 7.

2 Right-click the column that you want to appear to the right of the WBS field.

3 Click Insert Column.

■ The Column Definition dialog box appears.

4 Click the Field name ▾.

5 Click WBS.

6 Click OK.

CONTINUED ▶

WORK WITH WBS CODES (CONTINUED)

When you move tasks around in your project, sometimes Project renumbers WBS codes and sometimes does not. Project automatically renumbers WBS codes if you change the outline structure of your project because the codes are tied to the outline structure of your project. Likewise, if you promote or demote a task, Project assigns the task a new WBS code. However, Project does not renumber WBS codes for every move you make in your project. For example, if you drag a Level 1 task to a new Level 1 location, or if you drag a subtask to a new location beneath its original parent task, both tasks retain their original WBS code number.

At times, you may want to renumber the WBS codes, even when Project does not renumber them automatically. You can renumber the entire project or only selected tasks in the project. If you choose to renumber selected tasks, you must select the tasks before starting the renumbering process.

Project may not allow you undo WBS codes renumbering, so save your project before you start. If you do not like the results, you can close the project without saving it and then reopen it in the state it was before you renumbered it.

WORK WITH WBS CODES (CONTINUED)

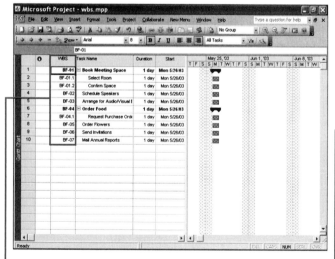

■ Project inserts a column containing WBS codes.

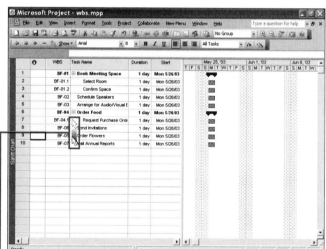

MOVING TASKS

1 Click and drag a task below another task

■ This example moved Order Flowers below Send Invitations.

■ Project does not renumber WBS codes.

Note: If, instead, you indent Order Flowers, Project does assign it to WBS Code BF-04.2 because you changed the task's outline level. Project does not change the codes of Send Invitations or Mail Annual Reports. WBS Code BF-05 will be missing.

Can I stop WBS codes from changing even if I change the structure of my project outline?

✔ Because WBS codes are tied to your project outline, they change if you restructure the outline. You can try using Outline codes, which are completely static. For more information, see the section "Define Custom Outline Codes" later in this chapter.

In the Sequence column, what does Characters (unordered) do?

✔ You use this choice to create a free-form WBS code. You can assign it for a portion of the code and maintain a structure for the rest of the code.

Can you give an example that uses Characters (unordered)?

✔ Suppose that you set up the WBS code with a first level of Numbers (ordered) Length 1, a second level of Numbers (ordered) Length 1, and a third level of Characters (unordered) Length 3. For any third-level task, you can enter any three characters that you want for the third part of the WBS code. In this example, when you enter a third-level task, Project displays a WBS of 1.1.***. You can change the last three characters to anything you want.

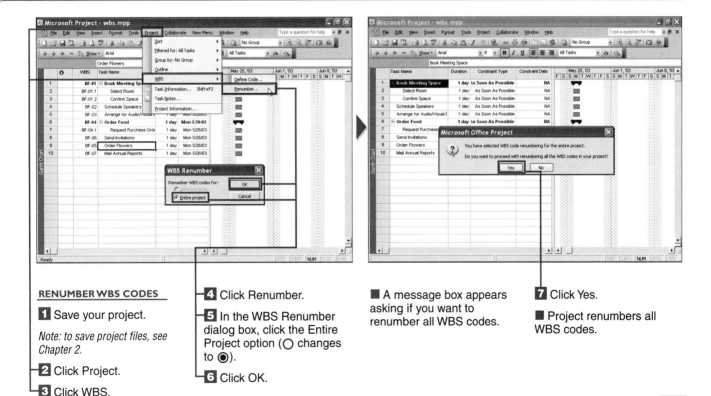

RENUMBER WBS CODES

1 Save your project.

Note: to save project files, see Chapter 2.

2 Click Project.

3 Click WBS.

4 Click Renumber.

5 In the WBS Renumber dialog box, click the Entire Project option (○ changes to ◉).

6 Click OK.

■ A message box appears asking if you want to renumber all WBS codes.

7 Click Yes.

■ Project renumbers all WBS codes.

DEFINE CUSTOM OUTLINE CODES

When you work on a project with a rigid, contractually agreed structure — perhaps in construction, government, or aerospace — you can use custom outline codes to create the structures in your project. Within a single project, you can use codes for accounts, as contract component identifiers, and to identify the group or department performing the work. If you use custom outline codes, you can

group, filter, and report on the project in different ways for different audiences.

Custom outline codes work well when you do not want the codes to change under any circumstances because they are completely static. Outline codes work like WBS codes work, but are static and not tied to the outline structure of your project. In addition to the government project example, you can use custom outline codes to

assign a department code to a task so that you can view the project organized by department. You can also use custom outline codes to assign a company cost code to a task so that you can view tasks by cost code.

In this task, you create a task custom outline code called Dept. Code. Like custom fields, you must display outline codes after you create them.

DEFINE CUSTOM OUTLINE CODES

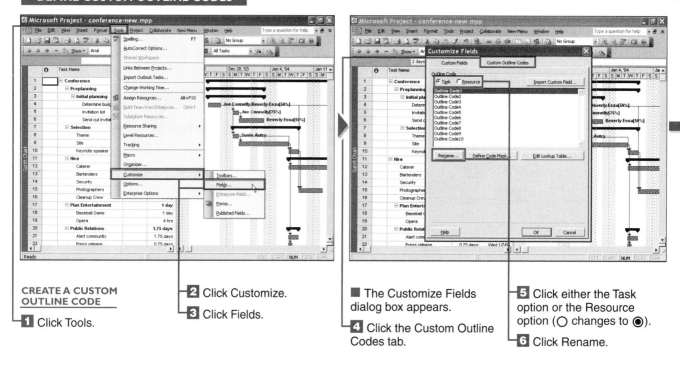

CREATE A CUSTOM OUTLINE CODE

1 Click Tools.

2 Click Customize.

3 Click Fields.

■ The Customize Fields dialog box appears.

4 Click the Custom Outline Codes tab.

5 Click either the Task option or the Resource option (○ changes to ◉).

6 Click Rename.

What does the Only allow new codes with values in all levels of mask option do?

✔ This option (☐ changes to ☑) ensures that the format of each code you type matches the format you define in the Outline Code Definition dialog box.

What does the Only allow codes listed in the lookup table option do?

✔ Clicking this option (☐ changes to ☑) ensures that you type values in the custom outline code field that appear in the lookup table. If you try to type a value that is not in the table, Project displays an error message stating that the code is not valid.

How many outline codes can I create?

✔ You can create up to ten custom outline codes for tasks and ten for resources.

Can I set up an outline code without using the Lookup Table?

✔ To create a format for the outline code so that users apply the correct format to outline codes, click OK in step 14 and proceed to the steps in the subsection "Display a Custom Outline Code" on the next page. You can select the Only allow new codes with values in all levels of mask option (☐ changes to ☑).

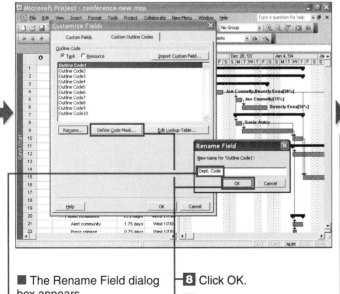

■ The Rename Field dialog box appears.

7 Type a new name for the outline code.

Note: You cannot use a name that Project already uses.

8 Click OK.

9 In the Customize Fields dialog box, click Define Code Mask.

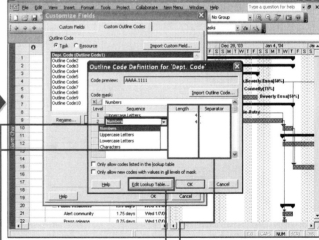

■ The Outline Code Definition dialog box appears.

10 Click in the Sequence column and select a value.

11 Click in the Length column to select a length for the code.

12 Click in the Separator column to select a separator.

13 Repeat steps 10 to 12 for each level.

14 Click Edit Lookup Table.

CONTINUED ▶ 193

DEFINE CUSTOM OUTLINE CODES (CONTINUED)

Once you define a custom outline code and display it on a sheet view, you can type values into the field that match the options you established while creating the field. For example, if you do not set up a Lookup Table by clicking either option at the bottom of the Outline Code Definition dialog box, users can enter any value in the outline code field; you, therefore, cannot enforce *standards*,

which are any common business practices consistently applied throughout the organization.

You establish standards when you create a Lookup Table for the custom outline code field because you provide a set of suggested values for the field. You optionally can organize the values in the lookup tables using levels, where level 2 is a subset of level 1 and level 3 is a subset of level 2 and so on.

You enforce standards when you click both options at the bottom of the Outline Code Definition dialog box, because values must conform to the format established in the Outline Code Definition dialog box. Take these actions if, for example, you are using a custom outline code for a government contract that specifies a particular list of WBS codes for deliverables and other tasks.

DEFINE CUSTOM OUTLINE CODES (CONTINUED)

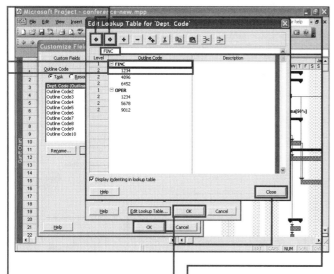

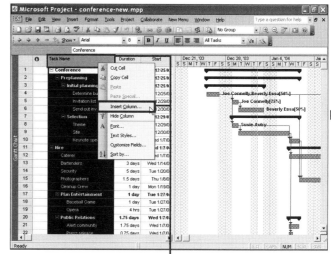

■ The Edit Lookup Table window appears.

15 Type a Level 1 outline code.

16 Type a Level 2 outline code.

17 Click the Indent button (■).

■ To supply another Level 1 code, type the code and click here.

18 Repeat steps 15 to 17 to finish entering codes.

19 Click Close and then OK twice.

DISPLAY A CUSTOM OUTLINE CODE

1 Display the table in which you want to display the custom outline code.

Note: For more on switching tables, see Chapter 7.

2 Right-click the column that you want to appear to the right of the custom outline code.

3 Click Insert Column.

If I forget to add a code to the lookup table, can I add it later?

✔ Yes. In the Edit Lookup Table dialog box, select the code that you want to appear *below* the code that you want to add, and then click the Insert Row button (⬚) at the top of the Edit Lookup Table dialog box.

Can I delete a lookup table code that is no longer valid?

✔ Yes. In the Edit Lookup Table dialog box, select the code and click the Delete Row button (⬚).

Can I assign both an outline code and a WBS code to a task?

✔ Yes.

How can I create a three-level outline code with a lookup table?

✔ Make sure that you define three levels in the Outline Code Definition dialog box. Then, in the Edit Lookup Table dialog box, type the code on a blank line below a Level 2 outline code, and click the Indent button (⬚).

Can I define a prefix for an outline code like you can for a WBS code?

✔ You can use the first level of the outline code to emulate the WBS Project Code Prefix.

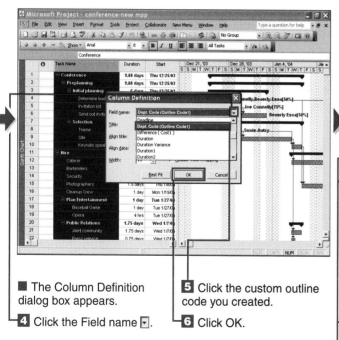

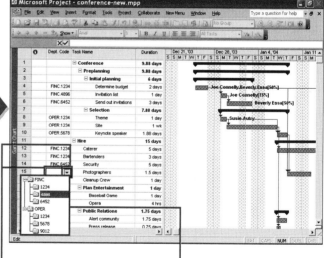

■ The Column Definition dialog box appears.

4 Click the Field name ▾.

5 Click the custom outline code you created.

6 Click OK.

■ Project inserts a column for the custom field.

7 Click an item in the new column (▾ appears).

8 Click the ▾.

9 Click an outline code for the task.

10 Repeat steps 7 to 9 for each task.

■ Project assigns outline codes to each task.

HOW TO APPROACH SCHEDULING PROBLEMS

Not only are scheduling problems unwelcome, but they are also inevitable. Scheduling conflicts can occur when your project takes longer than you planned, or when you overallocate your resources. In this chapter, you focus on identifying and resolving scheduling problems, while Chapter 11 addresses resource overallocation.

Identifying Scheduling Conflicts

Identifying a problem is half the battle. The various views and filters in Project are your greatest source of information. Changing views, switching tables, and filtering, sorting, grouping, and organizing information by using the techniques described in Chapters 6 to 9 can help you uncover problems. For example, you can spot some problems if you filter your project to view only incomplete tasks or slipping tasks. You can also unknowingly create a problem by using a task constraint.

Adding Resources

Project provides several techniques that you can use to resolve scheduling conflicts. If a task is effort driven, adding resources to a task can decrease the time that is necessary to complete the task because Project reallocates work among the assigned resources on effort-driven tasks. Be aware that adding resources to a task may increase the cost of the project. For more on Adding resources, see the section "Add Resources to Tasks."

Adding Time to Tasks

In some instances, you can resolve a scheduling conflict by increasing the duration of a noncritical, effort-driven task. Typically, you use this technique when you need one resource to complete two effort-driven tasks simultaneously and one of the tasks is not on the critical path. You can change a task's timing by increasing the duration of a task, and you may find that once-scarce resources are now available to complete the task. For more on this technique, see the section "Add Time to Tasks."

Using Overtime

If you are lucky, you have unlimited resources and you can add resources to effort-driven tasks to resolve scheduling problems. In reality, however, you do not have the luxury of unlimited resources, and adding resources may not be an option. If you cannot add resources, using overtime may be the best option to keep a task on schedule. Overtime work does not represent additional work on a task; instead, it represents the amount of time that is spent on a task outside regular hours. You can use overtime to shorten the time — duration — that a resource takes to complete a task, but because overtime work is generally charged at a higher rate, it can increase the cost of your project. For more on adding overtime, see the section "Using Overtime."

Identifying Tasks with Slack

If you have slack in your schedule, you can balance phases of the schedule that have no slack with phases that have too much slack by rearranging tasks. *Slack* is the amount of time that a task can slip before it affects another task's dates or the finish date of the project. Most projects contain noncritical tasks with slack, and these tasks can start late without affecting the schedule. For example, suppose that you are planning a birthday surprise party for your boss, and you have five days to plan the party. During this time, you need to get a card, and you estimate it will take you one hour to buy the card. The task of buying the card has 4+ days of slack built into it. Therefore, if your schedule contains slack, you can use tasks with slack to compensate for tasks that take longer than planned. For more on slack, see the section "Identify Tasks with Slack."

Identifying Constraints

When projects fall behind schedule, task constraints are often the source of the problem. For example, if you impose a Must Start On task constraint on a task with no slack time and with other tasks linked to it, you may cause a scheduling conflict. Project contains a Planning Wizard that warns you when you take an illogical action or an action that is likely to throw your project off schedule. For more on using the Planning Wizard, see the section "Identify Task Constraints."

Reviewing Dependencies

You can tighten up the schedule and eliminate scheduling conflicts by changing task dependencies. For example, if you link tasks that do not need to be linked, you may create a situation in which you do not have the resources to complete the tasks. As a result, the project schedule falls behind. For example, by linking two tasks that use different resources, the first resource may sit idle while the second resource works. If you had not linked the two tasks, both resources could be working. After you remove unnecessary dependencies, you can rearrange tasks and adjust the project to bring it back on schedule. For more on dependencies, see the section "Review Dependencies."

Dividing a Task

In situations where you cannot to complete a task on consecutive days, you can start the task, stop work on it for a period of time, and then come back to the task. Dividing a task is an effective way to resolve a scheduling conflict. You learn more about dividing a task in the section "Split Tasks."

Adjusting the Critical Path

The *critical path* shows the tasks that you must complete on schedule in your project for the entire project to finish on schedule. Tasks on the critical path are called *critical tasks*. If you can simply shorten the time frame that you originally allotted for the critical path, you can shorten the entire 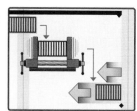 project and possibly resolve a scheduling conflict. Or, if any of the tasks on the critical path take longer than planned, then the duration of the project will increase.

ADD RESOURCES TO TASKS

I f a task is effort driven, adding a resource to a task can reduce the time you need to complete the task because Project reallocates work among the assigned resources on effort-driven tasks. What takes one resource two days to complete can, on an effort-driven task, be completed in one day by two resources. By reducing the time to

complete the task, you shorten the schedule and, hopefully, resolve the scheduling problem.

Be aware that this technique only works on effort-driven tasks such as fixed-work tasks, which are, by definition, effort driven. While Project creates fixed-unit and fixed-duration tasks by default as effort-driven tasks, you can change this

setting. You cannot assume that adding resources shortens a task's duration. As part of the process, you must first check that the task to which you want to add resources is an effort-driven task. For details on effort-driven, fixed-unit, fixed-duration, and fixed-work tasks, as well as how to handle task timing in general, see Chapter 3.

ADD RESOURCES TO TASKS

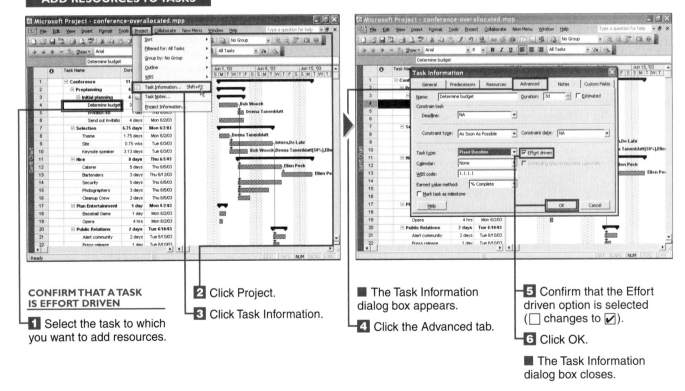

CONFIRM THAT A TASK IS EFFORT DRIVEN

1 Select the task to which you want to add resources.

2 Click Project.

3 Click Task Information.

■ The Task Information dialog box appears.

4 Click the Advanced tab.

5 Confirm that the Effort driven option is selected (☐ changes to ☑).

6 Click OK.

■ The Task Information dialog box closes.

If my task is not effort driven, how can I resolve a scheduling problem?

✔ You can focus on the following possibilities: adding time to the task, adjusting any slack the task may have, evaluating and possibly changing the task's constraints and dependencies, or splitting the task. All of these approaches are covered in this chapter.

How can I click Assign when it is gray?

✔ The Assign button turns gray after you assign a resource to a task, which is what you see in the figure. Prior to making or changing an assignment, the Assign button is available.

What does the indicator in the left column mean?

✔ Project displays an indicator whenever you add resources to or remove resources from a task, because changes like these can reduce the task's duration or keep the duration the same but increase total work or reduce the hours worked per day. If you click the indicator, Project displays an explanation of the indicator icon and options available to you for handling the effects of the change you made. In this example, because you are trying to resolve a schedule conflict, you want to reduce the task's duration.

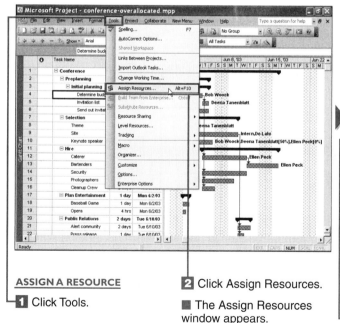

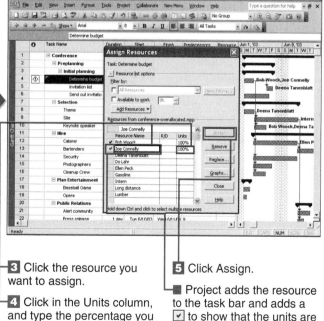

ASSIGN A RESOURCE

1 Click Tools.

2 Click Assign Resources.

■ The Assign Resources window appears.

3 Click the resource you want to assign.

4 Click in the Units column, and type the percentage you want to assign.

5 Click Assign.

■ Project adds the resource to the task bar and adds a ☑ to show that the units are assigned to the resource.

ADD TIME TO TASKS

When a schedule conflict involves using the same resource on two simultaneously scheduled effort-driven tasks, you can resolve the conflict by increasing the duration of one of the tasks. This technique works well when one of the tasks is not on the critical path. By increasing the duration of the noncritical task, you change the task's timing and possibly make once-scarce resources available to complete the task.

Suppose that you need to assign Mary to work full time on producing an invitation list, a one-day task, and a budget, a three-day task, for the grand opening of your new hotel. The budget task is on the critical path — you will not know how many guests to invite without the budget — but the invitation list task initially is not on the critical path. With the tasks scheduled to run simultaneously,

you do not have enough resources to complete both tasks as scheduled.

However, if you add three days to the invitation task, Mary can complete the budget — the critical task — and then complete the invitation list. All the work gets done, the project remains on schedule, and the total duration of the schedule does not increase.

ADD TIME TO TASKS

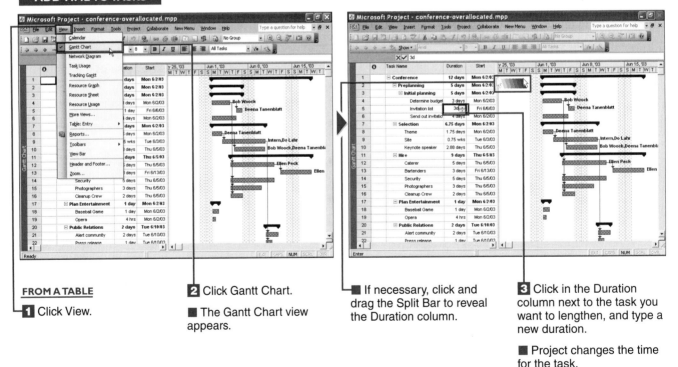

FROM A TABLE

1 Click View.

2 Click Gantt Chart.

■ The Gantt Chart view appears.

■ If necessary, click and drag the Split Bar to reveal the Duration column.

3 Click in the Duration column next to the task you want to lengthen, and type a new duration.

■ Project changes the time for the task.

How can I quickly open the Task Information dialog box?

✔ You can double-click the task you want to change, or you can select the task and click the Task Information button (🖼).

What happens if I try to lengthen a task on the critical path?

✔ You may resolve your scheduling conflict, but you may also lengthen the schedule, which increases the cost of the project. However, if your situation permits, or if you have no alternative, you can use this technique to solve a scheduling problem.

Am I really resolving a resource conflict instead of a schedule conflict?

✔ The issue is really one of perspective. It is rare to find a schedule conflict that does not involve a resource conflict. So, yes, you can think of resolving a schedule conflict by adding time to a task as also solving a resource conflict. The intent here is to focus on the method of solving the schedule conflict; consider it gravy that you are also solving a resource conflict.

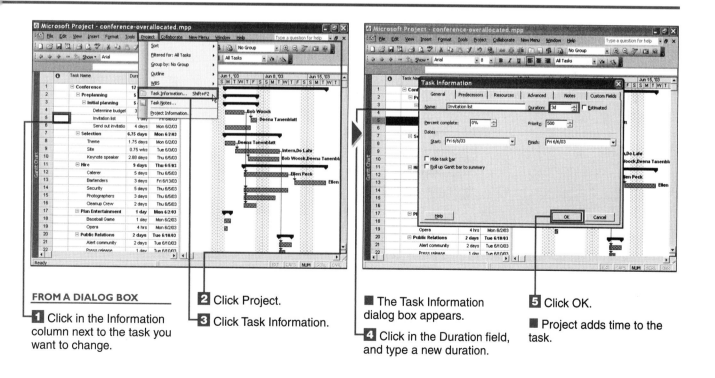

FROM A DIALOG BOX

1 Click in the Information column next to the task you want to change.

2 Click Project.

3 Click Task Information.

■ The Task Information dialog box appears.

4 Click in the Duration field, and type a new duration.

5 Click OK.

■ Project adds time to the task.

USING OVERTIME

Project defines *overtime* as the amount of work that you schedule beyond an assigned resource's regular working hours. Overtime work does not represent additional work on a task; instead, it represents the amount of time that is spent on a task outside regular hours. For example, if you assign 40 hours of work and 15 hours of overtime, the total work is still 40 hours. Of the 40 hours, 25 hours are worked during the regular work schedule, and 15 hours are worked during off hours. Therefore, you can use planned overtime to shorten the time that a resource takes to complete a task.

If adding resources is not an option, you can use overtime to keep a task on schedule. Using overtime has a cost, however, and it is not a hidden cost. It is a very obvious cost. Project charges overtime hours to the task at the resource's overtime rate just like it charges regular hours to the task at the resource's regular rate. So, while using overtime can help resolve a scheduling problem, it increases the cost of your project.

USING OVERTIME

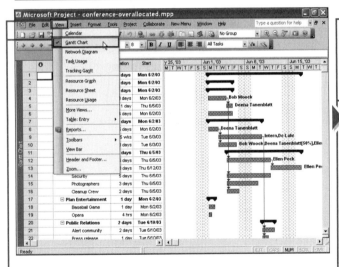

1 Click View.

2 Click Gantt Chart.

■ The Gantt Chart view of your project appears.

3 Click in the Information column next to the task to which you want to add overtime.

4 Click Window.

5 Click Split.

■ The Gantt Chart appears in the top pane, and the Task Form appears in the bottom pane.

How do I add overtime to a different task than the one I selected initially?

✔ Click in the upper pane that contains the Gantt Chart, and click a different task.

If I do not have enough resources to either add resources or assign overtime, what else can I try to resolve a scheduling problem?

✔ You can focus on the following possibilities: adding time to tasks, adjusting any slack that tasks may have, evaluating and possibly changing task constraints and dependencies, or splitting tasks. All of these approaches are covered in this chapter.

How do I close the Task Form pane when I finish entering overtime?

✔ Click Window, and then click Remove Split. You can also click and drag the horizontal split bar that divides the panes down to the bottom of the screen.

How do I add overtime for more than one resource to a task?

✔ In the Task Form pane, you can display other resources if you click Next or Previous, which appear after you click OK to save an overtime assignment.

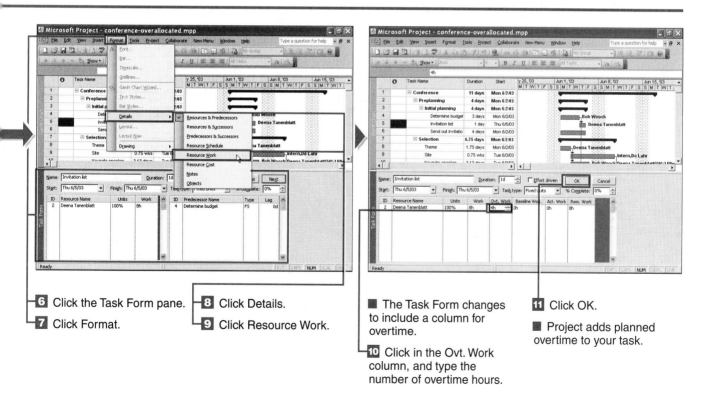

6 Click the Task Form pane.

7 Click Format.

8 Click Details.

9 Click Resource Work.

■ The Task Form changes to include a column for overtime.

10 Click in the Ovt. Work column, and type the number of overtime hours.

11 Click OK.

■ Project adds planned overtime to your task.

IDENTIFY TASKS WITH SLACK

If you have slack in your schedule, you can resolve scheduling problems by rearranging tasks and balancing phases of the schedule that have no slack with phases that have too much slack. *Slack,* also called *float,* is the amount of time that a task can slip before it affects another task's dates or the finish date of the project. In project management, there are actually two kinds of

slack. *Free slack* is the amount of time that you can delay Task One without delaying the next task that depends on Task One. *Total Slack* is the amount of time you can delay a task without delaying the project finish date.

Most projects contain noncritical tasks with slack, and these tasks can start late without affecting the project end date of the schedule. Therefore, if your schedule

contains slack, you can use tasks with slack to compensate for tasks that take longer than planned.

You may see positive or negative numbers when evaluating slack. Positive numbers identify the amount of time you can delay a task, while negative numbers identify the amount of time you must make up in the schedule to complete it on time. Tasks with 0 slack are critical tasks.

IDENTIFY TASKS WITH SLACK

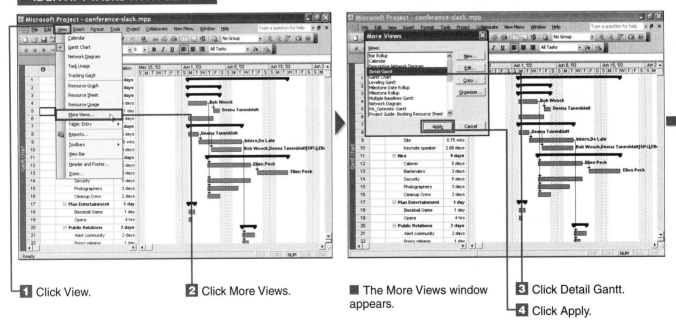

1 Click View.

2 Click More Views.

■ The More Views window appears.

3 Click Detail Gantt.

4 Click Apply.

Is there any reason to look for slack if I am not experiencing a schedule conflict?

✔ Yes. Slack values can help you identify inconsistencies in the schedule. For example, a negative slack value occurs when one task has a finish-to-start dependency with a second task, but the second task has a Must Start On constraint that is earlier than the end of the first task. In this case, the negative slack value does not mean that you need to make up time in the schedule; it means that you need to review dependencies and constraints.

How does slack happen?

✔ If you use the Must Start On constraint when you create your task, you usually create slack time. You can avoid creating slack if you use the As Soon As Possible constraint whenever possible.

Can avoid slack if I type a 0 in the Free Slack or Total Slack column?

✔ No. You you can rearrange tasks in your project to reduce slack and resolve scheduling problems. For more on moving or copying tasks, see Chapter 2.

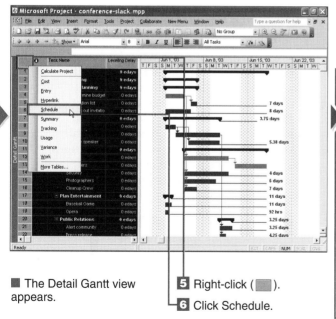

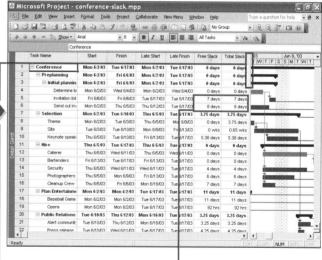

■ The Detail Gantt view appears.

5 Right-click ( ).

6 Click Schedule.

■ Project applies the Schedule table to the view.

7 Click and drag the vertical Split Bar until the Free Slack and Total Slack columns appear.

8 Look for tasks with slack greater than 0 and tasks with free slack greater than 0.

■ When adjusting the schedule, start by rearranging these tasks.

THE PLANNING WIZARD

Project contains a Planning Wizard that warns you when you are about to take an illogical action or an action that is likely to throw your project off schedule. This section explores two examples of when you can expect to see the Planning Wizard, and what to expect when you turn the Planning Wizard off.

Impose a Constraint

If you impose a constraint that may lengthen your project schedule, such as a Must Start On task constraint on a task with no slack time and with other tasks linked to it, Project displays the Planning Wizard because your action can cause a scheduling conflict.

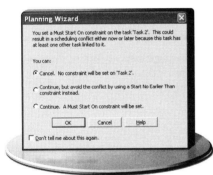

Impose an Illogical Start Date

You see another Planning Wizard dialog box if you impose an illogical start date on a task when recording actual dates. For example, you see a Planning Wizard dialog box if you accidentally enter a start date for Task 2 that is earlier than Task 1, and Task 2 is linked to and succeeds Task 1.

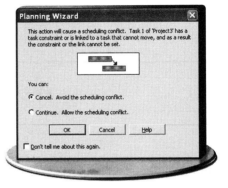

Turn Off the Planning Wizard

You can turn off Planning Wizard warnings if you find wizards popping up annoying. If you turn off the Planning Wizard, Project still displays warnings when you try to take actions that may cause scheduling delays, but the message is a little more traditional. Project makes suggestions concerning actions that you can take to avoid these kinds of conflicts, and these suggestions all refer to the predecessor task.

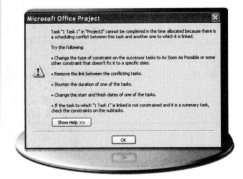

TURN ON THE PLANNING WIZARD

Because task constraints combined with task dependencies account for the majority of schedule conflicts, Project contains a Planning Wizard that can help you work more efficiently or warn you about illogical actions that you may accidentally try to take.

If you hate wizards, you can turn off the Planning Wizard when it pops up; the Planning Wizard boxes contain an option you can click that disables the wizard.

If you disable the wizard, Project displays more traditional message boxes when you enter illogical information or impose a constraint that can cause a scheduling conflict. The more traditional message boxes suggest actions you can take to resolve the problems, but they do not help you avoid the problems. If you turn off the Planning Wizard and regret it, you can turn it back on.

What kind of advice do I see if I click the Advice about using Microsoft Office Project option?

✔ You can view advice about faster or more efficient ways to use Project. For example, if you type the same duration in several consecutive tasks, a Planning Wizard box tells you about the fill handle.

TURN ON THE PLANNING WIZARD

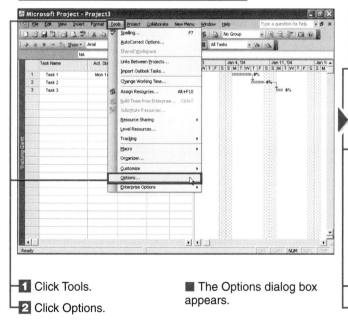

—1 Click Tools.

—2 Click Options.

■ The Options dialog box appears.

—3 Click the General tab.

—4 Click the Advice from Planning Wizard option (☐ changes to ☑).

■ The Planning Wizard includes several options that you can select to control the kind of advice Project gives you.

—5 Click OK.

■ Project saves your changes.

IDENTIFY TASK CONSTRAINTS

Task constraints are often the source of schedule conflict problems. For example, if you impose a Must Finish On task constraint on a task that has no slack time and other tasks linked to it, you may cause a scheduling conflict.

When you schedule your project from its start date, Project automatically assigns As Soon As Possible constraints — which are flexible — to each task,

theoretically starting each task on the first day of the project. Project defines flexible constraints as those not tied to specific dates; inflexible constraints are tied to specific dates. Project's flexible constraints are As Soon As Possible (ASAP), As Late As Possible (ALAP), Start No Earlier Than, Finish No Earlier Than, Start No Later Than, and Finish No Later Than.

Project's inflexible constraints are Must Finish On and Must Start On.

When you assign a constraint other than ASAP or ALAP to a task, Project displays an indicator next to the task to catch your attention. Inflexible constraint types typically cause a scheduling problem because constraint types require a specific date. You can position the mouse over each indicator to see information about the constraint, but that technique is tedious if used for more than a few constraints.

IDENTIFY TASK CONSTRAINTS

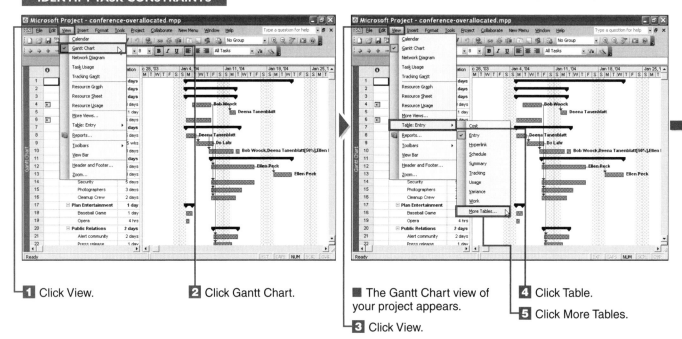

1 Click View.

2 Click Gantt Chart.

■ The Gantt Chart view of your project appears.

3 Click View.

4 Click Table.

5 Click More Tables.

How do I change a constraint?

✔ First, double-click the task. In the Task Information dialog box, click the Advanced tab and then the Constraint type ⊡ to select a different constraint type. Or you can apply the Constraint Dates table view. For more on switching tables, see Chapter 7.

What is the difference between a flexible constraint and an inflexible constraint?

✔ Unlike inflexible constraints, flexible constraints do not tie a task to a specific date. Think of all the flexible constraints except for ASAP and ALAP as soft flexible constraints. You can associate dates with them, but conditions in your project can move the dates.

What is the alternative to inflexible constraints when I want to target a particular date?

✔ Consider using a flexible constraint and entering a deadline for the task. The deadline icon alerts you visually. For details, see Chapter 3.

I did not set any constraints, but I see a constraint icon. Why?

✔ You probably manually entered a start or finish date or dragged the Gantt bar of a task. Projects scheduled from the start date are constrained to begin no earlier than the project start date. Projects scheduled from the finish date are constrained to begin no later than the date you type.

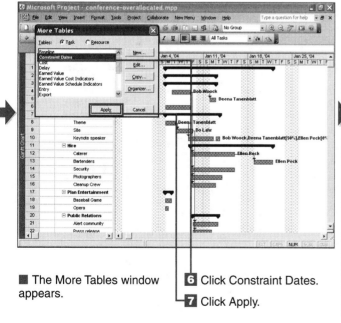

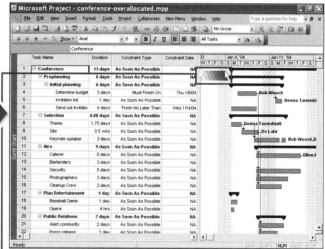

■ The More Tables window appears.

6 Click Constraint Dates.

7 Click Apply.

■ The Constraint Dates table appears.

8 Click and drag the vertical Split Bar to the right to reveal the table.

■ You can view each Constraint Type and any associated Constraint Dates.

REVIEW DEPENDENCIES

I n project management, dependency refers to the relationship between two tasks. A *dependency* exists when the completion of one task cannot happen unless the other task either finishes or starts.

Dependencies exist because all tasks in a project rarely can happen simultaneously. Some tasks must start or finish before others can begin. You cannot know the total time that you need to complete a

project until you establish durations and dependencies. For example, if your project is comprised of five one-day tasks with no dependencies among the tasks, the project takes one day to complete. However if the tasks must happen one after the other, the project takes five days to complete.

A task that must occur before another task begins is a *predecessor task*, and the task that occurs later

in the relationship is a *successor task*. If you inadvertently link tasks that you do not need to link, you may not have the resources you need to complete the tasks, which causes the project schedule to fall behind. If you discover unnecessary links, you can remove them, and you may find gaps in the project schedule where you can perform work.

REVIEW DEPENDENCIES

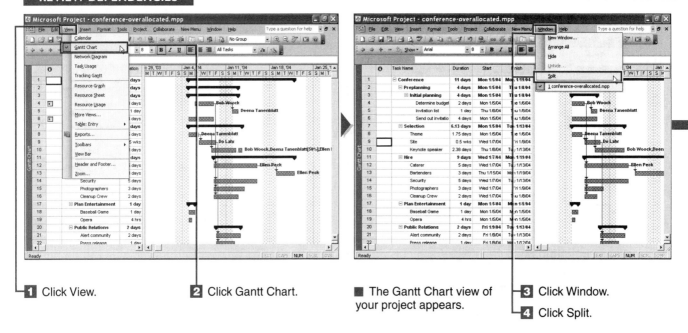

1 Click View.

2 Click Gantt Chart.

■ The Gantt Chart view of your project appears.

3 Click Window.

4 Click Split.

Is there a relationship between constraints and dependencies in Project?

✔ Constraints and dependencies are closely related. *Constraints* describe the relationship between a task and the project's start date or finish date, while *dependencies* describe the relationship between the start and finish dates of tasks. If a conflict exists between a constraint and a dependency, Project, by default, uses the constraint to drive the timing of the task; the task does not move from the constraint-imposed date. See Chapter 3 for more information on constraints and dependencies.

How do I eliminate a dependency?

✔ To eliminate a dependency, you eliminate the predecessor relationship. Click the successor task in the Relationship Diagram, and then click the Task Info button (🔳) to open the Task Information dialog box. Click the Predecessors tab. Click in the ID column of the relationship you want to eliminate, press Delete, and then click OK.

How do I get rid of the Relationship diagram pane when I finish?

✔ Click the Gantt Chart pane, click Window, and then click Remove Split.

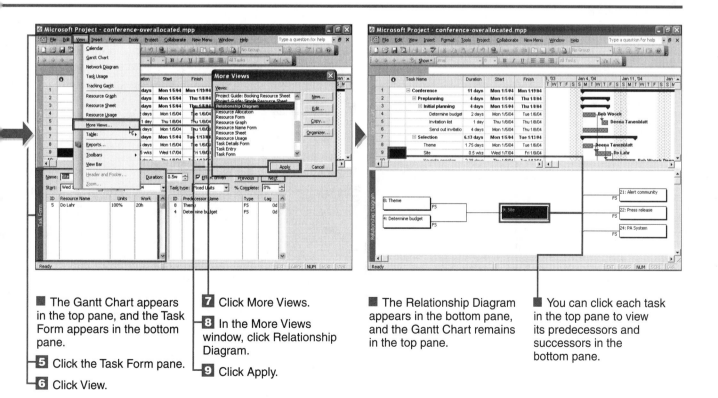

■ The Gantt Chart appears in the top pane, and the Task Form appears in the bottom pane.

5 Click the Task Form pane.

6 Click View.

7 Click More Views.

8 In the More Views window, click Relationship Diagram.

9 Click Apply.

■ The Relationship Diagram appears in the bottom pane, and the Gantt Chart remains in the top pane.

■ You can click each task in the top pane to view its predecessors and successors in the bottom pane.

SPLIT TASKS

By default, Project sets up every task to run from start to finish with no breaks in the schedule. Under ordinary circumstances, however, you may need to create a break in the schedule. For example, if the electric company needs to shut off the electricity in your building for two days while repairing code

violations identified by the fire department, your employees cannot come to work. You need to adjust the schedule to account for unavailable working time.

When you attempt to resolve a scheduling conflict, you can possibly split a task to resolve the conflict. When you split a task, you

create a gap between the task's start and finish dates without changing the task's work. For example, suppose that Joe needs to work on Task 1, which has one day of slack, for five days. On day 3, he also needs to attend a one-day seminar. You can split Task 1 so that work stops on day 3 while Joe attends the seminar.

SPLIT TASKS

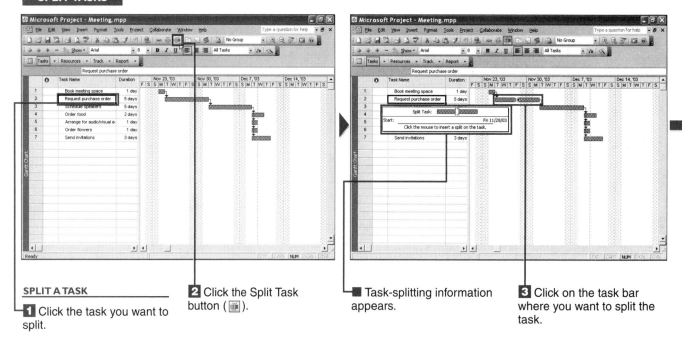

SPLIT A TASK

1 Click the task you want to split.

2 Click the Split Task button (▣).

■ Task-splitting information appears.

3 Click on the task bar where you want to split the task.

When should I use a split task instead of a task calendar?

✔ Use split tasks when you want a visual reminder in the Gantt Chart that work will cease for a specific time. Split tasks also work well in cases of unforeseen inactivity. Task calendars work best when a task runs on a different — but not necessarily interrupted — calendar than the rest of the project.

What happens if I click and drag the first portion of a split task?

✔ Project moves the entire task in the direction you dragged the first portion, retaining the split in the same logical position.

How do I split a task more than once or move a split?

✔ You can split a task as many times as you want by simply repeating the steps in this task. To move a split, follow the steps in Remove a Split, but do not join the bars.

Can I change the duration of one portion of a split without affecting other portions?

✔ Yes. Position ⌖ over the right portion of any split. Click and drag it to the right to lengthen the duration and to the left to shorten the duration of the split.

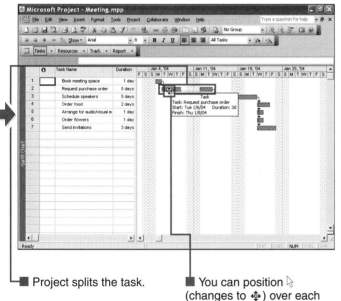

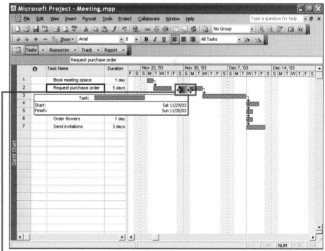

■ Project splits the task.

■ You can position ⌖ (changes to ✛) over each portion of the Gantt bar to view details for that portion of the task.

REMOVE A SPLIT

1 Position ⌖ (changes to ✛) over the right portion of the split.

2 Click and drag the right portion until it touches the left portion.

3 Release the mouse.

■ Project rejoins the portions of the Gantt bar and removes the split.

VIEW THE CRITICAL PATH

Suppose that your project contains five tasks, and each task takes three days to complete. Further suppose that a Finish-to-Start relationship exists for all tasks so that the tasks run consecutively. Your project completes in 15 days if you complete each task on time. If one task is late, the entire project schedule is late.

In this scenario, all five tasks are on the *critical path*. You must complete tasks on the critical path

on schedule in order for the entire project to finish on schedule. Tasks on the critical path are called *critical tasks*.

Assume that your organization uses the same resources on every project. It is possible that you can manage your project perfectly, but some other project's schedule can fall behind, making resources unavailable to you when you need them and when you planned to use them.

If you can shorten the time frame that you originally allotted for the critical path on your project, you can shorten the entire project and possibly resolve the scheduling conflict.

You can view the critical path in a number of ways to determine if you can shorten the tasks on it.

VIEW THE CRITICAL PATH

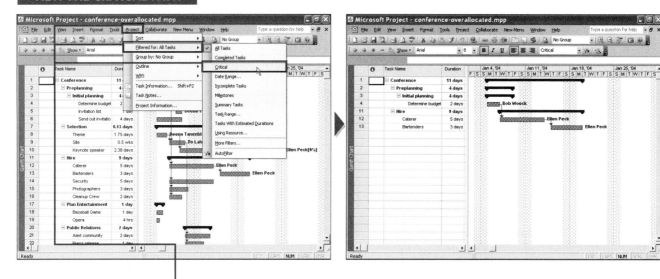

USING FILTERING

Note: This technique is most useful if you start from the Gantt Chart view.

1 Click Project.

2 Click Filtered for.

3 Click Critical.

■ Only the critical tasks in your project appear.

After filtering, how do I redisplay all tasks?

✔ Click Project, Filtered for, and then All Tasks.

Can I use AutoFilters and filter for the critical path?

✔ Yes. First, add the Critical column to a table. Right-click the column that you want to appear to the right of the Critical column, and click Insert. In the Column Definition dialog box, click Critical from the Field Name list. Click OK. Turn on AutoFilters and use the AutoFilter list to show only the tasks where the Critical column contains the value "Yes."

When I finish working with tasks grouped as critical and noncritical, how do I redisplay a regular Gantt Chart?

✔ Click Project, Group by, and then No Group.

Is there an easier way to format other than through the Bar Styles dialog box?

✔ Yes. You can use the Gantt Chart Wizard. See the section "Highlight the Critical Path with the Gantt Chart Wizard" later in this chapter.

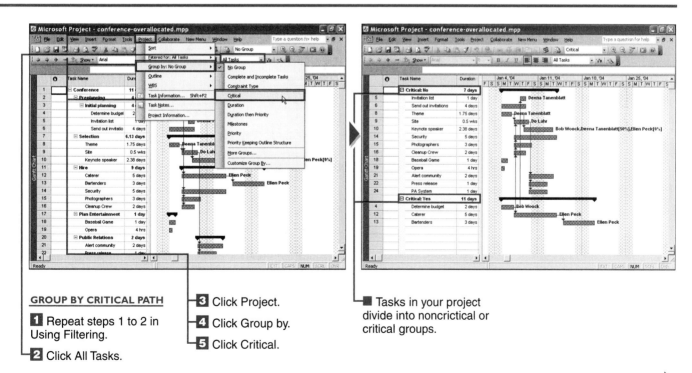

GROUP BY CRITICAL PATH

1 Repeat steps 1 to 2 in Using Filtering.

2 Click All Tasks.

3 Click Project.

4 Click Group by.

5 Click Critical.

■ Tasks in your project divide into noncritical or critical groups.

CONTINUED ▶

VIEW THE CRITICAL PATH (CONTINUED)

When you shorten the time on the critical path, you shorten your project's duration. As the project manager, you may also be responsible, in part, for the project's cost. Typically, the longer a project goes on, the more it costs. Therefore, shortening the critical path is often the project manager's goal.

Reducing a project's duration can mean one of two things: finishing earlier or starting later. The second alternative is riskier than the first, and if you are new to project management and not particularly confident in your estimates, you probably should not plan to start later. Instead, use your project management tools to help you evaluate the accuracy of your estimating skills. Experience can help you learn how accurate your estimates are, and then you can take the risk of starting a project later than initially planned.

The critical path of a project is not static. You may not find the same tasks on the critical path today that you found yesterday. Obviously, the critical path changes as critical tasks are completed. But, less obviously, the critical path can change because one or more noncritical tasks are delayed and suddenly become critical.

VIEW THE CRITICAL PATH (CONTINUED)

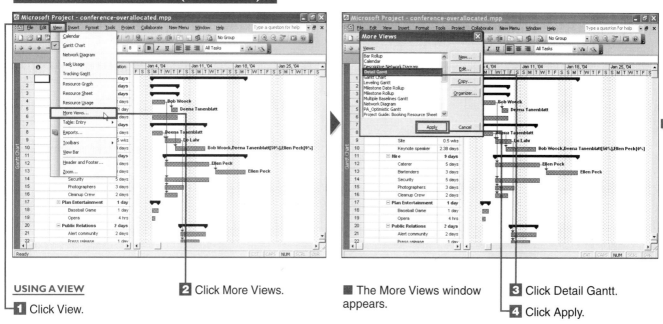

USING A VIEW

1 Click View.

2 Click More Views.

■ The More Views window appears.

3 Click Detail Gantt.

4 Click Apply.

Can I control how much slack Project allows for a task before it becomes critical?

✔ Yes. Click Tools, and then click Options. Click the Calculation tab and type the number of slack days you want to allow in the Tasks are critical if slack is less than or equal to box.

What is the best way to view the critical path if I want to make changes to it?

✔ The answer is really a matter of personal preference. For a suggestion, see the section "Shorten the Critical Path" later in this chapter.

When I apply a filter, does Project delete the information that does not meet the filter criteria?

✔ No. The information remains safely in your project file. When you filter a project, Project temporarily hides from view the information that does not meets the criteria. When you remove the filter, Project redisplays the information.

Can a noncritical task become critical?

✔ Yes. Noncritical tasks contain slack, so they can slip. If they slip too much, they can become critical.

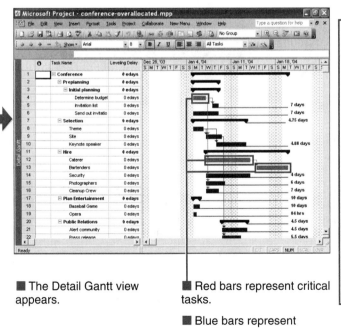

■ The Detail Gantt view appears.

■ Red bars represent critical tasks.

■ Blue bars represent noncritical tasks.

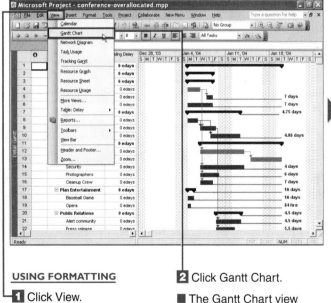

USING FORMATTING

1 Click View.

2 Click Gantt Chart.

■ The Gantt Chart view appears.

CONTINUED ▶

VIEW THE CRITICAL PATH (CONTINUED)

Once you identify the tasks on today's critical path, you can focus on reducing the time on the critical path. To reduce the time on the critical path, you can either reduce the duration of critical tasks or overlap critical tasks to reduce the overall duration of your project.

To reduce the duration of critical tasks, you can reassess estimates and use a more optimistic task

time. The PERT Analysis views can help you with this task. You can also add resources to a critical task so long as the task is an effort-driven task. Adding resources to a fixed-duration task does not reduce the time of the task. Last, you can add overtime to a critical task to complete it more quickly than originally estimated.

To overlap critical tasks, you can adjust dependencies and task date constraints. You also can redefine a finish-to-start relationship to either a start-to-start or a finish-to-finish relationship. Both of these relationships allow the tasks to run, for at least part of the time, simultaneously.

VIEW THE CRITICAL PATH (CONTINUED)

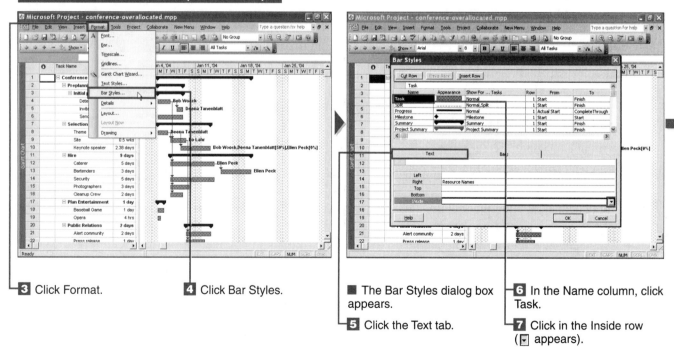

-3 Click Format.

-4 Click Bar Styles.

■ The Bar Styles dialog box appears.

-5 Click the Text tab.

-6 In the Name column, click Task.

-7 Click in the Inside row (appears).

What is on the Bars tab of the Bar Styles dialog box?

✔ You can use the Bars tab to apply different shapes, patterns, and colors shown in the top of the box to the beginning, middle, and end of Gantt bars. For example, you can apply a blue shape to the beginning, a blue bar to the middle, and another blue shape to the end of regular tasks. You can apply the same red formatting to summary tasks. You can use the Bars tab in conjunction with the top of the box to create special formatting for critical tasks.

How does the top portion of the Bar Styles dialog box work?

✔ You can use the Gantt bar definition table to define the appearance of various Gantt bar types. In the Name field, type a name for a type of bar. Project assigns the bar style shown for Task, but in black. You can click the Show For ⊡ to select the type of bar you want to appear with the formatting you are applying. You can change the Row field to give the appearance of double-spacing between tasks. You can set the From and To fields to any available Project field.

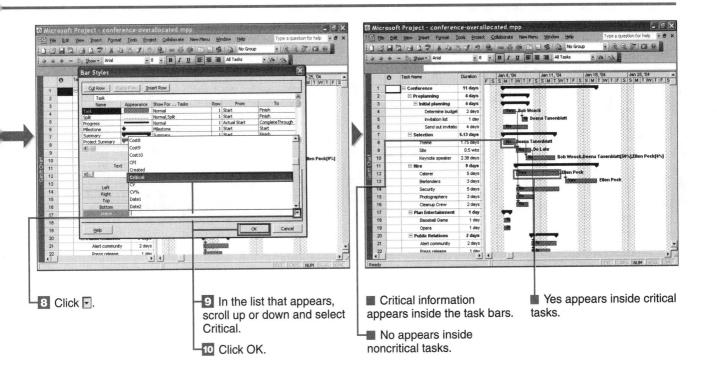

8 Click ⊡.

9 In the list that appears, scroll up or down and select Critical.

10 Click OK.

■ Critical information appears inside the task bars.

■ No appears inside noncritical tasks.

■ Yes appears inside critical tasks.

HIGHLIGHT THE CRITICAL PATH WITH THE GANTT CHART WIZARD

Y ou can use the Gantt Chart Wizard to format the Gantt Chart view to display the critical path and other information.

A *wizard* is the term Microsoft uses to describe a series of dialog boxes that prompt you for answers to questions or to make selections. As you walk through the Gantt Chart Wizard dialog boxes, a preview

appears that shows you how each option formats your Gantt Chart if you select it. When you finish the Gantt Chart Wizard, Project uses your input to format the Gantt Chart to display the critical path.

Because the Gantt Chart Wizard changes apply only to the project file that is open when you run the wizard, start by displaying the project that you want to format.

Using the Gantt Chart Wizard can be a fast, easy, and efficient way to highlight the critical path. Be aware, however, that you cannot undo the changes that Project applies to your schedule when you use the Gantt Chart Wizard. Save your project before you start. If you do not like what you see at the end, close your project without saving it and reopen it, or rerun the wizard and select the Standard format.

HIGHLIGHT THE CRITICAL PATH WITH THE GANTT CHART WIZARD

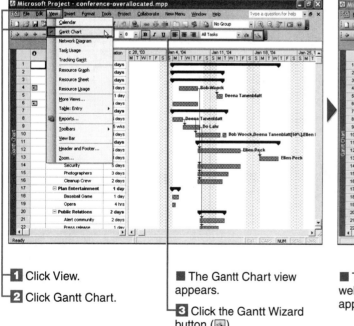

1 Click View.

2 Click Gantt Chart.

■ The Gantt Chart view appears.

3 Click the Gantt Wizard button (🔲).

■ The Gantt Chart Wizard welcome dialog box appears.

4 Click Next.

What does the Other option do on the second Gantt Chart Wizard dialog box?

✔ When you click this option (○ changes to ⊙), a ⊡ appears from where you can choose from a variety of formatting options for your Gantt Chart. As you select from the list, your choices appear in the Preview box.

What happens if I click the Custom task information option in the third Gantt Chart Wizard dialog box?

✔ Additional boxes appear that enable you to show separate Project fields on the left, right, and inside of task bars and summary bars. You also can display fields on either side of milestones.

When do I use the Custom Gantt Chart option (○ changes to ⊙) on the second Gantt Chart Wizard box?

✔ Several additional boxes appear as you progress through the wizard that show different types of bars for critical and noncritical tasks and display baseline and total slack information on the Gantt Chart. Other boxes let you select the color, patterns, end shapes, and bar styles of normal tasks, critical tasks, summary tasks, and milestones.

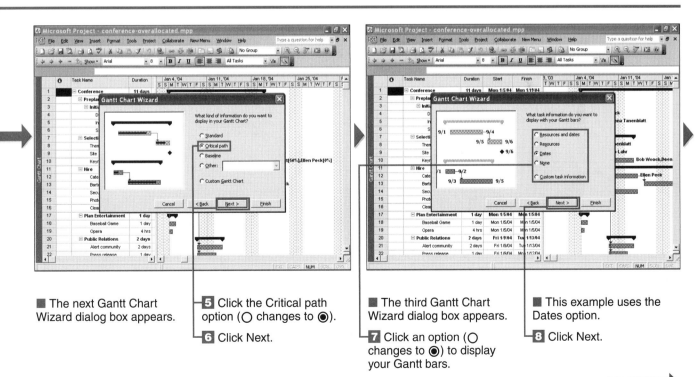

■ The next Gantt Chart Wizard dialog box appears.

5 Click the Critical path option (○ changes to ⊙).

6 Click Next.

■ The third Gantt Chart Wizard dialog box appears.

7 Click an option (○ changes to ⊙) to display your Gantt bars.

■ This example uses the Dates option.

8 Click Next.

CONTINUED

HIGHLIGHT THE CRITICAL PATH WITH THE GANTT CHART WIZARD (CONTINUED)

Y ou can run the Gantt Chart Wizard from either the Gantt Chart view or the Tracking Gantt view. The Gantt Chart Wizard can format a Gantt Chart view in other ways besides displaying the critical path. For example, the Gantt Chart Wizard can format the Gantt Chart to show baseline and actual information. You can also choose from a rather large selection of other formats for

your Gantt Chart. If you try other formatting through the Gantt Chart Wizard, you can run the Wizard again to return the Gantt Chart to its standard appearance.

You also can use the Gantt Chart Wizard to further customize the Gantt Chart. In addition to the options you select in this task, the Gantt Chart Wizard also enables you to create a highly customized

Gantt Chart that can show critical task bars formatted differently from noncritical task bars. You can also add baseline and total slack information to the critical path formatting. You can control the color, patterns, end shapes, and bar styles of normal tasks, critical tasks, summary tasks, and milestones by using the custom option.

HIGHLIGHT THE CRITICAL PATH WITH THE GANTT CHART WIZARD (CONTINUED)

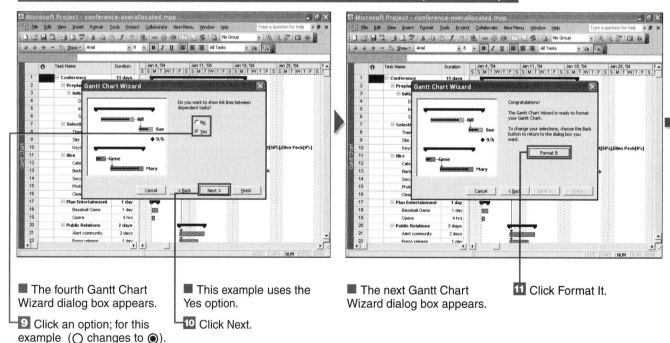

■ The fourth Gantt Chart Wizard dialog box appears.

9 Click an option; for this example (○ changes to ◉).

■ This example uses the Yes option.

10 Click Next.

■ The next Gantt Chart Wizard dialog box appears.

11 Click Format It.

For the example in this section, why did you select the Date option in the third Gantt Chart Wizard dialog box?

✔ Selecting the Date options (○ changes to ◉) makes Project display the start date and end date on either side of each task bar, eliminating the need to show the corresponding columns for start date and end date in the Gantt table. This can help you modify the size of your schedule printout.

What happens when you select the No option (○ changes to ◉) in the fourth Gantt Chart Wizard box?

✔ Task bars with no dependancy lines connecting them appear on the Gantt Chart.

What does the Standard option in the second Gantt Chart Wizard dialog box do?

✔ Click this option (○ changes to ◉) after you apply other formatting using the Gantt Chart Wizard that you no longer want. The Standard option returns your Gantt Chart to the appearance it had before you applied any formatting.

How do you use the Gantt Chart Wizard to show baseline and actual information?

✔ In the second Gantt Chart Wizard box, click the Baseline option (○ changes to ◉).

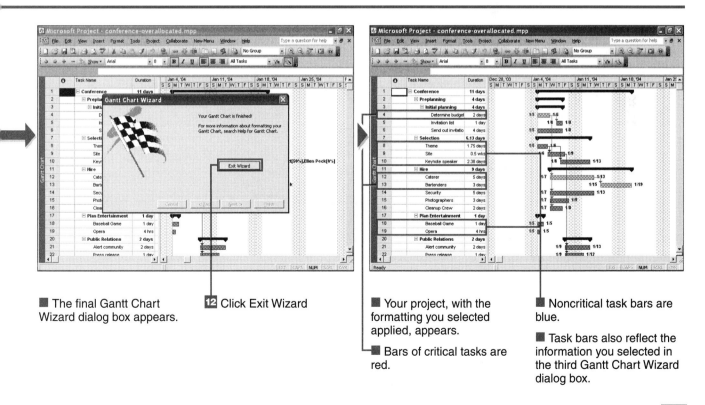

■ The final Gantt Chart Wizard dialog box appears.

12 Click Exit Wizard

■ Your project, with the formatting you selected applied, appears.

■ Bars of critical tasks are red.

■ Noncritical task bars are blue.

■ Task bars also reflect the information you selected in the third Gantt Chart Wizard dialog box.

SHORTEN THE CRITICAL PATH

I f you shorten the critical path of your project, you can shorten the duration of your project. Typically, costs are tied to tasks, and the longer a task takes, the more it costs. So, if you shorten the duration of tasks on the critical path, you can shorten the duration of your project and, possibly, its cost.

You can view the critical path using several different techniques, and the one you select is partly a matter

of personal preference and partly a matter of purpose. After all, viewing the critical path is one purpose, but taking action to shorten it is another.

To work on the critical path to try to shorten it, work in a view where you can see the path and the fields you are most likely to use to make changes. You may consider using the Task Entry view. This

combination view shows the Gantt Chart in the top pane and the Task Form in the bottom pane. Using this view, you see a graphic representation of your project in the top pane; the bottom pane contains most of the fields that you may want to change.

This section assumes that you start in the Gantt Chart view.

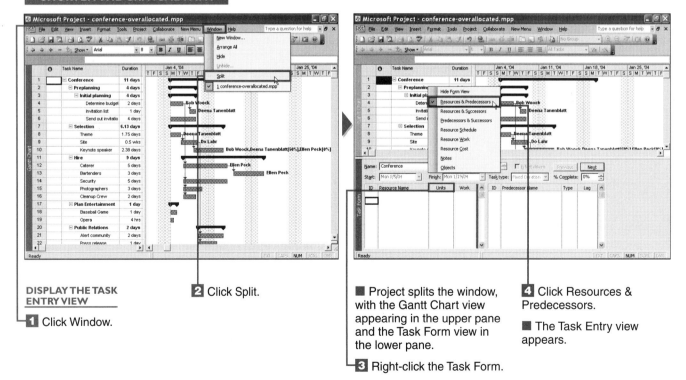

DISPLAY THE TASK ENTRY VIEW

1 Click Window.

2 Click Split.

■ Project splits the window, with the Gantt Chart view appearing in the upper pane and the Task Form view in the lower pane.

3 Right-click the Task Form.

4 Click Resources & Predecessors.

■ The Task Entry view appears.

How do I redisplay the Gantt Chart without the Task Form in the bottom pane.

✔ You can remove the split. Click Window and then click Remove Split, or you can double-click the split bar.

How do I split the view using the mouse?

✔ You can double-click the split bar, which appears at the bottom edge of the right scroll bar, or you can click and drag it to split the view. To positively identify the split bar, see Chapter 2.

Can I return the Task Entry view to viewing all tasks instead of just critical tasks?

✔ Yes. Click Project, Filtered for, and then click All Tasks.

Why do I use the Task Entry view when attempting to shorten the critical path?

✔ Besides trying to shorten the duration of tasks on the critical path, the other major goal is to remove tasks from the critical path, which you often accomplished by changing, whenever possible, predecessor information. The Task Entry view enables you to change the duration and predecessor information of any task.

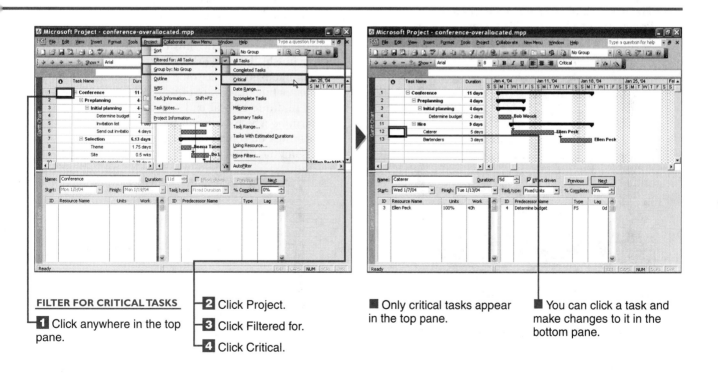

FILTER FOR CRITICAL TASKS

■1 Click anywhere in the top pane.

─■2 Click Project.

─■3 Click Filtered for.

─■4 Click Critical.

■ Only critical tasks appear in the top pane.

■ You can click a task and make changes to it in the bottom pane.

MULTIPLE CRITICAL PATHS

Not only does the critical path change as a project progresses; a project can actually have more than one critical path at a time. In fact, you can have a critical path for each network of tasks in your project. Because modifying the critical path impacts whether your project finishes on time, it is important to determine if your project has multiple critical paths. If your project does have multiple critical paths, you will want to evaluate each of them when you are trying to resolve scheduling problems.

Network of Tasks

Think of a network of tasks as the subtasks that comprise a task. Here, you can see four networks of tasks. The first network is comprised of Task IDs 2, 3, and 4. The next network is comprised of Task IDs 6 and 7. The network of tasks that comprises the Preparation task — the third network — are Task IDs 9 to 13. The last network of tasks is the Wrap Up tasks — Task IDs 15 to 18.

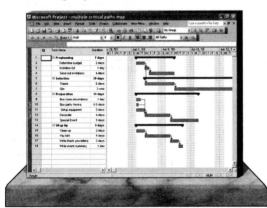

Viewing Multiple Critical Paths

Although by default Project displays only one critical path at a time, you can view more than one critical path. This feature comes in handy when you have lots of tasks that are driving other tasks and you want to find out which ones are truly critical to finishing the network of tasks on time.

When you display multiple critical paths, which are represented by crosshatched patterns in the figure, you see a critical path for each network of tasks. Project sets the late finish date of each task equal to its early finish date. When a task has no links, it is critical because its late finish is equal to its early finish. If a network of tasks contains slack, like Network 3, some tasks are not critical while others are critical. When you view multiple critical paths, you can determine which tasks within a network of tasks must be completed on time to avoid delaying the network.

DISPLAY MULTIPLE CRITICAL PATHS

By default, Project displays only one critical path for your project. When you view only one critical path, you view the tasks that you must complete to finish the project on time. These tasks have no total slack, total slack being defined as the amount of time that you can delay a task without delaying the completion of the project. The single critical path, therefore, focuses on completing the entire project.

Suppose, however, that your project contains numerous subtasks, and within the subtasks you have dependencies. You may start wondering, within a given network of tasks, which ones are really critical. In this case, view your project with multiple critical paths, where Project displays a separate critical path for each network of tasks.

With the exception of large projects with multiple of networks, when do I use multiple critical paths?

✔ If you combine several projects together, you create multiple networks of tasks. While the overall critical path of the project is of primary importance, the critical path of each network is also important.

DISPLAY MULTIPLE CRITICAL PATHS

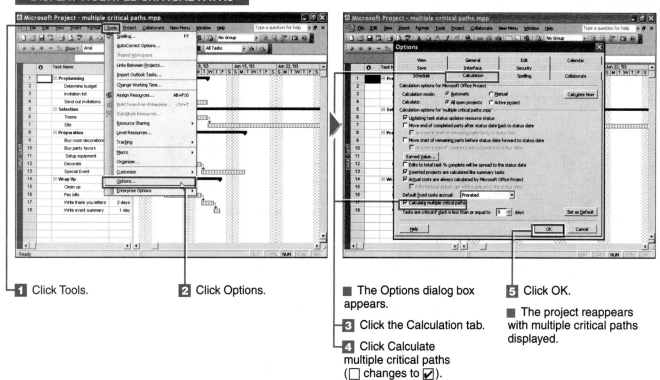

1 Click Tools.

2 Click Options.

■ The Options dialog box appears.

3 Click the Calculation tab.

4 Click Calculate multiple critical paths (□ changes to ☑).

5 Click OK.

■ The project reappears with multiple critical paths displayed.

RESOLVE CONFLICTS

The process of assigning resources is called *allocating* resources. Overallocation occurs when you assign more work to a resource than the resource can accomplish in the time available to do the work. To resolve resource conflicts, it helps to understand the process Project uses when you assign resources. Each time you assign a resource to a task,

Project checks the resource's calendar to make sure that the resource is working. However, Project does not assess whether the resource is already obligated to another task or project when you assign the resource to a new task; Project simply makes the assignment. Therefore, the additional assignment may overallocate the resource.

To calculate the scheduled start date for a task, Project checks factors such as the task's dependencies and constraints. Project then checks the resource's calendar to identify the next regular workday and assigns that date as the start date for the task. But when Project calculates the task start date, it does not consider other commitments that the resource may have outside of the current project.

Changing Resource Allocations

For effort-driven tasks, changing resource allocations can resolve resource conflicts. You can add a resource to reduce the workload, or you can substitute one resource for another to solve an overallocation.

Scheduling Overtime

You also can resolve a resource conflict by scheduling overtime for the resource. Overtime work does not represent additional work on a task; instead, it represents the amount of time that's spent on a task during nonregular hours. By scheduling overtime, the resource may finish the task faster and therefore eliminate the conflict.

Delay Tasks by Level Resource Workloads

If you have scheduled several tasks to run concurrently and you now find resource conflicts in your project, you can delay some of these tasks to spread out the demands that you are making on your resources.

Redefining a Resource's Calendar

If a salaried resource has a conflict and the number of hours in conflict on a given day is low enough, you can eliminate the conflict by changing the resource's calendar and increasing the working hours for the resource for that day.

Assign Part-time Work

Suppose that a resource is assigned to several concurrent tasks and is also overallocated. If adding or switching resources or adding overtime are not options, you can assign the resource to work part time on each of the tasks to solve the conflict, although the tasks may take longer to complete by using this method.

Control When Resources Start Work on a Task

For cases in which you have assigned more than one resource to a task, consider staggering the times that the resources begin working on the task to resolve resource conflicts.

Contour Resources

Contour is the term that Project uses to refer to the shape of a resource's work assignment over time. You can use different contours to control how much a resource is scheduled to work on a task at a given time and possibly resolve a conflict.

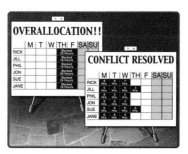

Pool Resources

Finally, you can try to solve resource conflicts by sharing resources in a resource pool, which is a set of resources that is available to any project. Read about pooling resources in Chapter 16.

IDENTIFY RESOURCE CONFLICTS

The potential for resource overallocation always accompanies resource assignment. Using a combination of *views* and *filtering,* you can identify resource conflicts. After you identify resource conflicts, you can resolve them.

You can review resource allocation using views in Project. Some views are more conducive to spotting resource overallocations than others.

For example, you can quickly identify resource overallocations on the Resource Sheet view or on the Resource Usage view. In these views, overallocated resources appear in red, boldface type.

The Resource Allocation view, a combination of the Resource Usage view and the Gantt Chart view, is useful for working with overallocations. The Gantt Chart in the lower pane shows the tasks

assigned to the resource that you select in the top pane. Tasks that start at the same time overlap in the Gantt Chart pane so that you can pinpoint the tasks that are causing the resource's overallocation.

Filtering is another simple technique that you can use to resolve resource conflict problems. If you filter the Resource Allocation view to display only overallocated resources, the problems become even more apparent.

IDENTIFY RESOURCE CONFLICTS

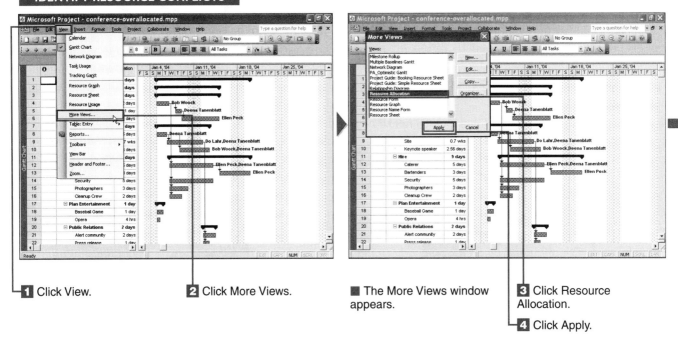

1 Click View.

2 Click More Views.

■ The More Views window appears.

3 Click Resource Allocation.

4 Click Apply.

How do I get rid of the combination view?

✔ Click Window, and then click Remove Split.

Are there any other views that I should look at when working with resource allocations?

✔ The Resource Usage Graph can show you the days on which a particular resource is overallocated and the total percentage allocation for the resource. The percentage allocation information can tell you how much time you need to assign to a different resource. For example, if a resource is allocated 200 percent, you know you need one more full-time person on that day.

When I spot a resource overallocation, how should I approach solving it?

✔ The approach you choose depends on many factors. For example, if you have other resources available, you can assign another resource. You also can assign overtime to the overallocated resource. The sections in this chapter cover the techniques you can try.

What does the Caution icon in the Indicator column mean?

✔ It signals an overallocated resource. Information about the overallocation appears if you position the mouse over the icon.

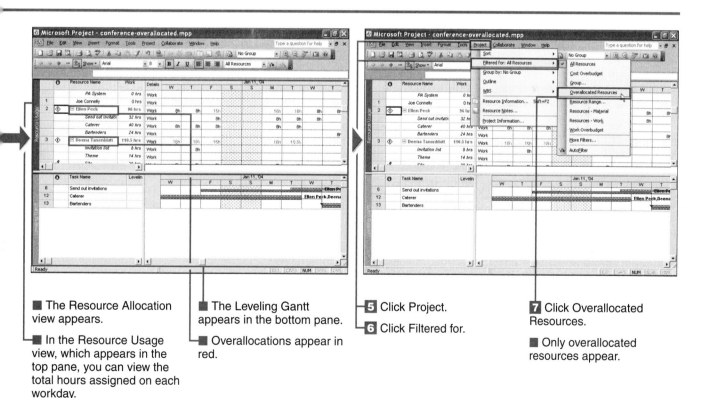

■ The Resource Allocation view appears.

■ In the Resource Usage view, which appears in the top pane, you can view the total hours assigned on each workday.

■ The Leveling Gantt appears in the bottom pane.

■ Overallocations appear in red.

5 Click Project.

6 Click Filtered for.

7 Click Overallocated Resources.

■ Only overallocated resources appear.

ADD A TASK ASSIGNMENT TO AN UNDERALLOCATED RESOURCE

An overallocation occurs when a resource does not have enough available time to complete all assigned work. If the overallocation appears on an effort-driven task, and you have an underallocated resource available, adding the underallocated resource to the task is one way to resolve the resource overallocation.

By adding an underallocated resource to help on an effort-driven task, you can shift the workload on the task, reducing the hours required from the overallocated resource and solving the resource overallocation.

Suppose Task 1 is an effort-driven task, that a resource conflict exists between Task 1 and Task 2, that the two tasks do not run concurrently — Task 1 continues when Task 2 starts — and that you need the same resource, Joe Connelly, to work on both tasks. If you add Cathy Frey to Task 1,

you reduce the amount of time needed to finish Task 1. If Task 1 finishes earlier, you can eliminate Joe's conflict between Tasks 1 and 2.

The steps in this section assume that you have identified the overallocation using the steps in the section "Identify Resource Conflicts" earlier in this chapter and know the task or tasks to which you want to add a resource.

ADD A TASK ASSIGNMENT TO AN UNDERALLOCATED RESOURCE

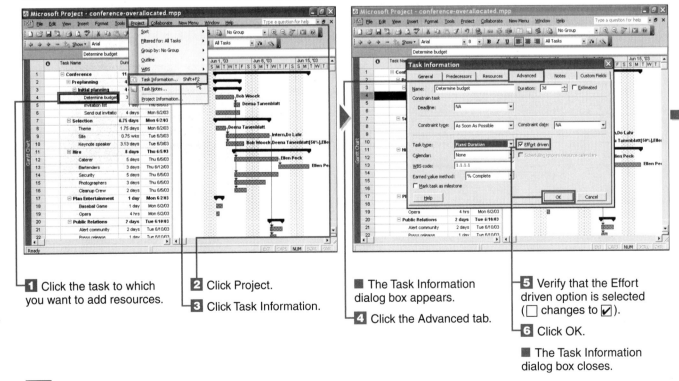

1 Click the task to which you want to add resources.

2 Click Project.

3 Click Task Information.

■ The Task Information dialog box appears.

4 Click the Advanced tab.

5 Verify that the Effort driven option is selected (☐ changes to ☑).

6 Click OK.

■ The Task Information dialog box closes.

In the Assign Resources window, what is the R/D column for?

✔ If you use Project Server and you intend to use the Resource Substitution Wizard, in the R/D field, type **R** for Request to indicate that any resource with the required skills can work on the task. You can also type **D** for Demand to indicate that the selected resource is specifically required to work on the task.

What does the Graphs button do?

✔ Click this button to display the Work, Remaining Availability, or Assignment Work graph for the selected resource.

What does the Available to work option do?

✔ You can use it to search for resources that are available to work a specified number of hours. If you use this feature, Project calculates the remaining available hours of each resource for the duration of the task and compares the result with the number of hours that you specified. Resources with available hours equal to or greater than the value that you supplied appear in the list, along with the resources that are already assigned to the selected task.

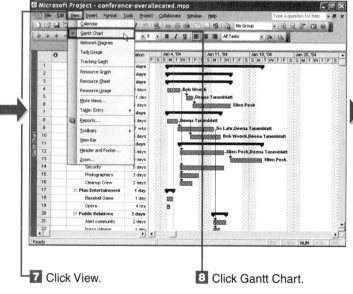

7 Click View.

8 Click Gantt Chart.

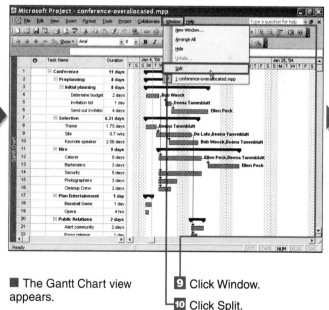

■ The Gantt Chart view appears.

9 Click Window.

10 Click Split.

CONTINUED ▶

ADD A TASK ASSIGNMENT TO AN UNDERALLOCATED RESOURCE (CONTINUED)

Adding a single resource to an effort-driven task may not remove an overallocation, but it can reduce the overallocation. As you add resources to an effort-driven task, you can see the number of overallocated hours on the overallocated resource go down.

Ideally, you want to know if you are about to overallocate another resource before you actually create a new

problem. From the Assign Resources window, three graphs help you select the best resource for the job. The graphs focus on the resource, not on any task for which you may consider a resource assignment.

The Work graph shows you, on a day-by-day basis, the amount of work assigned to the selected resource, regardless of the task.

The Assignment Work graph breaks down the total workload of the resource showing you the resource's workload on the selected task, other tasks, and the resource's total availability based on the calendar. This graph helps you determine if you will overallocate the resource by assigning it to this task.

The Remaining Availability graph shows you the resource's unassigned time.

.ADD A TASK ASSIGNMENT TO AN UNDERALLOCATED RESOURCE (CONTINUED)

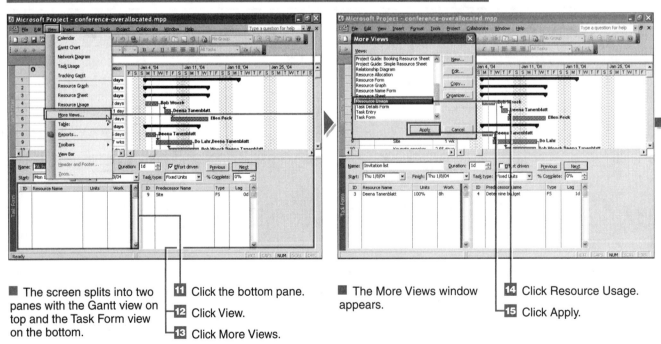

■ The screen splits into two panes with the Gantt view on top and the Task Form view on the bottom.

11 Click the bottom pane.

12 Click View.

13 Click More Views.

■ The More Views window appears.

14 Click Resource Usage.

15 Click Apply.

MASTER IT

Can I add resources if the task is not effort-driven?

✔ Yes, but adding resources to a task that is not effort-driven does not resolve resource overallocations. Project redistributes work only on effort-driven tasks.

When I assign units, what measure am I using?

✔ You are assigning units in percentages. You can assign any percentage of a unit that you want by simply typing the number; Project assumes percentages. If you want to assign 100 percent of the resource, do not type anything in the Units column; Project automatically assigns 100 percent of the resource.

If I need a resource for days instead of hours, should I convert the number of days to hours?

✔ No. Project makes the conversion for you. If you need a resource for 6 days, type **6d** in the Available to work field. Project converts the value to 48 hours.

How does Project calculate Available to work time?

✔ Project uses the resource's calendar to calculate the number of working hours for the selected task. Project then multiplies available working hours by the availability contour value and subtracts existing assignment work hours to determine Available to work hours.

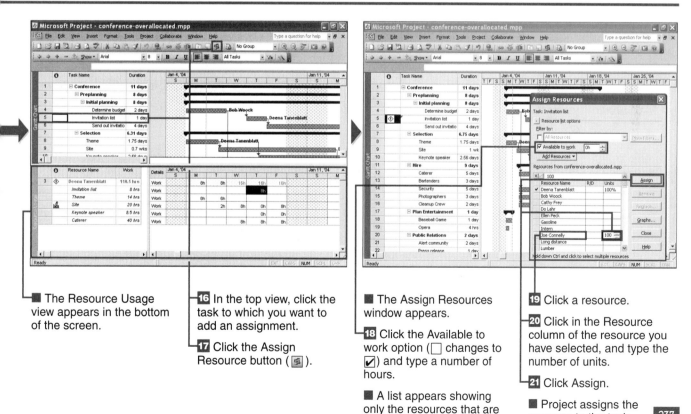

■ The Resource Usage view appears in the bottom of the screen.

16 In the top view, click the task to which you want to add an assignment.

17 Click the Assign Resource button (📇).

■ The Assign Resources window appears.

18 Click the Available to work option (☐ changes to ☑) and type a number of hours.

■ A list appears showing only the resources that are available to work.

19 Click a resource.

20 Click in the Resource column of the resource you have selected, and type the number of units.

21 Click Assign.

■ Project assigns the resource to the task.

237

MODIFY RESOURCE ASSIGNMENTS

When you discover an overallocation on an effort-driven task, a possible solution is to modify the resource's assignment. After reviewing the work required for the task, you may discover that you do not need the resource to work on that particular task; the other resources assigned to the task can handle the workload. You determine that the task will complete in the time allotted without the overallocated resource. Or, you may determine that the duration of the task will increase, but the task has sufficient slack that you can increase its duration without increasing the duration of the project. In this situation, you want to remove the overallocated resource from the task to eliminate the overallocation.

You may decide that the hours you require to complete the task cannot change, either because the task has no slack or because the task simply requires the number of person-hours you estimated. But perhaps a different resource can fill in for the overallocated resource. If you substitute one resource for another, you can possibly resolve the resource conflict.

MODIFY RESOURCE ASSIGNMENTS

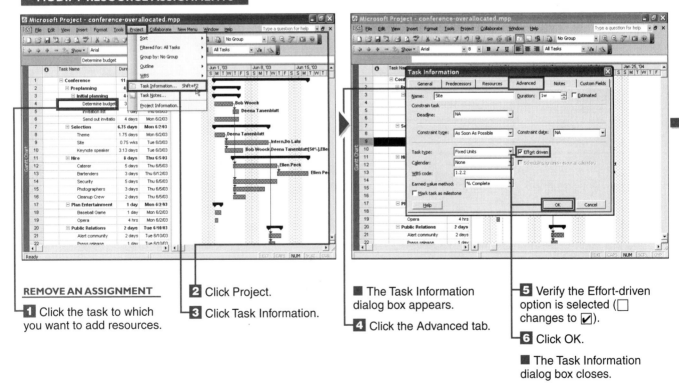

REMOVE AN ASSIGNMENT

1 Click the task to which you want to add resources.

2 Click Project.

3 Click Task Information.

■ The Task Information dialog box appears.

4 Click the Advanced tab.

5 Verify the Effort-driven option is selected (☐ changes to ☑).

6 Click OK.

■ The Task Information dialog box closes.

Why does a caution icon appear in the Indicator column after I remove a resource assignment?

✔ The warning icon (⚠) reminds you to decide how you want to handle the change you made to the work assignment. If you click ⚠, an option list appears. You can increase the duration so that you maintain the same total hours required for the task, or you can decrease the total work but keep the duration constant. You can also increase the hours worked per day by the assigned resource(s), keeping the duration and the total work the same.

Is there any reason not to delete a resource assignment for which I have recorded actual time worked?

✔ Yes. Deleting a resource assignment that contains actual work causes Project to list misleading information about the task. Suppose, for example, that you assign one resource to a task, the resource completes the task, and then you delete the resource assignment. Project shows the task as completed, but you will not see any work or actual work at the task level.

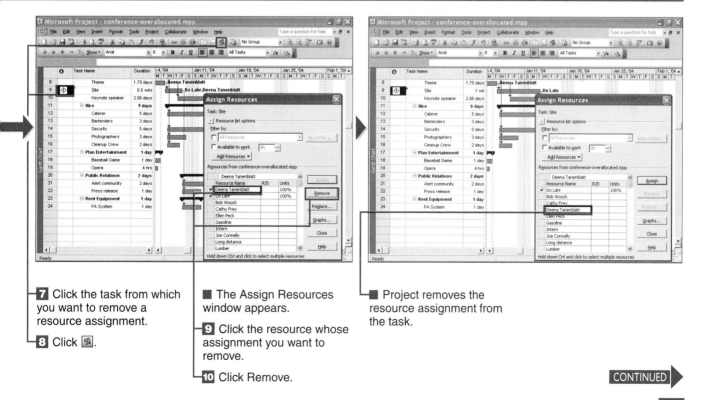

7 Click the task from which you want to remove a resource assignment.

8 Click 📇.

■ The Assign Resources window appears.

9 Click the resource whose assignment you want to remove.

10 Click Remove.

■ Project removes the resource assignment from the task.

CONTINUED ▶

MODIFY RESOURCE ASSIGNMENTS (CONTINUED)

Y ou also can resolve resource conflicts by switching resources. You can use this technique when one resource is overallocated, but you have another resource available that can perform the job. You switch resources by replacing resources on the task in question.

Before you start this process, identify the overallocated resource and examine the skills required to

do the job. Then, examine the resources available to you and determine if one of them is capable of performing the required work on the task. Last, determine if your substitution candidates are available. You do not want to assign a resource as a substitute for an overallocated resource and discover that you have solved one overallocation problem only to create another.

If you substitute John for Mary using the same number of units, you do not affect the work or duration of the task. Even if you substitute several resources for one resource, as long as you do not change the total units, you do not change the work or duration of the task.

MODIFY RESOURCE ASSIGNMENTS (CONTINUED)

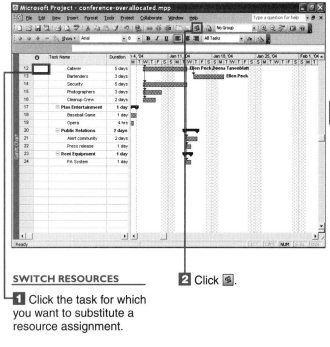

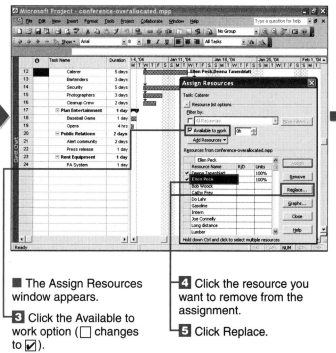

SWITCH RESOURCES

1 Click the task for which you want to substitute a resource assignment.

2 Click 🖳.

■ The Assign Resources window appears.

3 Click the Available to work option (☐ changes to ☑).

4 Click the resource you want to remove from the assignment.

5 Click Replace.

What is Active Directory?

✔ Active Directory is a Windows network feature. In a Windows network, the administrator can set up Active Directory to contain a list of people and their contact information.

If I make a replacement, how does Project handle the assignment units and the work amounts?

✔ Project tries to maintain the assignment units and the work amounts for the replaced resource.

Can I replace one resource with more or less of another resource?

✔ Yes. If the task is effort-driven, changing the amount of the resource assignment will affect the task's duration.

Can I replace one resource with several resources?

✔ Yes. In the Replace Resource dialog box, click each resource that you want to assign and supply a number of units for the resource. Project replaces one resource with all of the resources you select.

What happens if I replace one resource with several other resources and the percentages for the new resources do not equal the percentage for the original resource?

✔ If you are changing the assignments on an effort-driven task, Project adjusts the task's duration accordingly.

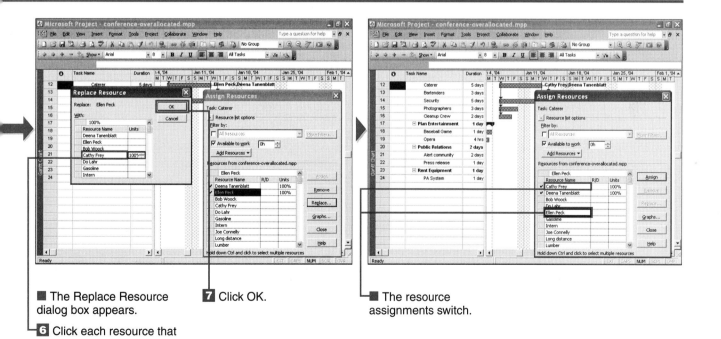

■ The Replace Resource dialog box appears.

6 Click each resource that you want to assign, and the number of units.

7 Click OK.

■ The resource assignments switch.

SCHEDULE OVERTIME

Y ou can resolve a resource conflict by scheduling *overtime* for the resource. Project defines overtime as the amount of work that you schedule beyond an assigned resource's regular working hours. Overtime does not represent additional work on a task; instead, it represents the amount of time that a resource

spends on a task during non-regular hours. For example, if you assign 40 hours of work and 10 hours of overtime, the total work is still 40 hours. In this example, the resource works 30 hours during the regular work schedule and 10 hours outside of regular working hours. Using overtime, you can shorten the time that a resource takes to complete a task. If the

resource finishes the task more quickly, your overallocation may resolve itself.

Overtime hours are charged, however, at the resource's overtime rate, which may make the task more costly than you first estimated. If your budget permits, you may possibly use overtime to resolve a resource conflict.

SCHEDULE OVERTIME

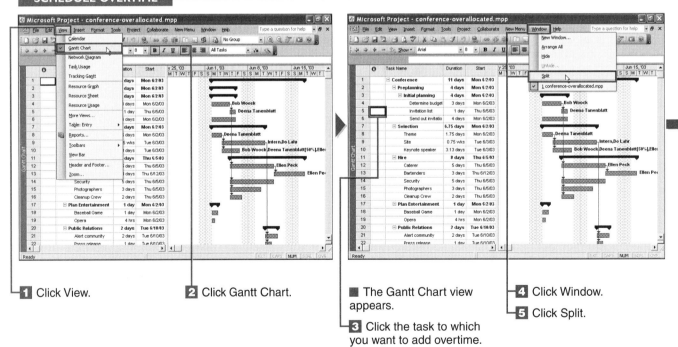

■ Click View.

■ Click Gantt Chart.

■ The Gantt Chart view appears.

■ Click the task to which you want to add overtime.

■ Click Window.

■ Click Split.

If I do not have enough resources to either add resources or assign overtime, how can I resolve a scheduling problem?

✔ You can focus on the following possibilities: add time to tasks, adjust any slack that tasks may have, evaluate and possibly change task constraints and dependencies, or split tasks. This chapter covers all of these approaches.

How do I add overtime to a different task than the one I selected initially?

✔ Click in the upper pane that contains the Gantt Chart, and click a different task.

How do I add overtime for more than one resource to a task?

✔ In the Task Form view, you can display other resources if you click Next or Previous, which appear after you click OK to save an overtime assignment.

How do I get rid of the Task Form pane when I finish entering overtime?

✔ You can click Window, and then click Remove Split. Alternatively, you can click and drag the horizontal split bar that divides the panes to the bottom of the screen.

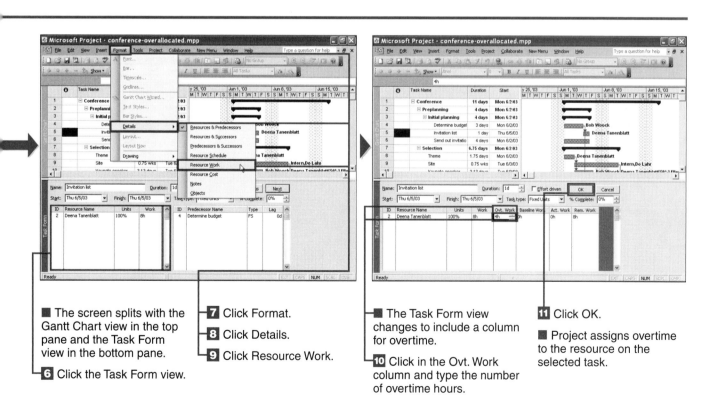

■ The screen splits with the Gantt Chart view in the top pane and the Task Form view in the bottom pane.

6 Click the Task Form view.

7 Click Format.

8 Click Details.

9 Click Resource Work.

■ The Task Form view changes to include a column for overtime.

10 Click in the Ovt. Work column and type the number of overtime hours.

11 Click OK.

■ Project assigns overtime to the resource on the selected task.

REDEFINE A RESOURCE'S CALENDAR

You can possibly redefine a resource's calendar so that nonworking hours become working hours. If the number of hours in conflict on a given day is low enough, you can eliminate the conflict by increasing the resource's working hours for that day.

Suppose that a resource needs two or three more hours on a particular day to complete a task. If the resource does not complete the task

on the specified day, a resource overallocation results. However, if you can increase the working day by two hours without adding cost to the task, you can resolve the resource conflict.

Project checks task priorities when it distributes work to a resource. When two tasks have the same priority and the same resource, Project selects the work that the resource completes, and it does not

always select the same work you would choose. However, if you set up priorities for the tasks, you can make Project assign the work so that the resource completes the correct task when you redefine the resource's calendar. In this section, leveling is set to manual; read more about leveling in the sections "Level Resources Automatically" and "Level Resources Manually."

REDEFINE A RESOURCE'S CALENDAR

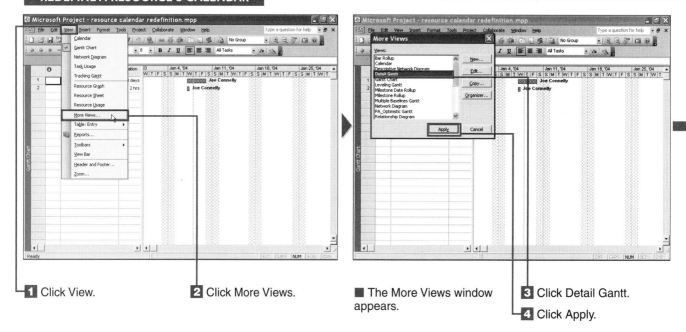

1 Click View.

2 Click More Views.

■ The More Views window appears.

3 Click Detail Gantt.

4 Click Apply.

Can you explain more about how Project uses priorities?

✔ While other factors influence how Project delays tasks, priorities contribute to the process. Project delays tasks with lower priorities before delaying tasks with higher priorities. In this example, to ensure that Project would schedule the two-hour task on the longer day, I gave Task 2 a higher priority than Task 1. That way, Project delayed Task 1 and not Task 2. For more information on how Project uses priorities, see the section "Level Resources Automatically" later in this chapter.

Does this technique still work if a task calendar exists for the task I want Project to assign to the resource on the day I redefine the resource's calendar?

✔ The answer depends on the way you set up the task calendar. If the Scheduling ignores resource calendars option is clicked, Project schedules the task without considering the calendars of any resources assigned to the task, and so this technique will not work. However, if you do not click the option, the technique will work.

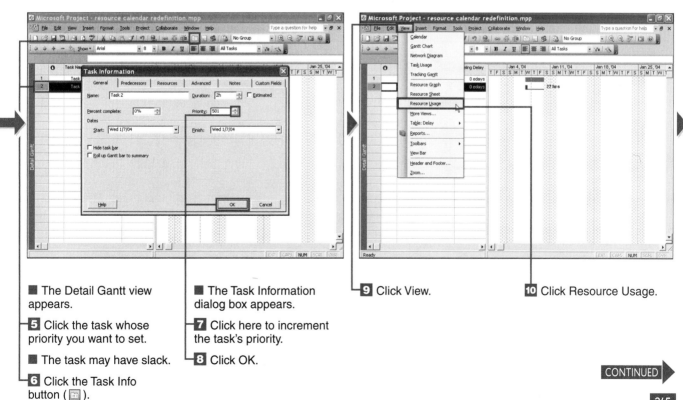

■ The Detail Gantt view appears.

5 Click the task whose priority you want to set.

■ The task may have slack.

6 Click the Task Info button (📖).

■ The Task Information dialog box appears.

7 Click here to increment the task's priority.

8 Click OK.

9 Click View.

10 Click Resource Usage.

CONTINUED ▶

245

REDEFINE A RESOURCE'S
CALENDAR (CONTINUED)

When redistributing work assignments while leveling, Project considers the priorities of each task and attempts to avoid delaying tasks based on their priority. In this example, you need to set the priority of the task that you want the resource to complete on the extended day to a higher number than the priority of the conflicting task.

You can make this kind of change for any resource, but you need to consider the effects on the cost of your project. Salaried employees typically do not have a separate, higher overtime rate, so adjusting the calendar of a salaried employee to allow the employee to work additional time outside of the regular work schedule — overtime — does not affect the cost of your project.

Nonsalaried employees, however, usually have a higher overtime rate. If you use an overtime rate for a resource who works during nonworking hours, redefining a resource's calendar to change nonworking hours to working hours is risky. Project calculates the cost at the regular rate without using the overtime rate. As a result, you may understate the cost of your project.

REDEFINE A RESOURCE'S CALENDAR (CONTINUED)

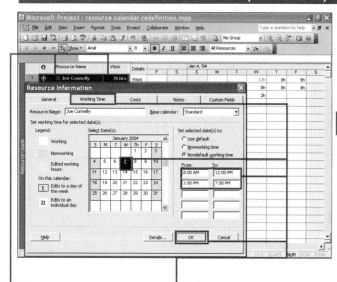

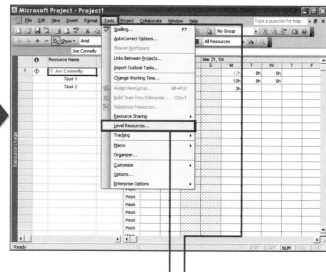

■ **11** In the Resource Usage view, note the date and number of hours the resource needs to work.

12 Double-click the resource name.

13 Click the Working Time tab.

14 Click the day to adjust.

15 Type the extended working hours.

16 Click OK.

■ The Resource Usage view reappears.

17 Click Tools.

18 Click Level Resources.

How can you see that the conflict disappeared?

✔ Using the Resource Usage view, you know the conflict has disappeared because the resource's name has changed from red, boldface type to black, normal type, and the hours on the conflicted day have changed from red to black. The names of resources with conflicts appear in red, boldface type. In addition, the total hours on the day of the conflict appear in red. The names of resources without conflicts appear in black, normal type, and total hours appear in black.

Why — and how — did you set leveling to manual?

✔ So that you could easily see the affects of redefining a resource's calendar to resolve a conflict. To change the leveling mode, see the section "Level Resources Automatically" later in this chapter.

Why should I start in the Detail Gantt view?

✔ The view you use to start must be a task view; otherwise, the view you choose is a matter of personal preference. You may prefer to use a view where you can see slack.

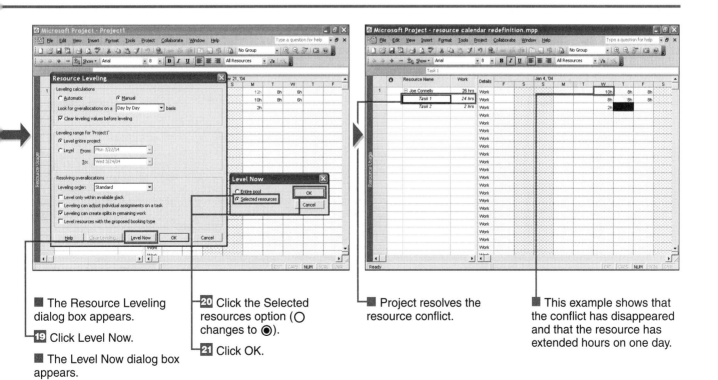

■ The Resource Leveling dialog box appears.

19 Click Level Now.

■ The Level Now dialog box appears.

20 Click the Selected resources option (○ changes to ⊙).

21 Click OK.

■ Project resolves the resource conflict.

■ This example shows that the conflict has disappeared and that the resource has extended hours on one day.

ASSIGN PART-TIME WORK

Y ou can assign part-time work to resolve a resource conflict. Essentially, you smooth out a resource's workload by having the resource work part time on more than one task simultaneously. While this technique may result in extending the duration of some tasks, it also can resolve conflicts when you have limited resources. Although it lengthens some of your tasks, it does not add cost to the project, because the resources continue to work at their regular rate.

For example, suppose that Mary needs to work on Tasks 1 and 2, which have a start-to-start relationship, with Task 1 taking three days and Task 2 taking one day. And, Joe cannot start work on Task 3 — a six day task — until Mary finishes Task 2. While no conflict exists per se, Mary's workload determines when Joe can start working. By assigning Mary to work on both of her tasks part time, you can reduce Joe's idle time because Joe can start working on Task 3 earlier than he would start the task if Mary worked full time on both of her tasks.

In this section, leveling is set to automatic. For more about leveling, see the sections "Level Resources Automatically" and "Level Resources Manually."

ASSIGN PART-TIME WORK

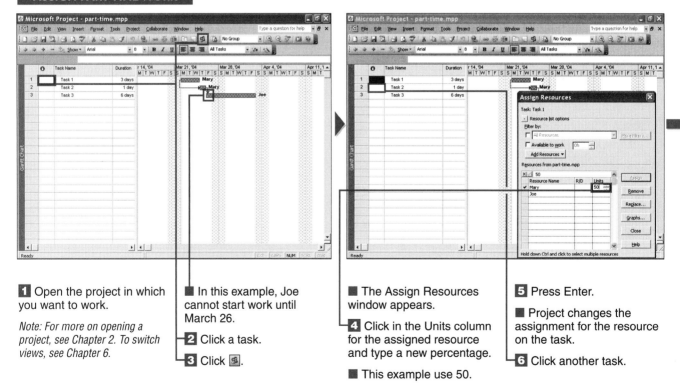

1 Open the project in which you want to work.

Note: For more on opening a project, see Chapter 2. To switch views, see Chapter 6.

■ In this example, Joe cannot start work until March 26.

2 Click a task.

3 Click 🖳.

■ The Assign Resources window appears.

4 Click in the Units column for the assigned resource and type a new percentage.

■ This example use 50.

5 Press Enter.

■ Project changes the assignment for the resource on the task.

6 Click another task.

What does the indicator next to the Task Name mean?

✔ When you change resource units, Project gives you the option to change the duration of the task or to change the task's total work. When you choose to change the duration, you indicate that you want resources to spend only the specified hours per day working on the task. When you change the task's total work, you indicate that you want Project to adjust the task's allotted work. By default, Project assumes that you want to change the task's duration.

If I know that I want to assign 50% of a resource to a series of tasks, is there a quick way to make the assignment?

✔ Yes. In the steps in this section, you select one task at a time to make the change. You can, however, select all of the tasks to which you want to make the same change. Then, in the Assign Resources window, change the units of the appropriate resource. Project changes the resource's assignment on all the selected tasks to the new amount you type in the Units column.

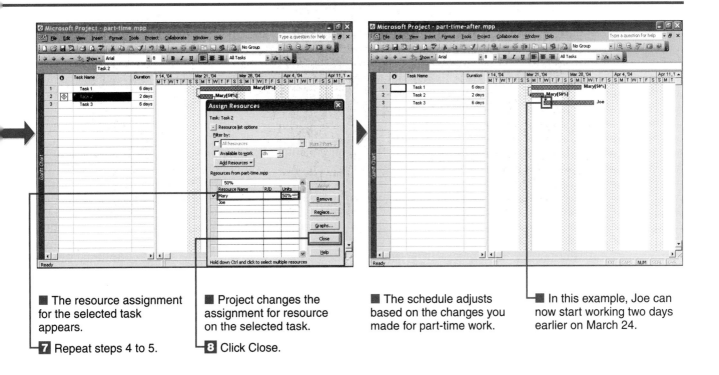

■ The resource assignment for the selected task appears.

7 Repeat steps 4 to 5.

■ Project changes the assignment for resource on the selected task.

8 Click Close.

■ The schedule adjusts based on the changes you made for part-time work.

■ In this example, Joe can now start working two days earlier on March 24.

STAGGER STARTING TIMES

If you have room in your project schedule and can afford some delay, you can consider staggering task start times in order to resolve resource conflicts. When you delay a resource's assignment on a task, Project recalculates the start date and time that the selected resource begins working on the selected task.

In the example shown here, Tom and Mary are working on the budget, a two-day task that begins

on January 8, 2004. Mary has a conflict because she is also working on the invitation list, a one-day task that also starts on January 8, 2004. After staggering the starting times, Tom begins work on the budget on the intended date but Mary begins on January 9, eliminating Mary's conflict on January 8. Tom finishes his work on the budget on January 9, but Mary's work completes on January 12. So this delays the task

by one day because of the staggered start times, but eliminates the resource conflict.

Although this approach extends the project schedule, it does not increase the labor cost, because you do not assign additional resources or require the resources to work overtime.

STAGGER STARTING TIMES

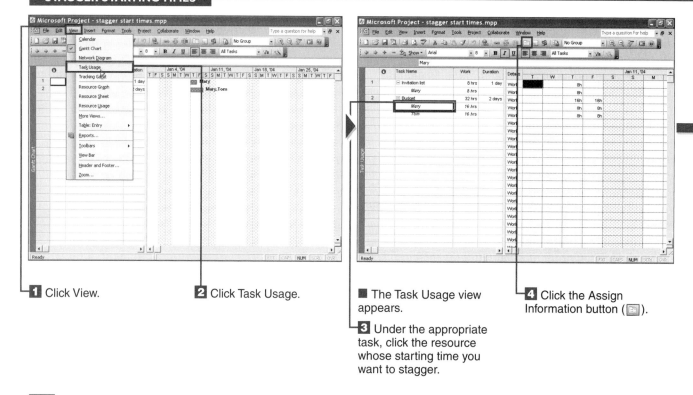

1 Click View.

2 Click Task Usage.

■ The Task Usage view appears.

3 Under the appropriate task, click the resource whose starting time you want to stagger.

4 Click the Assign Information button (▣).

To stagger the starting times for several different resources on several tasks, is there any easier way than opening the Assignment Information dialog box?

✔ Yes. You can use the Task Usage table, which appears automatically in the Task Usage view. Click and drag the vertical Split Bar to the right until you see the Start Date column. You can enter start dates directly in the table. When you click in the Start Date column, Project displays a 🔽 to let you select the start date from a calendar, the same as you do in the Assignment Information dialog box.

How can I monitor the task's cost while working in the Task Usage view, to ensure that I do not actually increase cost?

✔ You can add the Cost field to the Details section of the Task Usage view. After displaying the view, click Format, Details, and then click Cost. Project adds a row for every task so that the Task Name column looks as if it were double-spaced. In the Details section, you see Work in hours and Cost for every task, and every resource working on each task.

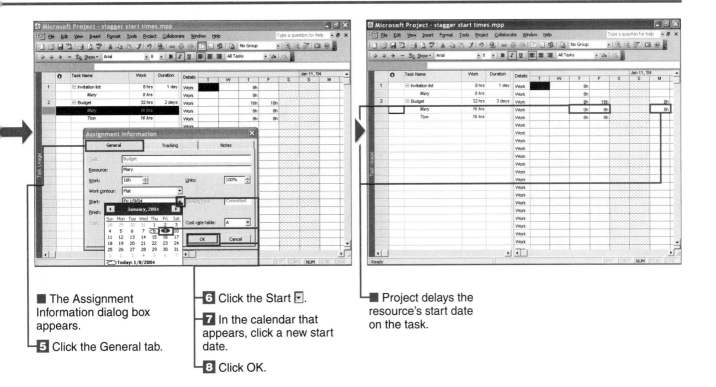

■ The Assignment Information dialog box appears.

5 Click the General tab.

6 Click the Start 🔽.

7 In the calendar that appears, click a new start date.

8 Click OK.

■ Project delays the resource's start date on the task.

LEVEL RESOURCES AUTOMATICALLY

eveling is the process of accommodating the schedules of assigned resources and resolving resource conflicts by delaying or splitting tasks. Leveling spreads out the demands that you make on your resources.

When Project levels, it redistributes a resource's assignments and reschedules them according to the resource's working capacity, assignment units, and calendar. Project also considers each task's

slack, predecessor relationships, dates, constraints, and priority.

You can use the Priority field in the Task Information dialog box to help control the order in which Project levels tasks. See the section "Redefine a Resource's Calendar" for more on the Priority field. In some circumstances, you want Project to level some tasks before it levels other tasks. To ensure that Project levels tasks in the correct order, you can assign different priority

levels to tasks. By default, Project assigns all tasks a priority of 500.

When you assign different priorities to tasks, Project avoids delaying tasks in order of their priority, from highest to lowest; that is, Project delays tasks with lower priorities before delaying tasks with higher priorities. For example, Project delays a task with a priority of 10 before it delays a task with a priority of 20. Before you level, consider how you want to prioritize tasks.

LEVEL RESOURCES AUTOMATICALLY

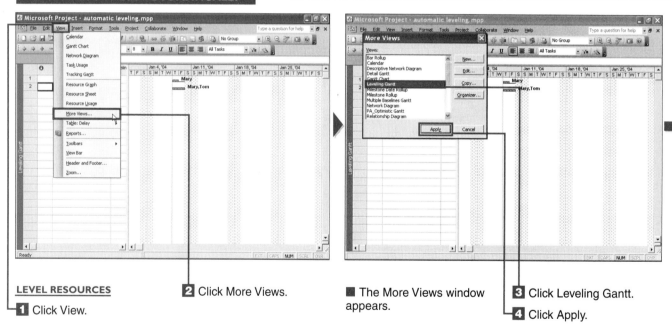

LEVEL RESOURCES

1 Click View.

2 Click More Views.

■ The More Views window appears.

3 Click Leveling Gantt.

4 Click Apply.

Why did you start leveling in the Leveling Gantt view?

✔ The results of leveling are most effectively viewed in that view. However, you can level from any resource or task view; if you level from a resource view, you see a dialog box after you click Level Now that permits you to level only resources that you select.

What happens if I clear the Clear leveling values before leveling option?

✔ If you leveled previously, Project starts by using the results from previous leveling. In this case, the scheduling for previously leveled tasks probably will not change.

Is there an easy way to set and view priorities?

✔ You can add the Priority column to any table view; that way, you can easily see the priorities of neighboring tasks. After prioritizing, but before leveling, you can sort tasks by priority to identify the tasks that Project is most likely to level.

Why did Project not level one particular task at all?

✔ You probably assigned a priority of 1000 to the task. Project treats the priority of 1000 in a special way; it does not delay any task to which you assign a priority of 1000.

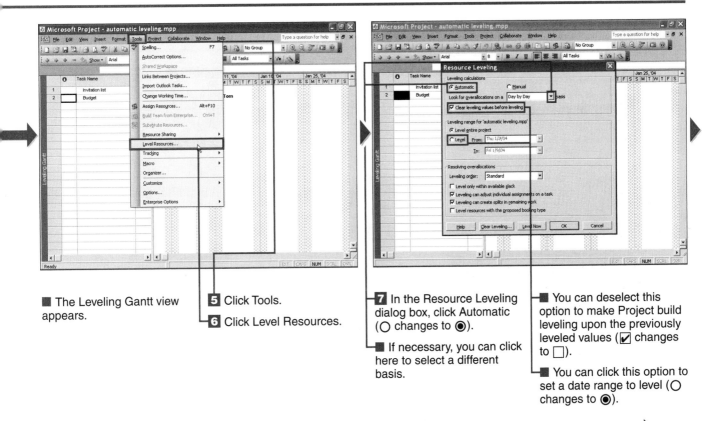

■ The Leveling Gantt view appears.

5 Click Tools.

6 Click Level Resources.

7 In the Resource Leveling dialog box, click Automatic (○ changes to ◉).

■ If necessary, you can click here to select a different basis.

■ You can deselect this option to make Project build leveling upon the previously leveled values (☑ changes to ☐).

■ You can click this option to set a date range to level (○ changes to ◉).

CONTINUED ▶

LEVEL RESOURCES AUTOMATICALLY (CONTINUED)

When you select a basis, you establish a time frame for Project to use to recognize overallocations and level resources, because a resource may appear overallocated for one time frame but not another. For example, you can assign the same resource to two two-day tasks that start and finish on the same date; in this scenario, the resource is overallocated on a daily basis by 16 hours. But, on a weekly basis, the

resource is not overallocated, because a week contains 40 working hours and the resource is assigned for only 32 hours for the week.

By selecting in the Leveling order field, you can determine the order in which Project delays or splits tasks. If you select ID Only, Project looks first at and delays task numbers with higher ID numbers before looking at any other leveling

criteria when selecting the best task to delay or split. If you select Standard, the default, Project looks at each task's predecessor relationships, slack, dates, priority, and constraints. If you click Priority, Standard, Project uses the same criteria as when you choose Standard, but moves Priority to the top of the list.

After leveling resources, Project may delay or split some tasks.

LEVEL RESOURCES AUTOMATICALLY (CONTINUED)

- ■ You can click here to determine the order in which tasks are leveled.
- **8** Click Level Now.
- ■ The results of leveling appear.
- ■ Project adds green bars above the original bars on the Gantt Chart that represent the duration of tasks before leveling.

What does the Level only within available slack option do?

✔ If you click this option (☐ changes to ✔), Project levels resource assignments without changing the finish date of your project. Unless you have built significant amounts of slack into your project, you do not see much effect when you level.

What does the Level tasks with proposed resources option do?

✔ Remember that you can assign resources to a task on a proposed basis. If you click this option (☐ changes to ✔), Project levels tasks with proposed resources as well as tasks with firm resource assignments.

What does the Leveling can adjust individual assignments on tasks option do?

✔ Clicking this option (☐ changes to ✔) allows Project to adjust when a resource works on a task regardless of when other resources are working on the same task.

What does the Leveling can create splits in remaining work option do?

✔ Clicking this option allows Project to split tasks to resolve conflicts.

When should I select level manually?

✔ Level manually when you do not want Project to level as you make resource assignments. See the "Level Resources Manually" section of this chapter for more information.

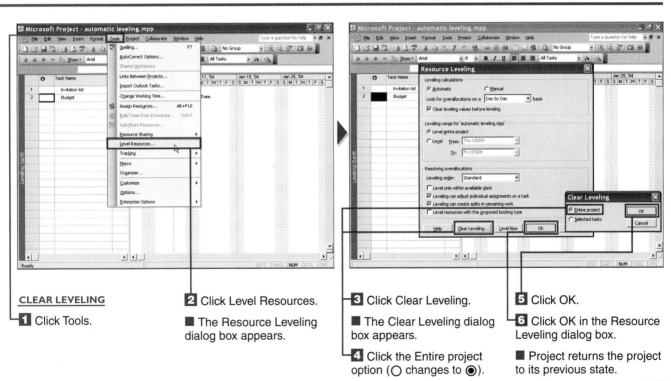

CLEAR LEVELING

1 Click Tools.

2 Click Level Resources.

■ The Resource Leveling dialog box appears.

3 Click Clear Leveling.

■ The Clear Leveling dialog box appears.

4 Click the Entire project option (○ changes to ●).

5 Click OK.

6 Click OK in the Resource Leveling dialog box.

■ Project returns the project to its previous state.

LEVEL RESOURCES MANUALLY

Y ou can manually level your project to control what and when Project levels. Manual leveling provides you with more control over the leveling that occurs in your project. Although you level manually, Project levels in the same way that it levels automatically. That is, priorities still come into play, along with predecessor and successor information, start and finish dates, slack, and constraints. The major difference between manual and automatic leveling is that you control when Project levels.

It is important to understand that leveling resolves conflicting resource assignments by delaying or splitting tasks to which resources with conflicts are assigned. Leveling does not substitute one resource for another to solve an overallocation, nor does it move tasks around in your project to solve an overallocation.

Similarly, leveling does not change the percentage of a resource's assignment; you do not see Joe's assignment change from 100 percent to 50 percent to resolve a conflict when you level.

The example shown in this section does not use the Resource Leveling dialog box; it allows you to type leveling values, offering you the most control possible over the amount of delay or split you introduce in your project.

LEVEL RESOURCES MANUALLY

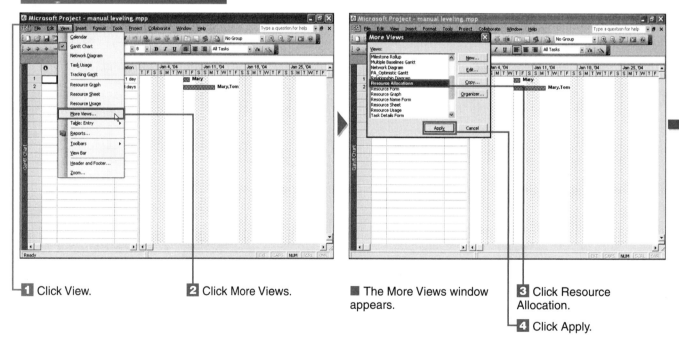

1 Click View.

2 Click More Views.

■ The More Views window appears.

3 Click Resource Allocation.

4 Click Apply.

Which leveling method lets me control when leveling happens but does not require me to type every leveling value?

✔ Project assumes that you want to level your project automatically, but you can change the state to Manual in the Resource Leveling dialog box, and when you are ready to level, you can let Project do the job for you. Perform the steps in the section "Level Resources Automatically" earlier in this chapter to open and set up that box and then click Level Now.

In the section, you clicked Mary's assignment to the Budget task. Why did Project delay both Tom's and Mary's assignment instead of just delaying Mary's assignment?

✔ When Project levels to remove a conflict, it delays the entire task without regard to other resources assigned to the task. That concept may make it seem that, by leveling, Project can introduce additional conflicts, and that is true if you level manually by typing values in the Leveling Delay field. If you simply control when Project levels, the leveling feature will not introduce additional conflicts.

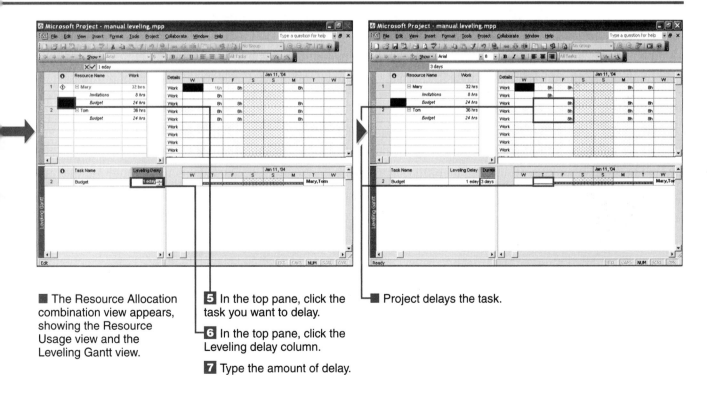

■ The Resource Allocation combination view appears, showing the Resource Usage view and the Leveling Gantt view.

5 In the top pane, click the task you want to delay.

6 In the top pane, click the Leveling delay column.

7 Type the amount of delay.

■ Project delays the task.

SET A CONTOUR PATTERN

You can possibly resolve a conflict by changing the contour of a resource's work assignment. If you plotted it on a graph, a resource's work assignment over time has a shape, which Project refers to as a *contour*. Project has different contours that help you control how much a resource is scheduled to work on a task at a given time.

To better understand contours, think of dividing each task into ten equal time slots. By using the various contours, Project assigns percentages of work to perform in each slot. Contours help you to assign work to a task based on when the task requires the effort. If a task requires less effort initially, consider using a Back Loaded contour. If a task requires the most

effort in the middle of the task, consider using a Bell, Turtle, or even an Early Peak contour.

By default, Project applies a Flat contour to each work assignment, which means that a resource works on the assignment for 100 percent of the maximum hours available each day — based on resource or task calendars, if they exist — for the duration of the assignment.

SET A CONTOUR PATTERN

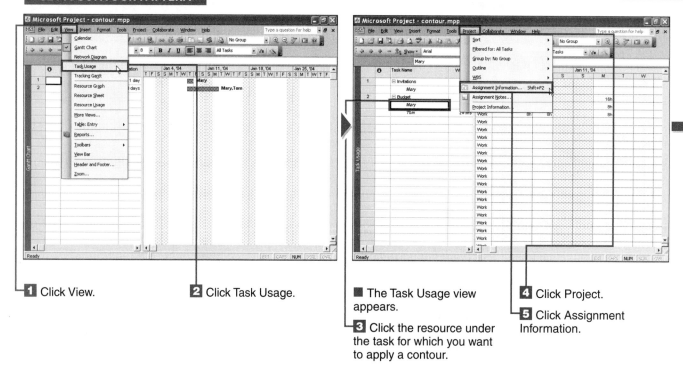

1 Click View.

2 Click Task Usage.

■ The Task Usage view appears.

3 Click the resource under the task for which you want to apply a contour.

4 Click Project.

5 Click Assignment Information.

MASTER IT

What happens if I add new total work values to the task after applying a contour other than Flat to the resource assignment?

✔ Project reapplies the contour pattern to the task and the resources by distributing the new task work values across the affected time span and then assigning new work values to the resources that are working on the task.

What happens if I change the start date of the task or the resource's work on the task after setting a contour?

✔ Project shifts the contour and reapplies it to include the new date, which preserves the pattern of the original contour.

What happens to the contour if I increase the duration of a task?

✔ Project stretches the contour to include the new duration.

What happens if I manually edit a work value on the portion of a view that displays the contour that I applied?

✔ You need to reapply the contour to redistribute the new values.

What happens to the contour if I enter actual work and then change the task's total work or total remaining work?

✔ Project automatically redistributes the changes to the remaining work values and not to the actual work.

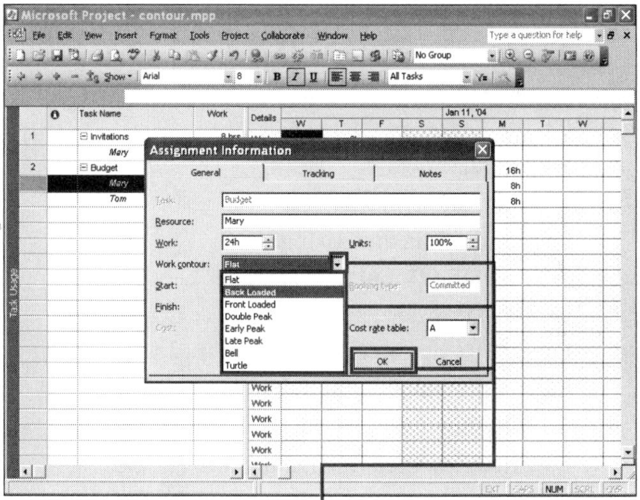

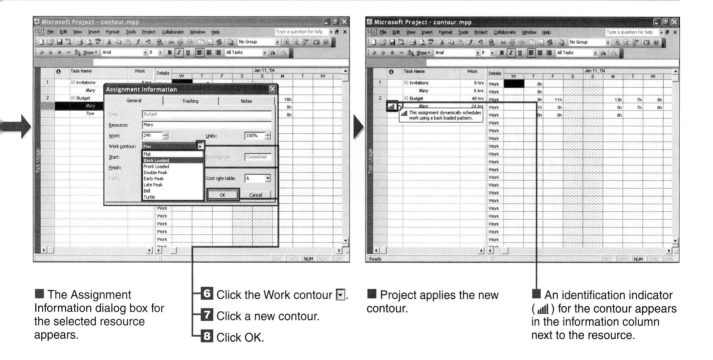

■ The Assignment Information dialog box for the selected resource appears.

6 Click the Work contour ▾.

7 Click a new contour.

8 Click OK.

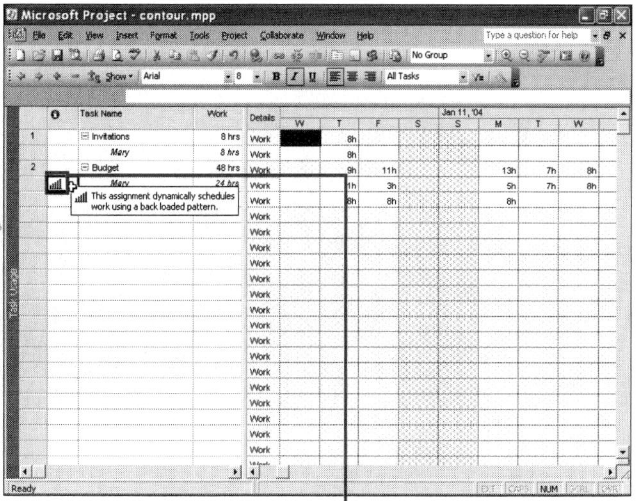

■ Project applies the new contour.

■ An identification indicator ( ) for the contour appears in the information column next to the resource.

SECTION IV

14) REPORT ON PROGRESS

15) ANALYZE PROGRESS FINANCIALLY

Project: Build a Pool

Task	Act. Start	Act. Finish	% Comp.	Act. Dur.	Rem. Dur.
Build a pool	6/02/03	NA	32%	3.51 days	7.49 days
Dig the hole	6/02/03	6/3/03	100%	1.88 days	0 days
Pour the pool	6/04/03	NA	40%	1.6 days	2.4 days
Build the deck	NA				

TIME CARD

	Mon	Tues	Wed	Thur	Fri	Sat	Sun
Regular	8	8	8	8	8		
Overtime	2	1	3	2	2		

REGULAR = 40   OVERTIME = 10

Bill
Time of task
= 2 hours
Cost = $50.00

THE PRINCIPLES OF TRACKING

Driving down the road may seem straightforward and simple, but while you drive you adjust to account for unexpected events. Project tracking is similar: You need to swerve and make adjustments for the changes in costs and timing that are virtually inevitable in any human endeavor. You must be prepared to adjust for unexpected events when establishing and tracking a project plan.

When you track your project, you compare what actually happens during your project to your estimates of what would happen. To track, you need to take a snapshot of your project schedule at the moment your planning is complete; this snapshot is called a *baseline*.

Estimates versus Actuals

Think of the project plan as your best guess of how long tasks may take, how one task affects another, how many resources you need to complete the work, and what costs you expect your project to incur. Good project managers become better project managers by keeping good records of their estimates and then comparing the estimates to the corresponding information. By comparing these two sets of data, you can see where your estimates were not accurate and then use this information to make your next plan more realistic. You also can use data on actual costs and timing to make the changes in your strategy that are necessary to keep you on track and meet your current project's goals.

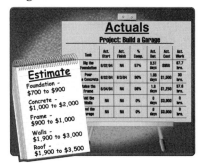

Actual Information

To track a project in Project, you enter "actuals" information such as the actual time that resources work and actual costs that the project incurs. When you record actuals, you record information about tasks in progress as well as about tasks that have been completed. By recording actuals, you also can generate reports that show management where your efforts stand at any given point in time. Using the real data on your project's status instead of your best guess, you can make persuasive bids to management for more time, more resources, or a shift in strategy if things are not going as you expected.

Project: Build a Pool

Task	Act. Start	Act. Finish	% Comp.	Act. Dur.	Rem. Dur.	Act. Cost	Act. Work
Build a pool	6/02/04	NA	32%	3.51 days	7.49 days	$1,550	67.7 hrs.
Dig the hole	6/02/04	6/3/04	100%	1.88 days	0 days	$750	30 hrs.
Pour the pool	6/04/04	NA	40%	1.6 days	2.4 days	$800	37.6 hrs.
Build the deck	NA	NA	0%	0 days	4 days	$0.00	0 hrs.
Screen the pool	NA	NA	0%	0 days	1 day	$0.00	0 hrs.

Adjust as the Project Progresses

Project managers usually track actual activity on a regular basis, such as once a week or every 2 weeks. You should not leave tracking until the end of the project, or even until the end of individual tasks. Tracking tasks in progress on a regular basis helps you to detect any deviation from your estimates. The earlier you spot a delay, the more time you have to make up for it. Project helps you make adjustments; for example, if Project determines that you are running late on a task, it automatically moves dependent tasks into the future.

As you track, Project shows the effect of unanticipated costs on the project's total budget. If the costs that you track on early tasks are higher than anticipated, Project displays your projected total costs based on a combination of actual costs and the remaining estimates. Project shows you exactly how much of your budget you have used and how much you have remaining, so you can revise your resource allocations to stay within your overall budget.

Tangible versus Intangible Results

With something tangible, such as a road under construction, you can look at the road and estimate, with some good degree of accuracy, how far along the project has progressed. Most projects, however, are not so straightforward. How do you estimate how far along you are in more creative tasks, such as coming up with an advertising concept? You can sit in meetings for weeks and still not find the right concept. Is your project 50 percent complete? Twenty-five percent complete? In these situations, completion is hard to gauge from other, similar projects you have worked on. It is very possible that, on the last project, you came up with the perfect concept in your very first meeting.

Monitor Project Progress

In Chapter 13, you learn how to record activity on a task by entering an estimate of the percentage of the task that is complete, actual resource time spent on the task, or actual costs incurred (such as fees or equipment rentals paid), or by entering the hours of work done per time period. Estimating the completeness of a task is not an exact science, and different people use different methods.

Money and Time

Avoid the trap of using money or time spent as a gauge. Unfortunately, it is easy to spend $10,000 on a task that you estimated to cost $8,000 and find you are still only twenty-five percent to completion. You probably have to use the same instincts that put you in charge of this project to estimate the progress of individual tasks.

Deliverables

Deliverables — items created because of or by the project — can be a good measure of completeness. As a deliverable, your project may create a component of a hard drive or you may need to write user documentation. If your project has individual deliverables that you can track, document them and use them consistently when you make your estimate.

UNDERSTANDING CALCULATION OPTIONS

The calculation options available in Project affect the "bottom line" of both the project's cost and the project's schedule. See the section "Set Calculation Options" later in this chapter to set the options described in this task.

Updating task status updates resource status

Select this option to have Project update resource status to correspond with any updated task status. This option works in reverse, as well. If you update a resource's status, Project also updates task status accordingly.

Calculation mode

You can control when Project calculates changes that you make to your project—automatically or when you take action. You also can choose to apply the calculation mode to all open projects or only to the active project.

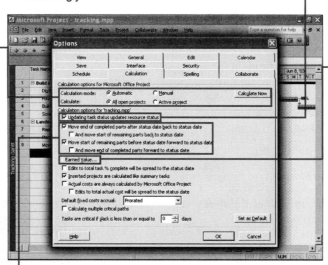

Earned Value button

Click the Earned Value button to set earned value options for the project. See Chapter 15 for more information about earned value.

Adjusting for late or early starts

When tasks begin late or early, Project does not change the task start dates or adjust the remaining portions of tasks. But you can change this behavior using these four options. These settings do not apply if you use timesheet information from Project Server to update your project.

Edits to total task % complete will be spread to the status date

Project distributes changes to the task percentage of completion to the end of the actual duration of the task by default. If you select this option, Project distributes the changes evenly across the schedule to the project status date instead.

Inserted projects are calculated like summary tasks

Project treats inserted projects like summary tasks when calculating the project schedule by default. If you deselect this option, Project treats inserted projects like separate projects.

Actual costs are always calculated by Microsoft Office Project

When you select this option, Project calculates actual costs, and you cannot enter actual costs until a task is 100% complete. If you enter actual costs before a task is 100% complete, Project overwrites the costs when you recalculate the project.

Default fixed costs accrual

By choosing this option, you can choose a method for Project to accrue fixed costs for new tasks.

Calculate multiple critical paths

When you select this option, Project calculates and displays separate critical paths in the project.

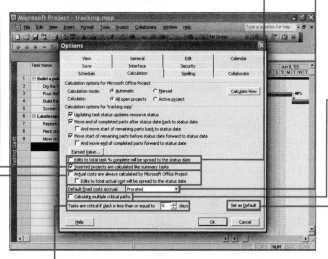

Set as Default

The calculation options listed at the top of the dialog box apply to all projects, but all other options apply only to the project you are currently viewing. Click this button to make all the other options apply to all projects.

Tasks are critical if slack is less than or equal to x days

By default, Project sets this option to zero; under these conditions, only tasks with no slack appear on the critical path. You can force tasks in your project onto the critical path by increasing this value.

SET CALCULATION OPTIONS

Project contains calculation options that you can set to affect the way Project calculates costs and the project's schedule. You can control whether Project automatically calculates changes that you make to your project, or whether you need to take action to update your project. Automatic calculation is the default, but if your project is very large, calculating can take quite a while. Under these circumstances,

you may want to switch to manual calculation to save time.

Project distributes changes to the task percentage of completion to the end of the actual duration of the task by default. If you prefer, you can have Project distribute the changes evenly across the schedule to the project status date.

When you allow Project to calculate actual costs, you want to wait until

a task is 100 percent complete before you enter or import any actual costs for the task, because Project overwrites any costs for uncompleted tasks when you recalculate the project.

Project also enables you to accrue fixed costs for new tasks at the start of a task or at the end of a task, or you can prorate the costs throughout the duration of the task.

SET CALCULATION OPTIONS

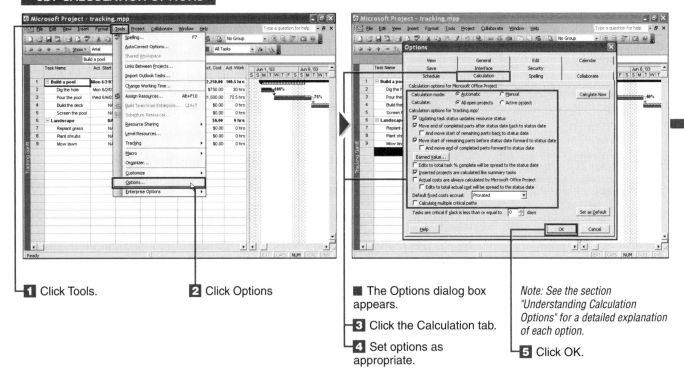

■1 Click Tools.

■2 Click Options

■ The Options dialog box appears.

■3 Click the Calculation tab.

■4 Set options as appropriate.

Note: See the section "Understanding Calculation Options" for a detailed explanation of each option.

■5 Click OK.

How does the Move end of completed parts after status date back to status date option work?

✔ If the project Status Date is December 9 and you have a four-day task with a Start Date of December 14 that actually starts on December 7, Project changes the task's start date to 12/7, sets the percent complete to 50%, and schedules the start of the remaining work for 12/16, creating a split task. If you also select the And move start of remaining parts back to the status date option (☐ changes to ☑), Project moves the start of the remaining work to 12/9.

How does the Move start of remaining parts before status date forward to status date check box work?

✔ If the project Status Date is December 9 and you have a four day task with a Start Date of December 1 that actually starts on December 7, Project leaves the task start date at 12/1, sets the percent complete to 50%, and schedules the start of the remaining work for 12/9, creating a split task. If you also select the And move end of completed parts forward to status date option (☐ changes to ☑), Project changes the task's actual start date to 12/7.

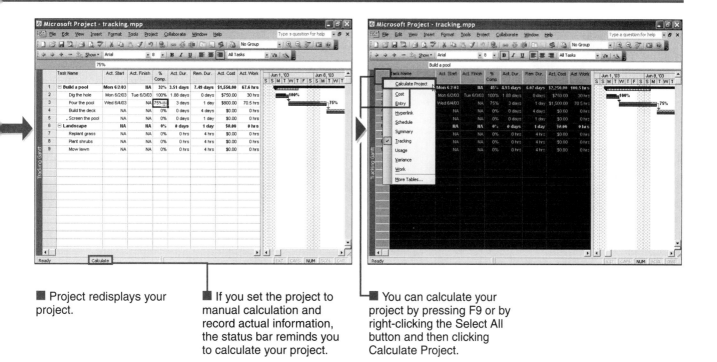

■ Project redisplays your project.

■ If you set the project to manual calculation and record actual information, the status bar reminds you to calculate your project.

■ You can calculate your project by pressing F9 or by right-clicking the Select All button and then clicking Calculate Project.

SET OR CHANGE A BASELINE

A *baseline* is a snapshot of your project at the point when you save the baseline. During the tracking phase of your project, you compare baseline information to actual information to help gauge the progress of your project and to identify slippage. Baselines contain a significant amount of information. You can save up to 11 baselines for your project; you typically save baselines during and at the end of the project-planning phase.

For a shorter project that closely approximates your estimates, you probably will set only one baseline. For longer projects, you may set several baselines to account for unforeseen circumstances such as changes to the scope of the project.

You do not want to change a baseline because it represents a moment in time against which you can use for comparison. If you change a baseline on a regular basis, you are defeating its purpose.

However, you may encounter circumstances under which you need to modify a baseline. After setting your baseline, you may realize that you left out a step, or that you need to break one step into two steps.

You can modify the baseline for the entire project, or you can modify the baseline estimates going forward from a particular point in the project.

SET A BASELINE

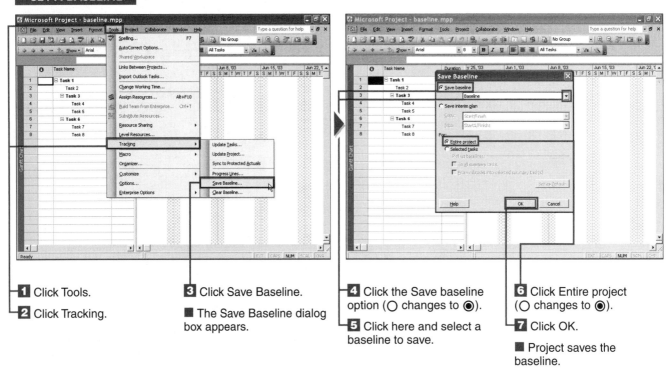

1 Click Tools.

2 Click Tracking.

3 Click Save Baseline.

■ The Save Baseline dialog box appears.

4 Click the Save baseline option (○ changes to ◉).

5 Click here and select a baseline to save.

6 Click Entire project (○ changes to ◉).

7 Click OK.

■ Project saves the baseline.

What information does Project store in a baseline?

✔ For tasks, Project saves duration, start and finish dates, work, timephased work, cost, and timephased cost. For resources, Project saves work, timephased work, cost, and timephased cost information. For assignments, Project saves start and finish dates, work, timephased work, costs, and timephased costs.

Can I display a baseline that I set?

✔ Yes. Click View and then click Tracking Gantt. The Tracking table provides lots of information, and the top portion of the Gantt bar represents actual while the bottom represents baseline information.

How do the options in the Roll up baselines section work?

✔ If you select Tasks 6, 7, and 8, and then select only the first option, Project rolls up baseline information from Task 6 to Task 1, ignoring baseline information for Tasks 7 and 8. If you select only the second option, Project rolls up the information from Tasks 7 and 8 to Task 6. If you select both options, Project rolls up baseline information from Tasks 7 and 8 to Task 6 and then rolls up that information to Task 1.

CHANGE A BASELINE

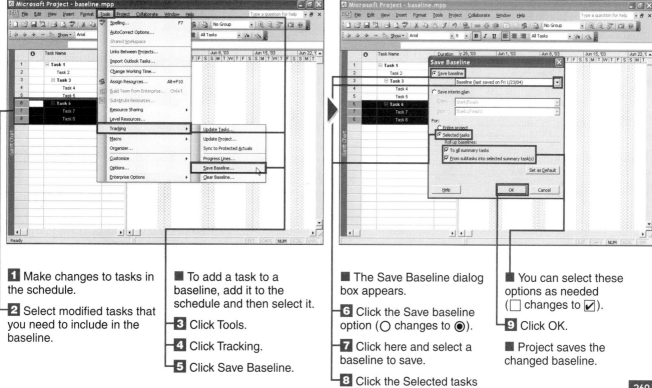

■ Make changes to tasks in the schedule.

② Select modified tasks that you need to include in the baseline.

■ To add a task to a baseline, add it to the schedule and then select it.

③ Click Tools.

④ Click Tracking.

⑤ Click Save Baseline.

■ The Save Baseline dialog box appears.

⑥ Click the Save baseline option (○ changes to ⦿).

⑦ Click here and select a baseline to save.

⑧ Click the Selected tasks option (○ changes to ⦿).

■ You can select these options as needed (□ changes to ☑).

⑨ Click OK.

■ Project saves the changed baseline.

SAVE AN INTERIM PLAN

Project enables you to save up to 10 interim plans, which are similar to baselines. You can compare interim plans to each other or to any baseline plan; the comparison can help you keep an eye on progress and alert you to shifts in the schedule that may cause slippage.

The distinction between baselines and interim plans in Project is the amount and type of information that Project saves. For baselines, Project saves approximately 20 pieces of information, including start and finish dates, durations, work and cost estimates, and totals and timephased information for assignments, resources, and tasks. For interim plans, Project saves only two pieces of information: the current task start and finish dates.

You can set interim plans for all the tasks in the project. However, you should save an interim plan only for tasks going forward. For example, if a labor strike pushes out a manufacturing project by two months, you should keep the baseline intact for all the tasks that were completed at the time the strike started, and save an interim plan for all the tasks that must still be performed when the strike ends.

SAVE AN INTERIM PLAN

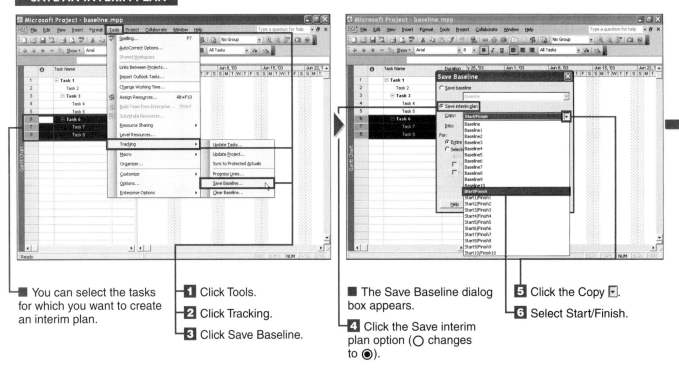

■ You can select the tasks for which you want to create an interim plan.

1 Click Tools.

2 Click Tracking.

3 Click Save Baseline.

■ The Save Baseline dialog box appears.

4 Click the Save interim plan option (○ changes to ◉).

5 Click the Copy ▾.

6 Select Start/Finish.

When should I save an interim plan?

✔ Save an interim plan during the tracking phase of your project when you are trying to monitor progress and you want to compare task start and finish dates at different points in time. Many people save interim plans at major milestones in their projects.

What is the difference between Start/Finish and Start1/Finish1?

✔ Start/Finish are the Start date and Finish date fields that store each task's current schedule information. Start1-10/Finish1-10 are custom fields that you use to hold start and finish date information for each task at other points in time.

How do I view the data stored in the various interim plans so that I can compare them?

✔ Add the appropriate custom fields to the Entry table of the Task Sheet view. To display the Task Sheet view, click View and then click More Views. In the More Views window, click Task Sheet and then click Apply. To display the custom fields as well as hide and insert columns, see Chapter 7.

When should I save a baseline instead of an interim plan?

✔ You should save a baseline during the project planning stages or when you want to compare information such as task, resource, or assignment information.

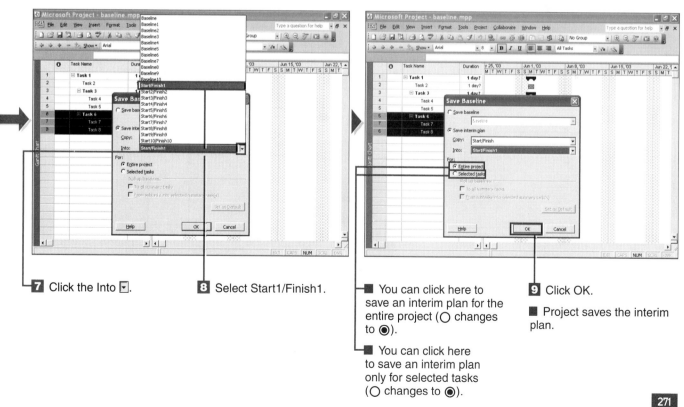

▬7 Click the Into ▾.

▬8 Select Start1/Finish1.

■ You can click here to save an interim plan for the entire project (○ changes to ◉).

■ You can click here to save an interim plan only for selected tasks (○ changes to ◉).

▬9 Click OK.

■ Project saves the interim plan.

CLEAR A BASELINE OR INTERIM PLAN

I nevitably, you save a baseline or an interim plan and then realize that you saved the baseline or interim plan prematurely. You may not have finished the planning stages of the project when you saved the baseline. Or, you may not have had all the information you needed when you saved the interim plan.

If you need to make changes that are not drastic, you may be able to

modify the baseline or the interim plan. For example, if you need to add a task or two to the original schedule, you can modify the baseline.

Under other circumstances, however, you may consider discarding a baseline or interim plan and starting again. Suppose, for example, that you finish the planning stage of a project that has not yet started, and you attend a

meeting in which you inform everyone that you are ready to start on Monday. Your announcement triggers discussion and, by the end of the discussion, the scope of the project has expanded considerably. You now need to rework the planning phase of your schedule; the baseline you saved previously is no longer valid and you need to clear it before you make changes.

CLEAR A BASELINE

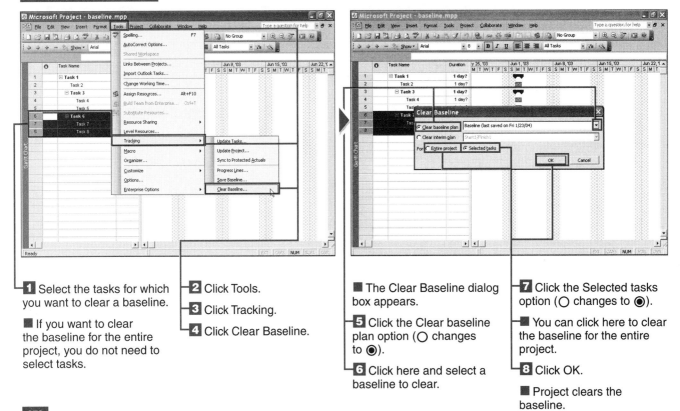

■1 Select the tasks for which you want to clear a baseline.

■ If you want to clear the baseline for the entire project, you do not need to select tasks.

■2 Click Tools.

■3 Click Tracking.

■4 Click Clear Baseline.

■ The Clear Baseline dialog box appears.

■5 Click the Clear baseline plan option (○ changes to ◉).

■6 Click here and select a baseline to clear.

■7 Click the Selected tasks option (○ changes to ◉).

■ You can click here to clear the baseline for the entire project.

■8 Click OK.

■ Project clears the baseline.

Can I change an interim plan instead of deleting it?

✔ Yes, you can change an interim plan by redefining it. Select the tasks to include in the interim plan and follow the steps in the section "Save an Interim Plan" earlier in this chapter. You overwrite the original interim plan by copying new information into the original interim plan custom fields.

Under which conditions should cost changes result in changing or clearing a baseline?

✔ If you save a baseline using a $50,000 budget and your budget is cut to $35,000, change your resources and costs, and then reset your baseline.

When should I change a baseline, clear it, and set a new baseline?

✔ Suppose that you actually start work three months later than you had planned. In this case, set a new baseline schedule before restarting. However, if you are six months into your project and it is put on hold for three months, modify the timing of future tasks and reset the baseline only for those future tasks; using this technique, you retain the ability to accurately assess your estimates.

CLEAR AN INTERIM PLAN

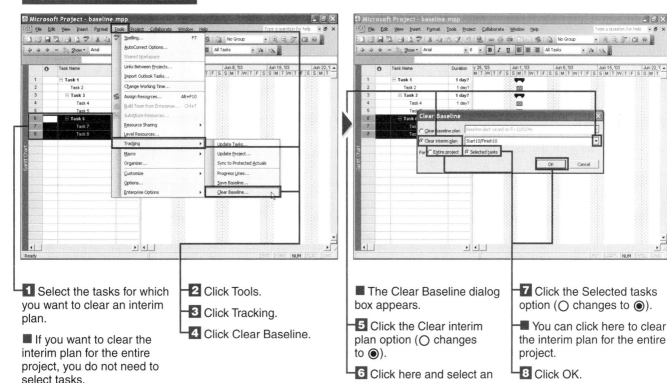

1 Select the tasks for which you want to clear an interim plan.

■ If you want to clear the interim plan for the entire project, you do not need to select tasks.

2 Click Tools.

3 Click Tracking.

4 Click Clear Baseline.

■ The Clear Baseline dialog box appears.

5 Click the Clear interim plan option (○ changes to ◉).

6 Click here and select an interim plan to clear.

7 Click the Selected tasks option (○ changes to ◉).

■ You can click here to clear the interim plan for the entire project.

8 Click OK.

■ Project clears the interim plan.

TRACKING STRATEGIES

I n Project, you can record actual information about the cost of a task and how much time was spent completing the task. When you record actuals, you enter information about what has occurred during your project.

Your tracking skills will improve as you use Project. However, if you follow certain basic principles of tracking, you can save yourself aggravation in your first few projects.

Handling Tracking

Tracking can become a monumental task because you must gather and enter information on each task's progress and costs using resource timecards information, reports from other project participants, and vendor invoices. However, the more often you update your schedule, the less the tracking data piles up, and the less likely it is to overwhelm you.

Consider assigning parts of the updating to different people on your project. If a particular person is in charge of one phase of the project, have that person track the activity on just that phase. You can then refer to Chapter 16, which provides ideas for compiling several schedules and managing schedules with workgroups.

An administrative assistant can also handle the tracking details. Make sure that you provide the assistant with appropriate training — and a copy of this book — so that he or she can track accurately and productively.

To remind you to track, enter tracking as a recurring task, occurring every week or two, within your project file.

Keep Track of Tracking

Using task notes to record progress and changes is another good tracking strategy. If an important change occurs that does not merit changing your baseline, use a task note to record it. When you reach the end of the project, these notes help you to document and justify everything from missed deadlines to cost overruns.

Establish standards for tracking in your organization. For example, how do you determine when a task is complete? How do you measure costs, and what is the source of information for resource time spent on a task? Project becomes a much more effective management tool if each project manager identically gauges progress and expenditures.

Setting multiple baselines is useful but requires a standard to determine when to save each iteration. Consider setting a different baseline for each major milestone in your project. Long projects typically have only four or five significant milestones, which occur after you accomplish a sizeable chunk of work.

Organize the Updating Process

Large projects with many resources can complicate the updating process. To avoid problems, establish efficient manual procedures for collecting information in a timely fashion, and determine the best ways to enter that information.

Individuals working on tasks should answer a few questions regularly. Is the task on schedule? How much is done? Is a revised estimate available on the duration of the task? Is a revised estimate available on the work that is required to complete the task?

If your organization has forms and processes that capture actuals and status information, use them as much as possible.

If your organization does not have forms and processes in place, consider creating a form for participants to use for their regular reports to provide the information that you need to update your project plan; you can use or customize one of the reports in Project.

Decide how often you must receive the collection forms. If you request the reports too frequently, your staff may spend more time reporting than working. If you do not receive the reports often enough, you cannot identify a trouble spot before it becomes a crisis.

You can use the timephased fields in Project to track actual work and costs on a daily or weekly basis. For more on using timephased fields for work or cost tracking, the section "Track Work with Timephased Fields."

When you receive the reports, evaluate them to identify unfinished tasks for which you need to adjust the planned duration, work, and costs. Remember that recording actual information enables you to compare estimates to actuals; this comparison can prove invaluable. To make this comparison, set a baseline for your project. See Chapter 12 for more information on setting baselines.

Methods to Update Tasks with Actual Information

Project provides several ways to enter the information: the Update Tasks dialog box, the Task Details Form view, the Tracking Table, and the Tracking toolbar. And, you can use a variety of techniques to record actual information in Project. For example, you can enter actual start and finish dates, actual durations, the percent complete for a task, or the work completed by a resource on a task.

In some cases, when you enter information into one field, Project calculates the values for other fields. For example, if you enter a percentage complete for a task, Project calculates and supplies an actual start date, an actual duration, a remaining duration, and an actual work value.

By recording actual information, you let Project automatically reschedule the remainder of your project if your task constraints permit rescheduling. You also provide management with a way to measure how well your project is going. Finally, You provide yourself with valuable information on your estimating skills, which is information that you can apply to the remainder of the current project and to your next project.

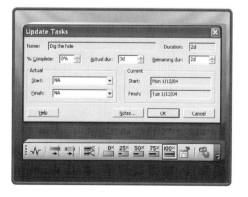

RECORD ACTUAL DURATIONS

T he *actual duration* of a task is the amount of time you need to complete the task. When you set an actual duration that is less than or equal to the planned duration, Project assumes that the task is progressing on schedule and sets the actual start date equal to the planned start date, unless you previously set the actual start date. In that case, Project leaves the actual start date alone. In either

case, Project calculates the percentage complete and the remaining duration for the task.

If you set an actual duration that is greater than the planned duration, Project assumes that the task is finished but that it took longer than expected to complete. Project adjusts the planned duration to match the actual duration and changes the Percent Complete field

to 100% and the Remaining Duration field to 0%.

You can use the Calculation tab in the Options dialog box to make Project update the status of resources when you update a task's status. If you set this option and then supply an actual duration, Project also updates the work and cost figures for the resources.

RECORD ACTUAL DURATIONS

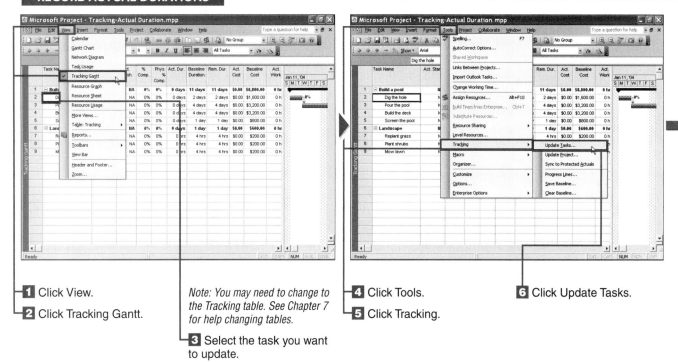

1 Click View.

2 Click Tracking Gantt.

Note: You may need to change to the Tracking table. See Chapter 7 for help changing tables.

3 Select the task you want to update.

4 Click Tools.

5 Click Tracking.

6 Click Update Tasks.

Can I see how Project updated the status of resources?

✔ When you set the Calculation option, Updating task status updates resource status, Project updates the Actual Work, Cost, Remaining Work, and Remaining Cost fields. To view these fields in relation to resources, switch to the Resource Usage view; see Chapter 6. Then, insert columns for the Remaining Work and Remaining Cost fields on the Usage table and in the Details section. Next, right-click and display the Actual Work and Cost fields to determine if Project displays values in these fields for the updated tasks.

If I use effort-driven scheduling, should I update the task's actual duration?

✔ No. You should update actual work. Remember that resource assignments affect the duration of effort-driven tasks. Use the techniques described in the section "Record Work Completed" or "Track Work with Timephased Fields" later in this chapter to record actuals.

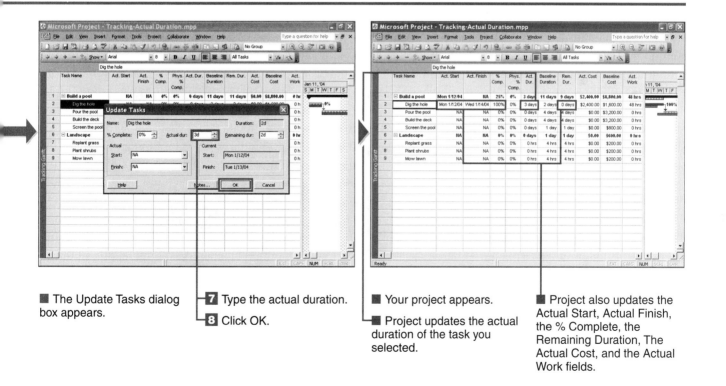

■ The Update Tasks dialog box appears.

7 Type the actual duration.

8 Click OK.

■ Your project appears.

■ Project updates the actual duration of the task you selected.

■ Project also updates the Actual Start, Actual Finish, the % Complete, the Remaining Duration, The Actual Cost, and the Actual Work fields.

SET THE PERCENT COMPLETE VALUE

You can establish the progress of work performed on a task by assigning a percent complete value to the task. Any value less than 100 indicates that the task is not complete. You can set a percent complete value from the Task Details form, from the Update Tasks dialog box, or from the Tracking Table view. Or, you can select the task from any task view and use the percentage buttons on the Tracking toolbar.

Use these buttons to set a task's actual progress at 0%, 25%, 50%, 75%, or 100% complete.

A value in the Percent Complete column also affects the Actual Duration and Remaining Duration values. When you set the percentage complete for a task, Project calculates the value for the Actual Duration column by multiplying the original planned duration by the percentage you

enter. Similarly, Project calculates the value for the Remaining Duration column by multiplying the original planned duration value by the percentage you enter.

When you assign a percentage complete to a task, Project also updates the Actual Start field and may also update the Actual Cost, Actual Work, and Actual Finish fields.

SET THE PERCENT COMPLETE VALUE

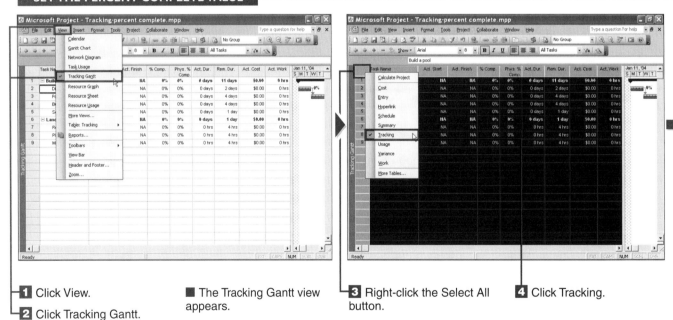

1 Click View.

2 Click Tracking Gantt.

■ The Tracking Gantt view appears.

3 Right-click the Select All button.

4 Click Tracking.

Under what conditions does Project update the Actual Finish field?

✔ If you assign 100% to the Percent Complete column, Project assigns the planned finish date to the Act. Finish field.

Does Project update the Actual Start Date field if I had previously entered a start date?

✔ Project only updates the Actual Start Date field if it does not contain information.

Can I override the Percent Complete value that Project calculates for summary tasks?

✔ Yes, but if you do, Project also adjusts the Actual and Remaining Duration fields and, if appropriate, the Actual Cost and Work fields.

Under what conditions does Project update the Actual Work and Actual Cost fields?

✔ Project updates these fields if you select the Updating task status updates resource status option on the Calculation tab of the Options dialog box.

My task is 100% complete, but it did not complete on the planned finish date. Can I still enter a Percent Complete for it?

✔ Yes, but Project assigns the wrong finish date to the task. You should enter an Actual Finish date instead of a Percent Complete value. See the section "Record Actual Start and Finish Dates" later in this chapter.

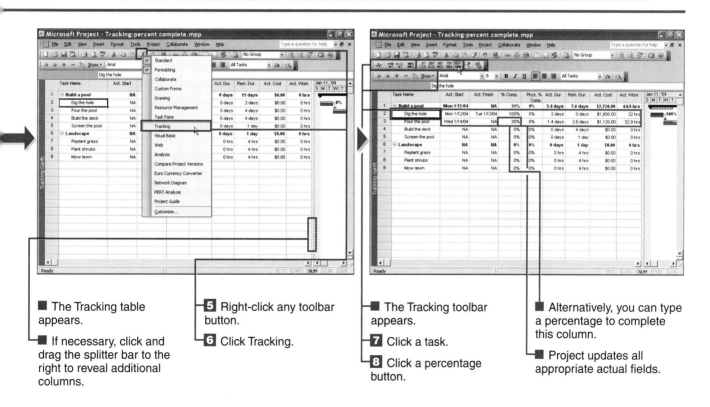

■ The Tracking table appears.

■ If necessary, click and drag the splitter bar to the right to reveal additional columns.

5 Right-click any toolbar button.

6 Click Tracking.

■ The Tracking toolbar appears.

7 Click a task.

8 Click a percentage button.

■ Alternatively, you can type a percentage to complete this column.

■ Project updates all appropriate actual fields.

RECORD ACTUAL START AND FINISH DATES

You can record actual activity by recording Actual Start Dates or Actual Finish Dates for tasks. When you plan your project, you typically enter durations for each task, and Project calculates a planned start date and a planned finish date. After you set your baseline, you can record Actual Start Date and Actual Finish Date values using, for example, the

Update Task dialog box, the Task Details Form view, or the Tracking table on any task view.

Project initially sets the Actual Start Date and Actual Finish Date fields to NA to indicate that you have not yet entered a date. When you update your project to provide actual start and finish dates, Project changes the planned start and finish dates to the actual dates that you enter. When you enter an

actual start date, Project changes only one other field — the projected start date. However, when you enter an actual finish date, Project changes several other fields: the Percent Complete field, the Actual Duration field, the Remaining Duration field, and possibly the Actual Work and Actual Cost fields. If you did not set an actual start date, Project also changes that field.

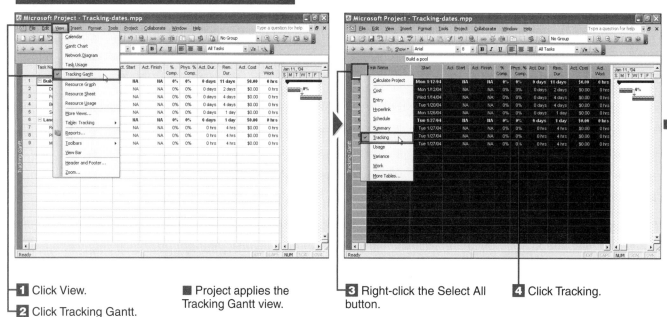

1 Click View.

2 Click Tracking Gantt.

■ Project applies the Tracking Gantt view.

3 Right-click the Select All button.

4 Click Tracking.

Under what conditions does Project update the Actual Work and Actual Cost fields?

✔ Project updates these fields if you select the Updating task status updates resource status option on the Calculation tab of the Options dialog box.

Project updated Actual Cost and Actual Work. How can I view the values Project assigned for Remaining Work and Remaining Cost?

✔ You can add the Remaining Work and Remaining Cost fields to the Tracking table or you can switch to the Work table and then the Cost table and review the values in the Remaining column.

Several tasks finished on time; is there an easy way to record the actual start and finish dates without entering each one individually?

✔ Yes. See the section "Update Tasks Simultaneously" later in this chapter.

How can I quickly compare baseline and actual start and finish dates?

✔ You can apply the Task Details Form view. You view one task at a time in this view, and, among other information, you see date fields. For each date field, you have Current, Baseline, and Actual option buttons. As you click an option button (○ changes to ◉), the dates associated with that selection appear.

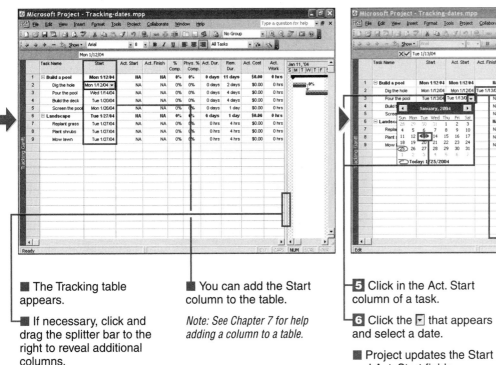

■ The Tracking table appears.

■ If necessary, click and drag the splitter bar to the right to reveal additional columns.

■ You can add the Start column to the table.

Note: See Chapter 7 for help adding a column to a table.

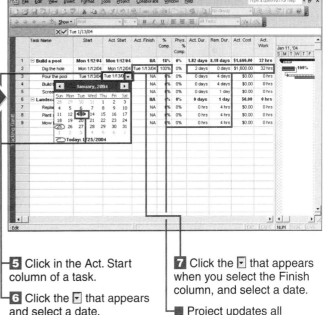

5 Click in the Act. Start column of a task.

6 Click the ⬇ that appears and select a date.

■ Project updates the Start and Act. Start fields.

7 Click the ⬇ that appears when you select the Finish column, and select a date.

■ Project updates all appropriate actual fields.

RECORD WORK COMPLETED

Sometimes you must schedule tasks based on the availability of certain resources. In these cases, tracking progress on a task is easiest if you update the work completed. Updating this value also updates the work that each resource is performing.

In the same way that Project calculates duration information when you fill in a duration field, Project updates the work remaining by subtracting the work performed

from the total work scheduled. Project also updates the percentage of work completed and, if the task is complete, the variance between baseline and actual work performed.

You can use the techniques described in this section whether you are scheduling tasks based on the availability of resources in general or the availability of specific resources. Use the Tracking Table view to enter information

into the Act. Work (Actual Work) column, but start in the Task Usage view so that you can enter actual work performed for specific resources or for tasks. When you record actuals based on the availability of resources in general, you enter values on the same row as the task, rather than on the individual rows for the resources. Project divides the actual and remaining work among the resources.

RECORD WORK COMPLETED

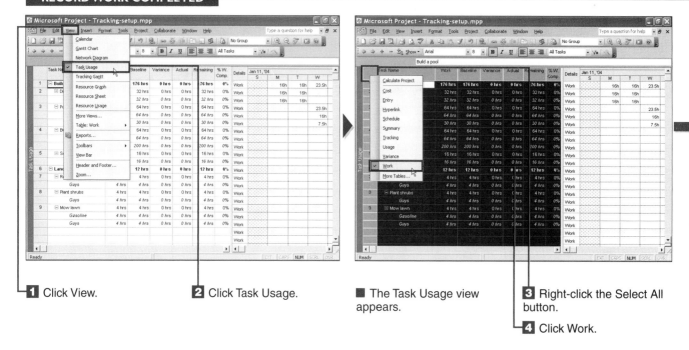

1 Click View.

2 Click Task Usage.

■ The Task Usage view appears.

3 Right-click the Select All button.

4 Click Work.

What happens if I type an amount on the line of the task name instead of next to a resource's name?

✔ Project distributes the amount you type among all resources listed for the task.

Should I use the Details portion of the Task Usage view?

✔ No. You can type actual information directly into the table as described. When you do not use the Details section of the view, Project distributes actuals to specific dates. For more information on using the Details section, see the section "Track Work with Timephased Fields" later in this chapter.

What is the advantage of typing work for specific resources instead of for the task as a whole?

✔ By typing work for specific resources, you can develop data that helps you estimate the speed with which a particular resource can complete a particular task. By typing work only for a task without assigning the work to a resource, you develop information that helps you estimate how long that task may take, but you do not account for the disparity in duration that having different resources work on the task introduces.

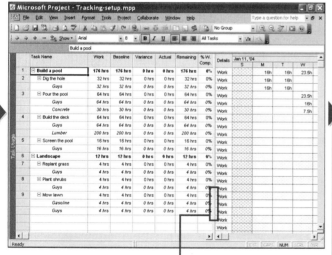

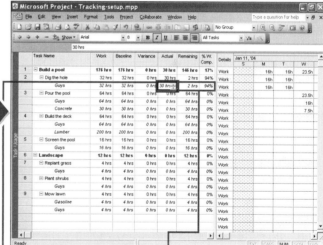

■ The Work table appears.

■ If necessary, click and drag the splitter bar to the right to reveal additional columns.

5 Type an amount in the Actual column for a resource under the appropriate task.

■ You can type the amount for the task instead of for a resource.

■ You can type an amount in the Remaining column instead of the Actual column.

■ Project updates the Remaining and % Work Complete fields.

TRACK WORK WITH TIMEPHASED FIELDS

You can accelerate the updating process with Project's *timephased* fields to update your project on a regular basis. Using Project's timephased fields, you can update the progress of your project regularly on a daily or weekly basis.

To use timephased fields to record progress information for resources, display the Worktable in the Resource Usage view. You can

customize the default table and Details section to make updating easier. Start customizing the table first.

You need to use most of the right side of the view, but on the left side of the view, you really need only the Actual Work column, which is hidden by the right side of the view. You can set up the table in a couple of different ways. For example, you can slide the splitter

bar over to the right, but you then lose the right side of the view. Or, after sliding the divider bar, you can hide all the columns between the Resource Name column and the Actual Work column, but to redisplay them, you must insert each of them.

To view the Actual Work column, insert it between the Resource Name and the Percent Complete column.

TRACK WORK WITH TIMEPHASED FIELDS

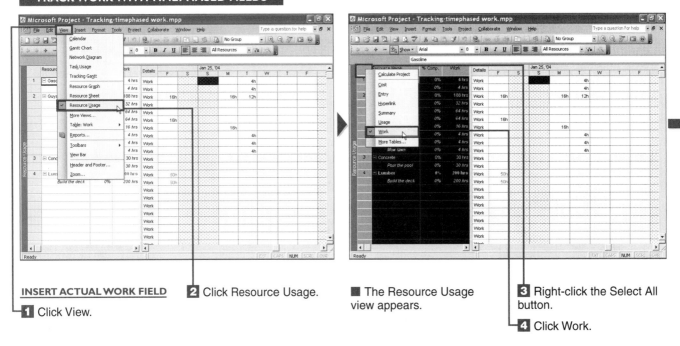

INSERT ACTUAL WORK FIELD

1 Click View.

2 Click Resource Usage.

■ The Resource Usage view appears.

3 Right-click the Select All button.

4 Click Work.

MASTER IT

What are timephased fields?
✔ Timephased fields show information distributed over time. When you use them in conjunction with the timescale, you can view information for any timeframe. You can view timephased fields in the righthand portion — the Details section — of the Resource Usage and Task Usage views. Project contains both work and cost-related timephased fields.

When should I use timephased fields?
✔ Timephased fields are very useful when you want to demonstrate trends over time. You can export timephased field information to Excel and graph it to effectively demonstrate your point. See Chapter 23 for more information.

If I decide I do not want a column on the table portion of the view, how can I remove it?
✔ Hide it. Right-click the column and select Hide Column from the menu that appears.

When I hide a column, does Project delete the data?
✔ Project hides the information from view, but the information still exists in your Project file. You can redisplay it at any time by reinserting the column. Right-click the column you want to appear to the right of the column you are reinserting and follow steps 6 to 9 for the column you want to display.

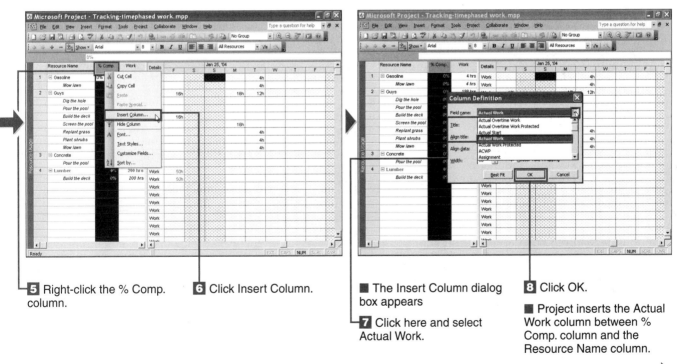

5 Right-click the % Comp. column.

6 Click Insert Column.

■ The Insert Column dialog box appears

7 Click here and select Actual Work.

8 Click OK.

■ Project inserts the Actual Work column between % Comp. column and the Resource Name column.

CONTINUED ▶

TRACK WORK WITH TIMEPHASED FIELDS (CONTINUED)

After you add the Actual Work column to the Work table, you can modify the timescale to reflect how often you want to record actuals. Then you can modify the Details section to include Actual Work. That way, you can enter Actual Work in either the table or the Details section. You enter Actual Work in the table when work began on the planned work date; Project will distribute

actual work figures across the planned work dates. More often than not, you enter Actual Work in the Details section to control the dates on which the work was accomplished.

If you decide that you want to update your project daily, you do not need to make any changes to the timescale on the right side of the window. But if you want to

update weekly — or with some other frequency — you must change the timescale. By default, Project shows two tiers for the timescale — the bottom tier shows each day, and the middle tier shows each week. To update weekly, you still use two tiers, but you change the bottom tier to show each week and the middle tier to show each month.

TRACK WORK WITH TIMEPHASED FIELDS (CONTINUED)

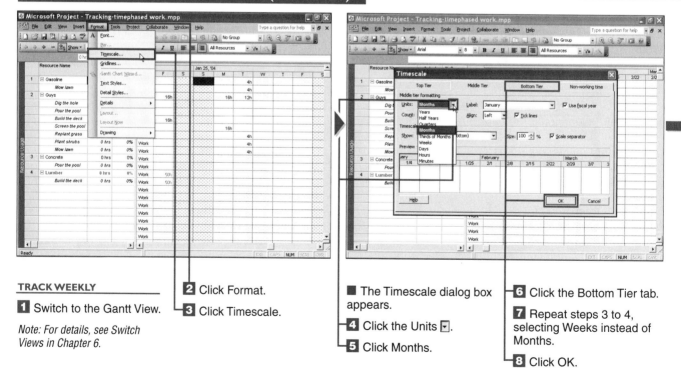

TRACK WEEKLY

1 Switch to the Gantt View.

Note: For details, see Switch Views in Chapter 6.

2 Click Format.

3 Click Timescale.

■ The Timescale dialog box appears.

4 Click the Units ▼.

5 Click Months.

6 Click the Bottom Tier tab.

7 Repeat steps 3 to 4, selecting Weeks instead of Months.

8 Click OK.

If I change the timescale to display weeks and enter Actual Work in a particular week in the Details section, what do I see if I change the timescale to display days?

✓ Project spreads the work across the week based on the task's assignment hours. Suppose that the timescale displays weeks and you enter 40 hours of work on a task with one resource assigned to work eight hours each day. If you change the timescale to display days, Project spreads the 40 hours over the entire week, allocating eight hours each day.

What does the Scale separator option do?

✓ If you select this option (☐ changes to ☑), Project displays a horizontal divider line between tiers. For example, if you use two tiers and show Weeks in one tier and Days in the other tier and select the Scale separator option, Project displays a horizontal line under the weeks and above the days. The Scale separator option affects all tiers; if you display three tiers and do not select the Scale separator option, Project does not display a horizontal line between any of the tiers.

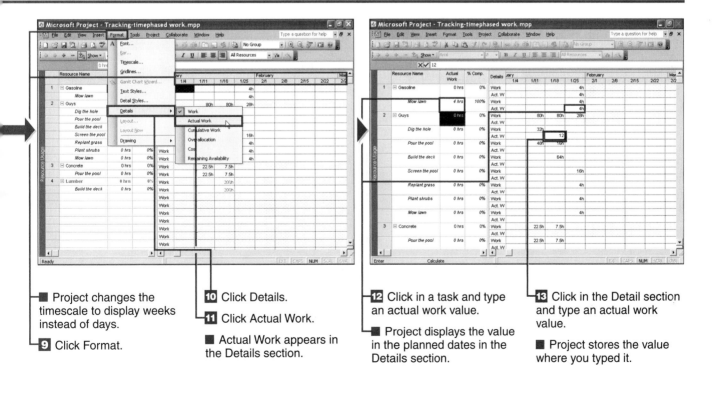

■ Project changes the timescale to display weeks instead of days.

9 Click Format.

10 Click Details.

11 Click Actual Work.

■ Actual Work appears in the Details section.

12 Click in a task and type an actual work value.

■ Project displays the value in the planned dates in the Details section.

13 Click in the Detail section and type an actual work value.

■ Project stores the value where you typed it.

ADD THE STATUS DATE FIELD TO THE TRACKING TABLE

Y ou can speed up the data-
entry process if you create a
custom Tracking table that
groups together the fields into
which you enter actual information.
You may consider including the
project's status date on your
Tracking table to help ensure that
you record information as of the
correct date.

You do not find the Status Date
field if you simply add a column to
the Tracking table, but you can add
a formula to a custom date field to
display the Status Date information
for the project.

In addition to adding the status
date to the Tracking table, you may
also consider adding the current
date; using both fields together, you
can easily find any tasks that you
do not have complete prior to the

status date. When you identify
these tasks, you identify work that
you must reschedule. See the next
section "Add the Current Date
Field to the Tracking Table" for
more information.

This section assumes that you start
in the Task Usage view using the
Tracking table. For switching to the
Task Usage view, see Chapter 6. To
switch to the Tracking table or to
insert a column, see Chapter 7.

ADD THE STATUS DATE FIELD TO THE TRACKING TABLE

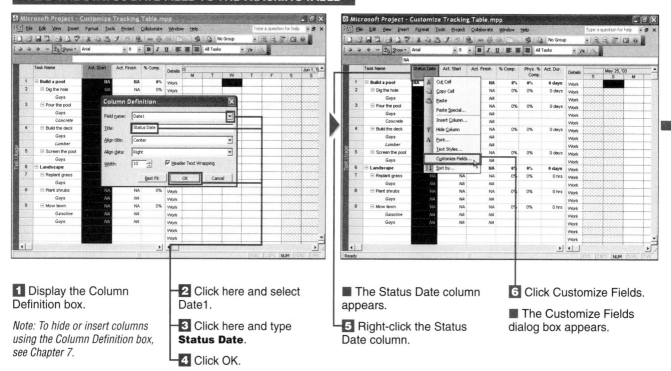

1 Display the Column
Definition box.

*Note: To hide or insert columns
using the Column Definition box,
see Chapter 7.*

2 Click here and select
Date1.

3 Click here and type
Status Date.

4 Click OK.

■ The Status Date column
appears.

5 Right-click the Status
Date column.

6 Click Customize Fields.

■ The Customize Fields
dialog box appears.

Why do I use the name Status Date for the custom date field when you named the column?

✔ The reason has more to do with the formula than with the column name. If you name a formula using words contained in the formula, Project displays an error indicating that you are trying to create a circular reference. To avoid the problem, use the full column name, which you see more often, and abbreviate the formula name. You also can fool Project and enter the formula before you rename the custom field.

Why do I receive an error message telling me that Project intends to replace the data in the field?

✔ The message you see when you click OK to save the formula is actually a warning message, not an error message. The warning explains that the values calculated by the formula will replace any existing data in the Date1 field. Because the Date1 field does not contain any information and because you want to place a calculated value in Date1, you can safely click OK.

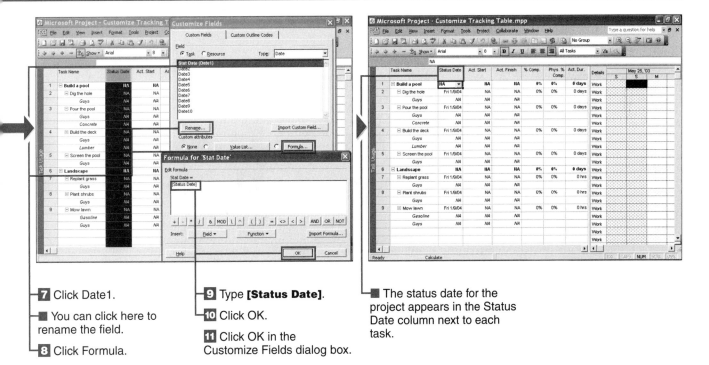

■7 Click Date1.

■ You can click here to rename the field.

■8 Click Formula.

■9 Type **[Status Date]**.

■10 Click OK.

■11 Click OK in the Customize Fields dialog box.

■ The status date for the project appears in the Status Date column next to each task.

ADD THE CURRENT DATE FIELD TO THE TRACKING TABLE

You can add a field to the Tracking table that displays the Current Date to make data entry easier and more accurate while recording actual information.

In the preceding section "Add the Status Date Field to the Tracking Table," you added a custom field to the Tracking table that displays the project's status date to help ensure

that you record information as of the correct date. When you also add the Current Date, you can use the two fields together to identify work that you must reschedule. See the section "Add the Status Date Field to the Tracking Table" earlier in this chapter for information on adding the status field to the Tracking table. Also see the section "Reschedule Uncompleted Work

Automatically" for details on rescheduling work.

You do not find the current date field if you simply add a column to the Tracking table, but you can add a formula to a custom date field to display the Current Date information for the project.

For help switching to the Tracking table, see Chapter 7.

ADD THE CURRENT DATE FIELD TO THE TRACKING TABLE

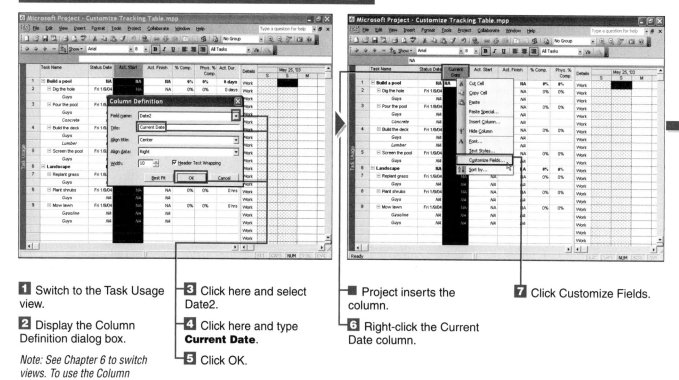

1 Switch to the Task Usage view.

2 Display the Column Definition dialog box.

Note: See Chapter 6 to switch views. To use the Column Definition box, see Chapter 7.

3 Click here and select Date2.

4 Click here and type **Current Date**.

5 Click OK.

■ Project inserts the column.

6 Right-click the Current Date column.

7 Click Customize Fields.

Why do I receive an error message telling me that Project intends to replace the data in the field?

✔ The message you see when you click OK to save the formula is actually a warning message, not an error message. The warning explains that the values calculated by the formula will replace any existing data in the Date1 field. Because the Date1 field does not contain any information and because you want to place a calculated value in Date1, you can safely click OK.

Why is it acceptable to name the custom field and the column the same for the Current Date but not for the Status Date?

✔ The conflict is not between the custom field name and the column name; the conflict arises when the custom field name also appears in the formula. The formula for the Status Date included the words *status date* while the formula for the Current Date did not include the words *Current Date*.

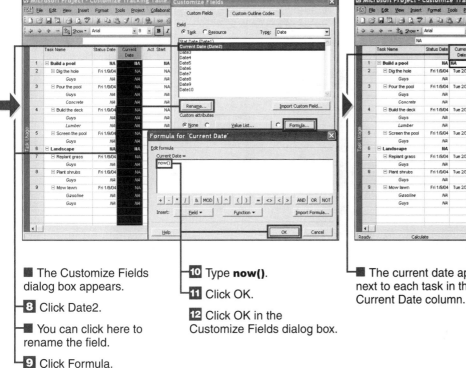

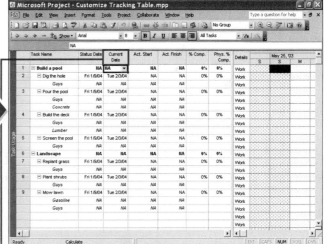

■ The Customize Fields dialog box appears.

8 Click Date2.

■ You can click here to rename the field.

9 Click Formula.

10 Type **now()**.

11 Click OK.

12 Click OK in the Customize Fields dialog box.

■ The current date appears next to each task in the Current Date column.

291

UPDATE TASKS SIMULTANEOUSLY

If you have several tasks that are on schedule or were completed on schedule, you can update the percentage complete for these tasks all at once. Using this method, you update the work that has actually occurred, based on the project's schedule. Project treats your scheduled dates as actual dates and sets the Percent Complete field accordingly.

To update the tasks you select, Project compares the scheduled start and finish dates with the date you supply in the Update Project dialog box. If a task's scheduled start date occurs after the date you enter, Project sets the Percent Complete field to 0% because it assumes that the task has not started. If the task's scheduled finish date occurs before the date you enter, Project sets the Percent Complete field to 100% because it

assumes that the task is complete. If the task's scheduled start date falls before the date you enter and the task's scheduled finish date occurs after the date you enter, Project assumes that the task is in progress and calculates the percentage of completion.

This technique only works well if your tasks are on schedule, because Project uses the scheduled dates to assign actual dates.

UPDATE TASKS SIMULTANEOUSLY

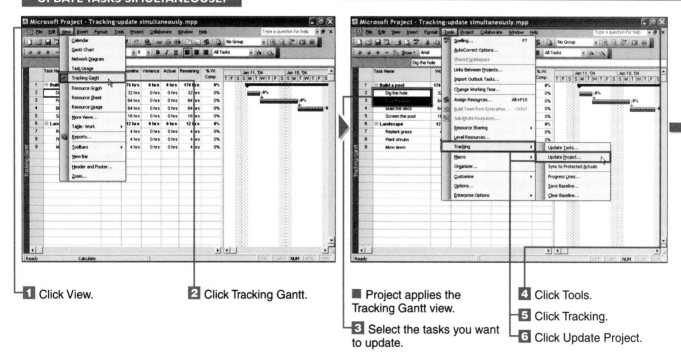

1 Click View.

2 Click Tracking Gantt.

■ Project applies the Tracking Gantt view.

3 Select the tasks you want to update.

4 Click Tools.

5 Click Tracking.

6 Click Update Project.

What is the difference between Set 0%–100% complete and Set 0% or 100% complete only?
✔ If you select Set 0%–100% complete, Project calculates the Percent Complete for each task. If you select Set 0% or 100% complete only, Project marks completed tasks with 100% and does not change the percent complete for incomplete tasks.

Why does nothing change when I followed the steps in this section?
✔ The period you selected does not have any planned activity for the tasks you selected.

How do I select contiguous tasks?
✔ Drag the mouse from the first to the last task. Or, click to select the first task, hold down Shift, and click the last task.

Am I setting a status date when I select a date in the Update Project dialog box?
✔ If you update the entire project, Project changes the project status date to the date you select in the Update Project dialog box. If, however, you update only selected tasks, Project uses the date you supply to calculate actual information such as the Actual Remaining and Percent Complete fields, but does not change the project status date.

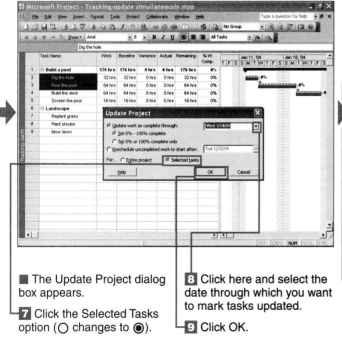

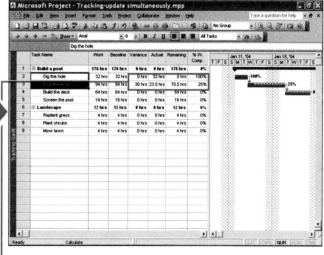

■ The Update Project dialog box appears.

7 Click the Selected Tasks option (○ changes to ◉).

8 Click here and select the date through which you want to mark tasks updated.

9 Click OK.

■ Project updates the Variance, Actual, Remaining, and % Work Complete fields for the selected tasks.

RESCHEDULE UNCOMPLETED WORK AUTOMATICALLY

I f your project falls behind schedule significantly, you can adjust the schedule by letting Project reschedule uncompleted work for you automatically. When you use this technique, you supply a new start date for the entire project or for selected tasks. Use this technique when you do not need to track details for tasks.

When you reschedule a task that has not started by the scheduled start date, Project sets the

scheduled start date to the date you specify and then applies a Start No Earlier Than constraint to the task. If the task is in progress but behind schedule, Project schedules the remaining duration to start on your specified date.

When you reschedule tasks automatically, Project sets the Stop and Resume fields, which this example adds to the Schedule table in the figures. Project enters the date of last reported progress in the

Stop field and rescheduled start date you specify in the Resume field.

When Project reschedules work automatically, it often splits tasks, which you may find desirable in your environment. You can control whether Project splits tasks that are in progress.

If you do not like the results you get when Project reschedules work, you can manually reschedule work.

RESCHEDULE UNCOMPLETED WORK AUTOMATICALLY

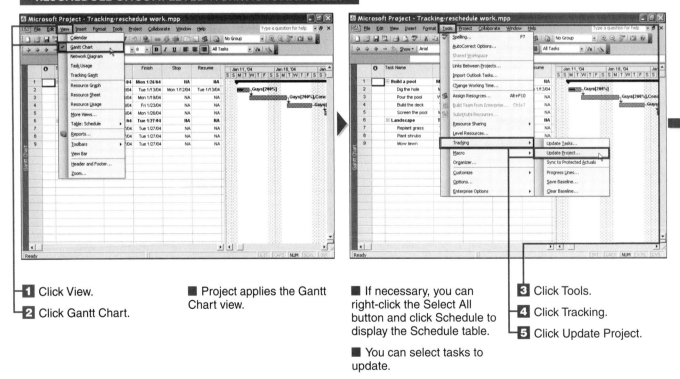

1 Click View.

2 Click Gantt Chart.

■ Project applies the Gantt Chart view.

■ If necessary, you can right-click the Select All button and click Schedule to display the Schedule table.

■ You can select tasks to update.

3 Click Tools.

4 Click Tracking.

5 Click Update Project.

MASTER IT

How can I control whether Project splits tasks in progress?

✔ Click Tools and then click Options. In the Options dialog box, click the Schedule tab. The Split in-progress tasks option is selected by default. If you deselect this option and reschedule work, Project does not split tasks in progress, nor does it reschedule them.

I have not changed the options on the Schedule tab, but my task does not split when I rescheduled. What did I do wrong?

✔ You probably have your project set to manual recalculation. Press F9 and Project splits your task.

How can I manually reschedule work?

✔ Drag the incomplete portion of a Gantt Chart task bar to the right. Project splits the task, starting the incomplete part on the date where you release the mouse. Be careful while dragging; dragging the finished part of the task moves the entire task, and dragging the end of the task extends its duration. Project alerts you if the task is partially complete and has a finish constraint that conflicts with the new start date. If the task has not started, Project replaces any constraint with the Start No Earlier Than constraint.

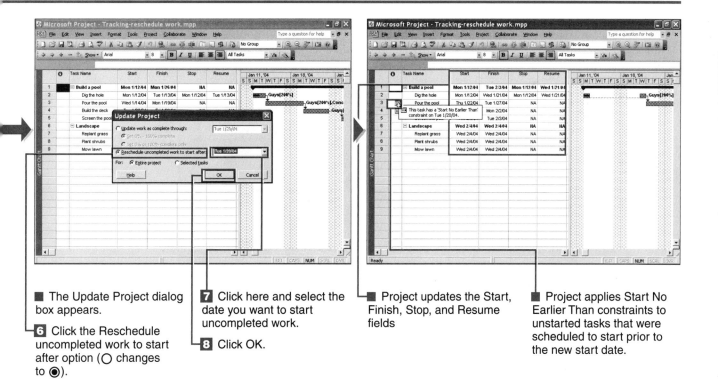

■ The Update Project dialog box appears.

6 Click the Reschedule uncompleted work to start after option (○ changes to ◉).

7 Click here and select the date you want to start uncompleted work.

8 Click OK.

■ Project updates the Start, Finish, Stop, and Resume fields

■ Project applies Start No Earlier Than constraints to unstarted tasks that were scheduled to start prior to the new start date.

UPDATE THE SCHEDULE USING REMAINING DURATIONS

You can specify the remaining duration of a task after you record an actual start date or an actual duration as of the status date information. Typically, you record remaining duration to adjust the schedule after you determine that an original estimate is not accurate based on work already completed.

The remaining duration column, called Rem. Dur. in the Tracking table, shows how much more time you need to complete a task. If you enter a value into the remaining duration column, Project assumes that you have started the work and that you will complete it based on the remaining duration value. Therefore, Project adjusts the actual duration and percent work complete values based on a combination of the remaining

duration value that you supplied and the original planned duration. If you set Project's options to update the status of resources when you update a task's status, Project updates the work and cost figures for the resources on the task.

Entering 0 in the Remaining Duration column tells Project that the task is complete and has the same effect as entering 100% in the Percent Complete column.

UPDATE THE SCHEDULE USING REMAINING DURATIONS

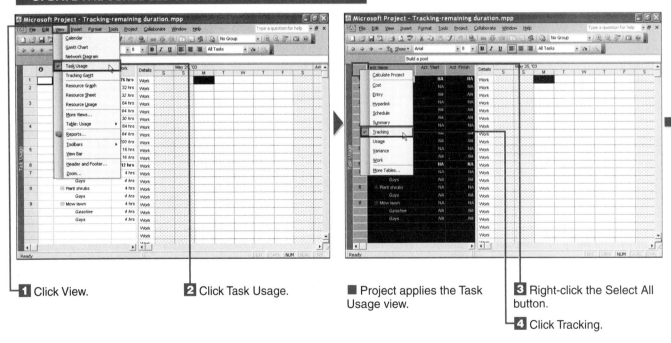

1 Click View.

2 Click Task Usage.

■ Project applies the Task Usage view.

3 Right-click the Select All button.

4 Click Tracking.

My task was scheduled for two days, but after two days I realized that it would take four days. I recorded the two days of actual work and then changed the remaining duration to two days. Can you explain the message that Project displayed?

✔ When you supplied the actual duration of two days, Project thought the task was complete. When you increased the remaining duration, Project assumed it had to assign new work. The message asks you how you wanted to assign the work.

If I increase the Remaining Duration value, how does Project use the information when it calculates Percent Complete for a task?

✔ If the task has not yet started, Project simply adjusts the schedule based on the new value you enter; Percent Complete is not affected because the task has not yet started. If the task has already started and you have entered an actual duration when you increase the Remaining Duration value, Project adds this new estimate to the previously calculated actual duration and adjusts the Percent Complete value.

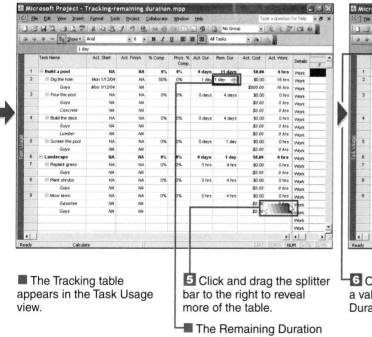

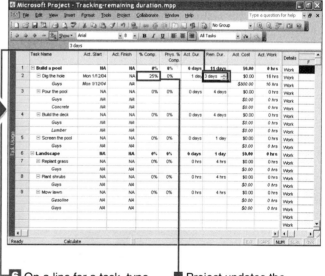

■ The Tracking table appears in the Task Usage view.

5 Click and drag the splitter bar to the right to reveal more of the table.

■ The Remaining Duration column is now visible.

■ **6** On a line for a task, type a value into the Remaining Duration column.

■ Project updates the percent complete values.

HOW PROJECT CALCULATES ACTUAL TASK COSTS

Project calculates the cost of your project using cost information it gathers from tasks. You can assign costs directly to a task and you can assign costs to resources that you then assign to tasks.

Cost information is very valuable. The cost-related information that Project provides helps you to verify the cost of resources and materials for any task, the cost of any phase of your project, and the cost of the entire project. This information can

help you predict when a project's costs accrue, which, in turn, helps you to schedule your bill payments. Last, cost information that you gather on one project may help you to calculate bids for future projects.

Resource Costs

When you create a resource, you can assign a standard rate, and possibly an overhead rate, and a cost per use rate to the resource. If you assign these rates to your resources and then assign the resources to tasks, Project calculates the cost of your project using these rates.

The standard rate that you assign to resources represents the rate for work performed by the resource during regular business hours. To calculate the standard rate, Project multiplies the number of hours times the cost per hour. Project calculates the default rate in hours, but you can charge a resource's work in other time increments. For example, you might charge $100 per day for a programmer. For material resources, think of the charge as per unit based on the unit you specify for the Material Label field.

The overtime rate that you assign to resources represents the rate for work performed by the resource outside of regular business hours. Again, Project calculates the default rate in hours, but you can change the default unit the same way that you changed it for the standard rate.

The cost per use rate that you assign to resources represents the cost that you charge for each use of the resource. You can think of the cost per use rate as a fixed fee that you charge each time you use the resource.

Task Costs

Some tasks are fixed-cost tasks. You know that the cost of a particular task stays the same regardless of the duration of the task or the work performed by any resources on the task. For tasks like these, you assign the cost directly to the task. If you assign a cost to a task, Project adds the fixed cost of the task to the cost of any resource work that you assign to the task when calculating costs for the project.

Remember that assigning a fixed cost to a task does not necessarily make the total cost of the task equal to the fixed cost that you assigned. You can, for example, assign a fixed cost and you can assign resource-based costs to a task.

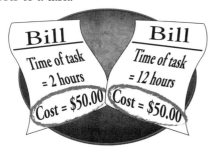

Project and Costs

Except for fixed-cost tasks, Project uses the cost of the resources that are assigned to the task over the duration of the task to calculate a task's cost. Project accrues the costs, and calculates the total project costs as the sum of all resource and fixed costs. Therefore, if you previously set up and assigned resources to your tasks, Project calculates and accrues the costs for you. All you need to do is review and analyze the costs.

Alternatively, you may have chosen not to assign resources to your tasks, or you may not have assigned rates to your resources. Or, you may have changed your default options so that Project does not calculate costs using the Calculation tab of the

Options dialog box. If you do not select the Updating task status updates resource status check box, Project does not calculate your project's costs. By default, this check box is selected, so, the chances are good that Project has been calculating the cost of your project as you have planned and executed it.

Cost Tables

You can review and update your project's costs from one of two cost tables: the Cost table for tasks or the Cost table for resources. You can also override the costs that Project assigns using these tables.

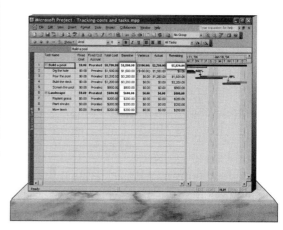

ENTER COSTS IN THE COST TABLE FOR TASKS

You can view cost information for each task in your project using the Cost table for tasks. This table shows you the baseline cost — the planned cost — the actual cost, the variance between planned and actual costs, and the remaining cost of the task.

Project uses the cost of the resources that are assigned to the task over the duration of the task to calculate a task's cost. If you assign a fixed cost to a task, Project adds the fixed cost to the calculated cost for the task. Project accrues the costs, and calculates the total project costs as the sum of all resource and fixed costs. Therefore, if you previously set up and assigned resources to your tasks, Project calculates and accrues the costs for you. All you need to do is review and analyze the costs.

You can display this table from any task view that also has a table. The Cost table for tasks is most useful if you saved a baseline view of your project, because it enables you to compare baseline costs with actual costs.

ENTER COSTS IN THE COST TABLE FOR TASKS

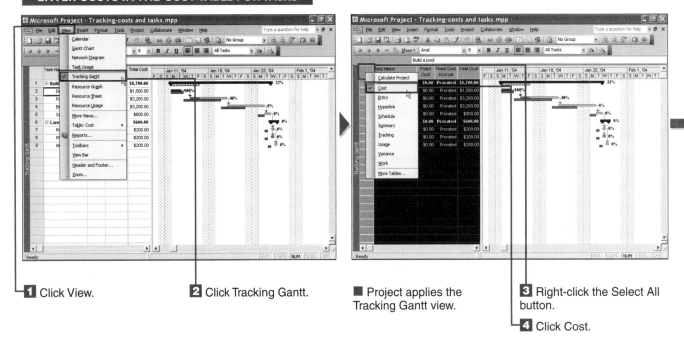

1 Click View.

2 Click Tracking Gantt.

■ Project applies the Tracking Gantt view.

3 Right-click the Select All button.

4 Click Cost.

How can I view tasks that are over budget?

✔ Display the Task Usage view and the Cost table. Then, click Project and click Filtered for. From the menu that appears, click Cost Overbudget.

What is the advantage of working in the Task Usage view?

✔ In the table portion of the Task Usage view, you can view total costs for a task on a resource-by-resource basis. In the Details section of the Task Usage view, you can view costs on a day-by-day basis.

How can I save a baseline view of my project?

✔ Click Tools, and then click Tracking, and then click Save Baseline. In the Save Baselines dialog box that appears, click the Save baseline ⬒ and select a baseline to save. Then, click OK. For more information on saving baselines, see Chapter 12.

What is a fixed cost accrual method?

✔ It determines when Project applies a fixed cost assigned to a task or resource. You can select Start, End, or Prorated; the last choice allocates the fixed cost over the duration of the task or the use of the resource.

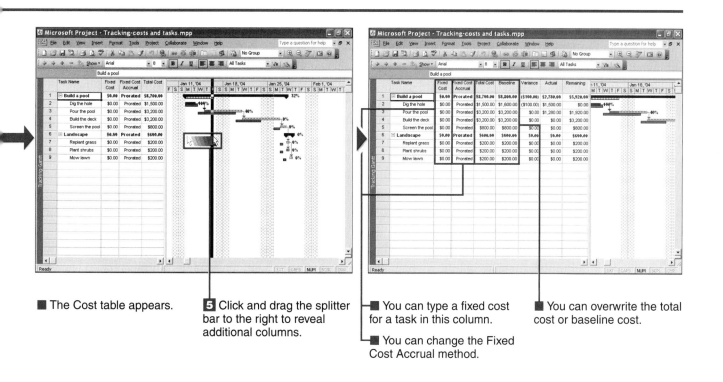

■ The Cost table appears.

5 Click and drag the splitter bar to the right to reveal additional columns.

■ You can type a fixed cost for a task in this column.

■ You can change the Fixed Cost Accrual method.

■ You can overwrite the total cost or baseline cost.

ENTER COSTS IN THE COST TABLE FOR RESOURCES

You can view cost information for each resource in your project using the Cost table for resources. This table shows, for each resource, the same information you see in the Cost table for tasks. You can display this table in any resource view that contains a table, but, if you display this table while viewing the Resource Usage view, you can view resource costs broken down by

task. The Cost table for resources is useful if you saved a baseline view of your project, because it enables you to compare baseline costs with actual costs.

When you create a resource, you can assign a standard rate, and possibly an overhead rate, and a cost per use rate to the resource. The standard rate represents the rate for work performed by the

resource during regular business hours. The overtime rate represents the rate for work performed by the resource outside of regular business hours. The cost per use rate represents the cost that you charge for each use of the resource. If you have already assigned these rates to your resources and then assigned the resources to tasks, Project calculates the cost of your project using these rates.

ENTER COSTS IN THE COST TABLE FOR RESOURCES

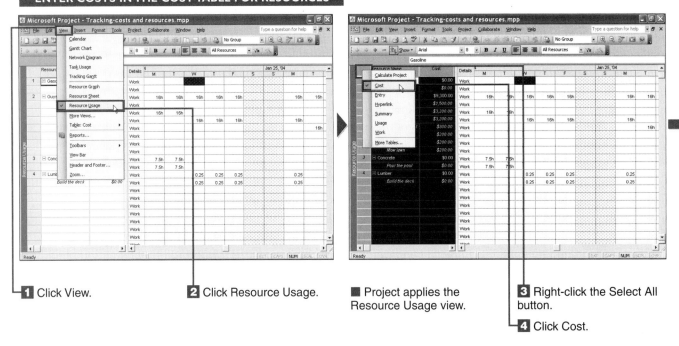

1 Click View.

2 Click Resource Usage.

■ Project applies the Resource Usage view.

3 Right-click the Select All button.

4 Click Cost.

How can I view resources that are over budget?

✔ Display the Resource Usage view and the Cost table. Then, click Project and click Filtered for. From the menu that appears, click Cost Overbudget.

The sum of the Cost column in the Gantt Chart view differs from the sum of the Cost column in the Resource Usage view. Why?

✔ You have entered fixed costs for a task, and fixed costs for tasks are not associated with any resource, so they do not appear on the Resource Usage view.

Can I view the total cost for my project?

✔ Yes, if you display a project summary task. Click Tools and then click Options. In the Options dialog box that appears, click the View tab. At the bottom of the tab, in the Outline options for section, select the Show Project summary task option (☐ changes to ☑). You also can review project costs from the Project Information dialog box. Click Project and then click Project Information. In the Project Information dialog box that appears, click the Statistics button to display the Project Statistics window.

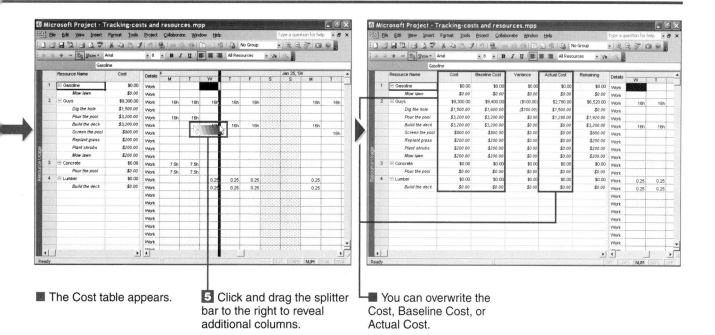

■ The Cost table appears.

5 Click and drag the splitter bar to the right to reveal additional columns.

■ You can overwrite the Cost, Baseline Cost, or Actual Cost.

OVERRIDE RESOURCE COST VALUATIONS

Project's default settings automatically update costs as you record actual activity on a task based on the value of the resources assigned to the task. Project uses the accrual method that you selected for the resource when you created the resource. For more information on the accrual method and how to create a resource list, see Chapter 4.

Alternatively, you can enter the actual costs for a resource assignment, or you can track actual costs separately from the actual work on a task. To do so, you need to wait until the task is complete and then enter costs manually to override Project's calculated costs. Before you can override the costs that Project calculates, however, you must turn off one of the default options.

When you turn off the default option to calculate costs, another option, the Edits to total actual cost will be spread to the status date check box, becomes available. The status of this box determines whether Project distributes the edits that you will make to costs through the status date or to the end of the actual duration of the task.

OVERRIDE RESOURCE COST VALUATIONS

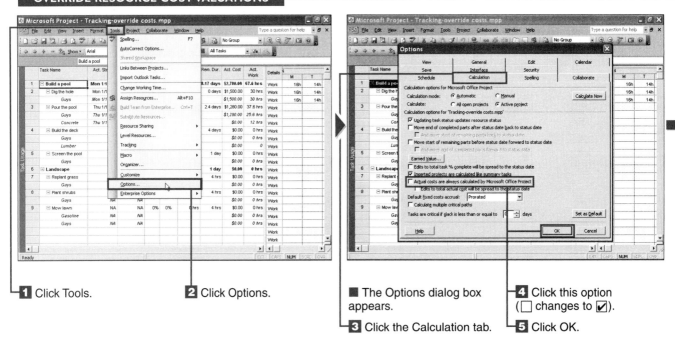

1 Click Tools.

2 Click Options.

■ The Options dialog box appears.

3 Click the Calculation tab.

4 Click this option (☐ changes to ☑).

5 Click OK.

Can I compare, day-by-day, baseline, and actual costs?

✔ Use the Task Usage view and the Cost table. Then, click Format and click Detail Styles. From the left side of the Usage Details tab, double-click Cost, Actual Cost, and Baseline Cost.

Can I control the way Project distributes manually entered costs?

✔ On the Calculation tab of the Options dialog box, the Edits to total actual cost will be spread to the status date option (☐ changes to ✔) controls how Project distributes your entries. If you do not select this option, Project distributes your entries to the end of the actual duration of the task.

I decided to override Project's cost calculations and now I have changed my mind. Can I have Project perform the calculations again?

✔ Yes. Reopen the Options dialog box and display the Calculation tab using Steps 1 to 3. Then, click the Actual costs are always calculated by Microsoft Office Project option (☐ changes to ✔). Project warns you that it will overwrite any manually entered costs when you click OK. Click OK, and Project recalculates your project costs unless you have set the Calculation Mode to Manual. Then press F9 to recalculate your project.

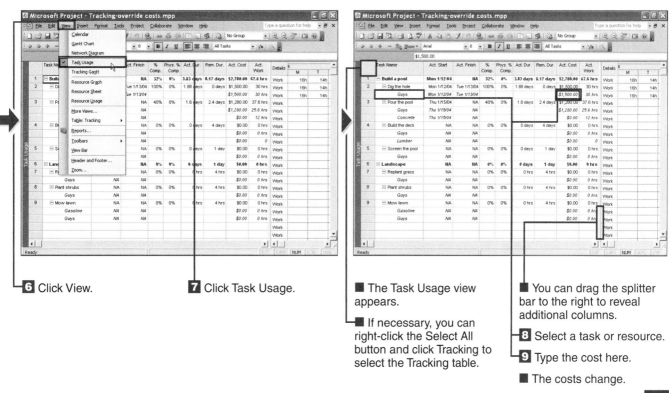

■ **6** Click View.

■ **7** Click Task Usage.

■ The Task Usage view appears.

■ If necessary, you can right-click the Select All button and click Tracking to select the Tracking table.

■ You can drag the splitter bar to the right to reveal additional columns.

■ **8** Select a task or resource.

■ **9** Type the cost here.

■ The costs change.

VIEW PROGRESS

Baselines, which you read about in Chapter 12, help you compare your estimates with actual activity in the project. Once you record actuals, you can view this variance both graphically, with baseline and actual task bars, and through data that appears in various tables. The Tracking Gantt view, in combination with various tables, helps you compare baseline and actual data to understand the status of your project.

Tracking Gantt View Entry Table

The Tracking Gantt view shows the Entry table by default, but you can add or remove fields — columns — or you can display other tables of information. The example shown includes the Baseline Duration and Baseline Cost fields to help compare estimated versus actual timing and costs. See Chapter 7 for more information about changing and modifying tables. See Chapter 15 for more information on earned value fields and calculations.

The Tracking table also contains the following information:

Field	Function
% Comp.	Shows the progress of various tasks in the schedule. In the figure, one task is complete.
Phys. % Comp.	Calculates BCWP, the Budgeted Cost of Work Performed. Project calculates the % Complete field for you based on Total Duration or Actual Duration values you enter, but Project allows you to enter a value for the Physical % Complete field. Use this field to calculate BCWP when the % Complete value does not accurately represent the real work performed on a task.

Field	Function
Rem. Dur.	Reflects the amount of time to complete an unfinished task. You can enter a value into this field or you can allow Project to calculate it for you by entering a value into either the Actual Duration field or the % Complete field. If you enter a value for Remaining Duration, Project calculates a new % Complete value and a new Duration value; Project changes the Duration value to equal the sum of Actual Duration and Remaining Duration, leaving Actual Duration untouched.
Act. Work	Shows the amount of work that has been performed by resources. There are Actual Work fields for tasks, resources, and assignments, as well as timephased Actual Work fields for tasks, resources, and assignments.

	Task Name	Act. Start	Act. Finish	% Comp.	Phys. % Comp.	Act. Dur.	Baseline Duration	Rem. Dur.	Act. Cost	Baseline Cost	Act. Work
1	⊟ Build a pool	Mon 6/2/03	NA	5%	0%	0.9 days	11 days	10.1 days	$0.00	$0.00	14.4 hrs
2	Dig the hole	Mon 6/2/03	NA	45%	0%	0.9 days	2 days	1.1 days	$0.00	$0.00	14.4 hrs
3	Pour the pool	NA	NA	0%	0%	0 days	4 days	4 days	$0.00	$0.00	0 hrs
4	Build the deck	NA	NA	0%	0%	0 days	4 days	4 days	$0.00	$0.00	0 hrs
5	Screen the pool	NA	NA	0%	0%	0 days	1 day	1 day	$0.00	$0.00	0 hrs
6	⊟ Landscape	NA	NA	0%	0%	0 days	1 day	1 day	$0.00	$0.00	0 hrs
7	Replant grass	NA	NA	0%	0%	0 hrs	4 hrs	4 hrs	$0.00	$0.00	0 hrs
8	Plant shrubs	NA	NA	0%	0%	0 hrs	4 hrs	4 hrs	$0.00	$0.00	0 hrs
9	Mow lawn	NA	NA	0%	0%	0 hrs	4 hrs	4 hrs	$0.00	$0.00	0 hrs

Tracking Gantt View Task Bars

You also can display the task bars by manipulating the divider between the table and chart areas to get a graphic view of progress on the project. The Tracking Gantt view displays various styles of task bars to indicate progress on tasks in the project.

At the top of the Gantt Chart, you see the summary task for the project, and below it, you see a black and white hatched bar. That bar represents progress on the summary task. The non-critical tasks appear in blue, and critical tasks appear in red. On all tasks that are not summary tasks, you see two bars; the top bar represents expected duration, and the bottom bar represents baseline duration.

The percentage indicator at the edge of a task reflects the percentage complete for that task. The top bars of completed tasks, such as the Dig the hole task, are solid in color, while the top bars of incomplete tasks, such as the Build the deck task, are patterned and appear lighter in color. The bars of partially completed tasks, such as the Pour the pool task, are solid on the left and patterned on the right.

You also can tell at a glance if a task is completed earlier or later than estimated. Look at the Dig the hole task; the top bar — the actual duration — is shorter than the bottom bar, which is the baseline duration.

The Task Variance Table

As you change the tables while displaying the Tracking Gantt view, you can view different information about your progress in the project. The Variance table, for example, highlights the variance in task timing between the baselines and actuals, showing you quickly if you are behind schedule.

You can easily compare the Baseline Start and Baseline Finish and the actual Start and Finish columns that show actual data for tasks on which you have tracked progress as well as baseline data for tasks with no progress. This table also contains fields to show you the Start Variance, which shows how many days late or early the task started, and the Finish Variance, which shows how many days late or early the task ended.

The Task Cost Table

The Task Cost table is most useful for pointing out variations in money spent on the project. At this point, the Dig the hole task exceeds its projected cost by $800. Project takes the following factors into account when calculating cost variations: actual resource time worked, the estimate of days of resource time you still need to expend to complete the task, and actual costs (such as fees and permits) that have been tracked on the task. For example, compared to a baseline estimate of $1600.00, the Dig the hole task is over budget.

The Task Work Table

The Task Work table of the Tracking Gantt view focuses on the number of work hours put in by resources that are working on tasks. To determine whether a task is taking much more effort than you estimated, check the Task Work table.

For example, the Baseline work for the Pour the pool task was 64 hours. However, the task is only partially complete and has taken 94 hours. Therefore, the Variance field, the difference between the baseline hours of work and the actual hours spent, shows a loss of 30 hours. On the other hand, the Baseline estimate for the Dig the hole task was 32 hours, and the task was completed in 30 hours. The Variance column shows a saving of 2 hours; the negative value indicates that fewer hours were used than were estimated in the baseline.

REVIEW PROGRESS WITH THE WORK TABLE

In Chapter 12, you learned to set and work with baselines and interim plans. In Chapter 13, you learned how to record actual information. After you set baselines and record actual information, you can view progress to view how your estimates differ from actual activity in the project. This helps you determine if work on your project is progressing as expected. You can compare work amounts for tasks as a whole, or for resources and their individual assignments. You can view this variance both graphically, with baseline and actual task bars, and through data that appears in various tables. The Work table focuses on the number of work hours being worked on tasks by resources.

The value in the Work field represents currently scheduled work, which is the total of actual and remaining work for tasks that have started, or the latest projected work value for tasks that have not yet started.

If you saved a baseline, then your original planned work amounts appear in the Baseline field, and you can compare work amounts in your original plan to currently scheduled work amounts. The Variance field shows the calculated difference between planned and scheduled work.

REVIEW PROGRESS WITH THE WORK TABLE

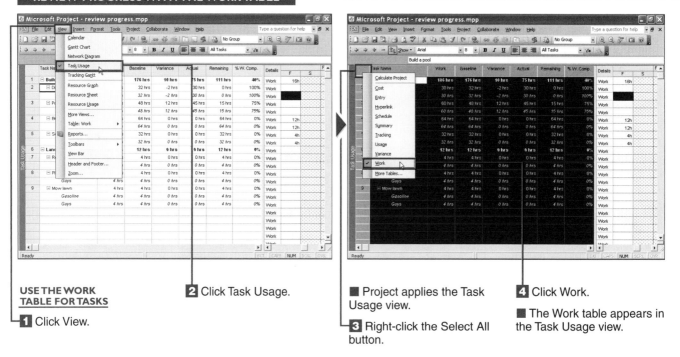

USE THE WORK TABLE FOR TASKS

1 Click View.

2 Click Task Usage.

■ Project applies the Task Usage view.

3 Right-click the Select All button.

4 Click Work.

■ The Work table appears in the Task Usage view.

When should I use the Work table in the Task Usage view instead of the Resource Usage view?

✔ The Task Usage view helps you examine tasks to determine whether their assigned resources are using more or less work than planned. The Resource Usage view helps you determine if a resource is doing more or less work than planned.

What does a negative variance mean?

✔ A negative variance indicates that planned work is less than the baseline estimate; essentially, you are ahead of schedule. A positive variance indicates that planned work is exceeding the baseline estimate and you are probably behind schedule.

Why did the Remaining column change to match the Work column after I updated the Work column?

✔ By updating the Work column, you updated the estimated amount of work still needed to complete the task. Project calculates the value in the Remaining column as the value in the Work column minus the value in the Actual column. If you record an actual amount, Project updates both the Remaining column and the % W. Complete columns appropriately.

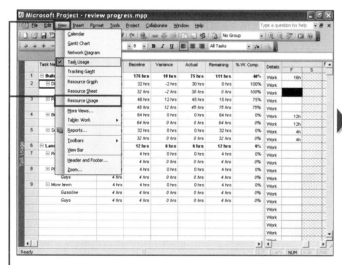

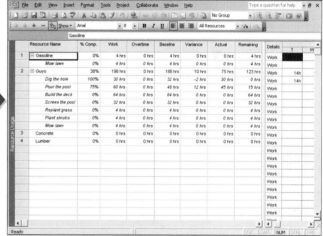

USING WORK TABLE FOR RESOURCES

■1 Follow steps 1 to 4 on the previous page clicking Resource Usage in step 2.

■ The Work table appears in the Resource Usage view.

REVIEW PROGRESS WITH THE COST TABLE

The Cost table helps you identify differences between planned and actual costs in your project. In some cases, you simply want to identify tasks that exceed the budgeted amount. In other cases, you may want to determine when your project began to exceed the budget as well as the task or tasks involved in the budget overrun.

In the Gantt view with the Cost table applied, you can review the Total Cost, Fixed Cost, Fixed Cost Accrual, Baseline, Variance, Actual, and Remaining columns. In the Task Usage view with the Cost table applied, review the Fixed Cost, Fixed Cost Accrual, Total Cost, Baseline, Variance, Actual, and Remaining columns. And, although not shown in this example, you also can use the Resource Usage view with the Cost table applied to review cost variances for assignments; review

the values in the Cost, Baseline Cost, Variance, Actual Cost, and Remaining columns.

You can also enter fixed costs for a task or a project from the Gantt view or the Task Usage using the Cost table. You may want to assign a fixed cost to an entire project if you are trying to apply overhead such as telephone service to a project. In this case, assign the cost to the project summary task.

REVIEW PROGRESS WITH THE COST TABLE

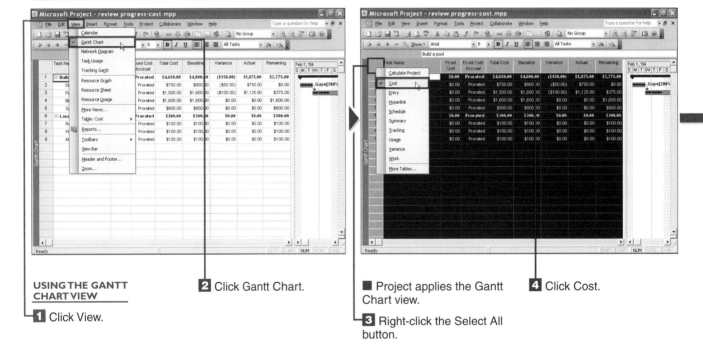

USING THE GANTT CHART VIEW

1 Click View.

2 Click Gantt Chart.

■ Project applies the Gantt Chart view.

3 Right-click the Select All button.

4 Click Cost.

Where is the project summary task that I should use to assign overhead costs?

✔ The project summary task does not appear by default. To view the project summary task, click Tools and then click Options. Click the View tab. In the Outline options section, select the Project summary task option (☐ changes to ☑). Click OK, and Project adds a row at the top of your project that summarizes the entire project. Assign the cost in that row.

What is the difference between the Cost and the Actual Cost fields in the timesheet portion of the Task Usage view?

✔ The value you see in the Cost field represents currently scheduled costs. Actual costs are those that have actually accrued. You can compare both fields with Baseline costs to determine how far planned costs have deviated from actual and scheduled costs. Similarly, the Total Cost field that appears on the Cost table with the Gantt Chart represents total scheduled cost; it is the sum of Actual and Remaining costs.

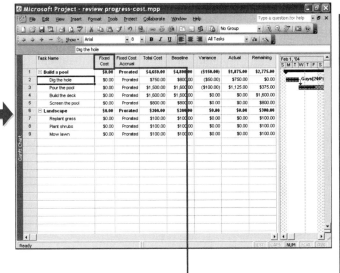

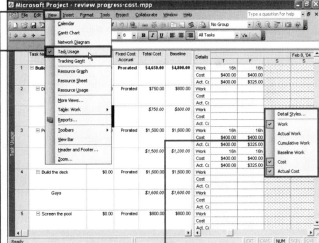

■ The Cost table appears in the Gantt Chart view.

■ You can type a fixed cost for a task in this column.

USING THE TASK USAGE VIEW

1 Follow steps 1 to 4 on the previous page, clicking Task Usage in step 2.

■ The Cost table appears in the Task Usage view.

■ You can right-click in the timesheet section to add rows to the section.

REVIEW PROGRESS WITH THE TRACKING GANTT

The Tracking Gantt view is most useful in viewing progress against your baseline estimates. The bottom bar in the graph portion of the view represents the baseline estimate, and the top bar represents progress on tasks. The Entry table appears by default in the view, but you can display other tables. The Tracking table, for example, contains the fields you need to record tracking information. In this section, the example shows how to display and use the Summary table for tasks and the Variance table.

The Summary table for tasks provides an overview of basic project information. You can determine how long a task is expected to take, its scheduled start and finish dates, the percentage of the task that is complete, how much the task has cost to this point, and how many hours of work are scheduled for the task. You can also find a version of this table available on resource views.

The Variance table highlights the difference in task timing between the baselines and actuals. You can easily compare the Baseline Start and Baseline Finish and the actual Start and Finish columns for tasks on which you have tracked progress as well as tasks with no progress.

REVIEW PROGRESS WITH THE TRACKING GANTT

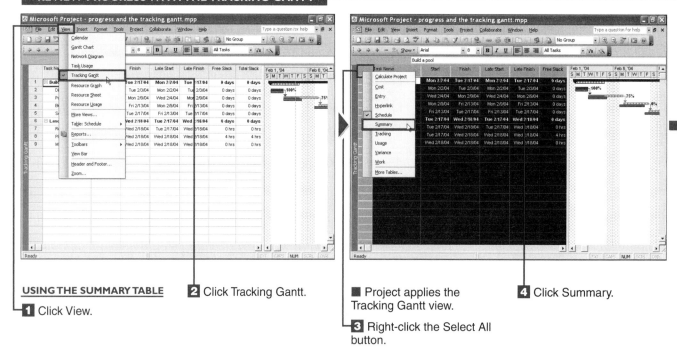

USING THE SUMMARY TABLE

1 Click View.

2 Click Tracking Gantt.

■ Project applies the Tracking Gantt view.

3 Right-click the Select All button.

4 Click Summary.

What do the Start Variance and Finish Variance columns on the Variance table show me?

✔ The Start Variance shows you how many days late or early the task started, and the Finish Variance shows you how many days late or early the task ended.

What information appears on the Summary table for resources?

✔ On the Summary table for resources, you can view an overview of project resource information, including the resource name and group, the standard and overtime rates, the maximum and peak units, and the cost and work for each resource.

If I could see the Actual Duration in the Variance table, I could use it both for tracking and reviewing progress. Is there a table that contains all the fields I want?

✔ You can create a new table based on the Variance table and add the Actual Duration to it. See Chapter 7.

What does the Work column on the Summary table represent?

✔ The Work column always represents scheduled work. The Work and the Actual Work column display the same value when a task is 100% complete.

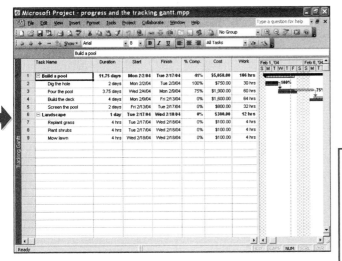

■ The Summary table for tasks appears.

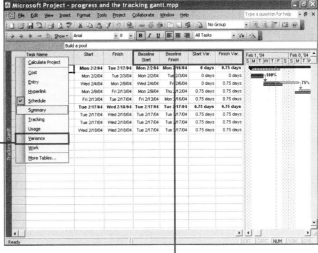

USING THE VARIANCE TABLE

1 Follow steps 1 to 3 on the previous page.

2 Click Variance.

■ The Variance table displays Baseline Start, Baseline Finish, Start Var., and Finish Var. columns.

PRINT A REPORT

Project contains various views that help you to evaluate the progress of your project, identify areas with problems, and even resolve problems. You can print views, but sometimes you need to present information in a format that is not available in any view. Under these circumstances, use the predefined task, resource, and crosstab reports you find in Project. You can adapt any of these reports to present the information you want.

All reports in Project have certain common characteristics. For example, you can print any report or you can review the report on-screen. Project organizes reports into categories of reports that are related to the same subject; for example, all the cost reports fall into the Costs category.

You can customize every report in Project to change the default font. You can customize many of the reports to change the information

that appears in the report. For example, you can choose whether to print task notes, predecessors, and successors. You modify the formatting in some reports by placing borders around details and gridlines between details. You can modify the order in which information appears on some reports, and you can limit the time frame of the information on some reports.

PRINT A REPORT

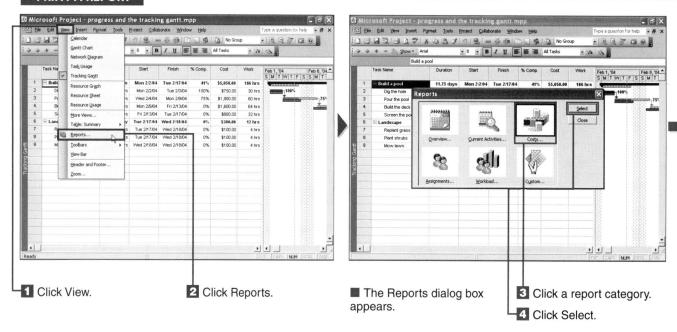

-**1** Click View.

2 Click Reports.

■ The Reports dialog box appears.

3 Click a report category.

4 Click Select.

What is a crosstab report?

✔ A crosstab report shows information about tasks and resources over a time period you specify. Project contains five predefined crosstab reports: the Cash Flow report, the Who Does What When report, the Task Usage report, the Resource Usage report, and the Crosstab report. The Task Usage and Resource Usage views also show information about tasks and resources over time.

How do I know which report to select?

✔ In Appendix B of this book, you find a sample of each predefined report in Project along with a description of the report.

How do I print a view?

✔ Display the view that you want to print. You can customize the view in any way — you can add columns to the table, change the formatting of bars, filter, or group information in the view. Once you have set up the view as you want it, click File and then click Print. If you want to preview first, click File and then click Print Preview. Project displays the view on-screen, and you can click the Print button to send the report to your printer.

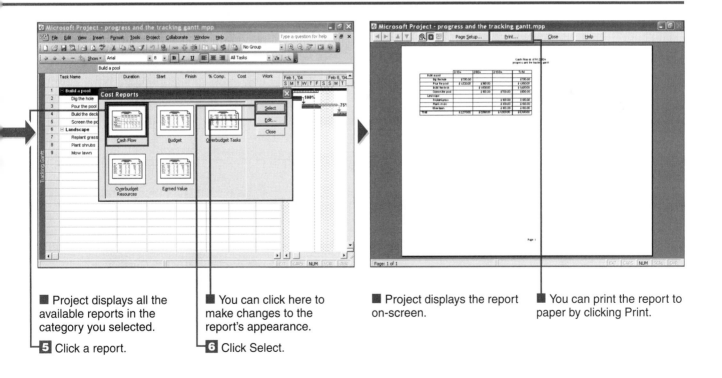

■ Project displays all the available reports in the category you selected.

5 Click a report.

■ You can click here to make changes to the report's appearance.

6 Click Select.

■ Project displays the report on-screen.

■ You can print the report to paper by clicking Print.

CUSTOMIZE A REPORT

Y ou can customize any of the reports you find in Project; you can see samples of these reports in Appendix B. In addition, Project contains three custom report formats. In the Custom Reports dialog box, you see all standard Project reports as well as the three custom report formats. You can customize and print any of the standard reports either from this dialog box or as described earlier in this chapter. To print any

of the three custom report formats, you must use this dialog box.

The three custom report formats you find in Project are the Task report, the Resource report, and the Crosstab report.

The Task report shows task information, such as the ID number, task name, indicator icons, task duration, planned start and finish dates, predecessors, and (if resources have been assigned) resource names.

The Resource report shows resource information including resource ID numbers; indicator icons; resource names, initials, and groups; maximum units; rate information; accrual information; base calendar information; code information; Overtime Rate; Cost/Use; Accrue At; and Base Calendar.

The Crosstab report is a tabular report that shows task and resource information in rows and time increments in columns.

CUSTOMIZE A REPORT

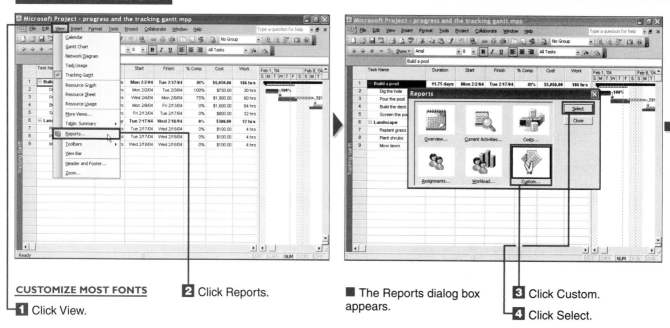

CUSTOMIZE MOST FONTS

1 Click View.

2 Click Reports.

■ The Reports dialog box appears.

3 Click Custom.

4 Click Select.

What kind of information do I find on the Crosstab report?

✔ You find that the Task Usage report and Resource Usage report contain much of the information that appears on the Crosstab report. Further, the Task Usage and the Resource Usage reports give you more formatting options than the Crosstab report. For example, on the Task Usage and Resource Usage reports, you can specify the period that the report covers and the table that is used in the report.

What does the Count field on the Definition tab do?

✔ This field works in conjunction with the Period that you select and controls the number of time unit intervals that Project prints on the report. For example, if you select Days for the Period and two for the Count, Project breaks the report down into periods of every other day.

Can I change a font color for a report?

✔ Yes. In the Report Text dialog box, click the Color ⊡ to select a font color for the selected Item to Change.

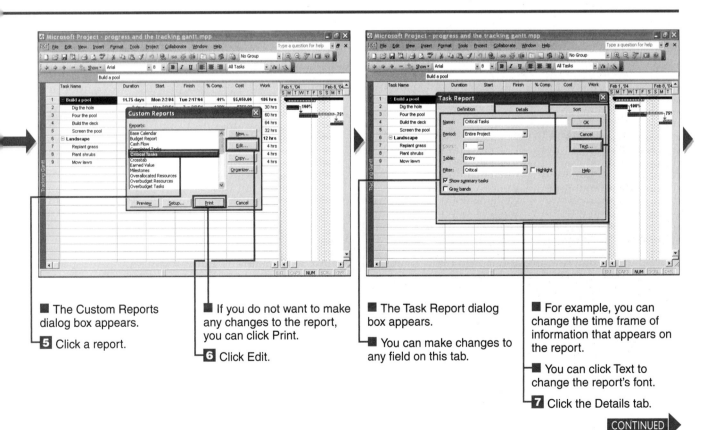

■ The Custom Reports dialog box appears.

5 Click a report.

■ If you do not want to make any changes to the report, you can click Print.

6 Click Edit.

■ The Task Report dialog box appears.

■ You can make changes to any field on this tab.

■ For example, you can change the time frame of information that appears on the report.

■ You can click Text to change the report's font.

7 Click the Details tab.

CONTINUED

CUSTOMIZE A REPORT (CONTINUED)

Project 2003 contains two variations of the Resource report, the Resource (material) and Resource (work) reports. Both reports look identical to the Resource report but one shows only material resources while the other shows only work resources.

You can customize every report in Project in some way. For some

reports, you can change the table or the task or resource filter to change the content of the report, or you can add details to the report or specify a sort order. For a few reports, such as the Working Days report, the only item that you can change is the font information that Project uses to print the report.

You can create your own reports from the Custom Reports dialog

box. When you define a new custom report, Project offers you four formats. Three formats are based on the custom report formats — the Task report format, the Resource report format, and the Crosstab report format. The fourth format, the Monthly Calendar format, functions just like the Working Days report. You can find a sample of the Working Days report in Appendix B.

CUSTOMIZE A REPORT (CONTINUED)

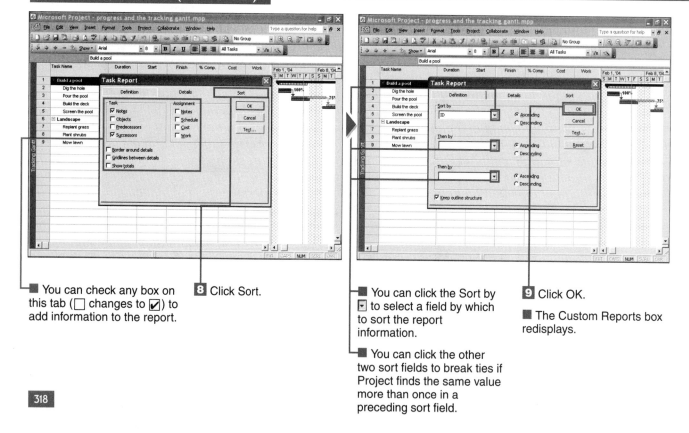

■ You can check any box on this tab (☐ changes to ☑) to add information to the report.

⑧ Click Sort.

■ You can click the Sort by ⊡ to select a field by which to sort the report information.

■ You can click the other two sort fields to break ties if Project finds the same value more than once in a preceding sort field.

⑨ Click OK.

■ The Custom Reports box redisplays.

Why do I see a different Definition tab than the one you show when I select the Crosstab report?

✔ The nature of a Crosstab report — showing information over time — dictates different options for customizing. For a Crosstab report, on the Definition tab, you can set the period and count as column headings and, for rows, you can select just about any task or resource field. You can filter and highlight filtered items, but you cannot apply gray bands. You can use the Details tab to show Summary tasks.

Why do I see a different Details tab than the one you show when I select the Crosstab report?

✔ You see different detail options for customizing because a Crosstab report shows information over time. For a Crosstab report, on the Details tab, you can choose to display summary tasks, row totals, column totals, and zero values. You also can display the first column on every page of the report and gridlines between tasks and between resources. Last, you can control the format of the date column on the report.

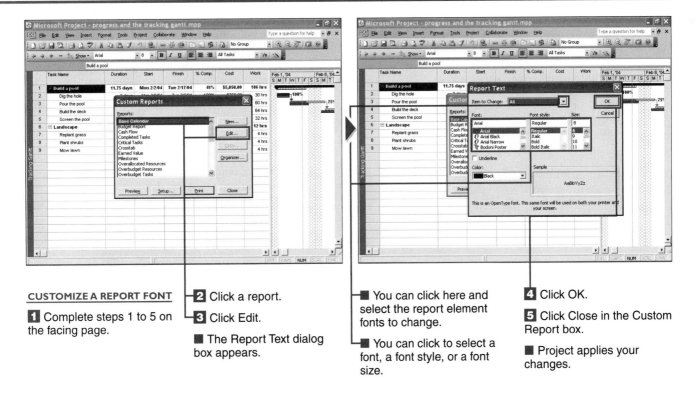

CUSTOMIZE A REPORT FONT

1 Complete steps 1 to 5 on the facing page.

2 Click a report.

3 Click Edit.

■ The Report Text dialog box appears.

■ You can click here and select the report element fonts to change.

■ You can click to select a font, a font style, or a font size.

4 Click OK.

5 Click Close in the Custom Report box.

■ Project applies your changes.

EARNED VALUE FIELDS

When you analyze the progress of your project, you must measure progress based on the costs that you incur as well as the progress of the schedule. In Project, you measure the earned value of your project.

Earned value is the measurement that project managers use to evaluate the progress of a project based on the cost of work performed up to the project status date. When Project calculates earned value, it compares by default your baseline cost estimates to the actual work performed to show whether your project is on budget. You can think of earned value as a measurement made by comparing the amount of the budget that you should have spent for the cost of the work performed thus far, to the baseline cost estimate for the task, resource, or assignment.

To work with and use earned value information effectively, you must first save a baseline for your project, assign resources with costs to tasks in your project, and complete some work on your project.

Understanding Earned Value Fields

The earned value fields in Project are currency fields that measure various aspects of earned value. Project uses a series of acronyms to represent earned value fields; the following table translates the acronyms.

Acronyms	Earned Value Fields
BCWS	Budgeted Cost of Work Scheduled
BCWP	Budgeted Cost of Work Performed
ACWP	Actual Cost of Work Performed
SV	Schedule Variance
CV	Cost Variance
BAC	Budgeted at Completion
EAC	Estimate at Completion
VAC	Variance at Completion

The Heart of Earned Value Analysis

Three fields are central to earned value analysis.

Budgeted Cost of Work Scheduled, or BCWS, measures the budgeted cost of individual tasks based on the resources and fixed costs that are assigned to the tasks when you schedule them.

Budgeted Cost of Work Performed, BCWP, indicates how much of a task's budget should have been spent given the actual duration of the task.

Actual Cost of Work Performed, or ACWP, measures the actual cost that is incurred to complete a task and, in Project, represents the actual costs for work performed through the project's status date.

Note that the Project Management Institute has replaced the terms BCWP, BCWS, and ACWP with Earned Value, Planned Value, and Actual Value, respectively.

Project and Earned Value Calculations

Project calculates BCWS, BCWP, ACWP, SV, and CV through today or through the project status date. The Schedule Variance, or SV, represents the cost difference between current progress and the baseline plan, and Project calculates this value as BCWP minus BCWS. Cost Variance, or CV, represents the cost difference between actual costs and planned costs at the current level of completion, and Project calculates this value as BCWP minus ACWP. Estimate at Completion, or EAC, shows the planned costs based on costs that are already incurred, plus additional planned costs. Variance at Completion, or VAC, represents the variance between the baseline cost and the combination of actual costs, plus planned costs for a task.

Project uses BCWS, BCWP, ACWP, SV, and CV as task fields, resource fields, and assignment fields. Project also uses timephased versions of each field. BAC, EAC, and VAC, however, are task fields only.

New Earned Value Fields in Project 2003

Project 2003 introduced new earned value fields; of these, CPI, SPI, CV%, and SV% are time phased.

Physical % Complete represents your estimate of a task's progress, regardless of actual work or duration, and is not a timephased field. Project calculates Physical % Complete by rolling up BCWP on subtasks to BCWP on associated summary tasks. You enter

Physical % Complete estimates, and Project applies the Physical % Complete to assignment data or Fixed Costs data for the associated summary task.

CPI stands for *Cost Performance Index,* and Project calculates CPI by dividing BCWP by ACWP. This field appears by default in the Earned Value Cost Indicators table.

SPI stands for *Schedule Performance Index,* and Project calculates SPI by dividing BCWP by BCWS. This field appears by default in the Earned Value Schedule Indicators table.

CV% stands for *Cost Variance %,* and Project calculates this field by dividing CV by BCWP and multiplying the result by 100. This field appears by default in the Earned Value Cost Indicators table.

SV% stands for *Schedule Variance %,* and Project calculates this field by dividing SV by BCWS and multiplying the result by 100. This field appears by default in the Earned Value Schedule Indicators table.

EAC stands for *Estimate at Completion,* and while not a new field, Project 2003 now calculates it by using the following formula: ACWP + (BAC − BCWP) / CPI. This field appears by default in the Earned Value for Tasks and the Earned Value Cost Indicators tables.

TCPI stands for *To Complete Performance Index,* and Project calculates this field by using the following formula: (BAC - BCWP) / (BAC - ACWP). This field appears by default in the Earned Value Cost Indicators table.

Note that Microsoft Project bases the remaining cost portion of the TCPI calculation on the BAC, BAC − ACWP, and not EAC. When using this value in reports or charts, reference the calculation as "TCPI (BAC)" to make sure the audience understands the calculation of the value.

SELECT AN EARNED VALUE CALCULATION METHOD

You can choose between two methods to calculate Budgeted Cost of Work Performed, BCWP. One method uses the value in the Percent Complete field, and the other uses the value in the Physical Percent Complete field. You should choose the method based on how you get paid for work performed.

Suppose you need to stack 100 cans in a supermarket display, with ten cans in each row. You place the

first row of cans in ten minutes, but each subsequent row takes an additional five minutes to place, because you must be careful not to knock down the display. You will complete the entire project in 325 minutes. Stacking 50 cans and completing 50% of the project physically takes 100 minutes or approximately one-third of the project's duration. Choosing your earned value method based on the can or the hour impacts earned value calculations.

You can record earned value using different methods for different tasks; you can use Percent Complete for some tasks and Physical Percent Complete for other tasks. You should set a default of the most commonly used method that Project applies to all new tasks. Then, you can set earned value methods on a task-by-task basis.

SELECT AN EARNED VALUE CALCULATION METHOD

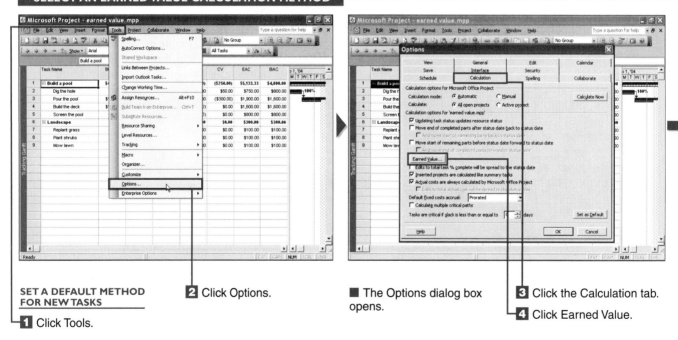

SET A DEFAULT METHOD FOR NEW TASKS

1 Click Tools.

2 Click Options.

■ The Options dialog box opens.

3 Click the Calculation tab.

4 Click Earned Value.

How does Project calculate Percent Complete and Physical Percent Complete?

✓ Project calculates Percent Complete by dividing actual task duration by total duration. Project does not calculate Physical Percent Complete; instead, you enter this value as your estimate of how complete a task is. The estimate you enter has no connection to duration.

Does Project calculate the budgeted cost of work performed for assignments?

✓ Yes, but Project calculates BCWP at the task level differently than it calculates BCWP at the assignment level. Use the task-level BCWP values because Project rolls the task-level BCWP values into summary tasks and the project summary task.

How do I change the earned value method for a lot of tasks?

✓ Insert the Earned Value Method column in a task table. Then, assign the method for one task and copy and paste it to other tasks. To copy and paste the information, click the cell containing the value that you want to copy and click the Copy button (🖻) on the toolbar. Then, select the cells where you want to paste the information and click the Paste button (🖻). For help inserting the column into a table, see Chapter 7.

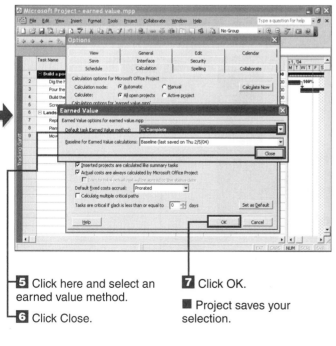

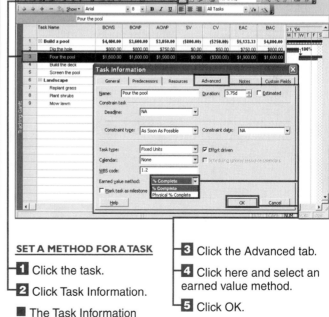

5 Click here and select an earned value method.

6 Click Close.

7 Click OK.

■ Project saves your selection.

SET A METHOD FOR A TASK

1 Click the task.

2 Click Task Information.

■ The Task Information dialog box appears.

3 Click the Advanced tab.

4 Click here and select an earned value method.

5 Click OK.

■ Project saves your selection.

CALCULATE BASIC EARNED VALUE

You can review the earned value fields and determine if your project will finish within the budgeted amount once you understand how Project calculates earned value.

Three fields are at the heart of earned value analysis: BCWS measures the budgeted cost of individual tasks based on the resources and fixed costs that you assign to the tasks when you schedule them. ACWP measures

the actual cost that is incurred to complete a task, and represents the actual costs for work performed through the project's status date. BCWP indicates how much of a task's budget should be spent given the actual duration, actual work, or percent complete of the task.

To illustrate how these values work, assume that you have two tasks, each scheduled to take four days with one resource assigned to each task at $25.00/day in a project

that starts on January 12, 2004. For one task, you calculate earned value based on the Physical Percent Complete, and for the other task, you calculate earned value based on the Percent Complete. You work in the Tracking Gantt view with a customized table. For more on the Tracking Gantt view, see Appendix A.

Project calculates earned value fields based on today's date or the status date of the project.

CALCULATE BASIC EARNED VALUE

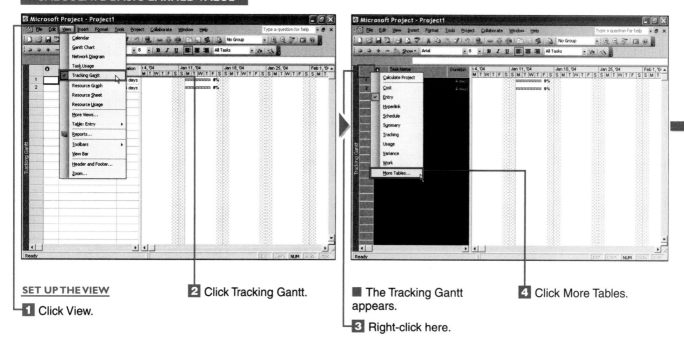

SET UP THE VIEW

1 Click View.

2 Click Tracking Gantt.

■ The Tracking Gantt appears.

3 Right-click here.

4 Click More Tables.

How do I change the order in which columns appear in the table?

✔ Click the column heading to select it. Then, point 📐 at the column heading and drag the column to a new position in the table.

How can I have Project automatically determine the width of the column so that I can see everything in it?

✔ In the Column Definition dialog box, click Best Fit. Or, double-click the right edge of a column's heading.

I inserted the column, but I cannot read all of its title. What should I do?

✔ You probably unselected the Header Text Wrapping option in the Column Definition box. Double-click the column heading to reopen the Column Definition dialog box and select (☐ changes to ✔) the Header Text Wrapping box. Otherwise, you can widen the column by dragging the right edge of the column heading.

What does the BAC column tell me?

✔ BAC stands for Budget at Completion and provides you with an estimate of the project's or task's total cost. BAC does not change unless you change the baseline.

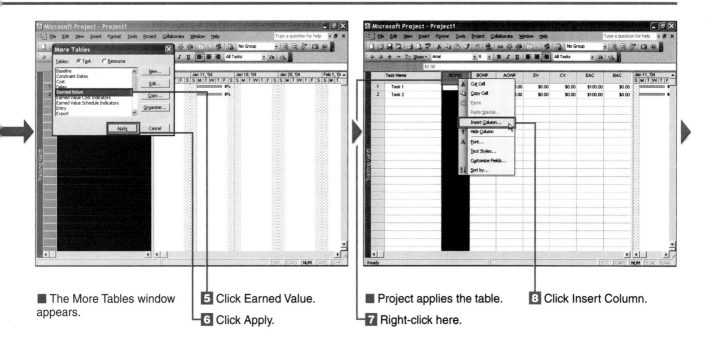

■ The More Tables window appears.

5 Click Earned Value.

6 Click Apply.

■ Project applies the table.

7 Right-click here.

8 Click Insert Column.

CONTINUED

CALCULATE BASIC EARNED VALUE (CONTINUED)

To understand the way that Project updates Earned Value fields as you work, create a custom table that contains columns for the Earned Value Method, BCWS, BCWP, ACWP, the Percent Complete, the Physical Percent Complete, the Actual Duration, and the Actual Work fields. If you do not want to calculate earned value using the Physical Percent Complete earned value calculation

method for any of your tasks, you can exclude either the Earned Value Method or the Physical Percent Complete columns in your custom table. The example in this includes these columns so that you can see the effect that Physical Percent Complete field values have on earned value calculations.

Project does not begin to calculate any of the earned value fields until

you set a baseline for the project. When you set a baseline, Project immediately calculates budgeted cost of work scheduled (BCWS) as the baseline cost of the task up through the status date or today's date if you have not set a status date. In this part of the exercise, the baseline was set on January 9, just before the project begins, so earned values will remain at $0.

CALCULATE BASIC EARNED VALUE (CONTINUED)

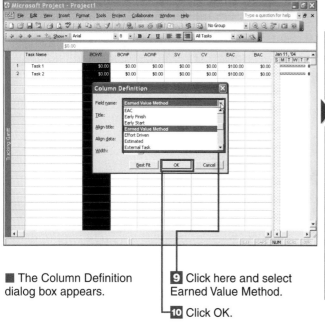

■ The Column Definition dialog box appears.

9 Click here and select Earned Value Method.

10 Click OK.

■ Project inserts the field.

11 Right-click the SV column heading.

12 Repeat steps 8 to 10 four times, changing step 10 to add % Complete, Physical % Complete, Actual Duration, and Actual Work.

■ Project inserts each column.

What information does Project store in a baseline?

✔ For tasks, Project saves duration, start and finish dates, work, timephased work, cost, and timephased cost. For resources, Project saves work, timephased work, cost, and timephased cost information with the baseline. For assignments, Project saves start and finish dates, work, timephased work, costs, and timephased costs.

What does SV tell me?

✔ SV stands for Schedule Variance and shows you the difference between the current progress of a task and the baseline plan for the task up to the status date or today's date if you did not set a status date.

What does EAC tell me?

✔ EAC stands for Estimate at Completion and is also called Forecast at Completion. EAC provides you with the expected total cost of a task or project given the work performed as of the status date and, in Project, is represented by the Total Cost field.

What does VAC tell me?

✔ VAC stands for *Variance at Completion* and shows you the difference between the budgeted project or task total cost — BAC — and the expected total cost of the project or task given the work performed as of the status date — EAC.

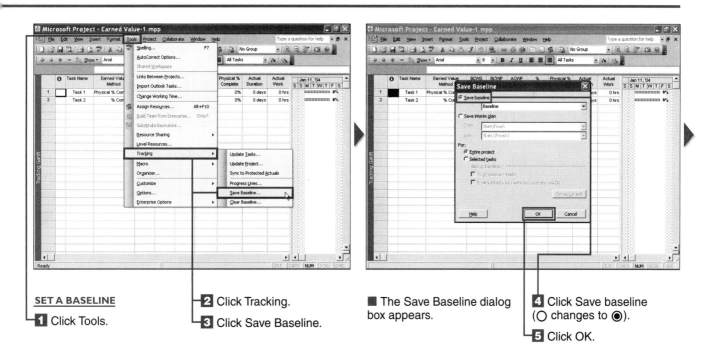

SET A BASELINE

1 Click Tools.

2 Click Tracking.

3 Click Save Baseline.

■ The Save Baseline dialog box appears.

4 Click Save baseline (○ changes to ◉).

5 Click OK.

CONTINUED ▶

CALCULATE BASIC EARNED VALUE (CONTINUED)

I f you set a status date, Project calculates earned value fields based on the project's status date; otherwise, Project calculates the values based on today's date. You can move the date forward and backward to determine earned values at any point in time.

Once you set a baseline, BCWS equals the sum of the baseline costs of the task as of the status date. If

the status date is later than the project start date, BCWS equals the amount that you schedule to earn up to the status date.

When you set a status date, Project assumes that the end of that day has occurred and includes that date in earned value calculations. Suppose that you have a task costing $25 per day scheduled to begin on Monday, January 12 and

end four days later. If you set the status date to Friday, January 9, 2004, then BCWS equals $0. If you reset the status date to Monday, January 12, BCWS equals $25. On January 13, BCWS equals $50. On January 15 and later, BCWS equals $100. When you set the earned value calculation date in this exercise, the current date is January 14.

CALCULATE BASIC EARNED VALUE (CONTINUED)

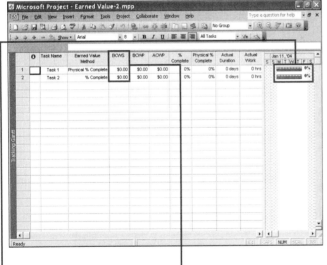

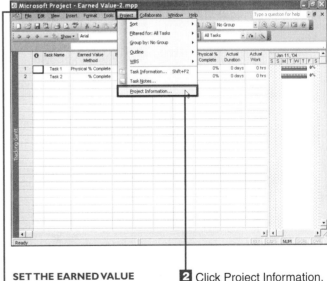

■ Project stores a baseline for your project and establishes a BCWS value equal to the total scheduled cost of the project as of the current date.

■ In this example, no status date was set and the current date is January 9, which is prior to the beginning of the project, BCWS equals $0.

SET THE EARNED VALUE CALCULATION DATE

1 Click Project.

2 Click Project Information.

What happens to earned value calculations if I clear the baseline?

✔ ACWP does not change. BCWS, BCWP, and SV reset to $0. EAC and VAC return to their pre-baseline values. Project recalculates CV based on the new SV value. Earned value calculations are really meaningful only if you have set a baseline.

What does CV show me?

✔ CV answers the question, "When I compare what I planned to do versus my performance so far, how am I doing with respect to cost?" Positive CV shows an under budget state and a Negative CV indicates an over budget state for the work done so far.

What does SV show me?

✔ SV stands for *Schedule Variance* and shows you the difference between the budgeted cost of work scheduled and the budgeted cost of work performed. You can use SV to help you determine whether your task or project is ahead of or behind schedule in terms of cost. If the SV value is positive, your task or project is ahead of schedule in terms of cost, but if SV is negative, your task or project is behind schedule in terms of cost.

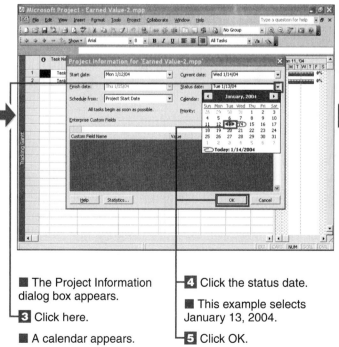

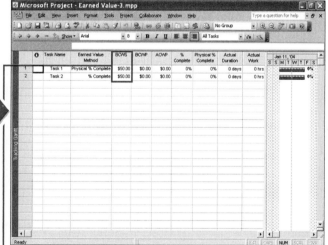

■ The Project Information dialog box appears.

3 Click here.

■ A calendar appears.

4 Click the status date.

■ This example selects January 13, 2004.

5 Click OK.

■ Project recalculates the BCWS value based on the status date.

■ In this example, BCWS equals one-half of the scheduled cost because the status date is one-half of the way to the task's scheduled finish date.

■ If you set the status date to January 14, BCWS equals 75% of the task's scheduled cost.

CONTINUED ▶

CALCULATE BASIC EARNED VALUE (CONTINUED)

Project updates the Budgeted Cost of Work Performed, BCWP, when you enter a value in the Physical Percent Complete field only if you set the earned value calculation method to Physical Percent Complete. To set the earned value calculation method, see the section "Select an Earned Value Calculation Method" in this chapter. Project calculates BCWP as the amount of the task's budget that you should have spent based on the status date and the earned value calculation method. If you use the Percent Complete earned value method, Project updates BCWP along with ACWP when you record actuals.

If you set a status date, Project calculates BCWP as of the status date; otherwise, Project calculates BCWP as of today's date.

Project updates the ACWP when you record a value for actual duration, actual work, or percent complete. If you have set a status date, Project calculates the ACWP as of the status date; otherwise, Project calculates ACWP as of today. Project calculates ACWP by multiplying the rates of resources assigned to the task by the value of actual work that you enter. Project also adds fixed costs to the calculation for ACWP.

CALCULATE BASIC EARNED VALUE (CONTINUED)

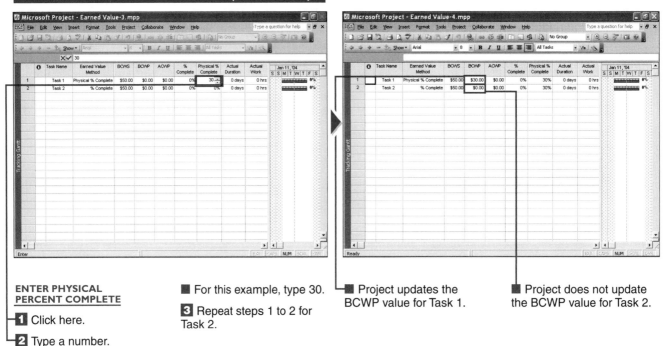

ENTER PHYSICAL PERCENT COMPLETE

1 Click here.

2 Type a number.

■ For this example, type 30.

3 Repeat steps 1 to 2 for Task 2.

■ Project updates the BCWP value for Task 1.

■ Project does not update the BCWP value for Task 2.

I entered a value into Physical Percent Complete and Project did not update BCWP. Why not?

✔ You set the earned value method of the task to Percent Complete, not Physical Percent Complete. When you use this method, Project does not calculate a BCWP value until you record actual work using either a Percent Complete value, an Actual Duration value, or an Actual Work value.

What does SPI show me?

✔ SPI, or *Schedule Performance Index,* represents the ratio of budgeted costs of work performed to budgeted costs of work scheduled. If the SPI value is over 1, your task or project is ahead of schedule.

What does CPI show me?

✔ CPI stands for *Cost Performance Index* and represents the ratio of budgeted costs of work performed to actual costs of work performed as of the status date. If the CPI value is over 1, your task or project is under budget. You can view this value distributed over time in the Task Usage view.

What does TCPI show me?

✔ TCPI stands for *To Complete Performance Index* and represents the ratio of budgeted work left to perform to unspent budgeted funds as of the status date.

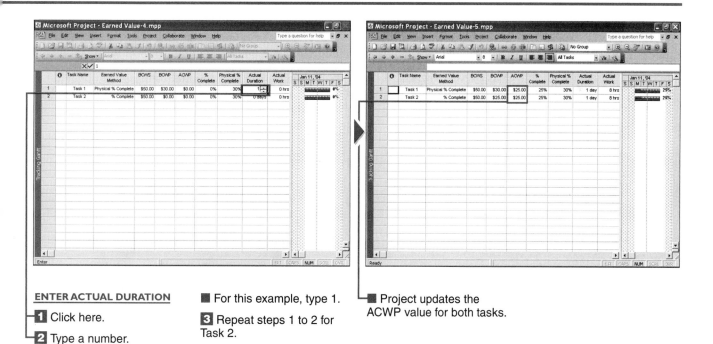

ENTER ACTUAL DURATION

1 Click here.

2 Type a number.

■ For this example, type 1.

3 Repeat steps 1 to 2 for Task 2.

■ Project updates the ACWP value for both tasks.

COMPARE EXPECTED TO ACTUAL COSTS

You can use the four Earned Value tables to forecast whether a task will finish within the budget based on the comparison of the actual costs incurred for the task to date and the baseline cost of the task. For detailed instructions on displaying a specific table, see Chapter 7.

The Earned Value Table for Tasks

When you use the Earned Value table for tasks, you can compare the relationship between work and costs for tasks. This table helps you evaluate your budget to estimate future budget needs and prepare an accounting statement of your project. You can use the information in the table to determine whether sufficient work is getting done for the money you are paying, or whether tasks need more money, less money, or should be cut. All the fields in this table are calculated except EAC and BAC. You can enter values in those fields to change information in the table.

	Task Name	BCWS	BCWP	ACWP	SV	CV	EAC	BAC	VAC
1	⊟ **Build a pool**	**$4,400.00**	**$3,600.00**	**$3,850.00**	**($800.00)**	**($250.00)**	**$5,133.33**	**$4,800.00**	**($333.33)**
2	⊟ Dig the hole	$800.00	$800.00	$750.00	$0.00	$50.00	$750.00	$800.00	$50.00
	Guys	$800.00	$800.00	$750.00	$0.00	$50.00		$800.00	$50.00
3	⊟ Pour the pool	$1,600.00	$1,600.00	$1,900.00	$0.00	($300.00)	$1,900.00	$1,600.00	($300.00)
	Guys	$1,200.00	$1,200.00	$1,500.00	$0.00	($300.00)		$1,200.00	($300.00)
4	⊟ Build the deck	$1,600.00	$1,200.00	$1,200.00	($400.00)	$0.00	$1,600.00	$1,600.00	$0.00
	Guys	$1,600.00	$1,200.00	$1,200.00	($400.00)	$0.00		$1,600.00	$0.00
5	⊟ Screen the pool	$400.00	$0.00	$0.00	($400.00)	$0.00	$800.00	$800.00	$0.00
	Guys	$400.00	$0.00	$0.00	($400.00)	$0.00		$800.00	$0.00
6	⊟ **Landscape**	**$0.00**	**$0.00**	**$0.00**	**$0.00**	**$0.00**	**$300.00**	**$300.00**	**$0.00**
7	⊟ Replant grass	$0.00	$0.00	$0.00	$0.00	$0.00	$100.00	$100.00	$0.00
	Guys	$0.00	$0.00	$0.00	$0.00	$0.00		$100.00	$0.00
8	⊟ Plant shrubs	$0.00	$0.00	$0.00	$0.00	$0.00	$100.00	$100.00	$0.00
	Guys	$0.00	$0.00	$0.00	$0.00	$0.00		$100.00	$0.00
9	⊟ Mow lawn	$0.00	$0.00	$0.00	$0.00	$0.00	$100.00	$100.00	$0.00
	Gasoline	$0.00	$0.00	$0.00	$0.00	$0.00		$0.00	$0.00
	Guys	$0.00	$0.00	$0.00	$0.00	$0.00		$100.00	$0.00

Using the Earned Value Table for Resources

When you use the Earned Value table for resources, you can compare the relationship between work and costs for resources. This table also helps you evaluate your budget to estimate future budget needs and prepare an accounting statement for your project. You can use the information in the table to determine whether the work is getting done for the money that you are paying or whether you need more or less of a particular resource. All the fields in this table are calculated, except BAC. You can enter values in the BAC field to change information in the table.

To display the Earned Value table for resources, start in any resource view, such as the Resource Sheet view.

	Resource Name	BCWS	BCWP	ACWP	SV	CV	EAC	BAC	VAC
1	Gasoline	$0.00	$0.00	$0.00	$0.00	$0.00	$0.00	$0.00	$0.00
2	Guys	$4,000.00	$3,200.00	$3,450.00	($800.00)	($250.00)	$4,950.00	$4,700.00	($367.19)
3	Concrete	$0.00	$0.00	$0.00	$0.00	$0.00	$0.00	$0.00	$0.00
4	Lumber	$0.00	$0.00	$0.00	$0.00	$0.00	$0.00	$0.00	$0.00

The Earned Value Cost Indicators Table

Project 2003 introduced the Earned Value Cost Indicators table Available only on task views, the Earned Value Cost Indicators table helps you compare the various budgeted and actual cost factors in your project. In this table, you find BCWS, BCWP, CV, CV%, CPI, BAC, EAC, VAC, and TCIP. At the heart of budgeted earned value analysis, BCWS measures the budgeted cost of individual tasks based on the resources and fixed costs that are assigned to the tasks when you schedule them, and BCWP indicates how much of a task's budget should have been spent given the actual duration of the task. CV represents the difference between how much a task or the project should have cost and how much it has actually cost. CV% compares cost variance to budgeted cost of work performed. BAC represents the baseline cost, while EAC represents the estimated cost at completion and VAC represents the difference between BAC and EAC. CPI and TCPI are both ratios. CPI focuses on work already performed and compares baseline to actual costs. TCPI focuses on what you have not yet completed and shows the relationship of work remaining to be done to funds remaining to be spent.

The Earned Value Schedule Indicators Table

Project 2003 also introduced the Earned Value Schedule Indicators table, which helps you focus on the effects of scheduling variances on the cost of your project. Also available only on task views, the Earned Value Schedule Indicators table contains BCWS, BCWP, SV, SV%, and SPI. SV represents the difference, in dollars, between the baseline schedule and current progress on the schedule. SV% compares schedule variance to budgeted cost of work scheduled. SPI compares the budgeted cost of work performed to the budgeted cost of work scheduled.

	Task Name	BCWS	BCWP	SV	SV%	SPI
1	Build a pool	$4,400.00	$3,600.00	($800.00)	-18%	0.82
2	Dig the hole	$800.00	$800.00	$0.00	0%	1
3	Pour the pool	$1,600.00	$1,600.00	$0.00	0%	1
4	Build the deck	$1,600.00	$1,200.00	($400.00)	-25%	0.75
5	Screen the pool	$400.00	$0.00	($400.00)	-100%	0
6	Landscape	$0.00	$0.00	$0.00	0%	0
7	Replant grass	$0.00	$0.00	$0.00	0%	0
8	Plant shrubs	$0.00	$0.00	$0.00	0%	0
9	Mow lawn	$0.00	$0.00	$0.00	0%	0

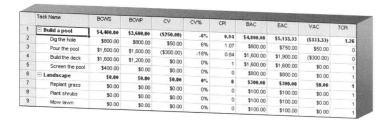

	Task Name	BCWS	BCWP	CV	CV%	CPI	BAC	EAC	VAC	TCPI
1	Build a pool	$4,400.00	$3,600.00	($250.00)	-6%	0.94	$4,800.00	$5,133.33	($333.33)	1.26
2	Dig the hole	$800.00	$800.00	$50.00	6%	1.07	$800.00	$750.00	$50.00	0
3	Pour the pool	$1,600.00	$1,600.00	($300.00)	-18%	0.84	$1,600.00	$1,900.00	($300.00)	0
4	Build the deck	$1,600.00	$1,200.00	$0.00	0%	1	$1,600.00	$1,600.00	$0.00	1
5	Screen the pool	$400.00	$0.00	$0.00	0%	0	$800.00	$800.00	$0.00	1
6	Landscape	$0.00	$0.00	$0.00	0%	0	$300.00	$300.00	$0.00	1
7	Replant grass	$0.00	$0.00	$0.00	0%	0	$100.00	$100.00	$0.00	1
8	Plant shrubs	$0.00	$0.00	$0.00	0%	0	$100.00	$100.00	$0.00	1
9	Mow lawn	$0.00	$0.00	$0.00	0%	0	$100.00	$100.00	$0.00	1

EXPORT AND CHART EARNED VALUE INFORMATION USING EXCEL

You can use Microsoft Excel to assist you in evaluating and charting earned value information. Pictures often explain a situation better than words, and, when looking at earned value information, you may find it easier to understand the information if you view a picture rather than study Project's Earned Value tables.

To enable Microsoft Excel 5.0 or later to create a chart, you first must export Project data to Excel. Doing so saves you from having to retype any earned value information into Excel. During the process of exporting earned value information from Project to Excel, you create an Excel workbook that contains a task ID, a task name, and various earned values for each

task. The earned values that you store in an Excel workbook in this section are the earned values that appear on the Earned Value table for tasks.

After you create the Excel workbook that contains your Project earned value information, you open it in Excel and create a chart.

EXPORT AND CHART EARNED VALUE INFORMATION USING EXCEL

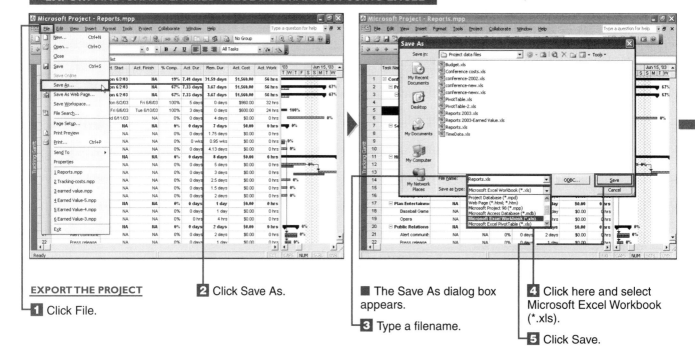

EXPORT THE PROJECT

1 Click File.

2 Click Save As.

■ The Save As dialog box appears.

3 Type a filename.

4 Click here and select Microsoft Excel Workbook (*.xls).

5 Click Save.

When do I identify the earned value fields I want to export?

✔ When you select the Earned Value map in the Export Wizard, Project automatically exports all the earned value fields that appear on the Earned Value table. If you want to export additional earned value fields, you need to modify the map to include those fields. Rather than modifying a predefined map, you should consider creating a new map that contains the fields you want to export. See Chapter 23 for details on reviewing the fields in a map.

Does it matter what view and table I am displaying when I export Project information to an Excel file?

✔ No. The map you choose automatically selects data from your Project file to include in the Excel workbook. You can view the Gantt Chart with the Entry table, and Project still exports earned value information when you select the Earned Value map.

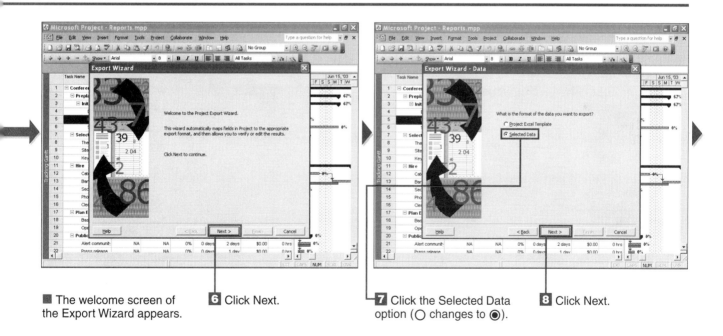

■ The welcome screen of the Export Wizard appears.

6 Click Next.

7 Click the Selected Data option (○ changes to ◉).

8 Click Next.

CONTINUED ▶

EXPORT AND CHART EARNED VALUE INFORMATION USING EXCEL (CONTINUED)

You use a predefined template called a *map* to select the earned value fields to export to Excel, and the map also contains information that formats the data into an Excel workbook. When you use the predefined map for earned value, you do not need to edit your data in Excel. Project automatically exports the task ID, name, and all the earned value fields you see in the Earned Value table. You can

export additional earned value fields by adding them to the map or by creating a new map that contains them. You can find more information about export maps in Chapter 23.

Once you create an Excel workbook containing the earned value information in your Project file, you can open the workbook in Excel, where you see the earned

values for the tasks in your project. Then, using Excel's Chart Wizard, you can create charts of earned value information. The Chart Wizard walks you through the process of creating a chart in a fairly painless way. The charts help to better illustrate the earned value data, making it easier for your audience to identify cost or schedule issues.

EXPORT AND CHART EARNED VALUE INFORMATION USING EXCEL (CONTINUED)

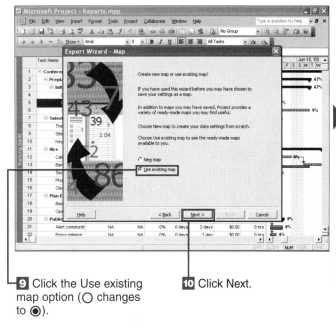

9 Click the Use existing map option (○ changes to ◉).

10 Click Next.

11 Click Earned value information.

■ You can continue through the wizard to change options of the Earned Value map.

12 Click Finish.

■ Project redisplays your project.

Why did I ignore the Project Excel template when selecting the export map?

✔ You ignored the Project Excel template because it is a predefined map that exports Project data to Excel. It does not, however, export earned value fields. Instead, it exports the Entry table fields to Excel.

Why did I not need to click Next after selecting Earned value information in the Export Wizard?

✔ When you select the Earned value information map, you give Project sufficient information to create an Excel file containing the earned value fields that appear on the Earned Value table for tasks.

If I click Next instead of Finish, what happens?

✔ First, a box appears where you can include earned values for tasks, resources, and assignments in the exported file. By default, the map selects tasks only. You also can include column headings and assignment rows in the file. By default, the map includes column headings but does not include assignment rows. You can add or remove fields from the exported file on subsequent screens. You can also reorder the information in the export file.

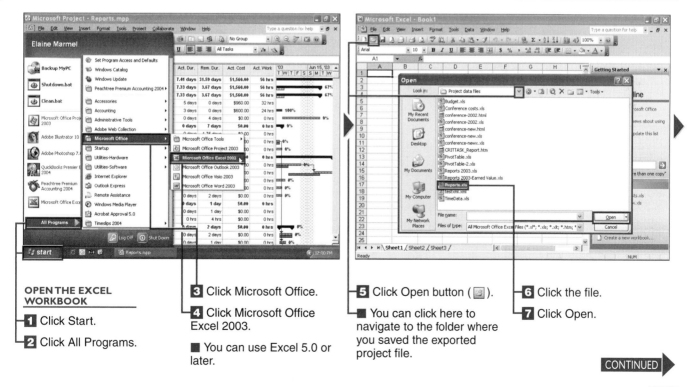

OPEN THE EXCEL WORKBOOK

1 Click Start.

2 Click All Programs.

3 Click Microsoft Office.

4 Click Microsoft Office Excel 2003.

■ You can use Excel 5.0 or later.

5 Click Open button (📷).

■ You can click here to navigate to the folder where you saved the exported project file.

6 Click the file.

7 Click Open.

CONTINUED

EXPORT AND CHART EARNED VALUE INFORMATION USING EXCEL (CONTINUED)

For each of Excel's 14 types of charts, Excel offers several sub-types that are variations of the chart type. For example, when you choose a column chart type, you can use a sub-type to cluster the bars next to each other or stack the bars on top of each other.

After you select a chart type, you identify the values that Excel should

include on the chart. Excel always places numbers on the Y (vertical) axis of a chart by default; you identify the information — called a *data series* — that should appear on the X (horizontal) axis of the chart. Think of a data series as a collection of data values. In the world of spreadsheets, a row is one data series and a column is another data series. In this example, all the information

for a given task appears on one row, and all earned values of a particular type appear in one column. In this example, you chart EAC and BAC for four tasks, so the data series you chart on the X-axis comes from columns in the workbook. In the following steps, the Series1 is already renamed to EAC and you see how to rename Series2.

EXPORT AND CHART EARNED VALUE INFORMATION USING EXCEL (CONTINUED)

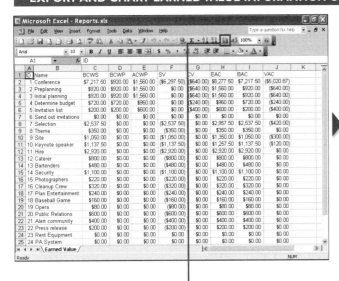

■ The earned value information from your project in an Excel workbook.

8 Click Chart Wizard (📊).

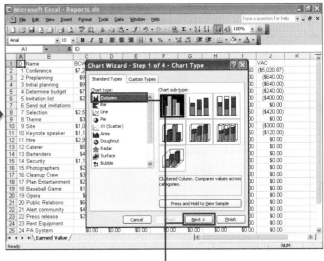

■ The first Chart Wizard dialog box appears.

9 Click Column.

10 Click Next.

Can I change the chart title without using the Chart Wizard?

✓ Yes. Click the title in the finished chart once to select it. Then, click again. Move the insertion point that appears as necessary using the arrow keys, the Backspace key, and the Delete key, and make changes to the title. Do not double-click the title. If you do, the Format Chart Title dialog box appears. In this dailog box, you cannot change the title, but you can change the formatting for the title, such as its font and alignment.

Can I preview the chart type I select?

✓ Yes. After you select the chart type, click Press and Hold to View Sample to preview the chart.

How do I change the chart type after I create the chart?

✓ While viewing the chart, restart the Chart Wizard by clicking the Chart Wizard button (🔲) on the toolbar. In the Chart Type dialog box that appears, select a new chart type and sub-type. Click Finish, and Excel changes the chart type without making any other changes.

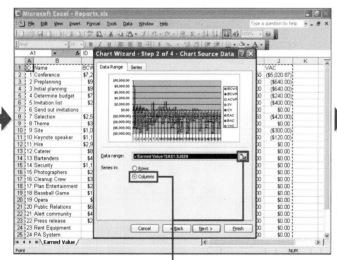

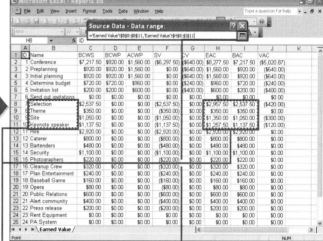

■ The Data Range tab of the Chart Source Data dialog box appears.

11 Click the Columns option (○ changes to ◉).

12 Click the Collapse button (🔳).

■ Excel hides the dialog box.

13 Select cells in the rows and columns containing the information that you want to chart.

■ To select non-contiguous columns, press and hold the Ctrl key while you drag.

14 Click the Expand button (🔲).

■ The Chart Wizard redisplays.

CONTINUED ▶

EXPORT AND CHART EARNED VALUE INFORMATION USING EXCEL (CONTINUED)

You can include column or row titles when you select data to plot. If you do, Excel uses the titles as labels. If you do not include titles when you select data — and sometimes it is not convenient to include them because they do not appear close to the data — you can specify the titles on the Series tab of the Chart Source Data box in the Chart Wizard. You can identify the titles either by selecting them in your

Excel workbook or by typing the titles. In this example, you type the titles yourself.

After selecting data series for the chart and labeling the data series, you can set a wide variety of chart options. For example, you can supply a title for the chart and individual titles for each axis of the chart. You also can add gridlines to the chart. By default, Excel displays

major gridlines that run horizontally across from whole numbers on the Y-axis. You can include major gridlines that run vertically on the chart from the X-axis, and you can include minor gridlines running in either or both directions. A note of caution here: too many lines on the chart obscure meaning.

EXPORT AND CHART EARNED VALUE INFORMATION USING EXCEL (CONTINUED)

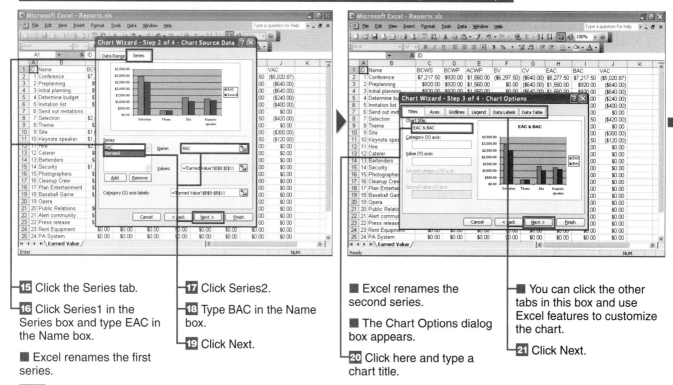

15 Click the Series tab.

16 Click Series1 in the Series box and type EAC in the Name box.

■ Excel renames the first series.

17 Click Series2.

18 Type BAC in the Name box.

19 Click Next.

■ Excel renames the second series.

■ The Chart Options dialog box appears.

20 Click here and type a chart title.

■ You can click the other tabs in this box and use Excel features to customize the chart.

21 Click Next.

If I make a mistake when selecting data series, how do I correct the mistake?

✔ Click the Chart Wizard button (image) on the toolbar to restart the Chart Wizard while viewing the chart. Click Next in the Chart Type dialog box to display the Chart Source Data dialog box. Then, follow steps 11 to 14 and, if necessary, steps 15 to 19 to make changes to the data series.

Can I change the values that appear in the chart?

✔ Yes. Change them in the workbook. Remember, though, the values do not change in Project.

What does the Data Table tab of the Chart Options dialog box do?

✔ When you click the Show data table box option (□ changes to ☑) on this tab, Project includes the data values Excel used to plot your chart on the chart. Deselect this box (☑ changes to □) to remove the effect.

What does the Data Labels tab of the Chart Options dialog box do?

✔ Using this tab, you can place labels on each data series on the chart. In this exercise, you can display the EAC and BAC dollar amounts at the top of each bar.

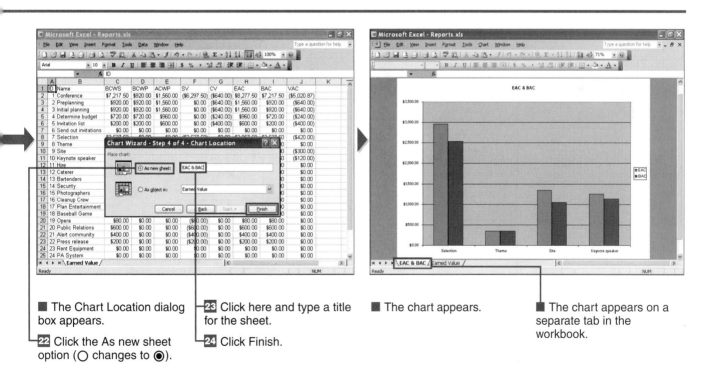

■ The Chart Location dialog box appears.

22 Click the As new sheet option (○ changes to ◉).

23 Click here and type a title for the sheet.

24 Click Finish.

■ The chart appears.

■ The chart appears on a separate tab in the workbook.

ANALYZE TIMESCALED INFORMATION

Y ou can send timephased earned value data from Project to Excel so that you can use Excel's features to chart the data. Charts provide visual representations of data that can clarify information that is not obvious when you look at the raw numbers used to create the chart. You may find it useful, for example, to compare budgeted cost of work performed to the actual cost of work performed for a particular

time period, as you do in the steps of this section. Comparing these values can tell you if your project is currently over or under its estimated cost.

You do not need to retype any Project timephased information into Excel; instead, you can use the Analyze Timescaled Data Wizard, which automatically exports information to Microsoft Excel version 5.0 or later. For more about

Project's capabilities to export and import data, see Chapter 23.

When you use the Analyze Timescaled Data Wizard, you identify the information in your project that you want to send to Excel; when you export the data, Project opens Excel for you and automatically creates a workbook containing the values you selected to export.

ANALYZE TIMESCALED INFORMATION

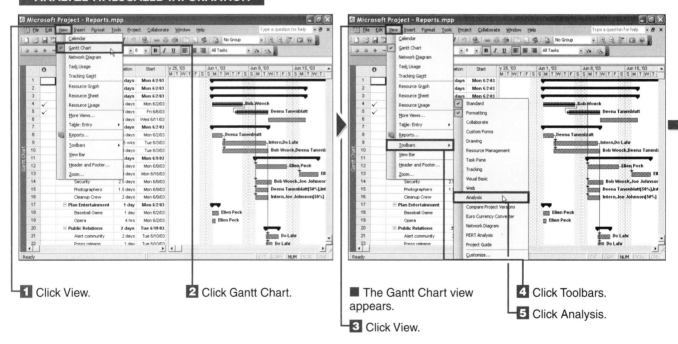

■1 Click View.

■2 Click Gantt Chart.

■ The Gantt Chart view appears.

■3 Click View.

■4 Click Toolbars.

■5 Click Analysis.

Can I create a chart for any time frame unit that I want?

✔ The choices in the Unit list include Hours, Days, Weeks, Months, Quarters, and Years. The time frame unit you use should relate to the date range you intend to chart. Your chart becomes difficult to read if you chart a six month date range in hours.

Can I create a chart for any date range that I want?

✔ Yes, but consider the units as well as the date range. If you want to create a chart that covers years, use Months or Years for the unit.

Can I add fields other than BCWP and ACWP?

✔ Yes, you can add any of the timephased fields that appear in the second box of the Analyze Timescaled Data Wizard. Be careful not to chart too many fields at the same time. Excel can handle as many fields as you can select, but the chart may become difficult to read.

Why did I select some tasks instead of the project?

✔ The example selects tasks for which actual work was performed to give the chart meaning because it was charting ACWP.

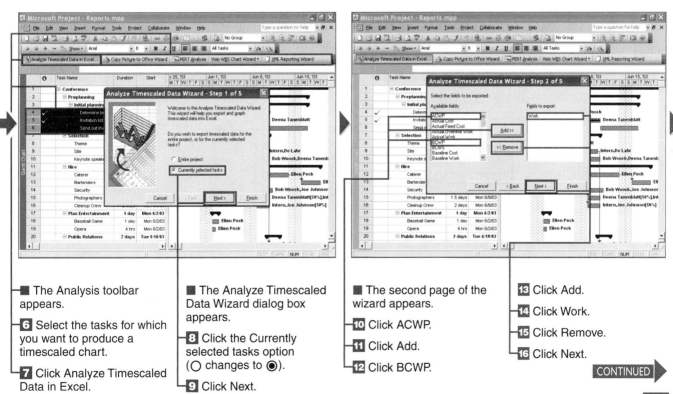

■ The Analysis toolbar appears.

6 Select the tasks for which you want to produce a timescaled chart.

7 Click Analyze Timescaled Data in Excel.

■ The Analyze Timescaled Data Wizard dialog box appears.

8 Click the Currently selected tasks option (○ changes to ●).

9 Click Next.

■ The second page of the wizard appears.

10 Click ACWP.

11 Click Add.

12 Click BCWP.

13 Click Add.

14 Click Work.

15 Click Remove.

16 Click Next.

CONTINUED

ANALYZE TIMESCALED INFORMATION (CONTINUED)

After the Analyze Timescale Data Wizard exports the information, the workbook that appears in Excel contains values for the fields that you selected to send over the time period you specified. For example, if you specify daily values for ACWP and BCWP, the worksheet will contain one column for each day of the time period; the rows will show the

ACWP and BCWP values broken down by task.

The Analyze Timescale Data Wizard gives you the option of producing a chart in Excel automatically. If you let the wizard produce the chart, Project bases the chart on the totals for ACWP and BCWP. In the worksheet, individual values for each task appear, but the chart is based on the sum of the individual task values.

Once the information appears in Excel, you can use any of Excel's features to manipulate the data. You can change the values in the worksheet or you can make changes to the chart settings, including changing the data series. Remember that any changes you make in Excel do not affect your Project file.

ANALYZE TIMESCALED INFORMATION (CONTINUED)

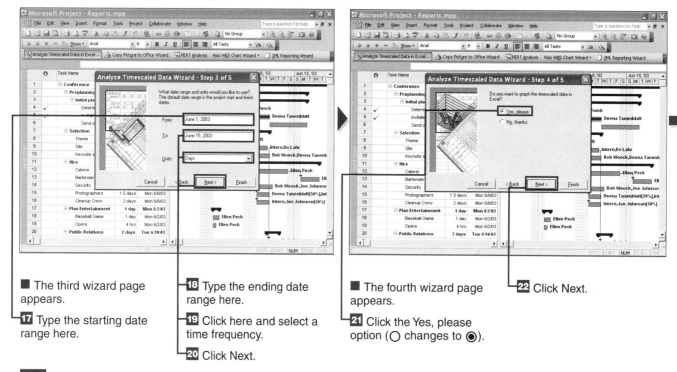

■ The third wizard page appears.

17 Type the starting date range here.

18 Type the ending date range here.

19 Click here and select a time frequency.

20 Click Next.

■ The fourth wizard page appears.

21 Click the Yes, please option (○ changes to ◉).

22 Click Next.

Can I save the Excel workbook?

✔ Yes, you can. By default, the file created in Excel is a temporary file named TimeData.txt, which is a text file, not an Excel workbook file. You can save the file as an Excel workbook the same way you save any workbook. Click File and then click Save As. Make sure that the Save As type box shows Excel Workbook (*.xls) and use the Save in box to navigate to a folder where you usually save Excel files or where you save your Project files. Then, click Save.

How do I change the chart type?

✔ The default chart is a three-dimensional line, but you can change it. While viewing the chart, click Chart and then click Chart Type. In the Chart Type box that appears, select the chart type you want from the lefthand column; in the righthand column, select the chart sub-type.

What does that box do that says Chart?

✔ You can use the Chart toolbar to make changes to the chart's options. For example, you can open the Chart Type box to change the chart type by clicking the third button from the left.

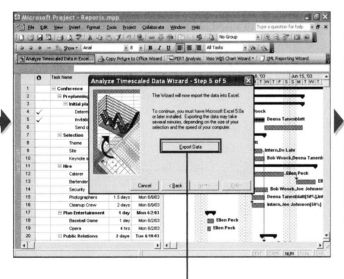

■ The last wizard page appears.

23 Click Export Data.

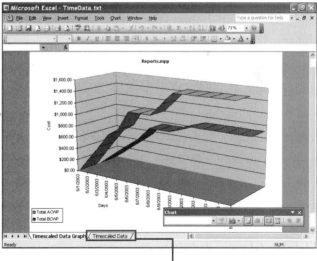

■ Excel opens and the selected data appears in a chart.

■ You can click the data to view the workbook from which the chart was created.

USING PIVOTTABLES FOR EARNED VALUE ANALYSIS

xcel *PivotTables* can be interesting and useful when you want to analyze Project earned value data. The PivotTable is an interactive table that summarizes large amounts of data in a cross-tabular format. You can rotate its columns and rows to view your data summarized in different ways. You also can display the details for some part of the data so that you can focus on that particular data.

You do not need to retype any Project earned value information into Excel; instead, you can export the earned value information in your Project file to Microsoft Excel version 5.0 or later. To learn more about Project's capabilities to export and import data, see Chapter 23.

You use the Export Wizard in Project to send earned value data to

an Excel workbook. When you create a PivotTable using earned value information, the Excel workbook contains two worksheets. On one sheet, you find the PivotTable worksheet, and on the other sheet, you find the data that Excel uses to create the PivotTable. You can start the process of creating a PivotTable using any view of your project.

USING PIVOTTABLES FOR EARNED VALUE ANALYSIS

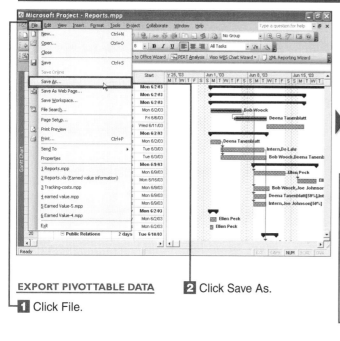

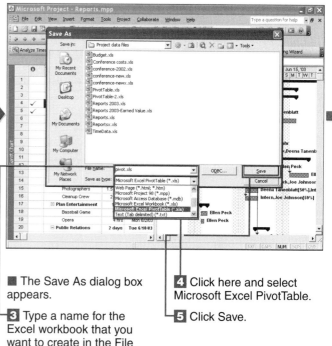

EXPORT PIVOTTABLE DATA

1 Click File.

2 Click Save As.

■ The Save As dialog box appears.

3 Type a name for the Excel workbook that you want to create in the File name box.

4 Click here and select Microsoft Excel PivotTable.

5 Click Save.

When do I identify the earned value fields to use in the PivotTable?

✔ When you select the Earned Value map in the Export Wizard in Project, Project automatically exports all the earned value fields that appear on the Earned Value table. If you want to export additional earned value fields, you must modify the map to include those fields. Rather than modifying a predefined map, consider creating a new map that contains the fields you want to export. See Chapter 23 for details on reviewing the fields in a map.

Does it matter what view and table I am displaying when I export earned information to create a PivotTable?

✔ No. When you select a map, Project automatically determines what data from your Project file to include in the Excel workbook. Project then uses this data when creating the PivotTable.

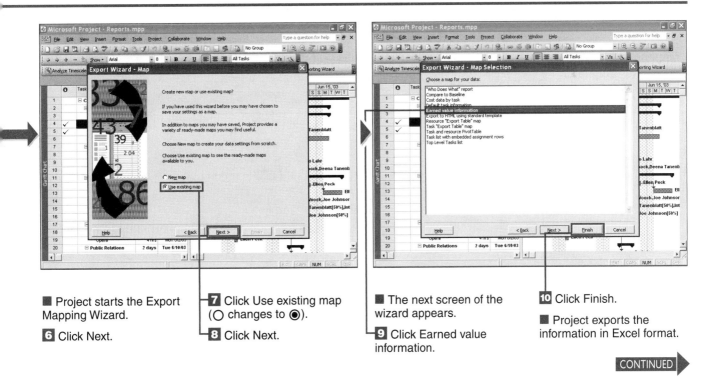

■ Project starts the Export Mapping Wizard.

6 Click Next.

7 Click Use existing map (○ changes to ◉).

8 Click Next.

■ The next screen of the wizard appears.

9 Click Earned value information.

10 Click Finish.

■ Project exports the information in Excel format.

CONTINUED ▶

USING PIVOTTABLES FOR EARNED VALUE ANALYSIS (CONTINUED)

PivotTables, also called PivotTable reports, are very useful when you want to analyze totals of related information. PivotTable reports are especially useful when you have a lot of figures to add up and you want to compare more than one fact about each figure. For example, you may want to analyze CV and SV for every task in the project. Although a spreadsheet shows lists of data, a PivotTable summarizes

the various pieces of information and lets you move those pieces around to see how they all relate to each other.

Because a PivotTable report is interactive, you can change the view of the data to view more details for a particular part of the table while hiding details for the rest of the table. You can also calculate counts or averages in the PivotTable. PivotTable reports help

you compare information, reveal patterns and relationships, and analyze trends.

The PivotTable received its name because you can rotate or "pivot" rows and columns into different arrangements to see different patterns. In a PivotTable report, each column in your source data becomes a PivotTable field that summarizes multiple rows of information.

USING PIVOTTABLES FOR EARNED VALUE ANALYSIS (CONTINUED)

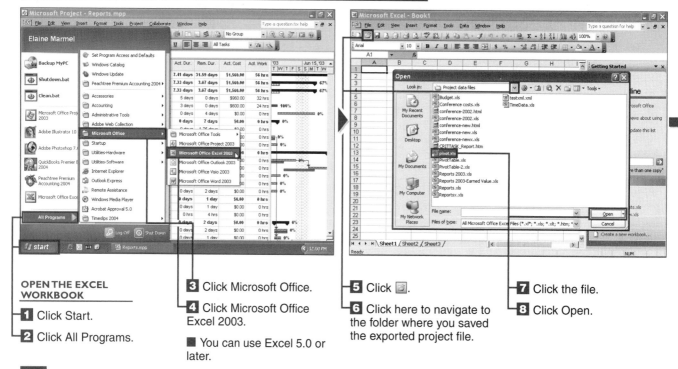

OPEN THE EXCEL WORKBOOK

■1 Click Start.

■2 Click All Programs.

■3 Click Microsoft Office.

■4 Click Microsoft Office Excel 2003.

■ You can use Excel 5.0 or later.

■5 Click 🗐.

■6 Click here to navigate to the folder where you saved the exported project file.

■7 Click the file.

■8 Click Open.

How can I rearrange information in a PivotTable?

✔ You can drag a column heading in the PivotTable up, down, left, or right to a new location, which changes the way Excel summarizes the information in the PivotTable. You also can use the PivotTable Field List to add fields to the table. By default, the PivotTable displays all the fields in the exported file as columns, but you can also add them as rows or rearrange them by dragging so that columns become rows.

How can I hide or display details?

✔ By default, you can view all details in the PivotTable created using Project data. To hide details, click the ⊡ next to a PivotTable column heading. A list of possible values for that column appears. To the left of each value is a check box. To hide details, deselect the check box next to any combination of values (☑ changes to ☐). To redisplay details, click the ⊡ again and check the boxes (☐ changes to ☑).

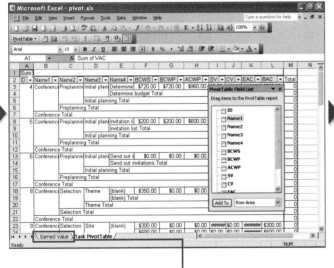

■ The pivot table sheet appears in the workbook.

9 Click the Earned Value tab.

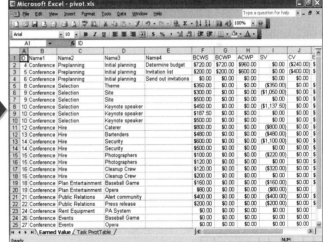

■ Excel displays the earned value data that it used to generate the PivotTable.

SECTION V

18) PROJECT SERVER AND THE PROJECT/RESOURCE MANAGER

19) PROJECT SERVER AND THE DAY-TO-DAY USER

20) PROJECT SERVER AND THE EXECUTIVE

CONSOLIDATE PROJECTS

Organization is a cornerstone of good project management, and in a large project, the sheer number of tasks makes the job of organizing the project more difficult than usual. You can use the concept of consolidated projects in Project to help you address the issue of organizing a large project. Essentially, when you use consolidation, you break large projects into smaller slices of the pie that you work in to schedule tasks, assign resources and costs to tasks, and generally perform all the functions you would perform in any project. You can link a task in one of the smaller projects to a task in another smaller project to retain relationships between the smaller projects in the overall project.

When you need to look at the bigger picture, you combine the smaller projects into one project — the consolidated project. In the consolidated project — sometimes called the *master project* — you can view multiple critical paths, report on the project as a whole, and address issues that affect the entire project.

Consolidate to Simplify

When you have a complex problem, finding the solution typically becomes easier if you can simplify the problem. Similarly, when you need to manage a complex project with many tasks, you may find it easier to organize the process if you deal with a limited number of tasks at one time. This allows you to focus on just the desired portion of the project. Subprojects appear as summary tasks in the consolidated project, and you can use Project's outlining tools to hide all tasks that are associated with any subproject.

Project makes it easy for you to take this approach to planning large, complex projects. By using Project's consolidation features, you can create subprojects, which you can think of as the tasks that constitute one portion of your large project. When you create a subproject, you save it as a separate project file. You can then assign resources and set up each subproject with links and constraints just as if the subproject were a separate project or the entire project instead of one part of a larger project. To view the bigger picture, you can consolidate the subprojects into one large project. When you consolidate, you insert one project into another; therefore, subprojects are also called *inserted projects*.

From the consolidated project, you can view, print, and change information for any subproject, just as if you were working with a single project. Because you insert the subproject into the consolidated project, Project retains a connection to the subproject while you work on it in the consolidated project — and updates the subproject, if you choose, with any changes you make while working in the consolidated project.

What Consolidation Can Do for You

Consolidation can help you achieve a number of objectives. For example, as often happens, different people manage different tasks in a project, and those tasks may be interdependent. By consolidating subprojects into a master project, you can create the correct dependencies to accurately display the project's schedule and necessary resources.

In addition, you may have a project that is so large that breaking it into smaller pieces can help you to organize it more effectively. By breaking the large project down into smaller segments, you may see relationships and even tasks that you may miss when working in one large project. You can refine the smaller projects so that they accurately reflect the work and resources you need to complete their tasks. Then, as needed, you can use consolidation to combine the smaller pieces and then view the big picture.

And, you may be pooling the resources of several projects and find that you need to level the resources. Consolidating enables you to link the projects sharing the resources so that you can level the resources. See Chapter 11 for information on leveling resources.

Project Server and Consolidation

If you are a Project Professional user who also uses Project Server, you may wonder if consolidation applies to you. Views in Project Server can roll up project information, but you still need consolidation techniques if you want to see one critical path across all consolidated projects.

You read about resource pooling in this chapter. Project Professional users who also use Project Server should take advantage of the Enterprise Resource Pool available through Project Server instead of using resource pooling. See Chapter 17 for more information on setting up and using the Enterprise Resource Pool.

If you are using Project Standard, you cannot take advantage of the Enterprise Resource Pool that is available in Project Server. Instead, you must use the resource pooling techniques described in this chapter.

If you are using Project Professional, you may want to consider using the Enterprise Resource Pool instead of using resource pooling as described in this chapter. To do so, see Chapter 19.

SET UP TO CONSOLIDATE PROJECTS

You must set up your projects to use consolidation when you decide to use Project's consolidation techniques. You may realize right away that the project is too large to handle in a traditional way, or you may discover that the project is bigger than you originally thought after you begin working on planning it. Suppose the Marketing department of a software company decides midway through the development

cycle to bundle various products under development. This introduces dependencies where none originally existed and provides an interesting opportunity for using consolidation.

If you decide to use consolidation before you start your project, simply create separate Microsoft Project files for various portions of the project. These files act as subprojects when you consolidate.

You must set up each subproject file so that it is complete, and you must create links within each subproject file, as necessary.

If you start a project and then decide that you want to use consolidation, you can create subprojects. Open the original large project that you created and use the techniques described in this section to create subprojects.

SET UP TO CONSOLIDATE PROJECTS

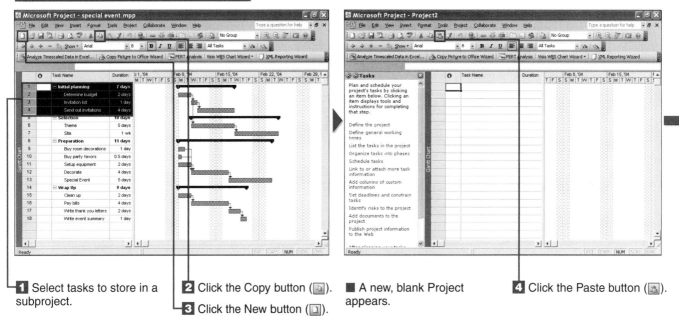

1 Select tasks to store in a subproject.

2 Click the Copy button (📋).

3 Click the New button (🗋).

■ A new, blank Project appears.

4 Click the Paste button (📋).

Do I need to set a project start date for each subproject?

✔ Because you will ultimately link together all of the subprojects, the start dates of subprojects after the first one will be driven by dependencies. You can assign a start date to the first subproject — the start date of the entire project. Or, you can simply wait and assign the start date to the consolidated project that contains all of the linked subprojects. If you intend to save the consolidated project, its start date will supersede any start date you assign to a subproject.

How do I set a project start date for the first subproject?

✔ You set the project start date for a subproject the same way that you would set it for any project — using the Project Information dialog box. Click Project, and then click Project Information to display the box.

Does the name I assign to the subproject matter?

✔ No. You can assign any name you want to any subproject or consolidated project, using Windows naming conventions.

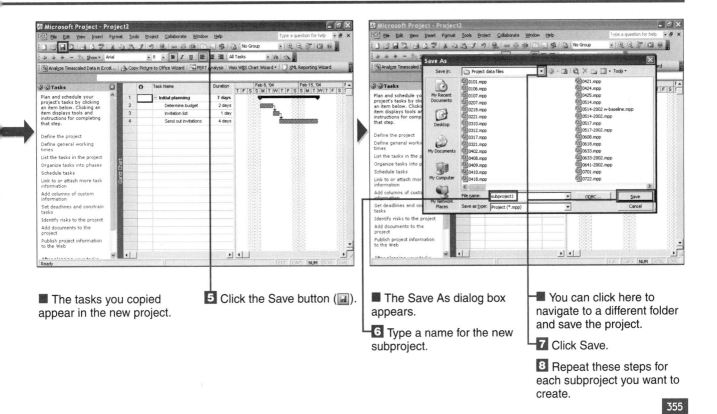

■ The tasks you copied appear in the new project.

5 Click the Save button (icon).

■ The Save As dialog box appears.

6 Type a name for the new subproject.

■ You can click here to navigate to a different folder and save the project.

7 Click Save.

8 Repeat these steps for each subproject you want to create.

CREATE A CONSOLIDATED PROJECT

After you set up the separate subprojects the way that you want, you can consolidate them into one large project. To consolidate project files, you insert projects into a host project file, often called the *consolidated project file* or the *master project file*. Each project that you insert appears as a summary task in the consolidated project file, and Project calculates inserted projects like summary tasks. An icon in the Indicator field identifies an inserted project.

You can insert projects at any outline level. The level at which an inserted project appears depends on the outline level that appears at the location where you intend to insert a project. Typically, an inserted project appears at the same level as the selected task. To produce a consolidated project in which the inserted projects line up at the highest outline level, make sure that you collapse the

preceding inserted project so that you cannot see its tasks when you insert the next subproject.

You can link inserted subprojects to their original files so that changes you make in the consolidated project will also update the subproject file.

The steps in this section assume that you are starting with a new project that will become the consolidated project file.

CREATE A CONSOLIDATED PROJECT

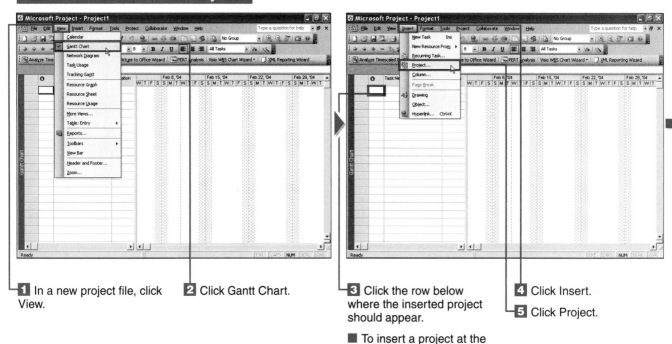

1 In a new project file, click View.

2 Click Gantt Chart.

3 Click the row below where the inserted project should appear.

■ To insert a project at the end of the consolidated project, click a blank line at the end of the project.

4 Click Insert.

5 Click Project.

I am not clear on the placement of an inserted project. Can you give more details?

✔ Project inserts projects above the selected row, just as it would a new task. If your consolidated project contains Subproject 1 and Subproject 2 that appear on consecutive rows, you can insert Subproject3 between them if you select the row containing Subproject 2 before you insert Subproject 3. To place Subproject 3 before Subproject 1, select Subproject 1 before inserting. To place Subproject 3 at the end, after both Subproject 1 and Subproject 2, select a blank line below Subproject 2.

Can I insert a subproject in between tasks of another subproject?

✔ Yes. Expand the subproject and follow steps 3 to 9 in this section.

Can you give some examples of the kind of indenting to expect when inserting projects?

✔ If the task above the selected task is indented further than the selected task, the inserted project appears at the same level as the task above the selected task. If the task above the selected task is at the same level or outdented further than the selected task, then the inserted project appears at the same level as the selected task.

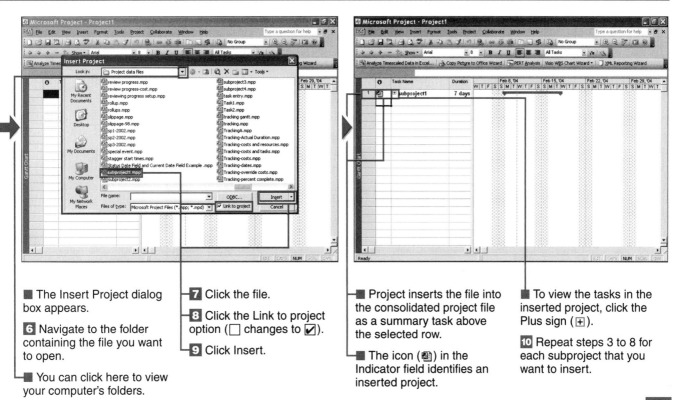

■ The Insert Project dialog box appears.

6 Navigate to the folder containing the file you want to open.

■ You can click here to view your computer's folders.

7 Click the file.

8 Click the Link to project option (☐ changes to ☑).

9 Click Insert.

■ Project inserts the file into the consolidated project file as a summary task above the selected row.

■ The icon (📷) in the Indicator field identifies an inserted project.

■ To view the tasks in the inserted project, click the Plus sign (⊞).

10 Repeat steps 3 to 8 for each subproject that you want to insert.

CONSOLIDATE ALL OPEN PROJECTS QUICKLY

Project contains a shortcut that you can use to create a consolidated project from several subprojects. This technique works well if you have several open subprojects, and helps you to avoid the Insert Project dialog box as you do in the section "Create a Consolidated Project." This technique also works well if you do not want to worry about placing the subproject in exactly the right location as you insert it.

Using this shortcut technique, you consolidate open subprojects using a dialog box. In the dialog box, you select subprojects to consolidate and Project creates a new consolidated project that contains the projects that you selected.

Project inserts the subprojects into the new consolidated project in the order in which the subprojects appear in the dialog box, and the

subprojects appear in alphabetical order in the dialog box, not in the order that you open them.

You do not need to consolidate all open projects; you can select only some open projects to include in the consolidated project.

Using this technique, Project links the subprojects in the consolidated project file to the individual subproject files. You cannot control this facet of creating a consolidated project.

CONSOLIDATE ALL OPEN PROJECTS QUICKLY

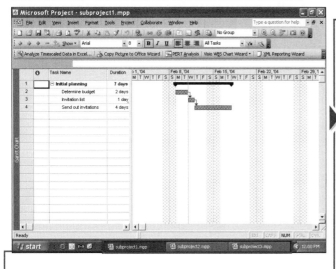

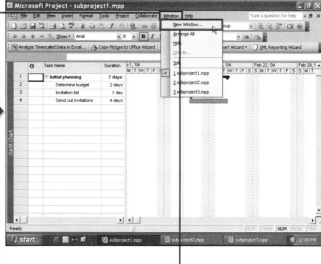

■1 Open all the projects that you want to consolidate.

Note: For more on opening projects, see Chapter 2.

■2 Click Window.

■3 Click New Window.

Can I control the order in which Project inserts the subprojects into the consolidated project?

✔ Project inserts the subprojects into the consolidated project in alphabetical name order. If you name your subprojects alphabetically so that they appear in the New Window dialog box in the order that you want them to appear in the consolidated project, Project then inserts them in the order you want. Even if you do not rename your subprojects alphabetically, you can still use this technique. Just rearrange them in the consolidated project. For more on moving tasks in a consolidated project, see the section "Reorganize a Consolidated Project."

How do I select all the subprojects in the New Window dialog box?

✔ You can press and hold Ctrl as you click each project in the Projects list. Or, you can click the first project and press and hold the Shift key as you click the last project in the list.

Is it important to link subprojects to a consolidated project file?

✔ Linking subprojects in a consolidated project to the stand-alone subproject helps ensure that you see the same information in the consolidated file that you see if you open the subproject separately.

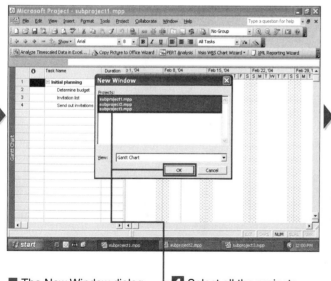

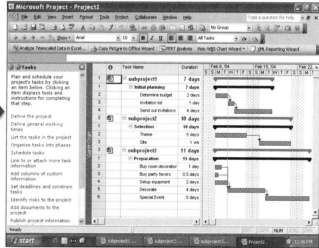

■ The New Window dialog box appears.

4 Select all the projects listed in the window.

5 Click OK.

■ Project creates a new project containing all the subprojects you selected.

UPDATE LINKS FOR INSERTED PROJECTS

In the preceding two tasks, subprojects that you included in the consolidated projects were linked to the original subproject files. Under these circumstances, if you make changes in the consolidated project, Project prompts you to update the subproject when you save or close the consolidated project. Similarly, if you open the subproject separately and make changes,

Project prompts you to update the consolidated project when you save or close the subproject.

If you do not link an inserted project to its source file, any changes that you make to the inserted project in the consolidated project file do not affect the source file. Similarly, any changes that you make to the source file do not affect the consolidated project file that contains the subproject.

The link you create when you insert a subproject works like any link that you create between two files in the Windows environment. If you rename the subproject file or move it to a different folder, you need to update the link or it does not work.

If you decide you do not want subprojects linked in a consolidated project, you can unlink them after inserting them.

UPDATE LINKS FOR INSERTED PROJECTS

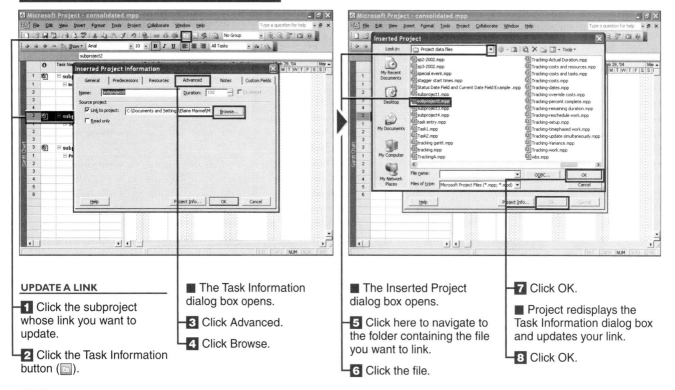

UPDATE A LINK

■1 Click the subproject whose link you want to update.

■2 Click the Task Information button (🗒).

■ The Task Information dialog box opens.

■3 Click Advanced.

■4 Click Browse.

■ The Inserted Project dialog box opens.

■5 Click here to navigate to the folder containing the file you want to link.

■6 Click the file.

■7 Click OK.

■ Project redisplays the Task Information dialog box and updates your link.

■8 Click OK.

MASTER IT

If I unlink my subproject and change my mind, is there any way to get the link back?

✔ You need to relink. You will lose any changes you make after unlinking unless you save the consolidated project, save the consolidated version, and then insert the subproject again so that your consolidated project contains two versions of the subproject — a linked version and an unlinked version. Use the information from the unlinked version to update the linked version, delete the tasks associated with the unlinked version, and resave the consolidated project and let Project update the linked subproject.

When would I not want to link subproject files in a consolidated project file?

✔ You do not need to link if you create a consolidated project file only to create dependencies between subproject files or to quickly generate a report. For more on creating dependencies, see the section "Create Dependencies in a Consolidated Project" later in this chapter.

Is there another way to fix a link because I moved the file?

✔ Click the plus sign (+) next to the subproject. Project displays the Can't Find Inserted Project dialog box, which looks like the Open dialog box. Navigate to the new location of the file and click OK.

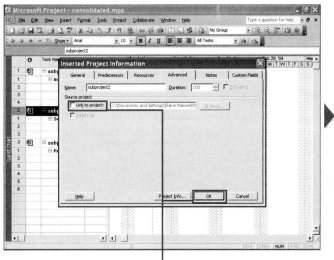

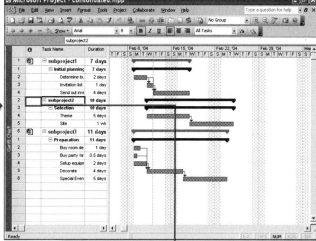

UNLINK A SUBPROJECT

1 Repeat steps 1 to 3 on the previous page.

2 Click the Link to project option (☑ changes to ☐).

3 Click OK.

■ The consolidated project appears.

■ The Indicator column no longer contains an icon for the unlinked subproject.

REORGANIZE A CONSOLIDATED PROJECT

Y ou can reorganize a consolidated project by moving tasks or subprojects around in it. This is useful if you must move a task from one subproject to another, or if you used the shortcut method of creating a consolidated project and Project did not insert the subprojects in the order you intended. For more on the shortcut method, see the section "Consolidate All Open Projects Quickly."

You can move tasks within the same subproject by dragging. You can move tasks from one subproject to another or you can move entire subprojects in the consolidated project by cutting and pasting. If you cut a summary task, the Planning Wizard appears.

Once you continue past the Planning Wizard dialog box, the summary task disappears, deleting the subproject and all its subordinate tasks. When you paste the subproject, Project places the

subproject immediately above the selected row. Therefore, in the Task Name column, you must click the task that you want to appear below the subproject. Then click the Paste button on the Standard toolbar. Project reinserts the subproject at its new location.

If you plan to move several tasks, consider selecting the Don't tell me about this again option to avoid viewing the Planning Wizard dialog box.

REORGANIZE A CONSOLIDATED PROJECT

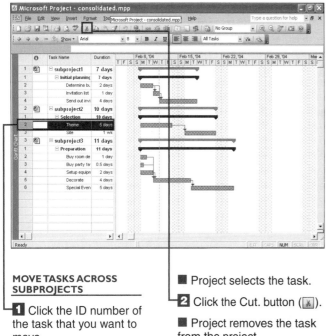

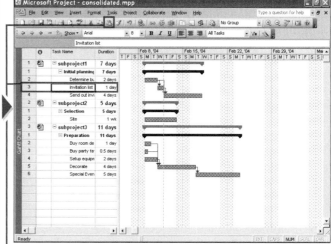

MOVE TASKS ACROSS SUBPROJECTS

1 Click the ID number of the task that you want to move.

■ Project selects the task.

2 Click the Cut. button (🔳).

■ Project removes the task from the project.

3 Select the task that you want to appear below the task you just cut.

4 Click the Paste button (🔳).

■ Project inserts the task in the row above the selected task.

362

Does Project display the Planning Wizard when I click and drag to move a subproject?

✔ No. The Planning Wizard only appears when you cut and paste.

Why does Project display the Planning Wizard when I move a subproject?

✔ Project treats subprojects the same way that it treats summary tasks, and it confirms that you really want to move all the information.

Why does Project prohibit me from dragging a task from one subproject to another?

✔ You must use the Cut and Paste method to move a task from one subproject to another.

If I turn off the Planning Wizard by clicking the Don't tell me about this again option, can I turn it back on again?

✔ Yes. Click Tools and then click Options. In the Options dialog box, click the General tab. In the Planning Wizard section, click the Advice from Planning Wizard option (☐ changes to ✔). Be sure that you see checks in the Advice about scheduling and Advice about errors boxes. You may also want to select the Advice about using Microsoft Office Project option (☐ changes to ✔) to see tips as you work about using Project.

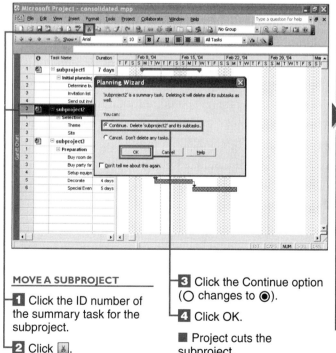

MOVE A SUBPROJECT

1 Click the ID number of the summary task for the subproject.

2 Click 📇.

■ A Planning Wizard dialog box appears.

3 Click the Continue option (○ changes to ◉).

4 Click OK.

■ Project cuts the subproject.

5 Click the task that you want to appear below the subproject once you insert it.

6 Click 📇.

■ Project inserts the subproject in the new location.

CREATE DEPENDENCIES IN A CONSOLIDATED PROJECT

In consolidated projects, you commonly find that you have one subproject dependent on tasks in another subproject. You can create links between subprojects in a consolidated file, and if necessary, you can change the links that you create.

You can create four different types of dependencies: finish-to-start, start-to-start, finish-to-finish, and start-to finish. In addition, these

types support lead and lag time. The process of linking tasks with dependencies across subprojects is much the same as the process of creating dependencies for tasks within the same project.

When you link tasks between projects, the task links look like standard links in the consolidated project. However, when you open the subproject files, Project inserts an external link, identifiable by its

appearance. The name and the Gantt Chart bar of each externally linked task appear gray. If you point at the Gantt Chart bar, Project displays information about the task, including the fact that it is an external task.

If you double-click the task name of the external task, Project opens the subproject that contains the task to which the external task is linked.

CREATE DEPENDENCIES IN A CONSOLIDATED PROJECT

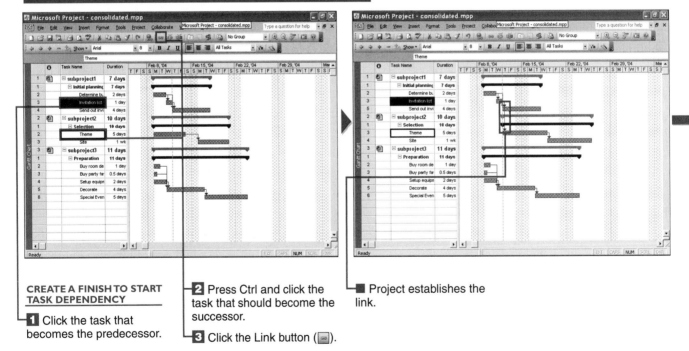

CREATE A FINISH TO START TASK DEPENDENCY

1 Click the task that becomes the predecessor.

2 Press Ctrl and click the task that should become the successor.

3 Click the Link button (🔗).

■ Project establishes the link.

Why does my link line point in a different direction than the one shown in the figure?

✔ You selected your tasks in a different order than described. The sequence in which you select tasks determines the direction of the links you create. You can tell which task was selected last. On-screen, the last task you select does not appear highlighted; a box, but no shading, appears around it.

Can I link tasks using other methods besides the Link button?

✔ Yes. For example, you can drag the Gantt bar of the predecessor task to the successor task.

Can I create an external link by typing in the Predecessors field?

✔ Yes, but this method can generate mistakes. If you decide to use it, type the link using the format *project name\ID#*. The project name should include the path to the location of the file as well as the filename, and you should make the ID# the same as the ID number of the task in that file.

How can I quickly select contiguous tasks?

✔ Click the first task, press and hold the Shift key, and click the last task.

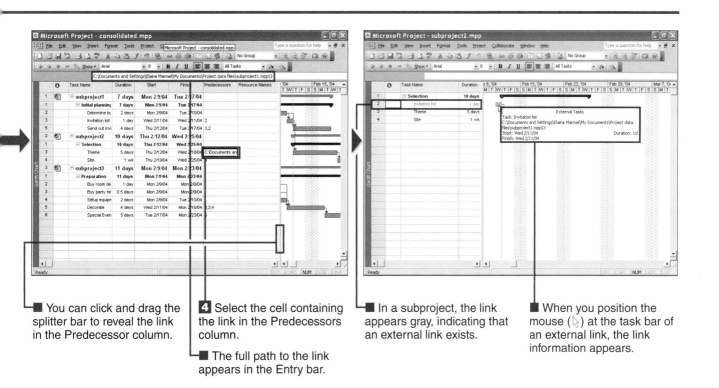

■ You can click and drag the splitter bar to reveal the link in the Predecessor column.

4 Select the cell containing the link in the Predecessors column.

■ The full path to the link appears in the Entry bar.

■ In a subproject, the link appears gray, indicating that an external link exists.

■ When you position the mouse (◊) at the task bar of an external link, the link information appears.

CHANGE DEPENDENCIES IN CONSOLIDATED PROJECTS

A fter you link tasks across projects, you may need to change information about the link. For example, you may want to change the type of dependency from the default finish-to-start link, or you may want to create lag time.

You can modify a link between tasks in different subprojects from either the consolidated project or from the subproject. As long as you linked the subproject when you

inserted it into the consolidated project, Project updates the dependency change in both files.

To make changes to dependencies, you work in the Task Dependency dialog box in either the consolidated project or in the subproject. However, the information that you can change differs, depending whether you work in the consolidated project or the subproject. If you make the change while working in the

consolidated project, you can change the type of link. For example, you can change a finish-to-start link to a start-to-start link. And you can also add lag or lead-time to the linked tasks.

If you make the change while working in the subproject, you can change the type of link, add lag or lead-time, and you also can change the path to the linked subproject file.

CHANGE DEPENDENCIES IN CONSOLIDATED PROJECTS

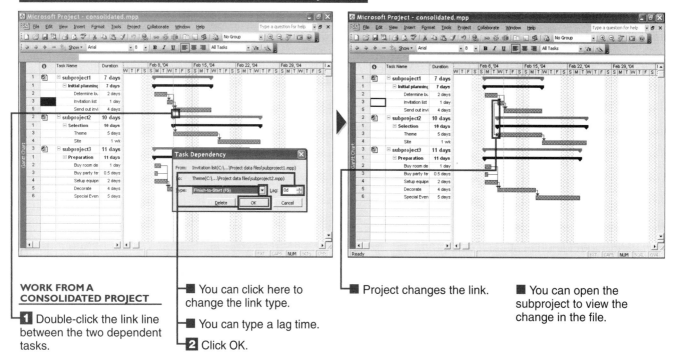

WORK FROM A CONSOLIDATED PROJECT

1 Double-click the link line between the two dependent tasks.

■ The Task Dependency box opens.

■ You can click here to change the link type.

■ You can type a lag time.

2 Click OK.

■ Project changes the link.

■ You can open the subproject to view the change in the file.

What information can I view in the Links Between Projects window?

✔ You can view the task ID number, the link type, the schedule date that affects either the predecessor or the successor, the percentage complete of the predecessor or successor, and any differences such as changes to start or finish dates for the predecessor or successor task that you have not yet applied by updating the subproject. You can control how Project updates link information on the View tab of the Options dialog box by selecting the Show Links Between Projects and the Automatically accept new external data options (☐ changes to ✔).

If I have numerous links between subprojects, is there an easy way to view information about all the links?

✔ You can click Tools and then click Links Between Projects to display a window that contains two tabs: An External Predecessors tab, and an External Successors tab. Subproject links can appear on either tab, depending on the timing of the linked tasks. Each link is represented by at least two rows in the window — the first row displays information about the task in the current project and succeeding rows contain information about the tasks in the linked file.

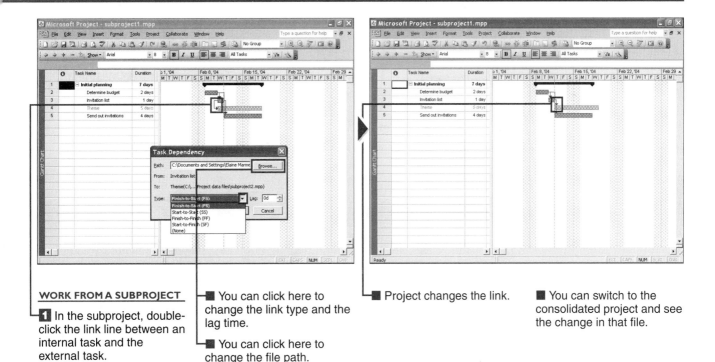

WORK FROM A SUBPROJECT

■1 In the subproject, double-click the link line between an internal task and the external task.

■ Project displays the Task Dependency box.

■ You can click here to change the link type and the lag time.

■ You can click here to change the file path.

■2 Click OK.

■ Project changes the link.

■ You can switch to the consolidated project and see the change in that file.

VIEW CONSOLIDATED PROJECTS

Creating a consolidated project makes your work easier because you can display and hide selected portions of your project. This section shows how you can use a consolidated project that contains three inserted subprojects. It demonstrates how you can focus on one particular area of

the project while keeping that area within the context of the rest of the project.

Suppose that you need to focus on the middle portion of the project. In the consolidated project, you can easily focus on the portion of the project that currently needs your attention.

Can I work in the subproject file and accomplish the same thing?

✔ Yes and no. Working in the subproject file does not let you easily view the effect of changes to the subproject on the rest of the project. Working in the consolidated project has the added advantage of updating the subproject if you keep the changes.

VIEW CONSOLIDATED PROJECTS

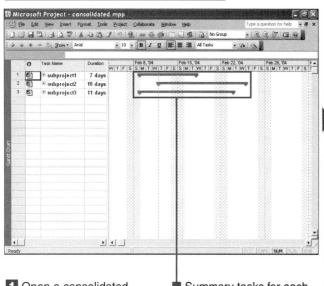

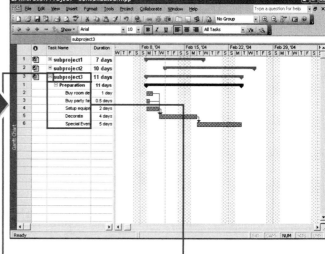

1 Open a consolidated project.

Note: For more on creating a consolidated project, see the sections "Create a Consolidated Project" or "Consolidate All Open Projects Quickly."

■ Summary tasks for each subproject appear.

2 Click ⊞ next to the subproject on which you want to focus (⊞ changes to ⊟).

■ Project displays the tasks in that subproject.

■ You can click ⊟ to hide the tasks for a subproject.

SAVE CONSOLIDATED PROJECTS

You can save consolidated project files, but you do not need to save them unless you want to keep them. Suppose that you create a consolidated project file using the steps described in the sections "Create a Consolidated Project" or "Consolidate All Open Projects Quickly," and you use it to create links and reports. You can save the consolidated project or you

can close it without saving it; regardless of your action, Project still asks if you want to save changes that you made to the subproject. If you save the subprojects without saving the consolidated project, the effects of the changes you made in the consolidated project appear when you open the subproject.

When I closed my consolidated project without saving, no prompt appeared to save the subprojects. Why?

✔ All subprojects were open when you closed the consolidated project. In this case, Project prompts you to save changes when you close the subprojects. If you save the consolidated project, Project prompts you to save changes to the subprojects.

SAVE CONSOLIDATED PROJECTS

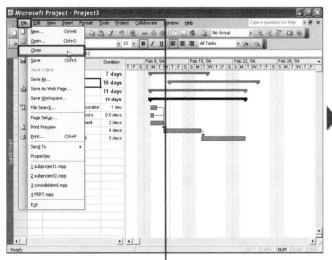

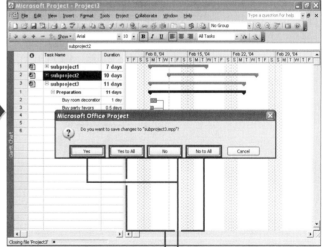

1 Open or create a consolidated project.

Note: For more on creating a consolidated project, see the sections "Create a Consolidated Project" or "Consolidate All Open Projects Quickly."

2 Make a change.

3 Click File.

4 Click Close.

■ A message appears asking if you want to save the consolidated project.

5 Click No.

■ Project asks if you want to save the subproject(s) with changes.

■ You can save or discard changes one project at a time by clicking Yes or No.

■ You can save or discard changes for all subprojects by clicking Yes to All or No to All.

VIEW THE CRITICAL PATH ACROSS CONSOLIDATED PROJECTS

By default, you view the critical path for the entire project in consolidated projects. You can, however, display the critical path for each inserted project.

When you consolidate projects, by default Project calculates inserted projects like summary tasks, which shows you, effectively, the overall critical path across all the subprojects because Project uses the late finish date of the

consolidated project to make calculations. This behavior can make subprojects within the consolidated project look like they do not have critical paths of their own.

Suppose that you want to see each subproject's critical path while viewing the master project. To do so, you can turn on multiple critical paths in the master project. That is the right idea, but you cannot view multiple critical paths using this

technique in a consolidated project, because Project displays multiple critical paths only for tasks that are owned by the project. In the case of consolidated projects, the subprojects own the tasks, not the consolidated project.

You can, however, instruct Project to stop treating subprojects as summary tasks. Under these circumstances, you are likely to see each subproject's critical path.

VIEW THE CRITICAL PATH ACROSS CONSOLIDATED PROJECTS

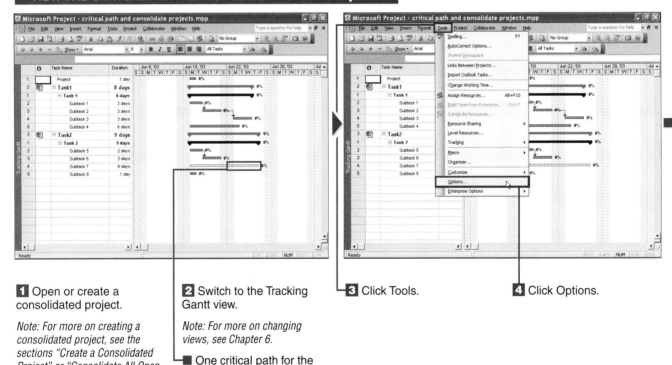

1 Open or create a consolidated project.

Note: For more on creating a consolidated project, see the sections "Create a Consolidated Project" or "Consolidate All Open Projects Quickly."

2 Switch to the Tracking Gantt view.

Note: For more on changing views, see Chapter 6.

■ One critical path for the project appears.

3 Click Tools.

4 Click Options.

How does changing this setting make Project calculate critical paths for each subproject?

✔ When Project does not calculate inserted projects as summary projects, it uses the late finish dates that subprojects send to the consolidated project to determine the critical path, showing you critical paths for each subproject.

How do I view only the tasks on the critical path in the consolidated project?

✔ The easiest way is to filter the consolidated project for critical tasks. Click Project, click Filtered for, and then click Critical. To redisplay the entire consolidated project, click Project, click Filtered for, and then click All Tasks.

Can I use the Gantt Chart Wizard to format the consolidated project and display critical paths for the subprojects?

✔ You can use the Gantt Chart Wizard to format the consolidated project, but that formatting does not display critical paths for each subproject.

How can I make the multiple critical paths feature work in a consolidated project?

✔ If you do not link the subprojects in the consolidated project, or if you break the links of the subprojects, you can use the multiple critical paths feature and not follow the steps in this task.

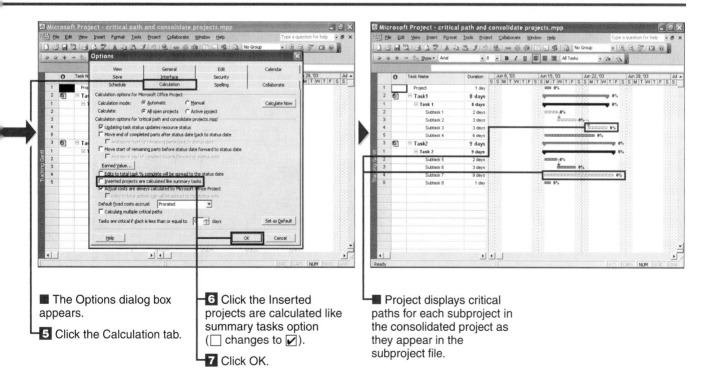

■ The Options dialog box appears.

5 Click the Calculation tab.

6 Click the Inserted projects are calculated like summary tasks option (☐ changes to ☑).

7 Click OK.

■ Project displays critical paths for each subproject in the consolidated project as they appear in the subproject file.

SHARE A RESOURCE POOL

I f your organization does not use Project Server, but shares resources on multiple projects, you can create a resource pool, which is a set of resources that are available to any project. You can use resources exclusively on one project, or you can share the resources among several projects.

Setting up a resource pool in Project can facilitate resource management, especially for

resources that are shared on several projects. To create a resource pool, you simply set up a project file that contains only resource information, and you make sure that the name of this project is easily identifiable so that all project managers can use it. Project managers then attach the resource pool to a project that needs resources. Typically, the resource pool project does not

contain any tasks, and the project that you attach to the resource pool does not contain resources.

If you have already set up a project that contains all the resources that are available, you can use that project as a model. Delete all tasks from it and save it as the resource pool project, assigning a name that makes it easily identifiable.

SHARE A RESOURCE POOL

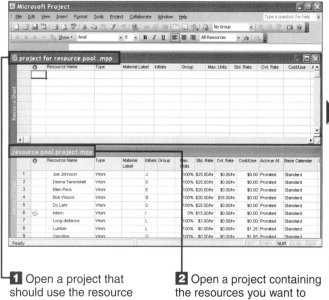

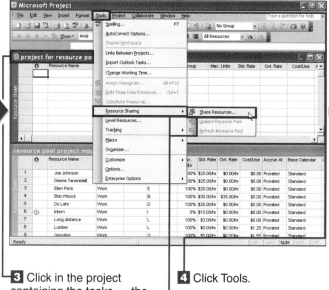

1 Open a project that should use the resource pool.

■ This project may contain tasks but does not contain resources.

2 Open a project containing the resources you want to share.

■ This project contains resources but no tasks.

3 Click in the project containing the tasks — the project to which you want to attach the resource pool.

4 Click Tools.

5 Click Resource Sharing.

6 Click Share Resources.

Do I need to create a separate file that contains only resources?

✔ While you do not need to delete all of the tasks to use a project as a resource pool to other projects, it is easier to manage the resource pool file if it only contains resource information. You can then name the resource pool file so that everyone can identify it, such as "Finance Department Resource Pool." This method also gives you a head start in preparing to use Project Server.

How do I make both projects appear on-screen simultaneously?

✔ Open both projects and then click Window and click Arrange All.

Must I display both projects on-screen simultaneously?

✔ No. I set up the projects this way so that you could see what was happening in the pictures.

What does the Pool takes precedence option do?

✔ You click this option (○ changes to ⊙) to tell Project that the resource calendars in the resource pool file take precedence when conflicts arise. If you select the Sharer takes precedence option (○ changes to ⊙), Project uses resource information in the file containing the tasks when conflicts arise.

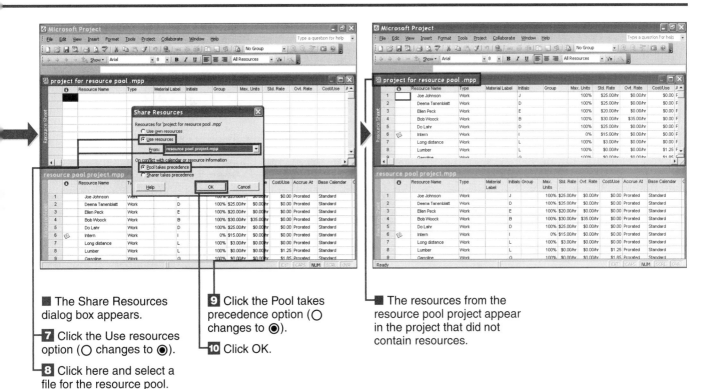

■ The Share Resources dialog box appears.

7 Click the Use resources option (○ changes to ⊙).

8 Click here and select a file for the resource pool.

9 Click the Pool takes precedence option (○ changes to ⊙).

10 Click OK.

■ The resources from the resource pool project appear in the project that did not contain resources.

OPEN A PROJECT THAT USES A RESOURCE POOL

When you set up a project to share resources, you must open both the project and the resource pool project. At some point, you will save and close your file and then come back to work on it at a later time. Once you have already set up your project to share resources, you do not need to manually open two files every time you want to work

on your project. When you open your file after you have set it up to share resources, Project displays the Open Resource Pool Information dialog box.

From this dialog box, you can choose to open the resource pool project file along with your project or you can leave the resource pool file closed and just open your project.

If you have not assigned resources to any tasks in your project, then, when the resource pool is not open, you cannot make any resource assignments. If you have made some resource assignments, you can make changes to those assignments in your project without opening the resource pool. You also can assign the resources you find in your project to other tasks in the project.

OPEN A PROJECT THAT USES A RESOURCE POOL

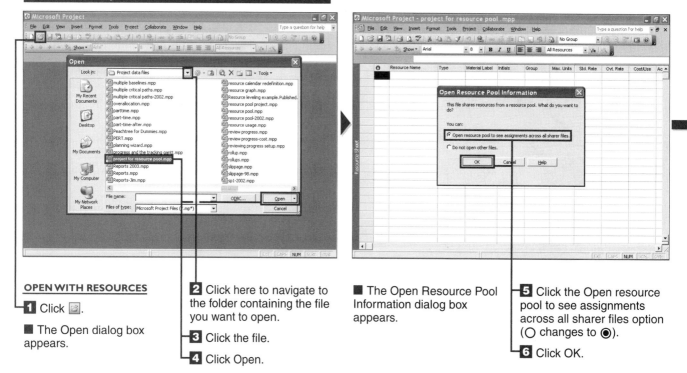

OPEN WITH RESOURCES

1 Click 🗁.

■ The Open dialog box appears.

2 Click here to navigate to the folder containing the file you want to open.

3 Click the file.

4 Click Open.

■ The Open Resource Pool Information dialog box appears.

5 Click the Open resource pool to see assignments across all sharer files option (○ changes to ⊙).

6 Click OK.

When should I open the project with the resource pool?

✔ Open both the project and the resource pool when you want to make or change resource assignments. When you open both your project and the resource pool, Project opens the resource pool as a read-only file, allowing other sharer files to also use the resource pool. You can view resource assignment in all project files that share resources by switching to the Resource Usage view.

How does Project handle assignment changes when the resource pool is closed?

✔ Project does not update the resource pool with your changes.

What is a sharer file?

✔ A *sharer file* is a project file that is sharing the resource pool file.

If I assign a resource from the pool and then later remove the assignment, what happens?

✔ If you are connected to the resource pool, you can update it with your changes. For more on updating information in the resource pool, see Chapter 17. Resources that you assign to your project appear on the Resource Sheet view of your project. And, the resources continue to appear in your project even if you remove the resource assignment in your project.

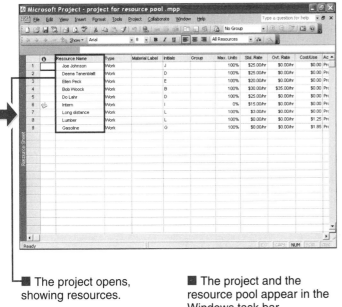

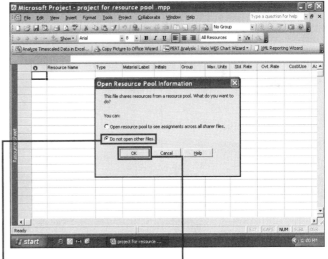

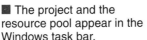

■ The project opens, showing resources.

■ The project and the resource pool appear in the Windows task bar.

OPEN WITHOUT RESOURCES

1 Repeats steps 1 to 4 on the previous page.

2 Click the Do not open other files option (○ changes to ◉).

3 Click OK.

■ The project opens without resources.

■ Only your project in the Windows task bar appears.

UPDATE INFORMATION IN THE RESOURCE POOL

If you make changes to resource information while you are working on your project, you must update the resource pool file so that others who are using the resource pool have the most up-to-date information. By default, when you open a project attached to the resource pool, Project prompts you to open the resource pool, too. If you do open the resource pool, Project opens it in read-only mode

so that others working in files attached to the resource pool can also update it.

To update the resource pool, make sure that you have the resource pool file, even in read-only mode. When you have both the project and the resource pool open, Project makes the Update Resource Pool command available.

If you open only your project and make changes to the resources, Project does not make this

command available. Furthermore, if you open only your project, save and close your project, and then open the resource pool file, Project still does not make this command available. To ensure that Project incorporates changes that you make to project resources in the resource pool, make sure that you open the resource pool file when you open your file.

UPDATE INFORMATION IN THE RESOURCE POOL

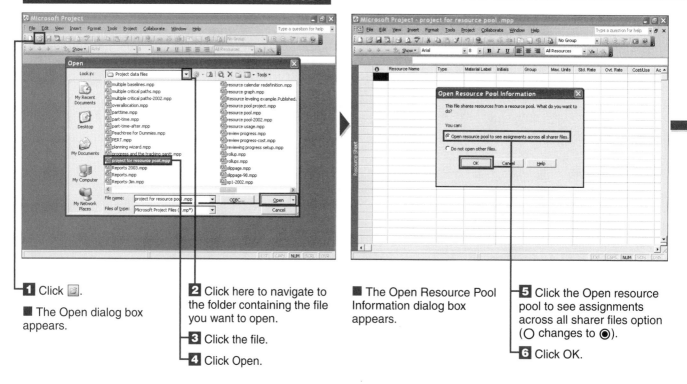

1 Click 📖.

■ The Open dialog box appears.

2 Click here to navigate to the folder containing the file you want to open.

3 Click the file.

4 Click Open.

■ The Open Resource Pool Information dialog box appears.

5 Click the Open resource pool to see assignments across all sharer files option (○ changes to ◉).

6 Click OK.

When do I use the other options that appear in the Open Resource Pool dialog box when I open the resource pool directly?

✔ You click the Do not open other files option (○ changes to ⦿) to open the resource pool and make changes to update resource information such as rates. To ensure consistency and avoid arguments in the workplace, make one group or person responsible for updating the resource pool. The third option opens the resource pool and all other Project files attach to it as one consolidated project file. Again, you can make changes to the resource pool. Use this option when you are trying to get "big picture" information about resource assignments.

If I forget to open the resource pool when I open my project, can I open it so that I do not lose the changes I made to resources in my project?

✔ Yes. You can open the resource pool file directly, the same way that you open any other Project file. The Open Resource Pool dialog box appears when you open the file; it contains three options for opening the file. You can click the first option (○ changes to ⦿), Open the resource pool as read-only, and use the steps in this task to update the resource pool.

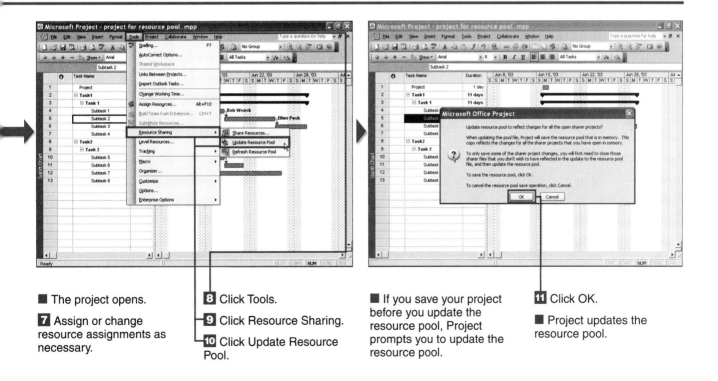

■ The project opens.

7 Assign or change resource assignments as necessary.

8 Click Tools.

9 Click Resource Sharing.

10 Click Update Resource Pool.

■ If you save your project before you update the resource pool, Project prompts you to update the resource pool.

11 Click OK.

■ Project updates the resource pool.

QUIT SHARING RESOURCES

There may come a time when you no longer want or need to share resources. For example, you may finish a project and want to disconnect it from the resource pool. Or, your organization may decide to begin using Project Server, which comes with its own version of the resource pool, called the Enterprise Resource Pool.

When you no longer want to connect a project to a resource pool file, you can disconnect that individual project from the resource pool while you have that project open. You can disable the resource pool entirely without opening all the files attached to it.

Even if you disconnect your project from the resource pool project, any resource assignments you made

from the pool still appear in your project. Furthermore, any resources you assigned to tasks in the project appear on the Resource Sheet of your project and you can assign the resource just as if the resource had never been part of a resource pool. And, if you change your mind after disconnecting the project from the resource pool, you can reestablish the connection.

QUIT SHARING RESOURCES

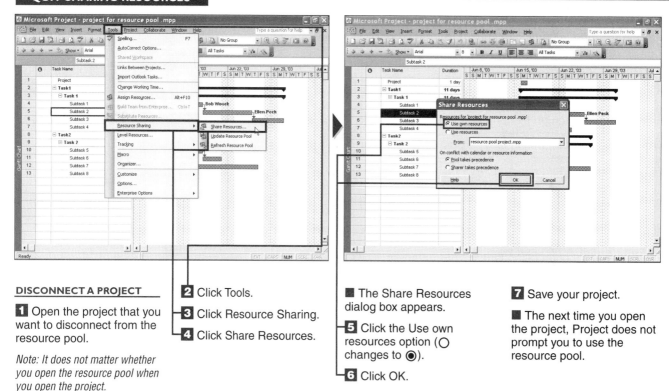

DISCONNECT A PROJECT

1 Open the project that you want to disconnect from the resource pool.

Note: It does not matter whether you open the resource pool when you open the project.

2 Click Tools.

3 Click Resource Sharing.

4 Click Share Resources.

■ The Share Resources dialog box appears.

5 Click the Use own resources option (○ changes to ◉).

6 Click OK.

7 Save your project.

■ The next time you open the project, Project does not prompt you to use the resource pool.

How can I reconnect my project to the resource pool after I disconnect the project from the resource pool?

✔ Follow the steps in the section "Share a Resource Pool" earlier in this chapter.

If I disconnect my project from the resource pool, does it affect any of the assignments in the project?

✔ No. You simply continue to use your project as if it had never been connected to a resource pool. Make assignments as necessary. If you need to add a resource to the project, use the Resource Sheet. For details, see Chapter 4.

What does the Refresh Resource Pool command on the Resource Sharing menu do?

✔ Because many projects can share a resource pool, you constantly need to update the resource pool. As you work on your project, others are making changes to their projects that affect the resource pool. Periodically, you must click Tools, Resource Sharing, and the Refresh Resource Pool to update the version of the resource pool that you have open. This allows Project to incorporate changes that you and others make. Remember, changes that others make can affect allocations in your project.

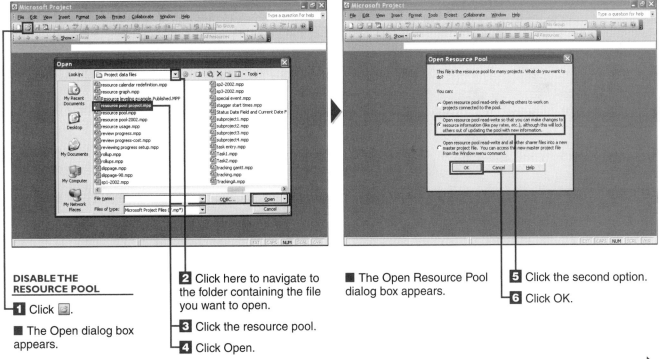

DISABLE THE RESOURCE POOL

1 Click 🗔.

■ The Open dialog box appears.

2 Click here to navigate to the folder containing the file you want to open.

3 Click the resource pool.

4 Click Open.

■ The Open Resource Pool dialog box appears.

5 Click the second option.

6 Click OK.

CONTINUED ▶

QUIT SHARING RESOURCES (CONTINUED)

W hen you disable the resource pool, you must open all files that are attached to it. However, you do not need to open each file individually; Project provides you with a way to open all the files at one time using the Share Resources dialog box.

Once you have all the files open, you can break their links with the resource pool project. Then, you

must save each file previously attached to the resource pool; otherwise, Project does not actually break the link between the files and the resource pool. Unfortunately, Project does not provide a Save All command, but you do have some choices. For example, you can use the Windows Task Bar to switch to each file and save it. Or, you can

close Project. Before Project closes, it prompts you to save each open file to which you made changes.

Disconnecting from the resource pool or disabling the resource pool does not affect any assignments you made in projects while connected to the resource pool.

QUIT SHARING RESOURCES (CONTINUED)

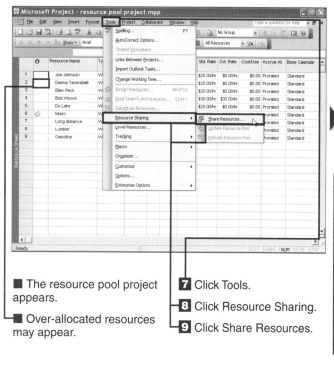

■ The resource pool project appears.

■ Over-allocated resources may appear.

7 Click Tools.

8 Click Resource Sharing.

9 Click Share Resources.

■ The Share Resources dialog box appears.

■ All the projects that share the resource pool appear.

10 Select all files listed in the Sharing links window.

11 Click Open.

■ Project opens all the selected files.

12 Click the resource pool project in the Windows Task Bar to switch back to it.

What effect does opening the resource pool read/write have?

✔ When you open the resource pool read/write, you have exclusive use and control the pool so that no one else can update it. While you have the resource pool file open read/write, others cannot use the Update Resource Pool command or the Refresh Resource Pool command. On the other hand, if you open the resource pool read-only, both you and other Project users can continue to work and update the resource pool with changes from your project.

How do I select all the files in the Sharing Links box?

✔ You can press and hold Ctrl as you click each file in the box, or you can click the first file you want to select, press and hold the Shift key, and then click the last file you want to select.

What does Open All do in the Share Resources dialog box?

✔ You can use it to simultaneously select all projects listed in the Sharing links box and open them.

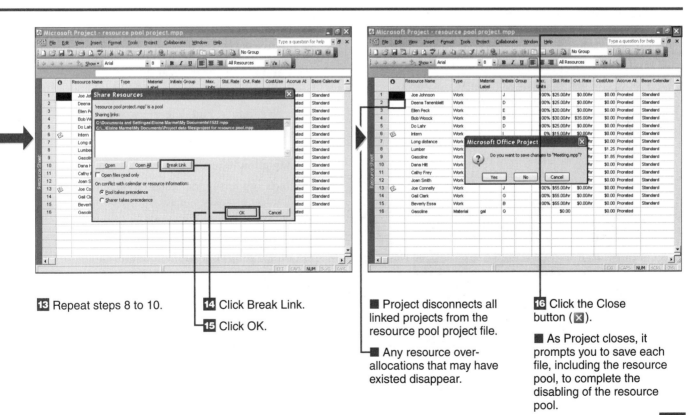

🔢 Repeat steps 8 to 10.

🔢 Click Break Link.

🔢 Click OK.

■ Project disconnects all linked projects from the resource pool project file.

■ Any resource over-allocations that may have existed disappear.

🔢 Click the Close button (🗙).

■ As Project closes, it prompts you to save each file, including the resource pool, to complete the disabling of the resource pool.

PROJECT SERVER AND PROJECT WEB ACCESS BASICS

Project Server is an edition of Microsoft Office Project that works in an enterprise environment — a networked environment where sharing of information occurs. The concept behind Project Server is that all the projects that your organization manages affect each other, making

the need for collaboration on projects greater than ever before. As the number of projects and the size of your organization grow, so does the need to manage the management of projects. Project Server enables you to store all projects and all resources for the organization in one central

database on your company's local-area network (LAN) or intranet so that you can match limited resources to projects. This chapter helps you understand the setup tasks that a project manager needs to perform to use the Project Server database effectively.

Project Server and Project Web Access Functionality

Only the project manager must actually install and use Project Professional. All other resources on the project use Project Web Access, a browser-based product that comes with Project Server, to view and update project data that is stored in the Project Server database. Using only Project Server

and Project Web Access, team members, managers, and executives can accomplish the following:

- Enter and view time sheet information
- View a project's Gantt Chart
- Receive, refuse, and delegate work assignments
- Update assignments with progress and completion information
- Attach supporting documentation, such as budget estimates or feasibility studies, to a project
- Receive notices about task status
- Perform project portfolio analysis and produce organization-wide reports
- Carry out basic issue and risk management
- Send status reports to the project manager

The Typical Scenario

When you consider the Project Server and Project Web Access environment, five roles come to mind: the administrator, the project manager, the resource manager, the day-to-day user, and executives.

The Project Server administrator role is labor-intensive as you create your Project Server database, but becomes far less demanding once you have the database up and running and people are using it. The Project Server administrator should be someone with good computer and networking skills along with a good foundation in project management. The administrator should work on the implementation team to understand the direction your organization takes when it designs the Project Server database. Your design team will identify, while defining requirements, custom fields, views, and categories your organization needs, along with security requirements. The administrator sets up user names and passwords, if appropriate, in the database and assigns permissions to users. The administrator also builds the Enterprise Resource Pool and makes modifications to the Enterprise Global. And, the administrator typically builds the OLAP cube and then maintains it for the organization. Once your database is implemented, the administrator's role becomes fairly routine.

The project manager creates web-based projects in Project Professional and uploads them to the Project Server database. In addition, using a variety of tools available through Project Professional, the project manager can assign resources to the project using the Enterprise Resource Pool –a company-wide pool of available resources — that are stored in the Project Server database. The project manager still tracks projects in Project Professional, but uses information supplied by team members using Project Web Access.

Resource managers do not need Project Professional to assign resources to a project from the Enterprise Resource Pool; they can use tools available through Project Web Access. For more information on the activities of project and resource managers, see Chapter 18.

Team members can see, in Project Web Access, the assignments that they have received and use Project Web Access to update work assignments, send status reports to the project manager, and even set up to-do lists. For more information, see Chapter 19.

Executives use Project Web Access to monitor progress on projects and attempt to identify bottlenecks and potential problems before they arise using the Portfolio Analyzer and the Portfolio Modeler. For more information, see Chapter 20.

PROJECT SERVER AND PROJECT WEB ACCESS BASICS (CONTINUED)

Project Server Software Requirements

You need a variety of software to use Project Server. For basic use of Project Server, you need, at a minimum, Windows 2000 Server with Service Pack 3 or above and Microsoft Internet Information Server (IIS) 5.0 or above. When you install Project Server, it sets up a connection between your database engine and IIS.

For your database engine, you need SQL Server 2000 with Service Pack 3 or higher. If you want to use the portfolio modeling features that are available in Project Web Access, you need SQL Server Analysis Services, which is included with SQL Server but must be installed separately.

Microsoft also recommends that you use Windows Server 2003 as the operating system platform for Project Server, and if you want to use the Documents and Issues features of Project Server, you *must* also run Windows Server 2003 and Windows SharePoint Services (WSS), formerly called SharePoint Team Services. Microsoft WSS is available for download at the Microsoft Web site. WSS requires the NT File System (NTFS).

To use e-mail notifications, both the server and client machines need Microsoft Exchange 5.5, 2000, or later or Internet SMTP/POP3, IMAP4, or MAPI-compliant messaging software.

Project Server Client Software Requirements

On the client side, the project manager needs Project Professional, but other resources need any of the following:

- Internet Explorer 5.01 with Service Pack 3
- Internet Explorer 5.5 with Service Pack 2
- Internet Explorer 6.0 with Service Pack 1

If you plan to import and export tasks between Project and Outlook, the client machine also needs Office 2000 with Service Pack 1, Office XP, or Office 2003. The process works most seamlessly using Office 2003.

Project Server Client Hardware Requirements

Microsoft recommends that each client machine have a 300-MHz processor, have 192MB of RAM, and use Windows XP Professional as the operating system. The minimum processor on a client machine is a Pentium 133-MHz. Each client machine should have a Super VGA (800 x 600) or higher resolution monitor with 256 colors and a Microsoft Mouse-compatible pointing device.

Project Server Hardware Requirements

Typically, you install Project Server on a Web server or on the company's server. If you are planning to use the bare-minimum hardware, you should load only Project Server on that computer. Other components, such as Windows SharePoint Services (WSS) and SQL Server, should run on separate computers.

Project Server also comes with some minimum hardware requirements. Microsoft recommends that you install Project Server on a computer with a minimum Pentium III processor that runs at 700 MHz and has 512MB of RAM. If necessary, you can run Project Server on a Pentium III, 550-MHz machine with only 128MB of RAM. This computer must also have a CD-ROM drive, a Super VGA (800 x 600) or higher resolution monitor, and a Microsoft Mouse-compatible pointing device.

For the computer on which you install Project Server, you need 50MB of available hard drive space. To install WSS, you need another 70MB of hard drive space and a minimum of 256MB of RAM, but 512MB of RAM is recommended.

To install SQL Server 2000, you need 250MB of hard drive space and 64MB of RAM — 128MB is recommended. If you also intend to install SQL Analysis Services, you need another 130MB of hard drive space and 64MB of RAM — 128 MB is recommended.

CONTINUED ▶ 385

PROJECT SERVER AND PROJECT WEB ACCESS BASICS (CONTINUED)

Project Server and Security

Because your project data is sensitive, the Project Server database has several levels of security built into it based on roles within your organization, and you can change the defaults if they do not work for you. Setting up the security in the Project Server database is the task of the Project Server administrator and beyond the scope of this book. However, you need to understand that your security level determines which of the various actions available in Project Server you can perform. For example, using the default security settings, you cannot edit the Enterprise Global Template unless you have privileges equal to or higher than a project manager. Similarly, you cannot edit the Enterprise Resource Pool unless you have privileges equal to or higher than a resource manager. If you try something and you see an error message, contact the Project Server administrator to determine if you have been given the privileges you need to do your job.

Project Server Advantages

Project Server enables you to store all projects for your organization in one common database; and, because the projects share a database, your organization creates consistent projects that use the same custom settings. Using the Enterprise Global Template, each project that you create contains all the same fields, maps, views, tables, reports, filters, forms, toolbars, groups, and calendars that are stored in the Global template file that is included in Project Professional, along with additional enterprise-only fields. Administrators can define whether fields are required or optional and can create look-up tables and value lists for fields. Because the settings are stored in the Enterprise Global Template, they can be used repeatedly without having to re-create information.

In addition, Project Server enables you to easily staff projects and manage resource assignments across projects using the Enterprise Resource Pool.

Project Server and Third Party Software

Project Server 2003 also integrates with third party systems, giving you added flexibility. For example, suppose that your organization already uses a system to capture timesheet information and the system works for you. In that case, integrate Project Server with your time-capturing system and transfer the information into Project Server, where you can perform the rest of the project management functions.

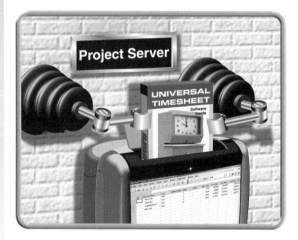

Or suppose that you need to update your general ledger with actual time worked. Again, you can integrate Project Server 2003 with your general ledger. Project Server 2003 contains a new feature that permits the Project Server Administrator to establish specific reporting periods and open and close the reporting periods to synchronize with the general ledger. Information transfers from closed periods in Project Server to the general ledger.

Do You Need Project Server?

The following is a list of scenarios where Project Server would work well:

- Your organization has determined that the time of project managers *and* resources time would be used more efficiently if resources could record their time directly in the project schedule instead of providing it to the project manager, who then updates the schedule.

- Your executives want better organization-wide reporting and analysis tools than you can currently provide.

- You manage many different projects using the same resources.

- Your organization is growing and has identified a need for tracking projects more accurately or utilizing resources more efficiently.

- Your managers need to model if-then scenarios.

- Your users need access to project data anywhere in the world.

CREATE A PROJECT SERVER LOGON ACCOUNT

As a project manager, although you create projects in Project Professional, you need a Project Server logon account that enables you to access Project Server. For example, to assign resources to your project, you use the Enterprise Resource Pool stored in the Project Server database. And, you need to store your projects in the Project Server database so that others in your organization can

view and update them. You may want to upload your projects into the Project Server database at several points in the project management process. For example, your organization may want you to upload a project before approval so that senior management can review the impact of the project on both resource management and company profitability.

You can easily create your own Project Server account from within Project after you know the URL for your Project Server database. Your Project Server administrator will most likely give you this URL, tell you your Project Server account name, and tell you which type of authentication to use when you create your logon account — Windows User Account or Project Server Account.

CREATE A PROJECT SERVER LOGON ACCOUNT

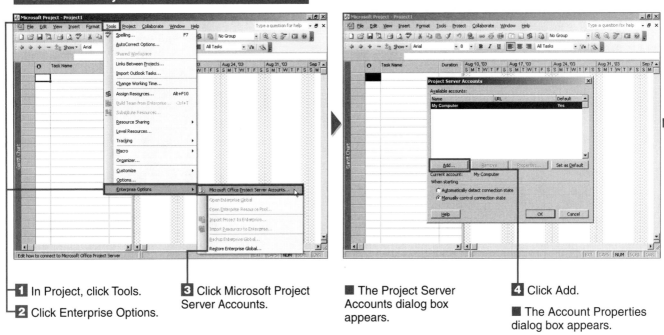

1 In Project, click Tools.

2 Click Enterprise Options.

3 Click Microsoft Project Server Accounts.

■ The Project Server Accounts dialog box appears.

4 Click Add.

■ The Account Properties dialog box appears.

What is the difference between automatically detecting and manually controlling the connection state?

✔ When you select automatic detection and open Project Professional, no dialog box appears from which you can select a Project Server logon account.

Are there restrictions on the name that I use for the Project Server logon account?

✔ Yes. You must use a name that no other user is already using, such as your own name.

Are there restrictions on the name I use if my organization uses Microsoft Project Server account authentication?

✔ Yes. You must use the name your Project Server Administrator gives you.

Why would I need more than one Project Server logon account?

✔ If your company uses more than one database in Project Server, you need more than one account to access the correct database.

What are the When connecting options on the Account Properties dialog box?

✔ To secure project data, most organizations require logon authentication. Project Server supports its own type of authentication, which is less strict than Windows authentication. Windows authentication uses your Windows logon account information.

What does the Test Connection button do?

✔ You click the button on the Account Properties dialog box to ensure that you type the URL correctly.

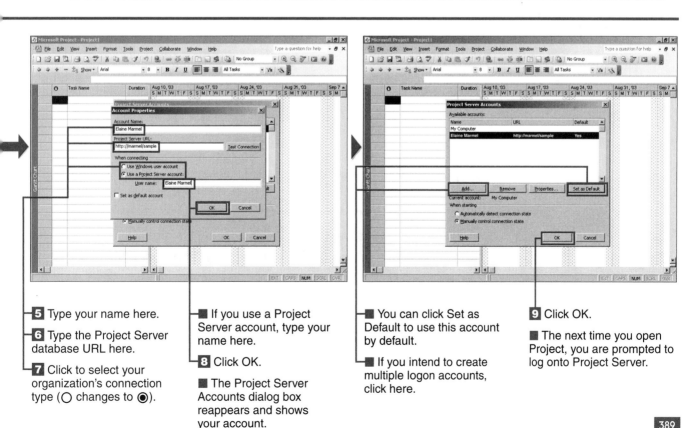

5 Type your name here.

6 Type the Project Server database URL here.

7 Click to select your organization's connection type (○ changes to ◉).

■ If you use a Project Server account, type your name here.

8 Click OK.

■ The Project Server Accounts dialog box reappears and shows your account.

■ You can click Set as Default to use this account by default.

■ If you intend to create multiple logon accounts, click here.

9 Click OK.

■ The next time you open Project, you are prompted to log onto Project Server.

LOG ON TO PROJECT SERVER

You can work with a project while connected to Project Server or in a stand-alone environment; you make that choice when you start Project Professional.

Suppose that you use Project from a notebook computer while traveling. During your time away from the office, you can keep track of the time that you spend working. If you manually control the connection state, discussed in the previous section, you can work offline. If you chose to automatically detect the connection state, you connect to Project Server when you start Project only if your computer is connected to the network.

This section assumes that you manually control the connection state and use a Project Server account to connect. When you automatically control the connection state and use a Windows account to connect, you do not see either of the screens shown here. Instead, Project simply opens.

How do I work offline when I manually control the connection state?
✔ Click My Compter and then click Work Offline.

Can I work offline when I automatically control the connection state?
✔ Yes. Disconnect from your network.

LOG ON TO PROJECT SERVER

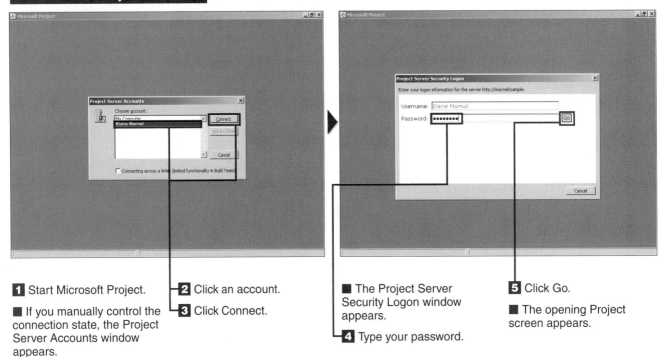

1 Start Microsoft Project.

■ If you manually control the connection state, the Project Server Accounts window appears.

2 Click an account.

3 Click Connect.

■ The Project Server Security Logon window appears.

4 Type your password.

5 Click Go.

■ The opening Project screen appears.

SET UP TO COLLABORATE

B y default, you cannot upload a project to the Project Server database unless you set options in the project to make it a Web-based project.

As the project manager, you use Project to build and maintain the project schedule and make task assignments. In addition, you must set up the project's Web communications options so that you can upload — also called *publish* —

the project to the Project Server database. These options include identifying the URL for the Project Server database and specifying a connection method of either Windows account or Project Server account, which you can read about in "Create a Project Server Logon Account." When setting options, you also decide if resources can delegate tasks, when to republish the project based on changes to it, and what information to publish.

How can I change the Microsoft Office Project user name option when it is grayed out on the General tab?

✔ You must open Project Professional without logging on to Project Server. Then, open the project and the Options dialog box. You can change the user name on the General tab.

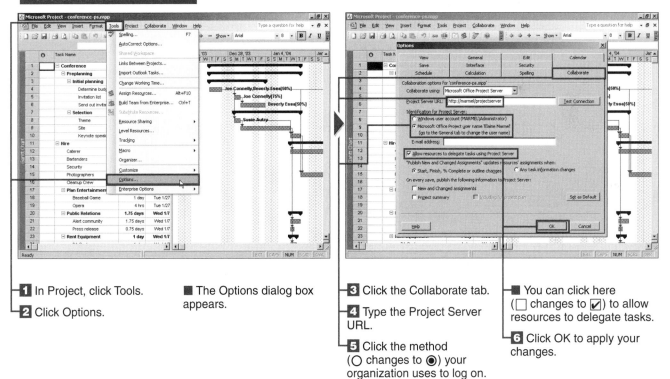

1 In Project, click Tools.

2 Click Options.

■ The Options dialog box appears.

3 Click the Collaborate tab.

4 Type the Project Server URL.

5 Click the method (O changes to ◉) your organization uses to log on.

■ You can click here (☐ changes to ☑) to allow resources to delegate tasks.

6 Click OK to apply your changes.

CREATE CUSTOM ENTERPRISE FIELDS AND OUTLINE CODES

Y ou create and use custom fields and outline codes to assign to resources, tasks, or projects to meet some specific need concerning the data stored in your organization's projects. Because Project Server stores custom fields in the Enterprise Global Template, you can enforce standards across projects by setting up custom fields for all project managers to use.

You can create custom enterprise fields and outline codes that use lookup tables — lists of predefined

values for the field. When you create a custom enterprise field or outline code, you can create *multi-value codes*, which enable you to assign more than one value to the same field. In this section, for example, you create a multi-value resource enterprise outline code to identify the language spoken by each resource. Because a multi-value field allows you to assign more than one value to the field, this code enables you to assign English and Spanish to the same

resource when you create resources in Create the Enterprise Resource Pool. You can use Enterprise Resource Outline Codes 20 through 29 as multi-value codes.

You need administrative privileges in Project Server to perform the steps in this section. This section also assumes that you are working in Project Professional and are connected to the Project Server database to customize the Enterprise Global Template.

CREATE CUSTOM ENTERPRISE FIELDS AND OUTLINE CODES

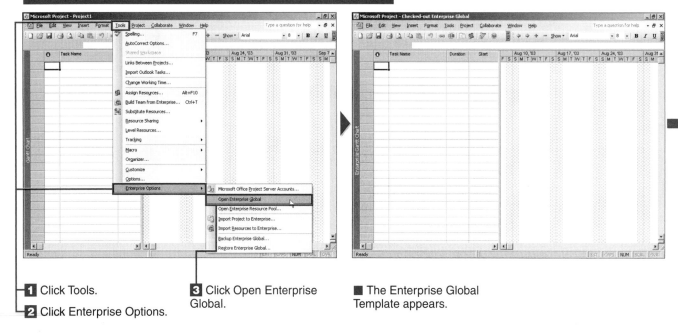

1 Click Tools.

2 Click Enterprise Options.

3 Click Open Enterprise Global.

■ The Enterprise Global Template appears.

Can you explain what the Enterprise Global Template is?
✔ The Enterprise Global Template in Project Server serves a similar purpose as the Global template in Project Professional — to store a collection of all default settings that projects use across your organization. Because each new project is based on the Enterprise Global Template, each project shares default settings and uses Enterprise features such as required custom fields in the same way, enforcing standardization across all the organization's projects.

Can I select any outline code and create a multi-value code?
✔ No. You can only use codes between Enterprise Outline Code 20-29.

Can I create a multi-value custom field or must it be an outline code?
✔ Multi-value codes must be outline codes.

Can I require that a custom outline code be filled in by users?
✔ Yes. On the Custom Outline Codes tab of the Customize Enterprise Fields dialog box, click the Make this a required code option (☐ changes to ☑).

What does the Import Custom Field option do?
✔ If you have created the custom field you want in a project, you can click this button to import it into the Enterprise Global Template.

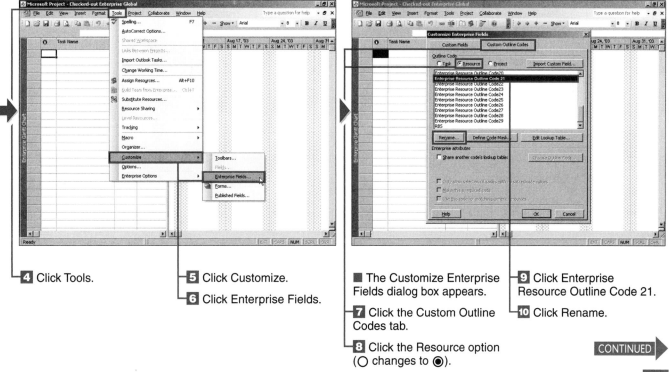

◄ **4** Click Tools.

5 Click Customize.

6 Click Enterprise Fields.

■ The Customize Enterprise Fields dialog box appears.

7 Click the Custom Outline Codes tab.

8 Click the Resource option (○ changes to ◉).

9 Click Enterprise Resource Outline Code 21.

10 Click Rename.

CONTINUED ▶

CREATE CUSTOM ENTERPRISE FIELDS AND OUTLINE CODES (CONTINUED)

You can use custom enterprise fields for many purposes. For example, your organization may want to set up a custom Enterprise field for Project Status and assign values such as Proposed, Awarded, In Progress, and Completed. Or, if your organization opts to use generic resources and wants to match the skills of a generic resource with a real resource that possesses those skills, you can

create a custom enterprise field and establish a value list for the field where each value represents a set of skills. Once you assign the appropriate value to each resource by using the custom enterprise field, you can use the code to match skill sets that are required by generic resources with skill sets that are possessed by real people when project managers run the Team Builder.

Lookup tables and code definition masks are optional for Enterprise custom fields and outline codes. Using a lookup table enables you to define accepted values for the field. Using a code mask enables you to define the format of the information entered into the field; you can define the types of information — characters, numbers, uppercase or lowercase letters — as well as the length of the value.

CREATE CUSTOM ENTERPRISE FIELDS AND OUTLINE CODES (CONTINUED)

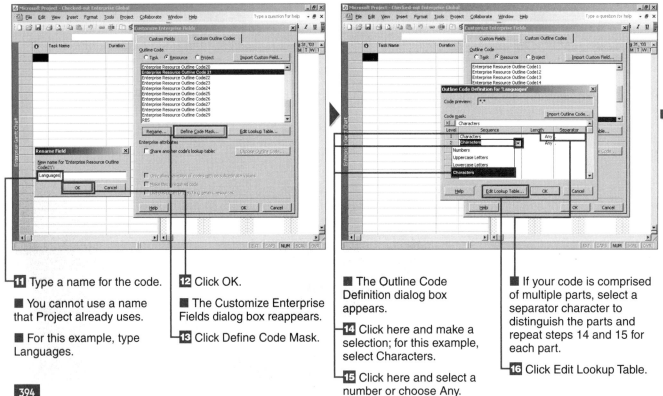

▐11 Type a name for the code.

■ You cannot use a name that Project already uses.

■ For this example, type Languages.

▐12 Click OK.

■ The Customize Enterprise Fields dialog box reappears.

▐13 Click Define Code Mask.

■ The Outline Code Definition dialog box appears.

▐14 Click here and make a selection; for this example, select Characters.

▐15 Click here and select a number or choose Any.

■ If your code is comprised of multiple parts, select a separator character to distinguish the parts and repeat steps 14 and 15 for each part.

▐16 Click Edit Lookup Table.

Can I use a lookup table that I defined for more than one custom outline code?

✔ Yes. On the Custom Outline Codes tab of the Customize Enterprise Fields dialog box, click the Share another code's lookup table option (☐ changes to ☑). Then, click Choose Outline Code to select the outline code lookup table that you want to share. The lookup table must exist in the currently open project file — in this example, the Enterprise Global Template.

How many enterprise outline codes can I create?

✔ You can create 30 Enterprise Task codes, 30 Enterprise Resource codes, and 30 Enterprise Project codes.

How many Custom Fields can I create?

✔ You can create 10 Enterprise Task codes for each type: Cost, Date, Duration, Flag, Number, and Text. Similarly, you can create 10 Enterprise Resource codes and 10 Enterprise Project codes for the same six types.

Besides the title bar, how is the Enterprise Global Template different from a regular project file?

✔ If you poke around, you find that certain commands, such as the Build Team from Enterprise command, are disabled.

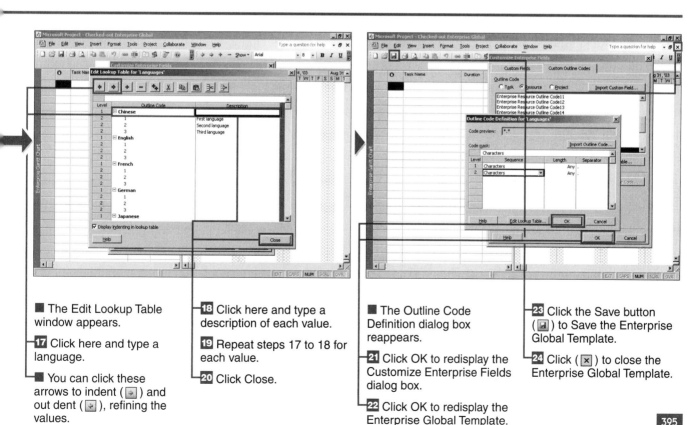

■ The Edit Lookup Table window appears.

17 Click here and type a language.

■ You can click these arrows to indent (⬆) and out dent (⬇), refining the values.

18 Click here and type a description of each value.

19 Repeat steps 17 to 18 for each value.

20 Click Close.

■ The Outline Code Definition dialog box reappears.

21 Click OK to redisplay the Customize Enterprise Fields dialog box.

22 Click OK to redisplay the Enterprise Global Template.

23 Click the Save button (🖫) to Save the Enterprise Global Template.

24 Click (⊠) to close the Enterprise Global Template.

CREATE CALENDARS IN THE ENTERPRISE GLOBAL TEMPLATE

Project Server uses calendars just like Project Professional does; you can assign a calendar to the Enterprise Global Template to enforce common workdays and work times across all projects. Resources in the Enterprise Resource Pool can use the calendar that is in the Enterprise Global Template unless you override that calendar by assigning a resource-specific calendar.

The Standard calendar automatically assigned to the Enterprise Global Template assumes a Monday to Friday, 8 a.m. to 5 p.m., 40-hour workweek that may not work in your organization. If your resources work different hours, change the calendar working day to match the workday of your resources. Or, you may want to update the calendar that all projects use to reflect holidays and company-granted days off, such as Christmas and Christmas Eve. To ensure that no

work is scheduled on holidays or other specified days, open the Enterprise Global Template, and update the Standard calendar to mark those days as unavailable. That way, project managers do not need to remember to update the calendar in their projects.

You must have administrative privileges in Project Server to open the Enterprise Global Template. For help opening the Enterprise Global Template, see "Create Custom Fields in the Enterprise Global Template."

CREATE CALENDARS IN THE ENTERPRISE GLOBAL TEMPLATE

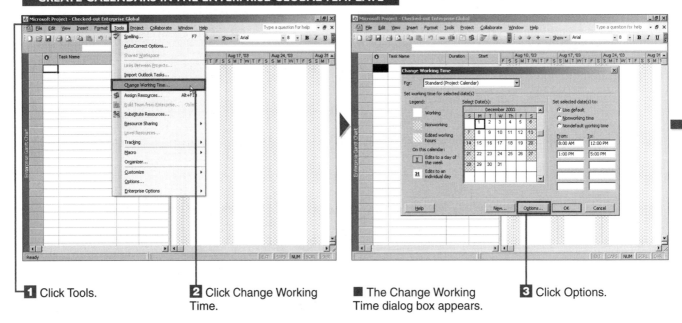

1 Click Tools.

2 Click Change Working Time.

■ The Change Working Time dialog box appears.

3 Click Options.

How can I select contiguous or noncontiguous days?

✔ To select contiguous days, click the first day, press Shift, and click the last day that you want to select. To select noncontiguous days, press Ctrl and click each day that you want to select.

I accidentally changed Sunday to scheduled working time. How do I change it back to nonworking time?

✔ Reselecting a date and clicking the Use default option (○ changes to ⊙) returns the date to its originally scheduled time on that date. Therefore, selecting Sunday and clicking the Use default option tells Project not to schedule work on Sundays.

I am using Project Professional, and sometimes I can create my own calendar; at other times I cannot. Why?

✔ Your organization uses Project Server and Project Professional. Project Standard users can always set their own base calendars. Project Professional users can create their own base calendars if they work offline and store the project locally, and not in a Project Server database. For projects stored in a Project Server database, you can create base calendars only if the administrator gives you the rights to do so. Also, the privilege to create base calendars does not permit you to change the Standard calendar.

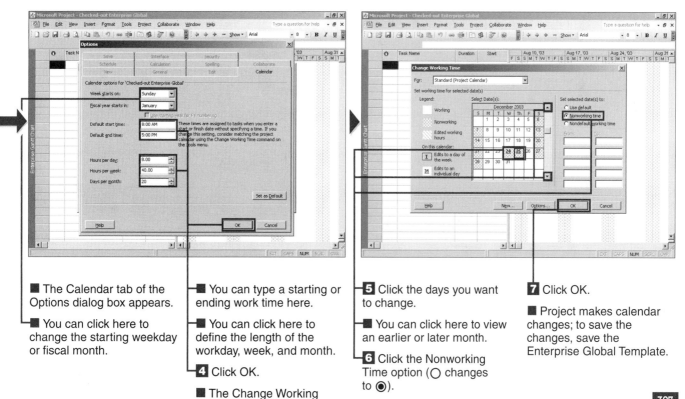

■ The Calendar tab of the Options dialog box appears.

■ You can click here to change the starting weekday or fiscal month.

■ You can type a starting or ending work time here.

■ You can click here to define the length of the workday, week, and month.

4 Click OK.

■ The Change Working Time dialog box reappears.

5 Click the days you want to change.

■ You can click here to view an earlier or later month.

6 Click the Nonworking Time option (○ changes to ⊙).

7 Click OK.

■ Project makes calendar changes; to save the changes, save the Enterprise Global Template.

CREATE THE ENTERPRISE RESOURCE POOL

The Enterprise Resource Pool is a single repository that project and resource managers can use when assigning resources to their projects. The Enterprise Resource Pool includes summary resource assignments, and resource base calendars; you also see any enterprise resource fields that you defined in the Enterprise Global Template.

Project managers "check out" a resource from the Enterprise Resource Pool to change attributes

for the resource. The Project Server administrator can set the permissions for others to add, edit, and delete resources from the Enterprise Resource Pool. Project Server manages the check-out/check-in operations.

You can create the Enterprise Resource Pool in one of two ways. You can open the Enterprise Resource Pool while logged onto Project Server and type in all the resources. Or, you can import resources from a project that

contains the resources that you want to store in the Enterprise Resource Pool. Using this second method, a wizard walks you through setting up the Enterprise Resource Pool.

For this section, make sure that you are logged onto Project Server and that the project file containing the resources you want to import is closed. You must have project manager privileges in Project Server to update the Enterprise Resource Pool.

CREATE THE ENTERPRISE RESOURCE POOL

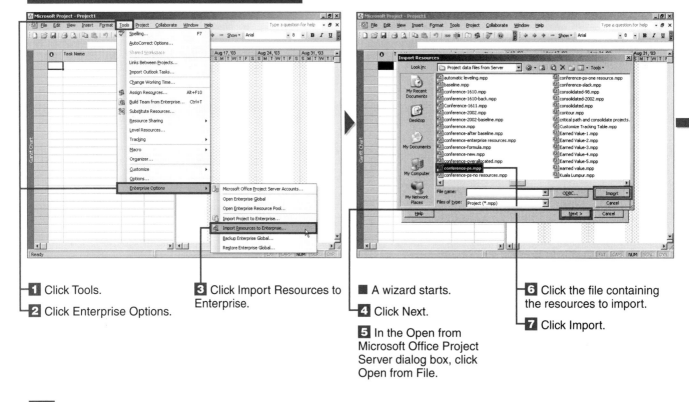

1 Click Tools.

2 Click Enterprise Options.

3 Click Import Resources to Enterprise.

■ A wizard starts.

4 Click Next.

5 In the Open from Microsoft Office Project Server dialog box, click Open from File.

6 Click the file containing the resources to import.

7 Click Import.

What do I do if my resources exist in several projects instead of one project?

✔ You can import several times, selecting a different project each time. On the last box of the Import Resources Wizard, you can click Import More Resources instead of Finish to start the process again.

If I do not already have my resources defined in a project file, how do I add them to the Enterprise Resource Pool?

✔ Click Tools, click Enterprise Options, and then click Open Enterprise Resource Pool. In the Open Enterprise Resources window that appears, do not check any resources; simply click Open/Add.

Can I still import resources if my resources exist in several Project files and some names overlap?

✔ Yes. When the Import Resources Wizard displays the resources to import, the names of those already in the Enterprise Resource Pool appear in red with an error of "Duplicate Name." Project Server does not allow you to import resources with errors.

What should I do if I receive a "Duplicate Name" message, but the resource is really different from the one in the Enterprise Resource Pool.

✔ Click Resource Information and change the resource's name.

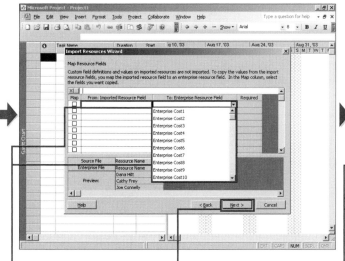

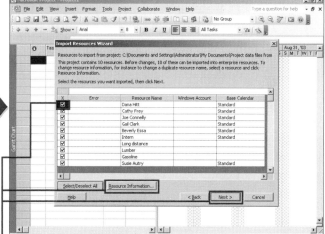

■ The Map Resource Fields Wizard dialog box appears.

■ You can click here to select resource fields to import.

■ You can click here to match them to Enterprise Resource fields in this list.

Note: Existing custom fields and values do not appear in the Enterprise Resource Pool unless you match them to enterprise resource fields.

8 Click Next.

■ The resources available to import appear.

■ You can click here (✓ changes to ☐) to not import a resource.

■ You can click here to change resource information.

9 Click Next.

■ Project Server displays a message stating that the import is complete.

10 Click Finish.

■ Project stores the selected resources in the Enterprise Resource Pool.

EDIT RESOURCES IN THE ENTERPRISE RESOURCE POOL

After you have stored a resource in the Enterprise Resource Pool, what happens if you find out that you need to make a change to that resource? Suppose, for example, that the resource's rate changes. You can edit the resource by checking out the resource from the Enterprise Resource Pool, making the change, and then checking the resource back into the Enterprise Resource Pool. For more on

creating a resource in the Enterprise Resource Pool, see the previous section.

As long as you have checked out the resource, no one in your company can make and save changes to the resource or assign work to that resource. Checked-out resources appear in the Resource Sheet view of the Enterprise Resource Pool. You make changes to checked-out resources either by editing on the

Resource Sheet or opening the Resource Information dialog box. After you make changes, saving the changes automatically checks the resource back into the Enterprise Resource Pool. And, once you check the resource back into the Enterprise Resource Pool, Project Server updates the resource information in the Enterprise Resource Pool so that anyone else who checks out the resource can view the updated version of the resource.

EDIT RESOURCES IN THE ENTERPRISE RESOURCE POOL

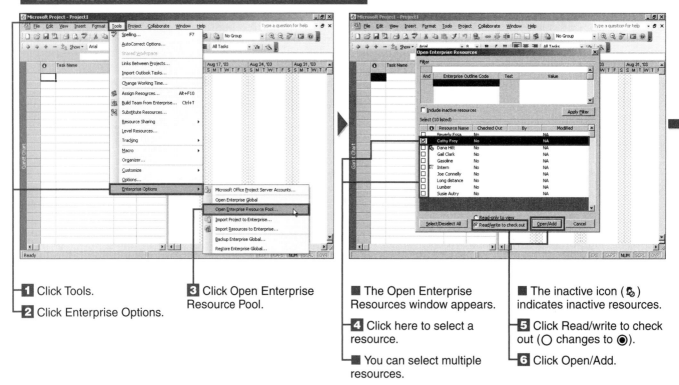

-1 Click Tools.

-2 Click Enterprise Options.

-3 Click Open Enterprise Resource Pool.

■ The Open Enterprise Resources window appears.

-4 Click here to select a resource.

■ You can select multiple resources.

■ The inactive icon (🐾) indicates inactive resources.

-5 Click Read/write to check out (○ changes to ◉).

-6 Click Open/Add.

What does the Apply Filter option in the Open Enterprise Resources window do?

✔ If your organization has set up Enterprise Outline Codes, you can use this button to help narrow the search for a resource. Select an Enterprise Outline Code and select a value for it. When you then click Apply Filter, you see only those resources who met the filter criteria in the Open Enterprise Resources window.

If the resource appears on the Resource Sheet of the Enterprise Resource Pool, why do I not see all the other resources in the Enterprise Resource Pool?

✔ You see only checked-out Enterprise resources.

If I want to make a change to a resource attribute that does not appear on the Resource Sheet, what should I do?

✔ You can double-click the resource to display the Resource Information dialog box for the resource or you can insert a column for the field you want to update. See Chapter 7 for help inserting columns.

What is an inactive resource?

✔ You do not delete enterprise resources; instead you make them inactive by checking the Inactive box on the General tab of the Resource Information dialog box. For more information on this dialog box, see Chapter 4.

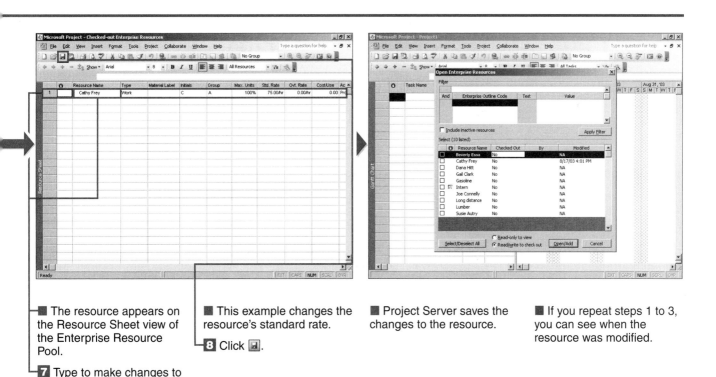

■ The resource appears on the Resource Sheet view of the Enterprise Resource Pool.

7 Type to make changes to the resource.

■ This example changes the resource's standard rate.

8 Click 🖫.

■ Project Server saves the changes to the resource.

■ If you repeat steps 1 to 3, you can see when the resource was modified.

ASSIGN A MULTI-VALUE FIELD TO A RESOURCE

After you create a multi-value custom outline code, you need to assign values for it. Earlier in this chapter, you created a Language multi-value resource outline code; in this section, you see how to assign values for it to resources. You can read more about creating custom fields and outline codes in Chapter 9 and in the section "Create Custom Fields in the Enterprise Global Template" in this chapter.

When you create a multi-value code, you create a lookup table for it that contains the values available for the code. For custom Enterprise outline codes that are *not* multi-value codes, you can assign only one value from the lookup table. The power behind a multi-value Enterprise outline code lies in the ability it gives you to assign more than one value to the same code.

When you assign a value to a multi-value outline code, you see two versions of the code — one with the original name you provided and one with -MV at the end of the name you provided. Using the original version, you can assign only one value for the code. But, using the other, you can assign as many values as you want.

This section assumes that you have started in Project Professional, and are logged onto Project Server.

ASSIGN A MULTI-VALUE FIELD TO A RESOURCE

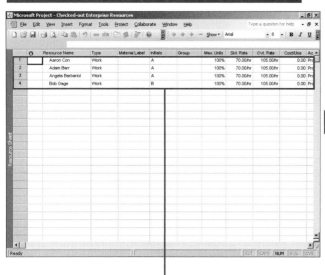

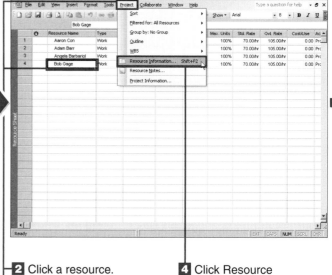

1 Check out the resources you want.

Note: To check out resources, see the section "Edit Resources in the Enterprise Resource Pool."

■ You can check out as many resources as you need so that you can assign values.

■ The checked-out resources appear on the Resource Sheet of the Enterprise Resource Pool.

2 Click a resource.

3 Click Project.

4 Click Resource Information.

Is there another way to open the Resource Information dialog box?

✔ Yes. You can double-click a resource or you can click the Resource Information button (🗒) on the Standard toolbar.

When would I use a multi-value outline code?

✔ Whenever you want to find resources, tasks, or projects that share common characteristics. For example, resources have many skills; suppose that your organization set up a multi-value field to assign skills such as C++ Programming and Database Development to the same resource. You can then search for resources based on the combination of skills you need in your project.

Is there a limit to the number of values I can assign to a multi-value field?

✔ Theoretically, however unlikely it may seem, you can assign every value available in a multi-value field's lookup table.

Must I structure the lookup table with levels?

✔ No. Your lookup table can be one long list of entries all at the same level.

Must I restrict the lookup table entries with a code mask?

✔ Not really. You can define a code mask that consists of only one part and you can allow any characters in that part.

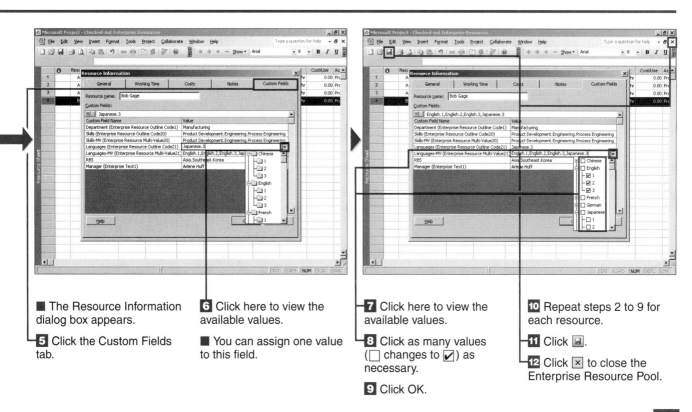

■ The Resource Information dialog box appears.

5 Click the Custom Fields tab.

6 Click here to view the available values.

■ You can assign one value to this field.

7 Click here to view the available values.

8 Click as many values (☐ changes to ✔) as necessary.

9 Click OK.

10 Repeat steps 2 to 9 for each resource.

11 Click 🗒.

12 Click ✕ to close the Enterprise Resource Pool.

STORE A PROJECT IN THE PROJECT SERVER DATABASE

For others to view and update a schedule, you must save it from your local hard drive to the Project Server database. When you do so, Project changes the name of your project in the title bar to include the word *Published* so that you know that you are viewing the version that you saved to the Project Server database. For example, if your original project name was *Conference*, the published version becomes *Conference.Published*.

Saving a project simply places a placeholder in the Project Server database for the project — it does not send any of the scheduling or summary information to team members or others so that they can view it using Project Web Access. To view the details of the project, you must *publish* information after you save the project. You can publish all information, new and changed assignments, the project

plan, or you can republish assignments.

This section assumes that you are logged on to Project Server as described earlier in this chapter and that you have the project that you want to store open. Instead of performing these steps, you can use a wizard. For more information, see the section "Import a Project into the Project Server Database."

STORE A PROJECT IN THE PROJECT SERVER DATABASE

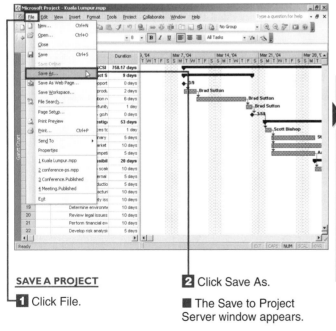

SAVE A PROJECT

1 Click File.

2 Click Save As.

■ The Save to Project Server window appears.

3 Type a name for the project.

■ You can assign a different name than the local file name.

4 Make sure that you assigned all custom fields.

5 Click Save.

Note: A message may appear; click Yes to All to replace local resources with enterprise resources.

■ The title of the project changes.

What does the Version option mean?
✔ Your organization establishes versions such as Published or Target.

What does the New and Changed Assignments command on the Collaborate menu do?
✔ The New and Changed Assignments command publishes changes to tasks, such as new start or finish dates. Resources receive notification in Project Web Access and via e-mail if your organization has set up Project Server to provide e-mail notifications and reminders.

What does the All Information command on the Collaborate menu do?
✔ The All Information command publishes both new and changed assignments.

What does the Republish Assignments command on the Collaborate menu do?
✔ This command forces Project to publish assignments, even if you have previously published them. You can choose to republish all or only some assignments.

What does the Project Plan command on the Collaborate menu do?
✔ When you choose this command, Project gives you the option to publish the entire plan or a summary of the plan. The summary includes only task and scheduling information, and the complete plan includes assignments. If you publish the summary only, you see the project in the Project Center of Project Web Access, but you cannot drill down and see details because they are not there.

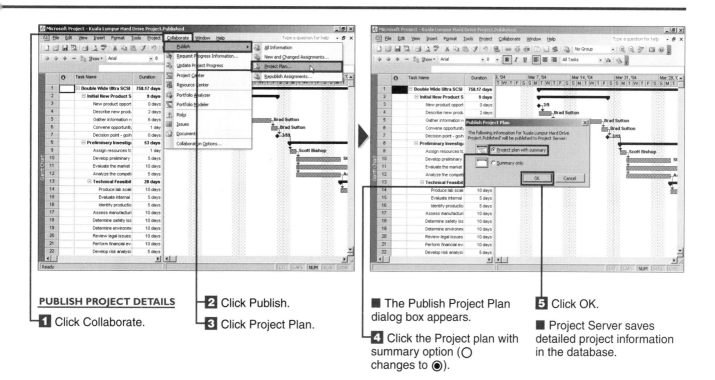

PUBLISH PROJECT DETAILS

1 Click Collaborate.

2 Click Publish.

3 Click Project Plan.

■ The Publish Project Plan dialog box appears.

4 Click the Project plan with summary option (○ changes to ◉).

5 Click OK.

■ Project Server saves detailed project information in the database.

IMPORT A PROJECT INTO THE PROJECT SERVER DATABASE

The section "Store a Project in the Project Server Database" demonstrated one way to upload a project to the Project Server database. If you prefer wizards, however, you can use the Import Project Wizard to save your project to the Project Server database. Do not open the project you want to import.

Once you start the wizard, you select the project to import. If any of the settings in your file are different from the settings in the Enterprise Global Template, you see a message; you should allow the Enterprise Global Template settings to overwrite the settings in your project. In the next wizard box, you can provide a name for the project that will appear in the Project Server database; you can make the name different from the local file name. You can also set enterprise custom field values.

The wizard enables you to map resources in your project to resources in the Enterprise Resource Pool if appropriate and, if necessary, task fields in your project to enterprise task fields.

Next, you see a summary of the settings that you have selected. The wizard also analyzes tasks in your project and reports any errors that it finds on this screen.

IMPORT A PROJECT INTO THE PROJECT SERVER DATABASE

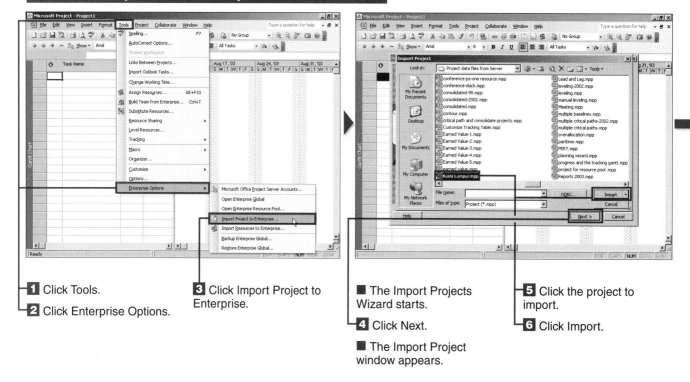

■1 Click Tools.

■2 Click Enterprise Options.

■3 Click Import Project to Enterprise.

■ The Import Projects Wizard starts.

■4 Click Next.

■ The Import Project window appears.

■5 Click the project to import.

■6 Click Import.

How do I set a value for an enterprise project custom field?

✔ In most cases, click in the Value column to select an acceptable value. If a custom field is calculated, you need to take whatever action your organization requires to calculate the field.

How do I map local resources to resources in the Enterprise Resource Pool?

✔ Click in the Action on Import column, and a list box appears from which you select the appropriate action. Click in the Calendar or Enterprise Resource column and select a resource.

How do I map local task fields to enterprise task fields?

✔ Click the option next to the field you want to map (☐ changes to ☑). Then click in the From: Task Field column, and a list box appears from which you select a local task field. Click in the To: Enterprise Task Field column, and another list box appears, from which you select the appropriate enterprise task field.

Can I import more than one project at a time using the wizard?

✔ No. However, at the end of the wizard, you can click Import More Projects to start the process again.

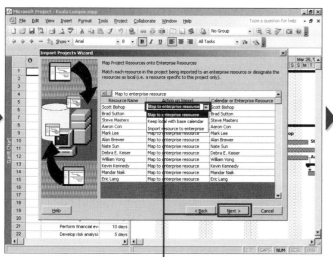

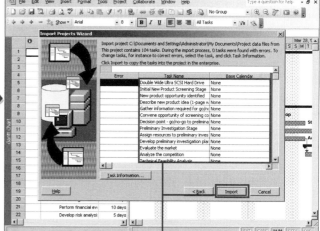

■ The project opens behind the next wizard box, which walks you through the process of assigning a name and values to the project's custom fields.

7 Click Next.

8 Click here to match local resources to enterprise resources as appropriate.

9 Click Next.

■ The wizard walks you through the process of matching local task fields to Enterprise task fields.

■ The tasks to import appear.

■ You can click here to assign task calendars.

10 Click Import.

■ The wizard walks you through the rest of the importing process.

OPEN A PROJECT STORED IN THE PROJECT SERVER DATABASE

Even if you are connected to the Project Server database, in Project Professional, you can open either the original project schedule or the version stored in the Project Server database.

When you open a project stored in the Project Server database, you see a published version of your project in Project Professional; the word representing the version appears at the end of the project name in the Project Professional title bar. For example, if the project name is

Data Center and you open a target version of it, you see Data Center Target in the Project Professional title bar.

With the project open in Project Professional, Project Server treats this project as *checked out*, and nobody else can open the project in Project Professional and save changes to it. You can identify who has opened each checked-out project in the Open from Microsoft Office Project Server dialog box.

When you close the project, Project automatically checks the project back in. If you do not close the project in Project Professional, it remains checked out; you can check it in from Project Web Access if you have appropriate security privileges, but any changes you made and did not save will be lost.

This section assumes you are starting in Project Professional and are logged onto the Project Server database.

OPEN A PROJECT STORED IN THE PROJECT SERVER DATABASE

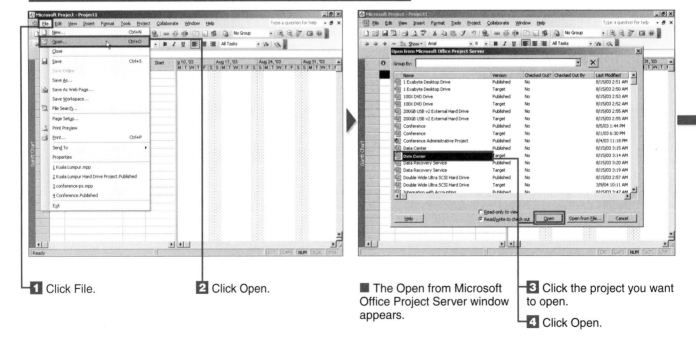

1 Click File.

2 Click Open.

■ The Open from Microsoft Office Project Server window appears.

3 Click the project you want to open.

4 Click Open.

Why would I open the local version of the project after I store it in the Project Server database?

✔ You may need to make major changes to a project you published because, for example, the project is in the planning stages and the start date changed. Open the original file instead of the version that is stored in the Project Server database by clicking the Open from File button in the Open from Microsoft Office Project Server window and update it. Make the necessary changes to the original file, and then republish it. If the project has started, you should never make changes and republish it.

After I upload a project to the Project Server database and others update it, how can I create an up-to-date local copy?

✔ Open the project using steps 1 to 4. Then click File and click Save As.

Once I make changes to the local version I created, how do I upload it?

✔ You cannot upload a project with the same name. To replace the file, use the Save As command to assign a new name to the project, upload it, and then delete the old published project using Project Web Access.

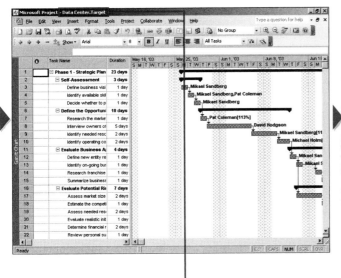

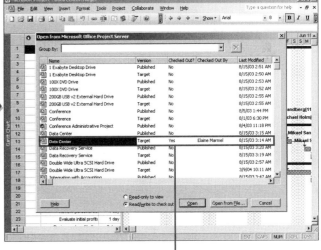

■ The project you selected appears in Project Professional.

■ The version appears appended to the file name in the title bar.

5 Repeat steps 1 to 2.

■ You see the status of all projects.

■ The project you opened appears checked out by you.

VIEW PROJECT SERVER PAGES IN PROJECT PROFESSIONAL

You can view the Project Center and the Resource Center pages of Project Web Access without leaving Project Professional. How much you see in these centers depends on your security settings.

In the Project Center, you see projects in the Project Server database. You can search for projects, filter to see projects that meet criteria you specify, and group projects in a variety of ways, including project name, version, duration, start date, finish date, and percent complete. For example, you might group by start date and then by project name to view projects scheduled to start around the same time. And, you can drill down into projects to see the details of the tasks in the project. While viewing details, you can focus on different aspects of the project based on the views defined by your organization.

In the Resource Center, you see resources in the Enterprise Resource Pool. You can view the availability of a resource. You can open the resource in Project — the equivalent of checking the resource out of the Enterprise Resource Pool — and, with proper privileges, you can make some changes to the resource in Project Web Access. As with projects, you can search for group, and filter resources.

VIEW PROJECT SERVER PAGES IN PROJECT PROFESSIONAL

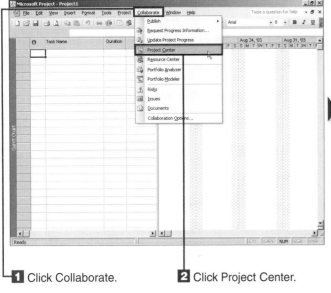

■ **1** Click Collaborate.

■ **2** Click Project Center.

■ The Project Center in Project Web Access appears.

■ One line represents each project.

■ You can click here to change views.

■ You can click View Options to change view options.

■ You can click here to search for, filter for, or group projects.

■ **3** Click here to return to Project Professional.

Why I do not see any projects or resources?

✔ You probably do not have proper security privileges; check with the Project Server Administrator.

Why do I see projects and resources but not all projects and resources?

✔ Again, your security privileges may be set to restrict the information you see; check with the Project Server Administrator.

How do I open a resource in Project Professional from the Resource Center?

✔ To the right of the View Availability button, you see an Open button. Highlight the resource you want to open and click that button.

When I click the Edit button next to the View Availability button, what fields can I change for a resource?

✔ You can change the current values for custom Enterprise resource codes that were established by your organization. To edit other fields, you must open the resource in Project.

I want to see information that does not appear in the views I see. Are there other views available?

✔ Typically, the Project Server Administrator creates views and assigns security privileges to use various views. Discuss the view you want to use with the Project Server database administrator.

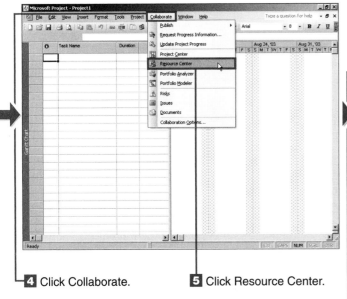

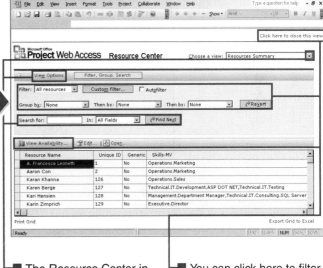

4 Click Collaborate.

5 Click Resource Center.

■ The Resource Center in Project Web Access appears.

■ You can click here to change views.

■ You can click here to specify search criteria.

■ You can click here to filter and group resources.

■ You can click here to view resource availability.

6 Click here to return to Project Professional.

SET UP ADMINISTRATIVE PROJECTS

Y ou set up administrative projects in Project Server to enable resources to account for non-working and non-project time. Project Server comes with a template administrative project containing tasks that represent reasons why a resource may not be available for work — vacation, sickness, bereavement, holiday, civic duty, military duty, family leave, training, and time off without

pay. You can add tasks to an administrative project as needed in your organization.

In an administrative project, you assign all resources you manage to all the administrative tasks. When you publish this project, Project Web Access displays these tasks at the bottom of each resource's time sheet with a work assignment of 0 hours. In Project Web Access, the

resource can assign time to these tasks as needed to report non-working or non-project time.

You start in Project Web Access to create administrative projects; you do not need to have Project Professional running, because Project Web Access automatically opens Project Professional to create the project. See Chapter 19 for details on logging onto Project Web Access.

SET UP ADMINISTRATIVE PROJECTS

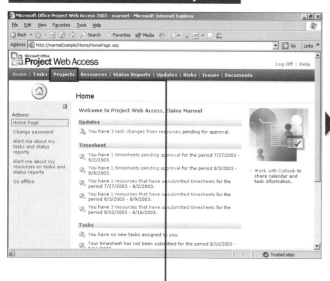

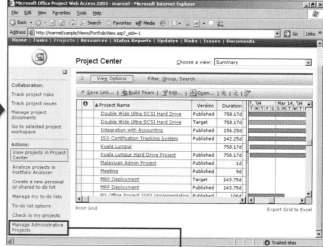

CREATE THE PROJECT

1 Open Internet Explorer and log onto Project Web Access.

■ The Project Web Access Home page appears.

2 Click Projects.

■ The Project Center appears.

3 Click the Manage Administrative Projects link.

Do assignments in administrative projects behave any differently than assignments in working projects?

✔ No. Project Server creates a resource assignment for every resource that you assign to an administrative task. The total number of resource assignments equals the number of projects to which a resource is assigned times the number of resources in a project. By and large, the more resource assignments you make, the longer it takes to open projects in Project Professional. Take this fact into account when your organization decides how to organize the use of administrative projects.

Are administrative projects included in the Portfolio Modeler?

✔ No. For more information on the Portfolio Modeler, see Chapter 20.

What is the best way to minimize the performance impact on Project Professional and use administrative projects?

✔ Try to organize the use of administrative projects in your oganization so that you assign each resource to as few administrative projects as possible.

What task types does the administrative project use?

✔ The tasks in the administrative project are not effort-driven; they are fixed duration tasks. And, you should not change that setting, because it accurately measures non-working time.

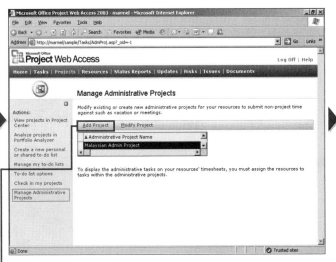

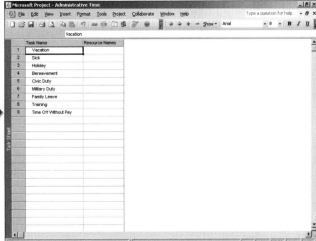

■ The Manage Administrative Projects page appears.

4 Click Add Project.

■ If you use Project Server security, the Project Server Security Logon window opens. Type your password and click Go.

■ Project Professional opens, showing the Administrative Time project.

CONTINUED

SET UP ADMINISTRATIVE PROJECTS (CONTINUED)

You can set up one administrative project per working project so that a resource can assign non-working or non-project time to the project on which he is working when he reports the non-working time. Other organizations have the resource manager create an administrative project that includes all resources he or she manages. A resource sees, at the bottom of his

timesheet in Project Web Access, non-working time fields for each administrative project to which he is assigned.

When the resource records non-working time by filling in time on any of the administrative tasks, you, as the resource's manager, receive notification. It is possible, however, that a resource you manage is assigned to a project that you do

not manage. In this case, you need to notify that project's manager of the change in the resource's availability, because Project Web Access no longer makes calendar changes based on working time changes. Instead, it changes a resource's availability. The project manager who is using your resource has no way of knowing that the resource reported non-working time unless you tell him.

SET UP ADMINISTRATIVE PROJECTS (CONTINUED)

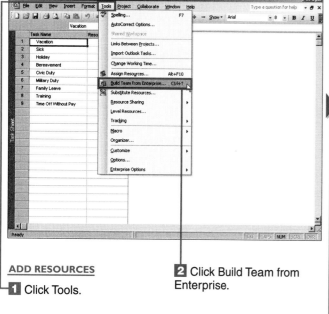

ADD RESOURCES

1 Click Tools.

2 Click Build Team from Enterprise.

■ The Build Team dialog box appears.

3 Click a resource.

4 Click Add.

■ You can click Customize filters (☐ changes to ☑) to set criteria to view only specific resources.

5 Repeat steps 7 to 8 for all of your resources.

6 Click OK.

■ The administrative project reappears.

Where can I read more about the Build Team dialog box?

✔ See Chapter 18. You use this dialog box to assign resources to a project and to replace generic resources with real resources, and Project Web Access contains a version of this dialog box that resource managers who do not use Project Professional can use.

In the example, why does only one resource appear to be assigned to each task?

✔ The Resource Names column was not wide enough to display all the resources assigned to the tasks. For more on widening columns or otherwise changing column appearance, see Chapter 7.

Because Project Server notifies the resource manager and not the project manager when a resource records non-working time, what is the best way to handle administrative projects and the communication required between project and resource managers?

✔ Your organization should standardize the way that communication and administrative projects are handled to minimize the manual intervention that administrative projects require. One technique your organization can employ is the status report available in Project Web Access. For more information on status reports, see Chapter 18.

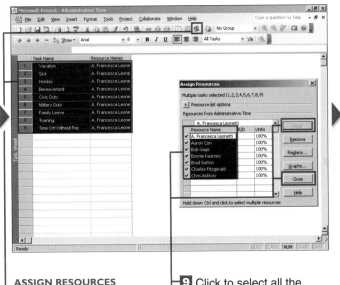

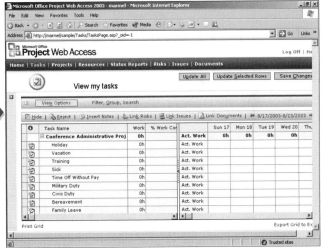

ASSIGN RESOURCES AND PUBLISH

7 Select all tasks in the project.

8 Click the Assign Resources button (🔲).

■ The Assign Resources window appears.

9 Click to select all the resources.

10 Click Assign.

■ Project assigns all resources to all tasks.

11 Click Close.

12 Publish the project.

Note: To publish a project, see the section "Store a Project in the Project Server Database."

■ When a resource in the project logs on and views the timesheet, the administrative tasks appear.

USING TO-DO LISTS

Project Server contains a to-do list feature that can help you manage small projects or personal projects. This feature is available in Project Server if the Project Server administrator enables the feature.

You name the to-do list and then you add items — tasks — to it that you need to accomplish. You can assign start dates and due dates to

the items, but you cannot link them or organize them outline-fashion or assign individual calendars to them like you can to tasks in Project Professional. You can assign resources to them, but you cannot define a task type, so any resource assignment does not affect the duration of the task. Further, the time that resources spend on to-do list tasks does not apply to any project.

You start and add to the list from the Project Center in Project Web Access, or PWA; see "Open and Close Project Web Access" in Chapter 19 for details. You can create to-do lists even if you do not have full privileges for the Project Center. If the items on the to-do list turn into a project, you can upload the to-do list information into Project Professional to use all of its scheduling and tracking features.

USING TO-DO LISTS

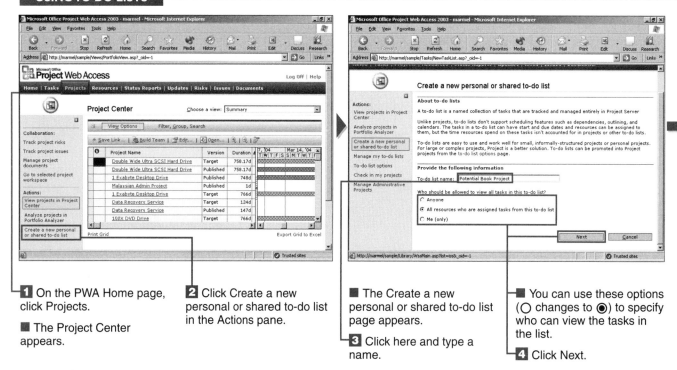

1 On the PWA Home page, click Projects.

■ The Project Center appears.

2 Click Create a new personal or shared to-do list in the Actions pane.

■ The Create a new personal or shared to-do list page appears.

3 Click here and type a name.

■ The Create a new personal or shared to-do list page appears.

4 Click Next.

■ You can use these options (○ changes to ●) to specify who can view the tasks in the list.

How many to-do lists can I create?
✔ As many as you want. Many people create a to-do list for each potential new project. You can create a to-do list of household chores, but be aware that to-do lists appear in the Project Center.

What happens if I click To-do list options in the Action pane?
✔ The To-do list options page appears where you select a to-do list to modify. You can rename the list, transfer the list to another resource, turn the list into a Project Professional project, delete the list, or change who can view it.

What kind of options can I set to filter, group, or search?
✔ You can filter to view only completed tasks, incomplete tasks, overdue tasks, or you can create a custom filter where you set criteria based on any field in the to-do list. For example, you can filter to view only tasks dated on a date you specify. You can group by to-do list or any field on the to-do list. You can search for any string in all fields on the to-do list or in any particular field.

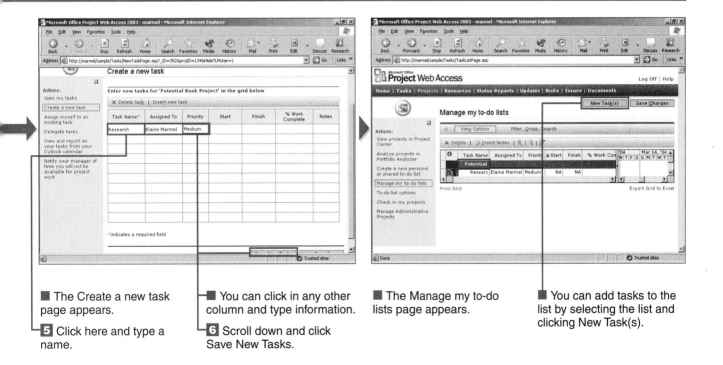

■ The Create a new task page appears.

5 Click here and type a name.

■ You can click in any other column and type information.

6 Scroll down and click Save New Tasks.

■ The Manage my to-do lists page appears.

■ You can add tasks to the list by selecting the list and clicking New Task(s).

ADD ENTERPRISE RESOURCES TO A PROJECT

Y ou can add resources to a Web-based project the same way that you add them to a stand-alone project, but you have some powerful tools available to you in Project Server that enable you to use the Enterprise Resource Pool to build a team for your project.

The Enterprise Resource Pool is a file that is available to all project and resource managers, and it provides a list of all resources that

are owned by your organization. In some organizations, the Project Server administrator initially builds the Enterprise Resource Pool, but, if you have appropriate permissions, you can add resources to the Enterprise Resource Pool.

As the project manager, you can use the Team Builder feature in Project Professional and the Enterprise Resource Pool to select resources that are appropriate for your project. You can also assign generic

resources to your project and then use the Team Builder feature to help you replace the generic resources with real resources. See the section "Replace Generic Resources with Real Resources" in this chapter for more information.

In addition, if you manage more than one project at a time, you can take advantage of the Resource Substitution Wizard to identify the best possible utilization of limited resources.

ADD ENTERPRISE RESOURCES TO A PROJECT

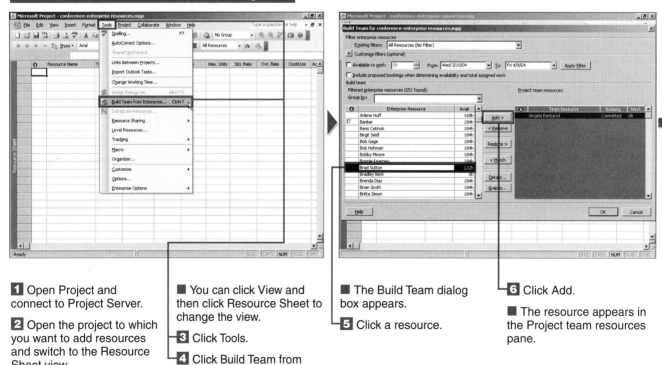

1 Open Project and connect to Project Server.

2 Open the project to which you want to add resources and switch to the Resource Sheet view.

■ You can click View and then click Resource Sheet to change the view.

3 Click Tools.

4 Click Build Team from Enterprise.

■ The Build Team dialog box appears.

5 Click a resource.

6 Click Add.

■ The resource appears in the Project team resources pane.

Did I need to switch to the Resource view to use the Build Team dialog box?

✓ No. You can add resources from the Enterprise Resource Pool from any view. However, you can view the results most easily in the Resource Sheet view.

Can I set more than one filter at a time?

✓ Yes. You can set as many filters as you want. By using the And choice, you reduce the number of possible resources that Project displays. By using the Or choice, you increase the number of possible resources that Project displays.

How do I create a custom filter?

✓ Click in the Field Name column to display a list of fields and select one. Click in the Test column and select a test like equals or greater than. Last, supply a value in the Value(s) column.

Can I indicate that I want to use a resource but I have not yet received approval for the assignment?

✓ Yes. When you select a resource, you can change the status from Committed to Proposed in the Booking column of the Project team resources pane to indicate that the resource assignment has not yet been approved.

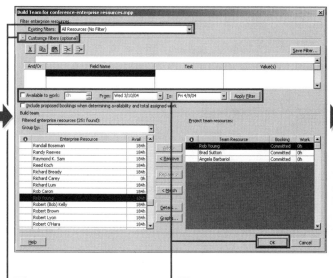

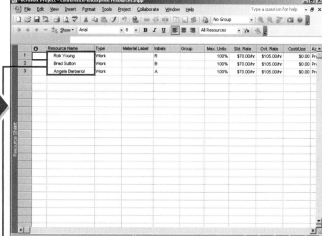

■ You can click here to filter resources based on values stored in a variety of Project fields.

■ You can click here to create custom filters.

■ You can click here to filter by available hours in a specified date range.

7 Repeat steps 5 to 6 until you add all the resources you want.

8 Click OK.

■ Your project reappears.

■ Your project includes the enterprise resources you added.

Note: To assign the resources to tasks, see Chapter 4.

Note: To publish your project to update Project Server with the resource assignments, see Chapter 17.

REPLACE GENERIC RESOURCES WITH REAL RESOURCES

I f your organization uses generic resources and has assigned skills to resources, you can use the Team Builder to match a generic resource in your project to a real resource that has the same skills assigned to the generic resource.

Some history: The person who creates enterprise custom fields — probably the Project Server administrator — created a multi-value enterprise resource custom

outline code to store skills needed by resources for projects performed by your organization — cleverly, the person who created the code may have called it Skills. The person in your organization who added resources to the Enterprise Resource Pool used the code to assign one or more skills to each resource. For details on adding resources to the Enterprise Resource Pool and using multi-value enterprise outline codes, see Chapter 17.

The same person who created the Enterprise Resource Pool also created generic resources, such as Accountant or Computer Programmer, and assigned values for the custom outline code to these generic resources.

Back to the present: Suppose, as you are building a team, you are not ready to assign real resources, so you assigned generic resources. Now, you need real resources; you can use the Team Builder to find them.

REPLACE GENERIC RESOURCES WITH REAL RESOURCES

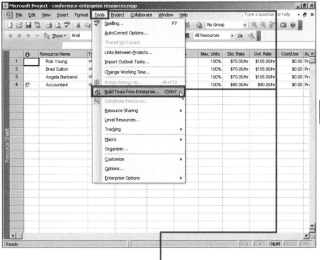
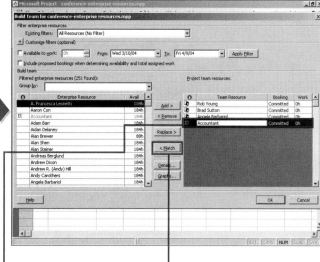

1 Open Project and connect to Project Server.

2 Open the project to which you want to add resources and switch to the Resource Sheet view.

■ You can click View and then click Resource Sheet to change the view.

3 Click Tools.

4 Click Build Team from Enterprise.

■ The Build Team dialog box appears.

5 Click the generic resource.

6 Click Match.

How can I view the skills of a particular resource?

✔ Check the resource out of the Enterprise Resource Pool — you can use the Read Only option. In the Resource Sheet, double-click the resource to view the resource's Resource Information dialog box. Click the Custom Fields tab and locate the multi-value custom field for skills — its name ends with –MV.

Who typically sets up the Enterprise Resource Pool?

✔ Your organization may assign the task to the Project Server Administrator or give privileges to project managers so that they can update the Enterprise Resource Pool. See Chapter 17 for details on setting up the pool.

What is the RBS code that appears at the bottom of the Custom Outline Codes tab of the Customize Enterprise Fields dialog box?

✔ RBS stands for Resource Breakdown Structure. The staff at Microsoft prenamed Enterprise Resource Outline Code30 to RBS. Conceptually, you can compare this code for resources to a WBS code for tasks. For more about WBS codes, see Chapter 9. Your organization may want to use the RBS code for skills or for a different purpose, such as assigning a resource's geographic location. The RBS code takes on whatever meaning your organization assigns.

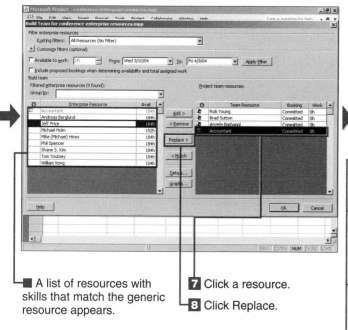

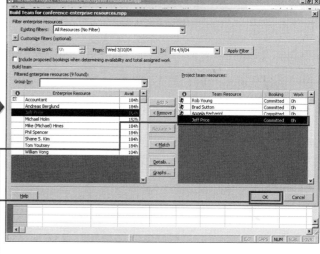

■ A list of resources with skills that match the generic resource appears.

7 Click a resource.

8 Click Replace.

■ Project replaces the generic resource with the real resource you selected.

9 Click OK.

■ The Resource Sheet in your project reflects the replacement.

10 Save your project and publish it to Project Server.

NOTIFY RESOURCES OF ASSIGNMENTS

After the project manager assigns work to resources, the resources need to know that work has been assigned. To notify the resources of the work assignments, the project manager publishes the assignments. At a minimum, the team members receive notifications in Project Web Access of new or updated assignments. If your organization chooses, team members may also receive e-mail notifications.

You can only view and process resource updates on assignments for which you are the manager. You can be the manager of one or more assignments without being the overall project manager. You become a manager, not by publishing the project plan, but by publishing an assignment for a task or assuming responsibility upon republishing assignments.

When you notify resources of assignments to tasks, you can make selective notifications if you want.

For example, if you make a change to an assignment on a task, you can select that task only and Project notifies the affected resources of the change in assignment on that particular task.

You notify resources of assignments in Project Professional from the project containing the resource assignments about which you want to send notifications.

NOTIFY RESOURCES OF ASSIGNMENTS

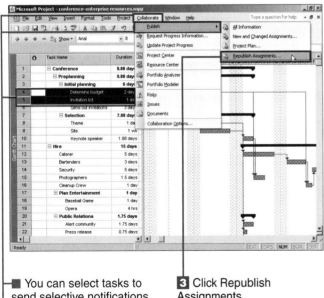

■ You can select tasks to send selective notifications.

■1 Click Collaborate.

■2 Click Publish.

3 Click Republish Assignments.

Note: A message may appear; click OK to save your project.

■ The Republish Assignments dialog box appears.

4 Click the Become the manager for these assignments option (☐ changes to ☑).

■ You can click the Edit message text option (☐ changes to ☑) to make any changes to the text that accompany the e-mail notification the resource receives.

5 Click OK.

Why select the Become the manager for these assignments option (☐ changes to ☑)?

✔ So that you can view and process any updates that resources make to these assignments. If you are not the manager of the assignments, you do not receive progress updates or changes made to these assignments or notifications about these assignments.

Why select the Republish Assignments command instead of New and Changed Assignments command?

✔ The New and Changed Assignments command, on the Publish menu, publishes changes to tasks, such as new start or finish dates. This command forces Project to publish assignments, even if you have previously published them.

What happens if I deselect the Notify all affected resources via e-mail option?

✔ When you select this option (☐ changes to ☑), resources receive notification in Project Web Access and via e-mail if your organization has set up Project Server to provide e-mail notifications and reminders. The resource does not receive notification of the assignment via e-mail if you deselect the option (☑ changes to ☐) or if your organiztion does not use e-mail notifications in Project Server. The resource still sees the assignment in PWA on the Home page and on the Tasks page.

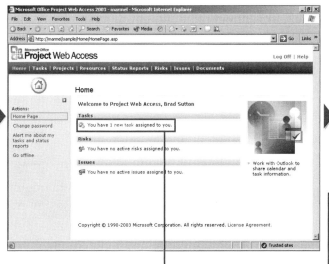

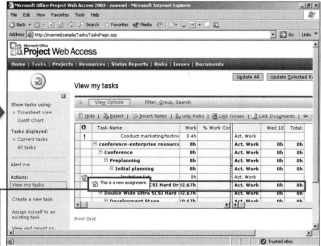

■ The Republish Assignments dialog box reappears.

6 Click OK.

■ When one of the resources views the PWA Home page, he or she sees notification of a new task assignment.

■ The resource can view the assignment on the Tasks page.

USING THE RESOURCE SUBSTITUTION WIZARD

S uppose that you manage multiple projects with the same set of resources and you want to try to smooth work assignments and reduce over-allocations across one or more projects. Or suppose that you assigned generic resources throughout a project and now want to find real resources to substitute. Use the Resource Substitution Wizard to find resources.

Earlier in this chapter, you saw how to use the Build Team dialog

box to replace a generic resource with a real resource. The steps in that section work best when you do not have much substituting to do and when the factors affecting the substitution are limited. For example, you can work successfully in the Build Team dialog box if you are trying to substitute only a few resources in a single project.

When you need to consider more complex factors, the Resource Substitution Wizard is a better choice because it can use different

criteria to substitute resources. The Resource Substitution Wizard enables you to substitute resources across multiple projects simultaneously and suggests a list of related projects that you can have the wizard consider while suggesting substitutions.

This section assumes that you have opened the projects that you want the Resource Substitution Wizard to consider before starting.

USING THE RESOURCE SUBSTITUTION WIZARD

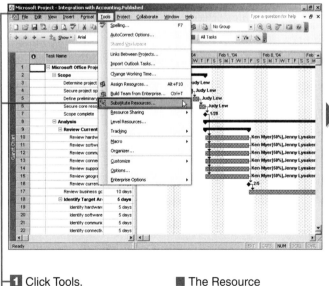

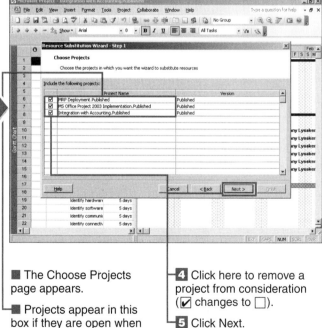

■1 Click Tools.

■2 Click Substitute Resources.

■ The Resource Substitution Wizard starts.

■3 Click Next.

■ The Choose Projects page appears.

■ Projects appear in this box if they are open when you start the wizard.

■4 Click here to remove a project from consideration (☑ changes to ☐).

■5 Click Next.

When I substitute resources, are the assignments committed or proposed?

✔ By default, the Resource Substitution Wizard uses committed resources only. However, you can include proposed resources as well if you click the Allow resources with the proposed booking type to be assigned to tasks option (□ changes to ✔) in the Choose Resources wizard box.

Can I make the Resource Substitution Wizard start substituting resources for tasks that start on or after a specific date?

✔ Yes. Type that date in the Resource freeze horizon list in the Choose Resources wizard box. By default, the resource freeze horizon appears as the current date.

What is the easiest way to assign a skill code to a task to identify the skills needed to complete the task so that I can staff using the Resource Substitution Wizard?

✔ Add the skills code to your project's tasks in the Resource Usage view. All tasks appear under the "Unassigned" resource before staffing, and you can add a column for the code to the view. Then, you can easily assign the code to each task, and the Resource Substitution Wizard will be able to add resources to your project based on the skills required to complete each task.

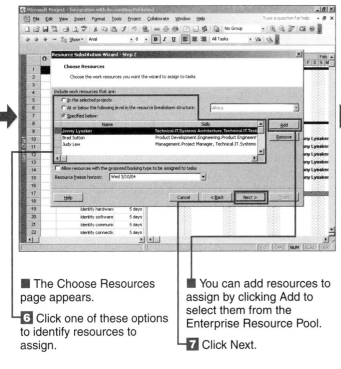

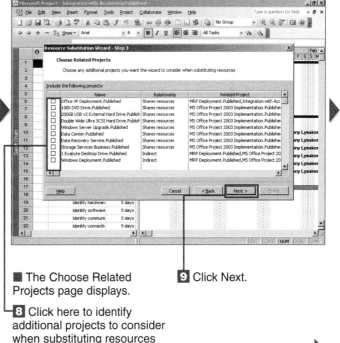

■ The Choose Resources page appears.

6 Click one of these options to identify resources to assign.

■ You can add resources to assign by clicking Add to select them from the Enterprise Resource Pool.

7 Click Next.

■ The Choose Related Projects page displays.

8 Click here to identify additional projects to consider when substituting resources (□ changes to ✔).

9 Click Next.

CONTINUED ▶

USING THE RESOURCE SUBSTITUTION WIZARD (CONTINUED)

Before you run the Resource Substitution Wizard, the Project Server administrator or some other designee should have created the Enterprise Resource Pool, defined the enterprise resource outline codes for resource skills, and assigned those resource skills to all enterprise resources. The Resource Substitution Wizard cannot, for example, compare the skills of resources unless the skill code has been defined and assigned.

Because the Resource Substitution Wizard does not work unless you assign these codes, you can double-check the code assignments of resources you want to consider by checking them out of the Enterprise Resource Pool and reviewing the code assignments by adding a column for the custom field to the Resource Sheet view. Note that you can review the skills outline code, but, without administrative privileges, you cannot add or change skills. For more on checking

out resources, as well as editing resources in the Enterprise Resource Pool, see Chapter 17.

After the wizard finishes, level the resources in the projects to see how the wizard's resource assignments change project finish dates and resource utilization. See Chapter 11 for details on leveling.

If you do not like the results of the wizard, simply close the affected projects without saving them.

USING THE RESOURCE SUBSTITUTION WIZARD (CONTINUED)

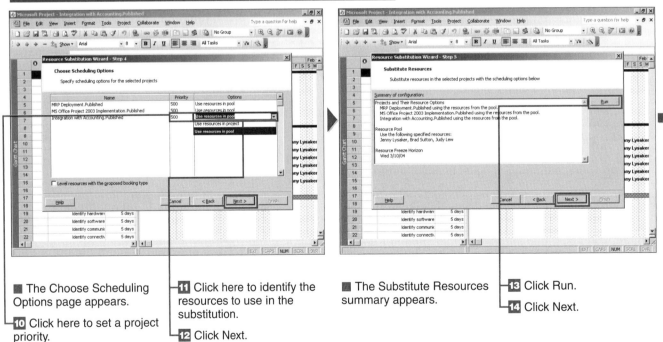

■ The Choose Scheduling Options page appears.

10 Click here to set a project priority.

11 Click here to identify the resources to use in the substitution.

12 Click Next.

■ The Substitute Resources summary appears.

13 Click Run.

14 Click Next.

What does the project priority in the Choose Scheduling Options box do?

✔ When making resource assignments, invariably, conflicts arise, and making resource assignments using the Resource Substitution Wizard is no exception. One of the techniques Project uses to resolve conflicts involves delaying. Project uses the priority of the project as one factor to determine which project to delay first when resolving conflicts. Project delays projects with lower priorities before delaying projects with higher priorities.

Does the Resource Substitution Wizard consider resource availability when making assignments?

✔ Yes.

When do I set a Resource freeze horizon date?

✔ Setting the Resource freeze horizon date is helpful when you want to retain current assignments in the short term but staff assignments further in the future.

On the Choose Related Projects page, what does the Relationship box tell me?

✔ The Relationship box tells you how the listed projects are related to your selected project — either the projects have linked tasks or they share resources. You can select a project in this page to add it to the projects being restaffed by the Resource Substitution Wizard.

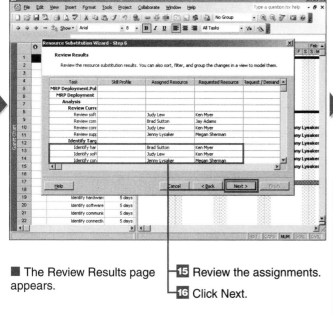

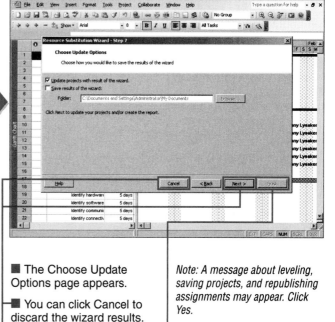

■ The Review Results page appears.

-15 Review the assignments.

-16 Click Next.

■ The Choose Update Options page appears.

■ You can click Cancel to discard the wizard results.

-17 Click Next to use the wizard results.

Note: A message about leveling, saving projects, and republishing assignments may appear. Click Yes.

-18 Click Finish.

ASSIGN RESOURCES USING PROJECT WEB ACCESS

A s a resource manager, you may not have Project Professional, but you can manage your resources using Project Web Access.

You can build a team for your project using Project Web Access. To find the resources you need, you can use filters. If your organization defined an enterprise outline code that describes skills, you can filter to find resources with specified skills. Similarly, you can replace generic resources with real

resources that have the appropriate skills needed for your project. And, you can specify whether you want the resources to be committed to the project or only proposed for the project. You also can check availability for a particular resource before you assign it to your project by viewing an availability graph of a resource.

The resource manager who does not use Project Professional works in the Project Center of Project Web Access to build a team and

manage resources. When you save resource assignments, a message appears indicating that no changes will appear in Project Web Access until the project manager republishes the project. When the project manager reopens the published project, the resources appear on the resource sheet, and the project manager can assign them to tasks.

ASSIGN RESOURCES USING PROJECT WEB ACCESS

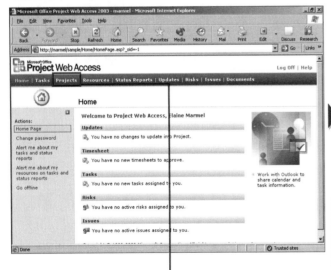

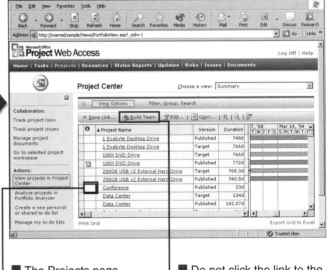

1 Log on to Project Web Access.

Note: For more on opening and closing Project Web Access, see Chapter 19.

■ You see the Project Web Access Home page.

2 Click Projects.

■ The Projects page appears.

3 Click the row of the project in the Information column.

■ Do not click the link to the project.

4 Click Build Team.

■ The Build Team page appears.

When I click View All, do I see all the resources in the Enterprise Resource Pool?

✔ You see only those resources you are permitted to see.

What happens if I click the link to the project?

✔ The project details appear, but the page contains no way to reach the Build Team page.

How do I assign resources to tasks?

✔ You do not. A project manager using Project Professional opens the project, which now contains the resources you assigned, and makes assignments.

How do I replace generic resources with real resources?

✔ Generic resources already in the project appear in the list on the right. Click the generic resource in the list on the right. Then click Match. From the resources that appear in the list on the left because they meet the criteria, select a resource and click Replace.

How do I quickly find a resource without filtering?

✔ You can click in the Filtered Enterprise Resources list and type the first letter of the resource's first name. Project takes you to the first resource whose name begins with the letter you typed.

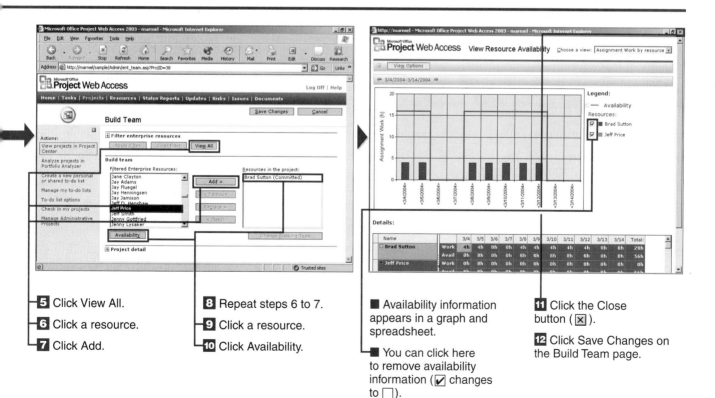

5 Click View All.

6 Click a resource.

7 Click Add.

8 Repeat steps 6 to 7.

9 Click a resource.

10 Click Availability.

■ Availability information appears in a graph and spreadsheet.

■ You can click here to remove availability information (☑ changes to ☐).

11 Click the Close button (☒).

12 Click Save Changes on the Build Team page.

SET UP STATUS REPORTS

After you upload a project to Project Server, you need to track its progress, and a status report is one technique you can use to effectively track progress. You can use a Project Web Access wizard to set up a status report template that contains the information you need to track the project; your team members can then use it to provide you with a status report.

As you can create the layout for the status report that you want to receive from your team members in Project Web Access, you identify the topics that you want included in the status report, and you can specify how often you want status reports. You also can select the team members who should submit status reports; you may not need to receive status reports from everyone because you may have structured reporting on your

project so that some team members report to other team members, who then report to you.

After you complete the report settings, you send an empty version of the report to the selected team members; they fill in the information you want and return it to you. This section assumes that you are starting in Project Web Access.

SET UP STATUS REPORTS

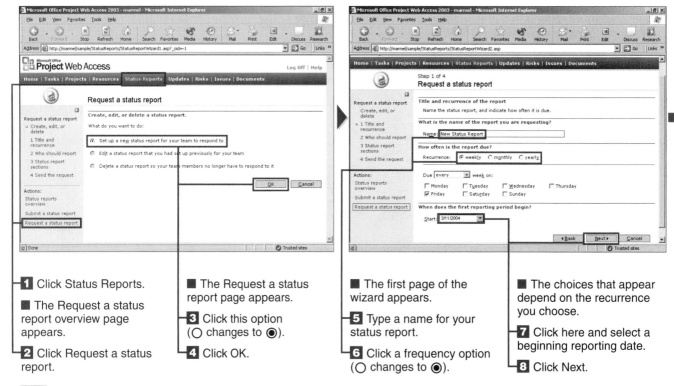

- **1** Click Status Reports.

■ The Request a status report overview page appears.

- **2** Click Request a status report.

■ The Request a status report page appears.

- **3** Click this option (○ changes to ◉).

- **4** Click OK.

■ The first page of the wizard appears.

- **5** Type a name for your status report.

- **6** Click a frequency option (○ changes to ◉).

■ The choices that appear depend on the recurrence you choose.

- **7** Click here and select a beginning reporting date.

- **8** Click Next.

When should I click Save and when should I click Send?

✔ If you click Send, Project Web Access both saves the report template and sends it to the selected resources so that they can use it to submit the report when required. If you do not want to send the report to the selected resources — perhaps because you may want to make changes — click Save.

How do I edit a status report?

✔ Follow the steps in this section again, clicking the Edit a status report that you had set up previously for your team option (○ changes to ◉) in step 3.

What does the Merge check box do?

✔ When you select this box next to selected resources (☐ changes to ☑), Project Web Access combines the reports of multiple resources into one report, essentially creating a status report for a group.

What choices appear when I choose to receive the report monthly?

✔ You can specify a specific date such as the 15th or as a floating date, such as the last Friday of the month. If you select yearly, you can specify a specific date or a floating date such as the first Wednesday of April.

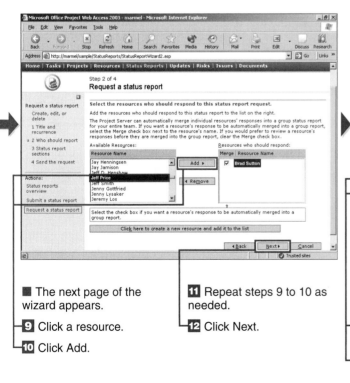

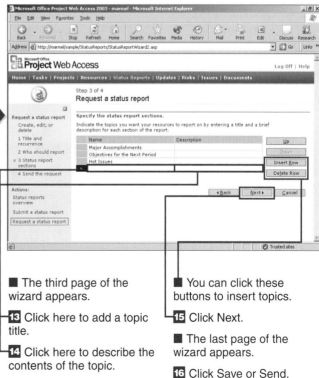

■ The next page of the wizard appears.

9 Click a resource.

10 Click Add.

11 Repeat steps 9 to 10 as needed.

12 Click Next.

■ The third page of the wizard appears.

13 Click here to add a topic title.

14 Click here to describe the contents of the topic.

■ You can click these buttons to insert topics.

15 Click Next.

■ The last page of the wizard appears.

16 Click Save or Send.

RECEIVE UPDATES FROM TEAM MEMBERS

Receiving updates from team members is critical to effectively tracking the progress of a project. When team members record time in Project Web Access, they see a message indicating that an update was sent to the project manager for approval of actual work recorded by the team member.

The project manager's home page in Project Web Access contains an Updates section that displays information about pending updates. This Updates section does not appear on a team member's home page. Using the Updates section, the project manager can view task changes submitted by resources and approve or reject the changes.

You, as the project manager, can accept or reject any individual update. If, after reviewing updates, you want to accept all updates you received, you do not need to individually accept the changes. Project Web Access contains a button that you can click, making it easy for you to accept all changes. If Project is not already running, Project Web Access launches it, opens the project from the Project Server database in Project, and updates the project. After updating has completed, you see a message indicating that you need to save your project.

RECEIVE UPDATES FROM TEAM MEMBERS

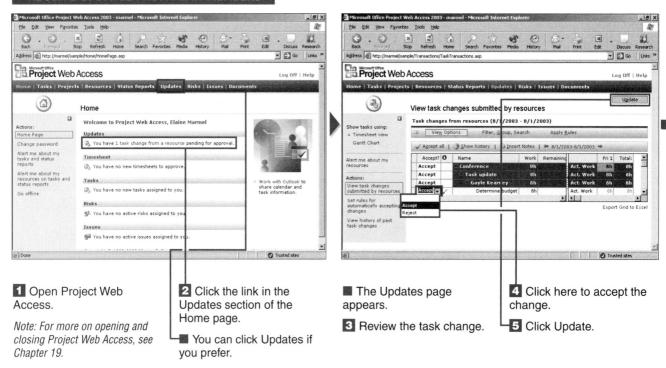

1 Open Project Web Access.

Note: For more on opening and closing Project Web Access, see Chapter 19.

2 Click the link in the Updates section of the Home page.

■ You can click Updates if you prefer.

■ The Updates page appears.

3 Review the task change.

4 Click here to accept the change.

5 Click Update.

What happens if I do not save the Project file?

✔ The updates remain in Project Web Access until you save the Project file.

Do I see anything in Project Web Access after I approve task changes?

✔ You see a message indicating that Project has updated approved task changes and has notified resources of rejected tasks.

Can resources submit calendar changes?

✔ Yes. If a resource submits a calendar change, the project manager sees the View changes to resource calendars page in Project Web Access.

Is there some way that I can speed up the process of accepting changes?

✔ Yes. You can set up rules for automatically accepting changes from selected users for selected projects. Click the Set rules for automatically accepting changes link in the Actions pane.

As a functional manager, can I also track and approve actuals that are recorded by resources who are working for me?

✔ Yes. From the Resource Center of PWA, click the Approve timesheets link in the Actions pane.

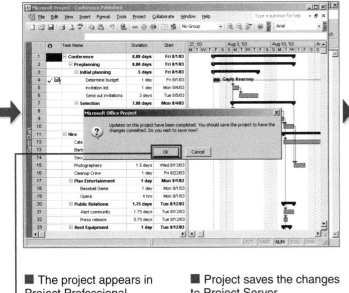

■ The project appears in Project Professional.

6 Click OK.

■ Project saves the changes to Project Server.

7 Switch back to Project Web Access.

■ A message appears indicating that Project successfully processed the updates.

8 Click OK.

ADJUST ACTUAL WORK

While in most cases, you should not change the work reported by a team member — accepting the values reported by a team member is simply good business practice — in some cases, you need to make adjustments to the actual work values that a resource reports. You can make these adjustments in Project Web Access if the Project Server administrator gives you the proper permissions.

You have the privileges required to adjust actual work if you see a link in the Actions pane of the Resource Center that enables you to navigate to the page where you make the adjustments. If you do not see the link and you believe you should adjust actual work values, contact the Project Server administrator.

To adjust actual work, you select a resource, and Project Web Access displays a grid with actual work

reported by the resource. You then find the value and make the change by supplying either a percentage on the left side of the grid or an hourly adjustment on the right side of the grid. Navigating away from the page saves the change.

ADJUST ACTUAL WORK

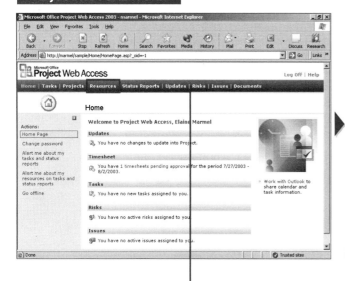

1 Log onto Project Web Access.

Note: For more on opening and closing Project Web Access, see Chapter 19.

2 Click Resources.

■ The Resource Center page appears.

3 Click Adjust actuals.

How do I save the adjustments?

✔ When you navigate away from the page, Project Server automatically saves the adjustments.

How can I filter and group resources on the Resource Center page?

✔ Using a custom filter, you can compare fields like Resource Name, Generic, Department, Type, Material Label, Maximum Units, availability dates, or enterprise custom multi-value outline codes equal to a test value. You can set a second and third level of the filter using the same fields to exclude even more resources. You can group by all of the same fields that you can use to create a filter.

I have permission to adjut actual work,but cannot see the link to adjust actuals in the Resource Center.Why not?

✔ Double-check with your administrator. You must not only have permission to adjust actual work, but you must also have permission to view adjusted actuals.

Where can I enter the adjustment as a percentage?

✔ On the last screen, where you can type the adjustment in hours, you need to use the scroll bar below the left side of the grid to navigate to the X column.

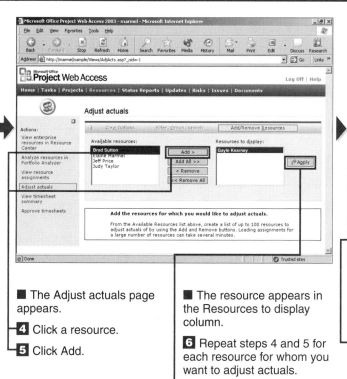

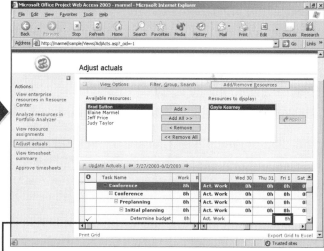

■ The Adjust actuals page appears.

4 Click a resource.

5 Click Add.

■ The resource appears in the Resources to display column.

6 Repeat steps 4 and 5 for each resource for whom you want to adjust actuals.

7 Click Apply.

■ The page expands to display actuals for the selected resources.

8 Click in a cell and type a new value.

9 Navigate to a new page by clicking the appropriate link at the top of the screen.

■ Project Web Access saves the changes.

TRACK ISSUES

Y ou can create and track issues that are associated with a project if your organization is using Windows SharePoint Services. Anyone with proper permissions can initiate issues, and the concept behind them is to promote collaboration on the project team.

Issues are unexpected things that occur on projects. They may be problems, or they may be

opportunities. When they arise, you can create an issue, let others on the team review the issue, assign the issue to someone to address, and monitor the progress of the issue.

Tracking issues is part of the larger Document Tracking feature provided by Windows SharePoint Services. When you track issues, you make sure that little things get addressed and do not fall through

the cracks during the mad rush to get everything done. The Document Tracking feature in Project Server enables you to attach documents to an issue. For example, suppose that a team member stumbles on a white paper that impacts the project. The team member can create an issue and attach the white paper to the issue so that everyone on the team can review the white paper and help come up with solutions to address the issue.

TRACK ISSUES

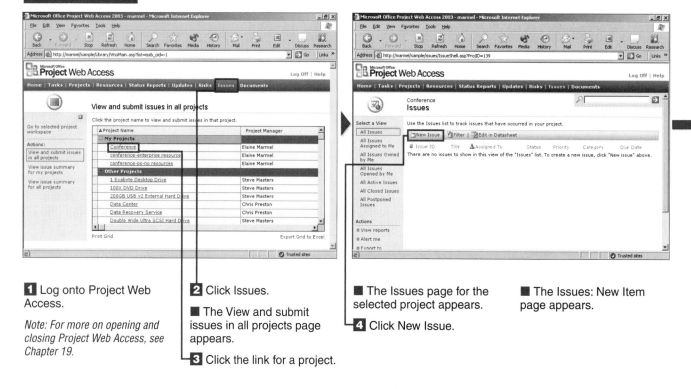

1 Log onto Project Web Access.

Note: For more on opening and closing Project Web Access, see Chapter 19.

2 Click Issues.

■ The View and submit issues in all projects page appears.

3 Click the link for a project.

■ The Issues page for the selected project appears.

4 Click New Issue.

■ The Issues: New Item page appears.

Why can I not create an issue?
✔ The Project Server administrator must give you rights to work with issues.

How do I view an overview of the number of issues on each project?
✔ Yes. Click the View issue summary for all projects link in the Actions pane on the left side of the View and submit issues in all projects page.

Is there anything else at the bottom of the Issues: New Item page?
✔ Yes. You have the opportunity to identify affected tasks, tasks that can help resolve the issue, other linked tasks, linked issues, and linked documents.

Is there a place for me to propose a resolution to the issue?
✔ Yes, at the bottom of the Issues: New Item page.

When I click Issues and see the View and submit issues in all projects page, do I really see all projects?
✔ No. You see the projects that you have security rights to view.

Can I attach documents to anything besides issues?
✔ Yes. You can attach documents to risks, projects, tasks, or to-do lists.

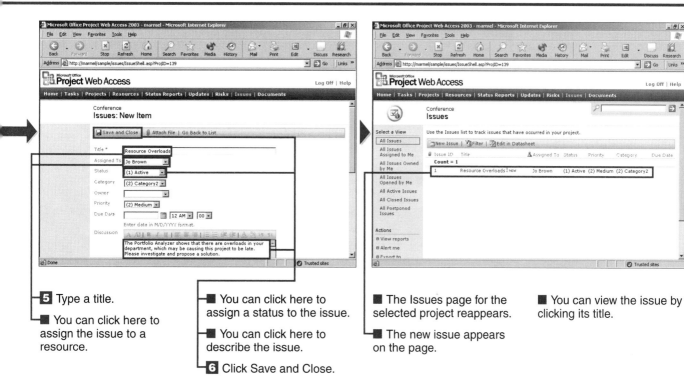

-5 Type a title.

■ You can click here to assign the issue to a resource.

■ You can click here to assign a status to the issue.

■ You can click here to describe the issue.

-6 Click Save and Close.

■ The Issues page for the selected project reappears.

■ The new issue appears on the page.

■ You can view the issue by clicking its title.

TRACK RISKS

You can create and track risks that are associated with a project if your organization is using Windows SharePoint Services. Anyone with proper permissions can initiate risks, and the concept behind them is the same concept behind tracking issues — to promote collaboration on the project team.

Risks are possible events or conditions that could negatively impact a project. Risks are events

that have not yet occurred but that *could occur.* Essentially, a risk is an issue before it happens.

Tracking risks, like tracking issues, is part of the larger Document Tracking feature provided by Windows SharePoint Services. When you track risks, you make sure that little things get addressed and do not fall through the cracks during the mad rush to get everything done. The Document Tracking feature in Project Server

enables you to attach documents to a risk. For example, suppose that a team member receives notification that the contract for the facility where your team is conducting the project is going to expire in 30 days. The team member can create a risk and attach the notification to the risk so that everyone on the team can review the notification.

TRACK RISKS

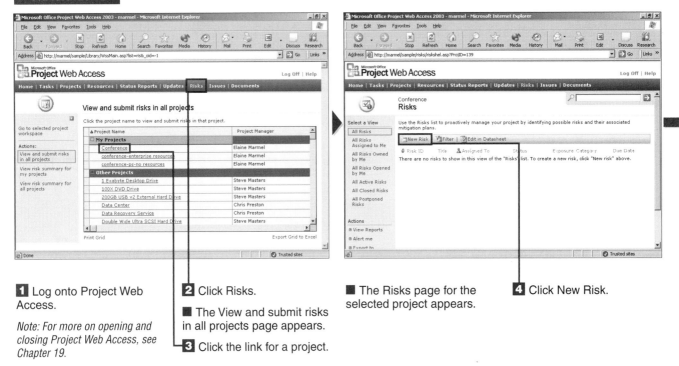

1 Log onto Project Web Access.

Note: For more on opening and closing Project Web Access, see Chapter 19.

2 Click Risks.

■ The View and submit risks in all projects page appears.

3 Click the link for a project.

■ The Risks page for the selected project appears.

4 Click New Risk.

I tried to create a risk, but I could not. Why not?

✔ The Project Server administrator must give you rights to work with risks.

Is there a place for me to propose a solution to the risk?

✔ At the bottom of the Risks: New Item page, you can provide a mitigation plan to try to lessen the risk, a contingency plan that serves as a fallback should the risk occur, a description of what might trigger the risk to occur, and a date on which the trigger might occur.

Is there anything else at the bottom of the Risks: New Item page?

✔ Yes. You have the opportunity to identify affected tasks, tasks that can trigger the risk, tasks that are part of the mitigation plan, tasks that are part of the contingency plan, other related risks in the project, and documents and issues related to the risk.

When I click Risks and see the View and submit risks in all projects page, do I really see all projects?

✔ No. You see the projects that you have security rights to view.

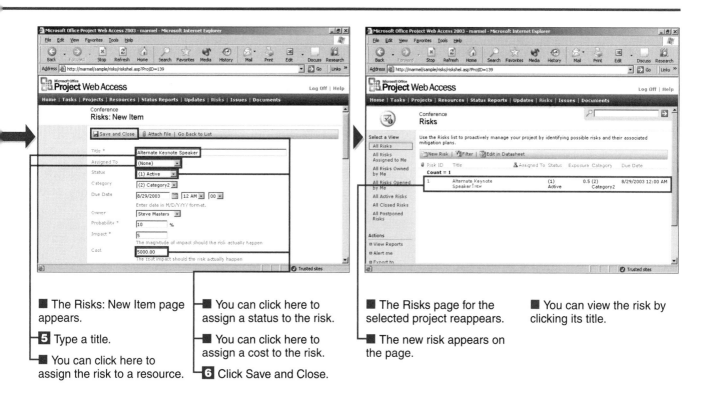

■ The Risks: New Item page appears.

5 Type a title.

■ You can click here to assign the risk to a resource.

■ You can click here to assign a status to the risk.

■ You can click here to assign a cost to the risk.

6 Click Save and Close.

■ The Risks page for the selected project reappears.

■ The new risk appears on the page.

■ You can view the risk by clicking its title.

USING VERSIONS

Your organization may decide to create a variety of versions that you can use when publishing projects so that you can compare variations of the same project. For example, your organization may create versions that enable you to compare variations of a project that include added and deleted tasks that were not saved in baselines. Making comparisons between snapshots of a project taken at different times can help you with trend analysis.

Or, your organization may want to use different versions of the same project so that, when modeling, you can evaluate different possible outcomes for a project.

Before you can create different versions of a project in the Project Server database, you must publish the project, and Project Server automatically defines a version called Published that you can use. You automatically publish your project when you save your

project to Project Server. If your organization wants to use other versions, the Project Server administrator must define the other versions that will be available to you.

When you open a project in Project Professional, you have the option of opening any available version for each project in the Open from Microsoft Office Project Server dialog box.

USING VERSIONS

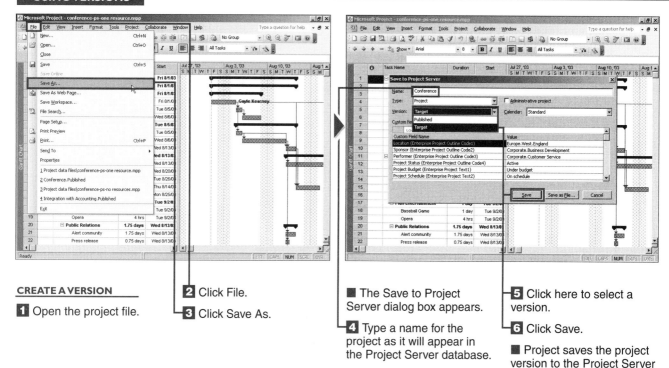

CREATE A VERSION

1 Open the project file.

2 Click File.

3 Click Save As.

■ The Save to Project Server dialog box appears.

4 Type a name for the project as it will appear in the Project Server database.

5 Click here to select a version.

6 Click Save.

■ Project saves the project version to the Project Server database.

440

When should I replace an existing version of a project using the method you just described, and when should I simply publish an alternate version?

✔ You should replace an existing version when it no longer has any meaning or use in your organization. For example, while the schedule may have changed — and so you published a new version — you may want to keep the original version for reporting or modeling purposes. If resource rates increase, publishing a new version of the project while keeping the original version enables you to compare the original project cost to the adjusted project cost.

When I tried to save the published version of my project back to the Project Server database, why does an error message appear?

✔ You did not do anything wrong; in fact, you demonstrated the purpose of versions. Versions help ensure that you never overwrite a published version of your project. By using versions, you preserve information as it was at the time you published the version. To replace an existing version of a published version, you must save the project using a different name and then delete the original version.

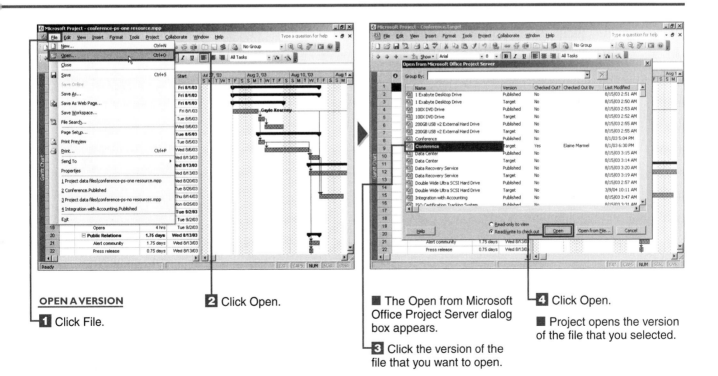

OPEN A VERSION

1 Click File.

2 Click Open.

■ The Open from Microsoft Office Project Server dialog box appears.

3 Click the version of the file that you want to open.

4 Click Open.

■ Project opens the version of the file that you selected.

OPEN AND CLOSE PROJECT WEB ACCESS

Team members can log on to Project Web Access, the browser-based interface that connects to the Project Server database, to view the tasks that they need to accomplish, report to the project manager, update the schedule with work completed, and even enter new tasks that may arise.

You log on to the Project Server database by using Project Web Access, or PWA. To open Project Web Access, a resource needs to know the URL for the Project Server database; the project manager should notify the resource of the URL.

Once you connect to the Project Server database using Internet Explorer, you can add the URL to your Favorites list. Or, if you use Project Web Access more than any other Web page, you can set it up as your Home page so that Project Web Access appears when you open Internet Explorer.

The window that appears when you enter the address for the Project Server database depends on the method that you use to log on to Project Server. If your organization uses Windows authentication, your Home page appears in Project Web Access. But, if your organization uses Project Server authentication, a Log On page opens.

OPEN AND CLOSE PROJECT WEB ACCESS

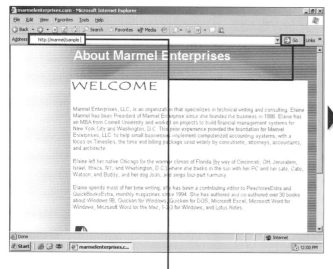

OPEN PWA

1 Open Internet Explorer.

■ You can click the icon in the Quick Launch tray or use the All Programs menu.

2 Type the address of the Project Server database.

3 Click Go.

■ Your Home page in Project Web Access appears.

Note: If you use Project Server authentication, a log on screen appears.

If I use Project Server authentication, what information do I need to provide to log on to Project Web Access?

✔ Your Project Server administrator should supply you with your user name and possibly with a password — or, the administrator may have left your password blank.

When I change my password in Project Web Access, why does a page appear telling me I cannot change it?

✔ Your organization uses Windows authentication to log onto Project Web Access; in your case, your Windows user name and password are supplied for you to Project Server when you log on. Only those who use Project Server Authentication can change passwords in Project Web Access.

What happens if I click the Alert me about my tasks and status reports link under Actions on the Home page?

✔ If your organization uses e-mail alerts, you can receive e-mail whenever you receive a new task or to-do list assignment, when your projects or to-do lists change, or when you receive a new status report request. You also can receive e-mail before your tasks start or are due. You can sign up for "nag" e-mails that arrive at specified intervals until your tasks or status reports are complete or become overdue.

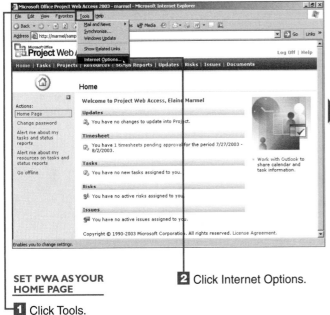

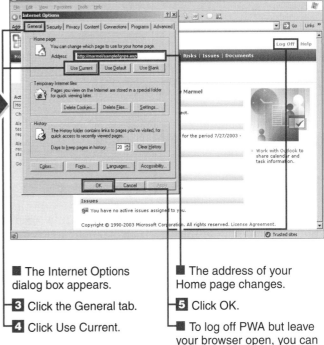

SET PWA AS YOUR HOME PAGE

1 Click Tools.

2 Click Internet Options.

■ The Internet Options dialog box appears.

3 Click the General tab.

4 Click Use Current.

■ The address of your Home page changes.

5 Click OK.

■ To log off PWA but leave your browser open, you can click Log Off.

REVIEW THE HOME PAGE

The Project Web Access Home page introduces you to Project Web Access and displays summary information, such as the number of new tasks that you have. It also provides you with links to navigate to other areas of Project Web Access.

Navigation links

The navigation links – Home, Tasks, Projects, Status Reports, Risks, Issues, Documents, Log Off, and Help – remain visible at all times. You click them to move to different areas within Project Web Access.

Actions pane

Enables you to view pages within a particular area. To move around in Project Web Access, you typically click a navigation link at the top and then a link in the Actions pane down the left side. You can hide the Actions pane via the small arrow (■) at the upper-right corner of the pane.

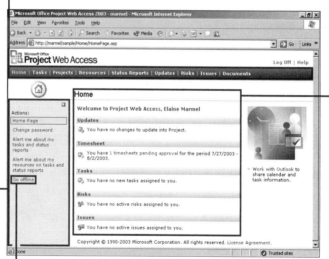

Home Page topics

What you see on your Home page depends on how your Project Server administrator set up the Home page. For example, in the center of the page, you may see notices of new events, tasks, risks, or issues.

Go offline link

When working away from the office using, say, a notebook computer while traveling, you can track the time you work. Simply click the Go offline link in the Actions pane and specify the date range you expect to work offline. While offline, you can only use certain features and can only view specific functions; for example, you can view, edit, and save changes to your timesheet only in the specified date range. When you reconnect in the office, you can upload information.

CHANGE YOUR PASSWORD

Those who use Project Server authentication can change the password they use when logging onto the Project Server database.

When you share plans for a project, you may run into security issues. For example, you may have resource rate information that you do not want everyone to see, or perhaps you want to make received project status messages for your

eyes only. Basic security starts with assigning a password to your user name when you log onto the Project Server database.

If you do not have a password — that is, your password is blank — when you log onto the Project Server database, you can use the method described in this section to set up a password of at least eight characters.

Why does Project Web Access keep prompting me to change my password?

✔ Your password is blank. As long as your password box remains blank, Project Web Access prompts you to set up a password to safeguard your project information from prying eyes.

CHANGE YOUR PASSWORD

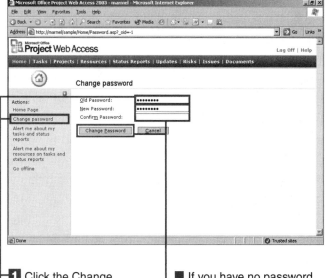

1 Click the Change password link.

2 On the Change password page, type your current password.

■ If you have no password, leave this box blank.

3 Type and retype your new, eight-character password.

4 Click Change Password.

■ Project Web Access confirms that your password has changed.

ENTER TIME ON TASKS

You can use the Timesheet view in Project Web Access to record any work that you have performed and report it to your project manager. When you save your work, you can update the Project Server database only, or you can also notify your manager that you have completed some work. If you notify your manager, Project Web Access confirms that your notification was sent.

Work assignments go from the project manager using Project Professional to team members via Project Web Access.

By default, all your tasks in the Timesheet view appear in Project Web Access. You can identify what you are viewing by looking in the Actions pane to see which option has the small box next to it — the small box identifies the selected view. From the View my tasks page, you also can view your tasks in a Gantt view.

Above the timesheet, you see two tabs: View Options and Filter, Group, Search. When you click the Filter, Group, Search tab, you see options that enable you to change the order in which tasks appear from the default order, which is by project to start date, work, or task name.

ENTER TIME ON TASKS

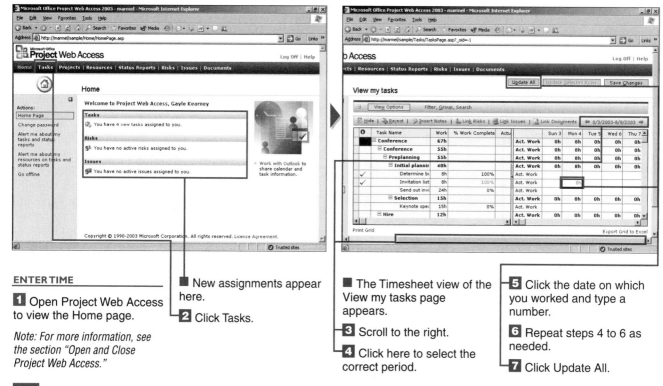

ENTER TIME

1 Open Project Web Access to view the Home page.

Note: For more information, see the section "Open and Close Project Web Access."

■ New assignments appear here.

2 Click Tasks.

■ The Timesheet view of the View my tasks page appears.

3 Scroll to the right.

4 Click here to select the correct period.

5 Click the date on which you worked and type a number.

6 Repeat steps 4 to 6 as needed.

7 Click Update All.

Is my Project Web Access Home page the only place to view notices of new tasks?

✔ If your organization chooses, the Project Server administrator can set up e-mail notifications so that Project Server generates e-mail notices and reminders of events, such as past due tasks. These e-mail notices and reminders appear in your regular e-mail client inbox.

In the Timesheet view can I view tasks only for the current period?

✔ Yes. Click the Current Tasks link in the Actions pane to filter out completed tasks and tasks that are far ahead in the future.

When I record actual work, do I enter hours or can I enter % Work Complete or Remaining Work?

✔ The numbers that you enter depend on the settings that your project manager or your organization selects. You may be able to fill in the % Work Complete and Remaining Work fields, the Total Actual Work and Remaining Work fields, or the Actual Work and Remaining Work fields.

What happens if I click Save Changes instead of Update All?

✔ You update the Project Server database, but you do not notify your manager of the changes. Consider saving changes daily even if you submit them weekly.

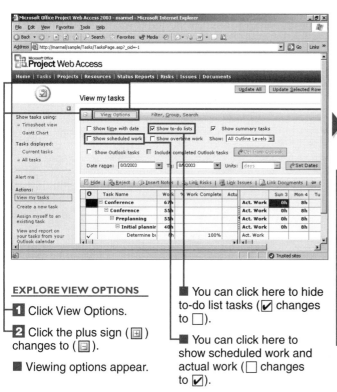

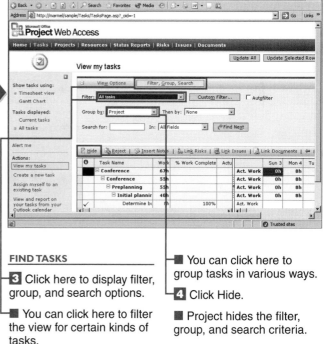

EXPLORE VIEW OPTIONS

1 Click View Options.

2 Click the plus sign (⊞) changes to (⊟).

■ Viewing options appear.

■ You can click here to hide to-do list tasks (☑ changes to ☐).

■ You can click here to show scheduled work and actual work (☐ changes to ☑).

FIND TASKS

3 Click here to display filter, group, and search options.

■ You can click here to filter the view for certain kinds of tasks.

■ You can click here to group tasks in various ways.

4 Click Hide.

■ Project hides the filter, group, and search criteria.

ADD TASK NOTES AND PRINT THE TIMESHEET

You can communicate with the project manager about a task by adding a note. The Timesheet view is actually divided in half. The left side shows a grid of fields such as Work, % Work Complete, Actual Work, and Remaining Work, and the right side contains timesheet data. The columns you see in either half of the Timesheet view depends on the

options that your manager or your organization chose for you to record updates.

At the bottom of the Timesheet grid, two links appear that enable you to either print your timesheet directly from Project Web Access or export the information to Excel. Clicking the Print Grid link makes PWA display a separate window where you can select columns to exclude when you print, reorder the columns, and set column

properties. After making your choices, you can print the information or you can export it to Excel.

You can export the information to Excel directly from the Timesheet view or from the separate view that opens when you click the Print Grid link. In either case, Excel opens and displays your timesheet on one tab of the workbook and the grid data on another tab.

ADD TASK NOTES AND PRINT THE TIMESHEET

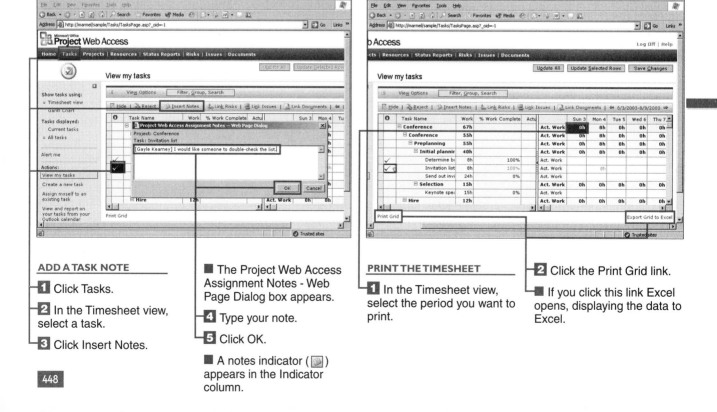

ADD A TASK NOTE

1 Click Tasks.

2 In the Timesheet view, select a task.

3 Click Insert Notes.

■ The Project Web Access Assignment Notes - Web Page Dialog box appears.

4 Type your note.

5 Click OK.

■ A notes indicator (📝) appears in the Indicator column.

PRINT THE TIMESHEET

1 In the Timesheet view, select the period you want to print.

2 Click the Print Grid link.

■ If you click this link Excel opens, displaying the data to Excel.

How can I edit a note after I save it?

✔ You cannot. Instead, add another note to the task by clicking the Insert Note link while the task is selected.

If I add a second note, do two note icons appear?

✔ No. If you add more than one note to a task, Project Web Access appends notes so that the project manager is not deluged with notes.

If I click Export to Excel while viewing the Gantt Chart, what happens?

✔ Project Web Access exports only the grid data to Excel.

If I click Print Grid while viewing the Gantt Chart, what happens?

✔ A separate window opens in Project Web Access, and it displays the grid data. From this version of the window, you have no option to switch to timesheet data. You can print the grid view and export it to Excel.

Can I make changes to the information in Excel?

✔ Yes, but any changes you make are not reflected in Project Web Access.

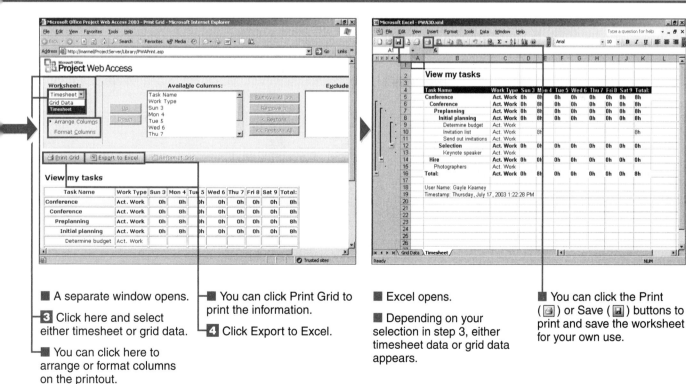

■ A separate window opens.

3 Click here and select either timesheet or grid data.

■ You can click here to arrange or format columns on the printout.

■ You can click Print Grid to print the information.

4 Click Export to Excel.

■ Excel opens.

■ Depending on your selection in step 3, either timesheet data or grid data appears.

■ You can click the Print ( ) or Save ( ) buttons to print and save the worksheet for your own use.

ADD TASKS

As a team member, you may realize that what you are doing requires more work than the manager anticipated. You can create new tasks that appear on your timesheet in Project Web Access and then notify your manager about the expected additional work. Because your manager has final approval, think of the task as a suggested task until you hear back from your manager.

When you create a new task, you select the project to which you need to add the task and a level for the new task in the outline. You also supply a name for the task, an optional comment that describes the task, the task's start date, and the amount of work that you estimate the task requires. When you save the new task, Project Web Access adds it to your timesheet; an icon appears next to it to remind

you to notify your manager of the additional work by updating your timesheet.

After you update your timesheet, the icon changes to indicate you have notified your manager but your manager has not yet approved the task and updated the project. Your manager can add the task to the project or reject the task.

ADD TASKS

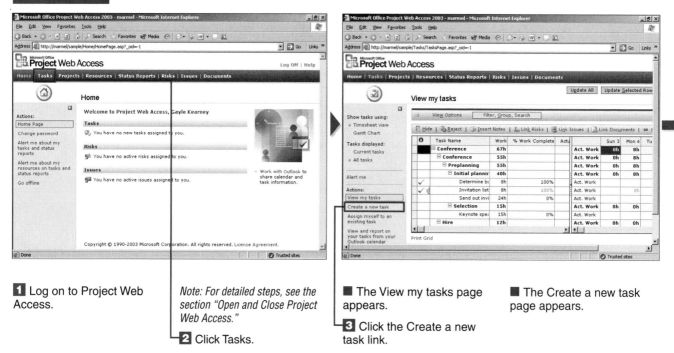

1 Log on to Project Web Access.

Note: For detailed steps, see the section "Open and Close Project Web Access."

2 Click Tasks.

■ The View my tasks page appears.

3 Click the Create a new task link.

■ The Create a new task page appears.

Should I assign myself to a new task that I create?

✔ Only if you have the time and are best qualified to do the task. Otherwise, leave the assignment to the project manager. Project notifies you if the project manager assigns the task to you or to someone else.

Do I need special permission to create a new task?

✔ No. Anyone can create a new task. It remains a proposed task and does not become part of the project until the project manager approves it.

What should I do if I realize, after creating a new task, that I made a mistake?

✔ You can attach a note to the task to notify your manager. For more information, see the section "Add Task Notes and Print the Timesheet."

When I click the Make the new task a subtask of list box, what happens?

✔ You can view a list of the subtasks in the project that you selected at the top of the Create a new task page.

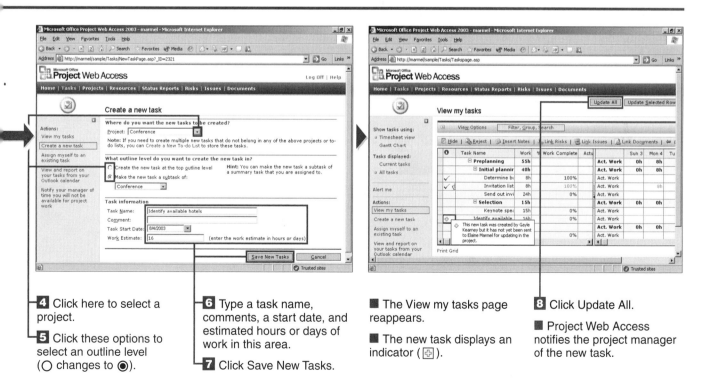

■ **4** Click here to select a project.

■ **5** Click these options to select an outline level (○ changes to ◉).

■ **6** Type a task name, comments, a start date, and estimated hours or days of work in this area.

■ **7** Click Save New Tasks.

■ The View my tasks page reappears.

■ The new task displays an indicator (⊞).

■ **8** Click Update All.

■ Project Web Access notifies the project manager of the new task.

VIEW OUTLOOK INFORMATION IN PROJECT WEB ACCESS

If you use Outlook 2000 or higher and your Project Server administrator has enabled Outlook integration, you can get a better handle on *all* the things you need to do by viewing them all on the View my tasks page in Project Web Access.

When you view Outlook tasks in Project Web Access, Project Web Access accesses Outlook for information. Because Outlook wins

the "Application Most Likely to Get Hit by a Virus, Worm, or Trojan and then Propagate It" award, Outlook developers have tightened security on the product. A message alerts you whenever any program tries to access Outlook and places a time limit on the program's access to Outlook information. The message appears when you set up Project Web Access to view Outlook tasks, and the language, while a little misleading, is meant

only to catch your attention and make sure that you really want to allow access to Outlook information.

The steps in this section show you how to view Outlook tasks along with Project Web Access tasks. To read about exchanging information between Project Web Access and Outlook, see the section "Exchange Information between Project Web Access and Outlook 2003."

VIEW OUTLOOK INFORMATION IN PROJECT WEB ACCESS

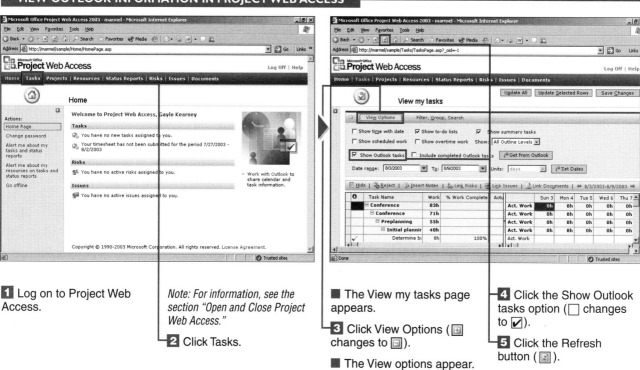

1 Log on to Project Web Access.

Note: For information, see the section "Open and Close Project Web Access."

2 Click Tasks.

■ The View my tasks page appears.

3 Click View Options (⊞ changes to ⊟).

■ The View options appear.

4 Click the Show Outlook tasks option (☐ changes to ☑).

5 Click the Refresh button (▣).

What happens if I click No when the message about a program trying to access e-mail addresses in Outlook appears?

✔ You see and must respond to the message for every Outlook task that will display on the Project Web Access timesheet. The tasks still appear even if you take this long way to display them.

Why is Project Web Access trying to access Outlook e-mail addresses?

✔ Project Web Access is not trying to access e-mail addresses; the message Outlook displays is a generic message that appears whenever any program tries to access any part of Outlook.

Why do I need to deselect the Show Outlook tasks option?

✔ If you keep this option selected (☑) and you log off Project Web Access, when you redisplay the View my tasks page, the message about a program trying to access Outlook appears. If you do not remember that you included Outlook tasks in the Timesheet view, you may mistakenly think that a virus is attacking you based on the content of the message. So, save yourself the heart palpitations and deselect the option (☐ changes to ☑).

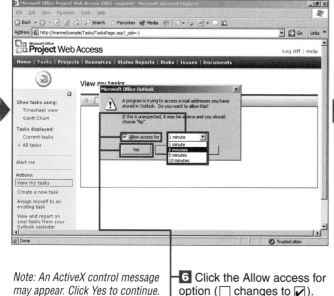

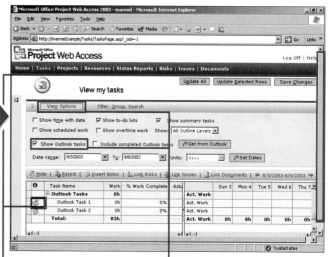

Note: An ActiveX control message may appear. Click Yes to continue.

■ A message appears indicating that a program is accessing Outlook.

6 Click the Allow access for option (☐ changes to ☑).

7 Click here and select a time frame.

8 Click Yes.

9 Scroll down.

■ Tasks from Outlook appear.

■ You can click the icon (✉) in the Indicator column to see the details of an Outlook task.

10 After viewing the tasks, click View Options.

11 Click the Show Outlook tasks option (☐ changes to ☑).

■ Outlook tasks disappear.

SET UP INTEGRATION BETWEEN OUTLOOK AND PROJECT WEB ACCESS

I f you use Outlook 2000 or later, you can display Project Web Access information in Outlook and exchange assignment information between Project Web Access and the Outlook calendar. This section describes the steps you need to take to establish the connection between Project Web Access and Outlook 2003 so that you can send Outlook calendar entries to Project Web Access and Project Web Access assignments to the Outlook calendar.

Note that, using Outlook 98, you can transfer Outlook information into Project Web Access, but you cannot display Project Web Access information in Outlook.

The appearance of Outlook changes when you set up integration between Project Web Access and Outlook. A Project Web Access toolbar appears in Outlook below the Standard toolbar, and on the Tools menu, you see a menu for Project Web Access.

To enable integration between Project Web Access and Outlook, you must download and install the Project Add-in for Outlook. Project Web Access walks you through this process; once you complete the process, you can open Outlook and establish the rules you want to use when you exchange information between Outlook and Project Web Access.

SET UP INTEGRATION BETWEEN OUTLOOK AND PROJECT WEB ACCESS

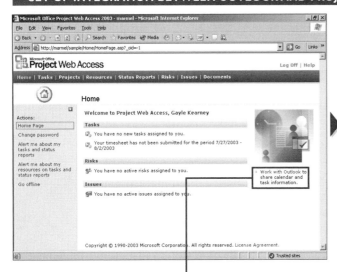

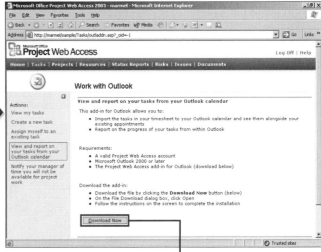

1 Log on to Project Web Access.

Note: For information, see the section "Open and Close Project Web Access."

2 Click the Work with Outlook to share calendar and task information link.

■ The Work with Outlook page appears.

3 Read the information on the page.

4 Click Download Now.

Note: An ActiveX control message may appear. Click Yes to continue.

What changes occur in Project Web Access after I download and install the Project Add-in for Outlook?

✔ None. The link remains on your Home page and you can still click the Work with Outlook page. You even can click Download Now. But, at that point, Project Web Access prompts you to either reinstall or repair the Project Add-in for Outlook installation or to uninstall it. All visible changes appear in Outlook. See the sections "Exchange Information between Project Web Access and Outlook 2003" for details on the visible changes.

If the Project Add-in for Outlook is safe, why do I see a security warning?

✔ Microsoft wants to give you one more opportunity to cancel the installation; in this case, the security warning is really just a safety net.

Is it necessary to establish integration between Outlook and Project Web Access?

✔ You need to establish integration between Outlook and Project Web Access only if you want to exchange information between the two products.

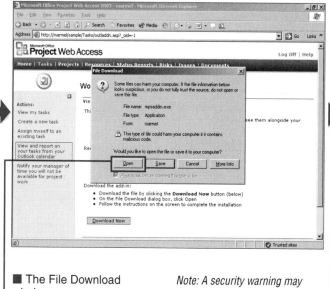

■ The File Download window appears.

5 Click Open.

■ The Project Add-in for Outlook downloads.

Note: A security warning may appear.

6 Walk through the installation.

■ This message appears after installation completes.

7 Click OK.

■ The Work with Outlook page reappears.

CONTINUED ▶

SET UP INTEGRATION BETWEEN OUTLOOK AND PROJECT WEB ACCESS (CONTINUED)

You have some choices about the way that updating occurs. By default, you manually import all assignments from Project Web Access to Outlook and all updates from your Outlook calendar to Project Web Access. You can import for a specific time period, and you can set up the updating process to occur automatically.

If you prefer to import assignments for a specific time period, change your Assignment Import settings in

Outlook on the Project Web Access tab of the Options dialog box. In the Date Range section, you can specify the time frame.

You can import assignments from Project Web Access to Outlook automatically based on a time frame. You can make similar choices about updating Project Web Access with information that you record on your Outlook calendar. When you access the Advanced Options button, you can determine

whether your updates from Outlook to Project Web Access affect only your Timesheet view in Project Web Access or also update your project manager. You also can control the Project Web Access behavior for creating reminders.

See the section "Exchange Information between Project Web Access and Outlook 2003" for details on exchanging information between the products.

SET UP INTEGRATION BETWEEN OUTLOOK AND PROJECT WEB ACCESS (CONTINUED)

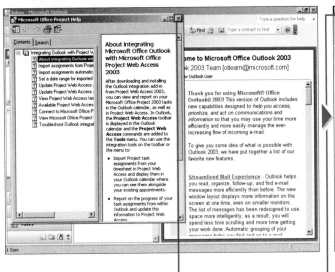

1 Open Outlook.

■ Outlook opens and displays a Help topic about integrating Outlook and Project Web Access.

2 Click the Help topic's Close button (☒).

■ The Help topic closes and shows the main window of Outlook 2003.

3 Click Tools.

4 Click Options.

■ The Options dialog box appears.

Why are some updating choices on the gray and not available?

✔ These options are available only when your organization uses Windows authentication instead of Project Server authentication. If your organization uses Project Server authentication, you can only update Outlook and Project Web Access manually.

What do the options do that are gray and unavailable on the Project Web Access tab of the Options dialog box?

✔ They enable you to schedule an exchange of information between Project Web Access and Outlook so that one or both products update automatically.

Can I send tasks from Outlook's Task List to Project Web Access?

✔ No. You can only send calendar entries from Outlook to Project Web Access.

What happens if I click the Enter login information button?

✔ A box appears enabling you to confirm the Project Server URL, the method you use to connect to the Project Server database — Windows or Project Server authentication — and your user name. You can also test the connection to the Project Server database from the Enter Login Information dialog box.

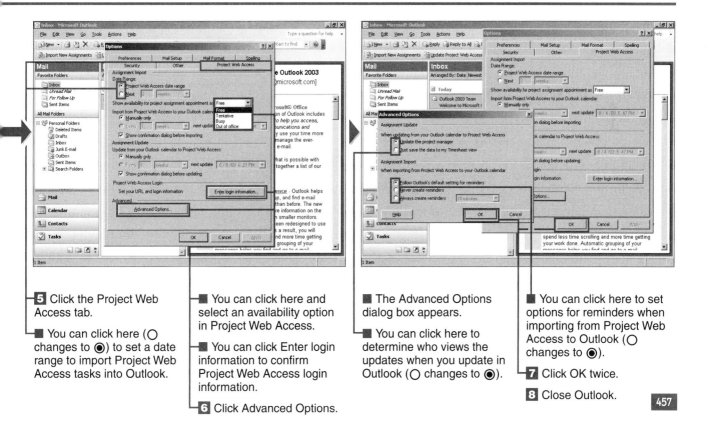

5 Click the Project Web Access tab.

■ You can click here (○ changes to ⦿) to set a date range to import Project Web Access tasks into Outlook.

■ You can click here and select an availability option in Project Web Access.

■ You can click Enter login information to confirm Project Web Access login information.

6 Click Advanced Options.

■ The Advanced Options dialog box appears.

■ You can click here to determine who views the updates when you update in Outlook (○ changes to ⦿).

■ You can click here to set options for reminders when importing from Project Web Access to Outlook (○ changes to ⦿).

7 Click OK twice.

8 Close Outlook.

EXCHANGE INFORMATION BETWEEN PROJECT WEB ACCESS AND OUTLOOK 2003

After you install the Project Add-in for Outlook and set integration options using the section "Set up Integration between Outlook and Project Web Access," you can import assignments from Project Web Access to the Outlook calendar. Then, in Outlook, you can record time spent on the assignments and export it back to Project Web Access.

Outlook imports assignments either based on the Project Web Access date range or over a period based on the integration options you set. You cannot selectively import assignments and they appear on the appropriate calendar date with no particular time.

In Project Web Access, you can record your work in the assignment's appointment window.

The appearance of the Project Web Access tab in the window and the method by which you update Project Web Access depends on how your organization records actuals.

This section's example is based on tracking hours of work done per day or per week; using this method, the time that you work on an assignment is saved directly in Project Web Access.

EXCHANGE INFORMATION BETWEEN PROJECT WEB ACCESS AND OUTLOOK 2003

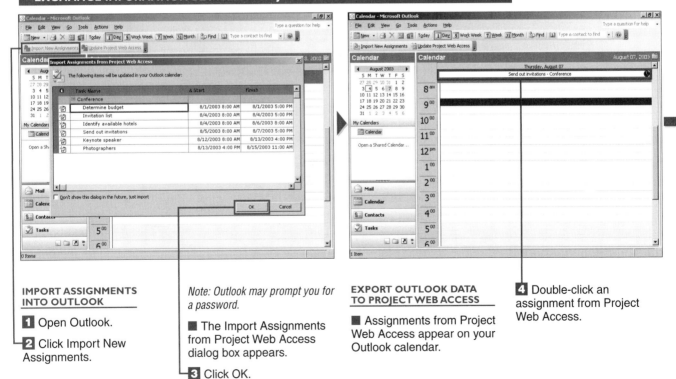

IMPORT ASSIGNMENTS INTO OUTLOOK

1 Open Outlook.

2 Click Import New Assignments.

Note: Outlook may prompt you for a password.

■ The Import Assignments from Project Web Access dialog box appears.

3 Click OK.

EXPORT OUTLOOK DATA TO PROJECT WEB ACCESS

■ Assignments from Project Web Access appear on your Outlook calendar.

4 Double-click an assignment from Project Web Access.

What behavior can I expect when the tracking mode is percent of work completed?

✔ You do not see the View my tasks page in the Project Web Access tab of an Outlook calendar appointment. Instead, you can view fields where you can specify a percentage. The time that you work on an assignment is saved in Outlook but not in the Project Server database; you must click Go To Timesheet in Outlook, or Update Project Web Access on the Project Web Access toolbar to send the information to the Project Server database.

What behavior can I expect when the tracking mode is Actual Work Done and Work Remaining?

✔ You also do not see the View my tasks page in the Project Web Access tab of an Outlook calendar appointment. Instead, you can view fields where you can specify Actual Work and Remaining Work. The information is saved in Outlook but not in the Project Server database; you must click Go To Timesheet in Outlook or Update Project Web Access on the Project Web Access toolbar to send the information to the Project Server database.

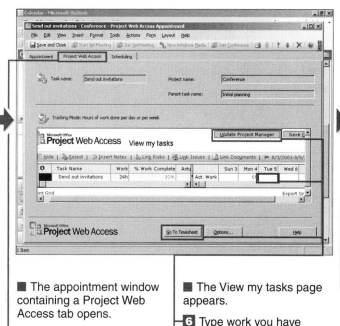

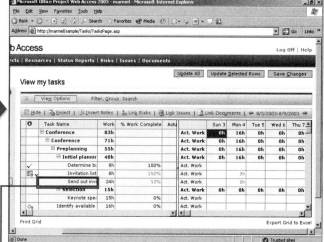

■ The appointment window containing a Project Web Access tab opens.

5 Click the Project Web Access tab.

■ If necessary, log onto Project Web Access.

■ The View my tasks page appears.

6 Type work you have performed.

7 Click Update Project Manager.

8 Click Go to Timesheet.

■ The update you made in Outlook appears in Project Web Access.

■ You can switch back to Outlook using the Windows Task Bar and close the appointment window.

NOTIFY MANAGERS OF WORKDAY CHANGES

Y ou can use Project Web Access to notify your manager of changes to your workday from Project Web Access. For example, if you were just selected for jury duty, or find yourself unavailable to work during the time that you were scheduled, you can notify your manager. Likewise, you can notify your manager if you anticipated an absence, but find yourself suddenly available to work. For example, the

case that you were to hear was settled out of court or the trial wrapped up earlier than expected and the jury was dismissed. You notify your manager of changes in your workday schedule from the Tasks page of Project Web Access.

When you notify your manager of a change in available working time, you do *not* create a calendar change; you are simply notifying your manager. If you are assigned

to a project that your manager does not manage, be aware that Project Web Access does not notify anyone of your workday change except your manager.

The behavior of the feature has changed between Project 2002 and Project 2003, and it is important to understand this distinction because of the obvious communication gap.

NOTIFY MANAGERS OF WORKDAY CHANGES

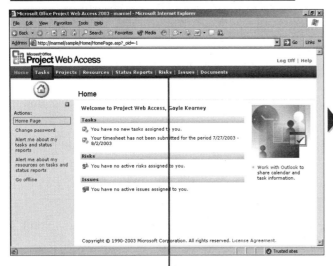

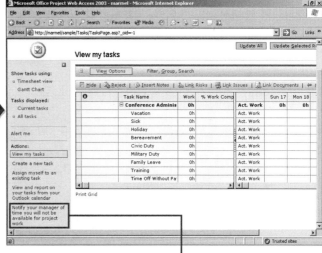

1 Log onto Project Web Access.

Note: For information, see the section "Open and Close Project Web Access."

2 Click Tasks.

■ The View my tasks page appears.

3 Click the Notify your manager of time you will not be available for project work link.

If I am working on a project that my manager does not manage, should I notify the project manager of changes to my workday?

✔ Yes, because any unexpected changes in your schedule could affect the overall project schedule, even if your current task appears unaffected.

I know that you said that my manager is notified of my workday change. Do I see any effects in Project Web Access of the notification?

✔ Yes. Once your manager approves the change, you can view the hours of administrative time that you recorded at the bottom of your timesheet.

Why do I receive an error message when I try to notify my manager of a change to my workday schedule?

✔ You were not assigned to any administrative projects. In Project 2003, managers in your organization need to create administrative projects that contain tasks for each type of nonworking time to which a user may need to assign himself. Once the administrative project is published, the tasks in it appear at the bottom of your View my tasks page, with no work assigned. You should contact your manager to resolve this problem.

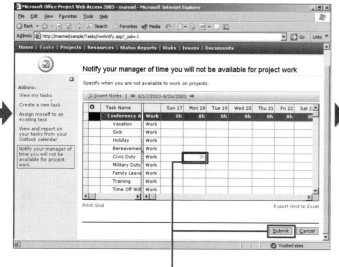

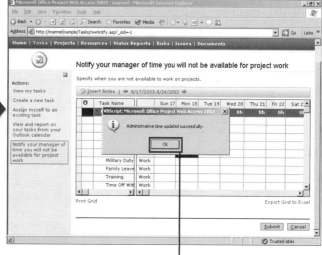

■ The Notify your manager of time you will not be available for project work page appears.

4 Type a number on the appropriate line and day.

5 Click Submit.

■ A message appears, indicating that Project Web Access successfully updated administrative time.

6 Click OK.

■ Your manager receives notification of your change in working days.

DELEGATE A TASK

What if you are overloaded with work, and you cannot possibly complete everything assigned to you, but management just approved your request to hire an intern to help you? Now you need to delegate some tasks and keep your project manager informed of the change in assignments.

You can use the Delegation Wizard in Project Web Access to delegate tasks from the View my tasks page.

You select the task that you want to delegate and start the Delegation Wizard. While delegating, you identify the resource to which you want to delegate the task and the role you want to continue to play. For example, you can continue to take the lead role on the task. You can delegate more than one task at the same time to the same delegate. If you delegate a summary task, Project Web Access delegates all subtasks.

The wizard then helps you send a message to the delegate and to your project manager to notify them of the action. New tasks appear in the Microsoft Project Web Access Task view of each affected recipient and the project manager. The person to whom you delegated can refuse the assignment. Unless you have appropriate security privileges, you cannot delegate tasks.

DELEGATE A TASK

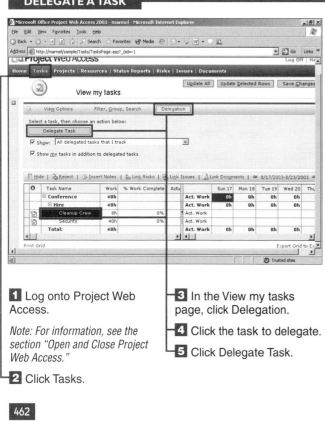

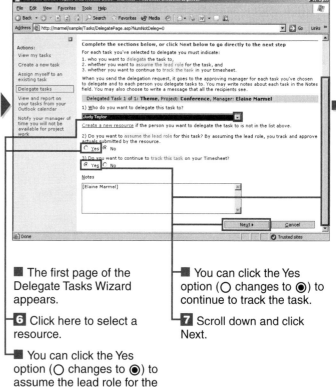

1 Log onto Project Web Access.

Note: For information, see the section "Open and Close Project Web Access."

2 Click Tasks.

3 In the View my tasks page, click Delegation.

4 Click the task to delegate.

5 Click Delegate Task.

■ The first page of the Delegate Tasks Wizard appears.

6 Click here to select a resource.

■ You can click the Yes option (○ changes to ●) to assume the lead role for the task.

■ You can click the Yes option (○ changes to ●) to continue to track the task.

7 Scroll down and click Next.

Can everyone delegate tasks?

✔ No. You must have the correct security permissions in Project Server to delegate tasks.

Why am I having trouble delegating a task when I have the correct permissions?

✔ You may not be able to delegate certain tasks because your manager does not permit you to delegate certain tasks, your manager has deleted the task, the task is a tracking copy of a delegated task or is a nonworking time entry, or someone has performed actual work and the manager's approval is still pending.

What else is on the bottom of the first page of the Delgation Wizard?

✔ A text box where you can write notes about the task you are delegating. An indicator for the note (🗐) appears in the Indicator column on the timesheet of the delegate. The delegate can click 🗐 to read the note.

How does a delegate refuse an assignment?

✔ When the task appears on the delegate's timesheet, the delegate clicks it and clicks Reject.

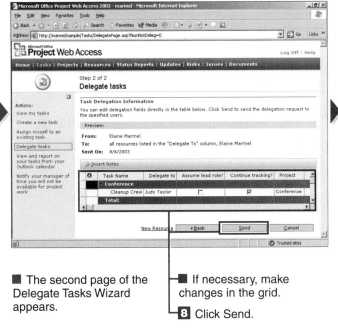

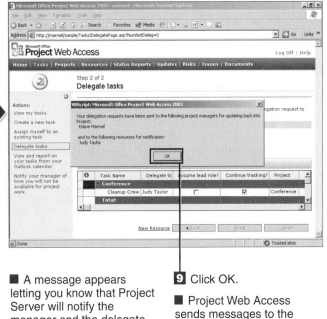

■ The second page of the Delegate Tasks Wizard appears.

━■ If necessary, make changes in the grid.

8 Click Send.

■ A message appears letting you know that Project Server will notify the manager and the delegate.

9 Click OK.

■ Project Web Access sends messages to the manager and delegate.

ATTACH SUPPORTING DOCUMENTS TO PROJECTS

I f your organization has Project Server using Windows SharePoint Services and gives you the correct permissions, you can view and attach supporting documents to a project, a task, or a to-do list.

You also can create and track issues and risks that you can associate with projects, tasks, or to-do lists. For more information on issues and risks, see Chapter 18.

You can link supporting documents to a project, a task, or a to-do list. This feature is useful, for example, when you have a budget justification or a feasibility study that you want on hand whenever the need arises. It also useful when other team members need to share the document to review it, either to edit it or because it impacts some other portion of the project. The Documents feature in Project Server enables you to create a

shared workspace where you can discuss the document with other team members.

You can view and post documents in the Public Documents folder, which is a public, company-wide space that anyone in the organization can access. Or, the documents for your project may appear in a project-specific space, where only those with access to the project plan also have access to the documents.

ATTACH SUPPORTING DOCUMENTS TO PROJECTS

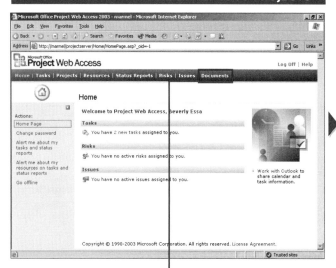

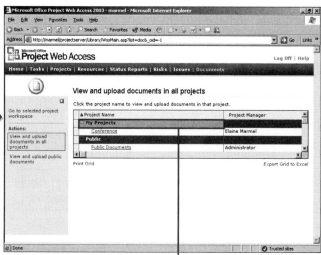

VIEW DOCUMENTS

1 Log onto Project Web Access.

Note: For information, see the section "Open and Close Project Web Access."

2 Click Documents.

■ The View and upload documents in all projects page appears.

3 Click a project link.

What is a shared workspace?

✔ A shared workspace is a location where multiple team members can work simultaneously. If you open a document in a shared workspace, the document appears in a Project Web Access window. You can invite other logged on team members to view the document and, together, you can edit the document using Word's revision tracking tools. You can insert discussions — comments — in the document; the discussions help you identify who said what. Periodically, you can update your version of the document to incorporate changes that other team members make.

What is the difference between checking out a Word document and editing it in Word?

✔ By checking out a document, you maintain exclusive use of the document while you can edit it. Although others can view the document while you work on it, they cannot save any changes to it until you check it back in. If you do not check out the document but simply open it in Word, another team member can check it out while you are editing it, and the other person's change will overwrite any changes you make to the document.

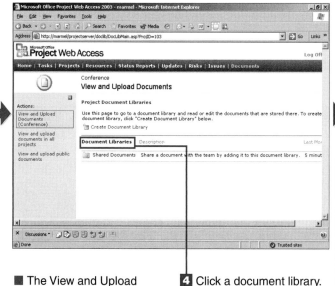

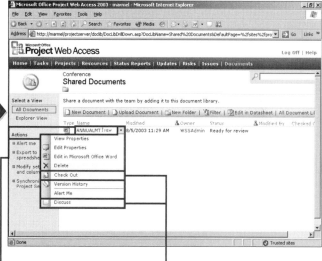

■ The View and Upload Documents page for the project appears.

4 Click a document library.

■ The library page for the project appears.

5 Position the mouse (↘) over a document (▾) appears.

6 Click here and select a Viewing option.

■ You can click Check Out to work on a document.

■ You can click Discuss to discuss the document in a shared workspace.

CONTINUED ▶

ATTACH SUPPORTING DOCUMENTS TO PROJECTS (CONTINUED)

I n addition to viewing documents, you can post documents so that team members have access to them. When you post documents, you place them in libraries, which are folders that contain items with something in common. All projects have a Shared Documents library, where the common element is nothing more than that your team shares the documents in the library. You can also create specific

libraries by subject, for example, to help organize your project's documents.

As you use the Documents feature, you may it helpful to set alerts that notify you when changes occur to a specific document or to a particular library. When you set an alert, you tell Project Server to notify you via e-mail whenever the type of change you specify occurs.

The opening Documents page in Project Web Access shows all the projects to which you have access. To add a document to a project, you select the project and the library within the project where you want to store the document. You can either post a previously created document from your hard drive or network, or you can create a new document.

ATTACH SUPPORTING DOCUMENTS TO PROJECTS (CONTINUED)

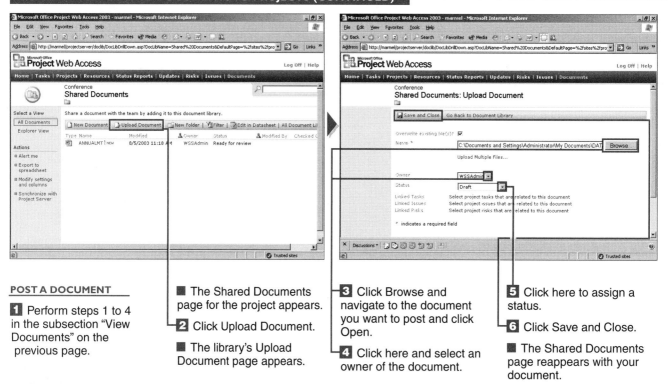

POST A DOCUMENT

1 Perform steps 1 to 4 in the subsection "View Documents" on the previous page.

■ The Shared Documents page for the project appears.

2 Click Upload Document.

■ The library's Upload Document page appears.

3 Click Browse and navigate to the document you want to post and click Open.

4 Click here and select an owner of the document.

5 Click here to assign a status.

6 Click Save and Close.

■ The Shared Documents page reappears with your document.

What happens when I click View Datasheet?

✔ You can view a grid-style view — think of Excel — of the document library that displays each document in the library on a row, with column headings for document type, name, date and time modified, owner, status, last modified by, and checked out. Each column heading has a ⬝ next to it; you can click ⬝ and set filtering criteria to view only those documents, for example, that are owned by a particular team member. You can return to the view shown in this section by clicking Show in Standard View.

How can I create a new library?

✔ From the project's View and Upload Documents page, click Create Document Library. On the New Document Library page that appears, type a name and description for the library. You can choose to display the library in the Actions pane on the Home page and whether Project Server should create a backup copy each time you edit a file in the document library. Last, you can select a template, such as Word document or Excel spreadsheet, that will serve as the default for new files created in the library.

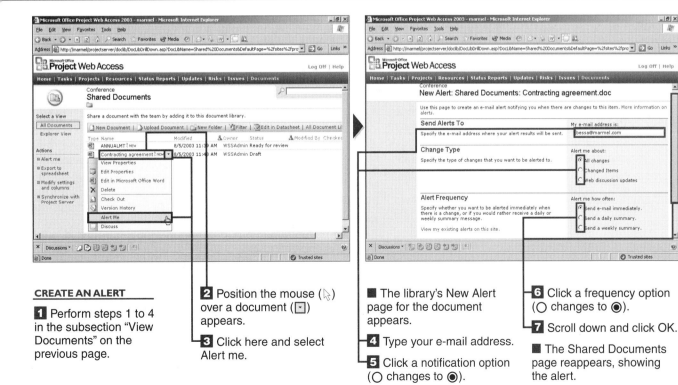

CREATE AN ALERT

1 Perform steps 1 to 4 in the subsection "View Documents" on the previous page.

2 Position the mouse (⟍) over a document (⬝) appears.

3 Click here and select Alert me.

■ The library's New Alert page for the document appears.

4 Type your e-mail address.

5 Click a notification option (○ changes to ◉).

6 Click a frequency option (○ changes to ◉).

7 Scroll down and click OK.

■ The Shared Documents page reappears, showing the alert.

VIEW ASSIGNMENTS

You may not work on only one project at a time. To help you manage your time, the Project Center in Project Web Access enables you to view tasks from more than one project at the same time.

In the Project Center, you can see individual projects, or you may see *Project Center views*, which are collections of projects. The administrator creates Project Center views and then identifies the team members who can view each Project Center view. You must have appropriate permissions from the Project Server administrator to view projects in the Project Center.

In the Project Center, you can view line-item entries that represent Web-based projects. Typically, you see entries for projects for which you have work assigned, but what you see depends on your security settings. On each line, a Gantt bar appears and shows you the duration of the project and progress that you have made on the project to date. When you find the particular project you want, you can drill down to view the details of your assignments on the project.

If you have the proper set of permissions, you also can view your assignments from the Resource Center.

VIEW ASSIGNMENTS

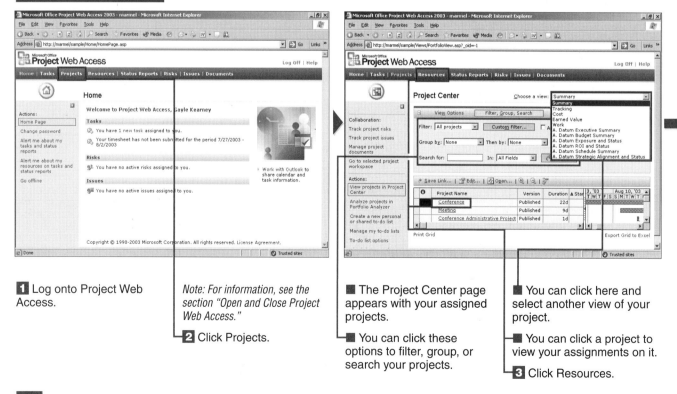

1 Log onto Project Web Access.

Note: For information, see the section "Open and Close Project Web Access."

2 Click Projects.

■ The Project Center page appears with your assigned projects.

■ You can click these options to filter, group, or search your projects.

■ You can click here and select another view of your project.

■ You can click a project to view your assignments on it.

3 Click Resources.

How do I access a view that does not appear in the view list?

✔ Typically, the Project Server administrator creates views and assigns security privileges to use various views. Discuss the view you want to use with the Project Server database administrator.

I do not see any projects or resources. Why?

✔ You probably do not have proper security privileges; check with the Project Server administrator.

I see projects and resources, but not all projects and resources. Why?

✔ Again, you probably do not have proper security privileges; check with the Project Server administrator.

How can I filter and group resources on the Resource Center page?

✔ Using a custom filter, you can compare fields like Resource Name, Generic, Department, Type, Material Label, Maximum Units, availability dates, or enterprise custom multi-value outline codes equal to a test value. You can set a second and third level of the filter using the same fields to exclude even more resources. You can group by all of the same fields that you can use to create a filter.

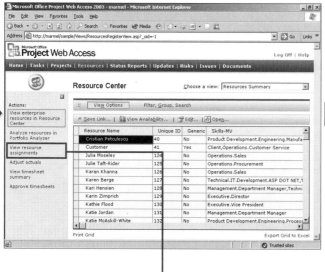

■ The Resource Center page appears.

■ The enterprise resource pool appears.

4 Click the View resource assignments link.

■ The View resource assignments page appears showing resources that you are permitted to view.

5 Click a resource.

6 Click Add.

7 Repeat steps 5 to 6 for each resource.

8 Click Apply.

■ Resource assignments appear at the bottom of the page.

REPORT STATUS

Project Web Access provides you with status reports that you can send to your project manager if the Project Server administrator has given you the proper permissions. Your manager can set up a standardized status report for you to submit on a specified frequency; in this case, you see a reminder on your Home page in Project Web Access when your status report is due.

You also can send an unsolicited status report to your project manager; this feature is useful when something unusual occurs and you want to call your manager's attention to the event.

In the section "Enter Time on Tasks," you saw how Project Web Access enables you to send updates from the View my tasks page. Status reports are different than task updates, because status reports are not tied to any one task.

You create solicited and unsolicited status reports from the Status Reports page. A status report is comprised of several text boxes where you provide information about key events on the project. Your manager may want information about your major accomplishments and any problems you faced during the status report period. The content of a status report is freeform.

REPORT STATUS

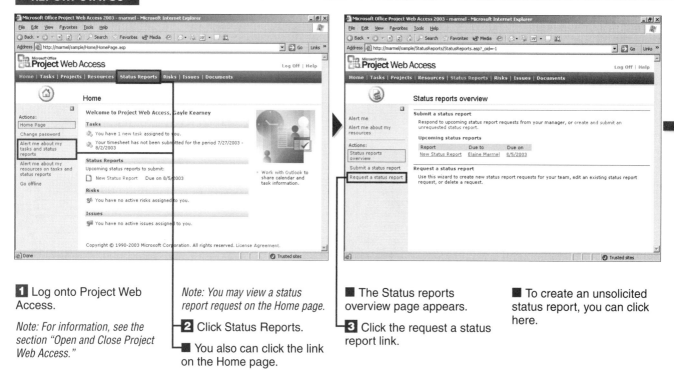

1 Log onto Project Web Access.

Note: For information, see the section "Open and Close Project Web Access."

Note: You may view a status report request on the Home page.

2 Click Status Reports.

■ You also can click the link on the Home page.

■ The Status reports overview page appears.

3 Click the request a status report link.

■ To create an unsolicited status report, you can click here.

What happens when I choose to create an unsolicited status report?

✔ Initially, you assign a name to the report, identify who receives the report, and specify the period the report covers. Then, you add sections to the report, supplying titles for the sections. As you create each section, you can fill it out; that way, when you finish creating the parts of the report, it is complete and you click Send to send it. If you want to use it again in the future, just add the sections without the information and click Save instead of Send.

I know I can submit an unsolicited status report when something unusual occurs, but what if the event needs both my manager's attention and the attention of other team members?

✔ You can send a copy to one team member. If your organization has implemented Windows SharePoint Services, you can create an issue or a risk; anyone on your project can view issues or risks, assuming the administrator has given all of you the proper permissions. See Chapter 18 for more information on issues and risks.

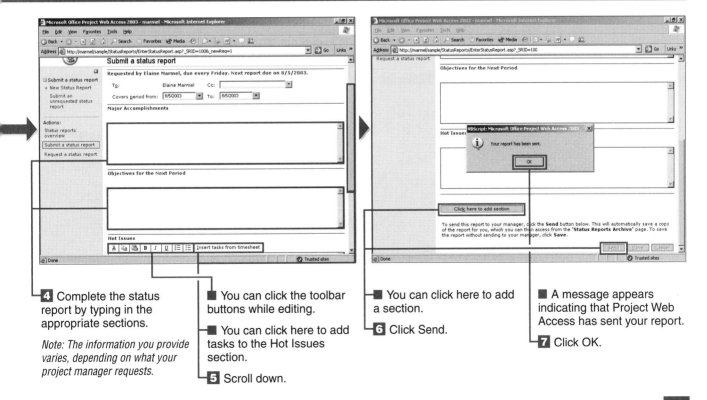

■ **4** Complete the status report by typing in the appropriate sections.

Note: The information you provide varies, depending on what your project manager requests.

■ You can click the toolbar buttons while editing.

■ You can click here to add tasks to the Hot Issues section.

■ **5** Scroll down.

■ You can click here to add a section.

■ **6** Click Send.

■ A message appears indicating that Project Web Access has sent your report.

■ **7** Click OK.

REVIEW A PORTFOLIO

As an executive, you can use Project Web Access to evaluate the portfolio of work that is happening across the organization. Begin in the Project Center, which provides a high-level picture of the projects that you have security permissions to view, and review your portfolio — a collection of projects. Your organization can create custom views for the Project Center, each providing you with different kinds of detail.

Project Server's sample database for A. Datum Corporation contains some good examples that can help you understand techniques for working with Project Server data.

The A. Datum Executive Summary view has been customized to include color indicators that help you determine, at a glance, projects that pose potential problems. As you move the mouse pointer over an indicator, you see a tip describing the meaning of that indicator.

You can drill down in any project and use additional views to see different kinds of detail. For example, if you see a project running behind schedule, drill down to pinpoint the problem. Find a task that is behind schedule. Then, use the Portfolio Analyzer, described in the section "Analyze a Portfolio," to determine why the task is behind schedule.

REVIEW A PORTFOLIO

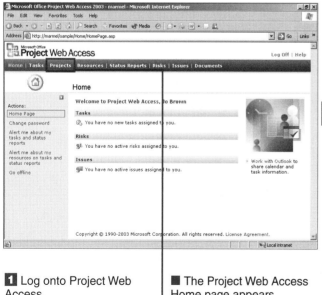

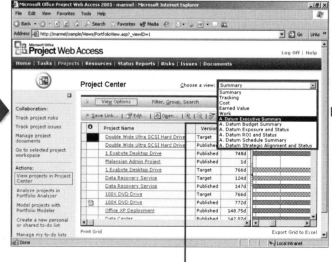

1 Log onto Project Web Access.

Note: For details on logging onto Project Web Access, see Chapter 19.

■ The Project Web Access Home page appears.

2 Click Projects.

■ The Project Center appears.

■ You can view all the projects that your security permits you to view.

3 Click here to select a view.

■ For this example, select A. Datum Executive Summary.

Who defines the information that appears in a view?

✔ Typically, the Project Server administrator sets up views, but, in most organizations, the various groups who use Project Web Access designs views based on their needs. Project managers, resource managers, portfolio managers, team members, and executives all require different information. The Project Server administrator also assigns rights to the various views so that both executives and team members can access the views that they most need.

If I determine that a problem's solution is a new project, can I create the project?

✔ You cannot create projects in Project Web Access. If you have and know how to use Project Professional, you can create the project. Otherwise, you may consider creating a to-do list to keep track of things that may turn into projects in the future. If you use the To-Do List feature, you can convert the items in the list into a project in Project Professional. For more information on the To-Do List in Project Web Access, see Chapter 18.

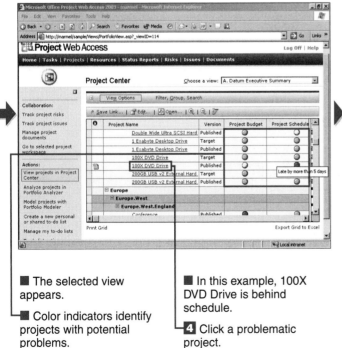

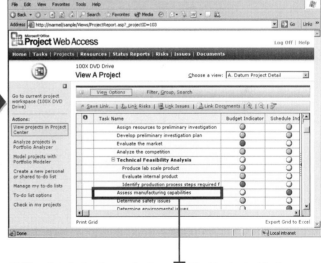

■ The selected view appears.

■ Color indicators identify projects with potential problems.

■ In this example, 100X DVD Drive is behind schedule.

4 Click a problematic project.

■ The details for the project appear.

■ The information you see depends on the view's definition.

5 Find tasks behind schedule.

■ You can click and drag the scroll bar to scroll down.

Note: To help resolve problems, see the section "Analyze a Portfolio."

ANALYZE A PORTFOLIO

Y ou can use the Portfolio Analyzer in Project Web Access to help resolve problems you see when you Review Your Portfolio. The Portfolio Analyzer is based on an Online Analytical Processing (OLAP) cube that your Project Server administrator creates. The cube consists of a chart and a PivotTable that help you analyze trends, spot the source of problems, and

possibly even identify a solution for the problem. This section shows you how to use the Portfolio Analyzer to determine why the 100X DVD Drive project of A. Datum Corporation — the sample company that comes with Project Server — is behind schedule so that you can attempt to correct the problem.

By default, the OLAP cube, which appears when you display the Portfolio Analyzer page, shows

information for all projects in your portfolio. Unfortunately, this amount of information is too large to help you analyze anything. You can narrow the information using views and by selecting only one project; or, if you are analyzing a problem that involves more than one project, you can include just the projects that you need to analyze.

ANALYZE A PORTFOLIO

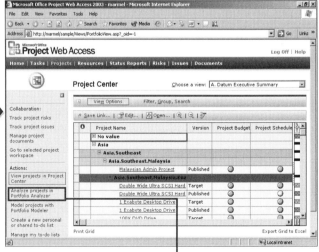

VIEW THE PORTFOLIO ANALYZER PAGE

1 Log onto Project Web Access.

Note: For details on logging onto Project Web Access, see Chapter 19.

■ The Project Web Access Home page appears.

2 Click Projects.

■ The Project Center appears.

■ All the projects in your portfolio appear.

3 Click Analyze projects in Portfolio Analyzer.

Why do I receive an error message when I try to view the Portfolio Manager page?

✔ It is possible that your Project Server administrator has not yet built the OLAP cube or that you do not have the proper security permissions to view the OLAP cube. Contact your Project Server administrator.

What kind of View Options are available on the Portfolio Analyzer page?

✔ You can display a list of fields that you can add to the PivotChart and PivotTable, and you can display a toolbar to help you manipulate the PivotTable and the PivotChart.

Can I transfer information into Excel?

✔ Yes. Display the PivotTable and then the toolbar. On the toolbar, you have a button available that sends the information to Excel.

When I send the information to Excel, do I get both the chart and the table?

✔ No, you can only view the table in Excel. You can, however, use Excel features to create a chart from the table.

Can I update the information in Excel and then upload it to Project Web Access?

✔ No. In fact, you cannot change the data in Excel because it is a read-only file.

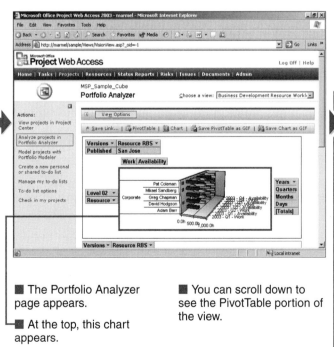

■ The Portfolio Analyzer page appears.

■ At the top, this chart appears.

■ You can scroll down to see the PivotTable portion of the view.

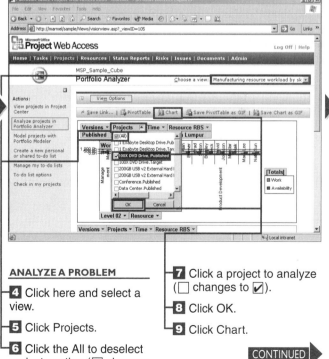

ANALYZE A PROBLEM

4 Click here and select a view.

5 Click Projects.

6 Click the All to deselect projects option (✓ changes to ☐).

7 Click a project to analyze (☐ changes to ✓).

8 Click OK.

9 Click Chart.

CONTINUED

ANALYZE A PORTFOLIO (CONTINUED)

When you first view the Portfolio Analyzer page, the chart for all your projects appears at the top of the page, and the PivotTable appears at the bottom. You can use buttons on the page's toolbar to view only the chart or only the PivotTable.

Once you identify the project or projects you want to review, you can use both the chart and the

PivotTable to help you in your analysis. The visual representation in the chart can help you quickly spot an issue like an overallocated resource, and the PivotTable provides numeric information that delineates the problem further. You can use the information in the PivotTable to narrow down — and therefore clarify — the information that appears on the chart.

If you identify a potential problem, you can draw attention to it using the collaboration tools that Windows SharePoint Services provides. You can create and monitor an issue or a risk. You also can respond to issues and risks. And, you can attach documents to projects, tasks, or to-do lists. See Chapter 18 for more information on issues and risks. See Chapter 19 for more information on document sharing.

ANALYZE A PORTFOLIO (CONTINUED)

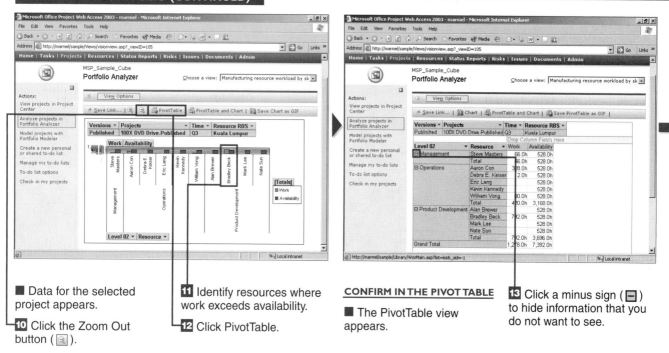

■ Data for the selected project appears.

10 Click the Zoom Out button (🔍).

11 Identify resources where work exceeds availability.

12 Click PivotTable.

CONFIRM IN THE PIVOT TABLE

■ The PivotTable view appears.

13 Click a minus sign (⊟) to hide information that you do not want to see.

How do I use the Fields list that can display as a view option?

✔ You can drag a field from the list to either the chart or the table, creating your own view as you work; you are not limited to viewing the details of your selected view.

What can I do with the toolbars that I can display as a view option?

✔ Using the chart toolbar, you can, for example, change the chart type or swap the rows and columns in the chart. Using the table toolbar, calculate totals and fields and send the table to Excel.

Can I save a view that I create by adding fields?

✔ Yes, in a way. You can click Save Link on the toolbar of the Portfolio Analyzer page. In the dialog box that appears, type a name that means something to you and click OK. The view you just created does not appear in the Choose a view list; instead, Project Web Access adds an entry to the Actions pane called Saved Links. By clicking the link, you access your newly created view. The link appears in the Actions pane whenever you click Projects in Project Web Access.

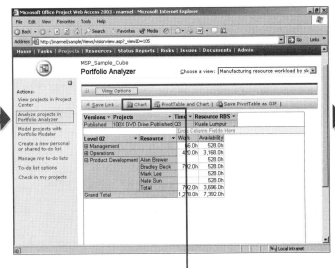

14 Review overextended resources where Work exceeds Availability.

15 Click Chart.

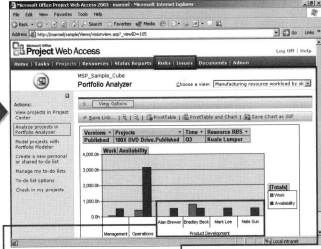

■ Hiding information that you do not want to view in the PivotTable cleans up the chart.

■ You can view other resources with the same skills that are available.

■ You can click here to create an issue or risk report to have a resource manager rebalance the workload.

ANSWER THE FAMOUS "WHAT IF" QUESTION

Managers often must ask, "What if this happens?" Using the Portfolio Modeler in Project Web Access, you can answer those types of questions, comparing different staffing and scheduling scenarios for projects to help identify the most efficient and effective use of resources to complete projects on-time and within budget.

The Portfolio Modeler can help you make resource allocation decisions.

You can select projects to include in a model and then interactively change tasks or staffing to view the impact on a project portfolio. Essentially, you can ask, "If I make these changes, what will be the impact?"

Suppose that you are an executive, portfolio manager, or resource manager who is considering a list of potential projects. You can use the Portfolio Modeler to determine if you have the resources to

perform the projects you have, given scheduling considerations.

You can find the Portfolio Modeler tool in the Project Center. Initially, you create a model and then you use it to perform the analysis. When you create the model, select the projects to include in the model and you identify the resources to use to staff the projects included in the model.

ANSWER THE FAMOUS "WHAT IF" QUESTION

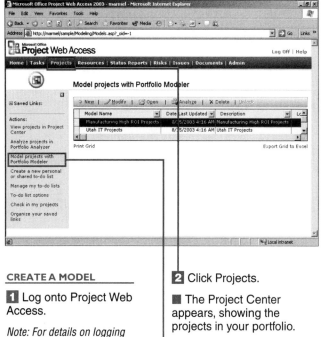

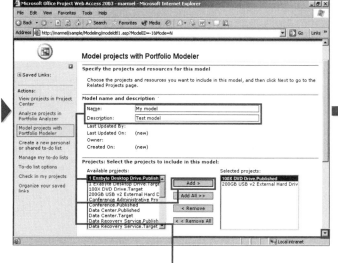

CREATE A MODEL

1 Log onto Project Web Access.

Note: For details on logging onto Project Web Access, see Chapter 19.

2 Click Projects.

■ The Project Center appears, showing the projects in your portfolio.

3 Click Model projects with Portfolio Modeler.

■ The Specify the projects and resources for this model page appears.

Note: Because each page of this wizard is called "Model projects with Portfolio Manager," the titles in this section refer to subtitles.

4 Type a name and description here.

5 Select a project.

6 Click Add.

7 Repeat steps 5 to 6 for each project.

8 Scroll down.

How do I view more than one resource on the resource allocation chart that appears at the bottom of the Specify the projects and resources for this model page?

✔ You can view a resource allocation chart for a combination of resources by holding down Ctrl as you click each resource that you want to include in the chart. Then, click the Refresh button ( ).

Can I delete a model?

✔ Yes. On the Model projects with Portfolio Modeler page, select the model and click Delete.

What is the difference between opening a model and modifying a model?

✔ When you open a model, a Gantt Chart helps you identify if the projects in the model are overallocated; Project also provides a resource assignment chart where you can view assignments for specified resources. But you cannot make any changes on this page. When you click Modify, you can make changes to any of the model's parameters — you can add or remove projects and resources and change scheduling options.

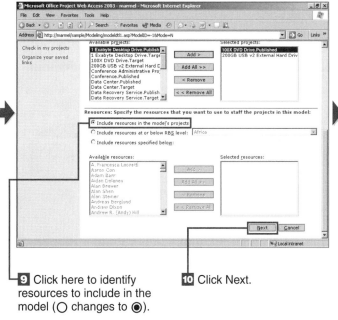

9 Click here to identify resources to include in the model (○ changes to ◉).

10 Click Next.

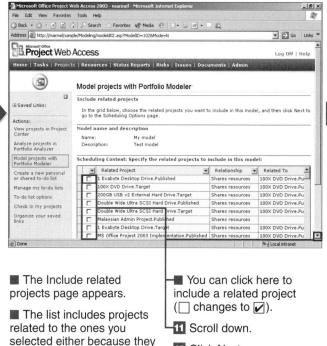

■ The Include related projects page appears.

■ The list includes projects related to the ones you selected either because they share resources or through an external link.

■ You can click here to include a related project (☐ changes to ✔).

11 Scroll down.

12 Click Next.

CONTINUED

ANSWER THE FAMOUS "WHAT IF" QUESTION (CONTINUED)

After you select additional projects to include in the model, you set scheduling options for the model. You can keep the dates and assignments that appear in each project or you can set up the model to reassign resources in the project or in the model.

At this point, Project Web Access saves your model. You can open it to review or the parameters to

include additional projects in the model, or change the start date, resources, or scheduling options you set for the model.

If you open the model that you created, a Gantt Chart displays summary statistics for each project that you included in the model. The colors of the bars represent the overallocated status of the project's resources during the specified time

frame. Green means that no resources are overallocated; yellow signifies that less than 10% of the resources are overallocated; and red means that more than 10% of the resources are overallocated.

At the bottom of the page, you can view a resource allocation graph for each resource that is included in the model.

ANSWER THE FAMOUS "WHAT IF" QUESTION (CONTINUED)

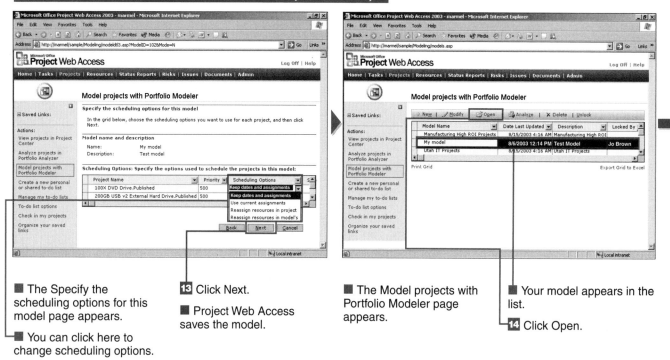

■ The Specify the scheduling options for this model page appears.

■ You can click here to change scheduling options.

⏹13 Click Next.

■ Project Web Access saves the model.

■ The Model projects with Portfolio Modeler page appears.

■ Your model appears in the list.

⏹14 Click Open.

Why do I see a resource name — my name — in the Locked column on the Model projects with Portfolio Modeler page?

✔ While you use a model, Project Web Access locks it so that nobody else can change it. You can unlock the model from the Model projects with Portfolio Modeler page. Select the model and click Unlock.

Can I compare one model with another model?

✔ Yes. Open the first model, and, on the page that appears, click Compare. A page appears where you can choose models to compare with the selected model.

If I forgot to include a project in the model, how can I add it after I create the model?

✔ You can add projects to the model by selecting a model on the Model projects with Portfolio Modeler page and clicking Modify. On the page that appears, you can add a project to the model by clicking it in the list of projects and then clicking Add. You also can remove a project from the model by clicking the project and then clicking Remove.

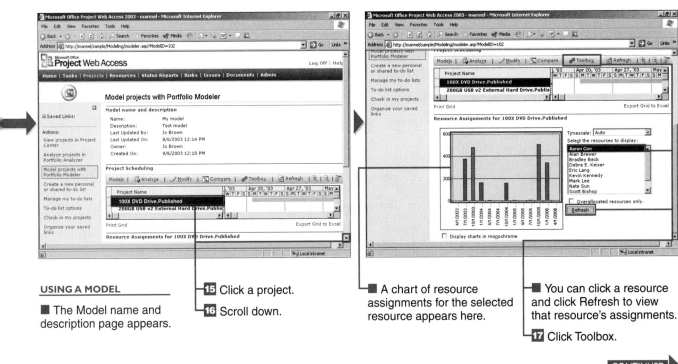

USING A MODEL

■ The Model name and description page appears.

⓯ Click a project.

⓰ Scroll down.

■ A chart of resource assignments for the selected resource appears here.

■ You can click a resource and click Refresh to view that resource's assignments.

⓱ Click Toolbox.

CONTINUED ▶

ANSWER THE FAMOUS "WHAT IF" QUESTION (CONTINUED)

When you analyze a model, Project Web Access produces a combined text and graphics report that describes the resource allocation in the model and makes staffing recommendations. The top portion of the report provides summary statistics for the shortest schedule and the modeled schedule. The shortest schedule assumes that you have an unlimited number of resources available to you.

In the middle of the page, Project provides a chart that compares time to work for three data series and tells you how efficiently the modeled project uses resources. The Demand data series shows you the work required to complete all projects in the model without considering resource availability. The Capacity data series shows you how much work resources can do while working on the modeled project without considering current assignments of the resources. And, the Utilization data series shows you the work that you still need to perform when current resource schedules are considered during modeling.

Your resources are underutilized when the Utilization data series is greater than the Demand data series. And, you are looking at a resource-deficit situation when the Utilization data series is greater than the Capacity data series.

ANSWER THE FAMOUS "WHAT IF" QUESTION (CONTINUED)

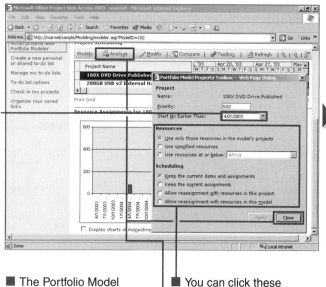

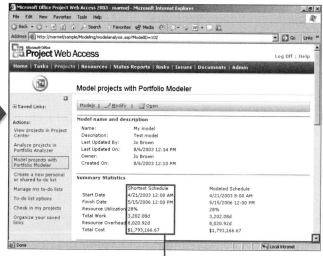

■ The Portfolio Model Property Toolbox window appears.

■ You can click here and select the start date for the model.

■ You can click these options (○ changes to ◉) to change the resources and scheduling properties of the model.

18 Click Close.

19 Click Analyze.

■ A text and graphics report appears, describing resource allocation and making staffing recommendations.

■ The summary statistics at the top describe both the shortest schedule and the modeled schedule.

■ The shortest schedule assumes unlimited resources.

20 Scroll down.

What should I do if the data in the model looks wrong?

✔ First, refresh the model to update it with any new information. If the data still looks wrong, Contact your Project Server administrator. The Project Server administrator builds an OLAP cube so that you can use the analysis and modeling tools in Project Web Access; periodically, the Project Server administrator should rebuild the cube to keep the information that is being analyzed and modeled up-to-date. The information you view may seem wrong because the cube is out-of-date.

How do I refresh the model?

✔ Open the model and click the Refresh button ([⬚]). A message asks if you really want to refresh the model because refreshing can take some time. Click Yes to continue.

Can I take information generated in a model and apply it to a project?

✔ At the present time, no, you cannot automatically transfer changes that you make in models to actual projects. You must manually reconstruct the information in Project Professional.

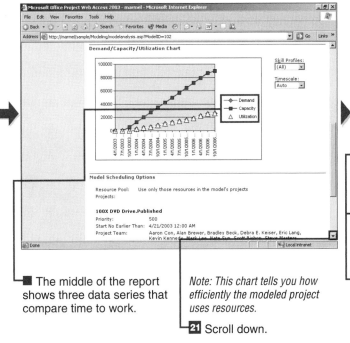

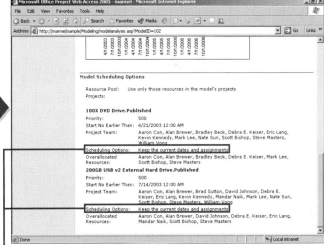

■ The middle of the report shows three data series that compare time to work.

Note: This chart tells you how efficiently the modeled project uses resources.

21 Scroll down.

■ The bottom of the report enables you to review scheduling options for all projects in the model.

SECTION VI

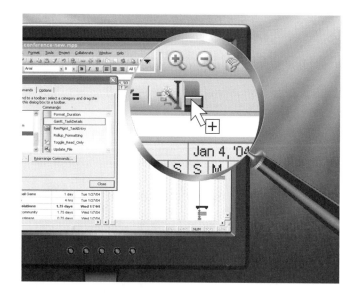

CONTROL THE WINDOWS TASKBAR ICONS

Do you yearn for the days when your Windows taskbar was not littered with icons representing every open Project file? You can take control of Project's behavior with respect to the Windows taskbar.

In Project 98 and earlier versions of Project, you saw only one icon on the Windows taskbar while Project

was open, regardless of the number of Project files that you opened. Starting in Project 2000, by default, one icon appears on the Windows taskbar for every open Project file.

If you open numerous files, the chances are good that you cannot readily or easily identify each file from the icon on the Windows taskbar. However, if you point the

mouse at the icon, a ScreenTip reveals the entire path and filename.

But suppose that you belong to the school of users who does not *want* an icon on the Windows taskbar for each open file; you believe that makes working harder, not easier. You can reinstate the behavior of Project 98 and earlier versions.

CONTROL THE WINDOWS TASKBAR ICONS

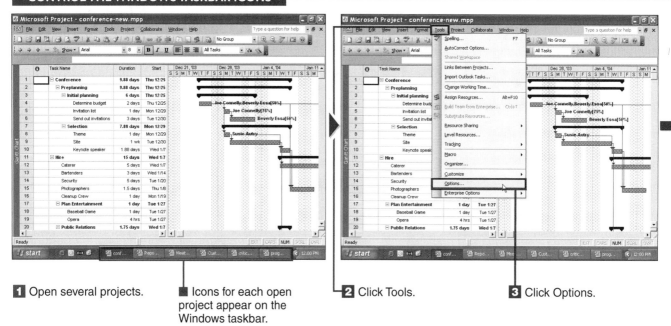

1 Open several projects.

■ Icons for each open project appear on the Windows taskbar.

2 Click Tools.

3 Click Options.

Can I view all the open projects on-screen simultaneously?

✓ Yes, but it is practical only if you have a large monitor and you display only two or three projects at the same time. Open the projects you want to view simultaneously, click Window, and click Arrange All. Project divides the monitor viewing area into equal size panes, each displaying one project.

What if I want icons to appear on the Windows taskbar for each open project?

✓ Repeat the steps in this task, but click the Windows in Taskbar option (☐ changes to ☑).

If all my projects are still open, how do I switch to another open project?

✓ In Project, click Window. All open projects appear in a list at the bottom of the menu. Click the one you want.

How do I make the taskbar bigger so that I can see filenames in the icons?

✓ You can make the taskbar bigger, but whether you can view the filenames depends on how many projects you open simultaneously. Place ⌖ over the top of the taskbar until you see ↕, and then drag upward. If you make the taskbar wider than you want, drag downward.

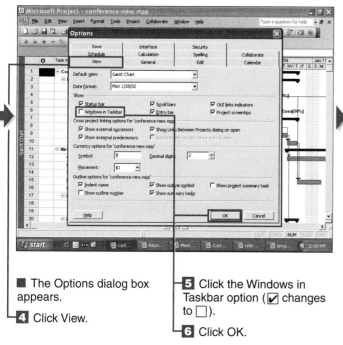

■ The Options dialog box appears.

4 Click View.

5 Click the Windows in Taskbar option (☑ changes to ☐).

6 Click OK.

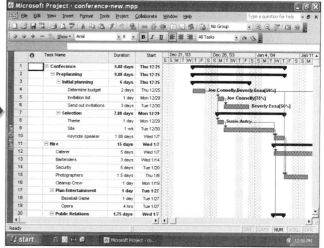

■ The icons for all open projects except the active project disappear from the Windows taskbar.

■ The other projects are still open; you simply do not see icons on the taskbar for them.

USING THE ORGANIZER

I f you have used the techniques described in Chapters 6, 7, 8, and 9 to create custom views, tables, combination views, and custom fields in a particular Project file, you may want to share these elements with coworkers or you may simply want to use them in other Project files. Project uses the Organizer to help you share views, tables, forms, reports, and more among projects.

You can use the tabs in the Organizer window to copy elements from the Global template,

Global.mpt, to the current project. You also can copy elements from the current project to the Global template, or you can copy elements between projects.

If you want to copy between Project files, open the Project file that contains the information you want to copy and the Project file into which you want to copy the information. To copy elements between a Project file and the Global template, you only need to open the Project file.

Why should I copy an element to the Global template?
✔ When you copy an element to the Global template, that element becomes available to all files that were created with your copy of Project.

USING THE ORGANIZER

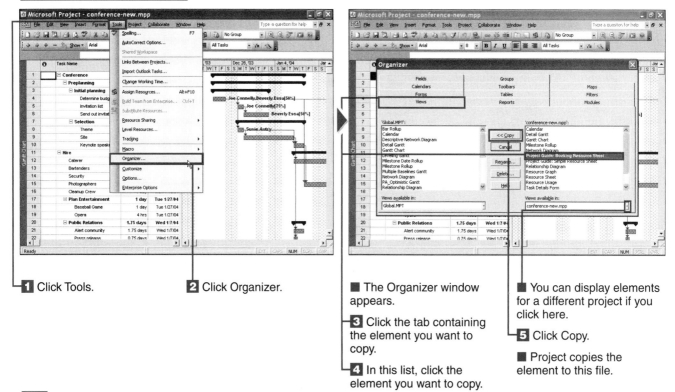

■1 Click Tools.

■2 Click Organizer.

■ The Organizer window appears.

■3 Click the tab containing the element you want to copy.

■4 In this list, click the element you want to copy.

■ You can display elements for a different project if you click here.

■5 Click Copy.

■ Project copies the element to this file.

COMBINE OR SEPARATE TOOLBARS

You can control whether Project's Standard and Formatting toolbars appear on one row or two at the top of your screen. Throughout this book, the Standard toolbar has appeared on a separate row from the Formatting toolbar, much like they appeared in Project 98 and earlier versions. When the toolbars appear on separate rows, you can view all the tools defined for the toolbars.

If screen real estate is vital to you and you want more vertical viewing space for your project, consider placing the toolbars on the same row. Project initially displays the tools that Microsoft thinks users most often use. If you need a tool that you do not see, you can click a button to display additional available buttons.

If I place the toolbars on one row, can I always display one of the tools that I initially do not see?

✔ You do not need to do anything except click the tool. After you use that tool, it appears on the toolbar, replacing the least-used tool, if necessary. As you work, the toolbars become personalized to your work habits, displaying the tools that you most often use.

COMBINE OR SEPARATE TOOLBARS

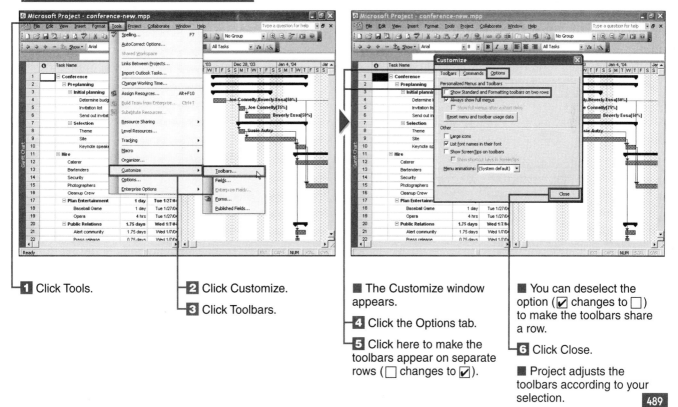

1 Click Tools.

2 Click Customize.

3 Click Toolbars.

■ The Customize window appears.

4 Click the Options tab.

5 Click here to make the toolbars appear on separate rows (☐ changes to ☑).

■ You can deselect the option (☑ changes to ☐) to make the toolbars share a row.

6 Click Close.

■ Project adjusts the toolbars according to your selection.

489

CONTROL MENU BEHAVIOR

By default, Project displays a limited set of commands in each menu — the set Microsoft thinks you use most often. If you prefer to view all of the commands available on a menu, however, you can modify Project's default behavior.

When you use the default settings for menus, Project personalizes the menus as you work to display the commands that you use most

frequently. When you open a menu while using the default settings, an abbreviated menu containing a limited set of commands appears. At the bottom of each menu, you can display the rest of the commands on the menu via an arrow.

When you use personalized menus, a vertical bar on the left side of the menu changes colors to help you distinguish between hidden commands and more frequently

used commands. If you select a hidden command, it becomes a frequently used command and appears on the abbreviated menu the next time that you open the menu.

Throughout this book, Project shows full menus. This section shows you how to change the setting that controls menu behavior and how to personalize how menus look and behave.

CONTROL MENU BEHAVIOR

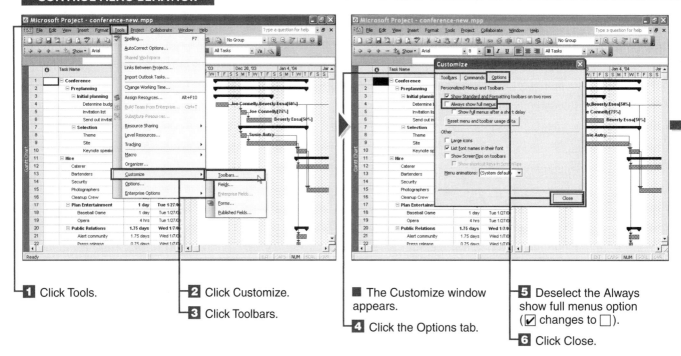

1 Click Tools.

2 Click Customize.

3 Click Toolbars.

■ The Customize window appears.

4 Click the Options tab.

5 Deselect the Always show full menus option (☑ changes to ☐).

6 Click Close.

How can I use personalized menus but still see all commands on the menu without clicking that arrow at the bottom?

✔ In the Customize window, select the Show full menus after a short delay option (☐ changes to ☑). With this option selected, Project first displays the shortened, personal set of menus. After a few moments, if you do not select a command, Project automatically expands the menu to display all its commands without your clicking the Expand arrow (⬇) at the bottom of the menu.

When should I use personalized menus and when should I use full menus?

✔ Your choice is exactly that — a choice. Use the types of menus that work best for you. Some people do not want to bother with commands that they never use; those people use personalized menus. Other people want to view all the available commands, in case they are looking for a way to accomplish a task; they think that seeing a particular command may generate an idea on how to accomplish the task.

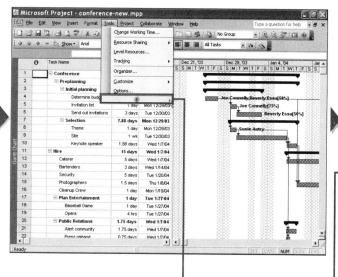

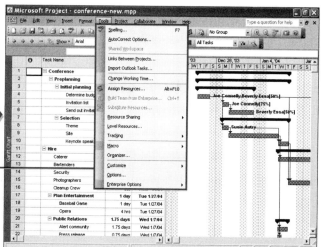

■ When you open a menu, it shows only some commands.

7 Click the Expand arrow (⬇).

■ Project displays the rest of the commands available on the menu.

ADD OR DELETE TOOLBAR BUTTONS

You can add or remove buttons from toolbars to make the toolbars most functional for your needs. Most of us want right at hand the buttons we use most. Similarly, we do not want buttons we rarely, if ever, use.

Microsoft provides a plethora of toolbars, but the odds are small that one toolbar in Project contains all the buttons you want available all the time.

For example, the Formatting toolbar includes commands to change the font and font size; apply bold, italic, and underline effects; and align tasks. But it does not include tools for modifying the timescale, gridlines, or bar styles. If you use those features often, you may want to add them to the Formatting toolbar. Or, you may simply want to add a tool for a

feature that you use all the time. For example, you may find yourself repeatedly right-clicking the Select All button to determine what table appears in the current view. You can add a toolbar button to any toolbar that shows you the name of the current table — and lets you switch tables.

ADD OR DELETE TOOLBAR BUTTONS

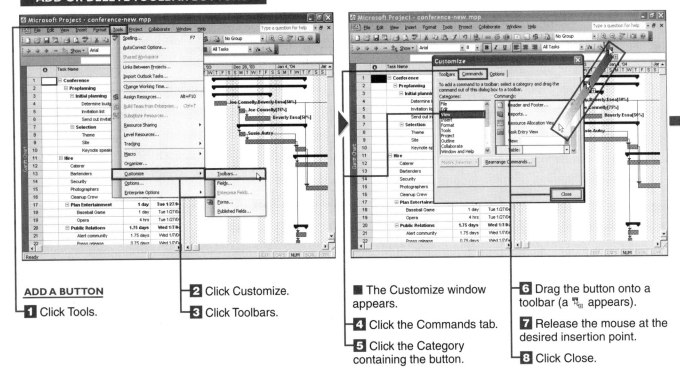

ADD A BUTTON

■1 Click Tools.

■2 Click Customize.

■3 Click Toolbars.

■ The Customize window appears.

■4 Click the Commands tab.

■5 Click the Category containing the button.

■6 Drag the button onto a toolbar (a ⬚ appears).

■7 Release the mouse at the desired insertion point.

■8 Click Close.

Does it matter which toolbar I select when adding a button?

✓ Not really. If you use the button all the time, add it to a toolbar that always appears on-screen; most people always display the Standard and Formatting toolbars. Be aware, however, that adding buttons to the toolbars that come with Project is not always a good idea. If you add a toolbar button to one of the toolbars that comes with Project and you reset that toolbar, the button that you added disappears because the toolbar returns to its original state when you installed Project.

What if I do not like the position of the button that I added to a toolbar?

✓ You can move buttons on a toolbar by clicking and dragging them to a new position when the Customize window is open. Or, you can click Rearrange Commands in the Customize window to display the Rearrange Commands window. In the Rearrange Commands window, you select a toolbar, select a button, and then move it. Moving the button up moves it to the left on the toolbar, and moving it down moves it to the right.

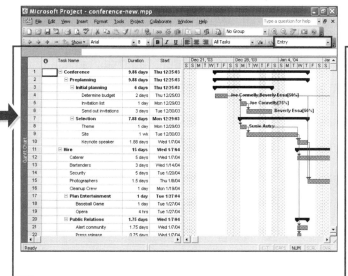

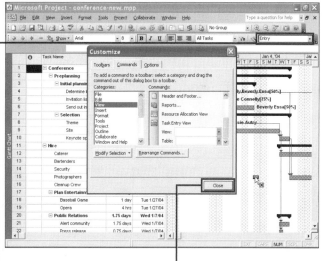

■ The button appears on the toolbar.

DELETE A BUTTON

1 Repeat steps 1 to 3 from the previous page.

2 Click and drag the button off the toolbar and drag it anywhere on your project (a appears).

3 Click Close.

■ The button disappears from the toolbar.

CREATE A CUSTOM TOOLBAR

The default toolbars contain buttons you use and buttons you do not use; instead of "getting by" with the default toolbars, you can create a custom toolbar that supports the way that you work. If you create a custom toolbar instead of editing an existing toolbar, you ensure that the buttons you add remain on the toolbar and appear in the order you specify. When you add buttons to or rearrange buttons on a toolbar

that comes with Project, you risk losing your changes if you reset the toolbar.

You do not need to limit the buttons on your custom toolbar to buttons that do not appear on an existing toolbar. You may find it useful, for example, to create your own version of the Standard toolbar and display it instead of the default Standard toolbar. On your version of the toolbar, you may include all

of the buttons on the default Standard toolbar except the File Search, Spelling, Format Painter, Insert Hyperlink, Publish All Information, and Copy Picture buttons. On your toolbar, you may want to include the File Close, Insert Column, Format Timescale, and Change Working Time buttons that do not appear on the default Standard toolbar.

CREATE A CUSTOM TOOLBAR

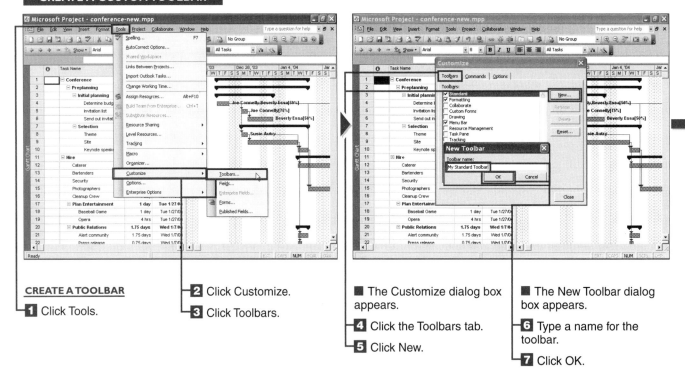

CREATE A TOOLBAR

-1 Click Tools.

-2 Click Customize.

-3 Click Toolbars.

■ The Customize dialog box appears.

-4 Click the Toolbars tab.

-5 Click New.

■ The New Toolbar dialog box appears.

-6 Type a name for the toolbar.

-7 Click OK.

MASTER IT

I created a toolbar that I want to use instead of the Standard toolbar. How do I make my toolbar the default toolbar?

✔ First, right-click the Standard toolbar. On the menu that appears, click Standard toolbar. The Standard toolbar disappears from your screen. To use your toolbar in the same place where the Standard toolbar appeared, click and drag your toolbar to the top of the screen. It automatically snaps into place. If you do not see your toolbar on-screen, right-click any toolbar and, from the menu that appears, click your toolbar.

How do I change the picture that Project uses for a button?

✔ You can edit existing button images or switch to a different, predefined image. Open the Customize window and then click the button whose image you want to change. Then, click Modify Selection. To modify the existing appearance of the button, click Edit Button Image to open the Button Editor window, where you can change the colors or erase portions of the button image. To switch to a different, predefined image, click Change Button Image and select a new image.

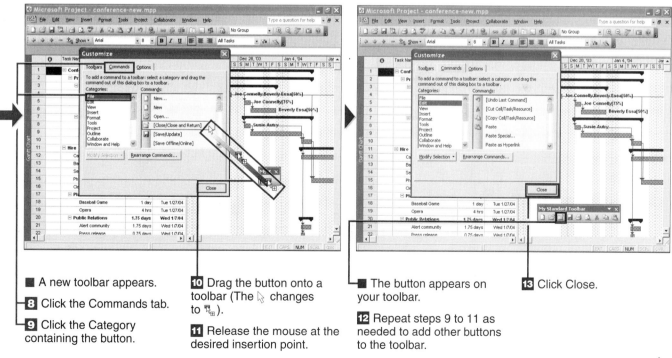

■ A new toolbar appears.

8 Click the Commands tab.

9 Click the Category containing the button.

10 Drag the button onto a toolbar (The ⌖ changes to ⌖).

11 Release the mouse at the desired insertion point.

■ The button appears on your toolbar.

12 Repeat steps 9 to 11 as needed to add other buttons to the toolbar.

13 Click Close.

CONTINUED ▶

CREATE A CUSTOM TOOLBAR (CONTINUED)

In addition to adding buttons to a custom toolbar, you can organize the toolbar by creating groups of buttons that, in your opinion, belong together. You may have noticed, on the Standard toolbar, for example, the vertical lines that appear periodically. These vertical lines visually group buttons. On your toolbar, you may want to group all the buttons that perform file operations, such as

New, Open, Close, and Save. You may also want to group Cut, Copy, Paste, and Undo, because you feel that they perform similar functions. Grouping buttons with similar functions helps you find the buttons quickly, but you may come up with a different organizational scheme that works better for you. You are limited only by your imagination.

You may realize that, while creating your toolbar, you did not place the buttons in the order you really want them to appear. You can reorganize them by dragging or, if you are not a fan of dragging, you can use the Rearrange Commands window to change the order of the buttons and to add or delete buttons from your toolbar.

CREATE A CUSTOM TOOLBAR (CONTINUED)

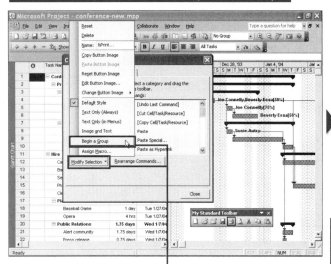

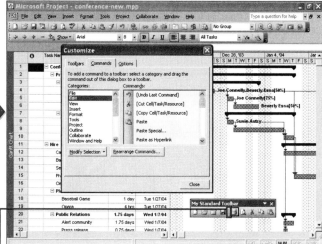

GROUP BUTTONS

1 In the Customize dialog box, click the button that you want first in the group.

Note: For more on opening this dialog box, see the section "Create a Custom Toolbar."

2 Click Modify Selection.

3 Click Begin a Group.

■ A vertical line appears to the left of the selected button.

How can I remove a group marker that I added by mistake?

✔ Because the Begin Group option toggles the mark on and off, you can repeat the steps in the subsection "Group Buttons" to add the group marker.

What happens if I click Add while viewing the Rearrange Commands dialog box?

✔ A dialog box appears similar to the Commands tab of the Customize dialog box from which you can add buttons to the toolbar without dragging. Click a category from the list on the left and a command from the list on the right and then click OK to add another button to the toolbar.

What does Modify Selection in the Rearrange Commands dialog box do?

✔ It functions exactly like Modify Selection in the Customize dialog box. For example, you can begin a group from the Rearrange dialog box window if you click the button that you want first in the group, then click Modify Selection and, from the menu that appears, click Begin Group.

What does Reset in the Rearrange Commands window do?

✔ It works like the Undo command; if you click it, Project discards any changes you made since you opened the Rearrange Commands dialog box.

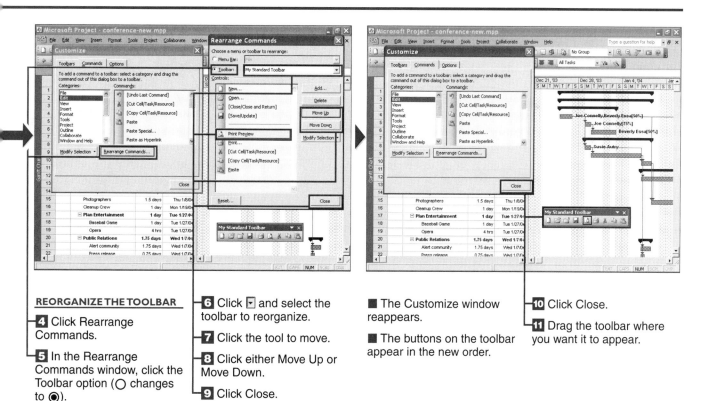

REORGANIZE THE TOOLBAR

4 Click Rearrange Commands.

5 In the Rearrange Commands window, click the Toolbar option (○ changes to ◉).

6 Click ▼ and select the toolbar to reorganize.

7 Click the tool to move.

8 Click either Move Up or Move Down.

9 Click Close.

■ The Customize window reappears.

■ The buttons on the toolbar appear in the new order.

10 Click Close.

11 Drag the toolbar where you want it to appear.

CUSTOMIZE PROJECT MENUS

I n the same way that the default toolbars contain buttons that you use and buttons that you do not use, the default menus contain commands that you use and commands that you do not use. And, in the same way that you can customize toolbars, you can customize menus to make them more suitable to the way you work.

You can create new menus and add commands to them or you can modify existing menus by adding

commands to or deleting commands from them. If you create a custom menu instead of editing an existing menu, you ensure that the commands that you add remain on the menu and appear in the order you specify. When you add commands to or rearrange commands on a menu that comes with Project, you risk losing your changes if you reset the menu.

You can add commands to a custom menu that already appear on some other menu. If you have a series of actions that you take regularly; you can place them on a menu together. That way, when you take the series of actions, you can simply click each command on your menu in the order that they appear on the menu.

CUSTOMIZE PROJECT MENUS

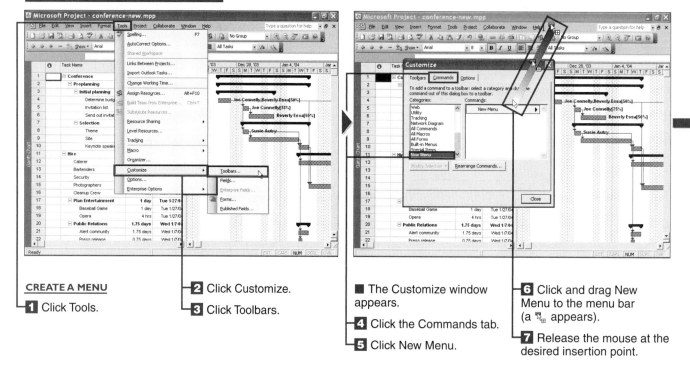

CREATE A MENU

1 Click Tools.

2 Click Customize.

3 Click Toolbars.

■ The Customize window appears.

4 Click the Commands tab.

5 Click New Menu.

6 Click and drag New Menu to the menu bar (a 🖫 appears).

7 Release the mouse at the desired insertion point.

Does my new custom menu appear automatically in Project or do I need to take some action to display it by default?

✔ As with toolbars, Project adds new menus to your Global template file, the default file on which all project files are based. Therefore, each time you open Project, your custom menu appears; in addition, your custom menu appears in all projects, even ones you created before creating the menu. And, changes that you make to menus or the menu bar affect all files that you create with this copy of Project.

How can I create a custom menu but not have it appear all the time?

✔ You can create a custom toolbar and drag the custom menu onto the custom toolbar. Then, the custom menu appears on the custom toolbar instead of the menu bar, and the custom menu becomes available only when you display the toolbar. To place a custom menu on a custom toolbar, display both the menu and the toolbar and open the Customize window. Then, drag the menu from the menu bar onto the toolbar.

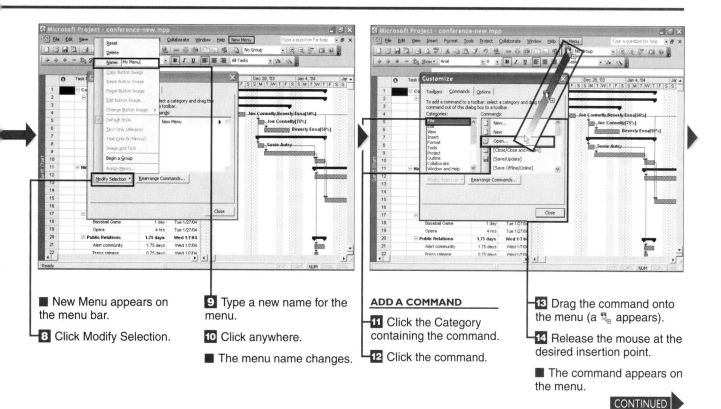

■ New Menu appears on the menu bar.

8 Click Modify Selection.

9 Type a new name for the menu.

10 Click anywhere.

■ The menu name changes.

ADD A COMMAND

11 Click the Category containing the command.

12 Click the command.

13 Drag the command onto the menu (a 🖫 appears).

14 Release the mouse at the desired insertion point.

■ The command appears on the menu.

CONTINUED ▶

CUSTOMIZE PROJECT MENUS (CONTINUED)

In addition to adding commands to a custom menu bar, you can organize the menu bar by creating groups of commands that, in your opinion, belong together. You may have noticed, on the View menu, for example, the vertical lines that appear periodically. These vertical lines visually group commands. On your menu bar, you may want to group all the commands that affect views, such

as View, Table, Column, and Timescale. You may also want to group Indent, Outdent, Hide Subtasks, and Show Subtasks, because you feel that they perform similar functions. Grouping commands with similar functions helps you find the commands quickly, but you may come up with a different organizational scheme that works better for you. You are limited only by your imagination.

You may realize that, while creating your menu bar, you did not place the commands in the order you really want them to appear. You can reorganize them by dragging or, if you are not a fan of dragging, you can use the Rearrange Commands window to change the order of the commands and to add or delete commands from your menu bar.

CUSTOMIZE PROJECT MENUS (CONTINUED)

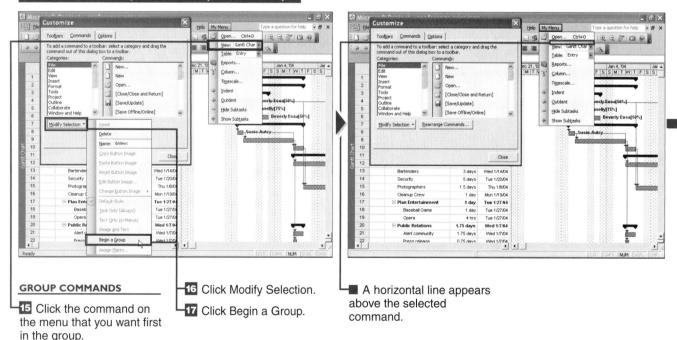

GROUP COMMANDS

15 Click the command on the menu that you want first in the group.

16 Click Modify Selection.

17 Click Begin a Group.

■ A horizontal line appears above the selected command.

How can I remove of group marker that I added by mistake?

✔ Because the Begin Group option toggles the mark on and off, you can repeat the steps in the subsection "Group Buttons" to add the group marker.

What happens if I click Add while viewing the Rearrange Commands dialog box?

✔ A dialog box appears similar to the commands tab of the Customize dialog box from which you can add buttons to the toolbar without dragging. Click a category from the list on the left and a command from the list on the right and then click OK to add another button to the toolbar.

Can I place a macro on a menu so that I can run the macro by clicking it on the menu?

✔ Yes. To assign a macro to a menu command, see Chapter 22.

How do I delete a menu that I created?

✔ Open the Customize window using steps 1 to 3 in the subsection "Create a Menu." Then, drag the menu off the menu bar and drop it anywhere on your project. You also can remove commands from a menu in the same way; with the Customize window open, drag the command off the menu and drop it anywhere on your project.

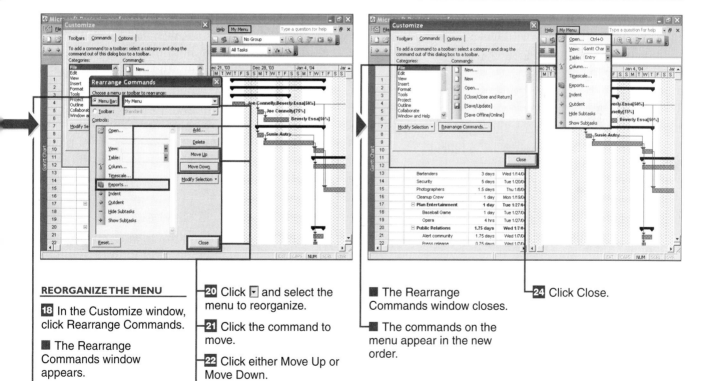

REORGANIZE THE MENU

18 In the Customize window, click Rearrange Commands.

■ The Rearrange Commands window appears.

19 Click the Menu Bar option (○ changes to ⦿).

20 Click ⬝ and select the menu to reorganize.

21 Click the command to move.

22 Click either Move Up or Move Down.

23 Click Close.

■ The Rearrange Commands window closes.

■ The commands on the menu appear in the new order.

24 Click Close.

UNDERSTANDING MACROS

Y ou can use *macros*, which are small programs, to help you execute repetitive tasks that you perform frequently. You may have used macros in a word processing program. Macros work the same way in Project as they do in your word processor.

Do not let the word *program* in the preceding paragraph deter you from getting to know macros. Although you can work with the macro programming language, Project provides an easier way for you to write a macro, which you learn about in this chapter.

When to Use Macros

Macros are most useful when you need to perform any repetitive task. For example, you can use Project macros to:

- Display or hide frequently used toolbars
- Display frequently used tables
- Display frequently used views
- Switch to a custom view
- Generate standard reports

As you become comfortable using Project, you will identify the steps that you take over and over again; these tasks are excellent candidates for macros.

```
Sub Format_Duration()

    On Error GoTo ErrorHandler

    Check_if_Project_Open

    frmFormatDuration.InitializeList
    frmFormatDuration.cboDurUnit.SetFocus
    frmFormatDuration.cboDurUnit.SelStart = 0
    frmFormatDuration.cboDurUnit.SelLength = frmFormatDuration.cboDu
    frmFormatDuration.Show

    Exit Sub

ErrorHandler:
    ProcessError Err
End Sub
```

Methods for Creating Macros

You can create a macro in one of two ways: You can enter the Visual Basic for Applications programming code — and that works well if you are a programmer, but most of us are not. You also can let Project record your actions as you take them; Project then translates your actions into Visual Basic programming code for you. Most of us use this latter approach, because it is easier than writing code.

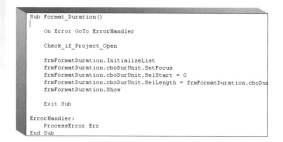

Running Macros

One you have created a macro, Project provides several ways to run the macro. If you do not use the macro often, you can run it from the Macro dialog box; you read about this method in the section "Run Macros."

Macros and Keyboard Shortcuts

If you run the macro often, you can assign a keyboard shortcut to the macro; when you press the key combination that you assign, Project runs the macro. You read about this technique in the section "Assign a Keyboard Shortcut to a Macro."

Macros and Toolbars

If you prefer, you can place it on a toolbar or on a menu; you read about these methods in the sections "Assign a Macro to a Toolbar Button" and "Assign a Macro to a Menu Command."

Sample Macros

Project ships with several sample macros. At the end of this chapter, you read about one of these macros — the Rollup Formatting macro. In Appendix A, you can read about rollup views, which roll up a project to summary task or even to the project level so that you can hide details and look at an overview of your project. The Rollup Formatting macro provides a shortcut method to format a Gantt Chart view using rollup formatting.

The sample macros come "as is" with no warranty from Microsoft that they will work. You should try them to see if they can help you in any way. In addition to the Rollup Formatting macro, you can find the following four macros:

Types of Sample Macros

Macro	Description
Format_ Duration	Sets a default duration unit in the project and reformats the duration of all of the tasks so that all of their durations are expressed in the same unit.
Toggle_ Read_Only	Switches a file's attributes between "read-only" and "read-write." If you open a read-only file, you cannot make any changes; you simply can read the information. You can make changes to a read-write file.
Update_File	If you make changes while viewing a read-only file, you can use this macro to restore the file to the most recently saved version. Update_File macro offers you the option to save the file by renaming it.
ResMgmt_ TaskEntry	Switches to the Task Entry view, a combination view that shows the Gantt Chart view in the top pane and the Task Form view in the bottom pane. For more on combination views, see Chapter 7.

RECORD MACROS

Although Project stores macros in the Visual Basic for Applications (VBA) programming language, you do not need to be adept at programming to create a macro. You can, instead, record a macro.

For example, if you find yourself often displaying a split view with the Gantt Chart on top and the Task Details Form below, you may find a macro useful. The steps you

take — and want to record in this macro — start in the Gantt Chart view and split the window. Then, you switch the Task Form in the bottom pane to the Task Details Form.

When you record a macro, you walk through the steps necessary to do whatever it is you want Project to do. Project then converts those actions into Visual Basic statements and stores the statements in a

macro. Later, when you want to take that action again, you run your macro. For more on running macros, see the next section, "Run Macros."

Before you record a macro, you should go through the steps that you want to take. You may even want to write down the steps. That way, you are less likely to make (and record) mistakes.

RECORD MACROS

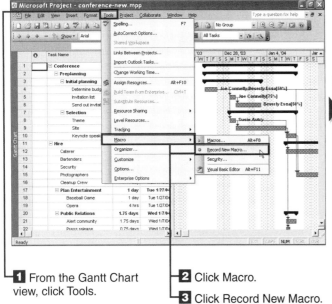

1 From the Gantt Chart view, click Tools.

Note: For more on switching view, see Chapter 2.

2 Click Macro.

3 Click Record New Macro.

■ The Record Macro dialog box appears.

4 Type a name for the macro.

■ You can type a letter to create a keyboard shortcut for the macro.

■ You can assign any letter key on your keyboard, but you cannot assign numbers or a special character.

■ You also cannot assign a key combination that Microsoft Project already uses.

Are there rules concerning macro names?

✔ Yes. You must make the first character of the macro name a letter, but you can make the other characters letters, numbers, or underscore characters. You cannot include a space in a macro name, so try using an underscore character as a word separator, or capitalize the first letter of each word.

Can I make the macro start in a particular view so that I do not need to remember to switch views?

✔ Yes. Record the steps to change to the correct view even if you are already looking at the correct view.

What do the options in the Row references and Column references sections of the Record Macro dialog box do?

✔ These options control the way that the macro selects rows and columns if the macro selects cells. For rows, the macro, by default, records relative references to rows. If you want a macro to always select the same rows, regardless of the position of the active cell, select Absolute (ID). For columns, the macro, by default, records absolute references to columns. If you want a macro to select the same columns, regardless of the position of the active cell when you run the macro, select Relative in the Column references section.

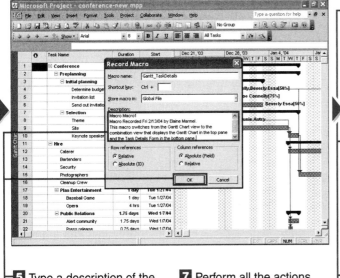

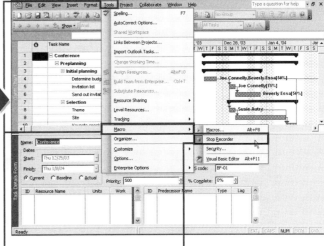

5 Type a description of the function that the macro performs.

6 Click OK.

■ Project redisplays your project and starts recording your actions.

7 Perform all the actions that you want to record.

■ For example, click Window and click Split. Right-click the bottom pane and click More Views. In the More Views window, click Task Details Form and click Apply.

8 Click Tools.

9 Click Macro.

10 Click Stop Recorder.

■ Project stores your macro.

RUN MACROS

Once you have recorded a macro, as illustrated in the section "Record Macros," you use the macro by running it. Some people refer to this action as *playing back* the macro because they associate recording and playing back with the process of recording a TV program on a VCR and then playing back the recording. There are several ways to run a macro; in this section, you see how to run a macro using the Macro dialog box.

If you expect your macro to make substantial changes to your project, you should save the project before you run the macro just in case the macro makes changes that you do not want or expect. You cannot undo the effects of a macro easily.

If the macro is not performing as I expected, can I stop a macro while it is running?

✔ You can stop a macro while it is running by pressing and holding Ctrl and then pressing Break on your keyboard. Be aware that this action works if your macro is long. If your macro is short, the macro will probably finish before you can stop it.

RUN MACROS

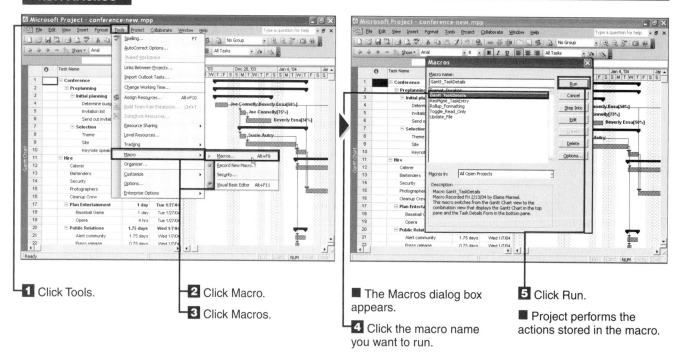

1 Click Tools.

2 Click Macro.

3 Click Macros.

■ The Macros dialog box appears.

4 Click the macro name you want to run.

5 Click Run.

■ Project performs the actions stored in the macro.

ASSIGN A KEYBOARD SHORTCUT TO A MACRO

Although you can run macros by selecting them from the Macros dialog box, if you use a macro on a regular basis, you may want to use a shorter method to run the macro. For example, you may be one of those people who like to keep their hands on the keyboard as much as possible. In your case, a keyboard shortcut for the macro is the answer. You assign a particular combination of keys to your macro; then, to run the macro, you press the combination of keys, bypassing the Macros dialog box completely.

In this section, you see how to assign a keyboard shortcut combination to a macro assuming that you did not make a keyboard shortcut assignment when you created the macro. If you change your mind and want to use a different combination or no keyboard combination at all, use the steps in this section to switch to a different combination or to remove the keyboard combination entirely.

Can I use any letter as a keyboard shortcut for my macro?

✔ You can use only letters that Project does not already use. If you try a letter that Project uses, Project asks you to try a different combination.

ASSIGN A KEYBOARD SHORTCUT TO A MACRO

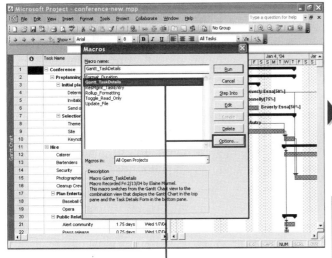

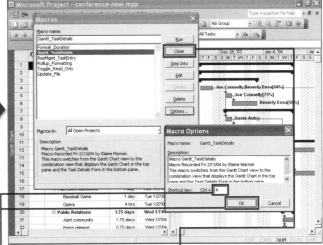

1 Complete steps 1 to 3 in the section "Run Macros."

■ The Macros dialog box appears.

2 Click the macro to which you want to assign a keyboard shortcut.

3 Click Options.

■ The Macro Options dialog box appears.

4 Type a letter for your shortcut.

5 Click OK.

■ In the Macros dialog box, Cancel changes to Close.

6 Click Close.

7 Press and hold Ctrl and type the letter you typed in step 4.

■ The macro runs.

ASSIGN A MACRO TO A TOOLBAR BUTTON

If you prefer toolbar buttons, you can create a toolbar button that you can click to make your macro run. Having a toolbar button that runs the macro is particularly useful if you use a macro on a regular basis, because it provides a quick and easy way to run the macro. You can by-pass the Macros dialog box and you do not need to remember a keyboard combination.

Be aware that adding buttons to the toolbars that come with Project is not always a good idea. If you add a toolbar button to one of the toolbars that comes with Project and you reset that toolbar, the button that you added disappears.

The steps in this section show how to add a button to the Standard toolbar and assign a macro to the button, but you can also add

toolbar buttons for macros to a custom toolbar that you create. To create a custom toolbar, see Chapter 21.

When you add a toolbar button to an existing toolbar, Project saves it in your Global template file. Any other project files that you open on your computer using that Global template file contain the new toolbar button.

ASSIGN A MACRO TO A TOOLBAR BUTTON

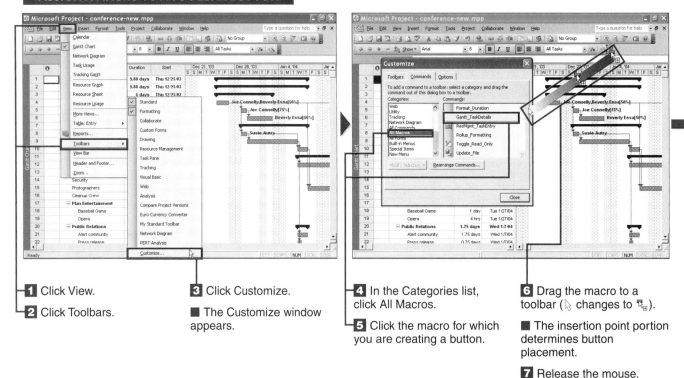

1 Click View.

2 Click Toolbars.

3 Click Customize.

■ The Customize window appears.

4 In the Categories list, click All Macros.

5 Click the macro for which you are creating a button.

6 Drag the macro to a toolbar (⟨⟩ changes to ▥).

■ The insertion point portion determines button placement.

7 Release the mouse.

If I change my mind and do not want the button on a toolbar, can I remove it?

✔ Yes. Reopen the Customize window using steps 1 to 3 in this section. Then, drag the button off the toolbar and drop it anywhere on your project. The button disappears from the toolbar, but the macro is still available for use.

What does Rearrange Commands in the Customize window do?

✔ It has nothing to do with macros; it enables you to rearrange the order in which commands appear on menus or buttons appear on toolbars.

Are there any limitations on the name I can give to a button?

✔ Yes. The ampersand underscores the character to its right, providing a hotkey character to use with the Alt key to select the button using the keyboard instead of the mouse. For example, instead of clicking Show, you can press Alt+S. To provide a hotkey character in your macro name, place an ampersand immediately before the character that you want to be the hotkey. Review the hotkeys on the toolbars first to ensure that the letter you select is not already in use by some other button.

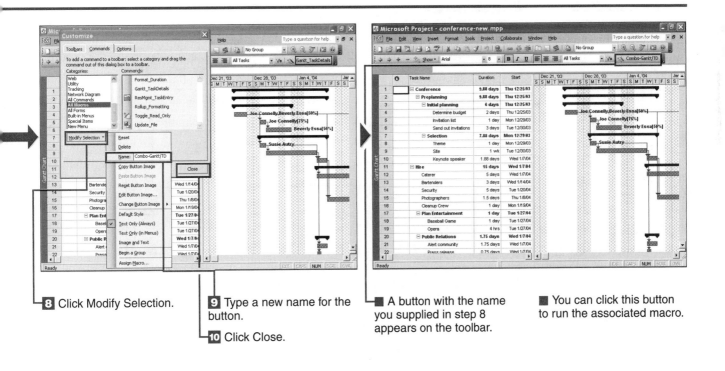

8 Click Modify Selection.

9 Type a new name for the button.

10 Click Close.

■ A button with the name you supplied in step 8 appears on the toolbar.

■ You can click this button to run the associated macro.

ASSIGN A MACRO TO A MENU COMMAND

Suppose that you are not a fan of toolbars, and you do not want to try to remember key combinations, but you still want a quick way to run a macro; for you, the answer may be to add a menu command to a menu and assign a macro to the menu command.

As with toolbars, adding commands to the menus that come with Project is not always a good idea. If you

add a command to one of the standard menus and you reset that menu, the command that you added will disappear.

The steps in this section explain how to add a menu command to one of Project's standard menus and assign a macro to that menu command, but you can also create custom menus and add menu commands for macros to those

custom menus. For more on customizing Project menus, see Chapter 21.

When you add a command to one of the default menus, Microsoft Project saves the command and the menu in your Global template file. Any other project file that you open on your computer using that Global template file contains the new menu command.

ASSIGN A MACRO TO A MENU COMMAND

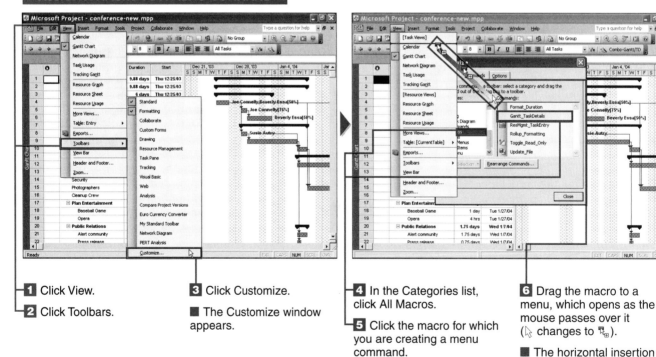

1 Click View.

2 Click Toolbars.

3 Click Customize.

■ The Customize window appears.

4 In the Categories list, click All Macros.

5 Click the macro for which you are creating a menu command.

6 Drag the macro to a menu, which opens as the mouse passes over it (⟨ changes to ⟨⟨).

■ The horizontal insertion point determines menu command placement.

7 Release the mouse.

If I change my mind and do not want the menu command on the menu, can I remove it?

✔ Yes. Reopen the Customize window using steps 1 to 3 in this section. Then, drag the menu command off the menu and drop it anywhere on your project. The menu command disappears from the menu, but the macro is still available.

Can I move a menu command after placing it on a menu?

✔ Yes. Follow steps 1 to 3 in this section. Then, open the menu on which the command appears and drag it to a new location.

Can I move any menu command or only macros that I place on menus?

✔ You can move any menu command as long as you are viewing the Customize window.

What does the Image and Text option on the Modify Selection menu do?

✔ You may have noticed images next to some entries in the Commands column on the Commands tab of the Customize window. For these entries, if you select Image and Text from the Modify Selection menu, Project displays both the text name of the command and the image associated with it.

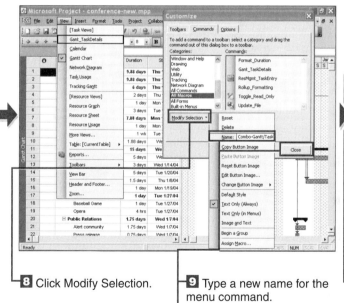

8 Click Modify Selection.

9 Type a new name for the menu command.

10 Click Close.

■ A menu command with the name you supplied in step 9 appears on the menu to which you dragged the macro.

■ You can click this menu command to run the associated macro.

CHAPTER 2

ROLLUP FORMATTING MACRO

You can use the Rollup_Formatting macro to help you view your project in a summarized way. Rolling up tasks in your project onto a summary bar can help you focus on the overall project, but still view some important task details. After you run the Rollup_Formatting macro, you can view your summarized project using the three rollup views in Project: Bar Rollup, Milestone

Date Rollup, and Milestone Rollup. To see samples of each of these views, see Appendix A.

When you run the Rollup_Formatting macro, Project displays, on the Gantt Chart view, a summary bar that contains symbols that represent tasks. In the Bar Rollup view, bars represent tasks. In the Milestone Rollup view, milestones represent tasks. And, in the Milestone Date

Rollup view, milestones and dates represent tasks.

A rollup view displays only the tasks that you format as rollup tasks. And, the Rollup_Formatting macro does not actually do anything unless you first mark tasks that you want to roll up. In this section, you see how to run the Rollup_Formatting macro, assuming that you have already marked tasks that you want to roll up.

ROLLUP FORMATTING MACRO

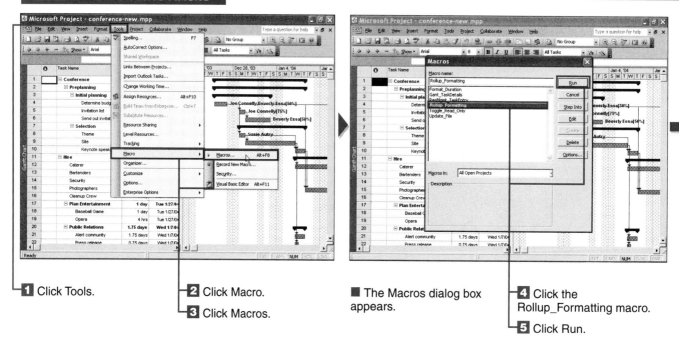

1 Click Tools.

2 Click Macro.

3 Click Macros.

■ The Macros dialog box appears.

4 Click the Rollup_Formatting macro.

5 Click Run.

How do I mark tasks so that they roll up when I run the Rollup_Formatting macro?

✔ Select the tasks and click the Task Information button (▣). On the General tab of the Multiple Task Information dialog box, click Roll up Gantt bar to summary (☐ changes to ☑).

How do I remove rollup formatting?

✔ You can deselect the tasks (◉ changes to ○) using the same steps described in the preceding tip; when you switch to a different view, such as the Gantt Chart view, you do not see the formatting. Or, you can close the project without saving it.

When I run in this section, why does my screen show task names that run together near the summary bar?

✔ When you roll up tasks that occur within a relatively short time frame, Project does not have enough space to display all the task names. So, the task names appear on top of each other. Rollup views are most effective when applied to tasks with longer durations or very short task names.

How can I see dates for the tasks?

✔ Apply the Milestone Date Rollup view. You can use this view even if you selected Bar in step 6.

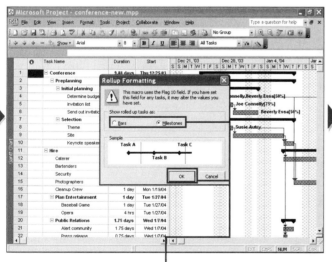

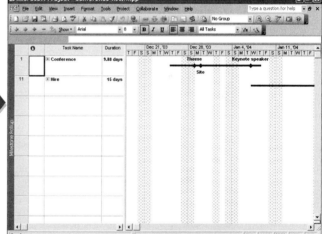

■ The Rollup Formatting dialog box appears.

──**6** Click the Bars option to format tasks as bars or Milestones to format tasks as milestones (○ changes to ◉).

──**7** Click OK.

■ Your project appears in rollup formatting.

■ If you selected Bars in step 6, the Bar Rollup view appears.

■ If you selected Milestones in step 6, the Milestone Rollup view appears.

APPENDIXES

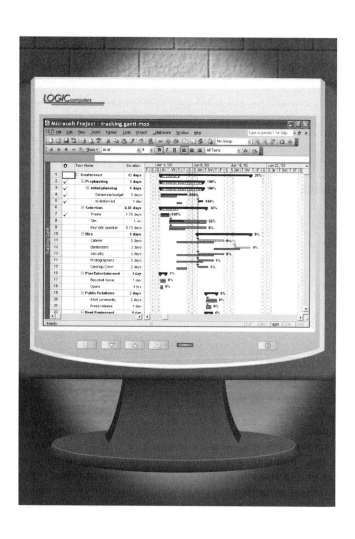

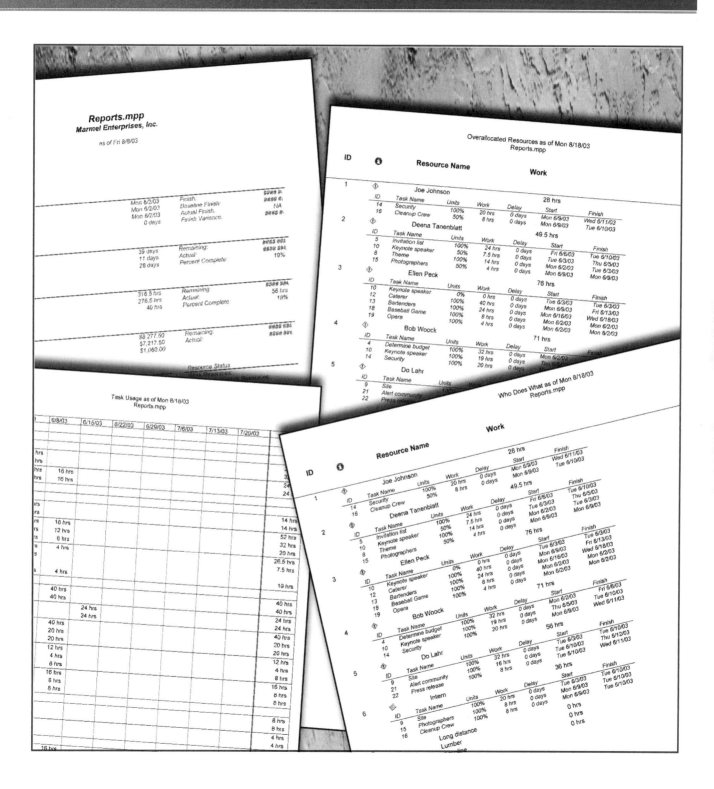

EXAMINE PROJECT VIEWS

You have many views available to you in Project Professional, and this appendix shows samples of most views and gives hints that describe how each view can help you. You can access these views via the More View dialog box, which you can open via the More Views command on the View menu. Remember that you can change the tables that appear in views that contain tables, and you can change the appearance of the Details section in views that contain a Details section. See Chapter 6 for detailed instructions on how to display views, for understanding the different perspectives that views give you in Project, and for details on making changes to changing tables and the Details section.

Calendar

The Calendar view makes it easy to enter a simple project and to reviewing what you tasks you need to perform on a given day. The familiar format of the Calendar view makes it easy to use; a black border highlights the current day. You can move from month to month by using the large arrow buttons in the upper-right corner of the view, across from the current month name. Using a monthly format, the Calendar view indicates the length of a task with a bar running across portions of days or even weeks. In the Calendar view, nonworking days are shaded. Although a task bar may extend over nonworking days, such as Saturday and Sunday in this example, the work of the task does not progress over those days. Remember that every project has a calendar — not to be confused with the Calendar view — that tells Project how to handle events, such as 24-hour shifts, weekends, and holidays off, over the life of your project.

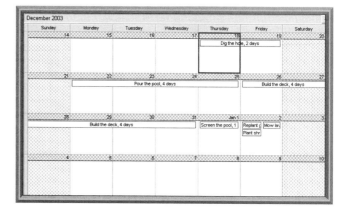

Gantt Chart

Chapter 2 covers the Gantt Chart view in detail. This view makes it easy for you to create a project, link tasks to create sequential dependencies, see how your project is progressing over time, and view tasks graphically while still having access to details.

Detail Gantt

The Detail Gantt view shows a list of tasks and related information. This view is most useful for evaluating slack and slippage, which it presents as thin bars between tasks. The default table in the Detail Gantt view is the Delay table.

You can think of *slack time* as flexibility in the schedule. *Slippage* results when you save a baseline on a project initially and then record actual dates or durations for tasks, and the resulting actual finish dates or durations

for the task are later than the baseline finish dates or durations.

You may want to incorporate the Task Details Form view in the bottom pane of the Detail Gantt view so that you can look more closely at the tasks that are associated with slippage or slack. Click Window and then click Split. Click a field in the Task Form view, click View, and click More Views. In the More Views dialog box that appears, click the Task Details Form view.

Slippage

The thin bar that appears at the left edge of the second task represents slippage of one day between the first task and the second task.

Slack

The thin bar that extends from the left edge of the third task shows slack time of one day between the second and third tasks. The number of days also appears.

Leveling Gantt

Leveling is the process of resolving resource conflicts or overallocations by delaying or splitting certain tasks. The Leveling Gantt view focuses on task delays. It provides a graphic representation of delayed tasks while still showing task detail information. In this example, the Site task shows a leveling delay. The default table that appears in the Leveling Gantt view is the Delay table. You can use the Delay table to add or remove delay time and see the effects of your changes. For more on resource leveling, see Chapter 11.

Leveling Delay Days

Shows detailed information concerning each task. In this example, the table indicates the number of days that the leveled task is delayed.

Table Before Leveling

Shows the effects before leveling.

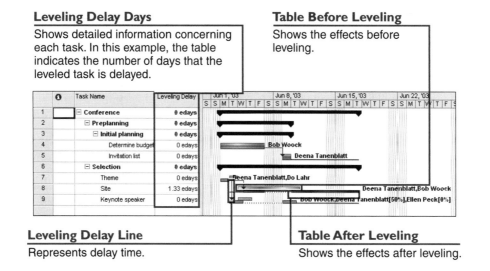

Leveling Delay Line

Represents delay time.

Table After Leveling

Shows the effects after leveling.

Tracking Gantt

The Tracking Gantt view, also based on the Gantt Chart view, provides a great visual way to evaluate the progress of individual tasks and the project as a whole. Although you can see progress on a standard Gantt Chart, you can examine progress more clearly in the Tracking Gantt view because this view shows you how your project has shifted from your original estimates. Knowing this can help you decide how to adjust your plans to accommodate delays.

A standard Gantt view of a project that has some activity shows the progress on tasks as a black bar within the baseline task bar. Tasks that depend on completed tasks move out to reflect delays in the actual work completed.

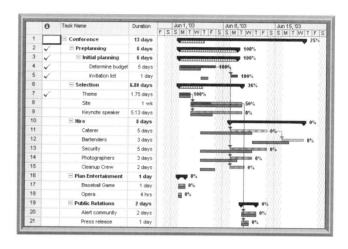

You can update your project with actual information using the Tracking table that appears by default when you view the Tracking Gantt. On the chart portion of the view, you see two bars for every task. The bottom bar shows baseline settings. The top bar reflects current scheduled start and finish dates if a task has not yet been started. If a task has been started — that is, if you have supplied some amount of work that has been completed — the top bar represents actual information and the bottom bar represents baseline information. Project fills in the top bar and makes it solid to represent completed work; a hatching pattern appears in the top bar to represent work that has not started or work in progress. The bottom bars represent baseline task bars that do not move; only the top bars push out to reflect delays in timing.

Multiple Baselines Gantt

The Multiple Baselines Gantt view is also based on the Gantt Chart view. The Multiple Baselines Gantt view enables you to see and compare the first three baselines you save for your project. Each baseline is represented by a different color. In this example, you see two baselines; two lines represent each task in the chart portion of the view. For more on baselines, see Chapter 9.

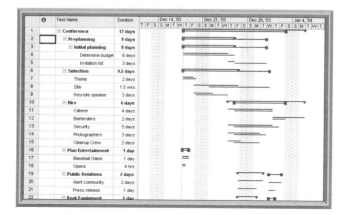

Network Diagram

The Network Diagram view has more to do with the general flow of work and the relationships between tasks in your project than with timing. This view makes it easy for you to evaluate the flow of your project and to check task dependencies.

Each node in the Network Diagram view represents a task and contains the task name, duration, task ID number in the sequence of the project outline, start date, finish date, and, if assigned, the resource(s). The thickness of the border and color of each node represent different types of tasks; that is, critical tasks are red and have thick borders, while noncritical tasks are blue and have thin borders. The lines that flow between the nodes represent dependencies. A successor task that must begin after another task is completed appears to the right or sometimes below its predecessor.

You can filter the Network Diagram. For more on filtering, see Chapter 6.

You also can group tasks in the Network Diagram view. Colored bands separate the nodes. For example, in the figure, you see tasks grouped by duration. You can group a project using the Group command on the Project menu.

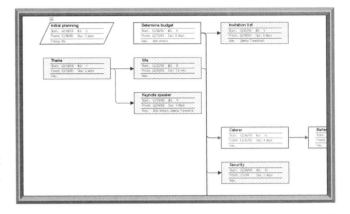

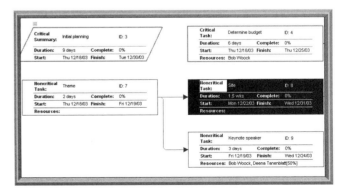

Descriptive Network Diagram

The Descriptive Network Diagram view, a cousin of the Network Diagram, focuses on the general flow of work and the relationships among tasks in your project.

Like the Network Diagram, each node in the Descriptive Network Diagram view represents a task in your project. If you compare the figure shown here to the figure in the preceding section, you can see more detail in the nodes of the Descriptive Network Diagram than you see in the Network Diagram. The Descriptive Network Diagram also indicates whether the task is critical and how complete the task is.

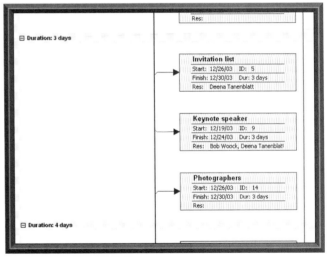

Relationship Diagram

Another cousin of the Network Diagram, the Relationship Diagram displays the current task in the center of the pane. The task's predecessors appear to the left and its successors to the right. When you are working on a

project with a complex relationship structure, this graphic view helps you to focus on one task and identify the tasks that are linked to it.

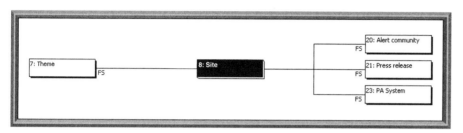

The PERT Analysis Toolbar

You can use the PERT Analysis toolbar, which appears just above the chart in each of the next four figures, to perform PERT analysis. To display the toolbar, right-click any toolbar, and then click PERT Analysis.

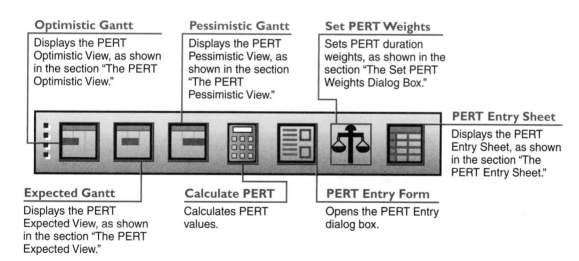

Optimistic Gantt

Displays the PERT Optimistic View, as shown in the section "The PERT Optimistic View."

Pessimistic Gantt

Displays the PERT Pessimistic View, as shown in the section "The PERT Pessimistic View."

Set PERT Weights

Sets PERT duration weights, as shown in the section "The Set PERT Weights Dialog Box."

PERT Entry Sheet

Displays the PERT Entry Sheet, as shown in the section "The PERT Entry Sheet."

Expected Gantt

Displays the PERT Expected View, as shown in the section "The PERT Expected View."

Calculate PERT

Calculates PERT values.

PERT Entry Form

Opens the PERT Entry dialog box.

The PERT Entry Sheet

The PERT Entry Sheet view focuses PERT analysis entirely on durations. Click the PERT Entry Sheet button on the PERT Analysis toolbar to display this sheet.

Using this sheet, you enter optimistic, expected, and pessimistic durations for each task. When you click the Calculate PERT button on the PERT Analysis toolbar, Project uses a weighted average of the numbers that you supply and calculates the probable duration of the task. Project displays the result in the Duration column for that task. Notice the duration of 1.58 days for the Theme task. Project calculated this duration by using the weighted average of the numbers in the Optimistic Dur., Expected Dur., and Pessimistic Dur. columns for the task.

	Task Name	Duration	Optimistic Dur.	Expected Dur.	Pessimistic Dur.
1	☐ Conference	9.25 days	4 days	8 days	12 days
2	☐ Preplanning	7.88 days	3.25 days	8 days	12 days
3	☐ Initial plannin	7.88 days	3.25 days	8 days	12 days
4	Determine b	5 days	3 days	5 days	7 days
5	Invitation list	2.88 days	2 hrs	3 days	5 days
6	☐ Selection	9.25 days	4 days	6.75 days	12 days
7	Theme	1.58 days	0.5 days	1.75 days	2 days
8	Site	1.03 wks	3.5 days	1 wk	1.5 wks
9	Keynote speak	6.13 days	3 days	1 wk	2 wks

The PERT Optimistic View

After you type optimistic, expected, and pessimistic durations in the PERT Entry Sheet view and click the Calculate PERT button, you can view the optimistic results for your entire project by clicking the Optimistic Gantt button on the PERT Analysis toolbar. As its name implies, the Optimistic Gantt view is a variation of the Gantt Chart view; the Optimistic case table is on the left side, and Gantt bars are on the right. You can use this view to type and evaluate the optimistic scenarios for completing your project.

Initially, you may not see bars in any of the PERT Gantt views. While displaying any of these views, click the Calculate PERT button on the PERT Analysis toolbar again, and the bars appear.

The PERT Expected View

You also can view the expected results for your entire project in the Expected Gantt view by clicking the Expected Gantt button on the PERT Analysis toolbar. The Expected Gantt view is a variation of the Gantt Chart view. You can use this view to enter and evaluate the expected scenarios for completing your project.

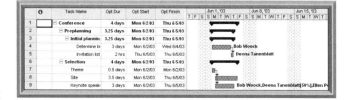

The PERT Pessimistic View

As with the Optimistic and Expected views, you can view the pessimistic results for your entire project in the Pessimistic Gantt view. Type optimistic, expected, and pessimistic durations on the PERT Entry Sheet view. Click the Calculate button, and then click the Pessimistic Gantt button on the PERT Analysis toolbar. The Pessimistic Gantt view is also a variation of the Gantt Chart view. You can use this view to enter and evaluate the pessimistic scenarios for completing your project.

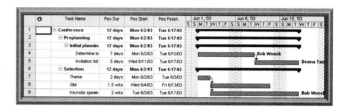

The Set Pert Weights Dialog Box

Project calculates a weighted average when you use PERT analysis. You can control the weights that Project applies to each scenario from the Set PERT Weights dialog box. Click the PERT Weights button on the PERT Analysis toolbar and type values that sum to 6. You can use different weights to change the emphasis that Project applies to its calculation of each scenario.

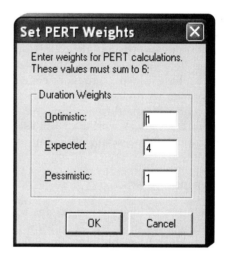

Resource Allocation

The Resource Allocation view is a combination view. The Resource Usage view appears in the top pane of the combination view and the Leveling Gantt Chart view appears in the bottom pane. You can use this view to simultaneously show the cost and allocation for each resource, to view each resource's work progress, and to help identify overallocated resources. For more information on the Leveling Gantt Chart view and the Resource Usage views, see the sections "Leveling Gantt" and "Resource Usage" in this appendix.

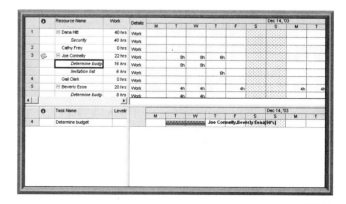

Resource Form

The Resource Form view displays assignment information about one resource at a time. You can use Previous and Next in the upper-right corner of the window to display different resources. If you have not sorted or filtered resources, Project shows them to you in resource ID number order. Use this view alone to quickly identify all tasks to which a resource is assigned. You also can use this view as part of a combination view. See Chapter 6 or more information on creating and using combination views.

Resource Name Form

The Resource Name Form view is a simplified version of the Resource Form view. None of the cost information appears in this view, nor do you view the resources' maximum units, base calendar, group, or code. You can use this view to set up basic information about resources for a project, and this view can give you a good idea about a resource's workload. You use the Previous and Next buttons to view different resources.

Resource Graph

Because the Resource Graph view highlights resource conflicts, looking at the Resource Graph view in a combination view can help you isolate overallocation problems. The Resource Graph view shows how a particular resource that you are using on a project. Project displays a resource's total work hours on any particular day as a bar. A bar that falls short of the 100 percent mark indicates that a resource is not working full time and may be underutilized. A bar that extends beyond 100 percent indicates that the resource is working too many hours in a day. The percentage of the workday that the resource is working appears at the bottom of the usage bars.

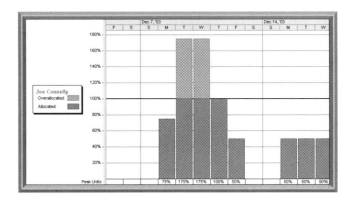

You can use the Resource Graph view to spot and correct resources that are inappropriately allocated. The Resource Graph view shows information for one resource at a time. To view a different resource, use the scroll arrows that appear below the left pane in this view. This view works well as part of a combination view.

Resource Sheet

The Resource Sheet view gives you a wealth of information about the resources that are assigned to your project such as standard and overtime rates, availability for overtime work, and fixed costs.

This columnar interface is a great way to create resources and prepare to assign them if, for example, you want to assign lower-cost resources to most tasks and higher-cost resources to certain mission-critical tasks. This view clearly shows to which group a resource belongs. If overallocations exist, the resource information appears in red, bold type, and a warning flag appears in the Indicator column in the far left of this view. Switch back to the Resource Graph to get resource-by-resource details on these problems.

By definition, the Resource Sheet is a table, and you can change the default columns in the table using the techniques described in Chapter 6.

Resource Usage

The Resource Usage view organizes task assignments by resource so that you can easily figure out what resource is performing what task, and when when he or she is performing that task. When you view resource assignments you can assign or reassign tasks to resources in this view by dragging the tasks among resources.

The Resource Usage view is also useful when you want to check resource overallocations, examine the number of hours or the percentage of capacity at which each resource is scheduled to work, view a resource's progress or costs, or determine how much time a particular resource has for additional work assignments. Add fields to the right side of the view by right-clicking the right side of the view and selecting a field to add.

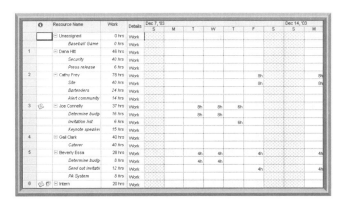

Rollup Views

When you enable rollup behavior and collapse the outline or any portion of it that contains subtasks, Project displays a summary task bar with marks that represent subtask dates.

You can roll up a project to a summary task or even to the project level so that you can hide details and look at an overview of your project. In the Gantt Chart view of your project, click Format and then click Layout. The Layout dialog box appears, which you use to enable rollup behavior for all tasks in your project.

Select the Always roll up Gantt bars option (☐ changes to ☑). If you do not want see the rollup bars when you expand the project outline to view all tasks, also select the Hide rollup bars when summary expanded option (☐ changes to ☑).

You can specify rollup behavior at the task level. Click the General tab of the Task Information dialog box so that Project does not roll up all tasks to summary bars when you collapse the outline. The changes you make in the Layout dialog box do not affect tasks whose rollup behavior you specified at the task level.

Once you have enabled rollup behavior, you can see the effects of the rollup behavior in the Gantt Chart view. The summary task for rolled up tasks appears as a segmented bar; each segment of the bar represents a rolled up task.

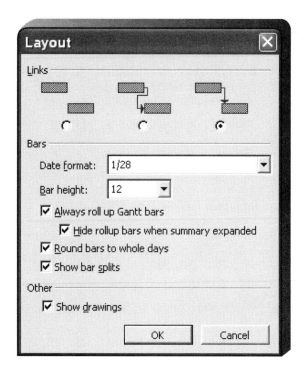

Bar Rollup View

And, Project contains three other views that you can use if you run the Rollup_Formatting macro. See Chapter 22 for details on running this macro.

The Bar Rollup view displays tasks for which you enabled rollup behavior as bars on top of their summary tasks. You see each task's name on a section of the bar.

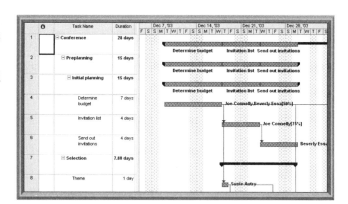

Milestone Rollup View

The Milestone Rollup view also groups tasks for which you enabled rollup behavior. However, in this view, the rolled up tasks appear as milestones on their summary task. On the Milestone view, each task's name appears at a milestone.

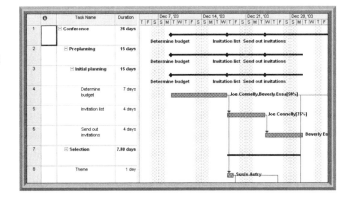

Milestone Date Rollup View

The Milestone Date Rollup view closely resembles the Milestone Rollup view; the major difference between the views lies in the information that appears near the milestone. ON the Milestone Date Rollup view, the task's name appears above the milestone, and the task's start date appears underneath the milestone.

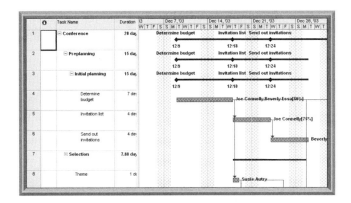

Task Details Form

The Task Details Form view closely resembles the Task Form view and the Task Name Form view. You can use the Task Details Form view to view and edit tracking information about one task at a time.

You can use the Previous and Next buttons in the upper-right corner of this view to switch from task to task. If you have not sorted or filtered tasks, Project displays them in order of ID number. The Task Details Form view works well as part of a combination view.

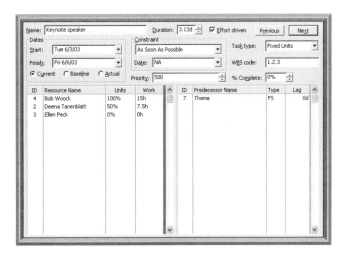

Task Entry

The Task Entry view is a combination view, with the Gantt Chart view appearing in the top pane and the Task Form view appearing in the bottom pane. To view information about a task in the Task Form view, select the task in the Gantt Chart view. Use this view when you want to view tasks graphically but also want to view detailed information about tasks and assignments.

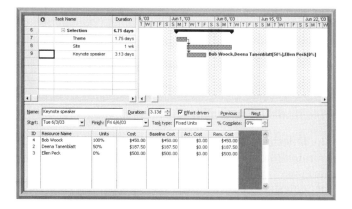

Task Form

The Task Form view appears on the bottom portion of the Task Entry view. The Task Form view closely resembles the Task Details Form view, which is shown earlier in this chapter. The Task Form view also closely resembles the Task Name Form view.

The Task Form view provides more resource information, such as costs, than the Task Details Form view, and the Task Details Form view provides more task information, such as predecessors, than the Task Form view. You can click Previous and Next to switch between tasks.

Task Name Form

The Task Name Form view is a cousin to the Task Details Form view and the Task Form view. This simplified version displays the basic characteristics of tasks, one task at a time. The Task Name Form view works well as part of a combination view.

Task Sheet

The Task Sheet view is the counterpart of the Resource Sheet view in that the Task Sheet view displays task information in a spreadsheet-like format. This view closely resembles the left portion of the Gantt Chart view and makes it easy to view tasks in chronological order. In this view, you can create tasks, link tasks, and even assign resources.

Task Usage

This powerful view shows resources grouped under the tasks to which they are assigned and enables you to focus on how resources affect the task. Use this view to organize resources by task, evaluate work effort and cost by task, and compare scheduled and actual work and costs.

In this view, you can change the table as well as the Details section that appears on the right side of the view. See Chapter 6 for information on changing the Details section.

REPORT SAMPLES

I n this appendix, you can view samples of each report that Project can create, along with a description of the report. Reports are organized by the following categories: Overview, Current Activities, Costs, Assignments, Workload, and Custom.

The Overview category includes these reports: Project Summary, Top Level Tasks, Critical Tasks, Milestones, and Working Days. The Current Activities category includes: Unstarted Tasks, Tasks Starting Soon, Tasks in Progress, Completed Tasks, Should Have Started Tasks, and Slipping Tasks.

The Costs category includes: Cash Flow, Earned Value, Budget, Overbudget Tasks, and Overbudget Resources, The Assignments category includes: Who Does What, Who Does What When, To Do List, and Overallocated Resources. The Workload category includes: Task Usage and Resource Usage

Project Summary

The Project Summary report shows top-level information about your project. This report presents summarized information about dates, duration, work, costs, task status, and resource status.

Meeting.mpp
Marmel Enterprises, Inc.

as of Fri 2/20/04

Dates

Start:	Mon 1/5/04	Finish:	Thu 1/15/04
Baseline Start:	NA	Baseline Finish:	NA
Actual Start:	NA	Actual Finish:	NA
Start Variance:	0 days	Finish Variance:	0 days

Duration

Scheduled:	9 days	Remaining:	9 days
Baseline:	0 days?	Actual:	0 days
Variance:	9 days	Percent Complete:	0%

Work

Scheduled:	0 hrs	Remaining:	0 hrs
Baseline:	0 hrs	Actual:	0 hrs
Variance:	0 hrs	Percent Complete:	0%

Costs

Scheduled:	$0.00	Remaining:	$0.00
Baseline	$0.00	Actual:	$0.00
Variance:	$0.00		

Task Status

		Resource Status	
Tasks not yet started:	6	Work Resources:	7
Tasks in progress:	0	Overallocated Work Resources:	0
Tasks completed:	0	Material Resources:	1
Total Tasks:	6	Total Resources:	8

Top Level Tasks

The Top Level Tasks report shows the summary tasks at the highest level in your project as of today's date. You can view scheduled start and finish dates, the percentage complete for each task, the cost, and the work required to complete the task.

Top Level Tasks as of Fri 8/8/03
Reports.mpp

ID	Task Name	Duration	Start	Finish	% Comp.	Cost	Work
1	Conference	39 days	Mon 6/2/03	Fri 7/25/03	19%	$8,277.50	316.5 hrs

Page 1

Critical Tasks

The Critical Tasks report shows the status of the tasks on the critical path of your project — those tasks that make the project late if you do not complete them on time. This report displays each task's planned duration, start and finish dates, the resources that are assigned to the task, and the predecessors and successors of the task. Although this example does not show the successors column, it appears on page 2 of the report, which is not shown.

Critical Tasks as of Fri 8/8/03
Reports.mpp

ID	🛈	Task Name	Duration	Start	Finish	Predecessors
1		Conference	39 days	Mon 6/2/03	Fri 7/25/03	
25		Events	3 days	Tue 7/22/03	Fri 7/25/03	
28	▦	Conference	0 days	Fri 7/25/03	Fri 7/25/03	

Page 1

Milestones

The Milestones report shows information about each milestone in your project. If you marked summary tasks to appear as milestones in the Task Information dialog box, summary tasks also appear in this report as milestones. For each milestone or summary task, Project displays the planned duration, start and finish dates, predecessors, and the resources that are assigned to the milestone.

Milestones as of Fri 8/8/03
Reports.mpp

ID		Task Name	Duration	Start	Finish	Predecessors	Resource Names
1		Conference	39 days	Mon 6/2/03	Fri 7/25/03		
25		Events	3 days	Tue 7/22/03	Fri 7/25/03		
26		Baseball Game	0 days	Tue 7/22/03	Tue 7/22/03		
27		Opera	0 days	Thu 7/24/03	Thu 7/24/03		
28		Conference	0 days	Fri 7/25/03	Fri 7/25/03		

Page 1

Working Days

The Working Days report shows the base calendar information for your project. You can view the name of the base calendar for the project and the working hours that are established for each day of the week, along with any exceptions that you defined.

Base Calendar as of Fri 8/8/03
Reports.mpp

BASE CALENDAR:	**Standard**
Day	Hours
Sunday	Nonworking
Monday	8:00 AM - 12:00 PM, 1:00 PM - 5:00 PM
Tuesday	8:00 AM - 12:00 PM, 1:00 PM - 5:00 PM
Wednesday	8:00 AM - 12:00 PM, 1:00 PM - 5:00 PM
Thursday	8:00 AM - 12:00 PM, 1:00 PM - 5:00 PM
Friday	8:00 AM - 12:00 PM, 1:00 PM - 5:00 PM
Saturday	Nonworking
Exceptions:	None

Page 1

Base Calendar as of Fri 8/8/03
Reports.mpp

BASE CALENDAR:	**Used for Microsoft Project 98 Baseline Calendar**
Day	Hours
Sunday	Nonworking
Monday	8:00 AM - 12:00 PM, 1:00 PM - 5:00 PM
Tuesday	8:00 AM - 12:00 PM, 1:00 PM - 5:00 PM
Wednesday	8:00 AM - 12:00 PM, 1:00 PM - 5:00 PM
Thursday	8:00 AM - 12:00 PM, 1:00 PM - 5:00 PM
Friday	8:00 AM - 12:00 PM, 1:00 PM - 5:00 PM
Saturday	Nonworking
Exceptions:	None

Page 2

Cash Flow

The Cash Flow report is a tabular report that shows, by task, the costs for weekly time increments. To change from a Weekly orientation to another time period such as monthly see Customizing Reports in Chapter 14.

Cash Flow as of Mon 8/18/03
Reports.mpp

	6/1/03	6/8/03	6/15/03	6/22/03	6/29/03	7/6/03	7/13/03	7/20/03	Total
Conference									
Preplanning									
Initial planning									
Determine budget	$960.00								$960.00
Invitation list	$200.00	$400.00							$600.00
Send out invitations									
Selection									
Theme	$350.00								$350.00
Site	$872.50	$477.50							$1,350.00
Keynote speaker	$1,137.50	$120.00							$1,257.50
Hire									
Caterer		$800.00							$800.00
Bartenders			$480.00						$480.00
Security		$1,100.00							$1,100.00
Photographers		$220.00							$220.00
Cleanup Crew		$320.00							$320.00
Plan Entertainment									
Baseball Game	$160.00								$160.00
Opera	$80.00								$80.00
Public Relations									
Alert community		$400.00							$400.00
Press release		$200.00							$200.00
Rent Equipment									
PA System									
Events									
Baseball Game									
Opera									
Conference									
Total	$3,760.00	$4,037.50	$480.00						$8,277.50

Page 1

Earned Value

The Earned Value report shows you the status of each task's costs when you compare planned to actual costs. Some column headings in this report may seem cryptic; see the following table for translations.

Project calculates BCWS, BCWP, ACWP, SV, and CV through the project status date. SV represents the cost difference between current progress and the baseline plan; Project calculates this value as BCWP minus BCWS. CV represents the cost difference between actual costs and planned costs at the current level

of completion; Project calculates this value as BCWP minus ACWP. EAC shows the planned costs based on costs that are already incurred plus additional planned costs. VAC represents the variance between the baseline cost and the combination of actual plus planned costs for a task. Note that even when you print this report in landscape format, you may not see all of the columns that can appear on this report. For more information about how Project handles earned value, see Chapter 15.

Earned Value as of Mon 8/18/03
Reports.mpp

ID	Task Name	BCWS	BCWP	ACWP	SV	CV	BAC
4	Determine budget	$720.00	$720.00	$960.00	$0.00	($240.00)	$720.00
5	Invitation list	$200.00	$200.00	$600.00	$0.00	($400.00)	$200.00
6	Send out invitations	$0.00	$0.00	$0.00	$0.00	$0.00	$0.00
8	Theme	$350.00	$0.00	$0.00	($350.00)	$0.00	$350.00
9	Site	$1,050.00	$0.00	$0.00	($1,050.00)	$0.00	$1,050.00
10	Keynote speaker	$1,137.50	$0.00	$0.00	($1,137.50)	$0.00	$1,137.50
12	Caterer	$800.00	$0.00	$0.00	($800.00)	$0.00	$800.00
13	Bartenders	$480.00	$0.00	$0.00	($480.00)	$0.00	$480.00
14	Security	$1,100.00	$0.00	$0.00	($1,100.00)	$0.00	$1,100.00
15	Photographers	$220.00	$0.00	$0.00	($220.00)	$0.00	$220.00
16	Cleanup Crew	$320.00	$0.00	$0.00	($320.00)	$0.00	$320.00
18	Baseball Game	$160.00	$0.00	$0.00	($160.00)	$0.00	$160.00
19	Opera	$80.00	$0.00	$0.00	($80.00)	$0.00	$80.00
21	Alert community	$400.00	$0.00	$0.00	($400.00)	$0.00	$400.00
22	Press release	$200.00	$0.00	$0.00	($200.00)	$0.00	$200.00
24	PA System	$0.00	$0.00	$0.00	$0.00	$0.00	$0.00
26	Baseball Game	$0.00	$0.00	$0.00	$0.00	$0.00	$0.00
27	Opera	$0.00	$0.00	$0.00	$0.00	$0.00	$0.00
28	Conference	$0.00	$0.00	$0.00	$0.00	$0.00	$0.00
		$7,217.50	$920.00	$1,560.00	($6,297.50)	($640.00)	$7,217.50

Page 1

Headings in the Earned Value Report

Heading	Translation
BCWS	Budgeted Cost of Work Scheduled
BCWP	Budgeted Cost of Work Performed
ACWP	Actual Cost of Work Performed
SV	Schedule Variance
CV	Cost Variance
BAC	Budget at Completion
EAC	Estimate at Completion
VAC	Variance at Completion

Budget

The Budget report lists all tasks and shows the budgeted costs as well as the variance between budgeted and actual costs. Unless you save a baseline for your project, this report has little meaning. The values in the variance column change from $0.00 as you complete tasks. The report also includes Actual and Remaining columns that do not fit on the same page as the other columns in the example.

Budget Report as of Mon 8/18/03
Reports.mpp

ID	Task Name	Fixed Cost	Fixed Cost Accrual	Total Cost	Baseline	Variance	Actual	Remaining
9	Site	$250.00	Prorated	$1,350.00	$1,050.00	$300.00	$0.00	$1,350.00
10	Keynote speaker	$0.00	Prorated	$1,257.50	$1,137.50	$120.00	$0.00	$1,257.50
14	Security	$0.00	Prorated	$1,100.00	$1,100.00	$0.00	$0.00	$1,100.00
4	Determine budget	$0.00	Prorated	$960.00	$720.00	$240.00	$960.00	$0.00
12	Caterer	$0.00	Prorated	$800.00	$800.00	$0.00	$0.00	$800.00
5	Invitation list	$0.00	Prorated	$600.00	$200.00	$400.00	$600.00	$0.00
13	Bartenders	$0.00	Prorated	$480.00	$480.00	$0.00	$0.00	$480.00
21	Alert community	$0.00	Prorated	$400.00	$400.00	$0.00	$0.00	$400.00
8	Theme	$0.00	Prorated	$350.00	$350.00	$0.00	$0.00	$350.00
16	Cleanup Crew	$0.00	Prorated	$320.00	$320.00	$0.00	$0.00	$320.00
15	Photographers	$0.00	Prorated	$220.00	$220.00	$0.00	$0.00	$220.00
22	Press release	$0.00	Prorated	$200.00	$200.00	$0.00	$0.00	$200.00
18	Baseball Game	$0.00	Prorated	$160.00	$160.00	$0.00	$0.00	$160.00
19	Opera	$0.00	Prorated	$80.00	$80.00	$0.00	$0.00	$80.00
6	Send out invitations	$0.00	Prorated	$0.00	$0.00	$0.00	$0.00	$0.00
24	PA System	$0.00	Prorated	$0.00	$0.00	$0.00	$0.00	$0.00
26	Baseball Game	$0.00	Prorated	$0.00	$0.00	$0.00	$0.00	$0.00
27	Opera	$0.00	Prorated	$0.00	$0.00	$0.00	$0.00	$0.00
28	Conference	$0.00	Prorated	$0.00	$0.00	$0.00	$0.00	$0.00
		$250.00		$8,277.50	$7,217.50	$1,060.00	$1,560.00	$6,717.50

Page 1

Overbudget Reports

Project contains two Overbudget reports: one for tasks and one for resources. Neither report prints, however, until you indicate that some tasks are at least partially completed.

The Overbudget Tasks report shows cost, baseline, variance, and actual information about tasks that exceed their budgeted amounts. In the example, the Actual and Remainings columns are missing because they do not fit on the first page of the report.

The Overbudget Resources report displays resources whose costs exceed baseline estimates, based on the current progress of the project.

Overbudget Tasks as of Mon 8/18/03
Reports.mpp

ID	Task Name	Fixed Cost	Fixed Cost Accrual	Total Cost	Baseline	Variance	Actual	Remaining
5	Invitation list	$0.00	Prorated	$600.00	$200.00	$400.00	$600.00	$0.00
9	Site	$250.00	Prorated	$1,350.00	$1,050.00	$300.00	$0.00	$1,350.00
4	Determine budget	$0.00	Prorated	$960.00	$720.00	$240.00	$960.00	$0.00
10	Keynote speaker	$0.00	Prorated	$1,257.50	$1,137.50	$120.00	$0.00	$1,257.50
		$250.00		$4,167.50	$3,107.50	$1,060.00	$1,560.00	$2,607.50

Page 1

Overbudget Resources as of Mon 8/18/03
Reports.mpp

ID	Resource Name	Cost	Baseline Cost	Variance	Actual Cost	Remaining
5	Do Lahr	$1,400.00	$1,100.00	$300.00	$0.00	$1,400.00
4	Bob Woock	$2,130.00	$1,770.00	$360.00	$960.00	$1,170.00
2	Deena Tanenblatt	$1,237.50	$837.50	$400.00	$600.00	$637.50
		$4,767.50	$3,707.50	$1,060.00	$1,560.00	$3,207.50

Page 1

Unstarted Tasks

The Unstarted Tasks report lists tasks, sorted by the scheduled start date, that have not yet started. For each task, Project displays the duration, predecessor, and resource information if you assigned resources.

Unstarted Tasks as of Fri 8/8/03
Reports.mpp

ID	❶	Task Name	Duration	Start	Finish	Predecessors	Resource Names
8		Theme	1.75 days	Mon 6/2/03	Tue 6/3/03		

ID	Resource Name	Units	Work	Delay	Start	Finish
2	Deena Tanenblatt	100%	14 hrs	0 days	Mon 6/2/03	Tue 6/3/03

ID	❶	Task Name	Duration	Start	Finish	Predecessors	Resource Names
9		Site	0.95 wks	Tue 6/3/03	Tue 6/10/03	8	Intern,Do Lahr

ID	Resource Name	Units	Work	Delay	Start	Finish
5	Do Lahr	100%	32 hrs	0 days	Tue 6/3/03	Tue 6/10/03
6	Intern	100%	20 hrs	0 days	Tue 6/3/03	Tue 6/10/03

ID	❶	Task Name	Duration	Start	Finish	Predecessors	Resource Names
10		Keynote speaker	4.13 days	Tue 6/3/03	Tue 6/10/03	8	Bob Woock,Deena Tanenblatt

	Resource Name	Units	Work	Delay	Start	Finish
2	Deena Tanenblatt	50%	7.5 hrs	0 days	Tue 6/3/03	Thu 6/5/03
3	Ellen Peck	0%	0 hrs	0 days	Tue 6/3/03	Tue 6/3/03
4	Bob Woock	100%	19 hrs	0 days	Thu 6/5/03	Tue 6/10/03

ID	❶	Task Name	Duration	Start	Finish	Predecessors	Resource Names
12		Caterer	5 days	Mon 6/9/03	Fri 6/13/03	4	Ellen Peck

	Resource Name	Units	Work	Delay	Start	Finish
3	Ellen Peck	100%	40 hrs	0 days	Mon 6/9/03	Fri 6/13/03

ID	❶	Task Name	Duration	Start	Finish	Predecessors	Resource Names
13		Bartenders	3 days	Mon 6/16/03	Wed 6/18/03	12	Ellen Peck

ID	Resource Name	Units	Work	Delay	Start	Finish
3	Ellen Peck	100%	24 hrs	0 days	Mon 6/16/03	Wed 6/18/03

ID	❶	Task Name	Duration	Start	Finish	Predecessors	Resource Names
14		Security	2.5 days	Mon 6/9/03	Wed 6/11/03	4	Bob Woock,Joe Johnson

ID	Resource Name	Units	Work	Delay	Start	Finish
1	Joe Johnson	100%	20 hrs	0 days	Mon 6/9/03	Wed 6/11/03
4	Bob Woock	100%	20 hrs	0 days	Mon 6/9/03	Wed 6/11/03

ID	❶	Task Name	Duration	Start	Finish	Predecessors	Resource Names
15		Photographers	1.5 days	Mon 6/9/03	Tue 6/10/03	4	Deena Tanenblatt[50%],Intern

ID	Resource Name	Units	Work	Delay	Start	Finish
2	Deena Tanenblatt	50%	4 hrs	0 days	Mon 6/9/03	Mon 6/9/03
6	Intern	100%	8 hrs	0 days	Mon 6/9/03	Tue 6/10/03

ID	❶	Task Name	Duration	Start	Finish	Predecessors	Resource Names
16		Cleanup Crew	2 days	Mon 6/9/03	Tue 6/10/03	4	Intern,Joe Johnson[50%]

ID	Resource Name	Units	Work	Delay	Start	Finish
1	Joe Johnson	50%	8 hrs	0 days	Mon 6/9/03	Tue 6/10/03
6	Intern	100%	8 hrs	0 days	Mon 6/9/03	Tue 6/10/03

ID	❶	Task Name	Duration	Start	Finish	Predecessors	Resource Names
18		Baseball Game	1 day	Mon 6/2/03	Mon 6/2/03		Ellen Peck

ID	Resource Name	Units	Work	Delay	Start	Finish
3	Ellen Peck	100%	8 hrs	0 days	Mon 6/2/03	Mon 6/2/03

ID	❶	Task Name	Duration	Start	Finish	Predecessors	Resource Names
19		Opera	4 hrs	Mon 6/2/03	Mon 6/2/03		Ellen Peck

ID	Resource Name	Units	Work	Delay	Start	Finish
3	Ellen Peck	100%	4 hrs	0 days	Mon 6/2/03	Mon 6/2/03

ID	❶	Task Name	Duration	Start	Finish	Predecessors	Resource Names
21		Alert community	2 days	Tue 6/10/03	Thu 6/12/03	9	Do Lahr

ID	Resource Name	Units	Work	Delay	Start	Finish
5	Do Lahr	100%	16 hrs	0 days	Tue 6/10/03	Thu 6/12/03

Page 1

Unstarted Tasks as of Fri 8/8/03
Reports.mpp

ID	❶	Task Name	Duration	Start	Finish	Predecessors	Resource Names
22		Press release	1 day	Tue 6/10/03	Wed 6/11/03	9	Do Lahr

ID	Resource Name	Units	Work	Delay	Start	Finish
5	Do Lahr	100%	8 hrs	0 days	Tue 6/10/03	Wed 6/11/03

ID	❶	Task Name	Duration	Start	Finish	Predecessors	Resource Names
24		PA System	1 day	Tue 6/10/03	Wed 6/11/03	9	
26	🔲	Baseball Game	0 days	Tue 7/22/03	Tue 7/22/03		
27	🔲	Opera	0 days	Thu 7/24/03	Thu 7/24/03		
28	🔲	Conference	0 days	Fri 7/25/03	Fri 7/25/03		

Page 2

Tasks Starting Soon

When you print the Tasks Starting Soon report, Project displays the Date Range dialog boxes so that you can specify the date range for the report using the mm/dd/yy format. On the report, Project includes tasks that start or finish between the two dates that you specify. The information that appears on the report is similar to the information that you find on the Unstarted Tasks report: the duration, start and finish dates, predecessors, and resource information, if you assigned resources. Completed tasks also appear on this report. They are identified by the check mark (✓) that appears in the Indicator column on the report.

Tasks Starting Soon as of Fri 8/8/03
Reports.mpp

ID	❶	Task Name				Duration	Start	Finish	Predecessors	Resource Names
4	✓	Determine budget				5 days	Mon 6/2/03	Fri 6/6/03		Bob Woock
	ID	Resource Name	Units	Work	Delay	Start	Finish			
	4	Bob Woock	100%	32 hrs	0 days	Mon 6/2/03	Fri 6/6/03			
5	✓	Invitation list				3 days	Fri 6/6/03	Tue 6/10/03	4	Deena Tanenblatt
	ID	Resource Name	Units	Work	Delay	Start	Finish			
	2	Deena Tanenblatt	100%	24 hrs	0 days	Fri 6/6/03	Tue 6/10/03			
6		Send out invitations				4 days	Wed 6/11/03	Mon 6/16/03		
9		Site				0.95 wks	Tue 6/3/03	Tue 6/10/03	8	Intern,Do Lahr
	ID	Resource Name	Units	Work	Delay	Start	Finish			
	5	Do Lahr	100%	32 hrs	0 days	Tue 6/3/03	Tue 6/10/03			
	6	Intern	100%	20 hrs	0 days	Tue 6/3/03	Tue 6/10/03			
10		Keynote speaker				4.13 days	Tue 6/3/03	Tue 6/10/03	8	Bob Woock,Deena Tanenblatt
	ID	Resource Name	Units	Work	Delay	Start	Finish			
	2	Deena Tanenblatt	50%	7.5 hrs	0 days	Tue 6/3/03	Thu 6/5/03			
	3	Ellen Peck	0%	0 hrs	0 days	Tue 6/3/03	Tue 6/3/03			
	4	Bob Woock	100%	19 hrs	0 days	Thu 6/5/03	Tue 6/10/03			
12		Caterer				5 days	Mon 6/9/03	Fri 6/13/03	4	Ellen Peck
	ID	Resource Name	Units	Work	Delay	Start	Finish			
	3	Ellen Peck	100%	40 hrs	0 days	Mon 6/9/03	Fri 6/13/03			
13		Bartenders				3 days	Mon 6/16/03	Wed 6/18/03	12	Ellen Peck
	ID	Resource Name	Units	Work	Delay	Start	Finish			
	3	Ellen Peck	100%	24 hrs	0 days	Mon 6/16/03	Wed 6/18/03			
14		Security				2.5 days	Mon 6/9/03	Wed 6/11/03	4	Bob Woock,Joe Johnson
	ID	Resource Name	Units	Work	Delay	Start	Finish			
	1	Joe Johnson	100%	20 hrs	0 days	Mon 6/9/03	Wed 6/11/03			
	4	Bob Woock	100%	20 hrs	0 days	Mon 6/9/03	Wed 6/11/03			
15		Photographers				1.5 days	Mon 6/9/03	Tue 6/10/03	4	Deena Tanenblatt[50%],Intern
	ID	Resource Name	Units	Work	Delay	Start	Finish			
	2	Deena Tanenblatt	50%	4 hrs	0 days	Mon 6/9/03	Mon 6/9/03			
	6	Intern	100%	8 hrs	0 days	Mon 6/9/03	Tue 6/10/03			
16		Cleanup Crew				2 days	Mon 6/9/03	Tue 6/10/03	4	Intern,Joe Johnson[50%]
	ID	Resource Name	Units	Work	Delay	Start	Finish			
	1	Joe Johnson	50%	8 hrs	0 days	Mon 6/9/03	Tue 6/10/03			
	6	Intern	100%	8 hrs	0 days	Mon 6/9/03	Tue 6/10/03			
21		Alert community				2 days	Tue 6/10/03	Thu 6/12/03	9	Do Lahr
	ID	Resource Name	Units	Work	Delay	Start	Finish			
	5	Do Lahr	100%	16 hrs	0 days	Tue 6/10/03	Thu 6/12/03			
22		Press release				1 day	Tue 6/10/03	Wed 6/11/03	9	Do Lahr
	ID	Resource Name	Units	Work	Delay	Start	Finish			
	5	Do Lahr	100%	8 hrs	0 days	Tue 6/10/03	Wed 6/11/03			
24		PA System				1 day	Tue 6/10/03	Wed 6/11/03	9	

Page 1

Tasks Starting Soon as of Fri 8/8/03
Reports.mpp

ID	❶	Task Name	Duration	Start	Finish	Predecessors	Resource Names
26	📅	Baseball Game	0 days	Tue 7/22/03	Tue 7/22/03		
27	📅	Opera	0 days	Thu 7/24/03	Thu 7/24/03		
28	📅	Conference	0 days	Fri 7/25/03	Fri 7/25/03		

Page 2

Tasks in Progress

The Tasks in Progress report lists tasks that have started
but not yet finished. You can view the tasks' duration,
start and planned finish dates, predecessors, and
resource information if you assigned resources.

Tasks In Progress as of Fri 6/20/03
Reports

ID	ⓘ	Task Name	Duration	Start	Finish	Predecessors	Resource Names
June 2003							
6		Send out invitations	4 days	Wed 6/11/03	Mon 6/16/03		Ellen Peck

ID	Resource Name	Units	Work	Delay	Start	Finish
3	Ellen Peck	100%	32 hrs	0 days	Wed 6/11/03	Mon 6/16/03

	Theme	1.75 days	Tue 6/3/03	Wed 6/4/03		Deena Tanenblatt

ID	Resource Name	Units	Work	Delay	Start	Finish
2	Deena Tanenblatt	100%	14 hrs	0 days	Tue 6/3/03	Wed 6/4/03

Page 1

Completed Tasks

The Completed Tasks report lists completed tasks. You can view the actual duration, the actual start and finish dates, the cost, the work hours, and the percent complete. The percent complete is always 100 percent. Partially completed tasks do not appear on this report.

Completed Tasks as of Fri 8/8/03
Reports.mpp

ID	Task Name	Duration	Start	Finish	% Comp.	Cost	Work
June 2003							
4	Determine budget	5 days	Mon 6/2/03	Fri 6/6/03		$960.00	32 hrs
5	Invitation list	3 days	Fri 6/6/03	Tue 6/10/03		$600.00	24 hrs

Page 1

Should Have Started Tasks

When you print the Should Have Started Tasks report you must supply a date by which tasks should have started. Project uses this date to determine which tasks appear on the report. For each task on the report, Project displays planned start and finish dates, baseline start and finish dates, and variances for start and finish dates. Successor task information appears when a task on the report has a successor defined.

Should Have Started Tasks as of Mon 8/18/03
Reports.mpp

ID	Task Name			Start	Finish	Baseline Start	Baseline Finish	Start Var.	Finish Var.
1	**Conference**			**Mon 6/2/03**	**Fri 7/25/03**	**Mon 6/2/03**	**Mon 6/16/03**	**0 days**	**28 days**
7	**Selection**			**Mon 6/2/03**	**Tue 6/10/03**	**Mon 6/2/03**	**Tue 6/10/03**	**0 days**	**0.25 days**
8	Theme			Mon 6/2/03	Tue 6/3/03	Mon 6/2/03	Tue 6/3/03	0 days	0 days
	ID	*Successor Name*	*Type*	*Lag*					
	9	*Site*	*FS*	*0 days*					
	10	*Keynote speaker*	*FS*	*0 days*					
9	Site				Tue 6/3/03	Tue 6/10/03	Tue 6/3/03	Tue 6/10/03	0 days	0 days
	ID	*Successor Name*	*Type*	*Lag*					
	21	*Alert community*	*FS*	*0 days*					
	22	*Press release*	*FS*	*0 days*					
	24	*PA System*	*FS*	*0 days*					
10	Keynote speaker			Tue 6/3/03	Tue 6/10/03	Tue 6/3/03	Fri 6/6/03	0 days	2.13 days
17	**Plan Entertainment**			**Mon 6/2/03**	**Mon 6/2/03**	**Mon 6/2/03**	**Mon 6/2/03**	**0 days**	**0 days**
18	Baseball Game			Mon 6/2/03	Mon 6/2/03	Mon 6/2/03	Mon 6/2/03	0 days	0 days
19	Opera			Mon 6/2/03	Mon 6/2/03	Mon 6/2/03	Mon 6/2/03	0 days	0 days

Page 1

Slipping Tasks

The Slipping Tasks report lists the tasks that you or your team have rescheduled from their baseline start dates. This report displays the same fields that you saw on the Should Have Started Tasks report, but the presentation of the information changes the focus of your attention to tasks that are projected to finish later than planned.

Slipping Tasks as of Mon 8/18/03
Reports.mpp

ID	Task Name	Start	Finish	Baseline Start	Baseline Finish	Start Var.	Finish Var.
1	Conference	Mon 6/2/03	Fri 7/25/03	Mon 6/2/03	Mon 6/16/03	0 days	28 days
2	Preplanning	Mon 6/2/03	Mon 6/16/03	Mon 6/2/03	Thu 6/5/03	0 days	7 days
3	Initial planning	Mon 6/2/03	Mon 6/16/03	Mon 6/2/03	Thu 6/5/03	0 days	7 days
6	Send out invitations	Wed 6/11/03	Mon 6/16/03	Mon 6/2/03	Thu 6/5/03	7 days	7 days
7	Selection	Mon 6/2/03	Tue 6/10/03	Mon 6/2/03	Tue 6/10/03	0 days	0.25 days
10	Keynote speaker	Tue 6/3/03	Tue 6/10/03	Tue 6/3/03	Fri 6/6/03	0 days	2.13 days
11	Hire	Mon 6/9/03	Wed 6/18/03	Thu 6/5/03	Mon 6/16/03	2 days	2 days
12	Caterer	Mon 6/9/03	Fri 6/13/03	Thu 6/5/03	Wed 6/11/03	2 days	2 days

	ID	Successor Name	Type	Lag
	13	Bartenders	FS	0 days

ID	Task Name	Start	Finish	Baseline Start	Baseline Finish	Start Var.	Finish Var.
13	Bartenders	Mon 6/16/03	Wed 6/18/03	Thu 6/12/03	Mon 6/16/03	2 days	2 days
14	Security	Mon 6/9/03	Wed 6/11/03	Thu 6/5/03	Mon 6/9/03	2 days	2 days
15	Photographers	Mon 6/9/03	Tue 6/10/03	Thu 6/5/03	Fri 6/6/03	2 days	2 days
16	Cleanup Crew	Mon 6/9/03	Tue 6/10/03	Thu 6/5/03	Fri 6/6/03	2 days	2 days

Page 1

Who Does What

The Who Does What report lists resources and the tasks to which they are assigned, the amount of work planned for each task, the planned start and finish dates, and any resource notes.

Who Does What as of Mon 8/18/03
Reports.mpp

ID	ⓘ	Resource Name				Work	
1		Joe Johnson				28 hrs	
	ID	Task Name	Units	Work	Delay	Start	Finish
	14	Security	100%	20 hrs	0 days	Mon 6/9/03	Wed 6/11/03
	16	Cleanup Crew	50%	8 hrs	0 days	Mon 6/9/03	Tue 6/10/03
2		Deena Tanenblatt				49.5 hrs	
	ID	Task Name	Units	Work	Delay	Start	Finish
	5	Invitation list	100%	24 hrs	0 days	Fri 6/6/03	Tue 6/10/03
	10	Keynote speaker	50%	7.5 hrs	0 days	Tue 6/3/03	Thu 6/5/03
	8	Theme	100%	14 hrs	0 days	Mon 6/2/03	Tue 6/3/03
	15	Photographers	50%	4 hrs	0 days	Mon 6/9/03	Mon 6/9/03
3		Ellen Peck				76 hrs	
	ID	Task Name	Units	Work	Delay	Start	Finish
	10	Keynote speaker	0%	0 hrs	0 days	Tue 6/3/03	Tue 6/3/03
	12	Caterer	100%	40 hrs	0 days	Mon 6/9/03	Fri 6/13/03
	13	Bartenders	100%	24 hrs	0 days	Mon 6/16/03	Wed 6/18/03
	18	Baseball Game	100%	8 hrs	0 days	Mon 6/2/03	Mon 6/2/03
	19	Opera	100%	4 hrs	0 days	Mon 6/2/03	Mon 6/2/03
4		Bob Woock				71 hrs	
	ID	Task Name	Units	Work	Delay	Start	Finish
	4	Determine budget	100%	32 hrs	0 days	Mon 6/2/03	Fri 6/6/03
	10	Keynote speaker	100%	19 hrs	0 days	Thu 6/5/03	Tue 6/10/03
	14	Security	100%	20 hrs	0 days	Mon 6/9/03	Wed 6/11/03
5		Do Lahr				56 hrs	
	ID	Task Name	Units	Work	Delay	Start	Finish
	9	Site	100%	32 hrs	0 days	Tue 6/3/03	Tue 6/10/03
	21	Alert community	100%	16 hrs	0 days	Tue 6/10/03	Thu 6/12/03
	22	Press release	100%	8 hrs	0 days	Tue 6/10/03	Wed 6/11/03
6		Intern				36 hrs	
	ID	Task Name	Units	Work	Delay	Start	Finish
	9	Site	100%	20 hrs	0 days	Tue 6/3/03	Tue 6/10/03
	15	Photographers	100%	8 hrs	0 days	Mon 6/9/03	Tue 6/10/03
	16	Cleanup Crew	100%	8 hrs	0 days	Mon 6/9/03	Tue 6/10/03
7		Long distance				0 hrs	
8		Lumber				0 hrs	
9		Gasoline				0 hrs	

Page 1

Who Does What When

The Who Does What When report also lists resources and the tasks to which they are assigned. This report, however, focuses attention on the daily work that is scheduled for each resource on each task.

You can change the timescale on the report from daily to some other increment, such as weekly. Also, if pound signs (###) appear in the body of your report, you can change the date format on the report to a wider format as this example shows. For more information on customizing reports, see Chapter 10.

Who Does What When as of Mon 8/18/03
Reports.mpp

	6/1	6/2	6/3	6/4	6/5	6/6	6/7	6/8	6/9	6/10	6/11	6/12	6/13	6/14	6/15	6/16	6/17	6/18
Joe Johnson									12 hrs	12 hrs	4 hrs							
Security									8 hrs	8 hrs	4 hrs							
Cleanup Crew									4 hrs	4 hrs								
Deena Tanenblatt		8 hrs	7 hrs	4 hrs	2.5 hrs	8 hrs			12 hrs	8 hrs								
Invitation list						8 hrs			8 hrs	8 hrs								
Theme		8 hrs	6 hrs															
Keynote speaker			1 h	4 hrs	2.5 hrs													
Photographers									4 hrs									
Ellen Peck		12 hrs							8 hrs	8 hrs	8 hrs	8 hrs	8 hrs			8 hrs	8 hrs	8 hrs
Keynote speaker																		
Caterer									8 hrs	8 hrs	8 hrs	8 hrs	8 hrs					
Bartenders																8 hrs	8 hrs	8 hrs
Baseball Game		8 hrs																
Opera		4 hrs																
Bob Woock		8 hrs	8 hrs	8 hrs	12 hrs	11 hrs			8 hrs	12 hrs	4 hrs							
Determine budget		8 hrs	8 hrs	8 hrs	4 hrs	4 hrs												
Keynote speaker					8 hrs	7 hrs				4 hrs								
Security									8 hrs	8 hrs	4 hrs							
Do Lahr			2 hrs	8 hrs	8 hrs	2 hrs			8 hrs	8 hrs	14 hrs	6 hrs						
Site			2 hrs	8 hrs	8 hrs	2 hrs			8 hrs	4 hrs								
Alert community										2 hrs	8 hrs	6 hrs						
Press release										2 hrs	6 hrs							
Intern			2 hrs	4 hrs	4 hrs	4 hrs			12 hrs	10 hrs								
Site			2 hrs	4 hrs	4 hrs	4 hrs			4 hrs	2 hrs								
Photographers									4 hrs	4 hrs								
Cleanup Crew									4 hrs	4 hrs								
Long distance																		
Lumber																		
Gasoline																		

Page 1

To Do List

The To Do List report lists, on a weekly basis, the tasks assigned to a selected resource. When you print this report, Project first displays the Using Resource dialog box, which contains the Show tasks using list box. The list box contains your resources, which you can select. The To Do List report shows the task ID number, duration, start and finish dates, predecessors, and a list of all of the resources that are assigned to each task.

To Do List as of Mon 8/18/03
Reports.mpp

ID	ⓘ	Task Name	Duration	Start	Finish	Predecessors	Resource Names
Week of June 8							
14		Security	2.5 days	Mon 6/9/03	Wed 6/11/03	4	Bob Woock,Joe Johnson
16		Cleanup Crew	2 days	Mon 6/9/03	Tue 6/10/03	4	Intern,Joe Johnson[50%]

Page 1

Overallocated Resources

The Overallocated Resources report shows the overallocated resources, the tasks to which they are assigned, and the total hours of work that are assigned to them. You can also view the details of each task, such as the allocation, the amount of work, any delay, and the start and finish dates.

Overallocated Resources as of Mon 8/18/03
Reports.mpp

ID	ⓘ	Resource Name		Work			
1	◈	Joe Johnson		28 hrs			
	ID	Task Name	Units	Work	Delay	Start	Finish
	14	Security	100%	20 hrs	0 days	Mon 6/9/03	Wed 6/11/03
	16	Cleanup Crew	50%	8 hrs	0 days	Mon 6/9/03	Tue 6/10/03
2	◈	Deena Tanenblatt		49.5 hrs			
	ID	Task Name	Units	Work	Delay	Start	Finish
	5	Invitation list	100%	24 hrs	0 days	Fri 6/6/03	Tue 6/10/03
	10	Keynote speaker	50%	7.5 hrs	0 days	Tue 6/3/03	Thu 6/5/03
	8	Theme	100%	14 hrs	0 days	Mon 6/2/03	Tue 6/3/03
	15	Photographers	50%	4 hrs	0 days	Mon 6/9/03	Mon 6/9/03
3	◈	Ellen Peck		76 hrs			
	ID	Task Name	Units	Work	Delay	Start	Finish
	10	Keynote speaker	0%	0 hrs	0 days	Tue 6/3/03	Tue 6/3/03
	12	Caterer	100%	40 hrs	0 days	Mon 6/9/03	Fri 6/13/03
	13	Bartenders	100%	24 hrs	0 days	Mon 6/16/03	Wed 6/18/03
	18	Baseball Game	100%	8 hrs	0 days	Mon 6/2/03	Mon 6/2/03
	19	Opera	100%	4 hrs	0 days	Mon 6/2/03	Mon 6/2/03
4	◈	Bob Woock		71 hrs			
	ID	Task Name	Units	Work	Delay	Start	Finish
	4	Determine budget	100%	32 hrs	0 days	Mon 6/2/03	Fri 6/6/03
	10	Keynote speaker	100%	19 hrs	0 days	Thu 6/5/03	Tue 6/10/03
	14	Security	100%	20 hrs	0 days	Mon 6/9/03	Wed 6/11/03
5	◈	Do Lahr		56 hrs			
	ID	Task Name	Units	Work	Delay	Start	Finish
	9	Site	100%	32 hrs	0 days	Tue 6/3/03	Tue 6/10/03
	21	Alert community	100%	16 hrs	0 days	Tue 6/10/03	Thu 6/12/03
	22	Press release	100%	8 hrs	0 days	Tue 6/10/03	Wed 6/11/03
				280.5 hrs			

Page 1

Task Usage

The Task Usage report lists tasks and the resources assigned to each task. It also displays the amount of work that is assigned to each resource in weekly time increments. You can change the time increment. See Chapter 10 for details on customizing reports.

Task Usage as of Mon 8/18/03
Reports.mpp

	6/1/03	6/8/03	6/15/03	6/22/03	6/29/03	7/6/03	7/13/03	7/20/03	Total
Conference									
Preplanning									
Initial planning									
Determine budget	32 hrs								32 hrs
Bob Woock	32 hrs								32 hrs
Invitation list	8 hrs	16 hrs							24 hrs
Deena Tanenblatt	8 hrs	16 hrs							24 hrs
Send out invitations									
Selection									
Theme	14 hrs								14 hrs
Deena Tanenblatt	14 hrs								14 hrs
Site	34 hrs	18 hrs							52 hrs
Do Lahr	20 hrs	12 hrs							32 hrs
Intern	14 hrs	6 hrs							20 hrs
Keynote speaker	22.5 hrs	4 hrs							26.5 hrs
Deena Tanenblatt	7.5 hrs								7.5 hrs
Ellen Peck									
Bob Woock	15 hrs	4 hrs							19 hrs
Hire									
Caterer		40 hrs							40 hrs
Ellen Peck		40 hrs							40 hrs
Bartenders			24 hrs						24 hrs
Ellen Peck			24 hrs						24 hrs
Security		40 hrs							40 hrs
Joe Johnson		20 hrs							20 hrs
Bob Woock		20 hrs							20 hrs
Photographers		12 hrs							12 hrs
Deena Tanenblatt		4 hrs							4 hrs
Intern		8 hrs							8 hrs
Cleanup Crew		16 hrs							16 hrs
Joe Johnson		8 hrs							8 hrs
Intern		8 hrs							8 hrs
Plan Entertainment									
Baseball Game	8 hrs								8 hrs
Ellen Peck	8 hrs								8 hrs
Opera	4 hrs								4 hrs
Ellen Peck	4 hrs								4 hrs
Public Relations									
Alert community		16 hrs							16 hrs
Do Lahr		16 hrs							16 hrs
Press release		8 hrs							8 hrs

Page 1

Task Usage as of Mon 8/18/03
Reports.mpp

	6/1/03	6/8/03	6/15/03	6/22/03	6/29/03	7/6/03	7/13/03	7/20/03	Total
Do Lahr		8 hrs							8 hrs
Rent Equipment									
PA System									
Events									
Baseball Game									
Opera									
Conference									
Total	#######	170 hrs	24 hrs						316.5 hrs

Page 2

Resource Usage

The Resource Usage report lists resources and the tasks to which they are assigned. Like the Task Usage report, this report shows the amount of work assigned to each resource for each task in weekly time increments, but this report focuses attention on the resource.

Project contains two variations of the Resource Usage report: the Resource Usage (material) and Resource Usage (work) reports. Both reports appear identical to the Resource Usage report, but one shows only material resources while the other shows only work resources. Both reports are custom reports; to print them, see Chapter 14.

Resource Usage as of Mon 8/18/03
Reports.mpp

	6/1/03	6/8/03	6/15/03	6/22/03	6/29/03	7/6/03	7/13/03	7/20/03	**Total**
Joe Johnson		28 hrs							28 hrs
Security		20 hrs							20 hrs
Cleanup Crew		8 hrs							8 hrs
Deena Tanenblatt	29.5 hrs	20 hrs							49.5 hrs
Invitation list	8 hrs	16 hrs							24 hrs
Theme	14 hrs								14 hrs
Keynote speaker	7.5 hrs								7.5 hrs
Photographers		4 hrs							4 hrs
Ellen Peck	12 hrs	40 hrs	24 hrs						76 hrs
Keynote speaker									
Caterer		40 hrs							40 hrs
Bartenders			24 hrs						24 hrs
Baseball Game	8 hrs								8 hrs
Opera	4 hrs								4 hrs
Bob Woock	47 hrs	24 hrs							71 hrs
Determine budget	32 hrs								32 hrs
Keynote speaker	15 hrs	4 hrs							19 hrs
Security		20 hrs							20 hrs
Do Lahr	20 hrs	36 hrs							56 hrs
Site	20 hrs	12 hrs							32 hrs
Alert community		16 hrs							16 hrs
Press release		8 hrs							8 hrs
Intern	14 hrs	22 hrs							36 hrs
Site	14 hrs	6 hrs							20 hrs
Photographers		8 hrs							8 hrs
Cleanup Crew		8 hrs							8 hrs
Long distance									
Lumber									
Gasoline									
Total	########	170 hrs	24 hrs						316.5 hrs

Page 1

INDEX

C

continued

INDEX

continued

INDEX

continued

continued

continued

continued

continued

Read Less – Learn More®

Visual

Visual Blueprint™

For experienced computer users, developers, and network professionals who learn best visually.

Extra

Apply It

"Apply It" and "Extra" provide ready-to-run code and useful tips.

Title	ISBN	Price
Access 2003: Your visual blueprint for creating and maintaining real-world databases	0-7645-4081-5	$26.99
Active Server Pages 3.0: Your visual blueprint for developing interactive Web sites	0-7645-3472-6	$26.99
Adobe Scripting: Your visual blueprint for scripting Photoshop and Illustrator	0-7645-2455-0	$29.99
ASP.NET: Your visual blueprint for creating Web applications on the .NET Framework	0-7645-3617-6	$26.99
C#: Your visual blueprint for building .NET applications	0-7645-3601-X	$26.99
Excel Data Analysis: Your visual blueprint for analyzing data, charts, and PivotTables	0-7645-3754-7	$26.99
Excel Programming: Your visual blueprint for building interactive spreadsheets	0-7645-3646-X	$26.99
Flash ActionScript: Your visual blueprint for creating Flash-enhanced Web sites	0-7645-3657-5	$26.99
HTML: Your visual blueprint for designing effective Web pages	0-7645-3471-8	$26.99
Java: Your visual blueprint for building portable Java programs	0-7645-3543-9	$26.99
Java and XML: Your visual blueprint for creating Java-enhanced Web programs	0-7645-3683-4	$26.99
JavaScript: Your visual blueprint for building dynamic Web pages	0-7645-4730-5	$26.99
JavaServer Pages: Your visual blueprint for designing dynamic content with JSP	0-7645-3542-0	$26.99
Linux: Your visual blueprint to the Linux platform	0-7645-3481-5	$26.99
MySQL: Your visual blueprint to open source database management	0-7645-1692-2	$29.99
Perl: Your visual blueprint for building Perl scripts	0-7645-3478-5	$26.99
PHP: Your visual blueprint for creating open source, server-side content	0-7645-3561-7	$26.99
Red Hat Linux 8: Your visual blueprint to an open source operating system	0-7645-1793-7	$29.99
Unix: Your visual blueprint to the universe of Unix	0-7645-3480-7	$26.99
Unix for Mac: Your visual blueprint to maximizing the foundation of Mac OS X	0-7645-3730-X	$26.99
Visual Basic .NET: Your visual blueprint for building versatile programs on the .NET Framework	0-7645-3649-4	$26.99
Visual C++ .NET: Your visual blueprint for programming on the .NET platform	0-7645-3644-3	$26.99
XML: Your visual blueprint for building expert Web pages	0-7645-3477-7	$26.99

Over 10 million Visual books in print!